Spain

A COMPANION TO SPANISH STUDIES

Spain

A COMPANION TO SPANISH STUDIES

edited by P. E. Russell

METHUEN & CO. LTD

First published in 1973
by Methuen & Co. Ltd
11 New Fetter Lane, London EC4P 4EE
First published as a University Paperback in 1976
Reprinted with revisions 1977
Reprinted 1982

© *1973 by P. E. Russell*

Printed in Great Britain by
Richard Clay (The Chaucer Press Ltd)
Bungay, Suffolk

ISBN 0 416 84110 4

Contents

II THE VISUAL ARTS IN SPAIN 473

O. N. V. Glendinning, Professor of Spanish, Queen Mary College, University of London

Preface

The present book is an entirely new version of the work of the same title, edited by the late Professor E. Allison Peers, which was first published in 1929. The success of *Spain: A Companion to Spanish Studies* during the following four decades demonstrated the correctness of Allison Peers's judgement that there was need for a work that would make available to students at sixth-form or university intermediate level and to others interested in things Hispanic, within a single pair of covers, relatively succinct descriptive and critical accounts not only of Spanish history and literature but also of the history of the visual arts and music there. The original book, twice enlarged and revised since 1929, ran through five editions. Volumes modelled on revisions of the pattern established by Allison Peers have been produced for Germany and France too. But, successful though *A Companion to Spanish Studies* has been, the erosive effects of time on chapters first written over forty years ago have now done their inevitable work. There has, since then, been a great increase in knowledge as well as many changes in critical values and in taste over the whole Hispanic field. Attitudes to and within the various disciplines involved have greatly altered and become more complex: there is more awareness of the relationship between the various arts themselves and between them and history. Equally important, the status of Hispanic studies in the British Isles has changed so drastically since 1929 that the sense of pioneering a still largely unknown culture that can be detected in some of the chapters of the original *Companion* serves only to date them.

The most obvious difference between the present book and its predecessor is one of length. The new *Companion* has more than double the number of pages of the latter. Much of this increase is accounted for by the fact that, nowadays, students and most other potential readers expect from historical and critical studies of the kind offered here greater depth of treatment and more evidence to support an individual historian's or critic's judgements than they did forty years ago. But it is hoped that the general reader, with no particular background or specialization in Hispanic studies, will also continue to find the book useful for reference; it has been written with his needs in mind as well as of those who wish to start or to extend an existing knowledge of Spain and its culture. Some knowledge of the Spanish language has been assumed, particularly in the chapters on literature, when textual quotation is attempted.

Chapter 1 now provides a great deal more detailed information about the history of the Spanish language (including Spanish as spoken in South America) than its predecessor was able to do. It is, however, still to this chapter that the reader should look for information about the physical geography of Spain and the history of the Iberian Peninsula before the coming of the Visigoths; linguistic history is an all-important contributor to our knowledge of the general history of those early periods. In the historical section proper a new chapter on the history of Muslim Spain, looked at largely through Muslim sources, has been added. This reflects the much greater interest these days in Muslim Spain as a historical and cultural phenomenon in its own right, as well as for the influence of its institutions and culture on Christian Spain. The chapters on Spanish history generally pay less attention to strictly political history and more to economic, social and institutional history than was formerly the case. Such an approach, as well as conforming more closely to modern attitudes to historical investigation, is more directly useful to students of literature and the other arts. In the literature section a chapter on medieval Catalan literature has been added – any survey of medieval Spanish literature that omitted literature written in Catalan would be both incomplete and, according to the way medieval Spaniards themselves looked at the culture of the Iberian Peninsula, anachronistic. An account of modern Catalan literature has been included in Chapter 9. The chapter on 'Golden Age' literature has been greatly extended in comparison with its predecessor; more attention is now given in it to the history of ideas and to those contemporary theories of literature and rhetoric which often decisively influenced the form and style of creative literature in the sixteenth and seventeenth centuries. Attention to minor literary figures of that period has been severely restricted to allow for a fuller treatment of major figures. A chapter on Spanish American literature has been added because it is believed that, thanks to the recent rapid growth of interest in this literature and the high quality of contemporary Spanish American writing, many potential readers of *A Companion to Spanish Studies* will find such a chapter helpful. Considerations of space have made it impossible to provide the same backing to this chapter in terms of history and the visual arts that are available to students of Peninsular Spanish literature in the volume.

In all the chapters on literature internal 'periodization' has provided the problems it usually does to those who seek to write about literature in a historical context. In many cases the subdivision or part subdivision of these chapters in terms of extra-literary factors (such as centuries or reigns) has, despite obvious disadvantages, often still seemed least likely to mislead. The reader should, however, not attach too much significance to these subheadings, except as means of conveniently dividing up the narrative.

The chapter on Spanish music now deals not just with modern music but with the history of music in Spain from the time of the Visigoths onwards. Apart from the intrinsic historical interest of Spanish music, the close relations between music and poetry, particularly in the Middle Ages and in the sixteenth century, also seemed to make this change appropriate. An account of the main visual arts has been combined in one chapter: painting, sculpture and architecture often illuminate and are illuminated by each other and, taken together, constitute a single unit in the history of artistic taste in Spain. In these two chapters, and particularly in that on music, care has been taken to avoid a merely belletristic approach so that the reader with some specialist knowledge of the arts concerned may find them useful, as well as those without such knowledge.

Apart from a common understanding about the kind of readers to whom this book is particularly directed and an acceptance of the need that, since it will be in print for some time, it should eschew what may be transient modishness or, particularly in the chapters on literature, any commitment to critical views that are uncertain to survive, no attempt has been made to impose consensus interpretations or identical patterns of treatment on individual contributors. The reader may, indeed, occasionally discover explicit or implicit contradictions between interpretations of the same facts when these are taken up in more than one chapter. In the long history of Spain and of Hispanic culture there are still many phenomena that are susceptible of differing interpretations, either according to the way they are approached, or simply because the facts about them are still too insufficiently known, or too near to us, to permit final conclusions. It seems no bad thing that the student, at however early a stage, should be made aware of this.

It is intended that each chapter should be a complete and independent survey of the subject-matter with which it is concerned but, by means of cross-references, the attention of the reader is also sometimes drawn to portions of other chapters which seem particularly relevant as an additional gloss on or elaboration of the matter in hand. No attempt to conclude the *Companion* with any sort of summing-up has been attempted. Most readers, it is presumed, will use parts of the book only, so that such a summing-up would be superfluous. In any case, in the last seventy-five years, subjective generalizing by individuals about Spain, the Spanish character and Spanish culture has been too common a pastime of scholars and critics, Spanish and foreign.

An attempt to supply full bibliographies has been made only for those subjects (such as the visual arts, music and some branches of history) where the reader is likely to find difficulty in securing access to up-to-date bibliographical information. Usually the bibliographies that follow each chapter make suggestions only for further general reading in the field concerned. In the bibliographies that follow the chapters on literature, critical works on individual authors have been included only when these also have a wider bearing on the writing of the period concerned.[1] In all the bibliographies some emphasis, when circumstances permit, has been given to works in English.

As was inevitable, a number of compromises between what would have been ideally desirable and what was possible have proved necessary. Thus, in the chapter on medieval Spanish history, the history of Portugal has not been dealt with except in so far as Portugal directly impinged on the history of her neighbours. This exclusion, as far as the Middle Ages are concerned, cannot be defended in terms of historical propriety; as late as the very end of the medieval period a dynastic union of the crown of Portugal with that of Castile and Aragon was still contemplated as an acceptable possibility, both in Portugal and in Spain. The history of medieval Portugal is not dealt with simply because to do so would have required the exclusion or cutting down of those portions of the book devoted to things we now classify as Spanish. Limits on space have dictated other exclusions – e.g. the thought and culture of Spanish Jewry.

My thanks are due, in the first instance, to those fellow scholars, all, with one exception, now teaching at universities in the British Isles,

[1] There are excellent up-to-date bibliographies of Spanish literature, including mention of articles as well as books, in each of the eight volumes of the Benn *Literary History of Spain* (London, 1971–2).

1 Spain and the Spanish Language

DOUGLAS GIFFORD

I Introduction

Spanish is nowadays the first language of more than 170 million people, over 140 million of them in Latin America. Outside the Peninsular boundaries of Spain (where, of course, Catalan, Basque and Galician-Portuguese are still the first languages of substantial minorities) Spanish is also spoken in the Canary Islands, in the two North African *plazas* (Ceuta and Melilla), and by a diminishing number of Jews in North Africa, the Balkans and Israel descended from those expelled from Spain in 1492. Behind these figures, both in Spain and in Latin America, there is a further substantial number of individuals who, while not speaking Spanish in their homes, have been educated in it or are obliged to use it because it is the official language of the states to which they belong.

In this chapter no attempt will be made to discuss Catalan or Galician-Portuguese, which belong to non-Spanish Romance language groups. Basque will be referred to only in so far as it affected the development of Spanish. The terms 'Spanish' and 'Castilian' are often used interchangeably. Historically speaking, 'Castilian' is the dialectal form of Spanish, originally spoken in Old Castile (north of the Sierra de Guadarrama), which became the 'standard' language of the Castilian and later the Spanish state. It is used with that meaning in this chapter.

Before discussing the early history of speech in the Peninsula it may be useful to remind the reader of some basic technical terms used when discussing linguistic history. *Phonology* is the description of the sounds of a language, together with the historical study of modifications of those sounds. *Morphology* deals with the study of the smallest meaningful units of language and of their formation into words; most considerations of grammar come under this heading. *Syntax* deals with the rules and relation of words to one another as expressions of ideas and parts of sentences. *Lexicology* deals with vocabulary. Here one must remember to distinguish between 'common' words ('horse', 'dog', 'sprat', etc.) and 'proper names' (personal names and place-names, for instance) which, in everyday use, have lost their descriptive function and are simply acoustic labels. Thus 'the green man' may describe a man who is unwell, or dressed in a green suit, or covered with leaves. 'The Green Man' as a proper name might mean nothing of the kind, and just serve to identify an inn.

Linguistic studies formerly set much store by written historical evidence about language as it was, but during the last fifty years or so an alternative attitude has emerged. This emphasizes the description and definition of language as it now is rather than trying to reconstruct it as it once was.

II Prehistory (to 218 B.C.)

To try to assess the linguistic history of pre-Roman Spain is like peering into the recesses of a dark cave. The further back one tries to look, the more vague the shapes and hollows appear, until one is left surmising mere outlines, indeed only guessing at what lies even further behind. The study of topography is important here, as is an awareness of the physical geography of the region to be studied and the ethnology and history of the peoples who lived in the Iberian Peninsula before, and after, the coming of the Romans. Climate and physical geography generally dictated the patterns of rural and urban life which, in their turn, help to explain linguistic history. That this is so can be seen by the linguistic history of even so small an area as the former Peninsular kingdom of Navarre, lying behind the western end of the Pyrenees. Along the Ebro valley, a hot, dry area where agriculture depended on irrigation, Navarre's linguistic history differs markedly from that of the rolling plains a little further north; a little further north still, in the Pyrenean foothills, linguistic situations are different again. In the mountains proper no invaders ever seriously interfered with the isolated Basque-speaking farmers. Roman settlers, however, moved both into the cereal-producing plains north of the Ebro and into the rich irrigated farms of the Ebro valley itself. Later the descendants of the Roman settlers were pushed out of the valley in their turn by Arabs and Berbers. Migration patterns like this must continually have occurred who agreed, it is hoped for the common good of Hispanic studies, to collaborate in writing this volume. Their task was more time-consuming and more difficult than might be supposed by those who have not undertaken similar tasks. The Editor's particular thanks are also due for advice and help on various matters received from Professor L. P. Harvey of King's College, University of London, and to my colleague, Mr F. W. Hodcroft of St Cross College, Oxford, who was generous as always of his time and his scholarship in helping me with various queries. I also owe a special debt of gratitude to Mr A. R. Pagden, who read a large part of the work in manuscript and made many useful suggestions, and to the secretaries of the Modern Languages Faculty Office for the care and patience with which they dealt with a good deal of retyping that proved necessary.

P. E. Russell

University of Oxford
20 June 1972

Note on the Revised Edition

The need to reprint the original edition of the book has presented an opportunity to bring bibliographies up-to-date and, where contemporary history and literature are concerned, to take account of events since 1972. Other corrections and emendations have been made where necessary, but the original pagination has been retained.

P. E. Russell

University of Oxford
1 July 1977

elsewhere in the Peninsula in pre-Roman times, producing a linguistic map much more complex than the tenuous concrete evidence we have suggests.

The physical geography of Spain therefore must be taken into account in any attempt to explain its early linguistic history. There is much which differs from the physical patterns of western Europe. Where rolling plains take up a large part of Germany, France or England, endowing them with an easy agrarian well-being, or where mountains predominate as in Switzerland or Austria, forcing human habitation into systems of valleys and pasturelands, Spain has a geographical character all of its own. As the highest country in Europe to possess a sea-coast (with an average altitude of over 2,000 feet) her 197,000 square miles of terrain include a huge interior tableland (nearly half the total area), the Meseta. The Meseta inclines gently towards the Atlantic, taking most of the larger Spanish rivers with it. Around the rims of this vast plateau is a fringe of mountain barriers which made ascent to and descent from the plateau an arduous business. Spanish rivers are not long by European standards, and carry little water: the Tagus (630 miles) hardly compares with such water-bearers as the Po or Rhône, not to mention giants like the Rhine or Danube. Mountain ranges (the Pyrenees and the Sierra Nevada) rise to over 11,000 feet in the north and south and there are notable mountain systems superimposed on the Meseta itself. The combination of these factors gives rise to an aridity which has always, in the past, concentrated human population in certain well-defined areas, such as those where either rainfall or irrigation can produce substantial crops or where mining and mineral wealth attract the industrialist. As the adage had it, 'En España la geografía manda.'

The mineral riches of a land can affect linguistic history by their power to attract fortune-hunting outsiders. The southern rivers of Hispania were known by the ancient world to produce gold; Cartagena was an outlet for silver, Huelva for copper, Andalusia generally produced tin and iron. Three main groups of peoples who came to these in search of metals can be discerned: the Phoenicians (together with their direct relatives and successors, the Carthaginians), the Greeks and the Iberians.

The Phoenicians came from the eastern Mediterranean in the eleventh century B.C. They were a seafaring people who set up trading-posts and mines in the south: e.g. *Gadir*, 'walled enclosure' > Cádiz (cf. Agadir in Morocco); *Asido* (the name of a god, possibly connected with the biblical Sidon) > (Medina) Sidonia; *Malaka* 'trading factory' > Málaga. Those who succeeded them, the Carthaginians (*c.* 500 B.C.), were those whom the Romans fought: Carthaginian place-names are *Cartago* > Cartagena; *Magonis* (after Hamilcar Barca's third son) > Mahón; *Ebusus* > Ibiza.

The Greeks also came to trade. Their presence is traceable in place-names on the Mediterranean coast such as *Emporion* > Ampurias, *Lucentum* > Alicante and *Rhode* > Rosas. It was through the Greeks and the Carthaginians that the vine and the olive, as well as the alphabet and writing, found their way to Spain.

Finally in this picture we can make out the Iberians (originally 'dwellers along the Iberus' > Ebro), probably land-hungry migrants from North Africa.

Minerals in the south, fertile land by the rivers and other economic attractions, then, brought immigrants to Spain. The picture takes on colour and form as we follow the rosary of small trading-posts down the eastern and southern coasts, all of which did a fair commerce with the farming or mining people in the interior.

Of the two types of settlers we have mentioned, traders in their sea-ports and miners or farmers inland, it is perhaps the latter whose traces are most useful to historians of language. The Iberians in particular have a recognizable culture; inscriptions at Alcoy, Mogente and Castellón contain much Iberian writing which has been deciphered but not under-stood, and knowledge about the language the Iberians spoke is as yet vague and ill defined. As usual, place-names can help us to a certain extent. From these we learn that the Iberians extended their settlements as far north as the Rhône delta and as far south as the area near Huelva; the river name Iberus, associated with the river Ebro, was extant in the Huelva area as well. Other place-names have even made scholars suspect that Iberian was the ancestor of modern Basque: there was an Iliberris near Granada which can be analysed by Basque *ili*, 'place', and *berri*, 'new', hence 'new place or town'. But however much Basque one knows, this knowledge has never helped satisfactorily to read Iberian inscriptions.

Pre-Roman words taken into Spanish Latin may well include *gordo*, 'fat'; *pizarra*, 'slate'; *becerro*, 'calf'; *manteca*, 'butter'; *bruja*, 'witch'; *cachorro*, 'puppy'; *guijarro*, 'pebble'; *vega*, 'river plain'; and *páramo*, 'high moorland'. The name Hispania (which of course gives us our Spain) has sometimes been ascribed to an Iberian Hispalis, a place-name which also comes down to us (through an Arabic form) as Sevilla.

As a people or peoples, the Iberians are not easy to define. It is possible that the name came to be a generic one for all non-Romans of the south and east, applied by classical geographers with rather the sense that we use when we talk of 'highlanders', or 'people of the bush', 'people of the interior' and the like. Whether one people or – what is more likely – a group of tribes with different remnants of distinct cultures, they represent the ethnic basis on which Latin had to build in southern and eastern Spain.

The pre-Roman languages of the north were destined to have far more influence on the evolution of Roman speech in Hispania than those of the south. The scarcity of evidence about the peoples of the north is, however, daunting: classical geographers incline to be too general, muddled or evasive, juggling forlornly with lists of tribal names without much idea of what they mean. 'The modes of all of them', says Strabo gloomily (c. 10 B.C., and speaking of the northern mountain tribes), 'are of like character. I shrink from giving too many of the names, shunning the unpleasant task of writing them down - unless it gives pleasure to someone to hear "Pleutaurans", "Bardyetans", "Allotrigans" and other names even less agreeable and of less significance than these.' Pomponius Mela, born in Hispania, speaks (c. A.D. 37) of 'some villages and rivers of the Cantabrians, whose names we cannot pronounce', while Martial, also born in Hispania (first century A.D.), mentions the 'most difficult names of our land'.

Two groups of peoples settled in northern Hispania are, however, important, and to these we shall now turn.

Few races have caused so much discussion and speculation as the Basques. Living in modern times on both sides of the western Pyrenees, their direct ancestors have been in that area for some four thousand years. Their language is pre-Indo-European, that is, prior in age to the emergence of the linguistic family which comprises Greek, Latin, Slavonic, Celtic and Germanic. Some half-million people still speak it today, and although the Basque linguistic area has contracted greatly during the last thousand years, there are traces of tribal and place-names of Basque origin as far east as Catalonia and as far west as Galicia. The Spanish Basque provinces today (the *Vascongadas*) are Vizcaya, Álava and Guipúzcoa.

The Basque language is at first glance difficult, but it is in reality only so when we try to fit on to it our own preconceived ideas of what grammar should be. It is agglutinative: that is, like many other languages in the world, its phrases and constructions are made up by the addition of particles or suffixes. Thus *etxe* (pronounced *etshe*) = 'house'; *etxeak* = 'the houses'; *etxearen* = 'to the house'.

This very ancient language is in every way quite unlike Spanish, yet its effect on the Romance of Spain has been significant. Apart from phonological influences (which we shall have cause to examine later) there is what W. J. Entwistle saw (not all students of language would agree) as:

> . . . a common mental outlook in the two languages. They eschew the negative and are forthright and concrete. What imagination they have is exercised on things rather than ideas; they refine on circumstances of action, such as time and person in the verb, and prefer only one voice; they are rich in auxiliaries, which are rather felt than logically distinguished. . . . In pronunciation there is a common basis of enunciation. It is not that Basque has imposed conditions upon those who learnt Latin in Spain; but rather that Latin, which presented alternative possibilities of treatment and development sufficient to give all the diversities of Romania, was subjected to the same mental control that had given Basque its special qualities. (W. J. Entwistle, *The Spanish Language*, p. 37.)

The Basques themselves call their language *Euskera*, and it is probable that the Latin noun Vascones was not based on an indigenous name but was an appellation given them by erroneous association with a tribe living on or near the river Ebro which is mentioned at the time of the Sertorian wars (75 B.C.).

If, when we consider the language of pre-Roman Spain, the Basques present a clearly identifiable element – at least in present-day terms – the Celtic contribution is harder to define. The Celtic migrations in Europe itself need little introduction, for all the west was violently affected by them. Britain, Gaul, Belgium, Germany, all recall Celtic tribal names (Brittoni, Galli, Belgae, Germani – not to mention the Alemanni and others). In Spain, two waves of Celtic migration seem to have occurred: one, around 900 B.C., penetrated what is now Catalonia, leaving however few traces. The other penetration, around 600 B.C., appears to have come at the other end of the Pyrenees. The names of many of the tribes involved, Belgae, Alemanni, Saefes, Germani, suggest they may have been southern offshoots of the tribes that also moved across northern Europe. Classical geographers are as vague about the Celts as they are about other peoples, but the richness of

Celtic place-names makes up for lack of information in historical sources regarding their movements.

It was in the north and west of the Peninsula that the principal Celtic tribes found attractive territory to settle, but they also spread to the Meseta itself. There they kept to the hilly regions, such as that around Teruel (whose name, connected with the Celtic tribal name Turolenses, can be found in such related forms as Tours in France and Thüringen in Germany), or in the Sierra Morena, where the Celtic tribe called the Germani settled.

Celtic place-names include elements such as *sego* or *segi*, 'victory' (Segorbe, Segovia); *briga*, 'fortress' (cf. German *burg*, English *burgh*), as in Coimbra (from *Conimbriga*); *dunum*, 'settlement or fort' (cf. Dundee, London), as in Berdún, Navardún. The well-known Celtic name 'Cluny' (cf. Forest of Clunie in Scotland, or the monastery of Cluny in France) appears in Coruña del Conde (Burgos). *Deva*, which has the same root as *deus* in Latin, meant river or god in Celtic (the Celts worshipped rivers – hence the synonymy) and appears in the river name Deva (occurring in both Guipúzcoa and Santander provinces) or in Riodeva (prov. of Teruel).

Celtic common-noun loan-words in Spanish were probably not directly acquired but came through Gaulish Romance: *camisa, cerveza, carro, camino, carpintero, cambiar, caballo, vasallo, cama.*

When referring to the head of the Ebro valley and the region adjacent to it, Roman geographers were wont to call the native tribes there 'Celtiberians', perhaps alluding to the fact of a racial symbiosis in that area between Iberians and Celts, rather like the Muslim–Hispanic fusions which were to take place in the same valley many centuries further on.

There were other ancient peoples connected with the Iberian Peninsula. Thus the Ligurians are thought to have settled in the centre, and they would seem to be related to the Ligurians of northern Italy. Toledo in Spain has a counterpart, Toleto, there; the place-name Langa appears in both areas, as does Berganza. The Ligurian suffix *-asca* or *-asque* comes into place-names in Piasca (prov. of Santander), Benasque (prov. of Huesca) or Tarascón (prov. of Orense) – all of which have parallels in northern Italy or the Rhône valley. If ever there was an established Ligurian culture, it was probably situated in the southern part of the Meseta in the second millennium B.C.

Lastly there were the Lusitanians in the western part of the Peninsula. These attacked the Romans in great force (148 B.C.). Their leader,

Viriathus, has been claimed as a local son of the province of Zamora, in whose capital a large statue proclaims him as the *Terror Romanorum*. And so he was, till treacherously assassinated by his own henchmen. The memory of the Lusitanians has helped to sustain the independence of Portugal.

III Latin in Spain

Spanish is essentially modernized spoken Latin. Italian is also a modernized version of the speech of the Romans, and so is French. The great differences between each Romance language are in part perhaps due to the influence on each of the languages spoken before the Roman settlers came (the linguistic 'substratum'), to differing historical and geographical factors, and to different influences in these regions subsequent to the Roman occupation.

Let us put ourselves in the place of a young Roman farmer in the valley of the Baetis (now called the Guadalquivir). The year is A.D. 400. He and his direct ancestors have irrigated and worked some fifty acres of good land for five generations, which is not a very long time, since the area itself has been inhabited by Romans since about 200 B.C. Our farmer is nominally a Christian like all the rest of his neighbours. Gone now are the bad days of the early Roman settlement when hillmen would descend from the mountains (now the Sierra Morena), when they were hungry and starving, to harass the farmers. True enough, they provided, these Germani, good cheap manual labour which was sorely needed at harvest time. Our Roman's great-great-grandfather had married a Lusitanian woman – not originally a particularly popular move in the family, but by now it was generally thought that some real indigenous blood in one's veins gave a sort of prestige. The Lusitanians were great fighters, and their women extremely good-looking.

Apart from the easy prosperity of these times (the place had not yet been plagued with wandering tribes of Vandals), if you had asked the farmer what he knew of Roman history what would he have told you? He would have first referred back to the civil wars, especially those in which Pompey took part. As far as early history was concerned, he would have known that there were people called Carthaginians who had tried to stop Roman expansion – an attempt which resulted in a war with them ending in 201 B.C. That was fully six hundred years ago (rather as if we were talking about the Hundred Years War, or Joan of Arc). He would perhaps know that the Roman settlements were originally confined to the Ebro and Baetis (Guadalquivir) valleys, with a thin connecting strip down the Mediterranean coast. Why those parts particularly? Because they most nearly approximated to the sort of terrain that emigrants from Italy had left. The pattern of settlements was often based on the system of the *conventus*, or association of groups of people with communal interests. These eventually gave rise to small townships from which, as in Italy, people would go out to work. Examples are *Italica*, founded 206 B.C., *Corduba* (156 B.C.) and others. Many old *conventus*-type towns later achieved municipal status. Many Roman urban nuclei too were superimposed on pre-Roman settlements by a generous infusion of time-expired Roman soldiers: e.g. *Caesar Augusta* (now Zaragoza (Saragossa)), *Emerita Augusta* (now Mérida). In 171 B.C. some 4,000 *hybridae*, sons of Roman soldiers and native women, petitioned Rome for a settlement of their own, and were given a colony at *Carteia* (near Gibraltar).

Our farmer would perhaps have known that, as far as Roman settlement went, the south was far more prosperous than the north in bygone days: Hispania Ulterior, centred on the Baetis valley, was colonized by Roman settlers over a wider area than Hispania Citerior. In the latter province settlement had been tentative at first, with settlers pushing their way up the valley of the Iberus (Ebro), but with the native element in the population persisting there too even after Roman occupation. Coins struck in the region bear legends in Iberian characters even when the minting was performed under Roman supervision. In Tarraco (Tarragona), at the mouth of the Ebro, bilingual inscriptions have been found; it too had Iberian coinage.

Later on, a major expansion of Roman settlement came in the time of Julius Caesar (102–44 B.C.), though again it was southern Hispania (or Ulterior) which benefited first. Caesar had served as *quaestor* in this province and when he returned to it again seven years later as *propraetor* he started a system of expansion by clearing the land to the north of its old boundaries as far as the Duero. This opened up what is now Portugal (an area later named 'Lusitania' by Augustus Caesar). The northern province followed suit. There the defeat of the Celtiberians at Numantia (near Soria) a long time before (133 B.C.) permitted the area round the Ebro valley to be settled far further up.

When Augustus (63 B.C.–A.D. 14) subdued the Asturians and Cantabrians he moved them from the mountains into the plains, where they would be more subject to Roman ideas and civilization. The mountains remained a bolt-hole for rebellious tribesmen, however. Right into

Visigothic times many rebellions originated in these cordilleras. The process of subjugation had been long: for nearly two hundred years the Romans had pursued a leisurely conquest of the Peninsula. Later, emperors such as Vespasian (A.D. 69–79) granted a wholesale extension of Latin rights to dozens of municipalities and Roman citizenship was granted to more and more of their inhabitants.

So much for our farmer's possible rough-and-ready knowledge of his country's history. Such persons' speech varied somewhat from region to region. But he was quite capable of speaking a good homely Latin: not for him the frills of the great writers, who after all were concerned with something different. There are instances of spoken Latin (often referred to as 'Vulgar Latin') in works like the *Appendix Probi* (sixth or seventh century, earlier thought to have been fourth century), which was a kind of spelling manual of the 'write this, don't write that' type, giving the 'correct' (i.e. written) form alongside the 'incorrect' form (in many cases the spoken one). In various letters such as that of Aetheria, a Spanish nun who went to Jerusalem on a pilgrimage (sixth century), we find good examples of spoken Latin. The walls of Pompeii, where graffiti are scratched, the plays of Plautus and works like the *Cena Trimalchionis* afford more instances.

But what were the principal distinctions between a Roman farmer's spoken Latin and that of the writer's 'literary' medium? In the main they were not very different from the gap between any spoken language and its written counterpart, but these differences are essential for any understanding of the history of any Romance language. The principal differences can be summarized as follows:

(1) In Vulgar or spoken Latin there was a stress accent – i.e. one of intensity, which may also have characterized the 'classical' language although there have been differences of opinion about this – and here it may be said that the soul of the word lay. The other syllables would be slurred over or even dropped, but the stressed element in a word remained, its vowel sometimes becoming a diphthong: thus Latin *térra*, *pórta* give Sp. *tierra*, *puerta*. Where the stress did not fall, the vowels became unstable and often disappeared: *óculus*, accusative *oculu(m)*, gives an intermediate stage *óclu* > Sp. *ojo*; *spéculum* > *spéclu* > Sp. *espejo*.

(2) One effect of the use of stress in words was to bring out the consonantal nature of *i* (or *y*) when it preceded a vowel: thus *dórmio* was pronounced *dórmyo*. This palatal *y* sound (not unlike that of *y* in English *yacht*) often affects the consonants just preceding it; the pheno-

menon is known to phoneticians as palatalization. Thus *ratióne(m)* (acc.) was pronounced **ratyóne* then **ratsyóne* > Sp. *razón*.

(3) Consonants which are unvoiced (i.e. where the vocal cords do not 'back' them), like *p, t, k*, often take on a voiced (i.e. vibrant) quality: *lócum* > *lógum* > Sp. *luego*. *Tótus*, accusative *tótu(m)* > Sp. *todo*; *apícula* > Sp. *abeja*. This voicing (i.e. vibrating of the vocal cords) occurred when the consonant came between vowels, that is, between two articulations of the vocal cords or voice.

Voiced consonants between vowels often merge into the vowels themselves and disappear: *frígidus*, accusative *frígidu(m)* > Sp. *frío*; *rívus*, accusative *rívu(m)* > Sp. *río*.

(4) Nearly all words of Latin origin in Spanish are, as the examples above have been implying, descended from the accusative form of Latin words, e.g. *pédem* (not *pes*) > Sp. *pie*, but the characteristic accusative final *-m* was lost in the spoken language long before it ceased to be written.

(5) Consonant groups were often written one way and pronounced another: *ménsa* (*mésa*), *ípse* (*íse*). The spoken form gave rise to Sp. *mesa, ese*.

(6) In the matter of gender spoken Latin seems to have become rather confused, recognizing in the end only a masculine and feminine so far as adjectives and non-abstract nouns were concerned, the Classical Latin neuter being dropped. Apart from pronouns all neuter forms ending in *-u* or *-o* became masculine, all in *-a* feminine, while such forms as those ending in *-en* as were neuter (*nómen, lúmen*) could become either, e.g. *el nombre, la lumbre*.

(7) The declension of nouns became confused because the final accusative *-m* was no longer pronounced, e.g. *páne*, and final *-o* and *-u* as well as *-e* and *-i* had become acoustically indistinguishable.

(8) The same vast simplification in the morphology of spoken Latin affected adjectives as well as nouns.

(9) Verbs in spoken Latin did not run to the number of tenses possessed by the Latin literary language and even the four conjugations were reduced to three. Irregular 'strong' verbs, i.e. verbs where the stressed stem changed (*facio, feci, factum*), gave way in the majority of cases to a 'weak' new form with an invariable stem. Thus the strong forms *divido, divisi, divisum* of literary Latin gave way in the preterite to **dividivi* > Sp. *dividí*. The future tense evolved from a periphrastic form, *cantáre habéo*, literally 'I am to sing' (> Old Sp. *cantar he*, modern Sp. *cantaré*). This wholesale disappearance of many classical

verb forms led to a simplification of spoken Latin which reminds one today of 'missionary Spanish' in a country like Bolivia, where only three tenses are used: the present (*ando*), past (*he andado*) and the periphrastic future (*voy a andar*).

Such are some of the main characteristics of that spoken Latin of Hispania which is the direct ancestor of modern Spanish. It must have been, syntactically, when spoken by the indigenous people of the Peninsula, a very simple language. But, whatever subsequent infusions of words or linguistic practices from non-Latin languages were to take place, the basic Latin framework was to remain. Modern Spanish *is* Peninsular spoken Latin brought up to date.

We have looked at pre-Roman Spain and we have seen how speech evolved in the time of the Romans themselves. Now we must follow the fortunes of Spanish Latin through the centuries when it was on its own and not politically dependent on Rome.

IV The Visigoths

The year 409 witnessed something the inhabitants of the Iberian Peninsula had not experienced since the Roman invasion: migrating tribes of Germans from Central Europe invaded Spain and settled there. The Swabians (Suevi) chose the north-west, and for a considerable time maintained an organized society side by side with the indigenous inhabitants of Galicia. Close by them the Asding Vandals settled too. The Alans, for their part, seem to have taken shallow root in what is now northern Extremadura (probably south of the Peña de Francia). The Siling Vandals chose for themselves the lusher Guadalquivir valley, much to the inconvenience of the Romans who had been cultivating these lands for centuries. It was possibly because of the protests from this particular region that help was sent from Rome itself. This came in 415 in the form of a large force of Visigoths, an East European tribe who had reached a political understanding with the Romans and who had recently settled around Toulouse, in southern France.[1]

The linguistic effect of these Germanic invasions was significant but almost exclusively lexical. There are about 2,400 place-names of Germanic origin in the Iberian Peninsula as a whole. The main influence of the Visigoths, who had become wholly or partly Latin-speaking by the time they entered Spain, is also strongly discernible in

[1] For a full account of the history of the Visigoths in Spain, see Chapter 3, section II.

the area of personal names, e.g. Alfonso (*hathus*, 'fight' + *funs*, 'ready' = 'all-prepared'), Fernando (*frithus*, 'peace' + *nanths*, 'bold' = 'daring ally'), Guzmán ('good man'), Elvira ('joyful and faithful'), Rodrigo ('famous and powerful'). There are a large number of others: Álvaro, Bermudo, Gonzalo, Manrique, Ramón. Place-names sometimes record the presence of other Germanic peoples who invaded the Peninsula before the Visigoths. Thus the Swabians of the north-west are remembered in Puerto de Sueve (prov. of Oviedo), Suevos (prov. of Coruña), Suegos (prov. of Lugo); the Alans left their mark in Villalán (prov. of Valladolid), Puerto del Alano (prov. of Huesca). The Vandals, it is generally supposed, bequeathed their name to Andalusia via Arabic *al-Andalus* as well as to such isolated places as Bandaliés (prov. of Huesca) and Campodevánol (prov. of Gerona).

At first, when a careful distinction was maintained between Visigoths and Romans, and any intermarriage prohibited, farms and settlements would sometimes show their racial character through their names, e.g. Romanos (prov. of Saragossa), Romanillos (Soria, Guadalajara, Madrid), Romanones (Guadalajara), Romancos (Guadalajara), as opposed to Toro (from (*Villa Go*)*thorum*, prov. of Zamora), Villatoro (Burgos). There were also dozens of place-names which incorporated Germanic personal names. Sometimes they were those of kings (e.g. Bamba (prov. of Zamora), Guitiza (prov. of La Coruña), which record the kings Wamba and Witiza respectively) or of a local Visigothic landowner, e.g. Casanande (Nandus), Castro Adalsindo (Adalsindus), Castrocontrigo (Guntericus), Castelladral (Aderaldus).

A fair number of common words in Spanish are of Germanic origin but most of these probably entered Late Latin or Old French before entering Spain. They involve social usage, e.g. *bastardo, alodio, embajador, feudal, gallardo, rico*; words connected with feelings and emotions such as *aleve, desmayar, escarnecer, fresco, lozano, orgullo, ufano*. Domestic and everyday life gave *blanco, ganso, guisar, sala, tapa*. Borrowings of warlike terms were frequent, e.g. *banda, bandido, espuela, estaca, estribo, guardia, guerra, heraldo, robar, rapar, tregua, yelmo*. Agricultural terms are few: *brotar, parra* ('vine'). Clothing terms include *cofia, falda*, O. Sp. *huesa* ('high boot'), *ropa*. One adjectival suffix is Germanic *-ing* > *engo*, which appears in the hybrid *realengo, abadengo*, or the medieval place-name *Villa Albarenga*.

V The Muslims

In 711 the Muslims began their occupation of Spain and nearly 300 years of Visigothic rule came to an abrupt end. This was the biggest single event in the history of Christian Spain.[1]

The immense impact of the Muslim occupation on the life of Christian Spain at all levels is naturally reflected in the language. The linguistic influence of Arabic on Spanish is most noticeable in the area of lexicography (some 4,000 words). Arabic terms often replaced Latin ones. Examples of Arabic loan-words in different fields are (1) administration: *aduana*, 'customs', *alcalde*, 'mayor', *alguacil*, 'constable'; (2) the sciences: *alambique*, 'still', *alcohol*, *algebra*, *alquimia*, 'alchemy', *auge*, 'meridian', *cenit*, 'zenith', *cifra*, 'cypher', *elexir*, *nadir*; (3) the home: *albornoz*, 'woollen cloak', *alfombra*, 'carpet', *alhaja*, 'jewel', *jarra*, 'jug, jar', *taza*, 'cup'; (4) agriculture and market-gardening: *aceituna*, 'olive', *acequia*, 'irrigation ditch', *albaricoque*, 'apricot' (Latin *praecoquus*), *albérchigo*, 'peach' (originally from Latin *malum persicum* but transmitted through Arabic), *alcachofa*, 'artichoke', *algarroba*, 'carob bean', *algodón*, 'cotton', *aljibe*, 'cistern', *arroz*, 'rice', *azafrán*, 'saffron', *azúcar*, 'sugar', *azucena*, 'white lily', *berenjena*, 'egg-plant, aubergine', *naranja*, 'orange', *noria*, 'irrigation wheel', *zanahoria*, 'carrot'; (5) architecture, art and music:[2] *ajimez*, 'arched window with central pillar', *albañil*, 'mason', *adufe*, 'timbrel, tambourine', *azotea*, 'flat roof of a house', *zaguán*, 'porch', *albogue*, 'shepherd's flute', *añafil*, 'trumpet', *laúd*, 'lute', *tambor*, 'drum'; (6) military terms which reflect centuries of raids, battles and campaigns between the Christians and Muslims and the adoption by the Christians of features of Hispano-Arabic military organization and tactics: *adarga*, 'leather shield', *alarde*, 'review of soldiers, parade', *alcaide*, 'governor of castle or fort', *alférez*, 'lieutenant, ensign', *atalaya*, 'watchtower', *rebato*, 'unexpected attack', *zaga*, 'rearguard'.

Adjectives are few, among them *baldío*, 'untilled, uncultivated', *carmesí*, 'crimson', *mezquino*, 'mean, poor'. Verbs include *halagar*, 'cajole, flatter', *recamar*, 'embroider', *acicalar*, 'polish'. Other words of Arabic origin are *hasta*, 'until', *ojalá*, 'would that . . .'. The great majority of loan-words, however, are nouns. Many of these, it will

---

[1] For historical accounts of the Muslim invasion of Spain and its consequences, see Chapters 2 and 3.

[2] For an account of Arabic musical instruments used in Christian Spain in the Middle Ages, see Chapter 12, section II.

have been noticed, start with *al-*, the Arabic definite article which was taken over together with the loan-word.

In the field of place-names the Arabic influence in Spain is also great. It is to a certain extent possible to use these place-names to distinguish different ethnic groups amongst the invaders – such as for instance the Berbers, whose settlements bear such names as Ginete, Mager, Zuares, Gomara, Orba – all Berber tribal names. Most place-names are descriptive: Alarba (prov. of Saragossa – 'the Wednesday', the understood meaning being 'the Wednesday market'), Albacete ('the plain'), Alcalá (appearing in ten provinces, with the meaning of 'the castle'), Alcántara (in three provinces – 'the bridge'), Alcázar (in five provinces – 'the palace'), Alcudia (in eight provinces – 'the hill'), Algeciras (Cádiz – 'the islands'), Algarbe (in two provinces – 'the west'), Almadraba (in three provinces – 'tunny-fishery'), Almoster (Tarragona – 'the monastery' – an example of a hybrid form, with Arabic article and Romance noun). The noun (*al-*)*calá* also appears in Calatayud ('Job's castle'), Calatañazor (prov. of Soria – 'castle of the eagles'). *Wadi*, 'river', appears in Guadalajara ('stony-bedded river'), Guadalquivir ('great river'), Guadalaviar ('white river'), Guadarrama ('sandy-bedded river'). Hybrid place-names also occur, e.g. with L. *lupus*: Guadalupe (prov. of Cáceres – 'wolf-river'), Guadalcanal (prov. of Seville – 'river adjoining the canal'). *Jabal*, 'hill', is also present in such names as Gibraleón (prov. of Huelva – 'hill of the springs'), Gibralfaro (Málaga – 'hill of the lighthouse' – another hybrid, including Romance *faro*) and Gibraltar ('hill of Tariq' – one of the first Muslim generals to cross the Straits to Spain in 711). Arabic *medina*, 'town', appears in Medinaceli (prov. of Soria – 'town of Salim'), Medinilla (in four provinces – 'little town'), or simply Medina (in four provinces). Other place-names allude to regions, such as La Mancha in Castilla la Nueva ('the high plateau'), or to parts of towns or estates, e.g. Rambla(s), Rambleta ('sandpit or sandy beach'; the latter two forms occur some ninety-five times in Spain).

It would be misleading to assume that loan-words and names form the only Arabic constituent element in Spanish. Especially in the thirteenth century, turns of phrase in written Spanish are traceable to Arabic constructions (e.g. *como sodes sabidor*; *dar salto* in the *Poema de Mio Cid*). In modern Spanish the majority of such calques have been lost, though some still exist (e.g. the emphatic construction *burla burlando, calla callando*).

VI The Emergence of Castilian

Castilian, destined to become the standard language of Spain and the Spanish empire in America, started as a local Spanish medieval dialect spoken in the county of Castile, originally a small region north of Burgos. In the Middle Ages four main dialects of Spanish can be distinguished. One was Mozarabic, the archaic form of Spanish Romance spoken by the Christians who elected after 711 to remain under Moorish rule. It is known to us mostly through place-names, through small fragments of song, and through Arabic borrowings from Romance. Because of its isolation it preserved for a long time features of Spanish as this was spoken in the Peninsula in late Visigothic times. Mozarabic disappeared as a result of the process of Christian reconquest. It persisted, however, among the Mozarabic community of Toledo into the thirteenth century.

Aragonese was the form of Spanish spoken in the Middle Ages in the territories of the kingdom of Aragon proper, whose capital was at Saragossa. Between it and the Mediterranean were the lands of the Catalan-speaking county of Barcelona. Aragonese was also spoken and written (along with Basque and, later, French) in the small Pyrenean kingdom of Navarre. To the west, beyond the county of Castile, was the region, more or less coextensive with the old kingdom of León, where the Leonese dialects were spoken over a wide area.

Aragonese and Leonese had many features in common as against Castilian, so that Castilian may be seen as a kind of wedge of linguistic and especially phonetic particularism driving ever deeper into the more or less uniform traditional speech patterns of the Peninsula and cutting off the language of León from that of Aragon. The linguistic expansion of the Castilian dialect was due to the political expansion of Castile. In the tenth century this dialect was spoken only in a restricted area running south from Santander to the banks of the Duero, south of Burgos. By the early thirteenth century it had been carried by the Reconquest far to the south of Toledo. Later in the same century, after the conquest and settlement of Andalusia by Ferdinand III of Castile, Castilian was spoken in most of Andalusia, too. At the same time it began to expand eastwards and westwards at the expense of the Aragonese and Leonese dialects respectively.

The reason why a dialect that was phonetically rather different from the rest of Spanish Romance developed in the county of Castile may be traceable to contact with Basque. The county bordered in the east on the Basque-speaking regions and the Castilians themselves were once, perhaps, Basque speakers. When they abandoned Basque for Spanish Romance they adapted, it is supposed, some features of the Basque phonemic system to Romance. Thus Castilian treats Latin initial *f-* in a special way. Basque did not possess this Latin sound. When it borrows from Latin it either drops the *f-* altogether (*ficu(m)* > Basque *iko*) or replaces it with a *b-* or a *p-* (*festa(m)* > Basque *pesta*). The Castilians, unlike the people of Aragon and León, also evidently had difficulty with Latin *f-*. The best they could usually do was to produce an aspirated sound, something like English 'h'. Thus *facere* > *hacer*, *fabulare* > *hablar*, with the *h-* strongly sounded. They evidently did not find the Latin initial *f-* so difficult when, for example, it was followed by a diphthong like *-ue-* from Latin accented *ŏ* (e.g. *fŏnte(m)* > *fuente*, *fŏru(m)* > *fuero*). Aragonese and Leonese can produce the Latin *f-* under all conditions, e.g. *fillo* (Cast. *hijo*), *fermoso* (Cast. *hermoso*). There are a number of other phonetic features which distinguished Castilian from Leonese and Aragonese. The Spanish diphthong from Latin stressed *ŏ* and *ĕ* (*ie* and *ue*) often does not occur in Castilian when a palatal 'yod' (*y*) sound is present immediately afterwards; Leonese and Aragonese diphthongization is not affected by this – e.g. Arag. *vienga* (Cast. *venga*), Arag. *nueyt* (Cast. *noche*). In Castilian the Latin initial consonant group *cl-* produces a palatal result, analogous to English *ly*, written *ll-*, but the other dialects may keep it or make it into a voiceless palatal sibilant, a sound like English '*sh*' in 'shall' or Portuguese *ch* – e.g. Arag. *clamar*, Leonese *chamar* (Cast. *llamar*). Castilian also palatalizes Latin *pl-* and *fl-* (*planu(m)* > *llano*, *flore(m)* > *flor*). The other dialects may keep the Latin group – e.g. Arag. *plano*. Another Latin consonant group, *-ct-*, palatalizes to give *-ch-* in Castilian. In Aragonese the process is only partly completed to give *-it-* – e.g. Arag. *feito* (Cast. *hecho*): *g-* before *e* and *i* and *j-* before all vowels were both pronounced [*y*] in Late Latin. Castilian often dropped this [*y*] but the other dialects did not (*januariu(m)* > Cast. *enero*, Arag. *genero*; *germanu(m)* > Cast. *(h)ermano*, Leonese *iermano*). The later stages of the palatalization by which Latin *-li-* eventually gives Castilian *-j-* did not take place in the other dialects – e.g. *filiu(m)* > Cast. *hijo*, Leonese *fillo*.

There were also marked morphological differences between Castilian and the other two dialects. Aragonese used *qui* for *que*. It had a possessive adjectival form *lur*, *lures* (Cast. *su*, *sus*) and a dative pronoun *li*, *lis* (Cast. *le*, *les*). It dropped final *-e* in adverbs to give *-ment*. It tended to regularize irregular verbal forms. Until the end of the fifteenth century Aragonese was the language of the chancery of the kingdom of Aragon and was used in documents issued at Saragossa even in the time of Ferdinand the Catholic before it was ousted by Castilian. In modern times the Aragonese dialect has virtually disappeared, surviving precariously only in some remote Pyrenean valleys.

Leonese, which included (and includes) a considerable number of sub-dialects, was always subject to the influence of Galician-Portuguese in the west and to ever-increasing linguistic pressure from Castilian in the east. Special features of Leonese include the development of diphthongized forms *ia* (Cast. *ie*) and *uo* or *ua* (Cast. *ue*). It shows a tendency to prefer *-u* for Cast. *-o* (*maridu*) and *-i* for Cast. *-e* (*esti*). It keeps the article with the possessive pronoun adjective. In modern Leonese the prepositions *con* and *en* are assimilated to the article: *ena* (Cast. *en la*), *conno* (Cast. *con lo*). A suffix form *-ín* is favoured (*sobrín*). The *-ra* forms of the verb still retain the pluperfect indicative meaning that it is largely lost in Castilian. The facts of geography served to keep Leonese alive and it has achieved some literary status. In the sixteenth century Spanish playwrights imitated for comic rustic effect the form of the dialect spoken by the shepherds near Salamanca (*sayagués*). The *montañés* of Santander is imitated by the nineteenth-century novelist Pereda. The poet Gabriel y Galán (1870–1905) tried to capture the essence of *extremeño* (the form of the Leonese dialect used in Extremadura) in his *El Cristu benditu*. The dialect, in its Asturian form (the most archaizing of all modern Spanish dialects), still survives in the valleys of the Cantabrian range and in some other pockets but, like Aragonese, it is in full retreat.

The development of Castilian as the literary language of most of Spain began in the thirteenth century. There then began to emerge a self-conscious attitude towards the vernacular which saw in it one of the marks of nationhood. Alfonso X of Castile ('the Wise', reigned 1252–84) played a considerable part in this movement. Until his time, serious works were still written in Latin but Alfonso caused historical writings to be written in the Castilian vernacular. His *Crónica general* involved much translation of earlier chronicles and other writings from the Latin and he also instigated the translation into 'el nuestro lenguaje de Castiela' of a variety of scientific and other writings. His chancery dropped the use of Latin so that Castilian now became the official written language of the administration. This association of nationalism with the use of the Castilian vernacular was not all gain. Latin was still the international language of European learning and of the Church but Spaniards seem increasingly to have thought that the vernacular was good enough for them; complaints of ignorance of Latin even among men of culture and ecclesiastics in Spain are increasingly heard during the later Middle Ages.

How did Castilian (which we may now properly refer to as 'Spanish'), as spoken at the end of the Middle Ages, compare with modern Spanish? In one way it was already surprisingly near the latter, for if we look at a piece of thirteenth- or fourteenth-century Spanish prose or poetry it is very much easier to understand on the basis of a knowledge of the modern language alone than a similar work in Middle English or Old French would be. Old Spanish did, however, contain then a number of consonantal sounds that were later to disappear. Thus -s- and -z- between vowels were pronounced 'voiced', like English z and dz respectively, e.g. in rosa as in Eng. pause, dezir as in Eng. adze. When voiceless, these sounds were represented in writing by -ss- and -ç-; -ç- had the sound of Eng. ts, or Italian -z- (as in forza). Voiceless -x-, as in dixo (modern dijo), had the sound of Eng. sh; its voiced equivalent, j, had the sound of Eng. j (as in jury) except between vowels when it perhaps sounded as the z in Eng. azure. The sounds of b and v were still distinguished. H- was still aspirated in large parts of Spain but the sound was already disappearing in Old Castile.

In the area of morphology and syntax late medieval Spanish differed quite substantially from its Golden Age and modern forms. In many cases various alternative ways of saying things still coexisted because a final choice had not yet been made. Literary works that consciously imitated popular speech, like the Archpriest of Hita's Libro de Buen Amor (c. 1343) or the Archpriest of Talavera's El Corbacho (c. 1438), use a language also substantially different from that used by writers who followed cultured or learned norms. Up to the end of the medieval period the third person dative pronoun ge (modern se) was in regular use. The Latin second personal plural verbal termination -tis > -des (fabulatis > fablades) began to disappear in the fourteenth century. Imperfect indicative endings in íe(n) were finally supplanted by the alternative and earlier form ía(n). The future subjunctive was still regularly used. The pluperfect indicative tense from the Latin was still used indicatively (amaveram > amara, 'I had loved') but it also occurs subjunctively in 'if' clauses implying negation. In Old Spanish the passive is normally formed by using ser with the past participle but the modern reflexive form as a substitute for a true passive form is already found.

Haber is not yet reduced merely to its present auxiliary function and still has the possessive and other meanings later enjoyed solely by *tener*. Throughout most of the medieval period *ser* and *estar* could both be used to indicate location or condition but towards the end of the Middle Ages there is a tendency to allocate to each its modern functions.

Medieval Spanish, in addition to its borrowings from Arabic, also borrowed extensively from French. These borrowings had historical and cultural causes. The ecclesiastical reforms instigated by French Cluniacs in the late eleventh century brought many French monks to Spain (*fraile, monje, deán*). Most of the pilgrims who thronged the pilgrim route to Santiago de Compostela were French-speaking (*mesón, vianda, manjar*). Another source of French influence on vocabulary was the French settlers (*francos*) attracted to Spain by the special privileges the Christian Spanish kings offered. Chivalry and courtliness also supplied medieval Spanish with many terms of French origin – *homenaje, linaje, fonta* ('dishonour'), *palafré, deleyt, vergel, doncel, damisela, madama, salvaje*. In the twelfth century French influence led, for a time, to a large-scale dropping of the *-e* after a consonant combination (*mont, cort, part*) but this extreme apocope was eliminated again in the fourteenth century. Not all these medieval borrowings from the French survive, e.g. *calonge* (*canónigo*), *follía* (*locura*), *sage* (*sabio*). One source of French borrowings in the literary language of the fifteenth century was the popularity of prose translations of French Arthurian romances and works written under the influence of French courtly practice, like Gutierre Díez de Games's *El Victorial*. Many of these borrowings, too, did not take permanent root in the language.

The great age of Spanish lexicographical borrowings from Italian was to come after the Middle Ages but significant numbers of terms concerning literature, the arts, military and naval warfare, and trade entered Spanish (sometimes through the medium of Catalan) in the fourteenth and fifteenth centuries: e.g. *novela, estrambote, soneto*, probably *belleza, lombarda/bombarda, cañón, piloto, esquife, brújula* (It. *bussola*), *ducado, florín* (It. *fiorino* via Catalan), *banco* (in its financial sense), *madona, micer* (It. *messer*), *lontano*. Catalan itself was also the source of a number of certain or probable borrowings: e.g. *remolcar, almete* ('helmet'), *rosicler, clavel, papel, entremés, pólvora, motejar*. Galician-Portuguese was, for a long time, the language in which lyric poetry was written even by Spaniards and this led to a degree of bilingualism. Old Spanish *portogalés* was replaced by Port. *portugués, Lisbona* by *Lisboa*. Spanish *alguien* is said to be from Port. *alguem, echar de menos* from Port. *achar menos*. Already some words connected with the sea and shipping were borrowed from the Portuguese – *pleamar* (Port. *prea mar* < Fr. *pleine mer*), *angra, almeja* (Port. *amêijoa*).

The most important source of loan-words borrowed by literary Spanish in the later Middle Ages was Classical Latin. In the fifteenth century, in particular, a veritable torrent of such Latinisms was incorporated into the language of literature. These learned borrowings (*cultismos*) are readily recognizable because they were transcribed from the Latin with the minimum of phonetic modification to fit Spanish Romance and do not exhibit the characteristic consonantal and vocalic modifications imposed by Spanish on orally transmitted words of Latin origin. The urge of Spanish fifteenth-century poets and prose-writers to Latinize the vocabulary (and syntax) of their language reflects an awareness (though not a very deep understanding) of the enthusiasm of the Italian humanists for following classical linguistic and stylistic models. This led, in Spain, to a demand for vernacular translations of the Latin classics which, in turn, brought recognition of the fact that the traditional language's vocabulary in particular was inadequate without enrichment to enable the task of translation to be adequately performed. But admiration for the Latin poetic classics also brought with it a desire (notably illustrated in the poetry of Juan de Mena, 1411–56) to dignify the poetic language by making it more Latinate in vocabulary and structure. Many of these fifteenth-century Latin loan-words passed permanently into the language then, or did so when they were taken up again by Fernando de Herrera (1534–97), in his search to dignify the language of poetry, and by the *culterano* poets of the seventeenth century. Examples of fifteenth-century borrowings of this kind are *disolver, estilo, rubicundo, nocturno, lento, digno, sublime, generoso* and a host of others. A considerable number of such borrowings reveal their origin because they bear the stress accent on the antepenultimate syllable, contrary to normal Spanish stress rules – *trémulo, ígneo, itálico, ínclito, ínfimo*. The Latinizing writers also showed a special fondness for Latinate adjectival suffixes like *-al* and *-ífico*. A number of these fifteenth-century borrowings from Latin did not, however, survive, Spanish eventually preferring the traditional alternative, e.g. *sciente* (*sabio*), *punir* (*castigar*), *menstruo* (*mensual*), *fuscado* (*oscuro*), *pluvia* (*lluvia*).

Parallel attempts to Latinize syntax are to be seen in the general tendency to shift verbs to the end of clauses and sentences and in other departures from the normal word order of Spanish (hyperbaton), such as the separation of adjectives from their nouns; Mena thus could write 'a la moderna volviendo me rueda' for 'volviéndome a la moderna rueda'. Another notable feature of the style of this time was its over-fondness for using linked pairs of synonyms when there was no logical call to do so – a device which weakened rather than strengthened thought. But this was derived from manuals of rhetoric rather than from imitation of Classical Latin texts. It may fairly be said of the Latinizers of the fifteenth century that they grasped only the surface of Italian humanism's linguistic attitudes and failed to understand what lay behind these. There was a lack of measure about their attempted linguistic innovations, which were too much for the language to absorb. They frequently, too, incongruously mingled medieval linguistic usages of the humbler sort with their Latinisms. Spain did not follow the Italian humanists in the latters' preference for using Latin, not the vernacular, as the language of learned and scholarly writings. But the movement did amplify Spanish vocabulary usefully and make it more flexible. Historically speaking, the premature attempt to Latinize the language anticipated the *culterano* movement of the seventeenth century in a striking way.

VII Golden Age Spanish

During the historical period 1474–1700 the Spanish language finally acquired the main phonetic characteristics it retains today. The aspirated *h-*, lost before the end of the Middle Ages in Old Castile, disappeared everywhere in the Castilian-speaking areas except for parts of Andalusia, where it is still kept. The aspirated sound was still recognized in the poetry of Luis de León and, in 1578, was described as a feature which then differentiated the speech of Toledo from that of Burgos; but it was finally lost early in the seventeenth century. The phonetic distinction between *b* and *v* was lost in Old Castile by 1558 and everywhere else in the seventeenth century. The distinction between voiced -*s*- and -*z*- on the one hand and voiceless -*ss*- and -*ç*- on the other was also lost, both voiced sounds becoming unvoiced so that the *s* in *rosa* now sounded like that in English *purse*, while the *z* of *dezir* (= Eng. *dz*) and the *ç* of *braço* (= Eng. *ts*), after losing their initial 'stop' (i.e. occlusive) element, merged as a single voiceless sibilant. The development was completed before the end of the sixteenth century: though the orthographical symbols -*z*- and -*ç*- continued to be used sporadically in print they no longer represented separate sounds. This sibilant is that which gave rise to the characteristic 'lisp' (*th* as in Eng. *think*) of Castilian *c* before *e* and *i* and *z* in all other positions. It may therefore, in the north of the Peninsula, have had an element of lisp about it from the beginning as its development there was different from that of the *s* in *rosa*. The lisp element seems to have been accentuated gradually at the expense of the sibilant quality so that both *z* and *ç*, in the seventeenth century, represented a kind of voiceless *th* sound. Thus Castilian *th* and *s* are now separate phonemes, save in most of Andalusia where *s* (if not aspirated) and *z/c* both sound as *th* or as *s* according to locality. In Castile *s* was itself pronounced with the tip of the tongue close to the upper gums giving it a sound something like a weak English *sh* as in *shame* (cacuminal *s*). In Andalusia the *s* generally was more like the *s* in English *silver*. This distinction between the speech of Castile and that of Andalusia also survives today.

X retained its medieval unvoiced palatal character (like *sh* in English *dish*) until the seventeenth century, as is shown by the transcriptions of the proper name Quixote into French (Quichotte) and Italian (Chisciotte) respectively. But, in vulgar speech, the point of articulation was already further back in the mouth producing the aspirated velar sound, like the *ch* in Scottish *loch*, of the modern Spanish *j*. By the end of the third decade this phonetic vulgarism had succeeded in imposing itself on the cultured language of Castile, the old medieval sound remaining only in some of the Spanish dialects.

Voiced *g* before *e*, *i* and *j* (as in English *George* or French *jour*) were also unvoiced. This change gave them the same value, from about 1550 onwards, as *x* (see above), whose history they thereafter followed. In general, then, the history of Spanish sounds in the Golden Age is one of the unvoicing of voiced sibilants and of the phonetics of Old Castile gradually imposing themselves on the whole Castilian-speaking area with Andalusia going its own independent way, particularly as far as the sibilants were concerned.

Only some of the main morphological and syntactical changes that Spanish underwent in the Golden Age can be indicated here. In the verbal endings the second personal plurals in *-ades*, *-edes* and *-ides* were entirely replaced by the modern forms *-áis*, *-éis*, *-ís* except when the ending was unaccented, when *-des* was retained (*amábades*, *dijéredes*, *viviéssedes*) alongside the reduced forms (*amábais*, *dijéreis*, *viviéseis*) until the late seventeenth century. In the imperative plural the metathesis of the verbal ending with a following pronoun was still normal – *dadnos* > *dandos*, *dadla* > *dalda*, *habladle* > *hablalde*. Analogously welded were an infinitive and a following pronoun object but here the infinitive -*r* and the *l*- of the pronoun were assimilated to give -*ll*- (e.g. *comello, decillas* for *comerlo, decirlas*). The nominative pronouns *nos* and *vos* were replaced by the forms, sporadically used in the later medieval language, *nosotros* and *vosotros*. The old third person dative pronoun *ge* disappears after *c.* 1530, being replaced by *se*. Unaccented pronouns at the beginning of a sentence or clause continue to follow the verb, e.g. 'hízolo así el amo', but the practice of putting them before the verb in these situations gradually extended. The demonstrative forms *aqueste, aquese,* vulgarisms in the modern language, remained in regular use in the Golden Age. The relative *quien,* formerly invariable, developed the plural form *quienes,* which, however, was regarded as inelegant until the seventeenth century. Modern Spanish uncertainty about the treatment of the accusative and dative pronouns *lo, la, le* in singular and plural situations is already apparent in the Golden Age. The medieval usage of *le, les* as the normal dative form continued in the sixteenth century but, in the courtly and literary language of the Golden Age, *le* is often also used in an accusative role while, especially in seventeenth-century literature, *la* and *las* are often found as feminine datives. During the sixteenth century the Latin superlative ending -*ísimo* became accepted. The diminutive -*uelo* was much more common in Golden Age Spanish than it is today.

The most important syntactical developments that occurred in Spanish during the Golden Age were those affecting the verb. At the beginning of the period both *haber* and *tener* were still more or less synonyms, *haber* sharing a transitive possessive meaning with *tener,* though Juan de Valdés (*c.* 1535) already regarded *haber* used transitively this way as archaic. By the seventeenth century this use of *haber* was no longer acceptable. As auxiliary verbs in active tenses employed with a past participle *haber* and *ser* (the latter only in the case of intransitive and reflexive verbs) also both continued to be used in the first half of the sixteenth century: Valdés thus wrote 'los moços son idos a comer y nos an dexado solos'. But, by the second half of that century, this auxiliary function was already largely reserved for *haber*.

The modern distinction between the functions of *ser* and *estar* was less firmly established than now. *Ser* was thus used occasionally to refer to situations of place even well into the seventeenth century. It could also still be used, with a past participle, to describe a completed passive state alternatively with *estar,* e.g. *es hecho, es escrito*; but this function gradually became restricted to *estar* as now. Examples of the characteristic Spanish 'reflexive' passive with *se* ('los vinos que en esta ciudad *se venden*' – *Lazarillo de Tormes*) had occurred in the language from the earliest times alongside the normal passive form – auxiliary plus past participle ('*son* vendidos'). This 'reflexive' form of the passive spread rapidly in the Golden Age.

In the medieval language verbal forms derived from the Latin pluperfect indicative (*amaram* > *amara*, 'I had loved') had retained their pluperfect indicative sense but quite early in the sixteenth century this use was censured as archaic, the composed form *había amado* being preferred. In the sixteenth century the *amara* form was still used in both halves of conditional sentences treating past unreality as a pluperfect subjunctive (*si tuviera, diera*) but, in the seventeenth century, composed forms of the pluperfect subjunctive made with an auxiliary (*hubiese amado* or *hubiera amado*) also increasingly took over. As this usage developed in the seventeenth century *amara* became increasingly used as an *imperfect* subjunctive alongside the traditional imperfect subjunctive form in *-ase, -iese*.

A new Golden Age usage concerns *en* followed by the gerund. In the earlier language this referred to a past action simultaneous with that in the main clause, e.g. *en llegando, vimos*, 'as we arrived, we saw'. In the Golden Age *en* plus gerund came to refer to an action immediately previous to that in the main clause, so that the same phrase meant 'having arrived, we saw'.

The custom of using *a* accusatively before nouns or pronouns referring to persons (or personified things) became increasingly frequent during the Golden Age, particularly where its absence led to doubts as to which was the subject and which the object (as in 'el varón prudente ama la justicia' cited by Juan de Valdés). But this 'personal *a*' was not yet mandatory, even in the first half of the seventeenth century. In Golden Age Spanish, too, the use of prepositions still differed quite considerably from modern usage. In general, compared with the modern language, Spanish syntax at this time was much less rigid in its ideas of correct usage; the influence of the spoken language on the written language was stronger than it would later be.

The history of forms of personal address in the Golden Age requires special attention; Spanish obsession with modes of address and their social implications at this time was such that the significance of forms of address in literature may otherwise pass unnoticed by the modern reader. The singular *tú* and the plural *vos*, at the beginning of the Golden Age, satisfied the requirements of direct address; *tú* was used to address familiars or inferiors and *vos* (used with the second person plural form of the verb even when only one person was involved) to address superiors, in formal correspondence and the like. When more than one person was involved the pronoun *vosotros* was employed to indicate plurality. Sometimes in literature, e.g. in *La tragicomedia de Calisto y Melibea, tú* is regularly used even when a servant is addressing a master, or the bawd Celestina a noble lady, but this is due to the influence of humanistic Latin usage. Quite soon, however, *vos* became devalued through over-use and was avoided except when addressing inferiors. *Vuestra merced* (with the third person of the verb) then became the most usual polite form of address. In the time of Juan de Valdés it was already shortened to *vuesa merced*. Because of the frequency of its use it is supposed that various further contractions were colloquially employed – *voacé, vuasted* (1617), *vusted* (1619) and *usted* (1620), the latter form finally being generally adopted – but the history of this development still presents unexplained problems. Other polite forms of address like *vuestra señoría* and *vuestra excelencia* were similarly abbreviated to *usía* and *vuecencia*.

Spanish vocabulary in the Golden Age was enriched by a great many borrowings of vocabulary from other languages. A distinction needs to be made here between the literary and the spoken language. As far as the language of poetry was concerned Fernando de Herrera (1534–97), in his attempts to ennoble poetic diction, took up again, though with infinitely more discrimination, the efforts of fifteenth-century Spanish poets and others to achieve linguistic dignity by copious borrowings from Latin; examples of this aspect of Herrera's poetic diction are words like *crespo, ejercer, hórrido, horrísono, languideza, luxuriante, opreso, riel* ('small gold bar'), *rígido, rutilar, toroso* ('full of muscle'), etc. Most of Herrera's borrowings genuinely and for the most part permanently enriched the poetic language with needed additions to the range of its vocabulary. Herrera was also concerned to Latinize the sound and appearance of the language; he thus was particularly addicted to the Latin-sounding adjectival ending -*oso*. A feature of Herrera's Latinizing, too, was his fondness for semantic *cultismos* – that is the use of traditional words but with the meaning their etymons had originally had in literary Classical Latin but had lost in Spanish Romance, e.g. *traducir* (in the sense of 'to transport'), *absolver* ('to finish'), *repetir* ('to go back to'), *ya* (in the sense of Lat. *jam*). A good many of Herrera's Latinisms in fact already existed in sixteenth-century Italian poetic diction and were taken by him from that source. Herrera, unsuccessfully, also sought to reform Spanish orthography to make it conform more closely to the way it was pronounced at the end of the sixteenth century, partly by introducing the use of the apostrophe, grave and acute accents, the elimination of Latin *h-* and so on.

It has been noted that many of the Latinisms which earned Herrera criticism from traditionalists had already been recorded in the language much earlier – some even before the fifteenth century. What caused criticism was the frequency of their use by him. The same is even more the case with the *culterano* movement in Spanish poetry associated particularly with the name of Luis de Argote y Góngora (1561–1627). The highly Latinized poetic diction of Góngora in his *culterano* poems has been shown, in fact, to contain very few words that had never before been used in Spanish (*intonso, adolescente, advocar* appear to be possible examples of the latter). What shocked Góngora's critics, too, was the sheer frequency of his use of these *cultismos* so that, as Góngora intended, his Spanish looked and sounded more like Latin than anything previously attempted. But the words that his opponents like Quevedo cited as an abusive use of Latinisms (e.g. *canoro, crepúsculo, nocturno, vulto, meta, homicida*) nearly all already existed in the Spanish poetic tradition. Góngora's attempt to close the gap between Latin poetry and Spanish poetic diction, however, involved a great deal more than borrowings of vocabulary from Latin and semantic Latinisms. He also made a determined attempt to Latinize Spanish syntax and Spanish poetic style; again, there were usually sporadic precedents for these characteristics of his work in earlier poetry. Very long statements, broken by the interpolation of parentheses (and sometimes parentheses within parentheses) and continuous transpositions of the logical order of words and phrases (*hyperbata*) made it necessary to 'parse' Góngora's poetry like Latin verse to get at its meaning. He made much use of the so-called 'Greek accusative' or accusative of respect (e.g. 'desnuda el pecho anda ella') and the ablative absolute ('herido el blanco pie del hierro breve' ('the white foot having been wounded'). Various syntactical formulae designed to add a symmetrical quality to the verse while at the same time making it possible to proliferate new images and ideas not required by logical statement were also a feature of Gongorine syntax: e.g. *A, si no B* ('que en voces, si no métricas, suaves'); *no B, sino A* ('al mar fiando, al viento, / no aromáticos leños, sino alados') and other similar permutations. The *culterano* style spread rapidly both during Góngora's time and after it, many of its most vehement critics ending up by adopting it. It is to be found in the language of some court preachers like Hortensio Félix Paravicino y Aliaga (1580–1633) and, as a form of preciosity, was used in the language of the lettered and ladies and gentlemen of the court. It became, to a greater or lesser degree, a general characteristic of poetic style in the seventeenth century.

French, an abundant contributor to medieval Spanish vocabulary, was a great deal less important during the Golden Age, but the influence of the French-speaking Burgundian court tradition from the time of Charles V was responsible for the introduction of terms like *ujier* (Fr. *huissier*), *banquete, moda, billete*, while military and nautical words like *carabina, bagaje, chalupa, babor* (Fr. *babord*), *estribor, echar a pique* and a few foods (e.g. *fresa* and *crema*) are borrowings from the French, as was *dintel* (Fr. *lintel*).

The influence of Catalan, too, was now very much reduced since Catalan had ceased to be an important language of literature or maritime trade. Portuguese was a more significant Peninsular contributor of neologisms to the Spanish Golden Age vocabulary. *Mermelada, caramelo, cariño* (probably) and the verb *despejar* are examples of Portuguese borrowings. After the annexation of Portugal in 1580 Portuguese became for a time a fashionable language at the Spanish court. Borrowings like *sarao* (Port. *serão*) and, probably, *vaivén* (Port. *vaivém*) belong to this period. Portuguese was naturally an important transmitter of Orientalisms to Spanish, e.g. Chinese *cha* (later replaced by *té* from another Chinese dialect, through Dutch), *biombo*.

It was, however, Italian which provided far and away the most important number of loan-words to Spanish during the Golden Age. These arose mostly from Spanish military and political involvement in Italy, and from Spanish familiarity at all levels with life there; most important of all, there was mass borrowing of terms relating to the arts. The first three causes supply *coronel* (It. *colonello*), *centinela, atacar, asalto, brigantín, fragata, salchicha* (It. *salciccia*), *cortesano, chulo* (It. *fanciullo*), *canalla, charlar, hipócrita, carnaval*. Technical and descriptive terms relating to all the arts entered Spanish in the Golden Age such as *novelador, esdrújulo, jornada* (in the sense of 'an act in a play'), *comedia, comediante, saltimbanco, diseño, modelo, claroscuro*, the colour *ultramarino, balcón, cúpula, galería, muralla* (It. *muraglia*), *pórtico, violín, concierto*, etc. A number of Italian loan-words do not lend themselves to classification, e.g. *aguantar, estropear* (It. *stroppiare*), *fracaso, bizarro* (in the sense of 'cholerical' or 'bold').

The most striking additions to Spanish Golden Age vocabulary were of course, the loan-words borrowed from the Amerindian languages by the Spanish discoverers and settlers. These reflect linguistically the historical fact that (except in Brazil) Spaniards were the first Europeans to establish and maintain culture contacts with the American Indians. Through Spanish many of these loan-words were to pass into the vocabulary of the other European languages. At first, as the Portuguese had done earlier in western Africa, the Spaniards, faced with the new flora, fauna, culture and political and religious institutions of America, tended to use those Spanish words in the traditional lexicon which seemed nearest the new object to be named. But soon the need for more exactness as well as greater awareness of the newness and difference of these objects led to the borrowing of the corresponding Indian words for them. It should be noted, though, that only a small proportion of the Indian loan-words commonly used in America by the Spanish settlers passed into the everyday speech of metropolitan Spain, though many more may be found in specialist books by historians and others concerned with the American scene. Reference here will only be made to those Amerindian loan-words which, in the sixteenth and seventeenth centuries, passed into the spoken and literary language of Spain.

The first of these borrowings were naturally made from Arawak, the native language of some of the main Caribbean islands. Arawak gave *canoa* and *cazabe* ('manioc bread') – both recorded in the year of the Discovery (1492). Other borrowings were *batata* ('sweet potato'), *bohío* ('Indian hut'), *cacique*, *hamaca*, *huracán*, *iguana*, *maíz* (from Arawak *mahís*), *(e)naguas* (originally describing the short cotton skirts worn by the Indian women of Santo Domingo), *sabana* ('savannah'), etc. Carib, the language of some of the Caribbean islands and parts of the adjacent mainland, gave a few words for objects not already accounted for by borrowings from Arawak, e.g. *manatí*, *piragua* and perhaps *caimán* ('alligator'). The most striking Carib borrowing was the racial name itself which occurs in the variant forms *caribe*, *caníbal*. The ferocious Caribs were supposedly eaters of human flesh and it is with this meaning that their name has passed into Spanish and many other languages. From Nahuatl, the lingua franca of the Mexican empire at the time of its conquest, many borrowings were made. Their origin is often indicated by the hispanization of the Nahuatl suffix -*atl* > Sp. -*ate*, e.g. *aguacate* ('avocado pear'), *cacahuete*, *chocolate*, *tomate*, etc. Quechua, after the discovery and conquest of Peru, supplied a great many loan-words to denote the flora and fauna and the Inca institutions of that region but few Quechua borrowings passed into everyday Peninsular Spanish; one example of a Quechua borrowing was *coca* ('coca plant') – from which *cocaína* is a derivative – and probably *quina* ('quinine plant'). Quechua borrowings are, of course, frequent in works that describe the Inca empire and its institutions like the *Comentarios reales* of El Inca Garcilaso de la Vega. The Quechua word for 'potato' – *papa* – crossed with the Arawak loan-word for 'sweet potato' – *batata* (1519) – to give Sp. *patata*. The large Tupi–Guaraní group of languages, spoken in the great river basins from the Amazon southwards, gave a number of loan-words to Golden Age Spanish, some of them through the Portuguese of Brazil. Examples are *ananás, jaguar* (replacing the older *tigre* used by the *conquistadores*), *maracá, tiburón* and, perhaps, *gaucho*.

Arising out of the great interest of Golden Age Spaniards in low life the language was also influenced by *germanía*, the argot of criminals and all those who lived collectively outside the law. The word probably originates in the Catalan of Valencia (*germá*, 'brother') and was first applied there to brotherhoods of thieves and professional ruffians. Later it came to be used to designate their private language. A few characteristic terms of *germanía* (e.g. *cadira*, 'chair') come from Valencian but the sources of this argot are many and include French and Arabic as well as many common Spanish words used with a specialized slang meaning. The first surviving appearance of *germanía* in literature is in a poetic dialogue by Rodrigo de Reinosa written very early in the sixteenth century. *Germanía* frequently appeared in Spanish literature thereafter, notably in Cervantes and Quevedo. Spanish borrowings from it include *columbrar* ('to spy out'), *garduño* ('sneak thief'), *hampa* ('the underworld'), *jácaro* ('rufián'), *jácara* (which first meant a gathering of rogues and was later also used to describe a comic ballad in *germanía*), *zafarse* ('to slip away').

Other low-life linguistic influences exploited by Spanish writers in the Golden Age include the Portuguese pidgin spoken by negro slaves, the dog Spanish of Moorish slaves and the rustic Leonese in which dramatists often made their peasant characters speak. Spaniards at this time were particularly sensitive to language and now had at their disposal a vastly expanded instrument of expression compared with that used by, say, their fourteenth-century forebears.

The way Spanish was used in Golden Age literature was naturally much affected by contemporary views about style and by the influence of rhetorical precept (studied as a matter of routine by all students of letters), as well as by current literary fashions. One example of the influence of a particular stylistic fashion on language – *culteranismo* – has already been discussed. Another long-drawn-out debate in the sixteenth century concerned the extent to which the literary language should or should not approximate to the language of everyday speech. In his *Diálogo de la lengua* (*c.* 1535) Juan de Valdés, in the Erasmian tradition, defended a simple natural style without affectation: 'escribo como hablo', he declared, though this must not, of course, be taken too literally. For Valdés the language of the Toledan courtiers was the authoritative norm. The popularity of the literary dialogue in the sixteenth century as a vehicle for the discussion of ideas gave continuing support to this naturalistic approach to the literary language. The latter was nowhere more pushed to extremes than in the writings of Santa Teresa, whose works represent the putting down on paper of the patterns of conversation of a gifted but comparatively uneducated woman seeking to express in colloquial language, as if she were actually speaking, difficult experiences and concepts. Her syntax frequently defies attempts to analyse it logically and her sentence structure reads more like recordings of improvised discourse than of an organized, controlled utterance. Her vocabulary is full of the phonetic and other vulgarisms of Old Castile in the sixteenth century.

Opposed to these developments were the many, like Antonio de Guevara (1480–1545), who held, in varying degrees, that the language of literature was, by definition, a very different instrument from the spoken language and should go out of its way to separate itself from the vulgarity of ordinary speech. Writers thus fashioned their style in accordance with the precepts of rhetoric using its 'flowers' and 'colours' to create a complicated prose often overladen with sheer weight of words piled up at the expense of clarity of meaning. Later in the period literary style settled down and much Spanish prose was modelled on the flowing, but balanced and controlled periods of Cicero. Ciceronian stylistic influence was furthered in the Jesuit schools and colleges; the Jesuits were heavily committed to Cicero as a master of style. Towards the end of the sixteenth century, however, the Ciceronian style was increasingly challenged by those who wished to imitate in Spanish the staccato, concise, epigrammatic style of Seneca, called in contemporary England 'the hopping style', where the object was to pack as much meaning as possible into as few words as possible. Rivalry between the disciples of Cicero's style and those of Seneca's style was common in Europe generally. Partly from a fondness for Seneca and Tacitus emerged the Spanish *conceptista* style of the seventeenth century to be seen, for example, in the prose and poetry of Francisco de Quevedo and in the prose of Baltasar Gracián. Here all the emphasis is on concision of language and the continuous employment of double or triple meanings for punning purposes. A particular mark of the *conceptista* style (closely related to the 'wit' of the English metaphysical poets) was frequent use of the rhetorical figure known as *catachresis* by which ideas or images apparently widely disparate in themselves, or in nature, are brought into forced association by logical sleight of hand, e.g. when Quevedo calls a galley-slave an 'escribano naval' because his oar can be imagined as writing on the water. But the explanation is never given. The reader must work out the conceit for himself. Though it is not, in practice, easy to distinguish between *culterano* and *conceptista* writing (Góngora was a master of *conceptismo* as well as of *culteranismo*), it is, very broadly speaking, true to say that *conceptismo*'s appeal was strictly intellectual while *culterano* writing, as seventeenth-century rhetoricians saw it, was a good deal concerned with external sensorial effects. Not all Spanish writers in the seventeenth century adopted either or both of these styles but it is notable how many of those, like Lope de Vega and Quevedo, who criticized the *culterano* style eventually ended up by using it. Not until the neo-classical movement of the eighteenth century rejected them did these two styles cease to be characteristic of much written Spanish.

VIII Peninsular Spanish since the Golden Age

The arrival of the French Bourbon dynasty on the Spanish throne (1700) prepared the way, under the influence of French rationalism, for an eighteenth-century reappraisal of the situation of the Spanish language as well as of Spanish institutions. The traditional literary styles inherited from the Golden Age were rejected by the innovators in accordance with the new cult of clarity, reason and elegant simplicity. Serious attention was given to establishing linguistic norms and to the study of the history of the language. The Real Academia Española, founded in 1714, at once set about producing its first dictionary (1726–39, six volumes), which became known as the *Diccionario de autoridades* because, for the first time, in addition to definitions, it gave some account of the history of usages by citing 'classical' Spanish writers as authorities, with supporting quotations. The Academy also sponsored spelling reforms and published a grammar of the language. Though never accorded the authority enjoyed by the Académie

Française, the Spanish Academy from the beginning helped to make educated Spaniards more linguistically self-conscious.

The prestige of French culture and French fashions in eighteenth-century Spain also led to a new large-scale introduction of French loan-words and expressions – a process satirized by contemporary writers like Iriarte and Cadalso. For those who admired the French prose style of the time, like Feijoo, traditional Spanish prose seemed marked by an 'afectación pueril'. Many of the eighteenth-century Gallicisms complained of, e.g. *alarmar, detalle, hacer ver, interesante, mamá, papá, resorte*, nevertheless took firm root in the language. Among eighteenth-century Gallicisms eventually rejected (at least officially though not always in common usage) were *arribar (llegar), comandar, jefe de obra (obra maestra), laqué, pitoyable*.

The Romantic movement of the nineteenth century also had a marked influence in particular on the language of literature. The popularity of the historical novel at this time, for example, brought with it a search for archaisms to supply a sense of period; the interest of the Romantics in popular culture led writers to cultivate the use of regional and dialectal vocabulary – a process carried to extremes in Estébanez Calderón's *Escenas andaluzas* (1847), a work often only partly intelligible to a reader unfamiliar with contemporary Andalusian speech. This interest in regionalisms and dialectalisms was to continue in the novels of Pereda and others and, notably with Gabriel y Galán (1870–1905), was taken up in poetry too. In the twentieth century, in a much more complex way, it is basic to the style of a novelist like Gabriel Miró (1879–1930), who exploited the resources of the regional-ist speech of the Levante. The Romantic movement in Spain witnessed, also, the disappearance after six centuries of the influence of traditional formal rhetoric on literary style: writers were no longer prepared to accept that what they set down on paper should be guided by and modelled on traditional paradigms and stylistic formulae handed down from the Latin tradition and believed to have universal application in supplying suitable 'forms' for any literary 'content'.

The development of the nineteenth-century realist and naturalist novel, too, also led to the entry into the language of literature of words, turns of speech, idioms and slang previously only heard in popular urban speech – a return, in a different way, to the traditions of Golden Age fictional prose writing. The realist author Pérez Galdós (1843–1920), when he came to write his novels, had complained that literary Spanish as he found it was ill equipped to reproduce, for example, the varied patterns and levels of everyday conversation. He did much to bring the two together. Conversely, notably in the verse of Rubén Darío, poets sought (as Herrera and Góngora had done) to renew from a variety of erudite sources a poetic diction which had come to seem too prosaic and conventional. Darío turned partly to Greek, e.g. *liróforo, propíleo, hipsípila, peplo,* as well as to other European languages in search of a new poetic vocabulary, often, too, using exotic proper names and place-names. Some members of the so-called Generation of 1898 also gave great attention to language: convinced that the authentic spirit of Spain was to be found in the Castilian countryside and in Spanish medieval and Golden Age literature they favoured *casticidad* in their language (a use of what was genuinely traditional and earthy). The process led to a fondness for archaisms and country terms and a desire to exploit the immense richness of the traditional language in names of things connected, in particular, with the countryside. Their style was deliberately low-keyed and was associated with a careful avoidance of anything except simple, direct forms of expression which were often, however, e.g. in the case of Azorín (1873–1967), the result of intense stylistic striving. The language of criticism and scholarship changed, too, at this time. It now sought precision, directness, simplicity and freshness while, at the same time, not fearing to coin neologisms when the existing vocabulary would not suffice. This victory is not, however, yet entirely won. A perhaps innate Spanish love of rhetoric (in its conventional sense) and a certain impatience with the need to define terms exactly is still discernible in some critical and scholarly writing and in oratory of all kinds. The influence of modern foreign philosophy in Spain and the need to express new abstract ideas has led to a perhaps excessive exploitation of the fact that, in Spanish, by placing the neuter article *lo* before an adjective or adjectival phrase, past participle, noun, etc., it is possible to create an abstract term, e.g. *lo verosímil, lo barroco, lo poeta* ('poetic genius'), *lo realista, lo existente.*

The pressure of French on the Spanish language continued all through the nineteenth century and still does. Notable areas dependent on French loan-words of the period are economics and finance (*cotizar, explotar, finanzas*); transport (*vagón, túnel*); food, drink and provisioning (*consomé, filete, flan, champán/champaña, menú*); clothing (*blusa, confeccionar*), and other words like *chófer, garaje* and a number of the parts of the motor car. It has been noted that even Spanish syntax has tended to be modified by French syntactical usage, e.g. the adjectival use of the gerund ('un decreto *otorgando* la creación') and the replacement, in expressions borrowed from the French, of the Spanish preposition *de* by French *a* ('un barco *a* vapor') or by *en* ('una maleta *en* cabra'). The tendency to use the adjective *pequeño* instead of the traditional Spanish diminutive suffixes has also been thought to be a Gallicism. But, nowadays, the pressure of English on Spanish everyday vocabulary and idiom, though not yet fully investigated, has, thanks to the importance of modern technology, of films and the circumstances of their dubbing, of television and the pull of North American life styles generally, probably become greater than that of French. At the same time distinctively Spanish American speech also exercises some attraction for metropolitan speech. Slang terms, too, sometimes borrowed from the *caló* of the gipsies, are accepted by educated persons (e.g. *chaval* (*muchacho*), *gachó* ('chap', 'bloke')).

Peninsular Spanish morphology, syntax and usage in the second half of the twentieth century – particularly as spoken – is quite often a rather different thing from what the grammars (Spanish or foreign) say it is, e.g. in the spread of *tú* at the expense of *usted*, the elimination of the definite article before the names of countries that used to require it (*Estados Unidos* for *los Estados Unidos*), the elimination of the preposition *de* in certain situations ('calle Goya' for 'calle de Goya', etc.), the written treatment of dates, etc. Though Old Castile still tends to preserve traditional phonemes, phonetic vulgarisms characteristic of the south are increasingly invading the speech of the capital: *yeísmo* (i.e. substituting for *ll* the sound *y*, as in *yo*, to give *caye*, not *calle*) is almost the norm in everyday speech, as is the dropping of intervocalic -*d*- (e.g. *equivocao* not *equivocado*) and of final -*d* (*Madrí* for *Madrid*). More far-reaching is the adoption of a phenomenon common to vulgar Spanish and to parts of Andalusia. This is the aspiration of -*s* at the end of a word or syllable so that *los hombres* becomes *loh* (*h*)*ombreh*, followed, sometimes, by loss of the aspirate, > *lo* (*h*)*ombre*. This process, in the case of feminine plurals (e.g. *las casas* > *lah casah* > *la casa*), can make it impossible to distinguish by sound singular from plural forms, though there is increasing evidence that, in Andalusia at least, a distinction is maintained by the quality of the final vowel. Spanish has always been a highly flexible language, where examples of actual use, even in literature, are often likely to prove disconcerting to those who too readily credit the existence of rigid rules of phonetics, morphology, syntax and lexicography.

IX American Spanish

Spanish as spoken in Central and South America exhibits wide regional divergencies in terms of phonetics, morphology, syntax, usage and vocabulary. There are, however, some features widespread enough to hint at some fairly general continental features. The gap between the spoken language and the written language is certainly greater in America than in the Peninsula, though the fissiparous tendencies of the spoken language there are combated in literature and other forms of serious writing both by the influence of the written tradition and, too, by the wish of Spanish American writers, generally speaking, to be intelligible to an educated public throughout their continent. The possible influence on American Spanish of the linguistic substratum represented by the large number of Indian languages and dialects spoken there has been much discussed – an analogy being sought with the supposed experience of Vulgar Latin in Europe when it was in contact with pre-existing non-Latin languages within the Roman Empire, for example the influence of Basque on the medieval Castilian dialect. But the situation of Spanish when it began its history in America was very different from that of Romance in the earliest stages of its contact with indigenous languages, and the proven influence of the Indian linguistic substratum on the phonetics of American Spanish is slight. The substratum languages do sometimes affect intonation. They have had some influence on morphology: the Nahuatl suffix -ecatl is responsible, in Mexico and Central America, for a fondness for the adjectival suffix -eco, -eca, while the Quechua possessive suffix y may, in speech, be added to a Spanish noun in regions like Peru, e.g. viday, 'my life'. But, on the whole, the history of American Spanish is rather discouraging to linguists inclined towards assigning a major role to substratum influences.

The phonetics of American Spanish as this is spoken in the mountains and highlands does tend to differ in substantial ways from that of the plains, the coast and the Caribbean islands; in this respect, and very broadly speaking, the language of the highlands is nearer Castilian and less like the speech of Andalusia than it is elsewhere. Attempts have been made to explain this by differing patterns of original settlement which involve supposing that settlers from the Castilian regions of Spain preferred the high ground, the Andalusians settling in the lowlands. There is little evidence that this was so. It has been said of American Spanish that, in the highlands, speakers tend to swallow (drop) vowels while on the coast they tend to swallow consonants – a situation said to be paralleled in the Peninsula, if we compare the Spanish of the Asturian mountain valleys with that of the Guadalquivir valley. It is suggested that the highlander has developed a greater lung capacity which affects his articulation, leading both to emphatic consonants and to the consequent loss of unaccented vowels. A parallel phonetic process seems to affect some highland Indian languages (e.g. the emphatic p', t', k' of Quechua). But this opinion is not universally accepted. Another explanation put forward to account for the greater phonetic proximity to Castilian of the Spanish of the uplands is the cultural influence in colonial times of highland capitals like Mexico City, Bogotá and La Paz, where literary and other evidence shows that influences favouring the maintenance of 'pure' (i.e. Peninsular) norms were strong. The existence of a phonetic difference between uplands and lowlands is certain but it cannot yet be said to have been satisfactorily accounted for.

Seseo is general everywhere in Latin America today, not only *s* but also *z* and *c* before *e* and *i*, all being pronounced as identical sibilants – more or less like English *s*. *Yeísmo* (*caballo* > *cabayo*) is also widely generalized. A tendency to aspirate *s* and to preserve the medieval Castilian aspirated sound that replaced Latin *f*- is common, e.g. *ihtoria*, *dehpuéh* (*después*), *jambre* (*hambre*), *jembra* (*hembra*), *jarto* (*harto*). These features coincide with the characteristics of some Andalusian speech today and it has usually been held that their presence in America is explained by a predominance of Andalusian influences on early settlement in America. This view has been challenged by some linguisticians in Spanish America who claim that the pattern of early settlement was not, in fact, predominantly Andalusian and that the phonetic characteristics referred to must have emerged independently on American soil. But this argument is difficult to sustain: the first colonial settlement (in the Caribbean islands) was certainly in the main an Andalusian settlement and, particularly important for linguistic history, Andalusian women were specially numerous among the settlers. The Spanish of the Canary Islands (settled before and during the conquest of America) is instructive in this respect. Andalusians from Seville played a major part in Canarian settlement, and the speech of the islands reveals all the characteristics under discussion.

A notable characteristic of American Spanish, found in Argentina, Uruguay, Paraguay and in Central America (though now extirpated from the cultured speech of Chile) is *voseo*. As we have seen (pp. 25–6 above), during the sixteenth century in the Peninsula, *vos* as a polite form of address was devalued and finally dropped. In the regions of America mentioned it remains, replacing *tú* as a form of familiar address. Despite this second person singular function, it is nevertheless used with second personal *plural* verb endings. Further complications are that these endings are not usually the modern Peninsular ones, e.g. *tenéis*, but the archaic second person plural endings dropped by Peninsular Spanish in the sixteenth century (e.g. *tenés*), while the accusative and dative and possessive pronominal forms of *tú* have not been forgotten and are frequently combined with *vos* (e.g. *ofrecerles un porvenir a vos y a tu hijo*, or imperative *vení(d) a tu casa*). Sometimes the regular second person singular form of the verb is also found with *vos* (*vos comiste*). An additional consequence of this development is that there is no familiar plural (*vosotros* being virtually unknown) so that *ustedes* (with, however, the third person plural forms of the verb) has to function as a familiar plural. The future of this curious phenomenon is uncertain as cultured influence has succeeded in curtailing its use in some parts of the Spanish American linguistic area, and it is a barbarism which plainly restricts rather than extends nuances of address.

Lexical borrowings from Amerindian languages have already been referred to (see pp. 28–30 above). Many Spanish words have undergone some semantic change to accommodate their meaning to American conditions, so that they no longer there have the meanings they have in Spain, e.g. *embarcarse* refers in America to the act of boarding any form of transport; *boleto* replaces *billete* ('ticket'); *vereda* replaces *acera* ('paved footpath'); *fletar* refers to the act of hiring any kind of transport. It has been noted, too, that where two exact synonyms exist, Spanish American often prefers to use one while Peninsular Spanish prefers the other (e.g. *flaco* rather than *delgado*, *estampilla* rather than *sello*, *plata* rather than *dinero*, *botar* rather than *tirar*). Throughout Spanish America, for a variety of social and economic reasons, there is much awareness of popular speech and popular slang. The very great number of words that in American Spanish have acquired an obscene meaning can have lasting effects on acceptable usage, eliminating from it a large number of words commonly used in Peninsular Spanish; for example *coger* cannot be used in parts of Latin America because of its obscene connotations so that *coger el tranvía* must be replaced by *agarrar el tranvía*; *madre* must be replaced by *mamá* even if inquiring of an elderly man about the state of his mother's health. This particular problem is made more complicated because the acceptable term in one part of Latin America may be a common obscenity in another.

In the past the regional peculiarities of American Spanish (notably those of Argentina) were sometimes defended as factors contributing to the development of a national sense. This attitude has now largely disappeared and, at least in intellectual circles, there is some attempt to protect the language from excessive invasion by vulgarisms of all sorts, and a concern to maintain standards of correctness. The success of the University of Santo Domingo in the Caribbean and of the nineteenth-century grammarian Andrés Bello in Chile in driving out *voseo* from educated use show what can sometimes be done. Spanish American and Peninsular academic bodies maintain close relations in the hope of defending their common language. But American Spanish, thanks to massive immigration from non-Spanish-speaking countries in certain areas, e.g. Argentina, has long been under much stronger pressures than is Peninsular Spanish. The present pressure of Anglicisms now invading Spanish in general is much stronger in Spanish America because of the cultural, economic and technological influence of the United States. In Puerto Rico, at certain levels, the influence of American English on Spanish seems overwhelming. American Spanish is also meeting a new indigenous challenge, notably from the revival of Quechua and Guaraní as languages of mass communication. No such challenge, at least, faces Peninsular Spanish. Peninsular Spanish and American Spanish, at any rate as far as the language of literature and the educated are concerned, are still evidently one language. The spread of universal education and the influence of other mass communications media may be seen as a factor likely to maintain unity. Immigrants from the countryside to the urban centres of America soon seek to divest themselves of their regional speech and vocabulary. But, against these factors, in Spanish America as in metropolitan Spain, linguistic purity of any sort seems a doubtful cause in an age when, for political and social reasons, linguistic authority like any other form of authority is challenged, and the language used by the media themselves, especially television, deliberately cultivates the introduction of loan words and other speech borrowings, particularly from English and French. The political fragmentation of Spanish America, as well as its dependence on (and hope of rivalling) the United States, make the future history of American Spanish specially difficult to predict.

Bibliography

GENERAL

COROMINAS, J. *Diccionario crítico etimológico de la lengua castellana.* 4 vols. Madrid, 1954–7. (Essential for the etymological history of Spanish words. There is a shortened version in one volume for non-specialists: *Breve diccionario etimológico de la lengua castellana.* Madrid, 1961.)

Enciclopedia lingüística hispánica. 3 vols: I–II and I (suplemento). Madrid, 1960–7.

ENTWISTLE, W. J. *The Spanish Language.* 2nd ed. London, 1962.

GARCÍA DE DIEGO, V. *Gramática histórica española.* 3rd ed. Madrid, 1970.

LAPESA, R. *Historia de la lengua española.* 6th ed. Madrid, 1962. (The most useful full-scale historical account of the development of Spanish.)

MACPHERSON, I. R. *Spanish Phonology: Descriptive and Historical.* Manchester, 1975.

SPAULDING, R. K. *How Spanish Grew.* Berkeley and Los Angeles, 1962. (A useful rapid survey of the history of the Spanish language.)

ZAMORA VICENTE, A. *Dialectología española.* 2nd ed. Madrid, 1967. (A full study of the history of the Spanish dialects, including American Spanish.)

MEDIEVAL SPANISH

GIFFORD, D. J., and HODCROFT, F. W. *Textos lingüísticos del medioevo español.* 2nd ed. Oxford, 1966. (A collection of texts to illustrate the characteristics of the various dialectal forms of medieval Spanish. Each section is preceded by a description of the linguistic features of the regional or other type of dialectal speech concerned.)

GOLDEN AGE SPANISH

ALONSO, A. *De la pronunciación medieval a la moderna en español.* 2 vols. Madrid, 1955–70.

ALONSO, D. *La lengua poética de Góngora.* 3rd ed. Madrid, 1961.

GARCÍA BLANCO, M. *La lengua española en la época de Carlos V.* Santander, 1958.

KENISTON, H. *The Syntax of Castilian Prose: The Sixteenth Century.* Vol. I. Chicago, 1938.

MENÉNDEZ PIDAL, R. *La lengua de Cristóbal Colón.* Madrid, 1942. (Contains the author's important articles 'El lenguaje del siglo XVI' and 'El estilo de Santa Teresa'.)

EIGHTEENTH CENTURY

LÁZARO CARRETER, F. *Las ideas lingüísticas en España durante el siglo XVIII.* Madrid, 1949.

AMERICAN SPANISH

In addition to the discussions of American Spanish included in the general studies of the Spanish language and its dialects listed at the beginning of this bibliography see:

KANY, C. E. *American-Spanish Syntax.* 2nd ed. Chicago, 1951.

—— *American-Spanish Semantics.* Berkeley and Los Angeles, 1960.

MALKIEL, Y. *Linguistics and Philology in Spanish America.* The Hague, 1972. (A readable account of all studies in this field.)

ROSENBLAT, A. 'Contactos interlingüísticos en el mundo hispánico: el español y las lenguas indígenas', in *Actas del Segundo Congreso Internacional de Hispanistas,* pp. 109–54. Nijmegen, 1967.

2 Muslim Spain (711–1492)

RICHARD HITCHCOCK

I The Invasion of Spain

Within a hundred years of the death of Muḥammad in 632, the Muslim empire had extended to North India in the east and to the Iberian Peninsula in the west. In the second half of the seventh century the Berbers, a light-skinned people of North Africa who were destined to play a major part in the Arab invasions of Spain, were gradually but inexorably subjugated by the advancing Arabs. Once their resistance had been broken, the Berbers, some of whom had adhered to Judaism, now became fervent converts to Islam, and enjoyed the full privileges accorded to Muslims in the Qur'ān. Simultaneously there began the process of their assimilation of the Arabic language and culture.

The circumstances of the invasion of Spain have been reconstructed largely on the basis of Arab chronicles and histories. Mūsā ibn Nuṣair, governor of North Africa since 705 for the Umayyad caliphate in Damascus, was the Arab authority most immediately concerned. The position of these Arab governors was frequently a difficult one. They had to ensure, on the one hand, that the newly conquered territories were being satisfactorily incorporated into Islam, that taxes were gathered there and soldiers conscripted. They had to see that further conquests, where appropriate, were undertaken. In July 710, Ṭarīfa, a Berber officer, took 400 men across the Straits of Gibraltar on what was little more than a raiding party. He returned with his spoils and reported encouragingly to Mūsā. In the summer of 711, Ṭāriq ibn Ziyād, the Berber governor of Tangier responsible to Mūsā, led a large expeditionary force of 7,000 men, mainly Berbers, across the Straits. This force defeated Roderic, the Visigoth ruler of Hispania, in a decisive battle near Medina Sidonia (prov. of Cádiz).

This military defeat can be explained by the endemic political instability of the Visigothic kingdom whose legal code decreed that there should be an elected and not a hereditary monarch and where Visigothic and Hispano-Romans had never been effectively unified. In 710, for example, Roderic, who had been elected king, had control of the capital, Toledo, and was in conflict with Achila, the son of the previous king, Witiza, who had died in 709. The nobility was thus split at the very moment when it needed to be united. Another factor in the downfall of the Visigoths was probably their treatment of the Jews. In 693 the Jews were forbidden to trade as merchants; they were to be compulsorily converted to Christianity; they could no longer be married according to their own laws. Though it was perhaps understood that judicious gifts would mitigate the reality of these prohibitions it was not surprising that, when the Arab invasion occurred, the Jewish subjects of the Visigoths regarded the invaders as deliverers. The seventeenth-century Arab historian al-Maqqarī, drawing on earlier Arab chronicles, states that whenever the Muslims conquered a town they put its Jewish population in control of the administration on their behalf.

After his victory over Roderic, Ṭāriq went on to capture Écija, Córdoba, Guadalajara and the Visigothic capital, Toledo. The ease with which these successes were accomplished encouraged Mūsā himself to enter Spain, which he did in 712, with an army of 18,000 men, mostly Arabs. This was a large percentage of the total number of Arabs who had entered Africa and reveals Mūsā's intention to colonize the newly acquired lands. He spent the winter of 713-14 in Spain, and having captured the important cities of Seville and Mérida, he united with Ṭāriq near Talavera (prov. of Toledo). In 714 a combined campaign achieved the surrender of Saragossa, and then, each following independent routes westward, Mūsā captured Soria and campaigned in Asturias, while Ṭāriq followed a more northerly route, capturing León and Astorga. Mūsā was then recalled to Damascus. After an initial hesitation, he obeyed, leaving his son, 'Abd al-'Azīz, as commander of the Arab armies. The reasons for Mūsā's recall are obscure. His departure meant the end of his career, since, although he took with him to Damascus captives as a living testimony of his conquests, he was punished and deprived of his position, perhaps for having exceeded his authority by campaigning in Spain without the caliph's orders.

'Abd al-'Azīz conquered most of the remaining cities of Spain, travelling between present-day Portugal and Barcelona, and extending his conquests as far as Narbonne. In March 716, after about two years in which he consolidated the achievements of the previous five years, he was murdered on the order of the caliph in Damascus, probably because his loyalty was called into question. Between 719 and 732 various Arab leaders led incursions from Spain into France, occupying temporarily several Frankish cities, including Carcassone and Nîmes. The defeat of the Muslim invaders by Charles Martel at Poitiers (732) effectively marked the end of further Muslim expansion north of the Pyrenees, although Muslim pockets in France survived for a considerable time. It is difficult to determine to what extent the doctrine of the *jihād*, or holy war against the unbeliever, was responsible for this persistent drive to acquire new territories in Europe.

For a brief while the Muslims controlled the whole Iberian Peninsula as far as the Cantabrian mountains, excepting the Basque and central Pyrenean areas. Soon, however, the northern boundary of Muslim-controlled territory became settled further south, and ran roughly along the line of the rivers Duero and Ebro but excluding the county of Barcelona after 801. Muslim Spain, for nearly three centuries, thus comprised something over two-thirds of the area of the Iberian Peninsula. From the time of the invasion the area controlled by the Muslims was known as al-Andalus. The term, derived by Arabic geographers from *al-Andlīsh*, the name given to the Vandals, only applied to Muslim-controlled territory. Christian areas were referred to by their regional names. The problem of the origin of the name al-Andalus is still unsolved.

II Al-Andalus (716–756)

Al-Andalus soon became the object of almost constant political scheming within the Arab world. It was governed between 716 and 756 by a rapid succession of Arab governors, nominally appointed by the caliph in Damascus, who were drawn from two main tribal groups that had settled in Spain: one from Syria and the other from the Yemen. The former were the most numerous, as the result of a sizeable emigration from Syria in 741. This, however, was the last big immigration of Arabs and the pure Arab element in the Peninsula soon diminished as a consequence of the widespread practice of intermarriage with the indigenous population. Syrians and Yemenites continually fought for precedence, and most governors, in order to retain their office, had to cope with numerous rebellions by the opposing faction. Two other factors contributed to this state of civil strife. The Berbers, including the original invaders as well as later colonizers, had mainly settled in the Duero valley and in Galicia. Their occupation of these regions ceased abruptly in 750, when a famine caused many to return to North Africa. They had long been dissatisfied with the treatment that they had received from their Arab overlords. Christian raids into al-Andalus had also been growing, causing the Berbers' tenancy to be more hazardous, and, indeed, wresting much loosely held territory from Muslim control. Campaigns undertaken by the Christian King of Asturias, Alfonso I, were responsible for the recapture of the entire north-west, including such cities and towns as Lugo, Oporto, León, Astorga and Zamora. As a result of his campaigns a kind of no-man's-land between Christian and Muslim became established along a frontier zone roughly following the line of the Duero. These zones, probably deserted and left untended, were known as the Marches (*ath-thughūr*). The Upper March comprised much of the Ebro valley; the Muslim garrison towns were Saragossa (Saraqusṭa) and Tudela. The city on which the defence of the Middle March was based was Toledo (Ṭulaiṭula); Mérida and Badajoz protected the Lower March.

As the Arabs gradually settled into the more favourable areas in the south, becoming perceptibly less inclined to pursue the *jihād*, they became more conscious of the indigenous population. As was the Arab practice with all conquered nations, the Visigoths and Hispano-Romans were given the choice of conversion to Islam or of pursuing their own religion, subject to certain rules and conditions, principally involving the payment of taxes as laid down in the Qur'ān. A text recorded by historians which exemplifies this statutory protection afforded to the indigenous population by the Muslims was contracted in 713 between 'Abd al-'Azīz and the Visigothic ruler of Murcia, Theodomir. It was agreed 'on the oath of Allah and his Prophet' that neither Theodomir nor any of his subjects should set aside the treaty or violate it; that they would not be deprived of their property; that they would not be killed nor reduced to slavery, nor separated from their wives or children; that they would be allowed to practise the Christian religion, that their churches would not be burnt, and that their lands would be left unmolested, as long as the following conditions were observed: that seven towns should be handed over to the Muslims; that they should not give refuge to exiles, neither should they interfere with the worship of Muslims, nor hold back information regarding the enemies of Islam; that they should each pay annually a poll-tax of one gold dinar as well as four half-gallon measures of vinegar, two of honey and two of oil, their servants paying half this amount. The earliest gold dinars of al-Andalus had a weight of 4·3 grams. The surrender of seven towns was doubtless intended to ensure that the Christian population would be kept to rural areas, a development that was to the obvious advantage of the early governors, as they sought to establish an Islamic urban framework.

The last governor of al-Andalus was an aged aristocrat of the Syrian faction who defeated the Yemeni aspirant to his position, but was himself defeated by a coalition of his opponents headed by 'Abd ar-Raḥmān I.

III The Independent Umayyad Emirate (756–929)

'Abd ar-Raḥmān b. Muʿāwiya, ad-Dākhil, 'the Immigrant', a member of the ruling Umayyad family in Damascus, was forced to flee to Egypt in order to avoid capture by the 'Abbāsids who had, in A.D. 750, occupied Damascus and overthrown the Umayyads. After much adroit political manœuvring he entered Spain, ousted the governor, proclaimed himself emir – temporal ruler of the Muslims – and established his capital in Córdoba (Qurṭuba). He quelled Syrian attempts to dispossess him, put down a number of independent rebellions, dealt with a Berber revolt and made a truce with the Asturians. For thirty years – he died at Córdoba in 788 – 'Abd ar-Raḥmān governed the new emirate and was responsible for imparting to it, for the first time, the elements out of which an independent Muslim civilization would develop. The political criteria he adopted were those that had been used by the now defunct Umayyad caliphate in Damascus, and which were of course acceptable to the majority of Arabs in al-Andalus, who were Syrians. He was his own chief minister, and he organized his state into provinces, each of which had a governor directly responsible to him. He encouraged a firm Islamic orientation in every facet of life. Schools for instruction in the Qur'ān were soon instituted. Many of the indigenous elements, both Christian and Jewish, who had not yet apostatized now became converts to Islam, enjoying immediately the same rights as other Muslims. 'Abd ar-Raḥmān was responsible for starting the construction of the Great Mosque at Córdoba. The part constructed during his emirate reveals a fusion of indigenous Hispanic with imported Arabic techniques. Thus, for example, the superimposition of one arch upon another in the style of a Roman aqueduct – the one at Mérida may have been an influence – was associated with characteristic aspects of the

Syrian mosques at that time. In literature 'Abd ar-Raḥmān I, to whom some famous verses full of nostalgia for his native Syria have been attributed, followed traditional Arab modes in his poetry. As a result of his patronage these survived in al-Andalus long after new forms of poetry had been introduced under the 'Abbāsids.

'Abd ar-Raḥmān's two immediate successors as emir continued his policies. The Mālikī law-school was introduced into al-Andalus at the end of the eighth century, and provided a basis of legislative theory and practice for the ruler, who was the supreme judge. The flexibility and orthodoxy of the Mālikī interpretation of Islamic law accounted for its popularity in al-Andalus, whose local traditions, thanks to it, could be legitimately incorporated into the corpus of law.

With the accession to the emirate of 'Abd ar-Raḥmān II (822–56) came a change of outlook. He refashioned Muslim society on 'Abbāsid models from the East, openly encouraging new cultural influences in his attempt to rival at Córdoba the brilliance of the 'Abbāsid court in Baghdad. Men of letters were attracted away from their Eastern home-lands to join those Arabs who had already found the beauty and fer-tility of al-Andalus alluring. An example of the deliberate fostering of the culture of the Muslim Orient in al-Andalus is afforded by the arrival there of the musician Ziryab in 822. He was given a large salary and an important position at court. Credited with having added a fifth string to the lute, he founded a music school in Córdoba and for thirty years instructed the Andalusīs in various civilized refinements – musical, vocal and social – setting the trend also as an arbiter of fashion. As the court at Córdoba began to acquire prestige in the Arab world, so there came to be gathered round it scholars, lawyers, grammarians and poets, after the style of the 'Abbāsid court in the East. Andalusī men of letters also visited the East and returned well acquainted with the latest trends in literature there, so that the principal poets and writers in the East came to be known and commented upon in al-Andalus.

'Abd ar-Raḥmān II also had to cope with the perennial military prob-lems facing the emirate. War continued on five main fronts: against the Gascons of Narbonne; the Franks, now independently established in the county of Barcelona; the Asturian Christians of the north, against whom he led a number of summer campaigns; the Norsemen, who conducted lightning raids on the coast of al-Andalus throughout the ninth century. He was also confronted by a revolt of the Mozarabs in Córdoba itself, the so-called 'martyr movement'.

The motives that provoked forty Córdoban Christians – monks and laymen – to curse Muḥammad publicly between 852 and 859 are difficult to unravel. The emirs had continued to honour the statutory protection accorded in the Qur'ān to Christians and Jews. 'Abd ar-Raḥmān II and his successor, Muḥammad I, who each reigned for over thirty years, were anxious to avoid outbreaks of communal dissension within the capital, and, in consequence, dealt warily with the indigenous population. The Mozarabs[1] knew that they were safe from persecution, as long as they desisted from public blasphemy against Muḥammad. It is established that the Mozarabic laity by the mid-ninth century were to a considerable degree Arabicized, customarily wearing Arabic clothes and speaking Arabic. They had their own civil head, the *comes*, who represented their interests, and whose appointment was approved by the Muslim authorities. As for the priesthood, it was split by the anthropomorphism taught by Hostigesis, Bishop of Málaga, and had largely lost even its awareness of the significance of ecclesiastical garments, preferring to wear Muslim dress. It has been argued that the decadence of the Mozarabic Church as an institution encouraged fervent believers to a public confession of their faith, but there may also have been provocation from the *muwalladūn*. These converts to Islam were eager exponents of their newly adopted religion, and also vehement opponents of their compatriots who had remained Christian. More intolerant than the ruling emirs, they may have sought, and perhaps created, opportunities for preferring charges of blasphemy against Mozarabs. The movement received great impetus from St Eulogius, whose writings, in particular his *De memoriale sanctorum*, praised the martyrs and included a vehement diatribe against Muḥammad and Islam. The Mozarabic civil hierarchy, led by their count, Gómez, and a sector of the clergy led by Reccafred, Metropolitan of Seville, saw their privileged position being rapidly undermined. An anxious *tête-à-tête* between representatives of the emir and Mozarab elders secured the calling of the Council of Córdoba (852). This was convened to condemn voluntary martyrs as guilty of suicide, and to prohibit public blasphemy against Muḥammad. But the speech of St Eulogius in defence of the martyrs effectively prevented a definite condemnation of those who had already died. He himself was invited to become metropolitan of Toledo in 858, perhaps because the Toledan Mozarabs saw in him a nominal leader for their scheme for ousting the

---

[1] From Ar. *musta'rab*, 'Arabicized'; 'having assimilated Arabic customs'. The word was used to denote non-Arabs living within Arab communities and came to be applied to those Christians who lived in al-Andalus.

Muslims from the city. Muḥammad I vetoed his election – a further indication of the gravity with which the situation was viewed by the Muslims, for the emir did not normally interfere in the internal elections of the Mozarabic Church. The 'martyr movement' reached its climax in 859, when St Eulogius himself was executed, in spite of efforts by prominent Muslims to persuade him to reconsider his position. The political embarrassment caused by the martyrs forced the emirs to adopt harsh measures against the non-Muslim population, thereby running the risk of inciting a popular revolt. The movement was obviously symptomatic of a religious *malaise* among the Mozarabs – perhaps an inevitable consequence of their separation for so long from contact with other Christians, though there may well have been other reasons involved of which we know nothing.

In the second half of the ninth century the authority of the emirs diminished. Rebellions in the Marches became more frequent. There was also friction among the Arabs in the major cities in the south, largely because of their personal ambitions for power. The gravest threat to the emirate, however, came from a *muwallad*, 'Umar ibn Ḥafṣūn. From his stronghold in Bobastro, in the mountains behind Málaga, 'Umar ibn Ḥafṣūn conducted a series of effective campaigns against the emirate between 879 and his death in 918. At one stage he threatened to capture Córdoba itself and overrun the entire south. A skilled tactician, he outwitted his opponents until 900, when he was apparently converted to Christianity. Hitherto he had relied on the support of the masses of *muwallads*, but his conversion must have entailed their defection from his army, thus significantly reducing the size of the forces under his authority. From then on, although still a formidable opponent, he did not constitute a direct challenge to the emirate.

With 'Umar ibn Ḥafṣūn's rising still a nagging sore, with several independent Muslim states forming themselves in the Marches, and also in Seville, the institutions of government at Córdoba experienced a period of severe crisis. The political and institutional remedies needed were almost all to be forthcoming from the last Umayyad emir 'Abd ar-Raḥmān III (912–61).

IV The Umayyad Caliphate (929–1031)

The tenth century was to turn out to be the century of greatest stability and of greatest splendour achieved in al-Andalus. 'Abd ar-Raḥmān III reigned for almost half this time and succeeded in creating a society whose brilliance was rivalled at this time neither in Baghdad nor in Egypt. He suppressed the dissident rebels in the Marches, destroyed what remained of the threat from 'Umar ibn Ḥafṣūn, kept the northern frontier with the Christians quiet and conducted a skilful diplomatic campaign in face of the Fāṭimid threat in North Africa. On 16 January 929 he proclaimed himself caliph, assuming the titles of Commander of the Faithful and Defender of the Faith of Allah. By this action he made himself the spiritual and temporal head of all believers in al-Andalus. He invested supreme authority in himself, not merely to emphasize that the 'Abbāsids in the East no longer retained, even theoretically, superior jurisdiction over the Muslims in the West, but also to counteract the claims of the Fāṭimids in North Africa. The problem presented by two caliphs reigning simultaneously posed problems for later jurists. The fourteenth-century historian Ibn Khaldūn maintained that two caliphs may be legal, provided that there was sufficient distance between them to prevent any conflict of authority. In practice interference from the Eastern caliphate was scarcely attempted after 'Abd ar-Raḥmān III's proclamation in 929.

The order and prosperity that 'Abd ar-Raḥmān established stemmed in large measure from the administrative stability that he succeeded in providing. The caliph himself held all the vital reins of power. He was sole commander of his armies, appointed all his ministers and ambassadors, and himself conducted all the important affairs of state. Second-in-command to the caliph was the *ḥājib* (minister of state) who was in charge of the central military and provincial administration, and was responsible for public security, under the constant direction of his caliph. The caliph chose as many advisers and ministers – *wazīrs* – as he wished, to take charge of particular departments of government. The all-important system of communications was controlled by the *ṣāḥib al-barīd* – the 'postmaster-general'. A postal system was responsible for transmitting official messages between government officials throughout the state. The post was probably carried by escorted couriers, who were mounted, by runners, or, for urgent messages, by carrier pigeon. The treasury department was managed by treasurers of whom there might be as many as six at any one time. These officials nearly all came from noble families established in Córdoba – they formed the acknowledged Arab aristocracy of al-Andalus although they were subject to summary dismissal by the caliph. Revenue for the public treasury, which was kept separate from the caliph's personal fortune, came from the taxes on personal wealth, from tithes on land, duties on imports and exports, taxes imposed on purchases made in the markets, and from the *jizya*, a tax each adult non-Muslim had to pay proportionate to his means. It amounted to about 2·5 per cent annually. Under 'Abd ar-Raḥmān III the level of the balance in the treasury was kept at about five and a half million gold dinars. The largest single factor responsible for this surplus was the extensive external trade of the caliphate and the consequent high receipts from customs duties on imports and exports.

Al-Andalus was, for the purposes of administration, divided into a number of territorial districts or *kūra*. An important town was the administrative centre of each: thus Seville (Ishbīliya) and Ronda (Runda), for example, were both 'provincial capitals' of their respective *kūras*. A provincial governor (*wālī*) lived in each of these capitals. He was appointed directly by the caliph and normally resided in the *qaṣāba* or citadel. The administrative system he had at his disposal was a replica in miniature of the central administration in Córdoba. Potentially the provincial governors had virtual autonomy, but under a firm caliph there were few who tried to exercise it. It was only later, towards the end of the caliphate, that the governors, profiting from the weakness of the central authority in Córdoba, established their own independence.

The chief justice, resident in Córdoba, was appointed by the caliph, though frequently with the popular consent of the community. He was an important figure in the caliphate, with a freedom of expression and an independence derived from the Muslim religious code that were zealously guarded. During al-Ḥakam's caliphate (961–76) the judge (*qāḍī*) became more of a political figure subordinate to the caliph's demands. Al-Manṣūr was later to use the office as a stepping-stone to political power. The *ṣāḥib ash-shurṭa* (literally 'head of police') had the function, both administrative and judicial, of dealing with offences against the private individual or the public interest. The *ṣāḥib al-madīna* (literally 'head of the city') had similar responsibilities within the city to which he was appointed. Special responsibility was also given to the *muḥtaṣib* (Sp. *motacén*) known also as the *ṣāḥib as-sūq* (Sp. *zavazoque*) – head of the market – to control the operation of the markets, to suppress fraud, to regulate trade, and to intervene in matters relating to sales, gambling, weights and measures, and public dress. Municipal administration in al-Andalus was well ordered and many of its offices were incorporated in the municipalities that were established in Christian Spain. As well as the offices of *alcalde* (Ar. *al-qāḍī*) and *almotacén*, that of *almojarife* (Ar. *al-mushrif*, 'superintendent of taxes') and *acequiero* (Ar. *ṣāḥib as-sāqiyya*, 'supervisor of canals') may be cited in this connection.

'Abd ar-Raḥmān III was responsible for the resumption, in A.D. 928, of the minting of the gold dinar. None had been minted in al-Andalus since A.D. 724, and one may suppose that his reintroduction of this coin was due in part to his assumption of the title of caliph with all the dignity this office implied; the legends on these dinars frequently make reference to his honorific titles. The silver dirham, with an average weight of 2·8 grams, had hitherto formed the principal currency minted in al-Andalus and copper coins were also used. The coin described as a dinar disappears from the coinage of al-Andalus during the thirteenth century, though it was adopted by the Spanish Christian kings, including Alfonso VIII, whose *maravedí* was an imitation of the Almoravid dinar. The gold and silver coinage of al-Andalus readily passed into circulation in the Hispanic Christian states and served to stimulate their economies from the eleventh to the fourteenth century. The gold *dobla* used in Castile had its origin in the gold pieces of 4·6 grams minted by the Almohads towards the end of the twelfth century.

Throughout the Umayyad caliphate the tribe was the unit of military organization until al-Manṣūr's accession to power in 979. Al-Manṣūr reorganized the army by abolishing the tribal regiments. By breaking down tribalism in the army he lessened the dangers of revolt, but in order to achieve his aim he had to bring in large numbers of Berbers from North Africa, and Slavs (*ṣaqāliba*) from Central Europe. This racial name was originally used to describe the inhabitants of the area from the Caspian to the Adriatic. It became the practice to capture them and sell them as slaves to the Arabs in Spain. During the caliphal period, however, the word *ṣaqāliba* acquired a wider usage and was applied to any slave at court who came from a Christian country. As the majority of such 'Slavs' arrived as children they were given an Islamic upbringing, and some achieved positions of distinction during the reign of 'Abd ar-Raḥmān III, both in the civil administration and as literary patrons. During this time it is estimated that there were some 7,500 *ṣaqāliba* in Córdoba alone, over half of whom were administrative personnel. Both Berbers and Slavs would later, as groups, become disaffected when there was no longer a firm central government to control them.

Military campaigns, known as *aceifas* from the Arabic word for 'summer', were usually begun in June; the soldiers, conscripted from the provinces, received their pay on their return. During the time of al-Manṣūr 500,000 dinars from the public treasury were set aside annually to defray the expenses of these expeditions. It is said that 'Abd ar-Raḥmān III never managed to raise more than 5,000 troops for any one expedition, which suggests that raiding tactics for plunder were adopted, rather than full-scale attacks aiming at the permanent occupation of Christian towns. Al-Manṣūr's expeditions in the final two decades of the tenth century were more destructive and had devastating consequences for the Christians.

As well as establishing a firm administrative system for the government and defence of his state, 'Abd ar-Raḥmān III was active in promoting a cultural splendour that had its centre at Córdoba. He caused to be constructed the vast, luxurious palace of Madīnat az-Zahrā', which was his official residence. It was sited about three miles from the city. The main hall, where ambassadors from the Christian north and from Byzantium were received, was decorated in the finest artistic style of the day, with marble of various colours, extracted from the sierras of Granada and Almería. This whole complex was destroyed by the Berbers during the struggle for the caliphate in 1013. In our own day excavations have uncovered much of the vast site. 'Abd ar-Raḥmān was, in other ways, a great patron of the arts, gathering round him poets, scholars, historians and musicians, all of whom thronged to his court, vying for his favour. The function of the poets was to compose verses eulogizing the sovereign, and their livelihood depended on their facility for doing this spontaneously. During the later years of the caliphate, especially under al-Ḥakam II (961–76), the main courts, Córdoba, Seville and Almería, all boasted resident poets, who were not only of Andalusī stock, but also sometimes had come from the Orient; literary culture was still largely based on Eastern models.

The Christians and the Jews in al-Andalus had by this time become largely absorbed into the Islamic administrative system, whilst retaining the practice of their respective religions. Both Christians and Jews were called upon to act as diplomats and translators. The services of the Christian Recemundus, described in a contemporary chronicle as 'adprime catholicus', and later appointed Bishop of Elvira (Ilbīra), were used by 'Abd ar-Raḥmān III, who sent him on missions both to the German and Byzantine emperors. Likewise the Jewish scholar and physician, Ḥasdai ibn Shaprūṭ, became an important minister in the caliphate, and also acted as ambassador for the caliph. In the eleventh century there were a number of Jews in prominent positions in all the major cities, particularly in Granada, which had long been known as the 'City of the Jews', and which was for a time in the effective control of two brothers belonging to the Nagrīla family. With political power came literary eminence, particularly, between A.D. 1000 and 1200, in the field of poetry. Although Arabic was both the spoken language of the Jews and the language used in their philosophical works, their poetry was written in Hebrew. This was because much of it was of a liturgical nature and because there was, at that time, a reawakened interest in the Hebrew Bible as the receptacle of the classical language. The poetry of Samuel ha-Nagīd, Solomon ibn Gabirol and Judah ha-Levi, the last the most prominent of the Jewish poets, is an important testimony both to the strength of the Hebrew tradition and to the influence of Arabic poetic themes and forms on Jewish poets.

The decline of the caliphate was almost as rapid as its rise. It collapsed in 1008, and after constant warring among numerous factions, was dissolved in 1031. One reason for its collapse was the centralization of power, particularly by al-Manṣūr, who, although not caliph, had contrived to gather the entire reins of government into his own hands. This led to inevitable quarrels amongst the Arab nobility eager to exploit the illegality of this situation for personal advantage. The friction became more intense when it was seen that al-Manṣūr, who had 'usurped' the caliphate, intended that his son, al-Muẓaffar, should succeed him. Throughout this time the legitimate caliph, Hishām II, was alive but powerless to act, and thus deprived of the awe to which the office of caliph entitled him. The Berbers and Slavs took advantage of the chaos after al-Muẓaffar's death in 1008 to establish independent dynasties centred on provincial capitals. Fierce conflict between these three factions, which included the sacking of Córdoba by the Berbers in 1013, led to the rapid and final disintegration of the Umayyad caliphate.

V The Ṭaifa Kingdoms (1031-1090)

'Ṭaifa' is the Arabic word for 'group' or 'party', and, in a Hispano-Arabic historical context, refers to the fragmentation of the Umayyad caliphate into twenty or so small states. Three ethnic groups now achieved ascendancy. The Hispano-Muslim group, which represented the fusion of Arabic with indigenous stock, was the most powerful; it established dynasties in Saragossa, Toledo, Seville and other cities. The Berbers, however, ruled in the important cities of Granada (Gharnāṭa) and Málaga, and the Slavs in the Mediterranean cities of Valencia

(Balansiya), Denia and Almería. Politically the Ṭaifa kingdoms continued to struggle amongst themselves, but the stronger states, such as Seville and Granada, gradually overcame the less powerful ones, centred on smaller towns. But the existence of the Ṭaifa kingdoms was ephemeral since they proceeded to weaken themselves by these internal conflicts at a time when two formidable enemies were assembling on the perimeter of al-Andalus. The Christians in the north, especially under Alfonso VI – who was encouraged by Pope Gregory VII's concept of the 'spiritual sovereignty of Spain' – made tributaries of many of the northern Ṭaifa states. Alfonso captured Toledo (a specially significant prize because of its place in the religious and political history of Christian Spain) in 1085. In the south, the Almoravids from North Africa, in response to an invitation from the ruler of Seville, entered al-Andalus and, taking advantage of the weakness of the existing states, conquered them.

The Ṭaifa kingdoms thus lasted a mere sixty years, but for all their endemic political debility they achieved a certain illusory splendour. Many of the states boasted courts where literature was seriously cultivated as it had been in Córdoba under the caliphate. The cultured Hispano-Muslims who had taken the place of the Arabs of pure Arabic stock no longer felt attached to the East by virtue of racial ancestry, and literary tendencies were consequently now apt to stress characteristics differing from those of the East. The popularity of the *muwashshaḥa* – a verse form whose final couplet included snatches of popular speech (both Arabic and Romance) – is an example of this; but more important was the realization among men of letters born in al-Andalus that poets and scholars of the East did not hold the monopoly of excellence in literary expression, as had hitherto been accepted. A poet attached to al-Muʿtamid's famous court at Seville in the second half of the eleventh century expresses this attitude: 'Eastern poetry, which has held our attention for so long, has now ceased to allure us. We can now get on quite well without it, for it is no longer necessary to have recourse to it, when Andalusīs themselves produce excellent pieces of prose, and poems of a quite original beauty.' This expression of pride in the literary excellence of the Andalusīs is matched by the praise bestowed upon Seville by a twelfth-century writer, ash-Shaqundī, who, writing of that city in the eleventh century, praised the grandeur of its buildings, the splendour of its gardens and parks, the excellence of its music, the variety of the musical instruments kept at court, the care taken in the upkeep of houses (which all, he claimed, had running water), the diversity of knowledge exhibited by its scholars, and the great number of its poets, who were of sufficient merit to enjoy the favour of wealthy patrons throughout the city.

VI The Almoravids and Almohads (1090–1212)

In the twelfth century the adherents of two Berber politico-religious reform movements originating in Africa overran al-Andalus. The Almoravids, whose name derives from Arabic *ribāṭ* – literally, frontier-post – combined mystical asceticism with practical warfare. Strict Muslims, they insisted on a literal interpretation of the Qur'ān, and were severer in the application of their religion than their more easy-going counterparts in al-Andalus. After overrunning the western Maghrib from their capital in Marrakesh, their emir, Yūsuf ibn Tāshfīn (d. 1106), led a major invasion of al-Andalus in 1085, and gained a prestigious victory over Alfonso VI at Zallāqa, near Badajoz, in 1086. By 1106 all the important cities of al-Andalus, except Sara-gossa, which fell in 1110, were occupied by the Almoravids. Almost immediately their power wilted. Originally nomadic, they soon suc-cumbed to the wealth and glitter of a sedentary life in the courts of cities such as Seville and Granada. The steadily growing strength of the Christian reconquerors was also a determining factor in their rapid loss of power. They lost Saragossa to Alfonso I of Aragon (1104–34) and were continually harassed by Alfonso VII of Castile (1127–51). They were finally ousted by Hispano-Muslim rebellions in 1145.

The second Berber invaders to control al-Andalus in the twelfth century were the Almohads ('unitarians'). The Almohad movement was originally a religious one that elaborated a theology based on the unity of all believers, and in conduct insisted on a literal acceptance of the teaching of the Qur'ān. Under their emir, 'Abd al-Mu'min (1130–63), they captured most cities in the south of al-Andalus, and by 1172 had overcome remaining resistance in Murcia and the east. They tried, but failed, to regain Toledo, and impelled by the spirit of the *jihād* sought to stem the tide of the Christian Reconquest. In July 1195 they defeated the Castilian king Alfonso VIII at Alarcos (prov. of Ciudad Real), but failed to take advantage of their victory. In 1212 the Almohads were decisively defeated by a combined force of Castilians, Navarrese and Aragonese, and thenceforward their power declined. The Christians, Castilians in the centre and Aragonese in the east, now swept south, and by 1248 al-Andalus had lost all her major cities, including Córdoba and Seville. Granada remained in Islamic hands and became the capital of the Naṣrid dynasty which was to survive until 1492.

The zenith of Almohad power in Spain had been from 1160 to 1210. This period was marked by firm administrative control of all the principal cities by the emir, who remained in Marrakesh. He crossed into al-Andalus only when military necessity demanded. The Almohads enforced strict adherence to the dogmas of the Qur'ān and discouraged the free-and-easy cultural attitudes that had existed during the Ṭaifa kingdoms, and which had been fatally alluring for the Almoravids. No non-believers were tolerated within Almohad territories, and the Mozarabs, who had already once been exiled to North Africa by the Almoravids (1125–6), were now given the choice of conversion to Islam, death or a second banishment. Many were killed, and many fled to Christian Spain, where they settled in Toledo (1147) and the surrounding area. The Almohads left their most famous monument in Seville – the minaret known as the Giralda, in which the decorative traditions inherent in Andalusī architecture were blended with Almohad formal severity to produce an impression of classical elegance. Two major philosophers lived in al-Andalus during the Almohad period: Ibn Ṭufail and the famous Ibn Rushd, 'Averroes' (1126–98) – the former the author of a celebrated allegorical story, and the latter responsible for important commentaries on Aristotle which, amongst other philosophical works, were translated into Latin and exercised an important influence (Averroism) on medieval Christian theology. Both philosophers were close advisers to the reigning emir, although Ibn Rushd was under attack from fundamentalists, and in 1195 suffered banishment for his vigorous defence of the possibility of reconciling the tradition of (Greek) philosophy with the teachings of Islam.

VII The Naṣrid Kingdom of Granada (1235–1492)

One of the Hispano-Muslim leaders to take advantage of the demise of the Almohads was Muḥammad ibn Naṣr, who established an independent state for himself around Jaén in 1231, and made Granada his capital in 1235. By the time of his death in 1273, the Naṣrid kingdom extended from Tarifa in the west to Almería in the east. It thus possessed some 240 miles of coastline and inland extended to include Ronda and Lorca. In its early years the kingdom depended for its continued existence on careful diplomacy with the Christian kings, especially Fernando III and Alfonso X; Muḥammad I became a tributary of the Christians as one of the means of maintaining his own position. Although Granada had the advantage of a strong position geographically and frontier towns such as Ronda were turned into major fortresses, it was diplomacy and gold that permitted the Naṣrid emirs to survive. Until the middle of the fourteenth century they were somewhat isolated from the rest of the Islamic world though dependent on Morocco for horses, food and other supplies which they mostly received through Ceuta. They were from time to time threatened by the Marīnid dynasty in Morocco until the disintegration of the latter in the late fourteenth century. The Portuguese capture of Ceuta (1415) added to the strategic and economic difficulties of Granada which, in the fifteenth century, became increasingly dependent economically on Genoa. The Castilians subjected the Naṣrid kingdom to constant pressure on its frontiers. There appears to have been, however, a considerable element of ambivalence in the relations between Castile and Granada so that the final solution (conquest by Castile) was endlessly put off. In the last twenty years of the fourteenth century, for example, there was an uneasy peace which corresponded with an epoch in which Muslim civilization in al-Andalus underwent a brief renaissance. The most luxuriant inner halls of the Alhambra – the word means 'reddish-coloured', reflecting the rock on which the building stands – were constructed during this time. By the time of its defeat at the end of the fifteenth century, the Naṣrid kingdom was very much an anachronism in a Spain which was by then fully integrated in European politics and on the threshold of forming her overseas empire. Contemporary sources help to explain the reasons for the survival of this anachronism – the economic importance of Muslim Granada to Castile, Genoese support for a state which increasingly became a Genoese economic colony and the belief that the Granadine frontier was an essential training-ground where the knights of Castile could learn the art of war and chivalry. One may suspect, too, that Naṣrid gold played its part in abating the crusading zeal of successive invading Castilian armies. In the fifteenth century Castile several times brusquely refused Portuguese offers of military help from Ceuta to put an end to Granada's existence. The fifteenth-century Castilian frontier ballads (*romances fronterizos*) plainly reveal the element of ambivalence in Castilian attitudes towards Granada until the Catholic Monarchs determined to end a situation that was highly damaging to Castile's international prestige.

Granada's population varied, but in the fifteenth century it had some

350,000 inhabitants, of whom about 50,000 lived in the capital. No Mozarabs survived in the state, but there was a small Jewish population, mainly residing in coastal towns like Málaga where they played an important part in trade with the Genoese. Some Jews pursued their traditional roles like those of physician and interpreter, which they had practised during the Umayyad caliphate and also carried on in Christian Spain. Although agricultural products, notably sugar, were exported, the wealth of the state was founded on its silk industry. The textile industry had been introduced from the East in the tenth century and was a source of considerable wealth by the eleventh century, as there was a continuous demand for silken garments that were produced from looms in Almería and Granada. The cost of living rose continuously throughout this final period, partly because of the tributes payable to the Castilians, though the need to meet these demands acted as a marked stimulus to economic development.

VIII Mudéjares

In the twelfth and thirteenth centuries, after the Reconquest of most of al-Andalus, many Muslims found themselves under Christian rule. They were known in Castilian as *mudéjares*, from the Arabic word for 'tributary'. The *mudéjares* were permitted to retain their homes and property and occupied a position in the Christian state in many respects similar to that occupied by the Mozarabs and Jews under the Umayyad emirate and caliphate, though, particularly in the Crown of Aragon, many of them were simply agricultural labourers. They maintained their religion and customs, and continued working their crafts. Some, of course, fled back into the Muslim-controlled regions or crossed into Africa, but many more coexisted with their Christian conquerors. In his *Siete Partidas*, Alfonso X, in the thirteenth century, had declared that 'by good words and appropriate preaching the Christians should seek to convert the Muslims and make them believe our faith . . . not by force or through bribery.' This attitude of spiritual tolerance, also applicable to the Jews, is reflected in the many *fueros* and privileges granted to reconquered towns. In this atmosphere *mudéjar* art flourished. Many churches, for example, were built by *mudéjar* craftsmen even late in the fifteenth century and reveal the extent to which these craftsmen applied their knowledge, traditionally acquired in the construction of mosques, hostels, palaces, baths and other buildings in Muslim cities, to the construction and decoration of Christian churches. The Christians who commissioned such work saw nothing unusual about it, even when the decoration included phrases in Arabic script. In the mid-sixteenth century, in Aragon, Morisco builders were still employed to build important public and private edifices in their characteristic style. It was much later, when the Muslims and the culture for which they stood ceased to inspire admiration, that the spirit of tolerance towards the *mudéjar* population, by then more affluent, gave way to resentment and hostility. The same change in attitude also affected, much more strongly, the lot of the Jewish population in Christian Spain.

IX Moriscos

The surrender of Granada by Muḥammad XI on 2 January 1492 marked a new era for the Muslims in Spain. Under the terms of the treaty with Muḥammad XI, the Muslims of Granada were given a complete guarantee of their safety if they elected to remain in the former kingdom. Those who wished to were free to depart with their possessions; Muslim prisoners were to be freed; Islamic law could continue to be observed amongst Muslim communities. These promises were soon broken by Ferdinand and Isabella, and in 1502, on the insistence of Cardinal Cisneros, a decree was passed offering the Muslims of Granada the same choice that had been given to the Jews ten years earlier – baptism or permanent exile.

The decree of 1502 did not apply to the *mudéjares* who had for long been settled in Aragon where they perhaps numbered one-fifth of the total rural and urban population. Many of the Muslims in Granada now grudgingly fulfilled the minimum of Christian religious duties imposed upon them by their outward conversion, and the Morisco problem was born. The Moriscos – the name given to Muslims who were baptized Christians – did not allow this nominal allegiance to interfere with their former way of life. In 1525–6, new decrees were issued forbidding the wearing of Muslim costume, the use of the public baths – a great deprivation – and the use of the Arabic language. These decrees, unlike that of 1502, also applied to the Moriscos of Aragon and Valencia and required their conversion, too. But, for forty years, they were not effectively enforced. The nobility of Aragon and Valencia, economically dependent on Morisco labour, for decades successfully protected their Moriscos from the attention of the Inquisition. Until 1566 the Moriscos were thus comparatively unmolested; they were permitted *taqiyya* – the observation of their religion in secret, an allowance made to Muslims in times of persecution – and they continued to wear their traditional dress and to speak Arabic. They were hard and skilful agricultural workers who cultivated to advantage even the unyielding soil of the Alpujarras of Granada. They were craftsmen, not only builders but also weavers, tailors, ropemakers, shoemakers and metalsmiths. Their 'literature', known as *aljamiado* (from an Arab word meaning 'non-Arabic', frequently used by the Arabs to denote the Romance languages in Spain, and later acquiring the general connotation of 'strange' or 'foreign'), was in Spanish, though written in Arabic script. This literature, which was extensive, circulated secretly where necessary, and consisted of works designed to counter the pressures to which their faith was subjected – expositions of canon law, polemical treatises, poems praising Muḥammad, folk-stories and legends based on popular figures in the Islamic religion. It contains few writings in the creative mould. Meanwhile the early evangelical attempts of Christian priests in Granada, who had learned Arabic in order to instruct Moriscos in the Christian faith, had little impact on the masses. When Philip II sought to enforce the decrees of 1526, he was confronted by open resistance from the Aragonese lords, and a serious Morisco rising of the Alpujarras in 1568–70. The Morisco forces in the Alpujarras were inevitably regarded as a kind of Muslim fifth column in Spain at a time when the Turks were all-powerful in the Mediterranean, though they in fact received no help from the Turks. Eventually Don John of Austria succeeded in defeating the Morisco rebels there and they were deported *en masse* to North Africa.

The departure of the southern Moriscos, with their special skills, deprived the region of a source of its prosperity. For a further forty years the Moriscos survived elsewhere. The greatest concentration of Moriscos was now to be found in the kingdom of Valencia. About a third of the city of Valencia's population were Moriscos at the turn of the sixteenth century, and nearly 120,000 were expelled from that kingdom in 1609, when the decree that 'all Moriscos should leave the country except six of the oldest and most Christian out of each village of a hundred souls' was implemented. In all, some 275,000 souls, about 3 per cent of the then total population of the Peninsula, left Spain as a result of this decision, the majority settling in North Africa, principally in Morocco. Near Tetuán a settlement of 10,000 Spanish Moriscos is recorded in 1613, consisting of refugees from the regions of both Valencia and Granada. Others reached Algeria and Tunisia. Nearly 50,000 also crossed the Pyrences and many were settled by the

French government near Saint-Jean-de-Luz. All these Moriscos, although Muslim, were culturally Hispanized. Their feelings are perhaps not inaccurately reflected by the remark of the Morisco Ricote in *Don Quixote*: 'Wherever we are, we weep for Spain, for after all, there we were born, and it is our natural fatherland.' The economic consequences of the Morisco exodus are difficult to evaluate precisely. Agriculture certainly suffered in Aragon as a result of the sudden disappearance of Morisco labour, and large expanses of the kingdom of Valencia were left entirely depopulated. Castile suffered less, as the gaps left by the departure of some 40,000 persons were spread over a far larger area. Various trades were certainly affected – the silk and paper industries in particular – but the expulsion of the Moriscos was only one contributory factor in the decline of the cities of Spain in the seventeenth century.

Any attempt to evaluate the historical role of Islam in Spain involves consideration of (i) the relationship of al-Andalus to the Muslim Orient and (ii) the impact of Islam on the history and culture of Christian Spain. The first evaluation can be more easily made than the second. Until the caliphate, Andalusī civilization was largely based in all respects upon Oriental models but this dependence on the Orient gradually diminished. 'Abd ar-Raḥmān III, as we have seen, drew indigenous Hispanic elements and traditions into the cultural ambit of the state he created, though that state was strictly Islamic. But his subjects, now thinking of themselves as Hispano-Muslims, no longer felt that al-Andalus was a poor relation of the Muslim Orient as far as its culture was concerned. The term 'Spanish Islam' is thus culturally as well as historically a meaningful one. The magnificent ex-mosque at Córdoba and the Alhambra of Granada still stand as obvious visual evidence of this fact.

To attempt to judge the influence of nearly nine centuries of contact with Islam on Christian Spain is, on the other hand, to come up against a series of imponderables that have been hotly but inconclusively debated by Spanish historians. That Christian Spain was considerably influenced in a host of ways by Islam is beyond dispute and, as the Reconquest gathered momentum, so this influence, though it tended to ebb and flow, grew stronger. It is apparent in the architecture of Christian Spain from the tenth century onwards, in the massive incorporation of Arabic words (and, to a certain extent, of other Arabic linguistic usages) into the nascent Spanish language, the adoption of

Islamic institutions and so on. But the exact extent of these and other Arabic influences has not yet been fully assessed, or even thoroughly examined, so that we can hardly yet answer the question whether Islam was or was not, in an infrastructural sense, an integral factor in the making of the Christian Spanish state that came into full existence at the end of the fifteenth century.

Bibliography

HISTORICAL

ARIÉ, R. *L'Espagne Musulmane au temps des Nasrides (1232–1492)*. Paris, 1973.

CAGIGAS, I. DE LAS. *Los mozáraves*. 2 vols. Madrid, 1947–8.

—— *Los mudéjares*. 2 vols. Madrid, 1948–9.

CARO BAROJA, J. *Los moriscos del reino de Granada*. Madrid, 1957.

CARRASCO URGOITI, M. S. *El problema morisco en Aragón al comienzo del reinado de Felipe II*. University of North Carolina, 1969.

CASTRO, A. *España en su historia: cristianos, moros y judíos*. Buenos Aires, 1948. English translation by Willard F. King and Selma Margaretten: *The Spaniards: An Introduction to their History*. Berkeley and Los Angeles, 1971.

CHEJNE, A. G. *Muslim Spain*. Minnesota, 1974.

DOZY, R. *Histoire des Musulmans d'Espagne*. First published 1861. Extensively revised by E. Lévi-Provençal 1932. Dozy's original work was translated into English by F. G. Stokes in 1913, and into Spanish twice. It is currently available in the 'Obras Maestras' edition, Barcelona, 1954. (Dozy's was a pioneer scientific study of the subject, replacing the earlier interesting, popular, but somewhat untrustworthy account by J. A. Conde, *Historia de los árabes en España*, first published in 1820–1. Dozy's work has, in its turn, now been superseded by that of Lévi-Provençal, but, with its anecdotal format, it still makes interesting reading.)

GABRIELI, F. *Muhammad and the Conquests of Islam*. World University Library, 1968.

GALLEGO Y BURÍN, A., and GÁMIR SANDOVAL, A. *Los moriscos del reino de Granada según el sínodo de Guadix de 1554*. Granada, 1968. (Interesting illustrations.)

GAYANGOS, P. DE. *The History of the Mohammedan Dynasties in Spain*. 2 vols. London 1840–3; reprinted 1963. (Translation of part of the *Nafḥ aṭ-Ṭib* of a seventeenth-century North African scholar, al-Maqqarī. The copious notes are excellent and the index at the end of Vol. II makes the work easy to consult.)

GUICHARD, P. *Al-Andalus – Estructura antropológica de una sociedad islámica en occidente*. Barcelona, 1976.

LÉVI-PROVENÇAL, E. *La Civilisation arabe en Espagne*. Cairo, 1938. (A rapid sweep of the civilization of Muslim Spain, consisting of three brief essays, with annotated bibliography. These essays were translated into Spanish by I. de las Cagigas (1950) and are currently available in the 'Austral' series, no. 1161.)

—— *Histoire de l'Espagne musulmane.* 3 vols. Vol. I: *La Conquête et l'émirat hispano-umaiyade 710–912.* Vol. II: *Le Califat umaiyade de Cordoue 912–1031.* Vol. III: *Le Siècle du califat de Cordoue.* New ed. 1950–3; reprinted 1967. (Only goes up to the fall of the caliphate. The massive general *Historia de España,* directed by R. Menéndez Pidal, contains (Vol. IV, 1950, 2nd ed. 1957) a translation of Vols I and II of the foregoing work; Vol. III is translated in Vol. V of Menéndez Pidal's *Historia.*)

READ, J. *The Moors in Spain and Portugal.* London, 1974.

SÁNCHEZ-ALBORNOZ, C. *La España musulmana.* 2 vols. Madrid, 1946. 2nd ed. 1960. (Illustrative extracts from contemporary sources, both Arabic and Latin.)

—— *España, un enigma histórico.* 2 vols. Buenos Aires, 1956.

VALDEAVELLANO, L. G. DE. *Historia de España.* 2 vols. Madrid, 1952; revised 1968. (Contains useful segmented bibliography, making it a helpful work of reference.)

VERNET, J. *Los musulmanes españoles.* Barcelona, 1961.

WATT, W. M. *A History of Islamic Spain.* Edinburgh, 1965. (The sections on literature are by P. Cachia.)

THE ARTS AND LITERATURE

BARGEBUHR, F. P. *The Alhambra.* Berlin, 1968. (An examination of the *Patio de los leones,* including numerous translations of Arabic and Hebrew poetry.)

BECKWITH, J. *Caskets from Cordoba.* London, 1960. (A discussion of the ivory boxes of the tenth century now in the Victoria and Albert Museum, throwing interesting light on the period.)

BEVAN, B. *History of Spanish Architecture.* London, 1939. (See especially Chapters IV, V, XI and XII.)

GABRIELI, F. 'The Transmission of Learning and Literary Influences to Western Europe'. *The Cambridge History of Islam,* Vol. II, pp. 851–89. Cambridge, 1970.

GARCÍA GÓMEZ, E. *Poemas arábigoandaluces.* Madrid, 1940. 4th ed. 1959.

GONZÁLEZ PALENCIA, A. *Historia de la literatura arábigo-española.* 2nd ed. Barcelona, 1945.

PÉRÈS, H. *La Poésie andalouse en arabe classique au XIe siècle.* Paris, 1937. 2nd ed. 1953.

TERRASSE, H. *Islam d'Espagne.* Paris, 1958. (The history of Muslim Spain seen through the art and architecture, with excellent photographs.)

TORRES BALBÁS, L. 'Arte califal'. In Menéndez Pidal, *Historia de España,* Vol. V, pp. 331–778. Madrid, 1957.

3 The Medieval Kingdoms of the Iberian Peninsula (to 1474)

R. B. TATE

I Introduction

We are still poorly informed about the first thousand years B.C. of Peninsular history. Of the Celts, who spread from Europe in two waves to the interior and the west from 900 B.C., we know little enough. The tribes called 'Iberian' which they met in the Peninsula have not been clearly identified. It was to the Carthaginian coastal settlements from the Pyrenees to Andalusia that the Romans were drawn when they were forced to make a decisive move against Carthage for the control of the western Mediterranean. In the end, after five centuries of activity, the Carthaginian traders yielded place to the Roman legions, and the Peninsula underwent, as the first Roman colony, its first fundamental cultural transformation. This first experiment in imperial administration carried Roman society, administration, laws and cults nearly to the utmost limits of the West, and in this way the local economy was drawn firmly into the larger Mediterranean commerce of wine and olive-oil, grain and metal.

The reaction of the native tribes was diverse. Some were absorbed into the Roman system; others held out against innovation and expropriation. Coastal penetration was naturally easier than control of the interior where roving pastoral bands harried Roman posts or the Meseta dwellers resisted behind elementary fortifications like those of Numantia. One can detect no coherent pattern of allegiance by other tribes whether to Scipio, Caesar or Augustus. By the time of the last, however, open warfare had given way to skirmishes and normal police operations.

The Golden Age of Roman colonial life in Hispania was during the

For genealogical tables of the rulers of Castile and León, and of the Crown of Aragon,
see pp. 568–70.

first two centuries A.D. – squarely in the middle of the 700 years the authoritative control of the Romans lasted. By A.D. 212 Roman citizenship was extended to the entire Peninsula. It is still uncertain how heavily the civilized superstructure bore upon the old tribal life outside the range of military or civil control but it is clear that, despite certain weaknesses which became evident from A.D. 300, the framework of Roman authority did not completely collapse until the Islamic invasion some four centuries later.

It was on the fertile areas of the periphery, with the aid of extensive irrigation, that the Romans developed an agrarian economy based on large estates worked by slave labour. Hispania, until then mainly considered to be a cereal-producing area, was now introduced to the cultivation of grape and olive, flax, esparto grass and cotton on farms which the proprietors often rented out to tenants or *coloni*. The most solid vertebrate structure was supplied by a net of small urban settlements such as Caesaraugusta (Saragossa), Tarraco (Tarragona), Cartago Nova (Cartagena), Hispalis (Seville). We do not know what percentage of the six million or so inhabitants of Roman Hispania lived in the towns, but the importance of the urban settlers as cultural transmitters was unquestionable. To the traffic of emigration and immigration to and from Rome itself we owe such figures as the two Senecas, Martial, Quintilian, Trajan, Hadrian and the spread of Christianity in the middle of the first century A.D. Prudentius and Juvencus were belligerent Christian poets in Latin, Orosius a belligerent historian; Hosius, Bishop of Córdoba, influential in the conversion of Constantine, presided at the Council of Nicaea.

Despite this, one should be wary of talking of a Peninsular unification imposed by Rome and Christianity. Hispania never reached a stage where the province displayed any self-conscious regional tendencies. Much less was there a common voice amongst its native writers. Hispania only existed with and because of Rome. When, subsequently, the rural world increased at the expense of the urban, the Roman heritage, although seriously impaired, was, however, never expunged.

By the same token, one should treat warily the tentative theorizing of cultural historians of our own age who would wish to uncover 'Iberian' or 'Hispanic' temperamental constants supposedly already dominant in these early periods. Such temperamental or racial characteristics do not seem significant enough to demand special treatment or to oblige the historian to set the Peninsula aside from the accepted norms of European and Mediterranean cultural evolution.

II The Visigoths

Politically, but not culturally, the Western Roman Empire disappeared as an entity by the end of the fifth century A.D., to be replaced by a series of barbarian kingdoms. This was due in part to tribal movement across Europe from east to west. The sifting of these northern Germanic tribes across the Pyrenees had gone on from the third century A.D., and can be attributed to various factors: the nomadic tradition, pressure from tribes further to the north, or the attraction of Africa which took the Vandals across Spain to Carthage. The terror and concern reflected in contemporary chronicles describing these invasions reveals the gulf between the urban settler and the invading nomad. The reputation of the Vandals persists until the present day. The last and most important of the barbarian movements into Hispania was that of the Visigoths, previously settled by the Roman government on the western coast of Gaul between the Loire and Garonne.

As federates of the imperial authorities they had owed Rome military service, but otherwise had lived under their own leaders, maintained their own customs, laws, religion and, one supposes, language. In 475 their king Euric (466–84), declaring his independence of Rome, expanded his authority to east and south so that by the end of the fifth century the Visigoths, operating from Toulouse, had straddled the Pyrenees and begun to settle in Hispania. After a serious defeat by the Franks in 507, they eventually shifted their capital, not to any point on the coastal plains as previous colonizers had done, but to Toledo in the centre of the Meseta.

Confined to four provinces in Spain and one in Gaul, they represented only a small minority of the Peninsular population. They may well have been outnumbered by about ten to one by the Hispano-Romans who, of course, possessed a much more advanced civilization. Some of the newcomers settled in the old Roman towns and cities; there was no such thing as a Visigothic city. Others – the majority – followed in Hispania the system of land appropriation operated for them by the Romans in Gaul by which they occupied two-thirds of the estates taken over.

The Visigothic kingdom of which Toledo was now the administrative centre reached the height of its power in the first quarter of the seventh century. By this time the Visigoths had turned from heretical Arianism to Catholicism and though two kings were assassinated in the early part of that century, despite what is sometimes said about the

Visigothic monarchy, not a single one was ever again murdered while on the throne. In the second decade of the seventh century the Goths were strong enough to defeat the Byzantine armies when these attempted to break out from the bridgehead they had erected in Málaga and Cartagena with the help of the Hispano-Romans. It is against these events that one must set the generous treatment of the Visigoths by their greatest scholar St Isidore (556–636) in his *Historia gothorum* (before 631).

There are still great gaps in our direct knowledge of the Visigothic period but enough is known to supply general answers to the problems arising from the coexistence of a relatively primitive people of nomadic origin alongside an almost wholly alien urban civilization. The ultimate basic principle of Visigothic rule was the maintenance of nearly complete separation of Goth and Hispano-Roman – a system the Goths themselves had experienced earlier at the hands of the Romans. Although the king and his highest officials were all probably Goths, both Goth and Roman lived on equal terms, and nowhere in the Western Provinces as much as in Spain did Roman life go on through the sixth century and most of the seventh century with so little change.

One could not expect this unusual type of symbiosis to be maintained in constant equilibrium. From Reccared's reign (586–601) onwards, Goth and Roman ceased to be divided by religious differences. In the reigns of Chindaswinth (642–53) and Recceswinth (649–72) the old Roman system of provincial government was abolished and definitive legal form was given to the Visigothic state in the *Liber judiciorum*, otherwise known as the *Lex visigothorum* or *Forum judicum* (654) (translated into Romance in the thirteenth century as the *Fuero juzgo*). The new code was intended to bind all the inhabitants of Spain alike without distinction. By it foreign (i.e. Roman) law was banned from the courts. We have no information to explain why the Hispano-Romans were deprived of practically all political, ecclesiastical and executive powers at this particular moment. Contemporary documents give no hint of dangerous tensions, and the reasons for the remarkable reforms of these two kings remain hidden from us.

This is not the only question without an answer. We know little about the language of common intercourse between the two races since no Gothic manuscripts or inscriptions in Gothic have been found in Spain. The Visigoths had brought their own legal code but Roman lawyers had drafted it. They initially worshipped the Christian God under the form of a Roman heresy. Their coins were Latin as were the inscriptions on their gravestones. Yet throughout all their concurrent history Goth and Roman evidently felt sufficiently distinct from one another never to feel the need to record that distinction in any precise form.

Some historians have suggested that the Church was a mediator between the Visigoths and the peoples of Hispania, controlling the monarchy through its ecclesiastical councils and eventually forging a national unity by means of the *Liber judiciorum*. There is no firm evidence for any of these propositions. Far from being a check on royal power, the Church councils were regarded by the kings as a support for their power. Seventh-century Spain was not, as has often been supposed, an example of clerical dictatorship. It was always the king and not the bishops who governed Church and country. There were of course great men amongst the prelates; their scholarship far surpassed anything in the contemporary West. But the view that the Visigothic monarchy was a theocracy derives from the historical writings of medieval clerics of a much later age who wanted to secure a more authoritative place for the Church in the state of their own day.

Much about the Visigoths that has been transmitted by medieval and modern historians contains a strain of myth. For this Isidore himself must be held partially responsible. We have no close study of the circumstances that led to the composition of his famous history of the Goths, a fact to be regretted, for this work encouraged the veneration of the Goths in Spain just as the Romans were revered in Italy. In the later Middle Ages Spaniards, as a result, believed the Goths to have been frank, sober, masculine conquerors of the decadent, power-hungry Romans; they were colonizers, it is true, but colonizers who fused with the early native tribes and, after rejecting a heretical Arian creed, were held to have been forthright crusaders for the spiritual and political unity of the Peninsula against such dissident and alien groups as the Jews and Byzantines. Only in the case of the Jews were the facts of later chroniclers correct. No contemporary power waged such a campaign of extermination against the Jews as the Visigothic monarchy did and it is almost certain that this alienated element effectively aided the Islamic invaders when, in 711, they swept across the Straits and all the way to the north of the Peninsula.[1]

[1] For an account of the Islamic invasion of Spain in 711, see Chapter 2, section I.

III Islam Triumphant: the Birth of the Northern Christian States

Information about the last decade of Visigothic rule in Spain and about the first few decades of the Islamic occupation is, from the Christian side, only available to us through a chronicler who wrote in 754. There were clear signs of weakness in the Visigothic state before the attack, in particular in the army, which consisted in certain areas mainly of conscripted slaves. If there was any lack of will amongst the forces whose task was to defend it, naturally there could be little hope of victory for the Visigoths against experienced Islamic armies which had travelled victoriously, for the most part meeting minimal resistance, across North Africa and were not to be halted finally until 732 by Charles Martel near Poitiers. Out of this confrontation between Christianity and Islam in the Iberian Peninsula there were born two sets of principalities which, like most frontier states, evolved in an atmosphere of both compassion and intolerance in their changing roles of victor and vanquished. Some modern historians claim that the true history of the medieval Christian kingdoms of the Peninsula begins at this point in time.

The death in battle of the so-called last king of the Goths, Roderic (710–11), the subsequent collapse of the Visigothic state and the Islamization of the greater part of the Peninsula did not extinguish all Christian resistance to the invader. Some Visigothic nobles in the south did manage to retain a degree of autonomy in their vassalage to Islam, but political resistance could only purposefully manifest itself in the high valleys of the Cantabrians and the Pyrenees – beyond the reach and interest of the permanent northern Muslim garrisons, which seem to have looked on the semi-nomad resisters more as foraging bandits than as a military or political threat. The Christians' composition is unclear. Perhaps some refugees from Roderic's army provided leaders for local tribes from among whom subsequent historians have chosen Pelayo (718–?37) as the symbolic victor of Covadonga (722). Led later by Alfonso I (739–57), a Christian principality in Asturias claimed by the reign of Alfonso II (791–842) to continue, as the 'kingdom of Oviedo', the old Visigothic state and its administrative institutions.

As far as we know no such political claims were made by the centres of Christian resistance established in the Pyrenees. These could count upon the protection of the Franks in the nearby kingdom of Aquitaine. Resistance here was most successful at the eastern end of the Pyrenees, where the campaigns which led to the Christian recovery of Barcelona

(801) also established a military frontier region known as the Spanish March. Thus, under the tutelage of the Franks, there emerged the Pyrenean counties of which the most important was Barcelona. Here Wilfred 'the Hairy' (d. 897) established a family dynasty which was to last unbroken through the male line for 500 years.

Having at first little contact or sense of common purpose and separated from the Muslims by open plateaux, all these early Christian states began their life like garrisons strung along the mountains from Asturias to the Spanish March. The most significant was the Asturo-Leonese kingdom which, by 914, had moved its capital forward from Oviedo to León. Further east was the kingdom of Pamplona, later to become the kingdom of Navarre. Then followed the county of Aragon, already a kingdom by the eleventh century. At the extreme east, the Counts of Barcelona, from the late ninth century, had extended their authority over smaller neighbouring counties.

The most significant event of the ninth and tenth centuries was without doubt the gradual repopulation of the Duero tableland, a first step in the continuous southward movement of the Christian kingdoms that has been labelled by later historians, for better or for worse, the 'Reconquest'. The Asturo-Leonese monarchs used every means to encourage settlement in the frontier zone which divided them from the caliphate. For his achievement in this respect Alfonso III (866–910) is known to historians as 'Alfonso the Great'. During his reign the advanced defence positions of the kingdom of León moved south to Coimbra, Astorga and Amaya with Burgos as a fortress on the eastern flank. In this latter area emerged the county of Castile which achieved independence of León in the late tenth century. Between these northern states and the lands of the caliphate a mosaic of small Muslim principalities ran from Badajoz across to Saragossa which the opportunist policy of Córdoba was just able to control. Motivated by its special sense of tradition, the chancery of the kingdom of León now started using the title *imperator* to refer to successive Leonese kings but the term is too ambiguous in its usage for it to be regarded as evidence of an aspiration to establish Hispanic unity under Leonese supremacy. There have been various theories to account for the appearance of the imperial title in León at this time but, whatever the explanation, it went on being employed. It was used with greatest justification by Alfonso VI, the conqueror of Toledo. With the death of his successor, Alfonso VII, in 1157 the imperial title disappeared from the political vocabulary of this state.

By the mid-tenth century the political initiative temporarily taken by the Christian kingdoms returned to the caliphate under the leadership of al-Manṣūr. Most of the main Christian cities and shrines, including Santiago de Compostela (997), were sacked. Al-Manṣūr's expeditions must not be interpreted as part of a renewed policy of Islamic territorial advancement; they were rather sallies by a power which recognized the legitimate existence of the northern kingdoms, but only as long as they operated within acceptable territorial limits. However, the repercussions of such grandiose Islamic *razzias* spread quickly through the north of the Peninsula and created concern beyond the Pyrenees.

IV The Expansion of the Northern States

The effectiveness with which the Moorish generals, when they put their minds to it, crushed forays from the northern kingdoms was only matched by the latters' capacity for self-preservation. Their inhabitants melted into the protective hills and valleys to emerge once again when the Moorish raiders withdrew. But there was no common policy or even amity in the Christian north. Nor can one legitimately point to any binding effects of a developing cultural life. Christian nobles fought as mercenaries for Moorish rulers – sometimes against their co-religionists – and at times carved out ephemeral areas of personal authority which persisted only because of the capricious balance of power between fluid frontiers. The political pattern in the north could well have remained like this indefinitely if it had not been for the continued and growing transformation of Europe beyond the Pyrenees, exemplified in the wide-reaching reforms of the Church instigated by the Benedictine abbots of Cluny in France. The thrust of Muslim power, spiritual, cultural and economic – which both fascinated and repelled – now provoked the counterthrust of Christendom into the western Mediterranean (until that date a Muslim sea) and into the Peninsula. The birth of what Spanish historians call the 'spirit of the Reconquest' is thus inextricably linked, in its initial stages, with developments beyond the Pyrenees. The Peninsular states which now responded most strongly to the crusading temper of Europe were the Pyrenean-based ones. The success of this response was immeasurably furthered by the contemporary internal fragmentation of the caliphate of Córdoba – up to then one of the most powerful political units in western Europe. By about 1020 it had broken up into a congerie of independent kingdoms of various sizes and substance known to Spanish historians as the 'reinos de ṭaifa'.[1]

The reforms initiated and disseminated through the Benedictine Order emerged from a complex of aspirations (not exclusively religious) and manifested themselves eventually in the call for a crusade against Muslim domination. In Spain hints of reformation appeared first in the abbey of Ripoll (in the eastern Pyrenees) but eventually found a more effective political base in the kingdom of Navarre, strategically situated as it was athwart the commercial and pilgrim routes at the western end of that mountain range. From the time of Sancho 'the Great' of Navarre (1000–35) marriage links with the French crown multiplied. At the same time Cluniac foundations extended their influence from such monasteries as San Millán de la Cogolla, San Pedro de Cardeña, San Salvador de Oña, San Juan de la Peña and Leire. Inheritance, marriage and conquest increased Sancho's dominions to a size far beyond those of the King of León. Several Pyrenean counties accepted his sovereignty, while his intervention in Leonese affairs brought Castile under his rule. This county – whose independence had been achieved half a century before under Count Fernán González (920–70) – Sancho enlarged at the expense of León, making it into a kingdom for his son Fernando. His other son, Ramiro, became the first King of Aragon (1035–63). This former county was also enlarged to include Ribagorza and Sobrarbe.

Under Fernando (Ferdinand) I (1037–65), ruler of the two kingdoms of Castile and León, the centre of political power on the Duero Meseta shifted definitively to Castile. Ferdinand exerted pressure on all his frontiers – both on Christian relatives and the Moorish Ṭaifa kingdoms. Of the latter, Badajoz, Toledo and Seville paid him some measure of tribute. All the region between the Duero and Coimbra was permanently occupied and its Moorish inhabitants driven away. The same pattern of rapid expansion southwards is evident in the reign of Ferdinand's second son Alfonso VI (1065–1109). Alfonso's territorial ambitions took him first in the direction of Saragossa, the rich Ṭaifa kingdom in the Ebro basin, then to Valencia on the Mediterranean and finally to the kingdom of Toledo, which fell to him in 1085. The old Castilian marches – centred on Soria, Ávila and Segovia – were now permanently resettled with immigrants from the north.

The Christian conquest of the kingdom of Toledo and the settlement of the area between the Duero and the Tagus were by far the most

[1] For an account of the break-up of the caliphate, see Chapter 2, sections IV and V.

significant historical events of the late eleventh century in Christian Spain. The circumstances of this expansion contributed to the formation of the future characteristic Castilian social structure by favouring the rise of military adventurers who were at once members of an emerging forceful minor aristocracy as well as mercenaries in search of personal aggrandizement.

In this period there was as yet no extreme Christian antagonism to Islam. The occupation of Toledo, the first major Moorish-controlled city in the Peninsula to fall into Christian hands, was marked by a certain Christian religious tolerance exemplified in the new title of Alfonso VI who, modifying earlier titles of the Leonese monarchy, now called himself on occasions 'Emperor of Spain and of the Two Faiths'. Such an attitude cannot have been easily comprehensible to the Christian immigrants – clerics, pilgrims, soldiers and traders – who were now coming from beyond the Pyrenees in increasing numbers. The period is marked, nevertheless, by increasing French cultural pressures on Christian Spain. Evidence of this is to be seen in the expansion of Cluniac foundations in the Peninsula, the appointment of French bishops to Spanish sees such as those of Palencia, Toledo and Valencia and the introduction of the new Roman liturgy in place of the old Spanish Mozarabic rite. In documents and books the old Visigothic script was replaced by the French Carolingian hand. In buildings a new style of architecture – Romanesque – appeared, of which the crowning example was the new cathedral at Santiago de Compostela. With these developments is associated, too, the emergence of whole urban quarters inhabited by Frenchmen (*francos*) in towns like Logroño, Burgos and Sahagún along the fast-developing pilgrim route to Santiago.

It was the diffusion of French culture in the broadest sense through Castilian border society that ultimately helped to preserve in the form of the vernacular epic (already flourishing in France) the deeds of the most famous of Alfonso VI's vassals, Rodrigo Díaz de Vivar, 'el Cid Campeador' (c. 1043–99). The Cid was a Castilian noble of modest stock from the Castilian frontier with Navarre. His earlier years were divided between service as a commander in the royal army of Ferdinand I, Sancho II and Alfonso VI and service as a mercenary under the Ṭaifa kings – against both Christian and Moor. Adopting the then current policy of Christian expansion towards the Levant, the Cid managed, by a combination of deft political expertise and military skill, to capture by siege the great Mediterranean city of Valencia a decade after the fall of Toledo. Christian the Cid might be, but, as ruler of the city, over which he established a protectorate, he was impartially lord over both faiths; in Valencia Muslims were allowed complete liberty of religion and in his absence the city was ruled by his Muslim lieutenant. This personal triumph proved ephemeral. It did not survive the Cid's death, when the city reverted to Muslim rule.

It would be hazardous to describe the recovery of land at this time up to and beyond the Tagus, or the thrust to the Levant, as an explicitly Castilian crusade. It can more prudently be described as an exploratory extension of Castilian political authority, not necessarily following an organized plan but depending more on the capacity of individual Christian leaders to take advantage of the mutual antagonisms of the Ṭaifa kings. Alfonso VI, as the Emperor of the Two Faiths, may be seen as a larger version of the Cid, intent on transforming the southern emirates into 'protectorates' under his control. However that may be, deepening Christian political penetration provoked a serious concern amongst the Muslims which now led to a challenging counter-attack from North Africa. This was the Almoravid invasion.[1]

The Ṭaifa kings of the Peninsula, concerned at Christian pressure on Saragossa and Valencia, did not arrive easily at a decision to invite the help of the puritanical, reformist, Berber Almoravids of North Africa against the Christian north. Nor did the Almoravids at first show much enthusiasm to engage in a campaign against the Christians in Spain. But their eventual acceptance of the Ṭaifa invitation and their invasion of the Peninsula led inevitably to a major battle between their army and a Christian army headed by Alfonso VI. This took place at Sagrajas (prov. of Badajoz) in 1086 – just one year after Alfonso's capture of Toledo. Alfonso's defeat at Sagrajas at the hands of the Almoravids was only the first of a series of agonizing military reverses which, amongst other things, cut short Castilian expansion towards the Mediterranean coast. By the beginning of the twelfth century Alfonso had also lost important territories recently gained by him south of the Tagus. His own son and heir fell in 1108 at the disastrous defeat at Uclés (prov. of Cuenca).

The military successes of the Almoravids petered out only to be succeeded by those of a second wave of reformers from Africa. The Almohads (or 'unitarians') were determined to finish what their predecessors had begun. By the mid-twelfth century they dominated all al-Andalus except Saragossa. Just as Cluny had provided backing for

[1] For an account of the Almoravids and their successors, the Almohads, see Chapter 2, section VI.

resistance against the Almoravids, so the Cistercians, another similar reforming group within the Benedictine Order, were prominent in stimulating resistance against the Almohads. They exercised jurisdiction over the newly founded Christian military orders of Calatrava (1158), Alcántara (1166) and Santiago (1170). These military-cum-religious foundations undertook defence at crucial strategic points along the Moorish frontier. But it is impossible, even so, to postulate the existence of any common front of the Christian kingdoms against Islam at this time. The twelfth century was, rather, a kind of Ṭaifa period amongst the Christian kingdoms. The Christian north was split by internecine strife in Galicia, in the county of Portugal (which declared its independence in 1143), in León and Aragon – all of which regions in various ways resisted, sometimes even with Moorish help (as in the case of León), a fragile Castilian assertion of Peninsular hegemony. This was briefly claimed in the title of 'emperor' assumed in 1135 by Alfonso VII of Castile and León (1126–57).

In terms of territorial expansion the twelfth century belongs to Aragon. Its warrior king, Alfonso I 'the Battler' (1104–34), pushed south to Tudela, Tarazona and Calatayud, taking the Aragonese frontier to the ragged eastern edge of the Meseta and investing the Moorish kingdom of Saragossa (1118) with the aid of French knights and the troops of the great European military orders. This fertile kingdom, the strategic opening to the Levant from the centre, was also coveted by Castile but, although Castile gained a somewhat empty and short-lived recognition by Aragon of her 'imperial' role, the Castilian crown lost any hope of conquering Saragossa, and Castilian pretensions edged the Aragonese into a definitive union with the Catalan county of Barcelona. This political association between the land-locked kingdom of Aragon and the maritime principality to its east created the unique federation known to historians as the 'Crown of Aragon'. The union was achieved through the betrothal in 1137 of the Aragonese princess Petronila to the Catalan Count of Barcelona Ramón Berenguer IV (1131–62). On the Atlantic side of the Peninsula Afonso Henriques (1114–85), grandson of Alfonso VI and ruler of the county of Portugal, thrust south after the battle of Ourique (1139) to Lisbon, vindicating his claims to kingship on the field of battle. He made the new kingdom of Portugal a papal fief to foil Castilian interference.

In the face of these internal divisions it is, then, difficult to sustain, as some scholars have tried to do, the notion that a concerted, conscious sense of Christian crusade, supposedly led by Castile, existed in the twelfth century. There is evidence here and there that the advantage of common enterprise was recognized – for example in the advance on Almería in 1147 in which the forces of Castile, Navarre, Catalonia, Genoa and Pisa participated. But what is most apparent at this time is the determination to carve three separate national spheres of influence in the western coastal plain, the central Meseta and the Levant fringe respectively. The first successful co-operative military action by the Christian kingdoms against Islam did not come until the great victory (1212) at Las Navas de Tolosa (prov. of Jaén) by the combined royal armies of Castile, Aragon and Navarre. This co-operation was in part due to an active canvass both of European monarchs and the papacy by the energetic and forceful Archbishop of Toledo, Rodrigo Jiménez de Rada (1170–1247), who instigated the marriage of Alfonso VIII of Castile (1158–1214) to Eleanor, daughter of Henry II of England, and engineered the bull of crusade granted by Innocent III in 1211. Archbishop Rodrigo, more than anyone else (because of his interest in fostering the power and influence of his see as against that of Compostela), forged a crusading emotion, in which he contrived to associate the ancient appeal of the name of Toledo, the history of Castile and the supposed tradition of the Reconquest.

The half-century from the victory of Las Navas to the occupation of Murcia in the east (1243) and Cadiz in the west (1250) marks the climax of the rapid territorial expansion of the main Christian Peninsular kingdoms. After the definitive union of León (politically now in second place) and Castile (1230) and the annexation of the Balearics (1229–35) and Valencia (1238) to the Crown of Aragon, those two states had very nearly achieved their final political form. The territorial limits and the military capacity of what remained of al-Andalus were reduced to vestigial proportions. The two monarchs chiefly responsible for this sustained drive to the south were Ferdinand III 'the Saint' of Castile and León (1217–52) and James I 'the Conqueror' of Aragon (1213–76), the most capable Christian leaders of the whole Spanish medieval period.

The slicing away of about 56,000 square miles from al-Andalus left in Islamic hands only the mountains and valleys and the coast of the future kingdom of Granada. The political centre of Castile now moved into New Castile, south of the Guadarrama range, and the Castilian speech of Toledo became the language of the royal administration. The lands of the Crown of Aragon were ruled from Barcelona. Aragonese, a Spanish dialect, was the language mainly used in the kingdom of Aragon proper and in the hinterland of Valencia. Catalan, the mother tongue of the royal family, was spoken in Catalonia, Valencia and the Balearics. It was also regularly used by the royal administration of the Crown of Aragon except in its dealings with Aragon proper.

The other significant event of the thirteenth century was the deflection of the Crown of Aragon from a trans-Pyrenean foreign policy to a Mediterranean one. Aragon's relations with Castile in the previous century demonstrate the indecisive nature of these two kingdoms' respective spheres of influence. It was thus a co-operative venture by both in 1177 which conquered Cuenca for the Castilians but the same co-operation also erased the nominal vassalage of Aragon to Castile; though the Treaty of Cazola in 1179 gave Castile the right to reconquer Mediterranean Murcia, it also finally disposed of any Castilian hopes of ever recovering Valencia – the Cid's former conquest. It is probable that such chess play, on the whole apparently disadvantageous to Aragon's future southern expansion at the expense of Islam, was influenced by Alfonso II's (1162–96) preoccupation with political affairs north of the Pyrenees, a preoccupation associated traditionally with the Counts of Barcelona. Alfonso, in fact, had brought both Provence and Catalonia temporarily under one crown, so that his influence extended from the Atlantic to Nice. But the Albigensian heresy ultimately provoked a confrontation between the crusading armies of France and the Aragonese monarchy which ended in the defeat and death of Alfonso's son Peter II (Pere 'el Catòlic', 1196–1213) at the battle of Muret in 1213, one year after Las Navas de Tolosa. From then on Aragon looked mainly to the south and to the Mediterranean.

V The Social and Economic Impact of the Reconquest

In any period during the five centuries between 800 and 1300, the rallies, thrusts and retreats of the Reconquest in the Peninsula can be shown to respond to a range of motives lying between the extremes of crusading zeal and material gain. The inhabitants of the various principalities south of the Pyrenees were no less moved by religious fervour, political opportunism or by more diffuse socio-economic pressures than were those other Europeans who attempted to exclude Islam from the eastern Mediterranean. The only signal difference was in the outcome. By the thirteenth century the western Mediterranean was a 'Christian' sea; the eastern basin remained largely in Muslim hands until Turkish power was broken in the sixteenth century at Lepanto.

The life style of the early Christian states in the north was, as one might expect, precarious – a local rural economy directed at satisfying immediate needs and whose outlets were blocked by difficult communications and the threat of raids. The centre of population was the *vicus* – the *villa* or fortified redoubt; the main occupations were cereal cultivation and livestock rearing, either on freehold or common land. It was from Asturias that the first thrust came to occupy the Duero basin – that enormous expanse of potentially rich territory which had lain abandoned during most of the eighth and ninth centuries. All reconquered land was deemed by tradition to belong to the king. It was occupied under the system known as *pressura* – a simple taking over of ownerless land by official or private enterprise stimulated by the crown. The crown could act either personally or through a representative to encourage settlement by *ingenui* (freemen), noble or monkish, according to their means. Such a procedure has left its mark permanently in the region, with its traditional small-scale holdings worked by pioneers within a fairly loose and 'democratic' social structure. At the eastern end of the Pyrenees the creation of a frontier area or march by the feudal French monarchy led to a similar process of resettlement there called *aprisio* – again consisting of a concession made by the prince to an individual or groups, lay or ecclesiastical, associated, however, with a framework of mutual obligations which by the tenth century had grown into a genuine feudalism indistinguishable from that of the rest of non-Hispanic Europe.

The second phase of resettlement can be called 'municipal resettlement'. This was carried out during the eleventh century when the new centres of population were granted royal charters (*fueros*) designating them as councils or municipalities. Under the reign of Ferdinand I these 'charter' towns edged forward to the line of the Guadarrama mountains and under Alfonso VI into areas which were not depopulated but supported the Mozarabs and Muslims of the old Moorish kingdom of Toledo and the frontier regions of Extremadura. The municipal councils (*concejos*) of such towns as Ávila, Segovia, Toledo, etc., acquired in the process large surrounding administrative areas (*alfoces*) in which new towns (*pueblas*) were in turn created and given particular privileges. From this period onwards reconquest and resettlement were firmly linked since extensive territorial gains could not be held without efficient, locally based defensive forces. To these gains may be added, in the twelfth century, the lands (*maestrazgos*) acquired by the military orders in the Tagus–Guadiana region, cultivated by groups of settlers dependent on the orders. The Order of Alcántara held the western part of Extremadura, that of Santiago the centre and that of Calatrava La Mancha the great central plain of New Castile. The system was that the king donated lands in perpetuity to the masters of the orders (*maestres*); under the masters the commanders (*comendadores*) organized the defence of the commanderies from fortified points, settled a labour force, usually immigrants from the north, and taxed the passing herdsmen.

In the third phase, resettlement was effected simultaneously by municipality, military order and the richer nobles or magnates, these last two receiving extensive territorial grants from the throne for services rendered. Colonization was now conducted on a more developed and controlled basis than under the older *pressura* system. The process of *repartimiento*, as it was called, can be defined as a redistribution by the crown of occupied territories and possessions calculated according to the social standing and degree of participation of an individual or group in the campaigns of conquest. In some areas the Muslim population continued to work the land, as in the Ebro basin and in Valencia. In others it was expelled, thus increasing security but disturbing cultivation. Around the frontier of Granada, in particular, arose a series of very extensive estates or *latifundia* belonging to the nobles and military orders which produced the powerful aristocratic clans of later centuries. While it may not be possible to connect directly the growth of the *latifundia* with the proliferation of royal gifts (*mercedes*), it is certainly clear that the orders were eager to extend their estates in the south where land was cheaper and more productive, even to the extent of exchanging their holdings in the north for such territories. The orders were equally interested in consolidating lands on the important trade and transhumance routes from north to south.

In Aragon and Navarre one can see similar phases in the repopulation of abandoned or lightly populated regions up to the early twelfth century. When, thereafter, Alfonso the Battler drove to Saragossa and the lands of the Ebro valley, closely worked by Muslim labour, the same system of *repartimiento* as that used in Castile and León was used to settle there Navarrese, Aragonese, Catalans and Franks. The more southerly zones of Valencia and Murcia presented special problems to the Aragonese crown because of the even higher density of Muslim labour. In both areas, Christian elements were deliberately interspersed amongst the Moorish residents at a fairly low density (a census of 1272 in the kingdom of Valencia reveals a ratio of 1:7). In this region, round the greater urban centres, a system of allotting individual parcels of territory was used, thus creating medium-sized properties still visible to the present day. In the hinterland of Valencia, however, lack of manpower compelled the crown to make large territorial cessions to the magnates – mostly Aragonese. Murcia, initially a Catalan conquest, also suffered from a shortage of settlers. The Crown of Aragon settled a significant proportion of its subjects there before ceding the region to the Castilian crown, which in turn settled the countryside lightly and towns more heavily.

Generally speaking the magnates were thus the principal beneficiaries of the opening-up of the new territories, and the trend was towards livestock-grazing rather than agriculture. The social structure of the parent kingdoms inevitably changed as a result; an aristocratic ethos emerged based on the experience of administering quasi-independent estates and disposed to resist any other source of authority, royal or municipal. This sense of autonomy often led easily to the sort of civil strife which was to bedevil the domestic history of the Crowns of Aragon and Castile right up to the late fifteenth century. The question of how far feudalism as a system of laws regulating social activities existed in either kingdom has been much debated. There is little precise evidence of feudalism in Castile in the early period; there land grants required confirmation by every new king and nobiliary jurisdiction in criminal justice was limited. Nor was military service a condition of such grants. But in practice, theory was often breached, especially in the later Middle Ages. Catalonia was the one area which knew feudalism in its common European form. In Aragon the term 'feud' was unknown too, but under Catalan influence, lordships eventually became hereditary.

Thus it can be seen that the repopulation of new territories had distinct consequences on the pattern of subsequent landownership according to whether it had been effected originally by individuals of modest means, like the freemen (*ingenui*), the knights (*equites*), or by the magnates, or by the ecclesiastical or military orders. In the earlier centuries, as in tenth-century Castile, the form of resettlement resulted in a pattern of small rural holdings with independent owners; from the eleventh century onwards larger properties (*señorios*) emerged, cultivated by those dependent on royalty, a lord, a monastery or a military order. In the centre and west a gradual process of incorporation slowly increased the dimensions of larger properties, giving rise to the so-called 'seigneurial regime' under which the lord exercised certain social, economic and juridical rights over the inhabitants of his lands, often scattered separately over a wide area. An example of a very early and powerful *señorío* was that created by the first powerful Archbishop of Santiago, Diego Gelmírez (bishop 1100–20; archbishop 1120–40). The increase in the number and extent of such properties coincided in time with the infiltration across the Pyrenees of feudal concepts and no doubt contributed to the strengthening of the power of the lord at the expense of that of the crown.

The focus of the *señorío* was normally the *villa* or manor, an area, usually the most fertile, in which were located the residence, granaries, mills, ovens, barns and workshops. The lord's own lands were worked by personal serfs, for slavery existed as an important component of society all through this period, or by day-labourers. The rest of his territory was divided into small units leased to peasants under a variety of tenancies, the most usual of which was the *precarium* (in theory for life but often in practice for longer) against rents of various types, taxes and certain services, military or agricultural, personal or collective. The freedom of movement of peasants under seigneurial dominion varied according to region. In Catalonia north of the river Llobregat, where their situation was worse than anywhere else in the Peninsula, they could not abandon their land except on payment of a sum called *remensa*, one of the six *mals usos* or onerous duties imposed on them. The lord also operated various monopolies in respect of common services such as milling, baking and forging, often the cause of friction between vassal and lord. His juridical powers also varied over the Peninsula. In the Crown of Aragon, but not in Castile or León, he could even impose and carry out the death penalty. However in areas of difficult and dangerous resettlement it was often the case that many of the standard duties owed to the lord were remitted.

In the majority of these regions an agrarian economy prevailed throughout the Middle Ages and, despite the modest rise in urban nuclei and the slow increase in commerce, this continued to be the case for many centuries, especially in León and Castile. This economy rested on the cultivation of cereals – wheat, barley, oats – and also, from the thirteenth century onwards, on extensive plantations of vine and olive. Enclosed areas were very rare. The rearing of livestock, side by side with crop-farming, was an inevitable consequence of the geography of the early Christian states. Their valleys and mountain pastures, the extremes of climate and the distribution of water were eminently suitable to transhumance. Moreover stock-rearing was less vulnerable than settled agriculture in the early phases of the Reconquest. Sheep-herding was already widespread in the north before the thirteenth century; it is known that, from the twelfth century, there was a constant seasonal movement of flocks on both sides of the Pyrenees. The needs of communal grazing on the *mesta* (public pasture) gave rise to small executive groups, also called *mestas*, whose duties eventually extended to the supervision of the transhumance routes which had inevitably become longer and longer as the Reconquest progressed. They were known as *cañadas* in Castile, *cabañeras* in Aragon and *carreratges* in Catalonia. These routes ran between fields and those using them were subject to local tolls. In the Pyrenean kingdoms long-distance grazing did not achieve similar importance. In 1273 Alfonso X of Castile conceded overall authority to a unified *mesta* organization throughout his lands, the 'Honrado Concejo de la Mesta'. This act facilitated a great increase in Castilian wool production. Exported from the Cantabrian coast to Flanders, Castilian wool competed successfully there with English wool because of its cheapness and high quality – the latter achieved by a dramatically successful cross between local stock and a North African merino strain.

The development of the Cantabrian ports is but one aspect of the so-called 'commercial revolution' in eleventh- and twelfth-century Europe as a whole. By the twelfth century León and Burgos showed recognizable signs of commercial activity, to be followed by towns such as Toledo and Saragossa, already thriving economic centres under Muslim rule. To the east, Barcelona, a point of contact between the Muslim and Christian worlds, had a long maritime history based first on the gold and slave trades and later on coastal commerce. The era of the pilgrimage contributed to the immigration and settlement of merchants along the pilgrim-route to Santiago.

As one might expect, the availability of agricultural and livestock products led to some local manufacture, particularly of cloth. This did not, however, reach an economically significant level of production. Raw materials tended to be exported – like Castilian wool or Basque iron ore or Catalan salt – for imported manufactured goods from northern Europe or from Venice. By the end of the thirteenth century foreign trade in the northern ports of Castile and the Basque country was sufficiently lively to bring about the creation of the 'Hermandad de las Marismas' (1282), similar in purpose to the German Hanseatic League. The even more dramatic expansion of the maritime trade of Barcelona due to the opening of the western Mediterranean will be dealt with later.

As in the rest of Europe, the increase in commercial activity, the development of urban nuclei and the improvement of living conditions in town and country involved an elaboration of organs of government at all social levels. From the late twelfth century, the name *Cortes* (or, in Catalan, *Corts*) was given to political assemblies under the presidency of the king and made up of representatives from the various estates of the realm (*estados* or *estaments*) each with its own peculiar juridical characteristics and social functions within the state at large. These bodies did not achieve their full status until the thirteenth century when the third, or non-noble, estate joined in deliberations with the magnates, knights and royal vassals of the noble estate and the prelates and abbots of the ecclesiastical estate. Scholars have, at different times, attributed widely differing powers to these assemblies, seeing them as examples of popular sovereignty or simply consultative bodies which in no way restricted the power of the monarch. The truth must lie somewhere in between, for although the king was endowed with full *imperium*, he could not in certain sectors act without the approval of the Cortes or annul the decrees promulgated there – a characteristic, however, more clearly marked in the operations of the Aragonese and Catalan parliaments than in the Castilian equivalent.

It is generally accepted that these Cortes developed from the royal *curia* and that the association of the third estate can be attributed to the growth in importance of the towns and the search by the monarch for political support from the *concejos* or municipalities. There were Cortes in each of the main political units, León, Castile, Aragon, Catalonia, Valencia. The first two fused in the fourteenth century, whereas those comprising the distinct units of the Crown of Aragon always maintained a separate existence. Without the royal convocation and the presence of the king, the Cortes could not function. On the other hand it could still act even if one of the estates were missing – a phenomenon only too frequent in the later fifteenth century.

The first estate consisted of the magnates or *ricos hombres*. At first an active element, the nobility lost interest during the fourteenth century and by the sixteenth century hardly attended at all. The same is true to a lesser extent of the ecclesiastical estate, comprising archbishops, bishops, abbots, priors and the masters of the military orders. Only the third estate attended with regularity, particularly during the fourteenth century when the crown sought the support of the *procuradores* (representatives) of the towns. But only towns situated in royal, not nobiliary, territory were entitled to representation, and the number of these settled eventually in the fifteenth century at the rather low figure of seventeen. These towns came to be represented by minor urban aristo-crats, so that by the reign of Henry IV the Castilian Cortes was in no sense a democratic assembly of citizen commoners.

The representative system in the Crown of Aragon was a little more complicated. There the king was obliged to convoke and personally attend separate meetings in each of the kingdom's constituent political units. No royal business could be transacted until he had first satisfied the complaints presented by the various estates. Moreover the Catalan Corts (also known as the *General* or *Generalitat*) had evolved a type of standing committee called the *Diputació* which, by the end of the four-teenth century, became a permanent body with steadily increasing powers, primarily of a fiscal nature.

Two important minorities were excluded from the parliamentary estates – Muslims and Jews. One of the most difficult issues to evaluate in the history of the Peninsular Middle Ages has been the impact of the Semitic element on Christian society, a feature of increasing importance as the Reconquest progressed and the Christian north was obliged to face the problem of incorporation into the state of these alien religious elements, the Muslim and the Jew. During the advance southward from the Tagus by the victorious Christian kingdoms increasing numbers of Moorish residents (*mudéjares*) came under Christian control from the mid-eleventh century. Despite the repressive decrees of the Church and the occasional outbursts of intolerance, there was no consistently hostile official attitude to these minorities. Both Muslims and Jews were active in the emerging urban settlements as merchants, members of the pro-fessional classes and artisans. The Muslims, too, constituted, in some regions, a rural proletariat of agricultural labourers. In cultural terms the Jews, despite their lesser numbers, left a deeper imprint on medieval Peninsular society, both as individuals and as transmitters of learning to the European north from the Islamic south.

In the eleventh century the Jewish population of al-Andalus, at that time the largest and wealthiest of Europe, started to drift north. There they were under the protection of the prince, as in the rest of Europe. Because of the slow growth of the Christian burgher class in the Hispano-Christian states, it was inevitable that the Jews, as in Germany, should contribute significantly to the social and economic development of the towns. Although the structure of the Hispano-Jewish com-munities during the period of the Reconquest was not entirely divorced from the soil, nevertheless there was not the same attachment to it as with Moor or Christian. The restrictions forced upon the Jews by religious edicts (which turned many into moneylenders and tax-gatherers) were not absolute until the late thirteenth century. Nor is it true to say that, in the Peninsula, these were the sole Jewish occupations. Such employments were, indeed, characteristic of a select minority within the community which, to the outsider, might appear to be representative of the whole, whereas, in fact, a high proportion of Hispano-Jews always earned their living as small shopkeepers and artisans.

The social status of the Jews in the Peninsula in the thirteenth century was certainly superior to that which they enjoyed in the rest of Europe. This was well illustrated in Castile during the thirteenth century. Whereas in thirteenth-century Aragon Jews were forced out of positions of influence, in Castile the dearth of public servants meant that a handful of Jews, mostly of Toledan origin, were employed by the crown to control the administration of taxes and other financial affairs for the whole kingdom. Such a position inevitably exposed them to the obloquy of the tax-paying classes whose representatives in the Castilian Cortes from the thirteenth century onwards tended to complain about the extent of Jewish involvement in the kingdom's financial affairs.

VI The Maturity of the Medieval Peninsular Kingdoms

As we have seen, the southward expansion into al-Andalus during the twelfth and thirteenth centuries led to some measure of co-operation between the main Peninsular kingdoms. The same period also saw the near-final elaboration of their mutual frontiers. In the aftermath of the collapse of Moorish power there emerged both the mercantile thalassocracy controlled by the Crown of Aragon and the stock-rearing aristocracy of the Castilian Meseta. If the former was to prove relatively rapid both in growth and in decline, the economic rise of the latter was slow but pervasive and, in its social, cultural and political consequences, decisive for the future of Castile.

In terms of Peninsular overseas trade one may regard the period from the late thirteenth to the early fifteenth century as a period of contest for dominance in the Mediterranean: in the fifteenth and sixteenth centuries the struggle was to be concerned with the Atlantic. When the battle of Las Navas finally broke the equilibrium between Christendom and Islam in the Peninsula it also opened the western Mediterranean to a whole range of revised interests. Both Castile and Aragon were now involved to a varying extent in trade with North Africa but only the Crown of Aragon (including the Balearics) was well placed geographically to exploit the two significant maritime passages, the so-called 'Mediterranean channel', fanning out from the northern ports of Morocco and Tlemcen to Majorca, and the easily navigable straits between Sardinia, Sicily, Malta and the North African coast generally.

The Crown of Aragon, by virtue of its frontiers and the characteristics of its constituent parts, had, over the years of its growth, accumulated an uncomfortably wide range of political choices. Two events in the thirteenth century narrowed this range considerably. The already mentioned defeat at Muret (near Toulouse) in 1213 marked the final loss of its possibilities of trans-Pyrenean expansion. The cession of Murcia to Castile by the Treaty of Almizra (1244) had put a final stop to Aragon's southern drive in the Peninsula but the Crown of Aragon was left with a long Mediterranean coastline and good ports. From this period onwards its human and material resources were directed to maritime expansion, thus shifting the political centre from the kingdom of Aragon and its capital, Saragossa, to Barcelona and Valencia. The House of Barcelona, too, produced in the thirteenth and fourteenth centuries seven monarchs of well above average talent, each with fairly coherent international policies designed to raise the Crown of Aragon to the status of a dominant power in the western Mediterranean. But this policy also provoked the century-long struggle with the House of Anjou which, from Provence, also planned an expansionist policy in the western Mediterranean aimed at the control of Sicily, the island-key to the control of the Mediterranean sea-routes. Peter III's (Pere 'el Gran', 1276–85) drive against Sicily massed against him Anjou, France, Pisa and Genoa, earned him the anathema of the Pope and brought crusading armies to the walls of Gerona.

Continued military and political threats, attempted bargains and compromises – including offers by the Pope to Aragon of Corsica and Sardinia – did not prevent the annexation of Sicily by the Crown of Aragon and the forging of political links with Italy that were not dissolved until the eighteenth century. The Aragonese determination to develop maritime contacts touched every shore of the Mediterranean and necessitated the backing of commercial enterprise by defensive forces grouped around what has been called the 'island diagonal' from Barcelona through Sardinia to Sicily. Catalan ships with their complement of marines (*almogávers*) were made available to other Mediterranean coastal powers – often in exchange for trading concessions. The most dramatic enterprise, undertaken independently of the Crown of Aragon, was the expedition in 1302 of some 6,500 Catalans offered to the Emperor of Constantinople, Andronicus II, for use against the Turks. This ended in the brief and bloody Catalan occupation of the Gallipoli peninsula, an act of intimidation directed against the emperor himself which also led to the acquisition in Greece of the duchies of Athens and Neopatria (1310–11) and the Morea (1315–16). The greatest moving spirit in the elaboration of the Aragonese Mediterranean maritime 'empire' was Peter IV (Pere 'el Cerimoniós', 1336–87), whose work involved the reincorporation of the Balearics into the crown (1344) and a more or less effective occupation of Sardinia (1386). In the fifteenth century this Mediterranean empire of the Crown of Aragon was completed with the conquest of the so-called Kingdom of the Two Sicilies (Naples and Sicily) by Alfonso V (1442).

To sustain this commercial expansion a variety of mercantile practices and institutions, mainly derived from the experience of the Italian city-states, were adopted. Alongside single merchant-adventurers, who hired ships for each new enterprise, there emerged joint-stock companies with capitalist tendencies, whose members could belong to a variety of classes, religions and nationalities. Barcelona was also intimately connected with the growth of the Marine Consulates, of which the first real example was founded in Valencia in 1283. These were professional corporations, similar to modern chambers of commerce, bringing together those bound by common concern for maritime trade. They also constituted tribunals with authority to resolve differences between trading parties. In the late fourteenth century such institutions were extended to most of the main ports of the Crown of Aragon. One of their most remarkable legacies was the code of maritime practice known as the *Book of the Marine Consulate* (*Llibre del consolat de mar*).

As far as Castile was concerned it was the reign of Alfonso XI (1312–50) that saw a great expansion of Castilian maritime trade – this time with northern Europe. By the mid-fourteenth century Castilian merchants, operating particularly from the Cantabrian ports, had benefited by the ambiguous neutrality of Alfonso in the early phases of the Hundred Years War. They now began their exploitation of the Flanders wool market. A sea battle off La Rochelle (1372) gave them a decisive victory over the English in the Atlantic zone, and by the end of the fourteenth century, Castilian merchants had not only won solid trading bases in

La Rochelle, Brittany, Rouen and Bruges – this last one of the richest markets in Europe for wool (the main Castilian export), iron, wine, wax, leather and olive-oil – and in England, but had also stemmed the southern penetration of the powerful Hanseatic League.

Internally, however, the Peninsular kingdoms during these two centuries of economic expansion overseas had to endure the social, administrative, political and military consequences of wars over territorial ambitions at each other's expense, dynastic quarrels, nobiliary dissension and the challenge to traditional social and political patterns presented by the growth of urban market centres and great ports like Seville. Constant intermarriage between the various royal houses, the exile or flight of dissatisfied cadet or illegitimate branches of princely families in search of support, long royal minorities disputed by members of regency councils, the shifting and kaleidoscopic confrontations of king, noble and representative assemblies, eventually led to changes of regime in Castile and Aragon in 1369 and 1412 respectively. The attempted annexation of Portugal by the Castilian crown in the 1380s led to a war that brought grave economic difficulties to both Castile and Portugal.

From the reign of Alfonso X of Castile to that of Henry IV (d. 1474) and of James I of Aragon to John II (d. 1479), the history of the two main kingdoms cannot be treated in isolation.[1] They were inseparably enmeshed by dynastic marriages, territorial rivalries and struggles to achieve Peninsular political hegemony at each other's expense. It is remarkable, though, that it was Castile – a kingdom riven by civil war and several times invaded by foreign armies – which emerged at the end of the fifteenth century politically and economically stronger than Aragon. The great fifteenth-century economic depression which ravaged both the Crown of Aragon and Portugal was only marginally felt in Castile. The pursuit of the Reconquest had by now become a marginal flourish, reduced, with few exceptions, to minor skirmishes in frontier areas. The one major battle in this period against Islam (Salado, 1340) – a joint victory for Portuguese and Castilian forces – signified the last serious attempt at interference by the Marīnids of North Africa in Peninsular affairs.

Royal authority *vis-à-vis* the magnates was seriously tested in both Aragon and Castile – particularly in the latter country – by a series of quarrels about the succession to the throne which brought into the open

[1] Nor ideally can that of Portugal, which has had to be omitted because of lack of space. See Preface, p. xiv.

the aggressive resistance to royal authority of nobiliary factions. It was mainly a question of marking out the boundaries of royal and seigneurial power, of the crown's resistance to feudal pretensions and of establishing the nature and limits of the political independence of the urban municipalities in respect both of the crown and of the great territorial magnates.

The armed struggle between the heirs of Alfonso X 'the Wise' of Castile (1253–84), followed by the turbulent minorities of Fernando IV (1295–1312) and Alfonso XI (1312–50), shaped the activities and the political philosophy of statesmen like Don Juan Manuel (1282–1348), nephew of Alfonso the Wise, who married into the Crown of Aragon, attempted to betroth his daughter to Alfonso XI of Castile and eventually married her to Peter I of Portugal. The Aragonese Crown for its part continually threatened the legitimate succession in Castile from the time of Alfonso X. In the fourteenth century it gave support to an illegitimate minor branch of the Castilian royal house, the Trastámaras, against the legitimate king Peter I (1350–69). The consequences of this Aragonese intervention eventually embroiled Portugal, France and England in Castilian politics and caused the Iberian kingdoms to become directly involved in the Hundred Years War. Peter I (and his heiresses after the king's assassination) were supported by England and, intermittently, Portugal and Navarre; associated with Henry of Trastámara's attempt to usurp the throne were France and Aragon. This protracted struggle culminated in the bloody murder (1369) of the legitimate king by the usurper. Peter was branded permanently in history as 'el Cruel' by the successful propaganda of the usurper Henry II (1369–79) and his French and papal supporters. Out of this contest there emerged in Castile a new clutch of second-class Castilian nobles who were rewarded for their support of the Trastámaras by lavish gifts of crown lands. Henry II's victory in the civil war, however, left Castile actively involved in the Hundred Years War on the side of France and at loggerheads with Aragon. The kingdom was twice invaded by English armies (1381 and 1387) and the dynastic crisis was not finally settled until 1388.

Throughout the fourteenth century the search for social and political adjustment between the various estates of the realm followed distinct patterns in Aragon and Castile respectively. The first serious attempt by the Crown of Aragon to exercise full *imperium* over the nobles by seeking the support of the expanding merchant class met with resounding defeat at the famous assembly of Egea (1285) when the Aragonese aristocracy contrived to limit the prerogatives of the crown and proclaimed themselves, not it, as the guardians of law – a situation unparalleled in the rest of western Europe. Half a century later this situation was reversed by Peter IV as a consequence of his victory at the battle of Epila (1348) when the king, backed by the now powerful urban patriciates of Barcelona, tore up the infamous 'Privileges of Union' of 1285 and destroyed the political power of the Aragonese nobles. For Castile, too, it has been argued that Peter I also attempted a similar alliance with the towns against the nobles, but this must remain at the level of hypothesis until more is known about the political history of the Castilian royal municipalities during a period not particularly rich in documentation. What is certain, however, is that in Castile the extensive territorial gains made in the south in the thirteenth century contributed to a progressive concentration of landownership in the hands of a selected group of favoured noble families. This concentration was effected and accelerated by a number of socio-economic factors: the great donations of land by the crown in Andalusia to certain nobles which established large estates or *señoríos* there on the periphery of the royal patrimony; the territorial acquisitions by the clergy and the military orders; the increasing practice of ceding lands in fee simple, transmissible to the eldest son only (*mayorazgos*), which caused the weight of inheritance to rest upon the shoulders of a single heir whilst the other sons sought their fortunes elsewhere.

Land by itself is, of course, no source of wealth; it is the products from it that create the wealth. As we have seen, the structure of the Meseta economy rested on the breeding of sheep and the sale of wool. During the fourteenth and fifteenth centuries circumstances external and internal continued to favour this activity. During this period the other main European supplier of wool, England, was involved in continuous strife with France, a situation the Cantabrian wool shippers had been quick to exploit. Furthermore, the ravages of the Black Death had significantly increased the cost of rural labour and this made it easier for the herder to take over from the arable farmer on marginal lands.

The dominance of a pastoral economy on the Meseta (two-thirds of that region were devoted to cattle- and sheep-raising by the fifteenth century) secured for Castile a very high return in terms of economic values. The additional privileges conceded by Alfonso XI to the Council of the Mesta abolished the classic obstacles to the movement of the herds and, through the *cañada* system, they permitted the creation of the first coherent network of communications from north to south since Roman times. The development of fairs like those of Medina del Campo, Villalón, Valladolid and Medina del Ríoseco on the wool routes made these main centres of trade. Wool from as far south as Extremadura was dispatched by land to the Cantabrian ports for export to Flanders so that the interior of Castile gradually became directly involved in international trade.

The beneficiary of these economic developments was the nobility, the landowning class. Nobility was therefore the one social level to which all with any interest in economic success or advantage aspired, and the possession of a *señorío* was the key to that success. From the Castile of the Reconquest was born the Castile of the Mesta. But, since Castile was self-sufficient in food supplies and was readily able to export raw materials for quick profit, there were no incentives to develop seriously the manufacturing sector. Only at the ports of the periphery or in the international market towns in the interior were to be found substantial urban concentrations, and those who accumulated wealth there as merchants and middlemen soon found that landowning was the most stable and profitable form of investment. It has been argued that, because of this, a self-conscious urban bourgeoisie had little chance of developing (still less of playing an influential political role) in Castile. In the absence of an urban middle class, at all events, the social and economic influence of the nobles was not balanced by any effective counterweight. Castile became a country of *hidalgos* – a society which was dominated by the virtues and the defects of this privileged land-owning class.

This complex of circumstances had particular significance for the situation of Jewry in Peninsular society from the thirteenth century onwards. The fourteenth century was, of course, a period of crisis for the Jews all over Europe. But whereas elsewhere the pressures against the Jews were strong enough to effect expulsion – for example in England and France where the communities were smaller – in Spain the pressure was first towards conversion. It is often argued that the indispensable administrative roles the Jews played in royal and local government and the contribution they made to the royal exchequer in taxes were responsible for this. In fact such a view is an over-simplification of the history of Spanish Jewry in the later Middle Ages. The pro-Jewish political opportunism of Peter I of Castile and the anti-Jewish opportunism of the usurper Henry II of Trastámara, for instance, brought the Castilian

Jewish communities near to economic destruction. Furthermore, the sharpening attacks by Jewish religious zealots at this period on the liberal attitudes of their own upper classes took place at a time when activities of Dominican and Franciscan reformers in particular were directed at dislodging the Jews from their traditional positions in government. Both movements weakened Jewish resistance to apostasy.

In 1391 a series of pogroms destroyed for ever the vitality of the Jewish communities (*aljamas*) in the Peninsula. During the interregnum after the death of John I of Castile (reigned 1379–90), Jewish synagogues and quarters in Seville were first set upon by the lower artisan classes and peasants incited by the friars. A wave of terror spread from there across New and Old Castile and into the Crown of Aragon, destroying the once-powerful *aljamas* of Seville, Toledo, Burgos and Barcelona. So many Jews sought baptism at this time that frequently, it is said, the supply of holy oil ran out. Although the Peninsular monarchs seriously attempted to bring the violent anti-Semitic trends in their lands under control from the 1420s onward, the former special situation of the Spanish Jews would never be restored. In Aragon the Saragossa community managed to survive but nearly everywhere the pogroms led to a dramatic reduction in the size of the communities and the Jewries of Barcelona and Valencia, for instance, could not be re-established at all.

The Jews did not now completely disappear from public life, especially in Castile, but their replacement either by Old Christians or by *conversos* became more frequent. The penetration of the *conversos* into many areas of government and finance at all levels was extensive and their presence there gave to the fifteenth century in Spain a special social and spiritual colouring. Their number ran into tens of thousands and the extent of their social influence within the Christian bourgeoisie and even on the nobility provoked distrust and suspicion in the lower levels of society, secular and ecclesiastical. The sincerity of Christian religious conviction manifested by individual *conversos* was remarkably varied; the response they evoked in the community at large could vary from active royal favour to peasant and townspeople's hatred. In the political and social struggles of fourteenth- and fifteenth-century Castile, charges of favour or antagonism to Jews and *conversos* (though the two were not always bracketed together) was inextricably interwoven with various other political prejudices and positions, as in the famous Toledo revolt of 1440. It has been argued that the traditional protection given to the Jews by the Castilian Crown led the *conversos* in the 1470s to back regimes that stood for strengthening the powers of the throne and this accounts for the support given by influential Jews and *conversos* to the marriage of Ferdinand and Isabella. If this is so both Jews and *conversos*, after 1474, were soon to be cruelly undeceived.

VII The End of the Middle Ages and the Rise of Castile

From the 1350s to the 1450s western Europe generally was embroiled in a long period of turmoil accompanied by a substantial transformation of European political, social, economic and intellectual structures. As is well known, it was a period of demographic and economic depression (aggravated by the consequences of the Black Death); of political and social instability (to which the Hundred Years War and peasant uprisings bear witness); of complex schisms in the Church; of heresies such as those of the Lollards and the Hussites. England, France, Flanders, Germany and Italy all experienced dynastic change, rebellion, civil war and dictatorship.

The Iberian Peninsula was in no way exempt from any of these European experiences. Each of its kingdoms experienced changes of dynasty; and each was beset by a factious nobility ready at times to use civil war to further its ends. Each experienced sporadic rural uprisings attributable to oppression and misgovernment and urban riots (provoked by clashes between lay and ecclesiastical authority). Each experienced violent pogroms carried out by the lower classes against the Jews. It was also a time of relative social mobility as well as of political reform – the latter brought about by the very civil strife mentioned above. The changes of dynasty also had repercussions beyond the frontiers of each state, modifying traditional alliances, increasing the tendency of the Peninsular kingdoms to interfere in each other's internal affairs and eventually leading to a Portuguese attempt to seize the Castilian throne.(in association with some Castilian magnates and influential churchmen) in the early years of the reign of the Catholic Kings.

Despite the achievements of Peter IV of Aragon, the prosperity of the Catalan Mediterranean empire was shortlived. The reasons for the rapid decline of the Crown of Aragon's thalassocracy have been much debated. According to some historians it was caused by demographic decline at home, by excessive commitments overseas and by a grave increase of piracy and privateering. Whatever the cause, by 1454 the tonnage of shipping using the port of Barcelona had decreased by over 75 per cent from the tonnage levels of half a century earlier.

In the Catalan countryside social conflict brought the peasants into a state of insurgence. This agrarian conflict lasted for decades and was not settled until 1486. In the Catalan towns production declined while the public debt grew. The guilds and artisans, supporters of protective tariffs and monetary devaluation, quarrelled with the mercantile oligarchy and the patricians. The Aragonese Crown itself became a subject of contention. Martin I (Martí 'l'Humà', 1395–1410) left no legitimate heir, and a number of pretenders contested the succession. Of these the two strongest were Ferdinand, co-regent of Castile, a Trastámara, who was the grandson on his mother's side of Peter IV, and the Catalan, James, Count of Urgell, a great-grandson of the same monarch. As the three national Cortes of the Crown of Aragon could not agree on a choice of successor to Martin I they appointed a commission which met at Caspe (1412) and offered the throne to the Trastámaran claimant, who reigned briefly as Ferdinand I of Aragon (1412–16). The election of a Castilian prince to the Aragonese throne did not create as much internal dissension as might have been expected but Ferdinand's extensive possessions in Castile and his political power there were to lead to constant intervention in Castilian affairs by his descendants.

The main preoccupation, however, of Ferdinand's eldest son, Alfonso V (1416–58), was with Italian politics and with his claim to the Kingdom of the Two Sicilies. He engaged in long and exhausting campaigns in Italy against France, the papacy and their Italian allies until he finally entered Naples in 1442. Alfonso settled in Naples for the rest of his life, immersed mainly in Italian politics and obsessed by the idea of a new crusade against the Ottoman Turks, who had slowly spread their rule through the eastern Mediterranean, conquering Constantinople in 1453. The Peninsular lands of the Crown of Aragon were ruled in his name by lieutenants.

The accession of Alfonso's brother, John II, already King of Navarre, to the throne of Aragon (1458–79) is usually taken to mark the reversion of the centre of gravity of Aragonese interests from Mediterranean expansion to the Peninsula. Under John II co-operation between the urban oligarchies of the Catalan coastal cities and the crown ceased. The fruitful association that had lasted three centuries was ruined in a decade of open civil war (1462–72) directed on the rebel side by the elected representatives of Barcelona. John II fought the Catalan rebels from a political and military power-base in the old Spanish-speaking kingdom of Aragon proper. No single cause explains this disastrous conflict, nor can it be simplified (as some have attempted) by calling it a clash between a supposed 'Castilian' and a supposed 'Catalan' mentality. A blend of social, economic and institutional crises went to its making. Nor can one isolate it from Peninsular and international politics in general. The rulers of rebel Barcelona attempted to persuade Portugal and Castile as well as the House of Anjou to provide candidates for the throne of Aragon. John II was obliged to make counter-efforts in the international arena to discourage his Catalan opponents' potential allies. His net stretched as far as England and Burgundy; his successful attempt to engineer a dynastic marriage for his son Ferdinand in Castile was part of his plan to secure his western frontier and leave him free to defend the Pyrenees against the French. The final triumph of John II over the Catalan rebels did not mean the destruction of Barcelona or a radical reconstruction of Catalan institutions; the victorious king did not act vindictively towards the defeated rebels. But the civil war marked the last chapter in the history of the medieval Aragonese state. It nevertheless left a distinct political legacy to the now united crowns of Aragon and Castile of which the main features were a long history of antagonism with France (Castile's close ally in the later Middle Ages), an all-important involvement in Naples and Sicily and an abiding interest in the North African coast.

Despite misleading appearances, Castile laid the foundations of her future leading role in the Peninsula during the fifteenth century. Seen superficially as an account of the vicissitudes of the royal dynasty, the history of the period looks disastrous. The assassination of Peter I, the implantation of the Trastámaras, followed in 1384 by an ill-conceived invasion of Portugal by John I of Castile (1379–90) – who attempted to annex the throne of that country and was defeated resoundingly by the Portuguese at the battle of Aljubarrota (1385); the two protracted minorities of Henry III (reigned 1390–1406) and John II (reigned 1406–54) and decades of civil war between crown and nobles and between different factions of nobles hardly looked like the prologue to an imperial destiny. But the court was not the kingdom, and for a key to the future one must look to that sector of Castilian society which had been accumulating benefits through the ownership of land and stock-rearing and to the economic expansion of Andalusian overseas trade.

The Castilian pastoral economy of the type already described had, as has been said, created a characteristic social structure of its own, its rulers and its entrepreneurs divorced from the earth but living off it. Associated with this phenomenon was the growth of a new and powerful aristocracy which owed its origins to but was by no means subservient to the Trastámaran dynasty. This new aristocracy was now decked out with all the European feudal titles of nobility (duke, marquis and count) but without the usual feudal obligations that went with such titles and without the full range of powers and privileges of European feudalism. A score or so of noble family groups, nostalgic about their past but equally dedicated to securing a prosperous future, ringed the royal territories on the central Meseta. The Velascos, for example, tried to reconstitute the old and powerful *señorío* of Lara, overshadowing the royal city of Burgos and lying athwart the wool route to Bilbao; the Manriques dominated the flat wheatlands of the Tierra de Campos from Palencia to the foothills of the Cantabrians. The passes and *cañadas* of the Mesta in the west were controlled by the Estúnigas and those to the east by the Mendozas of Guadalajara and Hita. Valladolid was the centre of power of the Enríquez family, who, with their cadet line, the Albas de Liste, commanded revenues greater than those of any other non-royal noble line in Spain. South of the Tagus stretched the territories of the military orders and such massive individual 'empires' as the marquisate of Villena, swinging in a great arc as far north as the Aragonese border and from Alicante in the south to the heart of Castile.

These great families were thus closely concerned with the development of Burgos in the north because it fed the wool routes to the northern ports such as Castro Urdiales, Laredo, Bilbao and the smaller Basque ports. The profits from the export of wool through these ports to northern Europe and the cultural contacts established there through it (there were important Castilian merchant communities in Bruges, London and Rouen) helped to give the fifteenth-century culture of Castile its at first sight unexpected north-west European colouring; Flemish paintings, for example, bought with such profits, established a taste for the style of the Flemish artists in Castile that, even in the sixteenth century, would prove extraordinarily enduring in the face of Italian Renaissance painting. The bourgeois painting of Flanders became the accepted style for Castilian nobles, for the Castilian court and for church art long before the advent of the Flemish emperor, Charles V. A taste for northern European architectural styles, fashions and the like followed.[1]

[1] For a detailed account of these Flemish influences on the artistic taste of Spaniards, see particularly Chapter 11, pp. 483–8.

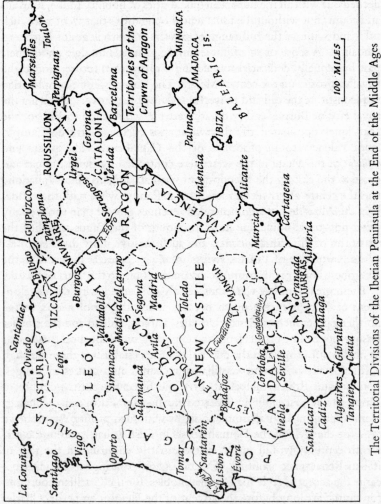

The Territorial Divisions of the Iberian Peninsula at the End of the Middle Ages

It would, however, be a great mistake to suppose that, at the end of the Middle Ages, Castile's maritime trade rested solely on the northern ports. Seville, the largest city in the kingdom of Castile, with perhaps some 80,000 inhabitants, had now become a great port and a financial centre of the first order. A string of other flourishing ports and centres of shipbuilding stretched along the Andalusian coast from the Guadiana estuary to Cadiz. The colonization of the smaller (and the attempted conquest of the larger) Canary Islands was pursued by the *sevillanos* as a private venture with the assent of the crown from the time of Henry III onwards. A duke of Medina Sidonia, aiming to compete with the Portuguese, secured from John II the donation of an extensive strip of Saharan coast. But the key to the prosperity of the Andalusian ports in the fifteenth century lay in the establishment in them, and particularly in Seville and Cadiz, of Italian merchants, notably the Genoese, with their special commercial expertise and their familiarity with the business of financing trade. Andalusia, indeed, now became a key factor in the overseas trade of the Genoese, supplying them with cereals, oil, salt, fish, wine, dyestuffs, leather, mercury and many other Spanish products. The Andalusian ports, under Genoese auspices, also became important transit markets for goods from North Africa reaching there by the trans-Saharan caravan routes – notably gold but also slaves, wax, gum arabic, indigo, malagueta pepper and the like. In the thirteenth and fourteenth centuries Iberian trade with North Africa had been largely in the hands of merchants resident in the lands of the Crown of Aragon but, though Valencia was still much concerned with this trade in the fifteenth century, the western movement of the trade of Genoa in the later Middle Ages found its most fruitful ground in Andalusia and in the Muslim kingdom of Granada which, in the fifteenth century, became a kind of economic colony of the Genoese supplying them with sugar, fruit and silk. Thus, while the northern ports of Castile carried on their all-important, well-organized and traditional trade in wool and other exports to northern Europe, the ports of Andalusia, long before the discovery of the Indies, were already acquiring an experience of a wider world of trade and exploration from which the great lords of the region were direct beneficiaries and in which they sometimes directly participated.

Castilian social history in the fifteenth century can thus be envisaged as a long process of aristocratization, which extended even into areas like municipal government previously controlled by commoners. The ultimate result was paradoxical. The crown in the end was able to recover liberty of action in the purely political sphere only by yielding to the nobility extensive administration and juridical control over large stretches of the kingdom. The main social consequence of this process was the failure of an energetic urban middle class to emerge. The conditions for such an emergence were certainly already present there in the fourteenth century but in the fifteenth century, as far as Castile was concerned, a middle class of any significance only existed in the ports and in market towns like Burgos and Medina del Campo. In its absence the political struggle was between the crown and the nobility. The struggle between these two groups has often been presented as if there were two permanent parties in unrelenting opposition. This is by no means accurate: the crown in Castile was never threatened by any viable institutional alternative. A large sector of the non-noble population saw royal protection as its only guarantee against abuse and oppression arising out of civil strife and nobiliary egoisms. Rewards from the crown in the shape of territorial grants and royal offices were, moreover, essential to the nobility. What the privileged classes by their shifting allegiances therefore sought to do was to hedge around the powers of the king, to reduce him to a *primus inter pares*, tying him by personal obligation to the immediate purposes of an unstable grouping, itself riven by intermittent antagonisms, but capable of uniting in opposition to any new promotion of titles by the crown.

The kind of balance of political power sought by Peter I was replaced by another one in the reign of Henry II, who tried to check the ambitions of his own relatives by giving them titles with no offices, and matching them against a lower-rank nobility with offices but no titles. This fragile equilibrium was disturbed during the Portuguese campaign of John I in the 1380s, by the English invasion of Galicia and León by the Lancastrian claimant to the Castilian throne, and during the minority of Henry III (reigned 1390–1406). All these events contributed to the elimination of the older nobility of Castile and the emergence of a minor nobility whose names later grace the imperial courts of the *Siglo de Oro*. The most powerful of the senior nobles in terms of possessions acquired by inheritance and marriage settlement was Henry III's brother, the future King of Aragon, Ferdinand of Antequera (so called because of his capture of Antequera, during a campaign against the Moors in 1410). His estates ran right across Old Castile from the frontiers of Portugal to Navarre and Aragon. Co-regent of Castile during the long minority of John II (reigned 1406–54), his political pragmatism and chivalric sense of duty restrained his own personal ambitions to the Crown of Castile but a remarkable array of descendants and relatives benefited from his position. When Ferdinand was raised to the throne of Aragon in 1412 after the Compromise of Caspe, his eldest son Alfonso thus became heir to that throne; another son, John, became King of Navarre; a third, Henry, Master of the Order of Santiago; a fourth, Sancho, was Master of Calatrava. Two of his daughters became queens.

Out of such a concentration of political and military power, not by any means homogeneous, emerged a party under the leadership of Henry and John of Navarre, the 'Infantes of Aragon', who, operating from Aragon, Navarre or from their estates within Castile, challenged the crown. A countervailing group was born during the second decade of the century led by an ambitious, clever and cultured minor Aragonese noble who became the royal favourite of John II of Castile. This was Álvaro de Luna (1390–1453) who used his position to plant a new list of nobiliary titles around the periphery of Castile. The manœuvring between these two (and other) noble factions was not restrained by the hesitations of John II who, a pawn rather than an arbiter of justice, suffered humiliation, insult and sequestration at their hands. For a short period during the 1430s and 1440s, Álvaro de Luna managed to govern Castile through an oligarchic regime controlled by six or more influential families. He reached the height of his career at the battle of Olmedo (1445) when he defeated the troops of John of Navarre and the Infante Henry of Aragon. His fall from power and his execution by John II's order only seven years later was the result of successful manœuvres by his noble enemies and the hostility of John II's Portuguese queen.

During the reigns of John II and his son, Henry IV, it is difficult to trace any pattern of committed allegiances on the part of any of the noble factions. The armed or political clashes between these shifting groups were usually neither brutal, decisive, nor politically significant; defeat usually meant only temporary withdrawal for recuperation. The possibility of disaster was, however, always present. No wonder that the theme of fortune became so prominent in the vernacular literature of the times. Towards the middle of the century the constant friction between noble and noble or king and noble increased demands from the population at large for the re-establishment of law and order at national and municipal levels.

Henry IV's reign (1454–74) began under more promising auspices. The Aragonese party had managed to eliminate Álvaro de Luna, executed by royal command in 1453, but they in their turn suffered a political defeat at the Peace of Ágreda (1454) which divested John of Navarre of his Castilian holdings. However, antagonisms created by Henry's proposals for reform, together with the new king's promotion of more *hombres nuevos* to positions of authority, reinforced the division between those magnates who favoured the by now established system of *privanza* (the existence of a royal favourite at court to oversee their interests there) and those in favour of some general formula for co-operation with the throne. The first party was represented by Juan Pacheco, Marquis of Villena, a creation of Álvaro de Luna, the second by Beltrán de la Cueva, Count of Albuquerque, a creation of the king. The former group went as far as sponsoring a more pliant claimant to the throne – Henry's step-brother Alfonso, a mere child. Henry was deposed symbolically in 1465 at Ávila, his brother being proclaimed king. The reasons given for this act of high treason were Henry's disregard of nobiliary privilege, the physical impotence of the king, the adultery of his Portuguese queen and the alleged illegitimacy of his daughter Juana (an imputation which had little to do with morals but much with rights of succession). The mutual mistrust of the conspirators, the death of Alfonso in 1468 and the inclination of Henry towards negotiation rather than force of arms against his enemies led to a temporary agreement in 1468 (Toros de Guisando) whereby the nobles recognized the king's authority in return for his acceptance of a new candidate, his half-sister Isabella, as heir to the throne.

Meanwhile these internal political struggles in the Castile of Henry IV were becoming progressively internationalized. Castile, with no male heir, was poised between the choice of an Atlantic or Mediterranean future. The lightning marriage of Isabella in 1469 to the Aragonese heir, Ferdinand, King of Sicily, provoked the Castilian king to disinherit his half-sister. He reinstated Doña Juana as his heiress and sought Portuguese support by offering to marry her to the King of Portugal, Afonso V. The offer presupposed that Afonso would be recognized as King of Castile after Henry's death. In 1474 the French invaded trans-Pyrenean Catalonia and, more importantly, the Portuguese invaded Castile in the name of Doña Juana, now betrothed (but never married) to Afonso V and recognized as Henry's legitimate heiress by an important group of magnates and ecclesiastics. Afonso was proclaimed King of Castile by his Castilian supporters at Plasencia in the presence of a large Portuguese army, and war broke out in Castile. At first the outcome of this campaign could not easily be foreseen but, although the immediate policies of those who supported Isabella were hardly aimed at such lofty ideological targets as the 'unification' of the Peninsula, nevertheless the result of the war would not only determine whose rights to the throne would be sustained but, in the longer term, what place Castile – and, indeed, Aragon – would occupy within the Peninsula and abroad, in the larger field of European politics.

It would be wholly erroneous to suppose that, in 1474, medieval Spain immediately ceased to exist in any significant way. But the death of Henry IV did presage the end of the international political map of the Iberian Peninsula in the way Spaniards had known it. Whatever the war's outcome the Crown of Castile would emerge either associated with that of Aragon or with that of Portugal.

Bibliography

GENERAL

BLEIBERG, G. (ed.). *Diccionario de historia de España.* 3 vols. 2nd ed. Madrid, 1968–9.
CASTRO, A. *The Spaniards. An Introduction to their History.* Berkeley, 1971.
GARCÍA DE VALDEAVELLANO, L. *Historia de España: de los orígenes a la baja edad media.* 2 vols. 4th ed. Madrid, 1968. (Up to 1212.)
JACKSON, G. *The Making of Medieval Spain.* London, 1972.
LIVERMORE, H. V. *The Origins of Spain and Portugal.* London, 1971.
MARAVALL, J. A. *El concepto de España en la edad media.* Madrid, 1954.
O'CALLAGHAN, J. F. *A History of Medieval Spain.* Ithaca and London, 1975.
SUÁREZ FERNÁNDEZ, L. *Historia de España: edad media.* Madrid, 1970.

INSTITUTIONS

GARCÍA DE VALDEAVELLANO, L. *Historia de las instituciones españoles: de los orígenes al final de la edad media.* Madrid, 1968.
SÁNCHEZ ALBORNOZ, C. *En torno a los orígenes del feudalismo.* 3 vols. Buenos Aires, 1945.
VAN KLEFFENS, E. N. *Hispanic Law until the End of the Middle Ages.* Edinburgh, 1968.

SOCIAL AND ECONOMIC HISTORY

Estudios sobre la sociedad castellana en la baja edad media. Cuadernos de Historia. Anejo III. Madrid, 1969.
GARCÍA DE VALDEAVELLANO, L. *Orígenes de la burguesía en la España medieval.* Madrid, 1969.
KLEIN, K. *The Mesta. A Study in Spanish Economic History (1273–1836).* Cambridge, Mass., 1920. Repr. 1964.
MOXÓ, S. DE. 'La nobleza castellano-leonesa en la edad media'. In *Hispania,* XXX (1970), 2–68.

STÉFANO, L. DE. *La sociedad estamental de la baja edad media española.* Caracas, 1966.

SUÁREZ FERNÁNDEZ, L. *Historia social y económica de la edad media europea.* Madrid, 1969.

VICENS VIVES, J. (ed.). *Historia social y económica de España y América.* Vols 1–2. Barcelona, 1957.

VICENS VIVES, J. *An Economic History of Spain.* Princeton, 1969.

ROMAN SPAIN

MENÉNDEZ PIDAL, R. (ed.). *Historia de España.* Vol. 2: *España romana (218 B.C.–A.D. 414).* Madrid, 1935.

SUTHERLAND, C. H. V. *The Romans in Spain, 217 B.C.–117 A.D.* London, 1939 Repr. 1971.

WISEMAN, F. J. *Roman Spain.* London, 1956.

VISIGOTHS

KING, P. D. *Law and Society in the Visigothic Kingdom.* Cambridge, 1972.

THOMPSON, E. A. *The Goths in Spain.* Oxford, 1969.

JEWS

BAER, Y. *A History of the Jews in Christian Spain.* 2 vols. Philadelphia, 1966.

NEUMANN, A. A. *The Jews in Spain: their Social, Political and Cultural Life during the Middle Ages.* 2 vols. Philadelphia, 1944.

TO THE END OF THE ELEVENTH CENTURY

KENDRICK, T. D. *St James in Spain.* London, 1960.

LACARRA, J. M. (ed.). *La reconquista española y la repoblación del país.* Saragossa, 1951.

LEWIS, A. R. *The Development of Southern French and Catalan Society, 718–1050.* Austin, Texas, 1965.

MENÉNDEZ PIDAL, R. (ed.). *Historia de España.* Vol. 6: *España cristiana: comienzo de la reconquista (711–1038).* Madrid, 1956.

PÉREZ DE URBEL, P. J. *Historia del condado de Castilla.* 3 vols. Madrid, 1945.

TWELFTH AND THIRTEENTH CENTURIES

BURNS, R. I. *The Crusader Kingdom of Valencia.* Harvard, 1967.

BURNS, R. I. *Islam under the Crusaders.* Princeton, 1973.

FOREY, A. J. *The Templars in the Corona de Aragón.* Oxford, 1973.

HILLGARTH, J. N. *The Spanish Kingdoms, 1250–1516.* Vol. 1: *1250–1410.* Oxford, 1976.

JAMES I OF ARAGON. *The Chronicle of James I of Aragon.* Trans. J. Forster. 2 vols. London, 1883.

LINEHAM, P. *The Spanish Church and the Papacy in the Thirteenth Century.* Cambridge, 1971.

LOMAX, D. W. *La Orden de Santiago (1170–1275).* Madrid, 1965.

MUNTANER, R. *The Chronicle of Muntaner.* Trans. Lady Goodenough. 2 vols. London, Hakluyt Society, 1920–1.

SHNEIDMAN, J. L. *The Rise of the Aragonese-Catalan Empire (1200–1350)*. 2 vols. New York and London, 1970.

SMITH, R. S. *The Spanish Guild Merchant: A History of the Consulado (1250–1700)*. Durham, 1940.

FOURTEENTH AND FIFTEENTH CENTURIES

DUFOURCQ, C.-E. *L'Espagne catalane et la Maghrib aux XIIIe et XIVe siècles*. Paris, 1966.

GIMÉNEZ SOLER, A. *Don Juan Manuel: biografía y estudio crítico*. Saragossa, 1932.

HIGHFIELD, R. (ed.). *Spain in the Fifteenth Century, 1369–1516*. London, 1972.

MACDONALD, INEZ F. *Don Fernando de Antequera*. Oxford, 1948.

MARTÍNEZ FERRANDO, J. E. *Jaime II de Aragón*. 2 vols. Barcelona, 1948.

MENÉNDEZ PIDAL, R. (ed.). *Historia de España*. Vol. 14: *España cristiana: crisis de la reconquista: luchas civiles (1350–1425)*. Vol. 15: *Los Trastámaras de Castilla y Aragón en el siglo XV*. Madrid, 1966 and 1964.

MILLER, T. *Henry IV of Castile (1425–1474)*. London, 1972.

RUSSELL, P. E. *The English Intervention in Spain and Portugal in the Time of Edward III and Richard II*. Oxford, 1955.

SUÁREZ FERNÁNDEZ, L. *Nobleza y monarquía*. 2a ed. corregida y aumentada. Valladolid, 1975.

VICENS VIVES, J. *Juan II de Aragón (1398–1479): monarquía y revolución en la España del siglo XV*. Barcelona, 1953.

—— *Fernando el Católico, príncipe de Aragón, rey de Sicilia (1458–1479)*. Madrid, 1952.

VILAR, P. *La Catalogne dans l'Espagne moderne*. Vol. 1. Paris. 1962.

4 Monarchy and Empire (1474–1700)

J. H. ELLIOTT

I Foundations

The civil war and Portuguese invasion which followed Isabella's accession in 1474 hardly seemed to be very auspicious auguries for the future of Castile. Yet within a generation Castile had not only become the dominant political unit in the Iberian Peninsula, but had also laid the foundations for an exercise in global power unprecedented in European history. The sixteenth and early seventeenth centuries were the age of the *monarquía española*, to use the title by which contemporaries referred to the great complex of territorial possessions owing allegiance to the Kings of Castile. Although the word 'empire' might have seemed more appropriate, this was reserved for that ancient European relic, the Holy Roman Empire, whose headship was momentarily combined with the crown of Castile in the person of Charles V (emperor 1519–58). But no one doubted the imperial characteristics of the Spanish monarchy of the sixteenth century. In the number and extent of its possessions, the magnitude of its financial resources, the prestige of its culture and the reputation of its arms, the Spanish monarchy was the first of the great empires to dominate the history of modern Europe. And the heart of this monarchy and empire was Castile.

The reasons why Castile should have risen so spectacularly to a position of pre-eminence after the long twilight years of disorder and confusion are not easy to determine. Geography, accident, personality all played their part in a process which even the most rigorous historical analysis finds it ultimately impossible to explain. It seems as if there occasionally comes a moment in the life of certain societies when divergent forces find their point of equilibrium, and the political and

For a genealogical table of the Habsburgs, see p. 571.

social order are uniquely harmonized. The new-found sense of unity creates, in turn, a sudden upsurge of confidence and releases pent-up energies. Such a moment came to Castile during the joint reigns of Ferdinand and Isabella (1474–1504), and it proved sufficiently exhilarating to generate an impetus which lasted for the best part of a century.

Later generations would look back to the reign of the 'Catholic Kings' (as Ferdinand and Isabella were called by Pope Alexander VI in 1494) as the true age of Castilian greatness. In part this reflected nostalgia for an age whose virtues were idealized and whose troubles were forgotten as it receded into history. In part, too, it sprang from an assumption about the nature of history – that all states were subject to a cyclical process of rise and decline – which itself had some influence on the course of events during the difficult days of the seventeenth century. Since presumably Spain was no more exempt from this process than any other state, it was not unreasonable, from the standpoint of the seventeenth century, to assume that its zenith had been reached under the Catholic Kings, and that their reign had been followed by a slow and inexorable *declinación*. No doubt there was an element of optical illusion in all this. Yet the achievements of Ferdinand and Isabella were solid enough to withstand the vagaries of fashion, and to justify their unique historical reputation as the creators of 'Spain'.

In 1474, on the death of Henry IV, they were no more than the rather precariously installed rulers of Castile. It took them five years of military effort and diplomatic manœuvre to establish Isabella's authority as legitimate Queen of Castile against the supporters of Juana '*la Beltraneja*', the allegedly illegitimate daughter of Henry's queen. Ferdinand's assistance proved to be of critical importance in this gradual assertion of his wife's claim to sovereignty. He brought to bear on Isabella's behalf not only his own expert gifts as a negotiator and politician, but also the military and diplomatic resources which he commanded as heir to the throne of Aragon. It was, for instance, his opportune reminders of the influence enjoyed by the Aragonese at the papal court which helped to swing the great family of the Mendozas, hungry for power and ecclesiastical preferment, behind the claims of Isabella. Even before Ferdinand's own accession as King of Aragon on the death of his father, John II, in 1479, the Aragonese marriage had shown itself to be a decisive element in the Castilian political struggle.

When Ferdinand and Isabella finally became joint rulers of Castile and Aragon in 1479, they also became, in the eyes of the world, the king and queen of *Spain*. *Hispania* had long been a geographical entity, and it had once been a political entity. It was not hard, therefore, to identify the united Crowns of Castile and Aragon as a reborn *Hispania*, even though Portugal, Navarre and the Moorish kingdom of Granada were still separate units. The identification was made all the easier by the fact that Castile and Aragon, having been rivals for so long, now spoke with a single voice in matters of international diplomacy. Irrespective of whether they were of Castilian or Aragonese origin, the ambassadors and envoys of the Catholic Kings worked together to promote the interests of *Spain*.

Domestically, however, the union of the Crowns was little more than nominal, except where matters of religion were concerned. Religious uniformity was all the more important when political and administrative uniformity were largely unattainable. A common devotion to a common faith could do much to unite heterogeneous peoples, especially when they contained in their midst non-Christian or dubiously Christian minorities. It was perhaps for this reason that a device originally intended to deal with a specifically Castilian problem was in due course extended to the Crown of Aragon. Because Castilian society was much exercised about the alleged deviation of the *conversos* – converted Jews and their descendants – Ferdinand and Isabella applied to Rome in 1478 for the establishment on Castilian soil of a tribunal of the Holy Inquisition. The Crown of Aragon had possessed, since the time of the Albigensian crusade, a rather ineffectual Inquisition of its own. Neither this fact, however, nor the absence of any serious Jewish problem in Aragonese territory, inhibited the Catholic Kings from extending the activities of the royal Consejo de la Suprema y General Inquisición to the Crown of Aragon in 1487. The measure met with bitter resistance; wealthy *converso* merchants fled from Barcelona; but the Crown had made its point. Purity of the faith should know no boundaries.

Elsewhere, however, the boundaries remained. Admittedly Castile's linguistic frontier was expanding into the territory of the old kingdom of Aragon proper – where the Aragonese dialect of Spanish, though now in retreat, survived – and gradually advanced into Catalan-speaking Valencia, but both Valencia and Catalonia continued to be governed by laws and decrees promulgated in their native tongues. The economic frontiers, too, remained. Throughout the sixteenth and seventeenth centuries the Crowns of Castile and Aragon were divided by customs barriers. The Crowns also maintained their independent monetary systems, although the great Castilian monetary reform of 1497 made the Castilian gold ducat (worth 375 *maravedís*) the exact equivalent of the highest denomination Catalan and Valencian coins, the *principat* and the *excel·lent*. Castile, however, reckoned in a money of account (the *maravedí*), while the Levantine states continued to reckon in pounds, shillings and pence.

There were equally striking differences in their governmental systems, although some administrative adjustment was unavoidable once the Crowns were united. Dual kingship and an itinerant court made it essential to devise a system by which the interests of the various kingdoms could be regularly and effectively represented in the royal presence. The old royal council of the kings of Aragon now took its place alongside the *consejo real* of Castile as a council attendant on the person of the monarch; and the traditional Aragonese institution of the viceroyalty became the standard device for the government of Catalonia, Aragon and Valencia during the long periods of royal absenteeism.

Although Ferdinand proved to be an almost permanently absentee ruler of Catalonia, he did succeed in restoring to the principality the peace and social order which had consistently eluded his father, John II. The Sentencia de Guadalupe of 1486 finally resolved the old Catalan agrarian question by abolishing, in return for monetary compensation, the 'six evil customs' traditionally exacted from peasants by their lords. The practical effect of this measure was to create in Catalonia a solid class of peasant farmers who were the effective masters of their land, and whose newly won security of tenure made them a stabilizing element in Catalan society for centuries to come. The equally difficult problem of the relationship between the ruler and the Catalan political establishment was also resolved in the 1480s, with Ferdinand's acceptance of the traditional Catalan constitutional system, based on the concept of a mutually binding contract. The laws were refurbished and the principality's representative institutions put into more effective working order; and Catalonia, along with Aragon and Valencia, entered the new age with its medieval liberties intact.

The constitutional system of the Aragonese lands contrasted sharply with that of Castile. The royal power in the Crown of Aragon was strictly limited. Taxes could be obtained only by vote of the Cortes of Catalonia, Aragon and Valencia, and any alleged violations of the law by royal officials were the subject of immediate inquiry by the standing committee of the Cortes in each of these states – the Diputación

– and in Aragon by that traditional defender of the kingdom's liberties, the Justicia. In Castile, on the other hand, the Cortes were dangerously vulnerable. They had failed to secure a share of the legislating power, just as they had also failed to establish the principle that redress of grievances should precede supply. Ferdinand and Isabella found them useful in helping to restore effective government in the early years of the reign, but thereafter they were primarily regarded by the crown as a convenient device for increasing royal revenues. This attitude in turn affected their composition. Since nobles and clergy were exempt from payment of the *servicios* (subsidies) voted by the Cortes, their interest in the proceedings was relatively slight. After a clash with the nobles in the Cortes of 1538 over the specific question of their tax exemption Charles V never asked them to attend the Cortes again. From this time, the Cortes of Castile came to consist only of the thirty-six representatives of the eighteen towns of the Cortes. Since they now represented only one estate of the realm, and that very inadequately, their effectiveness was correspondingly reduced, although they were still capable of mounting useful debates on matters of national concern. But they could do little to restrain the extravagant fiscalism of the crown, and their virtual demise in the later seventeenth century caused no tears to be shed.

It is true that there continued to be strong moral, as distinct from institutional, restraints on the exercise of kingship in sixteenth- and seventeenth-century Castile. Royal confessors and juntas of theologians acted as guardians of the royal conscience, and numerous sixteenth- and seventeenth-century treatises elaborated on the duties of kings and the limits of monarchical power. But the fact remained that the crown was much stronger in Castile than in the Aragonese lands – a fact with momentous implications for the Spain of the Habsburgs. The process of extracting subsidies from the Crown of Aragon was complicated, frustrating and often self-defeating. It is not, therefore, surprising that sessions of the Cortes of the Crown of Aragon should have become rarer as the sixteenth century advanced, and that the kings of Spain should have sought their revenues primarily in Castile, whose powers of constitutional resistance were slight.

There were, then, good constitutional reasons why the states of the Crown of Aragon should have come to count for less than Castile in the calculations of Spanish kings. But there were other and stronger reasons for the partial relegation of the Crown of Aragon to the margins of Spanish history in the sixteenth and early seventeenth centuries.

By the time of Ferdinand's accession Catalonia in particular was a tired society, its energies wasted by the social upheavals and recurrent epidemics of the later Middle Ages. Barcelona remained a busy port, but Catalan pre-eminence in the markets of the Mediterranean had passed to the Genoese, and Catalan merchants increasingly confined themselves to relatively safe commercial transactions with the crown's Italian territories.

Some of Catalonia's old economic vitality slipped southwards, to sixteenth-century Valencia; but during the reign of the Catholic Kings it became increasingly clear that the true vitality in the new Spain was to be found in Castile rather than in the Crown of Aragon. Castile, with a population which has been variously estimated at from $4\frac{1}{2}$ to 6 million inhabitants in the early sixteenth century, was not only much more populous than the Crown of Aragon (with little over a million inhabitants), but also more densely settled. It grew enough corn to feed its expanding population in good years, and its flourishing wool trade with the Netherlands had become an important source of wealth for northern and central Castile.

While the prosperous cities of Burgos and Bilbao competed for control of the Cantabrian trade with northern Europe, the central Castilian city of Medina del Campo, famous for its fairs, was already becoming from the mid-fifteenth century an international trading and financial centre. The same was also true of Seville, far away to the south, even before its prospects were transformed by the discovery in 1492 of a New World to the west. Genoese merchants, with their eyes on the gold trade of the Sahara, had long been installed in Seville, and they were quick to exploit the commercial possibilities of the overseas discoveries. But it would be a mistake to assume that Castilians and Andalusians of the late fifteenth and sixteenth centuries left everything to foreigners. The nobility of Seville was notorious throughout Spain for its active participation in the city's commercial life. Similarly, the rise of merchant dynasties, like the Ruiz of Medina del Campo or the Espinosas in Seville, suggests that there was no lack of commercial interest or aptitude in late fifteenth-century Spain.

Castilian economic life, then, displayed some buoyancy at the end of the Middle Ages. The merchants and *hidalgos* (lesser nobility) who dominated the life of Burgos or Segovia or Medina del Campo saw the opportunities for wealth and social advancement, and made the most of them. Castile's urban world of the late fifteenth century was the world of Fernando de Rojas's famous book *La Celestina* – a world which hankered after luxury, and in which money was believed to be capable of unlocking all doors, even the door to honour. But the prosperity of the towns depended on the capacity of the crown to create and preserve public order. It was this which the towns expected of Ferdinand and Isabella, and they were not disappointed.

Ineffectual kingship had bedevilled Castilian life during much of the fifteenth century, and it was only under the Catholic Kings that Castile at last succeeded in breaking out of the vicious circle of political weakness, aristocratic anarchy, and monetary and economic disorder. In reasserting their royal authority, Ferdinand and Isabella did not in fact have recourse to any very novel procedures. Indeed their attitude to the problems of Castilian society proved to be highly traditional. Their prime concern was to restore the old community of the realm, which had been disrupted by aristocratic faction and private greed. A proper community was, for them, one in which the crown was regarded, under God, as the supreme source of authority, rewarding the deserving with *mercedes* or favours appropriate to their social station, while punishing the guilty, irrespective of rank. The wishes of the crown would be transmitted through society in such a way that every man had justice. It was a society held together by ties of kinship, clientage and obligation; a society in which the community had precedence over the individual, and in which individuals belonged, wherever possible, to corporate groups whose privileges ultimately derived from the crown.

In a society of this type, the crown's principal instruments of power were fear, favour and prestige. Ferdinand and Isabella knew how to use all three. The military power at their disposal was limited, although the advent of artillery, which was too expensive for most private subjects, gave them, like other late fifteenth-century monarchs, an important advantage against unruly nobles. They could count, too, on the support of the popular militia of the *hermandades* – the citizen bands of the towns of medieval Castile, which were reorganized in the early years of the reign, and placed under the central control of a council or junta of the Hermandad. These civic militias, co-operating with each other under royal direction, proved reasonably effective deterrents to aristocratic depredations. By degrees order was restored in the country-side and the roads made safe for travellers. Later the *hermandades* dwindled into a modest rural police force, with neither prestige nor authority, but they showed themselves a valuable agency for the prosecution of royal policy in the opening years of Isabella's reign.

More settled times required more established procedures, and Ferdinand and Isabella found in the late medieval resident royal official known as the *corregidor* an ideal instrument for the exercise of their authority at the local level. In 1480 *corregidores* were appointed to all the principal towns of Castile. These *corregidores*, who were responsible to the Council of Castile, exercised administrative and judicial duties alongside, and increasingly on behalf of, the municipal governments of *alcaldes* and *regidores*. Since Castilian municipal government and jurisdiction extended far beyond the city walls, all Castile came in due course to be covered by the new pattern of local government. By the later sixteenth century the country was divided into thirty-six *corregimientos*; and although the Catholic Kings refrained from a direct assault on the numerous pockets of seigneurial jurisdiction throughout Castile, their insistence on the judicial primacy of the crown, backed up by the presence of the *corregidores*, gradually undermined the independent powers of seigneurial courts in all but the most trivial offences.

Fear of the crown and respect for its authority could not be instilled overnight, but the process could at least be accelerated by the intelligent deployment of another weapon in the royal arsenal – favour. Any fifteenth-century monarch – even if his resources were as depleted as those of the King of Castile – possessed great reserves of patronage, in the form of titles of nobility, offices in Church and State, and grants of land and jurisdiction. Successful kingship lay in the cunning exploitation of these reserves of patronage in order to elevate some families, depress others and keep the influential dependent on the goodwill of the crown. Ferdinand and Isabella proved masters of this art. The old territorial aristocracy were too firmly entrenched to be dislodged from their position of economic predominance, although the Act of Resumption of 1480 deprived them of lands and revenues usurped from the crown since 1464. But the Catholic Kings knew how to bind the great magnates to themselves by the golden chains of favour. To some extent this involved reinforcing their already powerful economic position with new grants and *mercedes*, but the process was partially counteracted by the crown's simultaneous extension of its own financial resources and political authority. In particular, Ferdinand and Isabella took the first steps towards incorporating permanently into the crown the masterships of the three great military-religious orders of Santiago, Calatrava and Alcántara. With their vast estates and revenues the orders could go far towards compensating the crown for the loss of its own lands to the magnates in the later Middle Ages. Moreover the 183 *encomiendas* of the orders, together with the numerous *hábitos* of knighthood, constituted a reservoir of patronage on which the crown would draw with great profit in the sixteenth and seventeenth centuries.

The great aristocrats of Castile emerged economically strengthened, but with their political wings clipped, from the reign of the Catholic Kings. Although they continued to occupy the great ceremonial posts, and to be given military and diplomatic appointments, Ferdinand and Isabella took care to exclude them from the central positions of power. As a result, the majority of them preferred to live like kings on their estates than to dance attendance at court. But their social and economic pre-eminence remained uncontested; and, given the size of their rent-rolls, nothing less could have been expected. By any standards, the great magnates of Castile were enormously wealthy, and their pre-eminence was openly recognized by Charles V when in 1520 he formally graded the aristocracy into a fixed hierarchy of rank, headed by twenty-five grandees (the *grandes de España*), who enjoyed such special privileges as the right to be covered in the royal presence. Beneath the grandees came the *títulos*, consisting of the remainder of the titled nobility of dukes, marquises and counts. The younger sons of this titled nobility – the *segundones* – bore no title, and tended to be the victims of the *mayorazgo* or entail system, which concentrated the family wealth and estates in the hands of the eldest son. They therefore had a strong incentive to serve the crown, in a military or other capacity, in the hope of building up an independent fortune, or at least of avoiding a gradual descent into the ranks of the lesser nobility – *caballeros* and *hidalgos* – who, like them, were distinguished from the plebeian tax-paying population, the *pecheros*, only by the prefix of Don. To all intents and purposes, then, the *grandes* and *títulos* – some sixty all told, with a combined rent-roll of over a million ducats – formed an exclusive caste, with a tendency to concentrate wealth in fewer and fewer hands through a carefully calculated policy of intermarriage and the use of *mayorazgos* to prevent the dispersion of property.

In spite of the overwhelming wealth of the handful of great Castilian families, the immediate future lay with men drawn from the middle ranks of society – the *hidalgo* and urban patrician families who had rallied to the support of the Catholic Kings. Ferdinand and Isabella were shrewd talent-spotters, and they knew how to be well served. They were quick to realize the need for a trained core of officials in government to act as councillors, secretaries and officers of justice. They expected the gentry and the upper urban classes to provide the bulk of these officials, and they relied upon the universities to train them. While the patronage of learning naturally accorded with the humanist inclinations of the Catholic Kings, they also had more utilitarian purposes in mind in patronizing and encouraging new educational foundations. At their instigation, or under the inspiration of their example, new colleges were endowed in existing universities, and new universities were founded. At the beginning of the sixteenth century there were eleven universities in Spain. A century later there were thirty-three.

The links between educational institutions and the state were strengthened by a law of 1493 which made ten years of university study in canon or civil law an essential qualification for many of the administrative or judicial posts under the crown. This meant that the way to promotion lay increasingly through the universities; and families would make great efforts to send a son to college, as the first and indispensable step on a career ladder which might eventually lead from some minor judicial or administrative appointment to a post in the legal chancellery of Valladolid or Granada, or even to membership of one of the royal councils. Since such promotion would in turn favour the fortunes of the entire family, education and public office were important devices for furthering social mobility. With social demand and the needs of the state working to the same end, the pressure for entry into the universities was consequently heavy, and it has been calculated that late sixteenth-century Castile supported an annual university population of 20,000 to 25,000 students – perhaps 6 per cent of its young male adult population.[1] In particular, the famous *Colegios Mayores*, of which there were four in the University of Salamanca, became the nurseries of a talented élite from which were drawn the scholars, the administrators and the clerics of Habsburg Spain.

A growing bureaucracy, university-trained and legalistic in its intellectual formation, was one of the most enduring legacies bequeathed by the Catholic Kings to their successors. It was this bureaucracy of *letrados* which administered, and held together, the expanding monarchy and empire of the sixteenth century. The *letrados* provided

[1] See Richard L. Kagan, 'Universities in Castile 1500–1700', *Past and Present*, 49 (1970), pp. 44–71. The reference takes account of private information supplied by this article's author subsequent to the publication of his article.

an indispensable counterweight to the old nobility and served as the bulwark of the crown's authority.

By selecting their servants from among the middle orders of society, and conferring their favours in Church and State without undue regard for rank and birth, Ferdinand and Isabella succeeded in revitalizing the conception of Castile as a coherent community, whose loyalties and aspirations were centred on the crown. This created new opportunities for the aspiring and released new energies for the service of the state. Ferdinand and Isabella set high ideals before their subjects – a revitalized society, a purified Church, a just administration – and because these ideals were widely shared, they succeeded in evoking a vigorous response.

High ideals, however, are difficult to sustain over long periods of time unless they are sanctified by success; and it was precisely because so many of their policies commanded success that the Catholic Kings enjoyed a unique prestige. They saw themselves entrusted with a providential mission, which included not only the restoration of justice and good government to Castile but also the advancement of the Catholic faith. Castile had a divine duty to expel the Moors from its soil, but it must show itself worthy of the great task that confronted it. This demanded a purification of the national Church. The Catholic Kings fought a tenacious, and ultimately successful, campaign against the papacy to ensure that they, and not Rome, should nominate to bishoprics. Their success in this campaign enabled them to place in high ecclesiastical office men who would forward the work of reform, on which Isabella had embarked under the guidance of her Hieronymite confessor, Hernando de Talavera (1428–1507). Talavera's successor, Francisco Jiménez de Cisneros (1436–1517), himself became Archbishop of Toledo in 1495. From his position of eminence he was well placed to direct the reform campaign in his own Franciscan Order, and to promote efforts for improving the learning and morals of the clergy of Castile. It was Cisneros who sponsored the Complutensian Polyglot Bible and founded the University of Alcalá.

A reformed and purified Church was the best defence against the subversive influences of heresy, and the reform programme of the Catholic Kings undoubtedly removed or diminished abuses which in other countries would have led to a break with Rome. Standards rose, if only slowly; and the vitality of Castilian Catholicism in the late fifteenth and early sixteenth centuries was enhanced by spiritual influences from outside the Peninsula – in particular the influence of regenerative and apocalyptic Italian Catholicism, and of Flemish devotional literature, which reached its climax in the immense popularity of the works of Erasmus. Such a church was well equipped to withstand heretical assaults, although it regarded the apparatus of the Inquisition as an essential protection against the pernicious Judaizing tendencies of insincere *conversos*.

In one area, however, the Church failed dismally, in spite of the opportunities which came its way. The long-interrupted process of the Reconquest was resumed again in 1482; and ten years later, on 2 January 1492, Granada itself finally surrendered, in return for a guarantee that the Moorish inhabitants would be allowed to retain their own laws, religion, customs and dress. Hernando de Talavera, chosen by the queen as first Archbishop of Granada, was anxious to win the Moors to Christianity by means of preaching and Christian example. But in the euphoria generated by the completion of the Reconquest, more militant voices demanded sterner measures, with their promise of quicker results. Cisneros, who arrived in Granada in 1499, impetuously insisted on a policy of mass baptism and forcible conversion, which drove the Moors of the Alpujarras of Granada to revolt. The suppression of the revolt was followed in 1502 by a pragmatic which went back on the word of the crown by ordering that all unconverted Moors should leave the country. Those who possessed the means left Spain for North Africa, but large numbers had no choice but to remain. Nominally they were now Christians, but the clergy made little effort to instruct them in their new faith, or to set an example which would encourage genuine conversion. In consequence, the Moriscos remained a sullen and resentful minority, clinging as best they could to the religious and ceremonial practices of their forefathers in a climate of Christian indifference.

For the majority of Christians the territorial conquest of Granada was itself enough, and the more exacting demands made by spiritual conquest were all too soon conveniently forgotten. With God's help they had overthrown Islam. Now, again with God's help, they must destroy those other enemies of the Church, the Jews. There were still many professing Jews in Spain, and these were untouched by the Inquisition, whose sphere of jurisdiction covered only their converted brethren. It was believed that the continuing presence of these Jews was dangerously attractive to the *conversos* and a cause of constant backsliding. In such circumstances, perhaps the most radical solution was the best; and in the elation caused by the fall of Granada there was little inducement to count its cost. On 30 March 1492, less than three weeks after the Moorish surrender, the Catholic Kings signed an edict ordering the expulsion of all professed Jews from their kingdoms within four months. Between 120,000 and 150,000 Jews (as well as some influential *conversos*) chose to abandon their country rather than their faith. The departure of so many merchants, professional men and skilled artisans left a gaping void which sixteenth-century Spain would never adequately fill, although Jewish talent, still surviving in the large number of *converso* families, was none the less to make a contribution of the first order to the civilization of Habsburg Spain.

Purified of its Jewish and Moorish strains, the Spain of the Catholic Kings felt itself free to pursue its providential mission on a wider stage. There were some, including Cisneros, who wished to continue the Reconquest across the Straits into Africa to the east of the territory there already occupied by the Portuguese, but the climate and terrain were unattractive, and Castile's Africa campaign never succeeded in advancing very far. There was more loot to be had in Italy, where Ferdinand's armies consolidated and extended the old Aragonese dominions against an ambitious French attack. There was, too, the prospect of even greater plunder and glory to be won among the hitherto unknown peoples of unknown lands.

In the afterglow of their victory at Granada Ferdinand and Isabella agreed to countenance the plans submitted by that tenacious Genoese seaman, Christopher Columbus (1451–1506), for a voyage to the west. The famous *capitulaciones*, signed with Columbus on 17 April 1492 in the camp city of Santa Fe outside the walls of Granada, named him hereditary Admiral of the Ocean Sea and viceroy and governor of such islands and lands as he should discover in it. In August Columbus set sail with his three ships and his crew of eighty-eight from the Andalusian port of Palos; and on 12 October he made his landfall in the Caribbean. The news of his success caused intense excitement. The Castile of the Catholic Kings could no longer entertain the slightest doubt that God's special favour rested upon it. First Granada, and now the Indies. Castile would carry its mission of conquest and conversion across the hitherto unsailed ocean, and before long its greatness would encompass the globe.

II Greatness

The discovery of the New World of America was in due course to transform the prospects both of Spain and of Europe, but the process of transformation occurred only slowly and took many generations to complete. By the bull *Inter Caetera* of 1493, Rome formally entrusted the Spanish crown with the task of evangelizing the peoples of the newly discovered lands. But the magnitude of Castile's spiritual mission overseas only began to be appreciated as new expeditions probed outwards from the island of Hispaniola and gradually revealed the existence of a vast land-mass which seemed to exist in its own right, and not as a mere extension of Asia.

With the exception of the land that fell within the sphere of jurisdiction allocated to Portugal by the Treaty of Tordesillas of 1494 between the Spanish and Portuguese crowns, any newly discovered territories were to be regarded as the exclusive preserve of Castile. But it was one thing to claim territory and quite another to establish effective sovereignty over it. Early sixteenth-century Castile invested heavily in the exploration, conquest and colonization of its American empire, and although the rewards proved to be great, they were often hard-won. The leadership and the guile of Castile's captains and the courage and stamina of its foot-soldiers were nowhere more brutally tested than in the tropical swamps of Central America or the harsh mountain landscapes of Peru. But by degrees the Castilians established their presence through the new-found continent. The Aztec empire of Montezuma fell to Hernán Cortés (1485–1547) between 1519 and 1521, and the Inca empire of Peru to his fellow Extremaduran, Francisco Pizarro (1476–1541), in 1531–2. From about 1540 the heroic age of conquest was over. The crown was now faced with the arduous task of imposing its own authority over the *conquistadores* and settlers. Only when this was achieved could crown and colonists begin to work together on the systematic exploitation of the resources – and especially the mineral resources – of the newly discovered lands.

For all the insistence of Cortés and his colleagues on the vast new opportunities which the conquest of the New World created for Castile, the priorities of the Spanish crown remained firmly European. America was regarded as a valuable bonanza for Spain, especially when it began to yield large quantities of gold and silver, but the key to Spanish greatness was assumed to lie in Europe. Here, Ferdinand's skilful diplomacy had secured for his country some remarkable successes. The trans-Pyrenean Catalan counties of Rosellón and Cerdaña were recovered from France by a treaty of 1493; the French recognized the Spaniards as the lawful possessors of the kingdom of Naples in 1504, after the Great Captain, Gonzalo de Córdoba (1453–1515), had scored a series of brilliant victories in Spain's Italian wars; and the southern half of the kingdom of Navarre was wrested from the hands of the native dynasty of Albret in 1512 and formally incorporated into the Crown of Castile three years later.

But Ferdinand's diplomatic efforts to isolate his old enemy, the French, led him to spin a web of international alliances in which the master spider himself was finally ensnared. The alliances, as was customary, were confirmed by royal marriages – to Portugal, England and the Empire. But the only son of Ferdinand and Isabella, Prince John, died in 1497. Death again intervened to cut short the hope of succession by the Portuguese marriage, and it was clear that the future of the line rested with the mentally unstable Infanta Juana (1479–1555), who was married to the Emperor Maximilian's son, the Archduke Philip (1478–1506). The Crown of Castile would therefore inexorably pass out of the hands of the Trastámaras into those of the House of Habsburg.

The prospect cast a dark cloud over the last years of Isabella. After her death in 1504 Ferdinand retired to Aragon, and Philip and Juana arrived in Castile in 1506 to take up their inheritance. But death again took a hand. Philip died soon after his arrival; his grief-stricken widow retired into a twilight world of solitude and madness; and her eldest son, Charles of Ghent, was only six years old. A regency council was set up under the presidency of Archbishop Cisneros, but the revival of aristocratic faction induced the Cortes of Castile to appeal to Ferdinand to return. Between them, Ferdinand and Cisneros succeeded in preserving the peace, and on his deathbed in 1516 Ferdinand reluctantly named Charles of Ghent as his heir, although his own preference was for Charles's Spanish-educated brother, Ferdinand.

The uncovenanted result of Ferdinand's diplomatic manœuvres was, then, to place on the thrones of Castile and Aragon a sixteen-year-old youth who had been brought up in the Netherlands and who seemed destined to succeed his grandfather, the Emperor Maximilian, on the imperial throne. The Castilians, who had come to think of themselves in recent years as subject to the alien domination of Ferdinand's Aragonese officials, now saw themselves condemned to a further period of alien domination, this time by Charles and his Flemings. A group of nobles hatched a conspiracy, which was foiled by the regent, Cardinal Cisneros, to proclaim Charles's brother Ferdinand as king; but when Charles finally arrived in the Iberian Peninsula from Flanders in the autumn of 1517 to take over the government of the country from the dying regent, he showed little awareness of the dangers that surrounded him. In particular, he allowed his Flemish entourage to load themselves with offices, booty and honours as they moved like a horde of locusts across Castile in his train. Castilian anxiety increased still further when news arrived of Charles's election in June 1519 as Holy Roman Emperor in succession to Maximilian. Was Castile then to be ruled by a permanent absentee, who would delegate his government in Spain to a band of Flemish rogues?

As the emperor-elect convened a new session of the Cortes to vote a fresh subsidy as a prelude to his proposed voyage to Germany, a wave of protest spread through the cities of central and northern Castile. On 20 May 1520 he sailed from Corunna, leaving his former tutor, Adrian of Utrecht, as regent in his absence; and, within a few days, Castile was in open revolt. The revolt was to last for the best part of a year. Not until the rebels went down to crushing defeat at Villalar on 23 April 1521 did Charles's authority run effectively again throughout Castile.

The revolt of the *comuneros* was a highly complex movement, which allows of no simple interpretation. By degrees it came to assume the character of a civil war, and the clues to many of its mysteries probably lie buried in the family hatreds and faction feuds of the fifteenth century. But it was something more original and more wide-ranging than a resumption of the civil wars of the reign of Henry IV, as the name *comunero* itself implies.

At least in its initial stages the movement consisted of a revolt of the communes of Castile, banding together in defence of the so-called *bien común*. Juan de Padilla (1484–1521) and his fellow *comuneros* claimed to be fighting, in the name of the community of Castile, for a public weal which in recent years had been betrayed. The immediate grievances were high taxation, royal absenteeism and the presence of foreigners in high offices of Church and State. The revolt can therefore be represented as a last stand by the old, traditionalist Castile against those forces, alien and innovating, which threatened to undermine its historical identity by linking its fate with foreign rulers and foreign lands.

Any attempt, however, to depict the revolt of the *comuneros* as a precursor of right-wing movements in modern Spanish history is liable to look as unsatisfying as nineteenth-century attempts to depict it as the precursor of liberal revolutions. Like the simultaneous rising in Valencia, known as the *Germanía*, the revolt of the *comuneros* was – or at least became – a popular rising against the rich and the privileged. Messianic and egalitarian voices were raised in both Castile and Valencia, and the urban mobs were whipped into a frenzy by demagogic friars. But the Valencian revolt seems to have had little political content, and was related less to the alleged iniquities of the new regime than to existing social tensions which became acute when the city of Valencia was struck by plague. The *comunero* cities of Castile, on the other hand, were deeply preoccupied by the implications of recent political changes and administrative measures, and formulated among themselves a political programme which was by no means purely negative in its approach. The *comunero* leaders were convinced that they were defending the idea of liberty, as understood in medieval Castile. Their thinking contained a strong contractual element, based on the conviction that the right of the community was, in the last resort, superior to the will of the king. 'When princes are tyrants, then communities must govern,' observed a *comunero* cleric.

This medieval Castilian doctrine of the superior rights of the community – a doctrine which Hernán Cortés was manipulating to his own advantage at almost the same moment in Mexico – was the most important principle at stake in the revolt of the *comuneros*. Municipalities were regarded as the living embodiment of community rights, whether in Castile or in New Spain; and it was because of this that not only the cause of municipal liberty, but also Castilian constitutionalism itself, met its death on the field of Villalar. At the national level the emperor was victorious; and at the municipal level his loyal servant, the *corregidor*.

The emperor returned in 1522 to a pacified country, in which the nobles, shocked by the violence of the populace, were ostentatiously displaying their loyalty, while prudent men concealed their earlier reservations and accepted Charles's government as a *fait accompli*. In any event, there were increasingly strong reasons for an accommodation between Charles and the political establishment of Castile. Charles himself returned to Spain with all the prestige of the imperial title. His Erasmian and humanist councillors had formulated for him an imperial programme which, with its visions of a regenerated Christendom under the aegis of the emperor, had a certain seductive attraction for native Spanish humanists. But the identity of interest was wider than this. The emperor offered his peoples of Spain a full share and a privileged place in his enterprises at a moment when their horizons were being dramatically extended by the victories of their soldiers on the battlefields of the Old World and the New. An imperial mission was being thrust upon Spain, and especially upon Castile, at a time when it had already been conditioned to think in terms of a providential mission on a global scale.

Charles, for his part, needed Spain. At least until the years around 1540 the Netherlands and Italy constituted the axis of his empire. But from the first he needed Spain's soldiers – the *tercios* of Castile – and more and more he would need its money as his expenses mounted and the alternative sources of revenue began to run dry. Castile, for all its barren tracts of land, had wealth – the wealth that came from modest economic growth at home, and from the rise of transatlantic markets in New Spain and Peru. The colonists of the New World were hungry for supplies from home, and they were prepared to pay for them with the gold and silver which America was beginning to yield in such abundance. And it was gold and silver, especially silver, which secured for Charles the credit on which he depended for the prosecution of his imperial policies.

Castile's function was therefore to sustain the world-wide empire of Charles V; and after seven years' residence in the Peninsula he felt sufficiently confident to leave it again, and to return thereafter only at infrequent intervals. During his long absences abroad he entrusted the government first to the Portuguese-born Empress Isabella (1503–39), and later to the only son of their marriage, Philip, born in 1527. But the day-to-day administration was left to one of the most able and devoted of his servants, Francisco de los Cobos (1477?–1547), a man of humble Andalusian origins who rose through the secretariat to become *comendador mayor de León* and the most powerful man in Spain. It was to Los Cobos that he turned whenever he wanted more money from Castile; and Los Cobos – and Castile – never failed him.

Castile accepted its role partly because, after Villalar, there seemed little alternative, and partly because the opportunities seemed considerable and the prospective prizes alluring. But the implications of Castile's involvement in the grand designs of the Habsburgs were to prove far-reaching, as a source at once of splendour and misery. Spanish history under Charles V and his Habsburg successors was in fact to be charac-

terized by a continuing interplay between the ambitions and commitments of a European-minded dynasty and the responses and resistances
of a relatively inflexible and still largely medieval society. The demands
of the dynasty imposed strains and distortions which ultimately crippled
Iberian development; but it would be a mistake to assume from this
that Castile was a permanently unwilling sacrificial victim on the
altar of Habsburg dynastic interests. There were, on the contrary,
some areas at least in which there existed a close coincidence of interest
between dynasty and people; and if the value to Castile of Italy,
Germany or the Netherlands was periodically called into question, the
crusading tradition was still sufficiently alive in the sixteenth century
to inspire Castilians with the sense that they were engaged in a holy
war against Islam or the Protestant heretics.

In the Mediterranean in particular the emperor's enemies were also
the enemies of Spain. As emperor, Charles had a holy mission to defend
Christendom against the Turk. But Ottoman power, allied to the
Barbary corsairs, was a permanent danger to Spanish interests. Spain's
garrisons in North Africa were vulnerable and its trade-routes to Italy
insecure. Worst of all, the Iberian Peninsula possessed, in its large
Morisco population, an unassimilated and potentially subversive
minority which looked on the Berbers and the Turks as its kin.

From the Granada rebellion of 1499 until the final solution of 1609-
14 when the Moriscos were expelled from the Peninsula, Spain was
haunted by nightmares of a Morisco insurrection aided and abetted by
international Islam. For this reason alone, it could not afford to ignore
the threat from Constantinople or Algiers. But the sixteenth-century
crusade against Islam lacked the clear-cut characteristics of the medieval
Reconquest. It was no longer concerned to free Iberian soil from
Moorish domination, and it was conducted more on the sea than on
land. In 1535 Charles led an expeditionary force which recovered
Tunis from the hands of Barbarossa, and in 1541 he tried, and failed,
to take Algiers. But such expeditions were the exception rather than
the rule. The Spanish–Turkish conflict was largely fought out on the
waters of the Mediterranean, and it proved to be episodic in its character
and indeterminate in its outcome.

Spain adapted with some difficulty to the demands of naval warfare
in the Mediterranean, and she was fortunate in being able to call on
the services of the Genoese fleet, in consequence of an agreement made
by the emperor with Andrea Doria in 1528. But when Philip II
succeeded his father on the Spanish throne in 1556 the Turks and

corsairs dominated the central Mediterranean basin, and threatened the coasts of Italy and even of Spain. The 1560s proved to be a highly dangerous and difficult decade. In 1565 the Turks laid siege to Malta, which was saved at the last moment by the arrival of a fleet commanded by the Viceroy of Sicily, Don García de Toledo (1514–78). The following year saw the first outbreak of troubles in the Netherlands, to which the great Duke of Alba (1507–82) was dispatched in 1567 at the head of an army which contained some of Castile's best soldiers. Then, with the Peninsula virtually denuded of troops, the worst happened: at Christmas 1568 the Granada Moriscos, goaded beyond endurance by recent attempts on the part of the Christian authorities to interfere with their traditional way of life, came out in revolt.

The second rebellion of the Alpujarras (1568–71) turned into a savage mountain war, which was all the more alarming because of its possible international implications. At any moment the Turks might send an expedition to help their brethren in distress. In the event, a Turkish invasion never materialized, although Spain was kept in a state of constant alert. Slowly the royal army, placed under the command of Philip's illegitimate half-brother Don John of Austria (1545–78), cleared the rebels from their mountain strongholds. As a punishment for their misdemeanour the Moriscos of Granada were driven from their homes and forcibly dispersed through the Peninsula.

The terrible shock administered by the Morisco rebellion galvanized Spain into a new and more vigorous drive against Turkish power in the Mediterranean. A Holy League was formed with Venice and the papacy, and on 7 October 1571 its combined fleets, commanded by Don John of Austria, routed the Turkish fleet in Greek waters, at Lepanto. The battle of Lepanto, in which Cervantes lost the use of an arm, was one of the great triumphs of Spanish and Christian arms, although its immediate consequences proved disappointing. Don John went on to capture Tunis in 1573, but it was lost again in the following year, and Spain never followed up its victory with a sustained offensive against the Turks. This was partly because of the character of naval warfare; partly because of the cost; and partly because of Spain's growing commitments elsewhere, with the rise of militant Protestantism in northern Europe. But the failure was less significant than it appears at first sight. The Turks, increasingly preoccupied with their Persian frontier, welcomed a respite on the Mediterranean front. As if by tacit agreement, therefore, the two great adversaries disengaged during the later 1570s and turned away from the Mediterranean to other theatres of war. In terms of territory won or lost there was little to show for the long years of conflict. But the Spain of Charles V and Philip II had succeeded in containing the Ottoman assault in the years when Constantinople was at its most aggressive; and the benefits of this containment were enjoyed not only by Spain itself but by Christendom as a whole.

Spain's involvement in other European theatres was more dubiously beneficial, even to itself. But in attempting any balance-sheet of profit and loss, it is important to remember that contemporaries looked upon foreign wars as a convenient form of blood-letting, purging the country of undesirable elements. If Castile under the Habsburgs enjoyed a domestic tranquillity that was remarkable by the standard of most contemporary states, this may be attributable in no small part to its persistent involvement in European and overseas enterprises, which deployed against foreign rivals energies which would have been difficult to contain at home.

The effect of these enterprises was to make Spain the dominant European power for the best part of a century. Under Charles V the rise of Spanish power was to some extent concealed by the fact that Charles was not only King of Spain but also Holy Roman Emperor. But Spanish armies fought for him in his wars against France, which in part at least were an Aragonese legacy, and in his campaigns against the German Lutherans. The result of Spanish military participation in these various enterprises was to make the name of Spain known, feared and hated in large parts of Europe; and it is no coincidence that the *leyenda negra* – the Black Legend of Spanish cruelty and rapacity – should have had its origins in Italy. For, by the middle of the century, Spanish power was dominant throughout the Italian peninsula: Sicily, Sardinia and the kingdom of Naples were all Spanish possessions. The duchy of Milan, which reverted to Charles V as an imperial fief on the death of its last Sforza duke in 1535, was vested in Prince Philip in 1540 and became a great Spanish military base. When the treaty of Cateau-Cambrésis of 1559 ended half a century of war between France and Spain, it effectively recognized the major Spanish military achievement of these years, the exclusion of French arms and influence from Italy.

It was, however, only in the reign of Philip II (1556–98) that Spain emerged from beneath the shadow of the Holy Roman Empire and became the dominant world power in its own name and under its own right. This emergence of the Spanish monarchy as a great imperial power corresponded to a structural transformation brought about by the abdication of the Emperor Charles V. Charles tried, and failed, to make Philip his successor on the imperial throne; and Philip had to be content with the Iberian Peninsula, together with Franche-Comté, the Netherlands, and Spain's Italian and American possessions, while Charles's brother Ferdinand secured the imperial title and launched the cadet branch of the Habsburgs on their independent, central European, career.

There could be no doubt where the centre of gravity lay in Philip's dominions, and he clearly recognized the realities of the situation when he left the Netherlands for Spain in 1559, never to return. In future Spain would be the centre of his monarchy, and, within Spain, Castile – its most powerful component part and the master of the New World, whose resources were indispensable for Philip's treasury. It was in Castile that Philip decided to fix his residence, and for the first time Spain acquired in 1561 a proper capital when he chose the unimpressive town of Madrid as the seat of his government. Two years later, work began on the construction in the vicinity of Madrid of the royal palace of the Escorial, which was completed in 1584. Where Charles had been an itinerant king, his son was to be the very opposite. Apart from three short trips to the Crown of Aragon and a period of residence in Lisbon in 1582-3 following his acquisition of the Portuguese crown in 1580, he spent most of his time at the geographical centre of the Peninsula, in or near Madrid.

While Madrid had much to commend it as a central vantage-point, its selection as the capital helped to increase Castilian influence in the government of the monarchy. Philip had chosen to live in the heart of Castile, surrounded by Castilians; and it was natural that his non-Castilian peoples should have grown to resent Castilian monopoly of the royal presence. It seemed to them that the Castilians already behaved as if they were the masters of the monarchy, and the king's close identification with them set up strains which could not be entirely contained even by a ruler as conscious of his obligations to his various peoples as Philip II. The states of the Crown of Aragon feared that their traditional laws and liberties would gradually be eroded by the activities of officious or malign servants of an absentee king. Certain incidents gave some substance to these fears, and in 1591-2 a revolt broke out in the kingdom of Aragon, nominally in defence of the sacred Aragonese *fueros*. Philip responded by sending an army into Aragon, but he was prepared to preserve the Aragonese constitutional system with only a few changes.

The indignation of the non-Castilian provinces of the Peninsula at Castile's monopoly of their prince was an inevitable outcome of Philip's style of kingship – a kingship that was sedentary where his father's had been itinerant, and bureaucratic where his father's had been personal. His decision to rule his dominions from a desk was partly a reflection of his own temperament, for Philip was a man more at home with paper than with people. But it reflected, too, the complexity involved in governing the dispersed dominions of a world-wide monarchy. In the second half of the century Madrid became the centre of a great imperial system, which extended from Sicily to Flanders and from Catalonia to Peru. Only by sitting at the centre of this system, at the receiving end of a constant stream of reports from his viceroys and officials, could Philip, or any other ruler of so large a monarchy, hope to keep abreast of events in all his territories.

The scale of the challenge was without precedent in European history, and it was one of the greatest, if least spectacular, achievements of the Spain of Philip II that it rose to the challenge with a considerable degree of success. Administrative procedures were devised which ensured the maintenance of a reasonable measure of justice and good government throughout the monarchy; and if the defects of the system were obvious, its virtues were none the less substantial. It operated, as it could only hope to operate, through a complicated machinery of checks and balances. Viceroys, bishops and judicial tribunals (the *audiencias*) all jealously guarded their rights while keeping a hawk-like watch on each other's activities. Their reports flowed back to Madrid, the seat of the councils which governed the monarchy. Some of these councils, like those of state, finance and war, had general responsibility for matters of common concern, while others – the Councils of Castile and Aragon, of the Indies and Italy – busied themselves with the affairs of their particular territories. Records of their deliberations, known as *consultas*, reached the king by way of the secretaries, who themselves often became influential figures in their own right. No king, not even Philip II, could read everything or know everything, and a royal secretary like Antonio Pérez (1540–1611), or even the less colourful Mateo Vázquez (1542–91), could play a role out of all relation to his nominal importance, simply through his inside knowledge of men and events.

The system was always open to abuse. Antonio Pérez, a totally unscrupulous character, was arrested along with the Princess of Éboli (1540–91) on the orders of the king in 1579, almost certainly for intrigues which were connected with the rebellion in the Netherlands and the delicate issue of the Portuguese succession. This was the kind of abuse which not even a king as naturally suspicious as Philip II could hope to prevent. There were other defects, too, which were inherent in the system. Corruption was rife, not least because salaries were inadequate and often in arrears; and business was subject to interminable delays, which were aggravated almost beyond endurance by the excessively cautious reflexes of Philip's own mental processes. Yet the cumbersome administrative machinery of the Spanish monarchy did succeed in holding it together, not merely during the reign of Philip II but also during the reigns of his feeble, and less conscientious, successors. Somehow it seems as if bureaucratic government achieved through its very inertia a momentum of its own, so that generations of routine-bound officials issued endless successions of royal orders which themselves helped to maintain an impression of close royal control.

Contemporaries were understandably impressed by the size and splendour of a monarchy governed with apparent impartiality by this vast administrative apparatus, and presided over by the enigmatic figure of a proverbially prudent king. Much, no doubt, depended on the person of Philip himself, and it is easy to forget that for a large part of his reign there was deep uncertainty about the succession. Don Carlos (1545–68), Philip's only child by his first marriage – to María of Portugal – grew up to be a mentally and emotionally unstable young man, totally unfitted to assume the awesome inheritance for which he was destined. By 1568 his behaviour was such that Philip was compelled to place him in custody, and he died in strange circumstances a few months later. There were no children of Philip's second marriage, to Mary Tudor, and only daughters by his third wife, Elizabeth of Valois. Of the male children born of his fourth marriage, to Anne of Austria, only one, born in 1578, survived childhood, to succeed his father as Philip III in 1598. Yet human uncertainties were an inevitable feature of life in sixteenth-century monarchies, and the Spanish monarchy under Philip II appeared more solidly grounded than many of its rivals.

It was, moreover, still growing. The Philippines were added to it in 1564, and in 1580 a far greater prize, Portugal and its empire. The death in 1578 of the young King Sebastian in a crassly foolish North African campaign left Philip in the direct line of succession to the

Portuguese crown. When Sebastian's successor, the aged Cardinal-King Henry, died in 1580, Philip moved with uncharacteristic decisiveness to take over his new inheritance. The kingdom of Portugal retained its laws and institutions and its own separate identity, but it became yet one more part of the Spanish monarchy; and the Trastámara dream of the entire Iberian Peninsula beneath the rule of a single sovereign was now triumphantly realized.

The acquisition of Portugal with its Atlantic seaboard, its merchant fleet and all the riches of its Far Eastern and African empire and Brazil brought an enormous accretion of strength to Philip and Spain. Until now, partly through temperament and partly through circumstances, Philip had tended to be sparing in the use of his power. Troubles in the Netherlands and war in the Mediterranean had kept him constantly preoccupied, and money for much of the time had been tight. But the years around 1580, when Portugal was added to his dominions, brought a dramatic increase in the quantity of American silver arriving in Seville for the Spanish crown. In 1575 it had been compelled to suspend payments to its bankers, but now, with two or three million ducats a year from America, its fortunes were visibly on the mend. As a result, for perhaps the first time in his reign, Philip was in a position to take and sustain large initiatives in foreign affairs.

To most European eyes, these initiatives were designed to achieve Spanish domination of the world; and as Spanish power grew increasingly inflated, so too did its constant companion, the Black Legend, swollen by gruesome tales of the horrors of the Inquisition and of Spanish atrocities in Mexico and Peru. But Philip saw himself as defending his own interests and those of the faith against a host of foreign enemies – Dutch rebels, French heretics, and English privateers who preyed on innocent Spanish shipping in the Channel, the Atlantic and even the Caribbean. He saw himself as the champion of the Catholic Church, beleaguered by the forces of heresy. His interests and those of Rome were identical – as long as Rome kept in its proper place. Resolutely determined to be the master of the Church in his own dominions, he would allow no papal interference, and expected the Popes to follow wherever he led. In the war against the heretics the decisions and the timing must rest with him, for he alone possessed the resources which would save the papacy and the Catholic cause. His monarchy was the greatest in the world because God so required it for His holy work.

III The Price of Greatness

For all the brilliance of Spain's achievements, it was becoming apparent by the later years of Philip II that the reckoning would be very heavy. No country committed to so vast and sustained a military effort as Castile under its first two Habsburg rulers – and least of all a country with so weak an economic infrastructure – could expect to emerge unscathed from such an exalting and exhausting ordeal.

The exaltation itself imposed strains which gradually took their toll. The commitment to a crusade, first against Islam, and then increasingly against the Protestants, created a religious climate of great intensity. Counter-Reformation spirituality naturally flourished in such a climate, and Catholic devotion achieved some of its greatest triumphs in the Castile of St Teresa of Ávila (1515–82).[1] Yet at the same time the championing of Catholic Christianity against its many enemies demanded an undeviating orthodoxy of those who marched beneath its banners. Such a demand created obvious problems for a country which had only recently, and not entirely adequately, dealt with the Jewish and Moorish minorities in its midst. Could Spain, the paladin of the faith, be sure that its own faith was beyond reproach? In search of an answer to this nagging question, Spanish society drove itself on a ruthless and ultimately self-defeating quest for an unattainable purity.

The appearance of Lutheranism in the German lands gave the Spanish Inquisition a new *raison d'être*. Although little was known in the Spain of the 1520s about Luther and his doctrines, this did not prevent the Holy Office from mounting a powerful attack on all those who might be conveniently tarred with a Lutheran brush. Special uneasiness was felt about the little circles of illuminists (*alumbrados*) and about the growing band of devotees of the writings of Erasmus. Erasmians and *alumbrados* were more concerned with an inner, personal religion than with the externals of the faith, and this helped to single them out as potentially dangerous deviationists.[2] In the late 1520s and early 1530s a series of spectacular trials showed which way the wind was blowing. No hint of deviation would be allowed in Habsburg Spain.

The Inquisition, whose necessity had only recently been questioned, now established an iron grip on the country, and maintained and perpetuated it through an apparatus of fear. There were some 20,000

[1] See also Chapter 8, pp. 294–6.
[2] See also Chapter 8, pp. 277–82.

familiars of the Holy Office scattered through Spain; informers pro-
liferated, and denunciations were frequent. The Inquisition both
created and fed on fear – the fear of nonconformist elements, engrained
in a society whose own inner cohesion and unity were still in doubt.
It was for this same reason that the problem of orthodoxy could not
exist in isolation, but became hopelessly entangled with that of ancestry.

With the expulsion of the Jews in 1492 the Jewish problem transformed itself into the *converso* question. Although many *conversos*
had become sincere and highly orthodox Catholics, and occupied
important positions in the ecclesiastical hierarchy, the *conversos* were,
by their very origin, objects of suspicion; and the fact that some of
them felt the attractions of Erasmian Christianity, with its scant regard
for outward forms, did nothing to lessen this suspicion in Old Christian
eyes. Castilian society as it emerged from the Middle Ages was obsessed
by the question of *honour*, which meant not only the inner worth of
a man and his family, but also how that worth was evaluated by
others and by society as a whole. The nobles were for ever preoccupied
by questions of honour, but the majority of them had a chink in their
own armour which could be exploited by those who were resentful
of their own lack of noble status. It was notorious that most of the
best families in Castile had intermarried with the Jews. If, then, the
noble harped on his honour, the jealous plebeian could counter with
a new, and perhaps superior, honour of his own – the honour that
derived from an immaculate ancestry.

From the middle of the fifteenth century certain corporations in
Castile were beginning to insist on purity of blood – *limpieza de sangre*
('Old Christian', i.e. non-Jewish descent) – as a criterion for membership. But it seems to have been during the reign of Charles V that the
popular movement against Jewish ancestry gathered real momentum.
In 1547 the cathedral chapter of Toledo, under pressure from its low-
born Archbishop Juan Martínez Silíceo (1486–1557), adopted a
limpieza statute which made racial purity an essential condition for
appointments to dignities and prebends. This Toledo statute set a
pattern which was followed by a whole succession of corporations,
both secular and ecclesiastical, until those suspected of Jewish ancestry
found themselves debarred from a wide range of offices, and smirched
with an indelible taint upon their honour and, by implication, their
orthodoxy.

The national obsession with an orthodox faith and an orthodox
ancestry, while a cause of great human suffering, is best understood

as a compulsive form of self-defence by a precariously united society which found itself caught up in the religious warfare of sixteenth-century Europe. An embattled Spain, well aware of the disruption caused elsewhere by religious disunity, was naturally determined to save itself from a similar fate. To do this, it took the most drastic preventive measures. In 1557 and 1558 the authorities reacted in a state of near panic to the discovery of allegedly Protestant cells in Seville and Valladolid. A pragmatic issued in 1558 prohibited the import of foreign books and established much more strict licensing regulations for books published in Spain. A new Spanish Index, more severe than its predecessors of 1545 and 1551, made its appearance in 1559; and, in the same year, Spanish students were forbidden to study abroad, except in specified colleges at Bologna, Rome, Naples and Coimbra.

These draconian measures were no doubt frequently evaded, or only partially obeyed, and Spain, in fact, continued to maintain strong cultural contacts with certain parts of Europe, especially Italy and Flanders. But they did mark the beginnings of an attempt to seal off the Peninsula from dangerous foreign influences, and they must bear their share of responsibility for the growing intellectual isolation of later sixteenth-century Spain. As it became more difficult to keep abreast of European intellectual movements, and as the sources of dissent were slowly stifled at home in pursuit of a conformism which came to be regarded as a national necessity, so the range of response to new situations was diminished, and Castile's adaptability to changing circumstances was correspondingly reduced.

Inevitably these were long-term rather than short-term results. In the short term, Castile was fortified and buoyed up by its sense of commitment to a providential mission, for which no sacrifices appeared to be too great. But increasingly under Philip II Spain experienced setbacks and misfortunes which suggested that it might not, after all, enjoy the full approval of the Lord. The unrest which broke out in the Netherlands in 1566 proved to have been only temporarily cured by the repressive measures of the Duke of Alba. From the time of the landing of the Sea Beggars at Brill in 1572 it was clear that Spain was confronted in the Low Countries with both religious subversion and organized revolt. Neither conciliatory measures by Don Luis de Requesens (1528–76), nor the brilliant military and political gifts of Alexander Farnese, Duke of Parma (1545–92), could smother the explosive combination of Calvinism and rebellion, which drew new strength from covert foreign help.

In attempting to uphold the Spanish and Catholic cause in northern Europe, Philip found himself caught up in an escalating conflict which placed an increasingly heavy strain on Spanish resources without providing the clear-cut victory for which his people yearned. During the 1580s the war spread to the whole Atlantic complex, as the England of Elizabeth sent assistance to the Dutch, while English privateers ventured deep into the Spanish Atlantic and raided Spain itself. In 1588 Philip's massive response – the great Armada – failed miserably in its attempted invasion of England; and in the early 1590s Spanish intervention in the French civil wars was unable to prevent the accession of the heretical Henry of Navarre to the throne of France. The northern heretics were, it seemed, more than holding their own in their struggle against Spain. Was it possible that God had abandoned His chosen people of Castile?

By the time of Philip's death in 1598 the sense of despair and dis-illusionment – *desengaño* – was running deep, especially in Castile, which had for so long borne the heat of the battle. Decades of warfare had imposed a cruel strain on a country which was anyhow poorly endowed with natural resources, and which had failed to fulfil such signs of economic promise as had been apparent in the opening decades of the century.

It was true that Castile had been able to call on the expanding economy of America for help, and the demands of the American market had for a time stimulated its economic growth. Seville, tied to the Indies by regular annual sailings of two great fleets, the *flota* and the *galeones*, had become a great emporium of European trade. Large quantities of American silver had reached Spain in a century when the shortage of liquid capital was one of the severest obstacles to economic growth. But too little of this capital had been invested in productive enterprises at home. Much of it inevitably went on conspicuous consumption; and an increasingly large proportion fell into foreign hands, and left the country without conferring any benefits on Castile's economy.

Castile was hampered in its attempts to capitalize on the growth of the American market by the fact that it proved to be the first and severest casualty of the general European price rise of the sixteenth century. Prices were everywhere being pushed up by the pressure of growing demand on relatively inelastic resources, and this situation was aggravated by the influx of silver from the American mines. Spain, as the first recipient of American silver, was early affected by the inflationary process, and its prices rose faster than those of its competitors. By the middle of the century foreign goods were undercutting native products in Castile's home market, and by the end of the century a sizeable proportion of Seville's export trade was controlled by foreigners.

The Castilian merchant community therefore found itself running into increasing difficulties as the century progressed. These difficulties were enhanced by the fiscal policies of the crown, dominated as they were by the need to obtain money for expensive foreign wars. Castile's tax burden, which had always been inequitable, became increasingly heavy, and the substantial merchant was naturally tempted to abandon his business enterprises and seek entry into the ranks of the tax-exempt *hidalgos*. Meanwhile, in order to raise loans, the crown gave special favours to its German and Genoese bankers at the expense of native Castilian merchants. It also sought to borrow on the domestic market by the issue of *juros*, or credit-bonds, on which it paid a regular annuity. Since these *juros* constituted a relatively safe form of investment compared with industry or trade, they were taken up in large numbers by the privileged sections of the community and by religious and charitable institutions, and consequently siphoned off wealth which might otherwise have been used for more productive purposes.

In 1599 and 1600 Castile and Andalusia, which were already suffering from the weakness of the native business community and from the lack of capital investment, were devastatingly struck by famine and plague. The plague, which may have claimed half a million victims, brought the population expansion of the sixteenth century to a sudden halt. The seventeenth century was to be a century of demographic stagnation, or even of some overall decline, with another disastrous plague ravaging Andalusia and the eastern regions of the Peninsula in 1647–51.

The immediate result of the plague of 1599 was to create a labour shortage in Castile and to push up wages at a moment when the reduction of costs was essential if international competitiveness were to be restored to Castilian industry. The situation was made more serious by the fact that the American market for Spanish and European goods was beginning to show signs of saturation. Although Seville's trade remained buoyant in the first decade of the seventeenth century, the growth of more self-sufficient economies in Mexico and Peru meant a diminishing demand for European products, and a consequent decline in the remittances of silver to pay for these goods. From around

1610–20, therefore, the whole elaborate economic system of the Spanish Atlantic was beginning to weaken, and Castile's chances of using the New World as a cushion against further economic hardship were correspondingly lessened.

Both the crown and Castilian society had grown accustomed to an age of easy money, and were likely to find difficulty in adapting to an age of reduced silver imports and a declining rate of inflation. Through all his difficulties Philip II had clung to a sound currency, but in 1599 the new government of Philip III authorized the minting of a *vellón* coinage of pure copper. The temptation to tamper with this coinage proved irresistible. Large sums of *vellón* were issued by hard-pressed governments, and nominal values were arbitrarily changed. In consequence, seventeenth-century Castile fell victim to acute monetary instability, as sharp inflationary movements were punctuated by dramatic falls in *vellón* prices as the crown attempted radical deflationary cures.

The miseries and uncertainties of life in early seventeenth-century Castile were a source of deep concern to thinking Castilians. It seemed to them as if they were living in a topsy-turvy society, which had got its sense of values hopelessly confused. It was a society characterized by extremes of wealth and poverty, in which the rich ate to excess while the poor starved. The poor were men of every rank, for appearances were deceptive. The *hidalgos* who flocked to the court of Philip III spoke loudly of their honour but often enough had scarcely a ducat to their names. In this society, luck was at a premium and work at a discount. It was, after all, easier to live on one's wits like a *pícaro* than to work long and hard for wages which were all too likely to find their way into the pocket of the tax-collector, or be reduced to nothing overnight by some sudden change in the value of money.

The effects of all this were particularly apparent in the countryside. Although the villages still had some substantial peasants, who fought hard to preserve their wealth and status, large numbers of peasants deserted the country for the towns, hoping to escape the attentions of the recruiting sergeant, the tax-collector and seigneurial officials. While the countryside was depopulated, some of the cities overflowed. Madrid in particular doubled its population, from 65,000 to 130,000, during the reign of Philip III. A parasitic city of courtiers and officials, servants and vagabonds, it sustained a brilliant if precarious civilization in a sea of poverty. It began to look as if the court, the Church and the bureaucracy were the only growth industries in a society which consistently neglected its agriculture and which penalized those who were most productively employed.

All this was acutely observed by the economic writers and projectors – the so-called *arbitristas* – who were concerned to save Castile from its own follies before it was too late. In a stream of books and pamphlets they inveighed against the iniquities of Castile's fiscal system and against the false values which lured Castilians away from agricultural and industrial occupations which constituted the only true basis of national wealth. There was, therefore, a consciousness of crisis in the Castile of Philip III – a sombre awareness of the contradictions in society which itself played its part in determining the general tone of seventeenth-century Spanish thought and civilization.

This extra degree of awareness may go a little way towards explaining the paradox of great artistic vitality in a nation threatened with economic collapse. What, after all, was real and what was illusory in a Castile so rich in gold and silver and yet so pitifully poor? There were great opportunities here for the keen observer of the social scene; and if traditional values themselves were rarely questioned, the actual behaviour of society was brilliantly observed and often mordantly portrayed. Acuteness of observation was not, however, confined to artists and imaginative writers. Some of the *arbitristas*, like Martín González de Cellorigo or Sancho de Moncada, were penetrating in their economic and social diagnoses, and at the same time capable of constructive suggestions. But would the ministers listen to what they had to say?

In practice, the years between 1600 and 1640 produced two types of governmental response, each of which proved inadequate. The crown could cut its commitments, or actively encourage reform, or – better still – do both at once. Philip III (1598–1621) was incapable of any personal initiative, and depended for most of his reign on the services of a favourite (the *valido* or *privado*), Francisco de Sandoval y Rojas, Duke of Lerma (1553–1625). Lerma, a Valencian noble, at least appreciated that Spain must reduce its burden of military expenditure. Philip II, shortly before his death in 1598, had ended his war with France by the Treaty of Vervins. In 1604 Lerma made peace with England. In 1609, following a fresh royal bankruptcy in 1607, he persuaded the council of state to agree to a twelve-year truce with the Dutch.

The gradual return to peace in the early years of the seventeenth century should have provided the opportunity for domestic reform.

But Lerma was the pawn of the Castilian high aristocracy, who were now beginning to abandon their estates for the pleasures of the court, and were insisting on a share in the government after the long years of exclusion under Charles V and Philip II. To keep his rivals at bay, Lerma distributed *mercedes* in lavish quantities. His henchmen in government – Rodrigo Calderón (1570–1621) and Pedro Franqueza (1547?–1614) – were notoriously corrupt; and the feckless extravagance of the court merely sharpened the sense of unreality which already pervaded the economic and social life of Castile.

Lerma's regime was clearly incapable of giving the country a new sense of priorities – a fact which was vividly confirmed by the issuing of a decree in 1609 for the expulsion of the Moriscos, on the very same day as the conclusion of the truce with the Dutch. No doubt the measure reflected the persistent failure of Spain to assimilate an alien minority, and in this respect it removed a possibly dangerous social irritant. But it also deprived Spain of some 275,000 citizens who were sober and industrious, if not the paragons of economic virtue which later ages believed them to be. Valencia, which lost a third of its population by the expulsion, was the hardest hit region of Spain. But Castile, for its part, could ill afford the loss of artisans, labourers and dockhands at a time when labour was tight and costs were high.

Amidst the frivolities of the Lerma regime, the opportunities provided by the return of peace were carelessly allowed to slip away. The peace itself was precarious, with the Dutch truce due to expire in 1621, and with war threatening in Central Europe after the Bohemian revolt of 1618. Although the government in Madrid was both passive and pacific, many of its servants abroad – men like Baltasar de Zúñiga (d. 1622) or the Duke of Osuna (1579–1624) – were deeply perturbed by the monarchy's humiliating weakness, so different from the reign of Philip II. In the autumn of 1618 Lerma was unseated in a palace revolution, while Madrid moved inexorably towards a military intervention in Germany which would prop up the Austrian branch of the Habsburgs and secure the vital 'Spanish road' from Milan to Flanders. But the imminent prospect of war gave new urgency to the demand for domestic reform.

Although the Council of Castile produced a famous *consulta* in 1619 analysing the troubles of Castile along lines which were already familiar from the works of the *arbitristas*, it was only after the unexpected death of Philip III on 31 March 1621 that it seemed as if words might be transformed into action. Philip IV (1621–65), although considerably more intelligent than his father, was equally lacking in confidence. But he chose as his favourite a vigorous Andalusian aristocrat, Gaspar de Guzmán, soon to become Count-Duke of Olivares (1587–1645), who breathed a new and impulsive life into the programme for reform.

The early 1620s were an astonishing time, when it seemed for a brief deceptive moment as if Castile, under Olivares's dynamic leadership, might yet enjoy the best of every world. The conflict with the Dutch was resumed, and Spain intervened with striking success in the opening phases of the Thirty Years War. Simultaneously the count-duke embarked on a series of ambitious plans for fiscal, administrative and economic reform which suggested that the advice of the *arbitristas* had finally been taken to heart. A campaign was launched against corruption in high places and Rodrigo Calderón was sent to the scaffold; the count-duke made increasing use of juntas of specially selected ministers to circumvent the cumbersome machinery of conciliar bureaucracy; pragmatics were issued to reform manners and morals and dress, and schemes were devised to stimulate economic life.

In the new and puritanical climate of purposeful change created by the Olivares regime, the central problem remained, as always, that of sustaining a massive military burden out of the shrinking resources of Castile. The war in the Netherlands, that perpetual drain upon the lifeblood of Castile, alone consumed one-third of the crown's annual budget. American silver was arriving in diminishing quantities, and Castile could not be expected to provide the rest from its waning resources. Admittedly Olivares had considerable success in finding new sources of revenue. By the use of ingenious fiscal expedients, such as 'voluntary' *donativos* and a *media anata* on the income from offices, he succeeded in taxing by indirect methods the traditionally privileged sections of Castilian society. But he was bound to seek external assistance if Castile were not to collapse from the weight of its war effort. This assistance could only come from those parts of the monarchy, and especially of the Iberian Peninsula itself, which were looked upon as under-taxed when compared with Castile.

Olivares's grand design for a 'Union of Arms', by which the different parts of the monarchy would raise and maintain fixed numbers of troops, was to end in disaster in 1640. Lerma had tried peace without reform. Olivares tried reform without peace. Castile's continuing involvement in war, culminating in open conflict with France from 1635, forced him to abandon one after another those plans for long-term reform which would have strengthened Castile by fomenting its economic growth. But at the same time it drove him to press ahead with the Union of Arms – with his schemes for the military and fiscal integration of the monarchy – which alone, in his eyes, could save Castile. Such schemes were bound to excite opposition in societies wedded to their own constitutional rights and deeply suspicious of Castilian designs. Both Portugal and Catalonia found themselves under increasingly heavy pressure to make a larger contribution to the costs of war. Catalonia, which was in the front line of the struggle with France, responded in the spring of 1640 by revolting; and in December of the same year Portugal followed suit.

The simultaneous revolts of Catalonia and Portugal ended any prospect of Spanish victory in the Thirty Years War. Castile, with wars on its hands both at home and abroad, had neither the money nor the manpower to redress the balance. Moreover, Seville's trading system, which had been exploited by the crown for fiscal ends, was temporarily disrupted in 1640, and American silver supplies for the crown slumped disastrously in the following years. In these circumstances it was surprising that the Spanish monarchy did not fare even worse. Olivares was given leave to retire from office in 1643, as a result of aristocratic pressures and the visible failure of his policies. His nephew and successor as first minister, Don Luis de Haro (1598–1661), navigated Spain with some skill through the peace negotiations in Westphalia, which ended with Spanish recognition of Dutch independence in 1648.

The monarchy faced, and survived, revolts in Sicily and Naples in 1647–8; and in 1653 the Catalans, disillusioned with French 'protection' and demoralized by war and plague, returned to allegiance to Philip IV on condition that their liberties remained untouched. Six years later, Haro at last made peace with France at the Treaty of the Pyrenees, and Philip's daughter, María Teresa, was married to the young Louis XIV as a symbol of reconciliation between Spain and France. Only the Portuguese question remained to be settled, but this proved to be beyond the powers of Castile. Enjoying French and English support, and drawing on the profits of an expanding trade with Brazil, Portugal under the restored dynasty of Braganza succeeded in beating off Castilian attacks. Eventually, in 1668, the Spanish crown reluctantly accepted the inevitable, and recognized Portugal as an independent state.

The survival of the Spanish monarchy, in spite of its battering in the middle decades of the seventeenth century, is itself something of a miracle. Through all these difficult times there was no revolt in Castile, nor in the American colonies. Apart from the loss of Portugal and the county of Rosellón, the monarchy emerged from the period of wars and revolts with its territorial integrity almost intact; and the inheritance which the sickly young Charles II (1665–1700) received from his father was not in fact substantially smaller than that inherited by Philip II from Charles V in 1556.

The clue to this apparently surprising resilience is to be found in the very structure of the monarchy. Loosely tied together by dynastic arrangements, it was not, as Olivares discovered to his cost, amenable to rapid and drastic change. Essentially it relied on its own inertia – on a system of equilibrium by which Madrid, the viceroys and the local aristocracies all enjoyed a share of power. So long as the equilibrium was not unduly disturbed, there was no great inducement in the provinces to make a bid for independence. Indeed, the dangers involved in any such attempt might well outweigh the benefits, as the Catalans ruefully found out for themselves after they had euphorically cut loose from Madrid. Foreign domination and social disorder were a heavy price to pay for the preservation of traditional liberties. By and large, therefore, the local élites in the different parts of the monarchy found that they could do better for themselves within the framework of the monarchy than if they struck out on their own.

After the traumatic experiences of the Olivares epoch, Madrid for its part was ready enough to oblige. Tampering with provincial liberties had proved to be a costly and dangerous enterprise. The age of heroics was over, and voluntary inertia became the order of the day. The provinces were left to their own devices while the Castile of Charles II was subjected to a succession of hopelessly inadequate governments which did nothing to relieve its miseries. Yet in spite of the distress caused by new wars with France, and the continuing uncertainty over the future of the dynasty, the last years of the seventeenth century were not, even for Castile, a period of unrelieved gloom. There were some signs of economic recovery in the peripheral regions of the Peninsula, especially in Catalonia, and even in Castile after 1680 the economic crisis seems to have passed its peak. For a moment, from 1685 to 1691, there was a fitful display of real government in Madrid during the ministry of the Count of Oropesa (d. 1707). But increasingly the future of Castile and of the Spanish monarchy and empire depended on decisions taken elsewhere, as the European capitals haggled over the succession to the childless Charles II.

On his deathbed in 1700 Charles II, for once in his life, made his own decision. The crown should go to Philip of Anjou, the grandson of Louis XIV and María Teresa; the Bourbons, for so long their enemies, were the legitimate successors of the Habsburgs on the Spanish throne. The dynasty which had directed Spain along its imperial pathway, and which had won such a heroic response from Castile at such a terrible price, was at last, after years of living death, on the point of extinction. True to itself, it ensured that legitimacy and traditionalism should triumph to the end. It was for the Bourbons to start again where Olivares had left off; to embark on the vast, and apparently hopeless, task of modernizing Spain.

Bibliography

GENERAL

DOMÍNGUEZ ORTIZ, A. *The Golden Age of Spain, 1516–1659*. London, 1971.
ELLIOTT, J. H. *Imperial Spain, 1469–1716*. London, 1963. Pelican Books, 1970.
LYNCH, J. *Spain under the Habsburgs*. 2 vols. Oxford, 1964 and 1969.
MERRIMAN, R. B. *The Rise of the Spanish Empire in the Old World and the New*. 4 vols. New York, 1918–34; reprinted 1962.
PARRY, J. H. *The Spanish Seaborne Empire*. London, 1966.

ECONOMIC AND SOCIAL

BENNASSAR, B. *Valladolid au siècle d'or*. Paris, 1967.
CARANDE, R. *Carlos V y sus banqueros*. 3 vols. Madrid, 1943–67.
CHAUNU, H. and P. *Séville et l'Atlantique*. 8 vols. Paris, 1955–9.
HAMILTON, E. J. *American Treasure and the Price Revolution in Spain, 1501–1650*. Cambridge, Mass., 1934.
KAGAN, R. L. *Students and Society in Early Modern Spain*. Baltimore and London, 1974.
LAPEYRE, H. *Une Famille de marchands: les Ruiz*. Paris, 1955.
—— *Géographie de l'Espagne morisque*. Paris, 1959.
SALOMON, N. *La Campagne de Nouvelle Castille à la fin du XVIᵉ siècle*. Paris, 1964.
VICENS VIVES, J. *An Economic History of Spain*. English trans. Princeton, 1969.
—— (ed.). *Historia social y económica de España y América*. Vols 2 and 3. Barcelona, 1957.

SPECIALIZED STUDIES

(a) The Catholic Kings
BATISTA I ROCA, J. *The Hispanic Kingdoms and the Catholic Kings*. The New Cambridge Modern History. Vol. 1. Cambridge, 1957.
MARIÉJOL, J. H. *L'Espagne sous Ferdinand et Isabelle*. Paris, 1892. English trans. New Brunswick, 1961.
TARSICIO DE AZCONA, P. *Isabel la Católica*. Madrid, 1964.

(b) Charles V and Philip II

BATAILLON, M. *Erasme et l'Espagne*. Paris, 1937. Revised and enlarged Spanish ed. *Erasmo y España*. 2 vols. Mexico, 1950.

BRAUDEL, F. *La Méditerranée et le monde méditerranéen à l'époque de Philippe II*. 2nd ed. Paris, 1966. English trans. London, 1972.

GOUNON-LOUBENS, J. *Essais sur l'administration de la Castille au XVIᵉ siècle*. Paris, 1860.

KAMEN, H. *The Spanish Inquisition*. London, 1965.

KENISTON, H. *Francisco de los Cobos*. Pittsburgh, 1960.

KOENIGSBERGER, H. *The Empire of Charles V*. The New Cambridge Modern History. Vol. II.

MARAÑÓN, G. *Antonio Pérez*. 2 vols. 6th ed. Madrid, 1958. Abridged English trans. London, 1954.

MARAVALL, J. A. *Las comunidades de Castilla*. 2nd ed. Madrid, 1970.

MATTINGLY, G. *The Defeat of the Spanish Armada*. London, 1959.

PARKER, G. *The Army of Flanders and the Spanish Road*. Cambridge, 1972.

PEREZ, J. *La Révolution des 'comunidades' de Castille (1520–1521)*. Bordeaux, 1970.

PIDAL, MARQUÉS DE. *Historia de las alteraciones de Aragón*. 3 vols. Madrid, 1862–3.

SICROFF, A. A. *Les Controverses des statuts de 'pureté de sang' en Espagne du XVᵉ au XVIIᵉ siècle*. Paris, 1960.

THOMPSON, I. A. A. *War and Government in Habsburg Spain 1560–1620*. London, 1976.

(c) The Seventeenth Century

CÁNOVAS DEL CASTILLO, A. *Estudios del reinado de Felipe IV*. 2 vols. Madrid, 1888–9.

DOMÍNGUEZ ORTIZ, A. *La sociedad española en el siglo XVII*. 2 Vols. Madrid, 1964 and 1970.

ELLIOTT, J. H. 'The Decline of Spain'. In *Past and Present*, 20 (1961).

—— *The Revolt of the Catalans*. Cambridge, 1963.

HAMILTON, E. J. 'The Decline of Spain'. In *Economic History Review*, VIII (1938).

HUME, M. *The Court of Philip IV*. London, 1928.

LOPEZ PIÑERO, J. M. *La introducción de la ciencia moderna en España*. Barcelona, 1969.

MARAÑÓN, G. *El Conde-Duque de Olivares*. 3rd ed. Madrid, 1952.

MARAVALL, J. A. *La teoría española del estado en el siglo XVII*. Madrid, 1944. French trans. Paris, 1955.

MAURA, DUQUE DE. *Vida y reinado de Carlos II*. 2 vols. 2nd ed. Madrid, 1954.

VALIENTE, F. T. *Los validos en la monarquía española del siglo XVII*. Madrid, 1963.

VILAR, P. 'El tiempo del "Quijote" '. In *Crecimiento y desarrollo*. Barcelona, 1964.

5 Spanish History from 1700

RAYMOND CARR

I The Coming of the Bourbons

The repeated crises of the seventeenth century had by the century's end left Spain economically weak and politically decomposed. But her huge empire in Latin America was intact, if threatened: she was still the greatest imperial power of the Western world. Her choice therefore lay between what may be called a Mediterranean or European policy – in particular, after 1714, the re-establishment of her position in Italy – and an Atlantic policy which would keep rivals away from the closed world of Latin America. Yet as a colonial power Spain was at a disadvantage: her enfeebled economy could not supply the imports needed by the Creole inhabitants of her American colonies. Britain was Spain's potential great rival in America, eager to penetrate a new market there. Spain lacked the naval power to keep the British out of South America; hence the alliance with Britain's colonial rival, France.

In 1700 Spain was still, too, a vital element in the European balance of power. When the dying Charles II (1665–1700) named Philip of Anjou (1700–46) as his heir, that balance tilted in favour of France. Thus the claims of Philip V (as the Duke of Anjou became) to the Spanish throne were contested by Britain and Austria in the War of the Spanish Succession (1700–14). The armies of the allied powers invaded Spain. In 1705 the Archduke Charles took Barcelona and set up his capital and court there; in 1706 the allies entered Madrid only to be decisively defeated at Almansa (prov. of Albacete) in 1707; after a series of defeats and a second entry of the allies into Madrid, Philip's Franco-Castilian army defeated the Anglo-Austrian army at Brihuega (prov. of Guadalajara) in 1710. By 1711 England had lost interest in

For a genealogical table of the Bourbons, see p. 572.

the war and by 1714 Philip's control of the Peninsula was complete.

The course of the war had itself ensured that this control should be exercised in an attempt to cure the inveterate defects of the Spanish state. Hence the initiation of the series of administrative and fiscal reforms which continued, on and off, throughout the eighteenth century; because of their association with the French advisers of the new dynasty they are called, rather misleadingly, 'the Bourbon reforms'.

The aim of the reformers was to create a rational administration within a unitary state. This meant the centralization of a monarchy that had grown by accretions and therefore retained privileges both for distinct regions and distinct social classes. To eighteenth-century bureaucrats such a state appeared a monster created by history: 'a monstrous republic', wrote one of them, 'composed of little republics which confront each other because the particular interest of each is in contradiction with the general interest.' The most striking examples were the regional charters or *fueros* of Aragon, Valencia, Catalonia, the Basque provinces and Navarre: these charters impeded the action of the central government while the cumbrous mechanism of the great Councils (Consejos) of State represented a historic policy of satisfying the claims of the nobility to influence within the framework of the monarchy.

The French experts who came with Philip V saw reform as a wartime necessity: only by breaking down local privileges could the maximum tax revenues be extracted from Spaniards and France freed of the financial burdens of defending Philip V. These views were shared, for different reasons, by a handful of Spanish civil servants, especially by Melchor Rafael de Macanaz (1670–1760), enemy of provincial privilege and aristocratic influence and the foremost exponent of regalism. Macanaz, obstinate and pedantic, sought by lengthy legal and historical argument to justify the regalist demand that the king control the Church. Like the French administrative technicians, he, too, disliked the cumbrous Councils, still dominated by the grandees. Like many eighteenth-century civil servants he was himself a minor provincial gentleman.

Reform was opposed by those who suffered from it: the higher aristocracy and the privileged regions. In wartime their opposition was treason. Thus when Aragon and Valencia resisted the crown's demands for troops and taxes – Saragossa even going as far as to resist the passage of royal troops – their ancient privileges were abolished and the property of the rebels confiscated (1707). When the Archbishop of Valencia resisted attempts to make priests of doubtful loyalty appear before royal courts, the regalism of Macanaz was given full course.

Castile was loyal to the new dynasty. The main centre of disaffection was Catalonia: the British and Austrian candidate for the throne of Spain, the Archduke Charles, had, as noted, set up his court in Barcelona (1705). When Philip V recaptured Barcelona (1714) the *furs* (*fueros*) of Catalonia, too, were abolished. To later generations of Catalan nationalists the 'Decrees of Nueva Planta' (1716) was the blackest day in Catalan history, marking, as they saw it, the beginning of the subjection of Catalonia, whose independent culture, civilization, legal system and political institutions lay under the heel of an absorbent, centralizing Castile. It has been argued that, in fact, integration, far from injuring the principality, was the prelude to economic advance since it 'opened' the domestic and, later, the American markets to Catalan enterprise. While Catalans came to talk of Castilian 'imperialism' the pushing, money-grabbing Catalan, clamouring for tariff protection at the expense of the rest of the nation, rapidly became a Castilian stereotype. Thus a major Spanish political conflict of modern times had its roots in the reforms of Bourbon centralizers.

After the suppression of Catalan privileges only the Basque provinces and Navarre retained their *fueros*; they had been loyal to Philip V and so escaped punishment. Their defence of their privileges against the second wave of reformers – the liberals of the early nineteenth century to whom centralization and uniformity were preconditions of constitutional liberty – was to set off a series of civil wars then. It was not till the 1870s that Spain finally became a unitary state.

Deserted by her French ally, Spain suffered severe mutilations at the peace settlements that ended the War of the Spanish Succession. She was stripped of her European possessions (Belgium, Luxemburg, Milan, Sardinia and Naples), had to hand over Gibraltar to Britain (1713) and was compelled to allow British merchants the right to send one ship a year to Spanish America.

Until the mid-century Philip V's policies veered between backing the desires of his dominating and difficult wife, Isabel Farnese, to re-establish her sons in Italy and a concern for Spain's position in America. The 'Italian' tendency triumphed with the installation of her son, Charles, as King of Naples (1734–59) where he served his apprenticeship as an enlightened despot. At home Philip V's reforming zeal declined sharply: thus Macanaz, arch-enemy of clerical privilege, was sacrificed to the Inquisition. Nevertheless a less dramatic but general tightening-up of administrative procedures continued: provincial administration was improved by the institution of captains-general and intendants. The captains-general were responsible for much public building; the intendants attempted to improve a hopelessly complicated taxation system.

The 'American-Atlantic' tendency was furthered by Spanish ministers with a particular interest in the navy and in foreign trade – Patiño, Ensenada and Carvajal. Towards the mid-century the Atlantic tendency became dominant. Since Britain was the great enemy in the Americas, the 'natural' ally seemed to be France. A consequence of this was the 'Family Pacts' of 1733 and 1743 based in fact not on dynastic sentiment but on common interest.

This new Atlantic interest was reflected in increased trade – the ancient system of dispatching fleets across the Atlantic was abandoned for individual sailings – the foundation of privileged trading companies, the construction of new naval arsenals at El Ferrol and Cartagena. There was an intimate connection between the commitment to an American policy and reform at home since only a strong metropolitan Spain could hold on to her imperial status: the Marquis of Ensenada (1702–81) was a great reformer whose single tax scheme, though it was broken by administrative inertia, long remained a model for reforming bureaucrats and liberals.

II Charles III (1759–1788)

Some historians of Spain have overemphasized the uniqueness of Charles III's reign as an era of reform. The reformers' king was a pious, hardworking, ruler much given to blood sports. His civil servants continued the work of predecessors like Macanaz or Ensenada: the rationalization and centralization of the administration and the increase of crown revenues.

There are, however, two important differences between these two generations of modernizing reformers. Firstly the civil servants of Charles III shared what can, with some exaggeration, be called a common philosophy. Only in part derived from the utilitarianism common to the European Enlightenment, this philosophy conceived the function of the state to be the generation of *felicidad* (happiness) defined in terms of material prosperity. Secondly, the Caroline bureaucrats emphasized the direct connections between prosperity, an efficient

SPANISH HISTORY FROM 1700 149

administration and high returns from taxation which would strengthen the state. This view of things was explicitly set out in a Royal Instruction of 1787. Too much attention had been paid to collecting taxes; they must not be merely collected but 'cultivated'. 'El cultivo consiste en el fomento de la población con el de la agricultura, el de las artes e industria y del comercio.'

State fostering of prosperity for revenue purposes thus came to imply the modernization of society, more especially by the removal of the *estorbos* ('hindrances' – a key word) which 'bad legislation' had put in the way of individual productive enterprise. Hence the onslaught on the great numbers of entailed estates (*mayorazgos*) which, by tying up land, inhibited the growth of a free market in land and of an agrarian sector stimulated by private profit. Hence, too, the attacks on the corporate privileges of the Mesta and the promulgation of laws permitting individuals to enclose their land. However, the desire to encourage what has been termed a bourgeois attitude to economic life could not extend to an attack on private property as such, since the application of the individual's efforts to his own property was considered by reformers like Gaspar de Jovellanos y Ramírez (1744–1811) as the 'engine of prosperity'. Thus, though all reformers recognized that the large, extensively cultivated, absentee estates of the great southern circle were an economic and social abuse, no real attack on these *latifundia* could develop. Agrarian reform had to wait until 1932.

The most notorious measure of Charles III was the expulsion of the Jesuits in 1767 and the consequent revival of regalism which was associated with the Count of Aranda (1719–98).

The Jesuits were held to have instigated the Madrid mob in 1766 against the king's Italian minister the Marquis of Esquilache, Leopoldo de Gregorio (?–1785).[1] They were expelled at short notice. Regalism was a political, not a philosophic, anti-religious attitude except for a few *esprits forts* such as Aranda himself (the subject of a laudatory if appalling poem by Voltaire). Caroline civil servants were rigid defenders of the superiority of royal jurisdiction over papal privilege – as the servants of Philip II had been. Reformers whose Catholic orthodoxy was impeccable resented the narrow-minded hostility of the clergy towards any attempt at modernization which threatened the clerical monopolies. Jovellanos, for example, was irritated by their

---

[1] That urban riot is an interesting example of the resistance of traditional society to 'enlightened' reform; the mob appears to have been organized by representatives of the privileged classes, including the Jesuits.

opposition to his schemes to set up a technical institute in his native province of Asturias.

The administrative and fiscal reforms of Charles III's time were not novel but represented a direct continuation of earlier Bourbon endeavours. Nor were they always successful. Thus the attempts to introduce Ensenada's single tax repeatedly failed and the government in the 1780s had to rely on the issue of paper money which brought a severe inflation. José Moñino, Count of Floridablanca (1728–1808), the most important of Charles III's ministers, did not succeed in by-passing the traditional Councils of State by means of a new, functionally organized, ministerial cabinet. The attempt to secure reform at the level of the municipalities by means of elected *síndicos* failed to deal with a major impediment to reform: the abiding administrative incompetence of impoverished, oligarchic municipalities. There were striking successes: for instance, a better road system – though bad communications and dependence on mule trains were to hold up the growth of the domestic market until the railways of the 1860s.

The imperial reforms of Charles III were central to his whole conception of the monarchy. He rightly saw that the true enemy of Spanish imperial greatness was Britain, and that against her there was only one conceivable ally – France. The 'Family Alliance' of 1763 was, therefore, not an outburst of dynastic sentimentalism but a piece of *realpolitik* – like the 'Family Pacts' of Philip V's time. The king was thus committed to helping France to defend her position in America against Britain. In the event, Spanish participation in the Seven Years War was disastrous to Spain and did not save Canada for France. At the Peace of Paris (1763) the Spanish crown lost all its territory between Florida and the Mississippi, gaining in return, however, the French territory of Louisiana. The opportunity for revenge soon came with the revolt of the American colonies against Britain (1775); but, with hindsight, we can see that to aid the rebel colonists of North America, as Spain now did, to create an independent nation was a dangerous step to take for an imperial power in America – as she was to learn after 1808 when her own American colonies revolted, influenced by the North American example.

Charles III was determined first to make the empire 'pay' and secondly to go on reserving its trade for Spanish subjects: only if the empire 'paid' could he afford the navy to defend it. By means of the intendant system and by the appointment of energetic viceroys the crown secured greatly increased revenues from America. But these innovations also set off a series of colonial revolts starting in 1780. The most striking success of Charles III was the opening of the American trade, hitherto confined almost entirely to Cadiz, to all important Spanish ports (1778). The proportion of Spanish goods exported and the volume of 'legitimate' trade now increased so rapidly that Britain became seriously alarmed at the prospect of a Spanish recovery that would exclude English merchants from a lucrative and developing market.

All Charles's civil servants were concerned to develop commerce, industry and what were then known as the 'useful arts'. How much of the increased prosperity of the late eighteenth century was due to government intervention is doubtful. An increase in population stimulated agricultural prices and production. The new Catalan cotton industry (started in 1746) owed little to direct government encouragement beyond the concession of a prohibitive protectionist tariff, the maintenance of which became the central concern of Catalonia. The foreign demand for brandy revolutionized Catalan viniculture and her long-standing mercantile tradition enabled her to exploit the growing markets in America. It is significant that population growth and the new prosperity were seated in the geographical periphery of Spain: the towns of Castile, for the most part, still vegetated; prices and wages moved less dramatically in the centre of the Peninsula than in the coastal regions. Here, then, were the beginnings of the modern tension between peripheral and central Spain which marks so much of modern history.

The philosophy of the Enlightenment (*las luces*) purported to supply an ideology for a progressive middle class which would become the driving force in economic progress. Yet the economic infrastructure for a middle class in Spain scarcely existed: this fact confined *las luces* to a minority of bureaucrats, a sprinkling of enlightened nobles and the small class of merchants and industrialists. The government, by fostering the 'Societies of the Friends of the Country' or 'Economic Societies' (that of the Basque country, founded in 1765, was the model), hoped to foster an interest in economic advance; but it would be false to talk in terms of a governmentally inspired 'bourgeois revolution'. The Caroline bureaucrats themselves were mostly provincial nobles; they might echo French polemical attacks on idle aristocrats but they had no conception of radical social change.

The Enlightenment in Spain was derivative; its interest lies in the application of the 'truths of political economy' to a traditional society.

Always opposed by traditional Catholics as foreign heresy, the ideas of the Enlightenment naturally became increasingly suspect after 1789.

III The Napoleonic Invasion and the War of Independence

The French Revolution and the Revolutionary and Napoleonic wars imposed heavy strains on the European states system. Nowhere were these strains more difficult than in Spain.

Neutrality in the wars of the French Revolution and the Empire was impossible for a weak power. Yet for Spain to ally herself with the traditional enemy, Britain, in the name of monarchical solidarity was to expose her to invasion from revolutionary France (1793–4); to ally with France was to allow Britain, as the greatest naval power, to cut Spain off from America and to penetrate the rich American market. The attempt to destroy the British navy at Trafalgar (1805) only destroyed the Spanish navy.

Charles III had died in 1788 and these strains were borne by Charles IV, a weak if amiable king. For most of the reign his Prime Minister was a young officer, his wife's favourite, Manuel Godoy (1767–1851), created Príncipe de la Paz after the Peace of Basle (1795), called the 'sausage maker' by his aristocratic enemies. Domestically Godoy weakened the reforming drive of Charles III's ministers, retaining 'only the external apparatus of Enlightened Despotism: ministerial omnipotence' (J. Vicens Vives). It was, however, his vacillating foreign policy (bedevilled in its later stages by his desire to win for himself the safe refuge of an independent principality in Portugal with the help of Napoleon) that ruined him and his master.

It was Napoleon's distrust of Godoy's vacillations and unreliability as an ally (he flirted with the anti-French coalition in 1805) that determined him to intervene directly in Spain. It was the 'dirty intrigues' of the heir to the throne, Ferdinand (1784–1833), Prince of Asturias, against his father that gave Napoleon the opportunity to place his brother Joseph Bonaparte (1766–1844; reigned 1808–13) on the Spanish throne and thus, he hoped, to secure the permanent subordination of Spain to the interests of French imperial policy.

By 1808 Godoy's 'dictatorship' was most unpopular. The lower classes suffered from the effects of inflation; the intellectuals he did not patronize and the court aristocrats to whom his presence was an affront laboured under injured pride. Hence the peculiar composition of the conspiracy which overthrew Godoy and forced Charles IV's abdication

(March 1808) and thus gave the throne to Ferdinand VII. The 'tumult of Aranjuez' represented the same combination of the mob and aristocratic conspirators which had appeared in 1766. Its success marked the end of the *ancien régime*: a Spanish king had been dethroned by 'the people'. The crisis also gave Napoleon the chance to summon Charles and Ferdinand to Bayonne where they renounced their rights to the throne. Napoleon then appointed his brother Joseph to succeed them.

Napoleon's calculation that Spain would accept a French dynasty proved a costly blunder. In general the upper classes and the constituted authorities at first either wavered or accepted Joseph's rule. Resistance came from the popular classes and seems to have been a continuation of the quasi-constitutionalist movement against Godoy's 'dictatorship'. The most dramatic of these popular movements was the rising of 2 May 1808 against the French occupation troops; it was put down with great severity; the executions were the subject of two of Francisco de Goya's (1746–1828) tremendous war paintings. In those parts of the country not occupied by French troops local gentry and town notables, supported by a populace outraged by the occupying troops' anticlerical vandalism, set up juntas to organize resistance.

The competing claims and quarrels of the provincial juntas made necessary some form of central government. It was inevitable that the weak Central Junta which sought to control provincial excesses should seek to legitimize and broaden the basis of its power by summoning the Cortes. The Cortes of Cadiz sat from 1810 to 1813. The debate as to its powers and functions, which began in 1809, was the first public political debate in Spanish history.

Conservatives stuck to the rigid view that the only task of the Cortes should be the provision of the sinews of war in the name of the absent king, Ferdinand VII, now in 'prison' in Talleyrand's château. Once the Cortes was summoned, the radical liberals were the only organized group and, as organized groups are wont to do, they imposed their views. In 1809 a wide body of informed opinion held that only a constitution could prevent the return of 'ministerial despotism' as practised by Godoy. The radical liberals founded this constitution on the sovereignty of the people.

The fact that these radicals – some from conviction, some for tactical reasons – chose to present their radicalism as derived from the constitutional tradition of medieval Spain, affected the form rather than the content of the Constitution of 1812. The 'sacred codex' of nineteenth-century democratic liberalism, as the Constitution of 1812 became, put severe restraints on royal power. Ministers were responsible to a democratically elected unicameral chamber – hardly a revival of medieval practice. The king was treated as 'a constitutional wild beast' and granted only a suspensive veto. It was the radicalism of this constitution which made its acceptance by *any* king worth his salt impossible; by 1837 all those radicals who wished to retain the monarchy saw that they could not retain the 'sacred codex' at the same time.

The liberalism of Cadiz went beyond constitutional reform. Although specific measures (for instance, hostility to entail) were inherited from the ministers of Charles III they were now part of a coherent liberal philosophy. The liberals aimed to create by legislation a modern bourgeois society based on a property franchise, which would give political power to the 'respectable' middle classes, and on the right to do what one liked with one's own property. Hence the legislation permitting the sale of municipal common lands, the abolition of guilds, and the right to enclose land or sell it 'subject only to the will of the contracting parties'. The rights of the individual were superior to the privilege of corporations.

It was the ecclesiastical settlement made by the Cortes of Cadiz that dissolved the general reformism of 1809 into a sharp division between liberals and conservatives. The abolition of the Inquisition decreed in 1813 and the sale of monastic property (now described as *bienes nacionales* after the French *biens nationaux* – a clear indication of French provenance) exposed the minority nature *in the country at large* of modernizing liberalism. The conservative, largely rural reaction against the radicalism of an élite provided the groundswell for the return to absolutism in 1814; the same phenomenon was to recur in 1823, even in 1936.

The collapse of the traditional monarchy in 1808–9 had its repercussions, too, in the American empire where it inevitably strengthened those tendencies making for independence. The Cortes of Cadiz also had, therefore, an imperial crisis on its hands. The liberals believed that the mere grant of representation in the Cortes itself would satisfy the Creole demand for self-government: 'From this moment, Spanish Americans, you see yourselves free men.' But the Creoles wanted effective self-government, not a limited voice in a centralized liberal empire. The setting up of juntas in Latin America which rejected the authority of metropolitan Spain was the real beginning of the movement which culminated in the independence of Latin America.

The primary task of the Cortes, however, was to organize a war effort to drive the French out of Spain. Three forces were involved: Wellington's army; the Spanish regular army; the guerrillas. Without Wellington's army it is hard to see how the French could have been defeated in the series of battles which culminated at Vitoria (June 1813). For the performance of his Spanish allies Wellington had only contempt: 'I have never known the Spanish *do anything*, much less do anything well,' he said. His criticisms of the regular army were justified; the victory of Bailén (July 1808) inspired Spanish generals with a mania for pitched battles in which their incompetence astonished even their enemies. Nevertheless the irregular operations of the guerrillas did help the operations of Wellington; moreover they forced Napoleon to commit valuable troops to mere police operations in occupied territory.

The guerrillas represented popular resistance in opposition to the collaborationism of a section of the official classes. Guerrilla warfare, therefore, had the overtones of a social conflict and in this respect parallels features of resistance movements in the Second World War. 'C'est, à proprement parler,' observed a harassed French general, 'la guerre des pauvres contre les riches.' The need to withdraw troops from Spain to Russia spelt the end of the French occupation. Madrid was finally evacuated in May 1813. After Wellington's victory at Vitoria a month later Joseph withdrew to France.

Not all Spaniards were patriots. Indeed, whole regions like Andalusia scarcely resisted at all. Respect for legality, timidity and opportunism provided Joseph with some partisans. The core of his pro-French party (the *afrancesados*) was made of nobler stuff. Some radicals believed in reform and regeneration by a French ruler as their grandfathers had in 1700. Some respectable administrators feared the popular risings that characterized patriot movements. Most calculated that resistance was useless and that co-operation was a better means of securing at least a nominal independence in face of French might. Napoleon's territorial rapacity ruined the *afrancesados'* programme of an independent Spain under Joseph, who made serious but ineffective gestures to 'win hearts'. The *afrancesados* went into exile with their French king in 1813. On 11 November of the same year Napoleon recognized Ferdinand VII, Charles IV's heir, as king.

The fact that cultured, reformist bureaucrats had co-operated with the 'intruder' confused the reformist tradition. It could be (and was) labelled 'anti-Spanish'. Given that, by and large, patriot liberals of

Cadiz shared many of the ideological assumptions and policies of the afrancesados (e.g. rational provincial divisions, uniform taxation, subjection of the Church to the State, and sale of monastic property), conservatives were able to cast a slur on liberalism as such as a foreign, anti-national, importation.[1]

IV Ferdinand VII (1813–1833)

The first years of Ferdinand's effective reign were dominated by four factors: (i) national bankruptcy; (ii) a politicized army; (iii) the struggle to recover the American colonies; (iv) the question of the future of liberalism, crushed in 1814 when 'El Deseado' ('The Desired One'), as Fernando was called, was restored to absolute power by the army. All were interconnected. Lack of money created military sedition. The colonies could not be recovered without an army which Spain could not afford. Thus, once assembled at Cadiz, the army which should have subdued America overthrew the absolute monarchy and restored the Constitution of 1812. The Spanish-American rebels subsidized liberal revolt.

The role of the army in politics in Spain deserves careful analysis since, henceforward, army officers were to be the final arbiters of Spanish political life. Political scientists have emphasized the role of armies in Latin America and Africa where the army constitutes the stablest institution in fluid political systems resting on a weak economy. While possibly true for the period 1833–75 this analysis, when applied to Spain, fails to take into account two factors: (i) the use of the army already in the eighteenth century as a normal instrument of civil government, and (ii) the peculiar conditions of the War of Independence and of the period 1814–20. During the war conflicts between the civilian juntas and the generals were frequent and acute. 'Can one deny', wrote an Asturian conservative, who had seen the Marqués de la Romana's fifty grenadiers dissolve the Asturian Provincial Junta,

[1] The differences between afrancesado liberalism and that of the patriots are, nevertheless, significant. While both shared a belief in the administrative rationalism and civil equality of the Napoleonic Code, only the liberal patriots insisted on political control of the executive by the legislature. In this respect they accepted the constitutional theories embodied in the 'Constitution of 1812' as opposed to the 'enlightened' but authoritarian 'Constitution of Bayonne' which was the official constitution of Josephine Spain. Thus the afrancesados could be utilized in Ferdinand VII's ominous decade because their enlightened views had no political consequences.

'that Spain is governed by soldiers? . . . How can I help seeing that this is the kind of government that threatens my grandchildren?'

Financial constraints after 1814 made it impossible for Ferdinand VII, a civilian monarch by temperament, to retain the large army that had fought the War of Independence. Guerrilla leaders soon staged the first *pronunciamientos* in favour of the liberalism defeated in 1814, less because they were convinced liberals than because they resented their demotion and retirement. All were unsuccessful until the mutiny led by Major Rafael de Riego (1785–1823) in January 1820 in the name of the Constitution of 1812. This succeeded because the troops assembled at Cadiz wished to escape service in a colonial war; because, through the secret societies, military sedition had at least some minimal civilian backing; and because the rest of the army proved unwilling to defend the monarch against even a handful of rebels. Riego's *pronunciamiento* already manifests what would come to be the classic form of such movements – from the *compromiso* (by which the officers bound themselves to act) to the *grito* (or 'electrifying' appeal to the troops) – so usual a proceeding that a handbook on military eloquence was later provided for officers.

The 'Constitutional Triennium' (1820–3), however, revealed once more the central weakness of liberalism: the narrowness of its social basis in a nation without a 'classic' middle class and where rural conservatism was a vital force. Nevertheless, in contrast with 1810–13, the liberal institutions of the Constitution of 1812 were applied, however superficially, to the whole country, and consequently more individuals became committed to their defence.

Nineteenth-century liberalism was destined to divide itself into a radical and a moderate stream. Radicals wished to take the doctrine of the sovereignty of the people to its logical extremes – universal suffrage, direct control of the executive. Moderate liberals held that the sovereignty of the nation should be exercised by those whose education and position enabled them to represent it with reason, i.e. the upper and upper middle classes. These divisions began to appear in the Triennium.

Political power during these three years was initially in the hands of the *doceañistas* ('men of 1812'), now, however, considered cured of the 'excesses' of 1812. Nevertheless it was through their own handiwork, the Constitution of 1812, that they had to operate, thus exposing themselves to control by the radicals in the Cortes and to the pressure of the radicals' allies in the street and the army. Francisco Martínez de la Rosa (1787–1862), the poet and dramatist, hoped for a constitutional revision on the lines of the French Charter of 1814: that is a workable constitution that would be backed by a humbled monarch and the upper middle classes. But Ferdinand was too much of an absolute monarch to work with ministers responsible to the Cortes or to support any form of constitutionalism. He characteristically betrayed a conspiracy of the Guards Regiments in support of constitutional revision (July 1822).

With the prospect of a moderate constitutional settlement ruined, power now fell to the radical *exaltados*. Their strength lay in that section of the army that had backed the revolution, and in the civilian clubs organized on Jacobin lines. The *exaltados* were a new class of politicians whose strength lay in their capacity to mobilize the urban masses. This strength, therefore, was confined to the great towns; the failure of the *exaltados* to appeal to the rural classes in the end proved fatal. A rural reaction developed in north-eastern Spain, backed by a French army – the 'Hundred Thousand Sons of St Louis' – sent into Spain to support Ferdinand by Louis XVIII. Reaction triumphed when the generals' support of liberalism disintegrated. 'They [the generals] behaved in this fashion', wrote Quintana, 'so that they might keep their jobs, remaining at the top of one system as they had been of the other.' The left wing of liberalism was committed to doctrinaire anti-clericalism. Whenever in power its attacks on the Church, especially on the regular orders, promoted a conservative reaction. Shootings and pillage, largely the work of military and civilian 'mushroom despots', appalled the 'respectable classes' in the towns and rural Spain. There was almost no resistance to the restoration of Ferdinand to absolute power by the French occupation troops (1823).

The 'ominous decade' (1823–33), as Ferdinand's second period of absolute power is called, saw the return to ministerial despotism. Liberal leaders went into exile; the army and civil service were purged. The only effective limitations on despotism now were financial and administrative; rigid conservatives could not negotiate European loans or run the government. Hence the use by Luis López Ballesteros (1782–1853), Finance Minister for the nine years after 1823, of *afrancesados* and his attempts to foster industry and commerce.

Traditional conservatives put up with these cautious 'liberal' measures because they put their hopes on the accession of the heir to the throne, Ferdinand's brother Don Carlos (1788–1855) – an uncompromising, bigoted 'apostolic', more at home in the sixteenth than the nineteenth century. He could be relied on to 'extirpate' both liberals and liberalism. But in 1829 Ferdinand married his niece María Cristina of Naples (1806–78). To secure her influence against the Carlist court faction, she persuaded the king to declare that, contrary to 'Salic Law', their child, *even if a female*, could inherit the crown. When Isabella was born, therefore, the hopes of Don Carlos and his supporters at court were defeated. After thwarting an attempt to force her to revert to the male succession, María Cristina used her power at court to put all the important military commands in the hands of generals who would support the rights of her daughter. This court feud was the origin of the Carlist War which broke out soon after Ferdinand's death on 29 September 1833.

V Isabella II (1833–1868)

One of the consequences of the Carlist rising in 1833 was the permanent recognition of some form of liberalism by the crown. In fighting for the rights of her daughter to the succession María Cristina – and through her the crown – was forced to ally itself with the liberals. It was an alliance not of conviction but of necessity, since only the liberals were prepared to oppose the Carlists. For the next century the crown would seek to escape the consequences of this alliance with liberalism by using its prerogative to keep in power what it considered to be the least dangerous brands of liberalism and to avoid the drift to the left implicit in liberalism itself. The monarchy was to be aided in this policy by the internal squabbles of the liberals. These enabled it to pick and choose among the liberal factions. But, in the end, the 'moderating power', as the crown's right to choose its own ministers was called, itself helped to dissolve the strong party system which is the basis of constitutional monarchy. It was a vicious circle: the personal politics of the rapacious María Cristina as regent till 1840 and her ichthyotic but sensual daughter Queen Isabella II (1830–1904) weakened the parties. Once the parties were weakened, then the crown was *forced* to meddle in politics in order to create a viable government. Both María Cristina and Isabella II further weakened their position by their private lives. María Cristina was forced to hide from hostile ministers repeated pregnancies resulting from her secret marriage to a sergeant. Isabella's fatal penchant for court clericals was in part due to her permanent combination of extramarital sexual adventures (she was married to a devout homosexual) with religious remorse.

The drift to the left was apparent by 1836. María Cristina could not avoid constitutionalism by the administrative reforms attempted in 1833. Nor could her moderate liberal ministers maintain the Royal Statute of 1834, a constitution designed to enhance the power of the crown, to keep power in the hands of the 'enlightened classes' and to guard against 'exaggerated pretensions', i.e. democratic radicalism. The radicals' strength lay in the urban militia recruited to support the army in the war against Don Carlos. A series of provincial urban uprisings in 1835, a sergeants' mutiny in 1836 and, finally, the *pronunciamiento* of General Baldomero Espartero (1793–1879) in 1840 swept the radicals to power. Their most important achievement was the sale of Church lands in 1836 by Juan Alvárez Mendizábal (1790–1853). These sales associated the anti-clericalism of the left with the necessities of war finance, for the proceeds of the sales were intended to meet the costs of the liberal army.

If, in the first instance, it was the 'contract' against Carlism that subjected the crown to a constitution, liberalism, in the broadest sense, became the dominant political creed of the nineteenth century because infrastructural changes in society now gave it the beginnings of an adequate social base. It even made some gains in the countryside where a class of landowners was created which owed part of its prosperity to liberal legislation. The economic and social consequences of Mendizábal's sales of Church lands, and of the sales of municipal and other common lands which followed them, are obscure. They have been made more obscure by the alliance between extreme left and extreme right opinion to condemn their social effects. In some areas, particularly in Andalusia and Extremadura, latifundism was strengthened; elsewhere it was the substantial peasantry which benefited. As in all such open-market sales of land it was the local 'powerful ones' who drove the marginal men to the wall. Not merely did the poor lose the benefits of access to common lands; the loss of revenue from municipal commons starved even the rudimentary local social services and compelled an increase in local indirect taxation, thus providing in its turn a source of urban unrest which ended in riots against the *consumos* (indirect taxes on consumption goods). One consequence of the great sales of land of the Mendizábal era is certain: the surge in cereal cultivation on the newly acquired land helped Spain to feed her greatly increased population. This rose from ten million to sixteen million between 1800 and 1860.

The basic strength of liberalism during the Isabeline period resided in the cities and it was the slow but marked growth of industry there after 1827 that produced both an urban middle class and an urban working class. In Catalonia, for example, the production of cotton doubled between 1830 and 1840; in the 1840s the rate of capital investment there increased eightfold and there was a spectacular change-over to steam power that altered the appearance of Barcelona from that of a port to a factory town. Built on colonial trade (with Cuba) and to meet the demands of the domestic market, the high-cost Catalan textile industry demanded tariff protection from Madrid. It was this demand which gave a new sense of separate interest to the 'differential factor' of Catalonia.

The alliance between urban middle class and liberal crown was already apparent in the support given by the industrialists of Barcelona to María Cristina as early as 1830. The radical political role of the new Catalan urban proletariat was apparent in the Luddism of 1836 and in the working-class agitation in Barcelona against Espartero after 1840. Whereas the rural regions of Catalonia tended to be Carlist, the urban artisanate and nascent proletariat were radical and gave a popular base in the Catalan cities to the Democratic Party – a crypto-republican grouping which was to have an increasing influence in revolutionary politics up to 1868.

The first Carlist War lasted from 1833 to 1839. It was a civil war of countryside against town, of clerical conservatism against the liberal *canalla*, of ill-supplied liberal armies against guerrillas, a war for the defence of the regional privileges of the Basque provinces and Navarre against centralizing liberalism. Carlism failed because it could not break out of its rural strongholds in the north and seize a major city. The siege of Bilbao cost the Carlist cause its greatest guerrilla leader, Tomás Zumalacárregui (1773–1836); the great Carlist expedition against Madrid turned back within sight of its walls (September 1837). To save what could be salvaged of the *fueros* the Basque Carlists then came to terms with Espartero, the most successful of Isabella's generals, in 1839. Just as the integration of Catalonia in 1715 was followed by industrial growth so now the abolition of the customs barriers between the Basque provinces and the rest of Spain was a precondition of industrial and financial development of the north.

From 1840 to Isabella's overthrow in 1868 political life turned on the balance of three factors: the crown; the parties that supported the dynasty; and the army. All were united against Carlists and Republicans.

It was the division of the 'Liberal Family' into two distinct streams that allowed María Cristina and (after her majority) Isabella to choose that group of politicians that suited them best: the Moderates. These oligarchs of liberalism – court aristocrats, bureaucrats, generals and the new *haute bourgeoisie* of business – believed in a property franchise and a strong executive as embodied in the Constitution of 1845. The heirs of the *exaltados* of 1820–3 were the Progressives. Although their preferred Constitution (that of 1837) was less radical than the 'sacred codex' of 1812 it was more of a democratic parliamentary constitution than that of 1845. Coming from lower reaches of the middle classes than the Moderates, the Progressives' political theory emphasized the right to have recourse to revolution as a counter to the crown's refusal to employ them in office. In consequence the Progressive leaders were forced into an uneasy alliance with the urban masses and lower-middle-class radicals – the only forces that could mount a revolution. However, whenever the attainment of office in a constitutional way by royal appointment appeared likely, the Progressive leaders were in the habit of abating their revolutionary zeal. It was the weakness of the Progressives in this respect which fostered the emergence of the Democratic Party. The latter sought, not compromise with the queen, but her overthrow.

All these parties – Moderates, Progressives and Democrats – shared the belief in 'progress' common to western Europe. The Moderates saw in material progress a cure for political radicalism; the Progressives believed that political liberalism, i.e. a system which would allow them a share of power, was a precondition of economic advance. The Democrats, with no hopes of power under the monarchy, held that progress could only come with the introduction of an unfettered individualism made possible by a republican constitution; though numerically insignificant, they were to give a radical, democratic, revolutionary tone to *pronunciamientos* in 1854 and 1868.

Like all wars, the Carlist War had enhanced the power of the military establishment. Generals acted as local despots, requisitioning supplies and imprisoning recalcitrant mayors. They then sought to translate this local predominance into power at the national level. There was, however, an important difference from the earlier *pronunciamientos* of the 1820s. The generals now became part of the political machine as party leaders. They did not act, as had Riego, from outside the system and against it. Thus, in 1840, General Espartero forced the resignation of María Cristina as regent. In 1843 his military rival, Ramón María Narváez (1800–68), in temporary alliance with

Progressives critical of Espartero's 'despotism', restored the Moderates. Narváez mastered sedition in the army and was able to use the army to suppress civilian sedition. Order gave the Moderates the opportunity to overhaul the kingdom's finances and push through a series of fundamental legal and administrative reforms (including the formation of the Civil Guard – the most effective rural police force in Europe). These reforms completed the structure of the liberal state; the Moderates crowned it with the conservative Constitution of 1845.

The settlement with the Church (the Concordat of 1851) reflected the Moderates' view of the Church as a useful buttress of the established order as long as it did not seek to upset the profits of anti-clericalism. The Church now accepted as a *fait accompli* the sale of Church lands in return for its recognition as a state Church paid for by the state. The Catholic religion was declared in 1851 the 'sole religion of the Spanish nation' and the Church was given control of education. The opposition Progressives, naturally, became committed to fight for religious toleration (to be provided by a 'neutral' state) and for lay control of education.

It was not, however, the strength of the Progressive–Democrat opposition to Isabella and the Moderates but the discontent of the military oligarchs which came near to dethroning Isabella in O'Donnell's *pronunciamiento* in 1854. Isabella's alienation of the Moderate generals in the Senate and her insistent hankering after some form of clericalist absolutism drove generals like Leopoldo O'Donnell (1809–67), later Duke of Tetuán, to combine with the excluded Progressives who had looked to Espartero to stage the Spanish equivalent of the European revolution of 1848; as it happened, the liberal Biennium of 1854–6, as the revolution came to be called, never lived up to the radical prospects it seemed to have in 1854.

If Espartero had been willing to follow the promptings of his Democratic allies and become 'the Washington of Spain', Isabella would have been dethroned in 1854 instead of in 1868. Instead, however, the Democratic clubs were shut down and the Biennium saw an uneasy alliance between Espartero and the more conservative O'Donnel. In July 1856 the queen forced Espartero's resignation; with the Progressives in the usual confusion which overcame them on the verge of armed action, O'Donnell dissolved the militia.

The Biennium was therefore a failure as a political revolution; its constitution was never operative. On the other hand its economic legislation (based on 'modern' *laissez-faire* premises, imported largely from France, as was so much of Progressive ideology) was to have important effects. There were fresh sales of ecclesiastical and common lands. A new company law and banking law provided the necessary legal framework for the new investment which was to underpin economic growth in the 1850s and 1860s.

The dynamic of this expansion was easy credit and foreign investment. The men of 1854 were infected by a Saint-Simonian belief in the role of credit, and it was the Pereire brothers who were responsible for the establishment of a Spanish equivalent of the *Crédit Mobilier*. The Catalan banks were joined by the beginnings of a new banking complex in the Basque country (Banco de Bilbao, 1855).

Much of this credit came from foreign investment – Belgian capital, for instance, was invested in zinc. Most spectacular was the French investment which made possible the creation of the Spanish railway network in the decade after 1853. Given that railway material came from abroad, the classic 'multiplier effect' of railway construction was lacking, in that it did not stimulate domestic iron and steel production; but the new railway network in Spain did provide the transport infrastructure for a national market. Textile production expanded as a modern wool industry grew up in Catalonia beside the older cotton industry. In the Basque country the archaic iron industry started its progress towards modernization.

Industrial expansion created a significant *haute bourgeoisie* (to become the most powerful single interest group in the country) whose craving for respectability in turn supported the beginnings of a Catholic revival. The new rich ranged from sober Catalan businessmen demanding protective tariffs to shelter their gains, to daring speculators like José de Salamanca (1811–83) who hired Napleon III's chef and installed the first private bathroom in Spain. They also included the successful generals – Narváez, with his diamonds, and Juan Prim y Prats (1814–70), the town chemist's son who married a Mexican heiress. Most of these new men were practising politicians whose riches were accumulated on the borderlands of business and politics. The less fortunate members of this society were the artisans and workers – suffering the early stages of industrialism – and the landless labourers. It was the former who were to support the Democratic Party and its Republican offshoots and to join the nascent trade unions in Catalonia in the 1850s and 1860s; the latter were to stage a violent, utopian rising at Loja (prov. of Granada), home town of Narváez (1861).

The politician who attempted to create a political system for the new society was O'Donnell, a dour, hard-headed, military politician who saw the social strength of liberalism and wished to absorb it within the monarchy. His receipt was a broad-based conservative-liberal grouping, called the Liberal Union, which should satisfy conservatives yet be 'open' enough to wean Progressives from sedition. This political hotchpotch was sustained in power by managed elections from 1855 to 1863. All the electoral techniques of *caciquismo* (see p. 169 below) were devised in the 1860s. O'Donnell's system eventually failed because the court did not support it and the oligarchs fell out among themselves. The court conservative governments which succeeded him contrived to provoke the revolution of 1868.

Court conservatism forced Liberal Union generals to join the Progressives against the dynasty. The loyalty of the Progressives could have been obtained by their participation in office; rejected by the crown, however, the Progressive leaders first staged a political strike (the *retraimiento*), and when that failed moved to military sedition. The chief Progressive conspirator was Prim. Though at the start ready to co-operate with Democrats and sergeants if no other allies were available, once the respectable generals of the Liberal Union were prepared to join the conspiracy he preferred to rely on the latter. Thus the 'Revolution' of September 1868 was made by generals who had been exiled to the Canary Islands and who were brought to Cadiz by Admiral Topete y Carballo – the only naval officer to play a major role in a *pronunciamiento*. It was the refusal of Isabella's armies to defend the monarchy in 1868 that forced the queen into exile and put Spain in the hands of a provisional government.

VI The Revolution of 1868

Though the Democrats did not 'make' the Revolution of 1868, it was their supporting role which made the dethronement of Isabella more than a successful army *coup d'état*. They set up revolutionary juntas in the main towns; it was their luminaries who gave the Revolution an intellectual content which, vague though it was, entailed a fundamental criticism, not merely of the monarchy but of traditional Catholic society. Men like the educationalist and philosopher Julián Sanz del Río (1814–69) and the republican orator and professor Emilio Castelar (1832–99) were concerned to change the value systems of Spain (mainly by introducing non-sectarian education). This was as important as the Democrat programme of universal suffrage; the fight for an educational system free of clerical control remained a distinctive programme of the Spanish left.

Democratic pressure certainly made the Constitution of 1869 a more radical document than the general-politicians wanted. In return for the provisional government's support for the retention of a monarchy, the Democrats secured universal male suffrage. Nevertheless, as long as the coalition of Prim and Francisco Serrano (1810–85) – a favourite of Isabella and now leader of the former Liberal Unionists – held together, the government could firmly repress the revolts of provincial radicals seeking to recover the radical republic of the provincial juntas jettisoned by the generals. With social peace restored by the army, the country looked fit to receive the centre-piece of the Constitution of 1869: a king. After a long search (which *en passant* ignited the Franco-Prussian War) one was found in the person of Amadeo of Savoy (1845–90), son of the King of Italy and thus a representative of a 'modern' dynasty, hostile to the claims of the papacy.

Amadeo tried to rule as a constitutional monarch without the existence of the essential ingredient of successful constitutional monarchy – a party ready to form a government and an opposition prepared to oppose without wrecking. His dilemma was that of Isabella II and Alfonso XIII. The September coalition of Progressives and Liberal Unionists, which had 'made' the Revolution, split; none of the fragments could form a stable government, nor would the separate factions permit a rival to rule. In February 1873 Amadeo abdicated and a republic was conjured into existence in order to fill the ensuing political vacuum.

The rapid descent of this first Spanish Republic into near anarchy was to have a profoundly negative effect on the future course of Spanish politics. Because of it a whole political generation put the preservation of an ordered society above all else. Yet the presidents of the Republic were dignified, respectable men who had fought against disorder and put constitutional legality above the implementation of their principles by violence. Like their successors in the Second Republic they were defeated by their intransigent supporters and by those on the right who capitalized on their failure to control their own extremist followers and the 'disorder' this produced.

The majority of the Republicans were Federalists. Following Francisco Pí y Margall (1824–1901), a disciple of Proudhon and President of the Republic (11 June to 18 July 1873), they envisaged a

Spain of provinces and towns bound together by 'synallagmatic' pacts freely entered into by the contracting parties. When the legalism of the Republican leadership in Madrid delayed the setting up of 'cantons', the extremists of the southern cities revolted. The cantonalist revolt, serious in Málaga and Cartagena, embarrassed a government that had by now lost the confidence of the army, whose discipline had been undermined by extremist Republican propaganda. It was a general who overthrew the First Republic (January 1874) in order to install a regime which could command the confidence of the officer corps.

The conservative successor regime, with General Serrano as presidential dictator of a unitary Republic, was faced with a new Carlist War. Because of the anti-clericalism and secularism of the regimes that issued from the September Revolution and the collapse of order which, to conservatives, seemed a logical consequence of the individualism enshrined in the Constitution of 1869, the Carlists grew in strength; only a return to traditionalist principles, they asserted, could save society. In the north they set about creating their own state with its capital at Estella, in Navarre, and with its arms factories, hospitals, postal service and customs organization. With the Republic's army enfeebled by indiscipline they won a series of striking victories in the north in 1874. Had Serrano been able to achieve a crowning victory against Carlism he might have survived longer. To most conservatives the restoration of the dynasty in the person of Isabella's son, Alfonso, seemed to present the only possibility of ending the war.

Nor was the Carlist War the only war confronting the governments after 1868. The severest drain on the political vitality of the regimes of the September Revolution was the Cuban war. Cuba (together with Puerto Rico and the Philippines) was all that remained of the Spanish empire. A guerrilla rising in Cuba which demanded independence for the island committed the Madrid governments to a costly war. As the war dragged on, so the revolutionary governments had to go back on what had been the most popular pledge of 1868 – the abolition of the arbitrary and unpopular form of compulsory military service (the *quintas*). *Quinta* riots fed radical discontent.

The man who was responsible for the growth of a party supporting a Bourbon restoration was Antonio Cánovas del Castillo (1828–97), a former Liberal Unionist. Highly intelligent, son of a schoolmaster, a hard-worker and early riser, Cánovas was no vulgar reactionary. His sceptical political philosophy was, in fact, strangely similar to that of Lord Salisbury. Opposed to military politics, he understood the strength of liberalism and the impossibility of a return to the rigid, Catholic conservatism of the old Moderate party; Alfonso must be restored by a popular movement. That he was in fact restored by the military rising of a young brigadier (Arsenio Martínez Campos, 1831–1900) at Sagunto (December 1874) irritated Cánovas.

As far as the intellectuals who had morally undermined the monarchy before 1868 were concerned, the Revolution was not merely a political failure but a spiritual disillusionment. Yet the September Revolution was both the culmination of the epoch of liberal revolutions and the crystallization of their heritage. The Count of Romanones (1863–1950), later a Liberal Prime Minister and a professional politician if ever there was one, recognized that what came to be called the liberal conquests of 1869 could 'never, never' be reversed. The assumptions of a Catholic monarchy sustained by conservative liberalism had been challenged by democracy and free thought. To Republicans the September Revolution was a religious revolution. In the narrow sense this was reflected in its crude anti-clericalism and, more importantly, in the assertion of complete religious toleration in the Constitution of 1869. The hostile reaction of the Church supplied Alfonsine conservatism with recruits; but even the restored monarchy could not revert to the position of 1868.

VII The Restoration (1875–1902)

Alfonso XII (1857–85) was a cadet at Sandhurst when he was called to the throne; he was to be an intelligent, popular king who resented but followed the strict counsels of his maker, Cánovas. Once the Carlist and Cuban wars were out of the way, the restored monarchy was destined to provide the framework for the longest period of relative political stability in the history of modern Spain – 'artificial' though the system has always seemed to its critics. It was buttressed by economic growth and by a religious revival which sought, without great success, to undo the ravaging effects of liberal indifference on a 'de-christianized' working class. It was untroubled by foreign complications until the renewed revolt of Cuba in 1895. It survived the death of Alfonso XII in 1885 and even the disaster of 1898. It was finally destroyed by the strains of the World War of 1914–18, by the political consequences of a disastrous colonial war in Morocco, by the growth of organized labour and by the failure of Madrid politicians to solve the Catalan question. It was these problems which made difficult an enlargement of political participation without upsetting the precarious balance of the system.

The aim of Cánovas was to bring within the Constitution of 1875 all those professional politicians who were not, on principle, opposed to the restored monarchy in the way the Republicans and Carlists were. He himself would marshall the conservatives, restraining those who wished to restore the Catholic exclusivism of the old Moderates, while Práxedes Mateo Sagasta (1827–1903), the ablest Progressive politician of the September Revolution, would bring into constitutional harness the left of the old September coalition. An 'open' liberal left was intended to wean extremists from attachment to the Constitution of 1869 by embodying within the system the so-called 'liberal conquests'. Once universal suffrage was granted (1889) only Catholic control of education remained to remind liberals that the Spain of Cánovas was not the Spain of Prim. By 1885 the system was in working order: Sagasta and Cánovas alternated in power as if they were chiefs of Liberal and Conservatives parties on the British model.

The essential mechanism of the *turno pacífico*, as this alternation was called, was wholesale electoral management. When the king was advised to change ministries then the new ministry must be sure of a working majority in the Cortes. This it achieved by 'making' the elections. Electoral management depended on a reliable connection between the Ministry of the Interior, the provincial governors and the network of local patronage and influence controlled by the local bosses or *caciques*. Thus the Liberal Party of Sagasta and his successors was completely dependent on manipulation of the liberal conquest of universal suffrage. Paradoxically the heirs of the urban Liberals of 1836 had become politically dependent on the control of rural votes.

This system of control, where political change came from above and did not reflect changes in the opinion of the electorate, could therefore survive the introduction of universal male suffrage. Nor was it threatened by republican conspiracies. Confronted by apathy and the political control of the monarchical politicians, the revolutionary guts went out of historic republicanism. It survived only on memories of 1873 until its revival as a mass party under Lerroux in the early twentieth century.

Until the later 1880s this political superstructure was sustained by economic prosperity, which ensured the support of the great landowners and of the *haute bourgeoisie* – in so many features an imitation of the French financial and industrial oligarchy – that had emerged in the 1850s.

While in 1875 there was a sharp political break with the revolutionary liberal tradition, socially and economically the Spain of the early Restoration was a culmination of the growth of the previous four decades. Railway construction picked up after the 1868 recession. The fiscal legislation of the Revolution – there is a parallel with 1854–6 – made possible a steep increase in foreign investment in mining. Spanish copper exports reached new levels and the iron of the Basque country was in strong demand in Great Britain after Bessemer converters came to South Wales (peak demand there came in 1899). After 1882 came 'the euphoria of cotton' – a rapid and risky expansion. Spain's own industrial production, largely channelled to the domestic market, still depended largely on the purchasing power of the agricultural sector. Wheat prices were high. The outbreak of phylloxera in France gave a stupendous boost to Spanish wine producers.

The economic boom broke in 1886–7. Phylloxera then invaded Spain and vineyards were abandoned; agricultural prices fell; the expanding metallurgical industry of Barcelona laid off hands. Economic optimism had turned to pessimism in 1887 – a factor often forgotten in emphasizing the dramatic effects of the disaster of 1898. The wheat-growers of Castile, the iron-masters of the Basque country, and the mill-owners of Catalonia clamoured for protection against foreign imports – in each case to compensate for the domestic high costs. The one liberal heritage decisively abandoned by Cánovas was free trade. Tariffs moved steadily upwards and the notions of autarky and of government interference in economic life gained ground.

VIII The Cuban Disaster and Alfonso XIII (1898–1923)

In 1895 a separatist rebellion broke out in Cuba. The Spanish forces there were defeated, not by the efforts of the Cuban guerrillas, but by the naval intervention of the United States in 1898. The Spanish fleet was destroyed outside Santiago (July 1898) and Cuba and the Philippines – last remnants of the once great empire – were surrendered at the Peace of Paris (10 December 1898). This humiliating defeat, known simply as 'El Desastre', gave strength both to those who wished to revitalize the Restoration system and to whose who wished to destroy it. The intellectual ferment of the so-called Generation of 98,[1] interesting in itself, was to have less political effect than the intensification of previous discontents and the reactions of already established political

[1] For a full account of the Generation of 98, see Chapter 9, section VII.

leaders. Fundamentally the Generation of 98 sought, or believed they sought, to persuade their fellow countrymen to adjust to the irrefutable proof that Spain was now a second-class power whose conservative society and archaic institutions had caused her to be humiliatingly defeated by the epitome of modernization, the 'barbarous' United States. To the majority of the Generation of 98, regeneration, therefore, could come only from some form of imitative modernization, some radical departure from things as they were.

Radical modernizers like the Aragonese polymath, Joaquín Costa (1844–1911), sought to introduce what he called the 'vital forces' (*fuerzas vivas*) within the political system to make that system correspond to the needs and desires of the progressive forces in Spain. *Caciquismo* must be destroyed before Spain could be modernized by democratic institutions, since it restricted political power to the 'ignorant and selfish oligarchy' that controlled local and central government alike. Costa's plea for regeneration failed; no new political force strong enough to break the monopoly of the two 'establishment' parties could be formed by an appeal to middle-class interest groups. After failing to create his new party (La Unión Nacional) Costa became a Republican.

The bid for regeneration that emerged from the political class itself has received less attention than it deserves. Reformist conservatives like Francisco Silvela (1845–1905) or Antonio Maura (1853–1925), rigid Catholics though they both were, and democratic liberals like José Canalejas (1859–1912) alike were aware that political apathy was the basic condition for the successful operation of *caciquismo*. They all hoped that a genuine appeal to the electorate would reinvigorate a tired political system. They were also aware that the most important challenge of the 'vital forces' to the two-party system and the electoral corruption that accompanied it was building up in Catalonia which, together with the Basque provinces, represented the modern sector of the economy. Only in 1909 did another threat appear – working-class agitation among a developing urban proletariat.

The economic demands of Catalonia now combined with that region's independent cultural and historic traditions to stake a claim for political regionalism: special treatment in the shape of some form of home rule. Catalan industrialists, as we have seen, had been demanding protection from foreign competition since the 1850s. The Catalan 'Renaixença',[1] a linguistic and literary revival of the eighties which,

[1] For a further account of the Catalan Renaixença, see Chapter 9, section V.

inter alia, emphasized the separate role of Catalonia in Iberian political, institutional and cultural history, gave emotional force to dry economic polemics. The cultural separatist movement ultimately provided an ideology for the political separatism which was to condemn Catalan regionalism to be perpetually misunderstood by Castilian patriots. The latter accused Catalans of wishing to destroy the 'unity of Spain'. Catalans in their turn accused the Madrid politicians of neglecting their moderate demands without any attempt at understanding the problems of Catalonia, thus strengthening separatism. The basic demands of the Catalan nationalists were set out in the 'Bases of Manresa' (1892); the demands for an autonomous government set out in the Bases remained the programme of political Catalanism.

The loss of Cuba by 'bungling' Madrid politicians, which had deprived Catalonia of a useful market, gave the Catalanists the possibility of a popular following. The Lliga Regionalista, founded in 1901 by conservative regionalists, sought to organize this support to force Catalan demands on the government by bringing out the vote for Catalanist candidates against the parties of the *turno pacífico*.

The conflict between the 'bourgeois' Catalanism of the Lliga and working-class demands precluded the emergence of a united Catalan party embracing all sectors of the population. The urban working classes – often of non-Catalan extraction – had no great sympathy with 'cultural' Catalanism. They were therefore available to radical Republicans who were anti-Catalan, or to Anarchists who were against any form of state.

Alejandro Lerroux (1864–1949) is usually dismissed as a vulgar demagogue. His violent and effective oratory was accompanied, however, by organizing talent and a realization that the doctrinaire squabbles of Republican leaders, living on memories of the Republic of 1873, must be replaced by a programme that reflected the discontents of the Barcelona workers. Between 1900 and 1909 the votes of Lerroux's party together with those of his political adversaries, the Regionalists, defeated the network of patronage which supported the old parties of the *turno* in Catalonia.

Anarchism had first entered Spanish working-class politics in 1868–73, when the old alliance of the working classes with the Democrats and later with the Republicans was replaced by a belief in direct proletarian action. Founded by Bakunin's disciples, the Spanish branch of the International veered from a belief in preparation for revolution by education and organization, towards faith in 'propaganda by deed', i.e. in terrorism as the midwife of a new society.

Anarchism appeared less organized and respectable than the Socialist Party (1874) and its trade union, the UGT (Unión General de Trabajadores, founded 1882). But socialism in Spain remained relatively unimportant. In Madrid its policies were dictated by the coterie of Pablo Iglesias (1850–1925) and much influenced by French Marxists. Its fighting strength lay in the industrial and coal-mining regions of the north. The regional division (Anarchism was strong in Catalonia and Aragon and among the landless labourers of the south) and the ideological disparity – the Socialists were Marxist social democrats, and the Anarchists libertarian revolutionaries – of these two working-class movements were to be a lasting source of conflict and weakness. It was only rarely possible (e.g. in the strikes of 1917) to get a semblance of proletarian unity.

The heirs of Sagasta in the Liberal Party offered no solution either to the 'social question' or to Catalan discontent.[1] The Liberals chose to expand their energy in an attempt to secularize education and to control the religious orders. The democratic programme of Canalejas foundered with his assassination (November 1912). The radical reformist element in liberalism tended to become republican with the formation of the Reformist Republican Party, moderate in tone and sympathetic to Socialist demands.

The most controversial attempt to rejuvenate dynastic politics came from Silvela and Maura (see p. 171 above), the conservative leaders who succeeded Cánovas (assassinated by an anarchist in August 1897). Both wished to end *caciquismo* and political corruption by 'sincere' elections; both were convinced Catholics. Maura failed to create a mass conservative Catholic party and his 'sincere' politics alarmed orthodox Conservatives who, like the Liberals, feared the results of a genuine appeal to the electorate. Nor could Maura solve the Catalan question in alliance with Cambó. Francisco Cambó (1876–1947), a brilliant businessman, was essentially a conservative who believed in solving the Catalan question 'within Spain'; yet he demanded more autonomy than Maura would give. Cambó's limited co-operation with Madrid,

[1] It was the centralism of the Liberal government of 1906 which gave Catalanism its most dramatic success. The government supported army officers who broke up the offices of a Catalanist newspaper. This led to the formation of Solidaridad Catalana, an electoral coalition which beat the established parties in Catalonia in 1906.

however, cut him off from the Catalan left and thus destroyed the electoral union Catalanist parties had achieved in 1906.

The crises of 1909 and 1917, both rooted in unsatisfied Catalanism and the 'social question' in Barcelona, deepened into a continuous crisis which lasted from 1919 until the *coup d'état* of 1923.

While the political problems thus became more severe, the political machinery became less able to deal with them. In 1902 Alfonso XIII became of age to perform the duties of king. With the parties in disarray his role became increasingly important: with neither clear verdicts from an independent electorate nor strong parties, the king could not act as a model constitutional monarch. He was forced either to bully the politicians into serving him, or to intrigue against them. Increasingly his critics accused Alfonso of irresponsible meddling in politics. He had, in fact, little alternative.

The first crisis was the most dramatic: the so-called 'Tragic Week' of July 1909 in Barcelona. The convent and church burning of the Tragic Week was set off by a call-up of troops for the first serious campaign in what was to be a long and costly war in Morocco. Anarchists and Radical Republican extremists combined in an ill-co-ordinated street rebellion which cut Barcelona off from Spain for a week. The Prime Minister, Maura, reacted strongly, shooting Francisco Ferrer (1849–1909), a well-known free-thinker, implicated in Anarchist conspiracies. The Liberals, prepared to ally with what Maura called the 'sewer' of Republican agitation in support of Ferrer, used Maura's unpopularity with the left in order to persuade the king to dismiss him.

The subsequent political crisis paralysed and divided the Conservative Party. Maura rejected the assumptions of the *turno*: the Liberals, far from acting as a 'lightning conductor' protecting the monarchy on the left, co-operated with anti-dynastic Republicans in attacking the king's ministers. Maura declared the Liberals political pariahs and refused to serve in alternation with them. The king and the less apocalyptic Conservatives rejected this view. Maura, said Lerroux, had 'torpedoed' the monarchy by weakening the Conservative Party, discrediting the Liberals and leaving the king with no proper instruments of government.

The European war of 1914–18 inflicted severe strains on weak Spanish governments which were in turn the expression of a party system in dissolution. Moreover the war not merely intensified political feuds related to the issue as to whether Spain should join the allies or Germany; it also intensified social tensions. Spain remained neutral in the war, and neutrality allowed industry to make huge profits; but wages did not rise with prices. Two classes suffered from this inflation: army officers on fixed wages, and the workers. Both went on strike and this combined with the discontent of Catalanists and Republicans to provide the elements for the serious political crisis of 1917.

The army strike took the form of the setting-up of Juntas de Defensa, a dramatic but novel reassertion of the army's political role. Novelty lay in the fact that, this time the juntas were controlled by junior officers. Cambó, though a conservative, was ready to ally both with army malcontents and Republicans. In Barcelona a convention of the discontented elements, organized by the Catalanist politicians, threatened to establish its own government. The crisis was surmounted partly because the conservative elements of the Lliga were scared by a general strike in which both the UGT and the CNT (see below) combined, partly by the formation of a national government under Maura.

The national government failed. Between 1918 and 1923 colourless combinations of Liberals and Conservatives were left to face two acute problems: the Moroccan War and the industrial unrest 1919–23.

The war in the Moroccan Protectorate, granted to Spain by France in 1912, produced a conflict between civilians who wished for pacification on the cheap and the soldiers who were left to fight the tribes with poor equipment. The *africanistas*, professional soldiers who were to play such an important role in the conspiracy of 1936, learned to despise civilian party government. So did Alfonso XIII. The crisis came to a head with the disaster to Spanish arms at Anual (1921): a total military defeat at the hands of the Rif chieftain, Abd el Krim.

The workers' unrest of the war years was not confined either to Catalonia or to the Anarcho-Syndicalists, but it was terrorism in Barcelona that prepared conservative opinion for a military takeover. Between 1919 and 1923 the struggle between the Barcelona employers and the CNT became the obsessive centre of national politics.

The great Anarcho-Syndicalist Union, the CNT (Confederación Nacional de Trabajadores), was founded in 1911. It combined uneasily a residue of anarchist belief in spontaneous revolution with the ambition of syndicalist leaders to build up a union disciplined enough to challenge employers directly. The early success of the great electricity strike of 1919 was a proof of the power of the new unionism; unfortunately for the moderate leaders, gunmen had infiltrated into the movement and into the employers' organizations. The employers' rejection of the

negotiated settlement of the 1919 strike ruined the moderate syndicalists. When the employers' viewpoint triumphed over the government's
attempt to strengthen moderate CNT leaders by negotiated settlements,
the social question became a vendetta of violence with the army
backing the employers.

Political confusions and social tensions were dramatically simplified
when Miguel Primo de Rivera (1870–1930), Captain-General of
Barcelona, rose against the government. His *coup* infused into the old-
style military *pronunciamiento* a new dimension – that disillusionment
with parliamentary government common to Latin Europe and
especially strong in Spain after 1898. This disillusionment accounts for
two important factors about Primo de Rivera's *coup*: the general support
he received in Spain – above all from the king – and the necessity the new
regime felt to formulate a new political and social theory. The generals
of the nineteenth century had operated with the commonplaces of
parliamentary liberalism. Primo de Rivera was forced to forge an
ideology, however primitive and eclectic it turned out to be, which
would be a *substitute* for nineteenth-century liberalism.

IX The Dictatorship of Primo de Rivera (1923–1930)

Primo de Rivera's personal rule lasted because powerful interest groups
initially supported him. These included the Catalan industrialists, the
army and large landowners on one side, and the UGT on the other.
He fell seven years later because these groups were alienated by his
erratic policies and because the economic prosperity of the twenties
withered away in the preliminary stages of the world depression of
the 1930s.

Initially economic growth was resumed after the severe post-war
economic crisis of 1919–22 had passed. Heavy industry and textiles
recovered; newer industries – electricity, cement and chemicals – grew
significantly. Nevertheless, the purchasing power of the economy and
the stability of the currency still depended on agricultural exports – for
instance Valencian oranges – and mineral exports. Thus the fall in the
price of primary products could have a serious effect on the economy
as a whole and on the standing of the peseta.

Primo de Rivera's attempts to foster prosperity combined a primitive
Keynesianism – heavy loan-financed expenditure on public works –
with an intensification of protectionism and government control.
State boards controlled activities from the dictator's all-important

hydro-electric schemes and his oil monopoly to the sale of rabbit skins.

At first the interest groups which benefited from governmental patronage supported the dictator. Increasingly, however, the complaint of those who did not benefit (e.g. the Catalan textile manufacturers, forced to buy expensive domestic cotton, and the private banks) grew. Thus government attempts to bolster up the peseta by heavy state purchases and the increasing dependence on high-cost loans for public works were fiercely criticized by opposition economists and bankers.

Nevertheless Primo de Rivera's fall is not solely to be explained by the collapse of the boom of the twenties. His failure was a political failure. He was unable to create a stable political system to replace the 'discredited' system of the Restoration.

His first intention had been to clear out the 'old' politicians by a brief period of military 'iron surgery'. The country could then be handed over to 'clean hands' who would run the old constitution. Unfortunately the 'corrupt' politicians did not repent and they found allies in the intellectual opposition led by Unamuno and Ortega. Nor could Primo de Rivera create a new political party – his Patriotic Union never got off the ground and remained the protective covering of committed supporters. Thus the attempt in the National Assembly (1928) to create a new constitution came to nothing because it was boycotted by all the significant political forces in the country. The regime was therefore dependent on the dictator's improvisation erected into a political system. A controlled press could not hide the erratic nature of a personal rule that lurched from regulating Spanish meals or prohibiting the import of foreign surgical instruments to a thorough overhaul of municipal government.

Primo de Rivera was, however, a courageous politician and a simple patriot. Resisting the pressure of the *africanistas* (they included the young Major Francisco Franco) for a forward policy in Morocco in 1924, he waited until the prospect of French military aid ensured the success of a combined naval and army landing at Alhucemas (1925). The Moroccan Protectorate was pacified in 1927 and the exhausting war which had bedevilled domestic politics liquidated. The Military Directorate was replaced by a Civilian Directorate. But the opposition of the 'old' politicians, of republicans, intellectuals and students was unconquerable. So was the hostility of Catalonia. Catalan conservatives and regionalists, alarmed by the strength of the CNT, originally supported the *coup d'état*. Once it was clear, however, that Primo's own brand of Spanish nationalism and rigid centralism constituted an irremovable obstacle to the hopes of Catalan autonomy, Catalonia turned against him. Similarly the tacit support of the UGT for a new deal in labour relations met with increasing hostility from the Socialist Party because of the latter's connections with 'bourgeois' republicanism. However, the regime might have withstood these forces longer but for the desertion of two critical elements: the king and the army.

The general-dictator's quarrel with the army was a curious result of his reformist streak and of the traditional hostility of the infantry and cavalry to the 'privileged' corps of the artillery and engineers. These corps enjoyed special privileges respecting promotion which stood in the way of a unified army with common norms of promotion. Primo's attack on these privileges drove the artillery officers to strike. Though many military reformers sympathized with the dictator's purpose, the destruction of 'the harmony of the military family' distressed the generals and appalled the king, who regarded his office as commander-in-chief of the army as his most important asset.

Alarmed at this erosion of support, Primo's last device was to consult the captains-general. Did he enjoy their support? The replies were not encouraging and the consultation, made without his consent, infuriated the king. He dismissed Primo (January 1930), who retired to Paris to die a broken man; Alfonso had 'Bourbonized' a faithful servant in difficulties in order to save the monarchy.

X The Second Republic (1930–1936)

Dropping the pilot did not save Alfonso. The politicians who had worked the system until 1923 never forgave the king for his desertion of the constitution and his early support for the dictator. This erosion of natural support left the monarchy undefended against a Republican movement; in August of 1930, at San Sebastián, a group of conspirators which ran from liberal Catholics through Catalanists to Socialists agreed on the overthrow of the monarchy. General Mola's memoirs reveal an impotent government dependent on inadequate, ill-equipped police forces battling against Republican conspirators, a revival of the CNT, the new belligerency of the Socialists and the continuation of a student revolt that had plagued the last months of Primo's rule.

The San Sebastián conspirators were ready to use force. They were saved from the consequences of a Republican *pronunciamiento* by the widespread feeling against Alfonso which was reflected in the victory of the anti-monarchical parties in the municipal elections of April 1931.

The great cities then voted Republican and, rather than face a civil war and the street pressure that was mounting in Madrid, Alfonso left the country. One factor deserves emphasis. The army took no positive stand, but the commander of the Civil Guard, General José Sanjurjo (1872–1936), made it clear that his forces would not support the king against the 'national will', i.e. the urban voters. This negative *pronunciamiento* was the decisive factor which dissuaded monarchists from a last-minute rally.

The history of the Second Republic falls into four distinct phases. The provisional government of the San Sebastián coalition survived for a few months until it was split asunder by Republican treatment of the Church (October 1931). The next phase was dominated by the coalition of Left Republicans and Socialists under Manuel Azaña (1880–1940) as Prime Minister. In the parliamentary elections of November 1932 a swing to the right gave power first to Lerroux's now conservative Radical Republicans and then to a coalition of Radicals and the new Catholic right under Jose María Gil Robles (1898–). It was the accession of Gil Robles to power that set off the revolution of October 1934, the crucial watershed. In the February elections of 1936 the Azaña coalition triumphed as the Popular Front; it was against this Republican government, which was supported by the Socialists in the Cortes, that the generals rose in July 1936.

Before examining those defects of Republican statesmanship which, with the advantages of historical hindsight, are so easy to detect, the achievements of the Republic in its early constructive phase deserve attention.

To Azaña's political toughness must go much of the credit for the settlement of the Catalan question. The campaign for autonomy after 1919 under the leadership of Cambó had been cut short by the Barcelona strikes and terrorism, and by 1931 political Catalanism had become the preserve of the Catalan left (the Esquerra), strongly organized in the middle classes and among the vine-growers. Its figurehead Colonel Francisco Macía (1875–1933), who had led a militant separatist movement, wished, on the downfall of the monarchy, to declare for a Catalan republic in a federal Spain. The Esquerra leaders were persuaded to wait on the cession of autonomy by Madrid. This was granted in the 'Catalan Statute' (1932) which gave the Generalitat de Catalunya control of its internal affairs. It was this settlement that ensured that Catalonia became a bastion of republicanism after July 1936.

The Socialist Party initially pledged itself to co-operation with the 'bourgeois' republic on a minimal programme, leaving for some more distant future the creation of a socialist society. Left Republicans like Azaña were prepared, on their part, to support new labour legislation. This legislation was the work of Francisco Largo Cabellero (1869–1946), the vastly experienced leader of the UGT. It created modern machinery for the settlement of labour disputes by joint committees of employers and workers. Azaña also undertook army reform. This was partly conditioned by his desire to get monarchist officers out of the army, partly by the aim of creating an efficient army without an over-large officer corps; officers could retire on full pay.

It is argued, with some truth, that these reforms shared a common defect: they alienated conservatives and radicals alike. Thus the Catalan Statute did not satisfy extreme Catalanists while it alienated conservative centralists. Much more important, the labour legislation of Largo Caballero met with the uncompromising hostility of the CNT. The CNT was increasingly dominated by the revolutionism of the Federación Anárquica Ibérica (FAI), a body of anarchist cells founded when the CNT was declared illegal by Primo de Rivera. Syndicalists regarded a labour code worked by governmental Socialists and employers as a heretical abandonment of direct action. The result was a trying series of bitter strikes and local risings.

Again, with the benefit of hindsight, it is now obvious that the treatment of the Church in the new Republican Constitution was a mistake. While it is true that the Vatican would have accepted a reasonable negotiated settlement separating Church and State, the historic traditions of Republicanism, apart from the pressure of the Socialists, made inevitable a modern edition of regalism: the assertion of the supremacy of the lay state and an attack on the religious orders. This was unacceptable both to Miguel Maura (1887–1971), Minister of the Interior, already shocked by a recrudescence of convent burning in the style of the 1830s (May 1931), and to the President of the provisional government, Niceto Alcalá Zamora (1877–1949).

This in itself would have been of no great importance, since Maura's and Alcalá Zamora's vision of a Catholic, Republican Centrist party was a non-starter politically. More important was Lerroux's increasing alienation from Azaña and the Socialists as he divined a political future in a Republican party able to rally the conservative middle classes. Above all, the Church settlement prepared the way for the emergence of a mass party of the right.

This party, Acción Popular, was the creation of Gil Robles. Committed to the revision of the Church settlement, it was in origin an imitation of European Christian Democratic parties in that its ideology included an intention – totally unattainable, given the previous commitment of the working class to the UGT or the CNT – to win over the 'de-Christianized' proletariat to a mild form of Christian Socialism. Theoretically Gil Robles was committed to 'accidentalism' – the doctrine, rooted in Leo XIII's encyclicals, that forms of government were indifferent to Catholics provided the vital interests of the Church were protected.

Gil Robles, whose father was a Carlist, drew some of his support and most of his campaign funds from Monarchists. Thus while his own accidentalism was sincere and he himself *preferred* a legal reversal of the Church settlement within the republic, the left Republicans and Socialists never accepted his legalism. To them he was either a covert Monarchist or a Fascist: his party was scarcely to be allowed a legal existence and certainly not to be permitted to exercise power within a republic. The ambiguities of Gil Robles's doctrine and the nature of his initial political support, together with the intolerant attitude of his opponents, were largely responsible for the erosion of the political foundations of the Second Republic.

By the time of the general elections of November 1932 the Azaña coalition was bankrupt. The Socialists opted out of the coalition at the polls and, given electoral laws which favoured combined lists, went down to defeat, as did their left Republican allies. The victors were Lerroux's Radicals and the CEDA, the newly formed electoral coalition of the Catholic right under Gil Robles. This victory revealed the recovering strength of conservative Spain, unnerved by April 1931. It reflected two crucial failures of the republic.

As 1936 was to show even more strikingly, the main appeal of the right lay in the failure of the left Republicans to maintain public order. Confronted by both CNT strikes and rightist conspiracies (Sanjurjo attempted a *pronunciamiento* in August 1932) Azaña used force. This did not end sedition but allowed the right and the Radicals to criticize Azaña's rule as 'a republic of mud and blood'.

By the end of 1932 further co-operation of left Republicans and Socialists was no longer possible. Mild 'bourgeois' reformism could no longer satisfy Socialists like Largo Caballero while it scared conservatives. Thus the moderate banking reforms of Indalecio Prieto (1883–1962) as Minister of Finance frightened capitalists but his orthodox taxation policies produced no revenues to deal with mounting unemployment, either by public works or some form of public assistance. Agrarian reform, which might have created a peasant basis for Republicanism, was limited by financial constraints, doctrinal differences between Socialists and Republicans, and by technical and legal difficulties; nothing could be done to clear up the menacing pool of rural unemployment or to satisfy the impatience of Socialists.

When the period of Lerroux's and Gil Robles's dominance is called the 'Two Black Years' (*Bienio Negro*) the term reflects, of course, the attitudes of Republicans and Socialists. To them the republic was not a *form* of government, but, as Azaña insisted, a *content*. On this view if the victors of 1933 reversed the legislation of 1930–2, then they were no longer 'within the ambit of the republic'; since Gil Robles was committed to the revision of the Church settlement by a parliamentary majority he could not legitimately enjoy power, even if he had gained it as the result of an election.

We can only understand the increasing militancy of the UGT and the left wing of the Socialist leadership in a European context; Fascism had long destroyed Socialism in Italy and more recently in Germany and Austria. Fascism was already a portmanteau term which tended to embrace all forms of anti-Marxism: 'an anti-Marxist Front is a Fascist Front'. There could be no questioning Gil Robles's anti-Marxism; ergo he was a Fascist. To stop Fascists taking power, armed rebellion was not merely legitimate but a necessary means of self-defence. That Gil Robles encountered constant difficulties in resisting his own violent, activist supporters in the name of Republican legalism was irrelevant.

Thus when, in October 1934, Lerroux had no parliamentary option but to call Gil Robles's majority party to power, the Republicans boycotted the government and the Socialists rose in armed rebellion. The rebellion was successful for a week in Asturias because the whole working-class movement there combined in a Workers' Alliance. In Catalonia the Socialists were joined by extreme nationalist and Esquerra leaders, the latter reluctantly driven to revolt by the belief that a conservative-rightist government would destroy Catalan autonomy.

The Asturias revolution divided Spain. As the right saw it the Socialists had revolted against a legal Republican government; miners had set up 'Soviets' and dynamited their way to local power. For the left the repression of the 'revolution' by the army and the punitive measures against the UGT and the left Republicans were unforgivable political crimes.

Instead of sponsoring resolute reaction, the CEDA–Radical governments between October 1934 and the elections of February 1936 exhibited an opportunistic conservatism aimed at reversing as much of the 'content' of the republic as they could get away with. Their performance did not satisfy the hard core of the right, which was rapidly losing patience with legalism. Rigid financial orthodoxy helped to drive down wages. Memories of the repression in Asturias provided the emotional foundation needed to reconstruct the Azaña coalition – now known as the 'Popular Front'. With the right in disarray, the Popular Front gained a majority in the general elections of February 1936.

XI Civil War (1936–1939)

It is important to realize that the new Popular Front government, installed immediately after the election results came through, did not include the Socialists. The Popular Front had agreed on a minimum programme; this was now to be implemented by a left Republican government.

The collapse of governmental authority which culminated in the rising of July 1936 is explained by the fact that neither the extreme left nor the extreme right accepted the premises of parliamentary republicanism. Given that Spain was almost equally divided, as the elections of February 1936 showed, each of the extremes, once it was clear that no central position was tenable, could count on the support of half the population. While there can be no doubt that the right must bear responsibility for the rising which set off civil war, it was the left which created the conditions without which rebellion would have been stillborn.

Although the CNT, at least in some areas, voted for the Popular Front, it did not drop its revolutionary intents. But the new factor in the situation was the 'maximalist' intransigence of those Socialists who followed the lead of Largo Caballero. Partly out of fear of losing militants to the CNT, partly under the influence of intellectuals who were fascinated by the Russian model, his language, if not his actions, against the 'bourgeois' republic became increasingly violent. While Prieto wished to strengthen the government by joining it, Largo Caballero wished to weaken it in order to establish a Socialist government and was ready both to tolerate violence as a means of pressure and to form an alliance with the Communist Party. The use of terms like 'dictatorship of the proletariat', the street activities of the Socialist Youth, a rash of strikes, all gave the impression to a hypersensitive right that it was about to see in Spain another October Revolution in the Russian manner. Largo Caballero did not *plan* such an insurrection; in so far as he had any plans for insurrection he probably saw it as a defensive reaction to a right-wing counter-revolution.

And that is precisely what happened. By this time Gil Robles's legalism was in rapid decline. The new force on the right was the National Block of José Calvo Sotelo (1893–1936). A former minister of Primo and influenced by French brands of Fascism, he sought to give the right a new look, making no secret of his belief that only violence could save Spain from Marxism. He openly appealed to the army. This new militancy was shared by the Carlists who had been training in the mountains of Navarre for a new crusade: they would never accept a lay republic in return for local self-government, as the Basques were to do.

Less significant as a political force was the Falange, the creation of the son of the former dictator José Antonio Primo de Rivera (1903–36). The role of youth movements in the pre-revolutionary period is significant and the Falange was primarily a student youth movement. Its ideology was a heady, quasi-poetic mixture of Spanish regenerationism and Italian corporate Fascism. Its aim was to win over the workers from Marxism to National Syndicalism and it cultivated a mystique of violence.

Neither the National Block nor the Falange nor the civilian right in general could hope to stage a successful counter-revolution without the army. There were many seditious generals – Sanjurjo had risen in 1932 to save Spain from Azaña and there had been monarchist plots; but as an entity the officers were slow to react and, after February 1936, the important military commands were held by loyal Republicans. Francisco Franco Bahamonde (1892–), a general with long experience in Morocco, former director of the Military Academy at Saragossa and Chief of Staff was prepared, in February 1936, to back a *legal* declaration of a state of war; but his later hesitations irritated the activists. These were the younger officers and it was not until March 1936 that they secured the backing of a group of generals whose relations with the most active conspirators – the Carlists – were difficult. It was the pressure of 'Reds' on the Republican government and the collapse of public order as officers conceived of it that drove the generals to resume a nineteenth-century role: 'picking up the government from the gutter' where civilians had thrown it. The murder of Calvo Sotelo on 13 July with the connivance of the government security forces was the final signal. On 17 July 1936 the army in Africa staged a *pronunciamiento*. General Franco, exiled to the Canaries, seized control of that archipelago. On 18 July the rising began in the Peninsula itself. This inevitably took on the character of a civil war once it was clear that the military *coup* had failed in large areas of Spain – above all in the great cities of Madrid and Barcelona.

Spain endured a civil war because the generals' takeover was initially successful only in Old Castile, in Navarre and in parts of Aragon and Andalusia. Of the larger towns, only Valladolid, Burgos, Saragossa, Seville, Córdoba, Granada and Cadiz fell to them. Galicia, Extremadura and most of Andalusia were, however, rapidly conquered. On 24 July a junta of generals was set up at Burgos. It proclaimed a crusade against Communism and took over the task of government of the 'Nationalist' regions. On 1 October General Franco was pro-claimed Generalíssimo and Head of State. In Madrid and Barcelona loyal security forces and a workers' militia, armed belatedly on 19 July by a government at first concerned to get a compromise settle-ment with the generals and fearful of mass pressure, had defeated the officers. Thus the Republicans held the centre, the industrial areas of the Basque provinces, Catalonia and the Levante. The 'Nationalists' held the food-producing areas – hence the acute food shortages in the Republican zone, which undermined morale there. But, for their part, the Nationalists were completely dependent on supplies of arms from foreign sources.

The role of the workers in defeating the military rising in the two great cities made the unions all-powerful. The official Republican government was by-passed by workers' committees which presided over the collectivization of industry and agriculture. In zones domin-ated by the CNT workers' control was almost complete; less dramatic where the UGT was powerful. The defence of this 'spontaneous revo-lution' was in the hands of the workers' militia, heterogeneous columns formed in the last weeks of July. Revolution in this form was distasteful both to the left Republicans and to the Communist Party. The latter rapidly grew in numbers and in political influence because it controlled the supply of arms from the Soviet Union. Largo Caballero became Prime Minister in September with the support of Communists as well as Socialists. In the name of an efficient war effort and the preservation of 'bourgeois' elements in the Popular Front, the Communists pressed for a popular army and central government control. The CNT was brought into the Catalan government and into Largo Caballero's ministry in Madrid – an astonishing move for a movement which had consistently rejected 'bourgeois' politics (September–November 1936). The CNT militants did not approve their leaders' 'surrender' and the dismantling of the militia-backed revolution.

The Communists used an uncoordinated rising (June 1937) of the POUM (Partido Obrero de Unificación Marxista), a small Marxist revolutionary party which rejected the 'bourgeois' Popular Front in favour of a workers' government, in order to suppress the POUM – described as 'Fascist *agents provocateurs*' – to weaken the CNT and to oust Largo Caballero as Prime Minister. He was replaced by Juan Negrín (1889–1956): Communist influence in the government and Communist domination of the republican army was now assured. It was used ruthlessly to eliminate political enemies. The great unions were now pushed aside by the political parties. This political in-fighting seriously weakened republican morale.

The Communists were correct in arguing that the committee-militia system had serious military defects. These had been apparent from the early days of the generals' rising in 1936 when General Franco's African army, ferried across to Andalusia protected by German and Italian planes, cut through the militia units 'like butter' and after capturing Toledo arrived outside Madrid by 7 November 1936. The successful resistance of the city, stiffened by the arrival of the International Brigades, Soviet tanks and aeroplanes, prolonged the civil war for more than two years.

On their side the Nationalists had, of course, a better-trained army and, thanks to foreign support, more abundant arms supplies. While the political situation in the Republican zone was bedevilled by acute party divisions, General Franco had by October 1936 established firm and unified political and strategic control in the Nationalist zone. In April 1937 he ruthlessly incorporated both the Falange and the Carlists into a unified movement under his personal leadership. Falangist radicalism was converted into paternalistic unionism and, together with the Carlist emphasis on Catholic orthodoxy, became the foundation of the 'new state'. Oppositional tendencies among the radical Falangists and the hard-line Carlists were quickly suppressed.

On the military fronts, once the Popular Army had 'militarized' the militia (hitherto responsible alike for the fall of Málaga to Italian troops in February 1937 and the defence of Madrid) the war lost its improvised

character and turned into a series of organized campaigns and operations. After his failure to capture Madrid, Franco transferred his effort
to the north, where the bombing of Guernica by German planes
outraged opinion in the democracies; by October 1937 he had possession of the Basque provinces, Santander and Asturias, thus securing
possession of important industrial areas. These victories, too, greatly
shortened his front. The Republicans' diversionary battles at Brunete
(outside Madrid) and in Aragon were costly and plainly revealed the
great weakness of the Republican Popular Army: its incapacity to
sustain an initially successful offensive.

The Nationalists' capture of the northern industrial zone in 1937
was decisive for the outcome of the Civil War. The battle of Teruel
(December 1937) proved the Popular Army was still capable of mounting an ambitious offensive; but Franco soon recovered Teruel, broke
through the Aragon front, reached the Mediterranean (in April 1938)
and thus cut the loyalist zone in two. Rather than driving north to
Barcelona, then virtually undefended, and thus ending the war,
Franco elected to turn against Valencia, where the Republican government had fled in November 1936. The campaign was long and difficult.
In July 1938 the Republic mounted its greatest battle when, achieving
surprise, it attacked the Nationalist-held territory across the Ebro. But
the Popular Army failed to exploit its breakthrough effectively and
the long and bitter battle destroyed it.

The final Nationalist campaign in Catalonia (1939) was relatively
easy. Barcelona fell to General Yagüe on 26 January 1939. Political
divisions on the Republican side became acute now all land contact
with the outside world had been lost. The Communists and Prime
Minister Negrín favoured continued resistance. On 7 March a civil
war broke out in Madrid between Communists and anti-Commun-
ists; on 28 March 1939 the Nationalist forces entered a starving capital.
The Republican seat of government, Valencia, fell on the 30th. The
Civil War was over and no peace terms existed to limit the victors'
freedom of action.

The Spanish Civil War had engaged the diplomacy of Europe. The
machinery of the Non-Intervention Committee, set up by France and
Britain, was intended to stop the war from becoming a European
conflagration by cutting off arms supplies to both sides. It did not stop
German arms deliveries (or the arrival of the German Condor Legion,
kept at a strength of 100 planes). Italian equipment, the Legionary Air
Force and Italian ground troops were even more important to the

Nationalists. Soviet tanks, planes and technical advice sustained the Republic until deliveries dropped off in 1938. France allowed spasmodic arms deliveries to the Republicans in the early days, but neither she nor Britain faced up to the repeated breaches of the non-intervention agreement by others.

The political emotions stirred up by the war caused bitter political divisions in the West. Catholic and conservative opinion supported the Nationalists; the left was pro-Republican. A whole generation of European leftist poets and writers was deeply committed until the sinister role of the Communists and their ruthless police methods in Spain disillusioned many of them.

XII Franco's Spain (1939–   )

The first decade of General Franco's government was harsh. Economic hardship was matched by political repression. The aid given during the war tied Franco to his Axis benefactors until 1945 and brought the hostility of the Allies in the war itself and the diplomatic isolation of Spain after 1945. Recovery after 1939 was made difficult by the destruction of the Civil War, by a severe loss of skilled labour, by a series of severe droughts (especially in 1949), by the restrictions on the import of capital goods imposed by the Second World War. Economic isolation enforced state-fostered industrial development within a protected economy, and this began to show results only after 1947. By 1940 the national income had dropped back to the levels of 1900 and real wages were halved compared with 1936. The early forties were the years of the black market, of rural misery and a flight to the towns.

During the war, though Spain remained neutral, Franco's sympathies, and those of his Foreign Minister, lay with Germany and Italy to whom Spain gave some material and moral support. But Franco successfully resisted attempts by Hitler to engage him actively in the war against the Allies (on whom he was dependent for vital imports). He did, however, make the war against the Soviet Union part of his anti-Communist crusade, dispatching the 'volunteer' Blue Division to Russia, where it fought from 1941 to 1943. Franco's aim, once it became clear in 1943 that the Allies would win the war, was to support the idea of a separate peace between the Allies and Germany which would isolate the Soviet Union. After the end of the European war and the establishment of liberal-leftist or Communist governments everywhere, Franco found his isolation as the only 'Fascist' ruler in Europe complete in 1945. His speedy fall was confidently expected but the economic and political isolation imposed on Spain by foreigners proved to be a boomerang, securing some reluctant support for the regime from middle-of-the-road patriotic Spaniards and from all those who feared more than anything a new civil war.

The hostility of the victorious democratic powers to the Franco regime did give new life for a time to the forces opposed to it. Don Juan, son and heir of Alfonso XIII, saw himself as leader of an opposition coalition, which would include the CNT, the Socialists and the constitutional monarchists but would exclude the Communists. The opposition (which was, of course, illegal) failed to secure any direct support from the Western democracies. Guerrilla operations in Spain (1944–8) against the regime were limited in scope and easily suppressed and the opposition soon divided. Franco successfully used his ostracism by foreign countries both to solidify opinion in Spain in his favour while attempting to give his regime a more liberal look. In fact the regime was now based on the support of the Church and the army; the Falange, which supplied the ideology of the regime, never achieved power; the Carlists, despite their valuable contribution to the Nationalists' victory, were cold-shouldered.

General Franco's chance to end isolation and to achieve international respectability came with the intensification of the cold war and the strategic importance of Spain to the West. In 1953 the United States signed an agreement which gave Spain significant economic and military aid in return for US bases in Spain. The opposition was now powerless. 'At last', Franco could declare, 'I have won the Civil War.'

Politically the regime was secure after 1953 and political stability was matched by rapid economic growth. Indicative planning allowed a relaxation of tight state control; foreign investment and rapidly increasing revenues from tourism improved the balance of payments. Rural unemployment in the *latifundio* districts was 'solved' by emigration to the cities and abroad. In spite of inflation, damped down by stabilization and devaluation in 1959, the Spain of the sixties was relatively prosperous and some of this prosperity was shared by most Spaniards.

The governmental crises of 1944–6, 1956–7 and 1969 represented changes within the balance of forces that supported General Franco – for instance, the growing power of the technocrats of the Opus Dei (a lay Catholic organization) as against the old hands of the Falange. It was these technocrats who were responsible for the turn from state control towards a neo-capitalist market economy.

The system provided no safety-valve for opposition from those not committed to the regime. This opposition came from students, Basque Nationalists and those workers dissatisfied with the Falangist union structure; the workers and the Basques enjoyed some sympathy from young radical priests. Opposition assumed quite serious proportions in the spring of 1968. Nevertheless General Franco rode every crisis, unruffled.

Uncertainty about the succession to General Franco remained until, in July 1969, he nominated the son of the Spanish Pretender, Prince Juan Carlos, as heir to the throne and his successor as Head of State. This implied the rejection of the constitutional liberalism represented by the Pretender himself and symbolized the Caudillo's confidence in the system he had created. There was no need to change it; 'I do not find the burden of rule heavy,' he once remarked. 'Spain is easy to govern.'

This confidence was misplaced. With the death of the Caudillo (November 1975) it became apparent that the 'institutions' would not survive the death of their creator. King Juan Carlos moved his first governments rapidly towards the introduction of a Western democratic system, hindered only by the efforts of the extreme Right and the terrorist Left to 'destabilize' the situation and ruin the prospects of peaceful evolution.

Bibliography

KAMEN, H. *War of the Succession in Spain 1700–1715*. London, 1969.
HERR, R. *The Eighteenth Century Revolution in Spain*. Princeton, 1958.
CARR, R. *Spain: 1808–1939*. Oxford, 1966.
FONTANA, J. *La quiebra de la monarquía absoluta*. Barcelona, 1971.
BRENAN, G. *The Spanish Labyrinth*. Cambridge, 1950.
ARTOLA, M. *La burguesía revolucionaria*. Madrid, 1973.
KERNAN, V. G. *Revolution of 1854 in Spanish History*. Oxford, 1966.
HENNESSY, C. A. M. *The Federal Republic in Spain*. Oxford, 1962.
MALEFAKIS, E. E. *Agrarian Reform and Peasant Revolution*. Yale, 1970.
MARTÍNEZ CUADRADO, M. *La burguesía conservadora: 1874–1931*. Madrid, 1973.
ROBINSON, R. *The Origins of Franco's Spain*. Newton Abbott, 1970.
JACKSON, G. *The Spanish Republic and the Civil War 1931–39*. Princeton, 1965.
THOMAS, H. *The Spanish Civil War*. London, 1961. Penguin Books, 1968.
HILLS, G. *Franco: The Man and his Nation*. London, 1967.
MEDHURST, K. N. *Government in Spain*. Oxford, 1973.

6 Spanish Literature and Learning to 1474

IAN MICHAEL

I Introduction

The literary works which began to be written in the Spanish vernacular from the end of the twelfth century did not arise *ex nihilo*; they had been preceded by almost twelve hundred years of works in Latin written by inhabitants of the Iberian Peninsula. Furthermore, the rise of vernacular literature did not immediately affect the continuity of the Latin writings, although these cannot be compartmentalized nationalistically as 'Spanish', because any Latin work written anywhere in the world became part of the literary patrimony of all the peoples of the former Roman Empire. The Spanish literary scene was greatly complicated by the Muslim invasion and the growing importance of the Jews, which meant that from the eighth to the thirteenth century classical Arabic, and, to a much smaller extent, Hebrew, achieved the cultural position in the centre and south of the Peninsula that Latin held in the north and beyond the Pyrenees.

The first literary men born in Spain wrote most of their works in imperial Rome. Three of them were members of the celebrated Annaei family from Córdoba: Seneca the Elder (or the Rhetor) (*c*. 55 B.C.–A.D. 37), Seneca the Younger (or the Philosopher) (4 B.C.–A.D. 65) and Lucan (A.D. 39–65). The epigrammatist Martial (A.D. *c*. 40–*c*. 104) was born near Calatayud, and Quintilian (A.D. *c*. 36–*c*. 96) came from Calahorra. Although these were not really *Spanish* authors in any important sense, they were certainly to be regarded as such by Alfonso X and much later writers. A number of short commemorative and elegiac poems of this early period have been recovered from inscriptions found in Spain – fragmentary, anonymous, they may be indicative of a widespread literary activity that otherwise went unrecorded.

II Early Christian Latin Authors

The rapid spread of Christianity throughout the Empire and the edict issued in favour of the Christians by Constantine the Great in A.D. 313 produced an ideological crisis among men of letters which was to continue well into the sixth century. Trained in rhetoric and weaned on the classics, they found much of the latter incompatible with Christian thought, while they considered the language of the Bible barbarous and uncivilized. It was a Spanish priest, Caius Veccius Juvencus, who first attempted to resolve the crisis by putting the Gospels into Virgilian hexameters in his *Evangeliorum libri IV* (c. 330) in order to make them acceptable to cultured people. While the traditionalists considered the Latin *auctores* beyond criticism, the Christians, obsessed with the decadence of society, thought that rhetoric could be put to more edifying use than to serving pagan literature. It was this period, then, that witnessed the beginning of a radical change in the concept of what writing was for: from the aesthetic to the moralistic; literature was not to recover fully from this onslaught until the Renaissance.

Theodosius the Great (Emperor of the East 378–95, sole Emperor from 392) was born in Spain c. 346, son of General Theodosius; he appointed to high office a fellow countryman, Prudentius (Aurelius Prudentius Clemens) (c. 348–*post* 405), born in Calahorra (prov. of Logroño), who, at the age of fifty-seven, entered the cloister and began to write poetry which is among the best of the age. It is staunchly Christian yet has a lyrical quality which recalls the classical poets. His *Cathemerinon*, consisting of twelve hymns, contains the outstanding poems on 'Easter Evening' and 'The Burial of the Dead'; his *Peristephanon* is a lively book of martyrs, composed in a variety of metres, which Menéndez Pidal called 'un romancero sagrado'; his *Apotheosis* is a defence of the Trinity and the divinity of Christ and his *Hamartigenia* deals with the origin of sin. His best work is undoubtedly the *Psychomachia* ('Battle of the Soul'), which describes a battle between the virtues and the vices; the figure of Luxuria in particular is finely drawn (lines 310–20). This allegorical poem was widely read during the Middle Ages.

The fall of Rome to Alaric's hordes in 410 and the invasion of Gaul and Spain by the Swabians and the Vandals marked the end of the political Empire, although the new Germanic leaders behaved as though it continued to exist, and the new spiritual Roman Empire steadily increased in power in the following centuries, while the literary crisis remained unresolved, even among the Fathers of the Church; both Augustine and Jerome confessed their difficulty in ridding themselves of their love of the classics.

The temporary chaos brought about by the invasion of Spain by the Germanic tribes was the reason for the journey of Paulus Orosius – a priest from Braga – to Hippo in 414, where he discussed with St Augustine not only the problems of the Pelagian and the Priscillianic heresies but also the pagan allegation that Christianity was the cause of the downfall of the Empire. On St Augustine's advice, Orosius travelled to Jerusalem to study with St Jerome. On his return to Europe he composed his *Historia adversus paganos* (418), a universal history in which the secular tradition of Greek and Roman historiography was abandoned and the newer concept of a providential plan governing the rise and fall of empires was propounded; he sought to show that the ravages suffered by mankind had been worse before Christianity. His work was well known to St Isidore, Bede and most of the later historians and theologians, and continued to have a profound influence in the medieval period.

Up to the time of the conversion of the Visigothic King Reccared to Catholicism at the Third Council of Toledo in 589, there were few writers of note in Germanic Spain, one possible exception being St Martin of Braga (*c.* 515–79), who had come to the Swabian part of the Iberian Peninsula from Palestine around 550 and who wrote a number of pastoral works, including *De correctione rusticorum, De ira* and *Formula vitae honestae*, a work on Christian ethics, though entirely based on Seneca. Reccared was converted from Arianism to Catholicism by St Leander (San Leandro), Bishop of Seville 584–600, brother of the famous St Isidore, both sons of an important Hispano-Roman family from Cartagena (prov. of Murcia). St Leander demonstrated his considerable rhetorical skill in his *De institutione Virginum et de contemptu mundi*, which he dedicated to his sister, St Florentine. The most erudite and influential scholar of the Visigothic period was St Isidore (*c.* 560–636), who succeeded his brother as Bishop of Seville in 601. He performed a great task of synthesis, collecting and ordering the learning of the past but interpreting it in an orthodox Christian manner. Though thoroughly trained in rhetoric (his library contained the works of Horace, Virgil, Ovid and Lucan), he was condemnatory of pagan literature; yet he would have 'rather grammar than heresy'. His many works include *Sententiarum* (on theology), *De numeris* (on the symbolic interpretation of numbers in the Scriptures), *Quaestiones* and *Allegoriae* (on biblical typology), *De ecclesiasticis officiis* (on Church organization), *Differentiae* and *Synonyma* (on synonyms), *De natura rerum* (on philosophy), *De haeresibus* (on the history of heresies), *Historia Gothorum* (containing the well-known 'De laude Hispaniae' or 'Praise of Spain'), *De viris illustribus* and *Chronica majora* (a history of the world up to 615). His most influential work was the vastest: *Etymologiae* (or *Origines*) in twenty books. Here every aspect of human knowledge was investigated by an etymological procedure. The fact that an extraordinary number of manuscripts of this work have survived from the medieval period demonstrates St Isidore's position as the encyclopedist *par excellence*. Although he might be charged with causing the neglect of the originals from which he worked by providing a Christianized pot-pourri of them, it is certain that he saved much knowledge for the medieval scholars that otherwise would have been unknown to them. After him came St Braulio (San Braulio) of Saragossa (*c.* 585–651), whose *Vita Sancti Aemiliani* provided the source for Gonzalo de Berceo's *Vida de San Millán*; St Hildefonsus (San Ildefonso) of Toledo (607–67), who wrote *De cognitione baptismi*, *De virorum illustrium scriptis*, *Libellus de Virginitate Sanctae Mariae contra tres infideles* and a number of hymns; St Eugenius (San Eugenio) of Toledo (*c.* 600–58), one of the few poets of this period, who wrote on religion and the natural world in various metres; and St Julian of Toledo (*c.* 642–90), among whose works were *De perpetua Virginitate Sanctae Mariae*, *De contrariis* (an attempt to resolve apparent contradictions in the Scriptures) and an *Ars grammatica*.

The Eighth Council of Toledo in 653 saw the completion and approval of the great legal code, *Forum judicum*, which combined the Visigothic laws and the Roman code (*Lex Romana Visigothorum*) and which remained as the basic secular code for Christians until the thirteenth century.

If the seventh century was an age of saints, the eighth can be called an age of heretics. Many of the intellectuals of this period exercised themselves over the Adoptionist heresy upheld by Felix, Bishop of Urgel (*fl.* 783), and Elipandus, Bishop of Toledo 780–*c.* 802. They maintained that God adopted Jesus as his son at the moment of his baptism in the Jordan, and they spread this heresy among the people, Felix in the Pyrenean region and the south of France, and Elipandus in north-west Spain. They were immediately opposed by Heterius, Bishop of Osma, and Beatus, Abbot of Liébana, in their *Heterii et Sancti Beati ad Elipandum epistola*; the battle was also joined by Pope Hadrian I and by Charlemagne, and numerous Church councils were summoned before the new movement was eradicated. Beatus of Liébana is more famous for his *Beati in Apocalipsim* (*c.* 776), a fine commentary on Revelation.

A few chronicles were written in the eighth century, the most celebrated being the *Continuatio Hispana* (754), but the Muslim invasion of 711 had disrupted intellectual life and led to the emigration of a number of Spanish scholars.

It seemed at first that, paradoxically, Muslim Córdoba in the mid-ninth century was to see a Christian literary rebirth equal to that of the Isidorian school in the seventh century: St Eulogius of Córdoba visited a Navarrese monastery in 848 and brought back copies of some classical authors, including Horace, Virgil and Juvenal, the reading of which may have improved his style, though the content of his work is solidly orthodox: *Documentum martyriale*, *Memoriale sanctorum*, *Apologeticus sanctorum martyrum*. His sister Flora was denounced to the Muslim authorities for apostasy and Eulogius and his more famous colleague Paulus Alvarus of Córdoba, in their defence of Flora, preached a doctrine of voluntary martyrdom among the Mozarabic population of Córdoba which led to many executions.[1] This politico-religious opposition to Muslim rule was brought to a halt by St Eulogius's own martyrdom in 859. Alvarus, who was of Jewish stock, wrote a life of Eulogius (860), a *Confessio* and the well-known *Indiculus luminosus*, a fierce attack on Islam. His rhetorical style is violent and showy, even to the extent of introducing rhymed prose; he complained that few of the Mozarabic churchmen knew enough Latin even to write a letter, while nearly all of them could display their skill at Arabic verse. The Christians who lived under the caliphate spoke in the Mozarabic dialects (the most conservative of the Romance vernaculars) and in Vulgar Arabic, but the educated members of their society used Classical Arabic for official purposes, including literary purposes, though they retained an uncertain hold of Classical Latin. About the year 840, John, Bishop of Seville, had written a biblical commentary in Arabic, and later, in the mid-eleventh century, the very canons of the Church were to be treated likewise.

Already Arabic scientific works were being translated into Latin, particularly in Catalonia, during this period, and it was in the monasteries of Ripoll and Vich that Gerbert of Aurillac (*c.* 940–1003), who was later to become Pope Silvester II, spent three years studying mathematics, astronomy and music, which made him 'the inscrutable

[1] For a discussion of this period of Mozarabic history, see Chapter 2, section III, pp. 46–8.

master of all sciences'. The tenth century witnessed the Muslim culture of the caliphate reaching its zenith, but it also saw the nadir of creative work in Latin, although there was increased activity in the copying of books in the monasteries.

III Christian Authors of the Eleventh and Twelfth Centuries

It was in the eleventh and twelfth centuries that the Latin translators of Oriental works came into their own, because of the eagerness of European scholars to participate in the superior science and philosophy available to the Muslims.

Petrus Alphonsi (Pedro Alfonso) (c. 1062–c. 1135), born Moshe Sephardi, a Jew of Huesca, became physician to Alfonso I of Aragon. On his being received into the Catholic Church on St Peter's Day 1106, the king agreed to be his sponsor, and these two circumstances account for his new Christian names. He later went to England where he became physician to Henry I. He wrote a polemical treatise in Latin against Judaism and translated Arabic works on astronomy, but his most influential work was his *Disciplina clericalis*, based on Arabic literature and on the sayings of the classical philosophers, which was the first book of tales produced in Spain. The framework for the thirty-four tales, which consists of a father giving advice to his son, is the earliest example of this literary form in western Europe. The book received wide acclaim and was translated into French in the twelfth century and into other European languages later. Although the twelfth-century Latin translators of Arabic reworkings of Greek philosophy and science carried out their task in Barcelona, Pamplona, León and the south of France, Toledo was to become the most important school. Scholars travelled to Spain from all parts of Europe – Rudolph of Bruges, Adelard of Bath, Gerard of Cremona, all of them desirous of securing the scientific knowledge of the Greeks.

Reaching Navarre as early as 1033, the French Order of Cluny (reformed Benedictines) began to bring far-reaching changes to the Spanish monastic, ecclesiastical and cultural scene. The Visigothic form of the liturgy, known as the Mozarabic Rite, had seemed to Pope Alexander II (1061–73) not entirely free of heresy, and under the influence of Pope Gregory VII (1073–85) the Council of Burgos in 1080 ordered its abolition in favour of the Roman liturgy (or French Rite), which had been adopted in Catalonia (under the influence of the see of Narbonne) from at least the ninth century. Some of the chronicles give an amusing account of the trial by fire of the contending rites: according to one, the books of each rite were cast on the fire at Alfonso VI's command, it having been agreed that the book which escaped the flames would be adopted. The Mozarabic Rite jumped out of the flames, but the king angrily kicked it back, exclaiming 'Allá van leyes ó mandan reyes' (or 'Ad libitum regum flectantur cornua legum' as the *Crónica najerense* puts it). Four years before the city yielded to him in 1085, Alfonso VI had asked Gregory VII to raise the see of Toledo to an archbishopric, and the Pope's nominee was a French Cluniac, Bernard de Sédirac; his appointment was confirmed by Pope Urban II in 1085. The new pope lent Bernard special protection, foreseeing the difficulties he would face in carrying out the reform of the antiquated customs of the Spanish Church, and brought the sees of León, Oviedo and Palencia under his control. Archbishop Bernard recommended the appointment of six other French Cluniacs to bishoprics; among them was Raimundus, who became Bishop of Osma in 1109 and succeeded to the see of Toledo in 1126 on Bernard's death. From then until his death in 1152 he gathered in Toledo a great library of Oriental manuscripts and a famous school of scholars and translators, among them Dominicus Gundisalvi, Archdeacon of Segovia, and a Jew, Selomo ibn David, who, on being christened, adopted the name Juan Hispalense: it was these two men who made Avicenna's *De anima* available to European scholars.

The Cluniac reform was accompanied by a change in the making of books: the Carolingian (or French) book-hand soon completely ousted the ancient and cramped Visigothic script. This change led to a great deal of recopying and, because the Visigothic script became difficult to read, to a partial break in the cultural tradition of the centre and west of the Peninsula (Catalonia had adopted the Carolingian script much earlier). French cultural influence now became ascendant, though the Cluniac and papal reforms did not go entirely unopposed: García de Toledo (*fl.* 1099) wrote a parody on the finding and the translation of holy relics entitled *Garsuinis* (or 'The Garcineid'), with echoes of Terence, Horace and Juvenal; it contains sharp caricatures of Urban II and 'Grimoardo' (Bernard), Archbishop of Toledo. Another work, also anti-French in tone, is the *Historia silense* (*c.* 1115), which, despite its title, has no connection with the monastery of Santo Domingo de Silos (prov. of Burgos) and appears to be a Leonese production. The anonymous Latin chronicler provides an account of the destruction of Spain through the folly and heresy of the Gothic kings and sees the

Muslim invasion as divine retribution. The work breaks off at the death of Ferdinand I (1065). It is in the latter part that the author charges the Franks with possessing vices similar to those of the Goths. His Latin style has echoes of Sallust, Virgil and the *Ilias latina*.

The Cluniac reform led also to a general improvement in the quality of written Latin which is reflected even in notarial documents. An early fruit of this flowering was the *Registrum*, or *Historia compostelana* (*c.* 1140), compiled on the orders of Diego Gelmírez, the Cluniac Bishop (and, later, Archbishop) of Santiago from 1100 to *c.* 1140, who was instrumental in making his shrine one of the most important centres of pilgrimage in the Middle Ages. The *camino francés* or pilgrim road to Santiago enormously increased the French influence on Spanish culture, particularly on the emerging vernacular dialects and the later vernacular literature.

The chief political figures of the disturbed years after 1067, Alfonso VI, Minaya Albar Fáñez, Rodrigo Díaz de Vivar ('el Cid') and Alfonso VII, are portrayed in several Latin chronicles and poems of the twelfth century. The *Historia* or *Gesta Roderici* (*c.* 1110, though it may be much later), written in Aragon, provides an account of the Cid's career, presenting him as 'vir bellator fortissimus et campidoctus'. Also from the east of the Peninsula (monastery of Ripoll) and perhaps from the same period is the *Carmen Campidoctoris* (1093–4?), a Latin panegyrical poem on the Cid. The *Chronica Adefonsi Imperatoris* (1147–9), probably written in León (possibly by Arnaldus, Bishop of Astorga), recounts Alfonso VII's capture of the Moorish city of Almería in 1147. It has a fluid Latin style containing many biblical expressions and occasional classical touches. The same author may have written the Latin poem known as the *Poema de Almería* (*c.* 1152), which, in occasionally faulty hexameters, presents Alfonso VII almost as a classical epic hero and the march on Almería as a holy crusade. The much debated lines 215–26 appear to refer to some version of the *Chanson de Roland*, but do not well support the hypothesis that a version of the *Poema de Mio Cid* existed in this period. The Cluniac monastery of Santa María de Nájera (in Upper Rioja) was the home of the compiler of the *Crónica najerense* (*c.* 1160), which provides a history of the world from the Creation up to Alfonso VI. The section relating to Sancho II and the battle of Vulpejera may be a prosification of a Latin poem in hexameters which has not otherwise been preserved, but the further hypothesis that this lost poem was in turn based on a lost vernacular epic is extremely shaky. The *Najerense* betrays its Cluniac connections by its account of the intervention of St Hugo, Abbot of Cluny, with Sancho II to obtain the release of Alfonso VI.

The persistence of the Mozarabic Rite in the centre and west of the Peninsula may have had the effect of depriving those areas of liturgical drama, which was developing in Catalonia, France, England and Germany, perhaps initially as a dramatic elaboration of parts of the Roman liturgy on important feasts (Christmas, Epiphany, Easter); nor did the Cluniacs introduce drama with the Roman Rite.[1] There is one surviving twelfth-century example from Santiago de Compostela, called the *Visitatio sepulchri*, which was probably the result of foreign influence. It is a *tropos* intended to be performed before the altar on Easter Day, beginning with the question 'Ubi est Christus meus . . .' and only a few lines later ending with the last response 'Non est hic, surrexit sicut predixerat . . .', which is followed by 'Alleluia! . . . Te Deum laudamus . . .', etc. A similar stark primitive effect is to be found in the first Spanish vernacular text, which was found at Toledo, the *Auto de los Reyes Magos*, which may date from the last half of the twelfth century. It is, perhaps, somewhat ironical that vernacular Spanish literature should begin with a mediocre religious play, but the *Auto* is a fragment of only 147 lines (though there probably was not much more of it). Its polymetric rhyming couplets, the likelihood of Gascon influence on its language, its similarity to the Orléans mystery play and the popular vernacular style suggest that it was a French importation intended for performance outside the church on the Feast of Epiphany. It is essentially a dramatization of Matthew 2 : 1–9, and has some typological interest in the scene where Herod's learned men are unable to find the truth about the arrival of the Messiah even in their best books, which are made ineffective by that event. In contrast to some of the Latin works of the twelfth century, the *Auto* does not possess much literary value, but its popular language provides the first indication of the imminent rise of vernacular literature and the slow decline of Latin literature which the next century was to bring.

Brief mention must be made of the Mozarabic lyric poems known as *kharjas*, the earliest of which was written down not later than 1042. They are contained in Arabic poems called *muhwashshahas*, a form found only in Muslim Spain. These are stanzaic and multi-rhymed, the Arabic *muhwashshahas* being written in Classical Arabic, apart from the *envoi* or *kharja* at the end of the final stanza, which is in Vulgar Arabic or Spanish Romance. The form passed early to Judaeo-Spanish poetry,

[1] But see note at end of chapter (p. 245).

where the main part of the poem was written in Hebrew, with the *kharja* in Spanish Romance. The *kharjas* were popular verses on which the *muhwashshaha* poets built their poems, although the adjustment of the *kharja* was not always perfect. The same *kharja* was sometimes used by more than one poet. The *kharjas* are most commonly love-laments, placed in the mouth of a Christian girl. There have so far been found 43 Arabic *muhwashshahas* which contain Romance *kharjas*, and 22 Hebrew *muhwashshahas* all with Romance *kharjas*. Hardly any of the Arabic *muhwashshahas* were included in the Classical Arabic verse anthologies, either because their hybrid origin and bilingual form put them in an inferior class, or because their diffusion was so popular that they were placed apart from the more learned classical poetry. Nevertheless, some of the *kharjas* possess a simple lyricism of great emotional intensity. They have, however, come down to us in such faulty form and the transcription of those contained in the Arabic *muhwashshahas* is so open to question that literary judgements have to be made with great caution.

IV The Early Thirteenth Century

Literature in Spanish really began with the thirteenth century, but Latin continued for some time to be the normal language written by churchmen, scholars, courtiers and lawyers. The late appearance of vernacular literature in Spain is in striking contrast to the position in France, where vernacular works of the highest quality were produced in the twelfth century. The early flowering of French literature was clearly due to the different socio-economic and political conditions, yet Latin literature continued to reach high peaks there (e.g. the works of Gautier de Châtillon in the second half of the twelfth century). The Cluniac reforms with their emphasis on the improvement of Latin, the lack of lay patrons owing to the political and military commitments of the Spanish nobles and the consequent continued monopoly of the Church over all intellectual matters, all these may be the reasons for Spain's belatedness in terms of vernacular literature. The enormous French cultural influence on Spain in the thirteenth century was not only to make the vernacular respectable for literary purposes but also to provide many of the forms and themes for Spanish literature. Although much poetry was now to be written in the Spanish vernacular, the clearest evidence of a decline in the importance of Latin in Spain is provided by the Romance prose translations of historical and legal works, which indicate the existence of literate men who knew little or no Latin, whereas in the previous centuries to learn to read had meant to learn to read Latin.

The earliest work of the century appears to be the *Disputa del alma y el cuerpo* (c. 1201), based on a French *Débat du corps et de l'âme*. The Spanish poem was discovered at the monastery of San Salvador de Oña and consists of a fragment of seventy-four lines in rhyming couplets of irregular Spanish octosyllables. On a sabbath eve the poet sees a vision of a lamenting soul returning to a corpse which is covered with a new shroud (the idea of this weekly revisitation derives from the so-called *Vision of St Paul*). The soul berates the body for its sins and failure to do penance. The end of the fragment has an early example of the 'ubi sunt' theme (lament for things past and gone). From the same period is the *Diálogo* or *Disputa entre un cristiano y un judío*, a prose text derived from a Latin source. The *Liber regum*, a brief chronicle of the kings of Spain written in Aragonese, is also considered to date from the beginning of the thirteenth century.

The best-known work of the thirteenth century is the *Poema de Mio Cid*, which modern linguistic and historical researches suggest may belong to the first decade (1201–7?). Literary criticism of the poem has suffered from its steady involvement in the controversies over the origin of medieval epic poetry, from the nineteenth-century Romantic theory (L. Gautier), via the individualist (Bédier), the 'neo-traditionalist' (Menéndez Pidal) and the 'oralist' (Parry and Lord) theories to the latest reassessments. The poem survives in a single manuscript copied some time in the fourteenth century which bears such clear signs of scribal tradition that it cannot have been the result of dictation by an illiterate singer. There is some evidence in the poem that the author may have been a notary, who possessed some detailed knowledge of the eastern part of Castile bordering on Aragon, especially the San Esteban de Gormaz and Medinaceli area, but who was also associated with Burgos and the monastery of San Pedro de Cardeña. The poem is written in Castilian and has the usual epic features of assonating *laisses* of varying length and lines with a strong central caesura. The assonances are not always perfect and the hemistichs usually contain between six and eight syllables, though some have as few as four and others as many as fourteen. This irregular metre cannot, however, be regarded as totally anisosyllabic, because its irregularity lies within quite strict limits; thus it is more irregular to the eye than to the ear. Direct address and epic epithets are actively used, but the percentage of formulae used appears to come nowhere near the level considered by

Lord to be necessary as proof of oral composition. The poem was never-theless intended for recitation to an audience and such a performance may well have been sung or chanted.

The poem opens with its hero, Rodrigo Díaz de Vivar, 'Mio Cid', abandoning his home at Vivar (near Burgos). The reason for his banish-ment by Alfonso VI is only very vaguely given as the poem progresses, and this fact has reinforced the view that the first part is missing (per-haps some fifty lines); in artistic terms, however, it is difficult to imagine better opening lines than those we have. The Cid's reaction to his exile, 'Be joyful, Alvar Fáñez, that we are banished!' (line 14), epitomizes the heroic resignation and the glad acceptance of the chance to prove his worth that he expresses on later occasions. Although the poet is often faithful to historical fact and eschews fantastic material, he departs from history at the outset by making Minaya Alvar Fáñez the deuteragonist of the poem, the Cid's right-hand man throughout most of the action, when in fact he was a follower of Alfonso VI rather than of the Cid. The poet also takes an early opportunity of connecting the Cid with the cathedral of Santa María in Burgos and with the nearby monastery of San Pedro de Cardeña, devoting much space to the Cid's leaving Doña Jimena and his daughters in the abbot's care, his promise of financial endowment, and the set piece of Doña Jimena's prayer in the church of the abbey, which ends with a plea for St Peter's inter-cession (lines 330–65). Thus at the beginning of the poem the poet establishes the Cid as a pious Christian, a devoted husband and father, and a loyal leader who is, moreover, divinely approved (by the Archangel Gabriel, who appears to him in a dream). He then demon-strates his hero's military prowess and his generosity to the defeated, by raising the unattested skirmishes of Castejón and Alcocer into major en-gagements. He ends the first *cantar* with the Cid's capture of Ramón Berenguer, Count of Barcelona; the count's hunger strike and the earlier fraud the Cid perpetrated on the Jewish moneylenders constitute the two comic episodes in this first part. So far, then, we are presented with a courageous and prudent hero in middle life, a paragon of the medieval virtues of *sapientia et fortitudo*, who has been unjustly treated and who is winning his way to fame and favour. But we are afforded interesting glimpses of his violent and hotheaded youth, of how he had struck a relative of the Count of Barcelona at the latter's court (lines 962–3), and later, in the final *cantar*, of how he had insultingly pulled Count García Ordóñez's beard at the Castle of Cabra (lines 3,287–90). The second *cantar* crowns the Cid's military success with his capture of

Valencia and resolves the banishment with his reconciliation with Alfonso VI. Again the ecclesiastical element is present with the Cid's nomination of Jerónimo, a French cleric, as Bishop of Valencia. The structure of the poem now takes a new turn with the king's insistence on the marriage of the Cid's daughters to the Leonese Infantes of Carrión; thus a feud is introduced that is both personal and national. In the third *cantar* the Infantes of Carrión reveal their malice and cowardice, and the climax is reached when they whip and abandon the Cid's daughters in the oakwood of Corpes. The poem ends with a majestic court scene, in which the Cid amazes the onlookers with his fierce bearing and his grasp of complex legal procedure. Redress is obtained, judicial duels are won, and new, royal, marriages are arranged for the daughters.

The poem departs from history on a number of occasions: the second banishment is not mentioned, the first marriages and most of the events of the third *cantar* are unhistorical, the names of the Abbot of Cardeña and the Cid's daughters are changed, the Cid's son is not mentioned, and the time sequence is poetic only. Yet, if art is truly a process of selection, what is surprising is how much historical detail has remained. The skilful structure of the plot, the occasional examples of interweaving of simultaneous episodes and the use of *laisses similaires*, the oblique cross-references and allusions and the careful hints and foreshadowings would all appear to rule out composition by an illiterate or semi-literate *jongleur*. Apart from the division into three *cantares*, the form is similar to that of the (earlier) French epic poems, and we do not have to assume a tradition of orally transmitted versions of the poem that are lost to us. One of the poet's purposes may have been to connect the Cid's fame with Burgos and particularly with the monastery of Cardeña, while another could have been to inspire recruits for the military commitments of Castile in Andalusia.

Legends had also grown around other figures: Bernardo del Carpio, the seven Infantes of Lara (or Salas), Fernán González, the Treacherous Countess, Prince García and Sancho II. There doubtless existed *cantares* and *fablas*, which the chroniclers condemned for their historical inaccuracy and from which the narrative poets dissociated themselves, just as many councils of the Church had branded the *joculatores et histriones* as rascally vagabonds (the terms *juglar* in Spain and *jongleur* in France regularly had pejorative connotations), but we have no clear idea of the nature, length or structure of these productions. The scholarly attempts to reconstruct the lost epics from the vernacular chronicles of the thirteenth and fourteenth centuries have shown that they possessed the usual characteristics of assonance, formulae, epithets and use of paragoge, but the 'oralist' case, that the medieval *juglares* were not mere reciters of poems composed by more learned poets but, rather, impromptu composers who used methods similar to those of the modern Yugoslav singers of tales, has not been conclusively made out. Since the lost *cantares* went on being recited long enough for them to be used by the vernacular chroniclers, it is remarkable that not a single one of them was recorded for posterity, when the *Poema de Mio Cid*, their alleged counterpart, was copied more than once as the evidence of scribal tradition in the single extant manuscript suggests. If they were of such poor quality that they did not seem worth preserving, then the *Poema de Mio Cid* may have been noticeably different and of higher quality and greater usefulness.

Apart from the late *Mocedades de Rodrigo*, the only other epic poem of which we have direct evidence is the *Roncesvalles* fragment of just over a hundred lines, discovered in 1916 inside the binding of a book in the Archivo General of Navarre in Pamplona. It consists of the latter part of a Spanish version of the *Chanson de Roland*, and recounts Charlemagne's lament over Roland's corpse. The manuscript folio dates from the fourteenth century, but the poem was probably composed in the thirteenth century. It is written in assonating *laisses* and in the same irregular metre as the *Poema de Mio Cid*, but its language shows traces of the Navarrese dialect.

The *Razón de amor*, written in irregular octosyllabic rhyming couplets, dates from the early thirteenth century. The manuscript of the poem is contained in a collection of Latin sermons which probably originated in the south of France. The *Razón* is followed by a poem entitled *Denuestos del agua y del vino*, together with a short Spanish prose commentary on the ten commandments. Modern research has suggested that the *Razón* and the *Denuestos* are thematically connected. The superficial story is mysterious: the poet says that he is a scholar who has 'suffered' ('ovo tryança') in Germany and France, and dwelt in Lombardy in order to learn 'courtesy'. He finds himself in a paradise garden, lying in an olive grove. He sees amid the top branches of an apple grove a silver vessel containing clear red wine, placed there by the mistress of the garden for her lover; the wine possesses health-giving properties. On top of the apple grove he sees another vessel containing cool water, but he is afraid to drink it in case it is enchanted. He rests in the meadow and takes off his clothes near a cool fountain, from which

he drinks. A lady, who is not the lady of the garden, then appears singing a love song, and he recognizes her as his beloved because she is
wearing the tokens he has sent her. They converse in amorous tones,
but the lady soon has to depart and the poet is left disconsolate. A dove
appears, fluttering over the fountain, and it finally tips the vessel of
water into the vessel of wine. The *Denuestos* that follow consist of a
debate between the wine and the water, in which the wine accuses the
water of weakening it, and the water accuses the wine of disturbing
men's reason. In their final *ripostes*, the wine boasts of being used in holy
communion, but the water prides itself on being used for baptism. The
language of the work has Aragonese features, and the author was
clearly influenced by Provençal literature. The *Razón* could be taken
to be a courtly love poem having no connection with the *Denuestos*, but
much of it would then not make good sense. The work appears therefore to be allegorical or cryptographic, and several interpretations have
been put forward. For Leo Spitzer the poems form an *amorosa visione*
and the connection between them is thirst (sexual and physical), the
water representing pure love and the wine sensual love; the theme of
the work is *concordia discors*, the harmony of chastity and joy. For
Enrique de Rivas the poem is related to the Catharist sect, which was
active in northern Italy, and in southern France (its adherents there
being the Albigensians). Thus the mistress of the garden and the vessel
of wine could represent the Catholic Church, while the poet's beloved
and the vessel of water could represent Catharism. Many of the other
details may also have a special significance: the dove (divine grace?)
appears to choose the water, and the water is given the last word in the
Denuestos (unlike the Latin model, the *Denudata veritate*). Rivas's
suggestion is that the poet was a secret Catharist who was passing on
his heretical message in veiled form. Both the heresy and the courtly
lyric flourished in the south of France and they may not have been unconnected; but the serious weakness in putting forward an explanation
of the *Razón* in these terms is that the Cathars do not appear to have
used water in their ritual, replacing baptism by the *consolamentum* (or
laying-on of hands).

A number of thirteenth-century poems were written in the irregular
Spanish adaptation of the octosyllabic rhyming couplets which had
proved a fine vehicle in France for Chrétien de Troyes. The Spanish
handling of the metre is much inferior, the lines usually containing from
seven to nine syllables, with enneasyllables predominating. The longest
and best of the poems written in the short metre is the *Vida de Santa*

María Egipciaca (*c.* 1215), which survives in a single manuscript. It recounts the life of St Mary of Egypt and is an adaptation of the French *Vie de Sainte Marie l'Égyptienne*. The legend was developed from the life of Mary Magdalene, and the clear purpose of the work is to exhort sinners to repentance, the case of St Mary being presented both as a warning and as an inspiration. The tale is entertainingly told: Mary, a beautiful Alexandrian prostitute, decides one day to board a pilgrim ship bound for Jerusalem. Her shipboard companions, like the men of Alexandria earlier, are completely overwhelmed by her charms, which she bestows on them all. But when she tries to enter the Temple in Jerusalem on Ascension Day, a host of angels disguised as knights bearing swords bar her way; she is conscience-stricken and prays to an image of the Virgin who tells her that her penance must be to spend many years in the wilderness. Mary takes to the desert with only three loaves of bread, and her changed appearance is skilfully contrasted with her earlier sinful beauty. After wandering for forty-seven years, by this time reduced to eating grass, she meets Gozimás, a monk, who recognizes her saintliness, especially when she levitates before him and crosses the Jordan by walking over the surface of the water. After making her confession she receives communion from him and later dies. Divine writing appears in the sand to instruct Gozimás how she is to be buried, and a lion is providentially sent to help dig the grave. Despite an occasional clumsiness, the story is told with considerable verve.

In 1219 the first prose annals in Castilian were completed, the *Anales toledanos*, which were based on the Latin *Annales complutenses*, but with some interpolations and a continuation. Another vernacular prose text, *La fazienda de Ultramar*, has strong Aragonese linguistic features and appears to belong to the first third of the thirteenth century, despite a recent editor's claim that it is a twelfth-century Castilian text. It consists of an itinerary of the Holy Land, interpolated into translations of parts of the Bible, which for the most part appear to have been made from the Hebrew. It is prefaced by a letter from Raimundo, Archbishop of Toledo, to a certain Almerich, Archdeacon of Antioch, and Almerich's reply, which implies that the work was composed at Antioch at Raymond's request. It seems extraordinary that a French cleric at Antioch should compose a text in a Spanish vernacular dialect for another French cleric, especially for one who was a patron of the famous Toledan school of Latin translators. It is more likely either that the letters are spurious or that the extant text is a translation of a lost twelfth-century Latin work. The *Fazienda* is contained in one well-preserved manuscript in the Library of the University of Salamanca, and, apart from its linguistic importance, the partial biblical translations have on occasion a movingly simple style superior to that of the Spanish Bibles translated from the Vulgate in the late thirteenth and fourteenth centuries.

Ferdinand III (1217–52) commissioned a Castilian translation of the *Forum judicum* for the Council of Córdoba of 1240 and this, the *Fuero juzgo*, not only served as the basic code of law for the reconquered territories but also began the process whereby Castilian was to become the official language of the united lands. Ferdinand also seems to have commissioned, for the edification of his children, the translation from Arabic of the *Libro de los doce sabios* (or *Tratado de la nobleza e lealtad*), which is a collection of maxims and apologues told by a group of wise men.

The first vernacular poet in Spanish whose identity is known to us was Gonzalo de Berceo, born in Berceo, presumably towards the end of the twelfth century, and educated at the monastery of San Millán de la Cogolla, where he later seems to have served as notary to the Abbot Juan Sánchez. Ten of his poems have survived: four are lives of saints, three are in praise of the Virgin Mary and three are doctrinal or liturgical. Of the lives of saints, the first he wrote was *La vida de San Millán de la Cogolla* (*c.* 1230), based principally on St Braulio's *Vita Beati Aemiliani*. This was followed by *La vida de Santo Domingo de Silos* (*c.* 1236), based on Grimaldus's *Vita Beati Dominici*. Later came the incomplete *Martirio de San Lorenzo*, which probably derived from some lost *Passio Sancti Laurentii*, and in his old age he wrote *La vida de Santa Oria*, based on the lost *Vita Sanctae Aureae* by a certain Muño. Almost all his verse is in the fourteen-syllable Spanish alexandrine, arranged in four-line monorhymed stanzas, a form known as the *cuaderna vía*. As far as can be ascertained, Berceo was the first Spanish poet to use this form, the line being an adaptation of the French alexandrine, but the origin of the stanza form probably lay in medieval Latin verse. None the less he proved a more accurate master of this form than his successors, his verse being correct both to the eye and to the ear, though its regularity tends to produce a hypnotic effect, such as is produced by the limerick, while many of the fourth lines of the stanzas have a sometimes comic predictability.

His life of St Aemilianus and most of his other works are vernacular versifications of Latin prose texts, in which he did not hesitate to employ *jongleuresque* techniques to entertain and instruct those who knew no

Latin. Yet his prime purpose was a combination of the devout and the economic: his monastery had begun to suffer from the effects of competition from other newly founded houses, and was making great efforts, including the forging of ancient privileges, to ward off the attempts of neighbouring bishops to gain a share in its tithes, and to increase the catchment area of the latter. Berceo therefore popularized the founder of the monastery and its associated saints, while emphasizing the necessity of paying the proper dues for its upkeep. His presentation has a fresh and direct quality that his material hardly deserved. San Millán is presented with the attributes of the 'sancto cavallero' (56c) and of the 'leal obrero' (32c); Santo Domingo is an 'adalid caboso' (441a) and a shepherd (29a). In depicting his saints as military heroes on the one hand and as honest workmen on the other, he must have struck a chord of sympathy among the faithful: these saints began as farmworkers, they went on to display the prowess so much admired in the secular heroes, and they crowned their lives with sanctity and performed posthumous miracles. This proved a most successful formula, both for the finances of the monastery and for the fame of Berceo.

His three Marian poems are also connected with the monastery in that its church was dedicated to the Virgin: *Loores de Nuestra Señora*, *Milagros de Nuestra Señora* (*post* 1252), *Duelo que fizo la Virgen*; it was the second of these that was to be considered Berceo's greatest poem. It begins with an allegory in which the poet finds himself in a paradise garden, which represents the Virgin; it is watered by four springs, which are the Gospels; the shade of the trees represents the Virgin's prayers for sinners; the trees are her miracles; the birds singing there are the Fathers of the Church, the prophets, martyrs and confessors; the flowers of the meadow are the names of the Virgin. This is the fine preface to the twenty-five miracles that follow, many of them told in the most entertaining fashion, more entertaining indeed than the Latin *Miracula* which are the source of nearly all of them. Berceo's doctrinal works consist of the *Himnos*, *El sacrificio de la misa* (a symbolic exposition of the Eucharist) and *De los signos que aparesçrán ante del juicio* (a lively account of the Last Days).

The *Libro de Alexandre* (c. 1240?) appears to be the work of a *clérigo d'escuela* or schoolman, to judge by the breadth of his sources, which included the *Alexandreis* of Gautier de Châtillon, the French *Roman d'Alexandre*, the *Ilias latina* and some versions of the *Historia de proeliis*. In addition he used the *Etymologiae* of St Isidore, Josephus's *Antiquities of the Jews*, Quintus Curtius, Julius Valerius, the *Physiologus* and Ovid.

Neither Berceo nor any of the later narrative poets came near to the *Alexandre* poet in sheer erudition. The work is also the most extensive (10,700 lines) of all medieval Spanish poems. It survives in two manuscripts, one of the early fourteenth century (Osuna-Madrid) which claims to have been copied by one Juan Lorenzo de Astorga and the language of which exhibits Leonese characteristics, and the other of the fifteenth century (Paris), which claims to have been composed by Gonzalo de Berceo and which shows Aragonese features. Both the authorship and the place of composition are uncertain, but it is highly unlikely that Berceo wrote it. Its author may have been a schoolman who composed at Salamanca or Sahagún. The poet does not handle the alexandrine with such accuracy as Berceo, but he manages to produce a less jingly and more austere effect. He incorporated the story of Troy within the Alexander story, building a complex structure in which the feats of the Trojan heroes become a standard by which Alexander's deeds are judged. The author complicated matters further by turning Alexander into a medieval king, a paragon of wisdom, valour and other proper royal attributes, but a man who falls into the sin of pride; by this moral downfall the early collapse of Alexander's achievements is explained. There is a tension in the poem between this moralistic outlook which originates with the author and the eulogy of Alexander's fame which comes from the sources, but all the action of the poem is subjected to Christian morality. The poet culled many descriptive passages from his sources, which he carefully distributed throughout his composition to relieve the long stretches of narration. The work can be regarded as a mirror of princes, but it is also clearly intended to edify a wider readership. Unlike the *Poema de Mio Cid* and Berceo's poems, which appear to have had only local diffusion, the *Alexandre* left its mark on a number of later works, including the *Libro de Apolonio*, the *Poema de Fernán González* and the *Libro de buen amor*, and it is quoted as late as the fifteenth century by the Marqués de Santillana.

The *Alexandre* poet occasionally used *jongleuresque* techniques, though less frequently than Berceo, yet in the second stanza of his poem he was careful to distinguish his learned craft ('mester . . . de clerezia') from 'joglaria'. This has led to the artificial distinction in the histories of literature between the 'mester de juglaría' (*Poema de Mio Cid*, *Roncesvalles* fragment and the lost epics) and the 'mester de clerecía' (Berceo, *Alexandre*, etc.), but this interpretation assumes that the *Alexandre* poet knew and perhaps despised the *Poema de Mio Cid*, when it may be that he was referring to the shoddier songs of the *juglares*. The possible common denominators of the so-called 'mester de clerecía' poems are that they were popularizations of Latin works and that they were basically didactic or moralistic; but the *Fernán González* appears to have had mainly a popular source, while the *Apolonio* is only superficially didactic or moralistic and the other works vary considerably in the lessons they are trying to impart. The *Poema de Mio Cid* uses a popular metre and lacks overt moralization, yet it contains firm ethics and nationalistic propaganda. Nor is the *cuaderna vía* verse form an adequate defining factor for 'clerecía'; the *Vida de Santa María Egipciaca*, as we have seen, and a number of other poems were written in an irregular Spanish adaptation of the French octosyllabic rhyming couplets.

One of these short-metre poems is the *Libre dels tres reys d'orient* (c. 1250), which is preserved in the same manuscript as the *Vida de Santa María Egipciaca* and the *Libro de Apolonio*, and which also exhibits Aragonese features in its language. In only 242 lines, the anonymous poet recounts the story of the Magi, Herod's massacre of the innocents, and the flight into Egypt, which provides the opportunity of introducing the legend of the two robbers who beset the holy family. This episode accounts for most of the poem. Parts of the story derive from the apocryphal gospels, but the exact arrangement of the details may have been original. One of the robbers plans to kill the holy child, but the other saves the family from his wicked partner and offers them shelter. The good robber's wife weeps bitter tears as she bathes the infant Jesus and tells Mary that her own newly born son is leprous. Mary then bathes the leprous child, Dimas, in the same water, which bestows grace on him and he is healed. The poet then moves swiftly to Herod's arrest of Dimas, now a fully-fledged robber, and his partner in crime, Gestas, who is the son of the wicked robber. They are crucified with Christ at Golgotha, and Dimas at his right side begs for Christ's forgiveness and is saved, while Gestas is damned. The legend is told in great haste, and, apart from the brief scene where the children are bathed, the author lacks the skill of the poet of the *Santa María Egipciaca*.

The *Libro de Apolonio* (c. 1250) is written in the *cuaderna vía* and has Aragonese linguistic features. The anonymous poet's source was a version of the *Historia Apollonii Regis Tyri*, a Latin account of the adventures of Apollonius (Pericles), which achieved great popularity in medieval Europe. The tale is of the Byzantine type and follows the usual pattern of the separated members of a family undergoing various vicissitudes until they meet once more, recognize one another and live happily thereafter, a formula which under various guises has continued to enjoy the most remarkable success up to the present day. The Spanish poet wields the verse form quite freely, though some of the *enjambements* are somewhat violent. He fully exploits the convolutions of the plot, and, although he injects more moralization than is to be found in the Latin and French versions of the tale, the moralizing is by no means as extensive or important as that of the *Libro de Alexandre*.

The last important *cuaderna vía* poem of the thirteenth century was the incomplete *Poema de Fernán González* (*c.* 1260?), apparently written by a monk of the monastery of San Pedro de Arlanza (though this has been disputed). One of its purposes is to connect the first Count of Castile with the foundation of that monastery, but its wider purpose is nationalistic. It has survived in only one manuscript and is in a very faulty state, but there is enough of it for us to see its general lines. It begins with a long account of the history of Spain and its conquest by the Moors up to the birth of Fernán González, which is based on the Latin *Chronicon mundi* of Lucas de Túy (1236). This first section ends with a eulogy of Spain (stanzas 146–59) derived from St Isidore's 'De laude Hispaniae'. The purpose of these preliminaries is to place the deeds of Fernán González in historical and moral perspective. The account of the count's career is based probably on a lost *cantar*; there are certainly numerous examples of *jongleuresque* technique. There is much praise of fame and military prowess, though there are appropriate saintly visitations on the battlefield. The loss of the latter part of the poem makes it difficult to judge the skill of its overall structure: it has been alleged that it is based on a numerical principle, a sequence of tripartite divisions and subdivisions, but this is far from being 'un fait acquis à la science'.

Vernacular works increased by the mid-thirteenth century, but Latin was by no means dead. By 1236, Lucas of Túy (el Tudense) had completed his *Chronicon mundi* and in 1240 Herman the German, one of the Toledan translators, finished his translation of Averroes's commentary on the *Ethics* of Aristotle. In 1243, Archbishop Rodrigo Jiménez de Rada (el Toledano) (*c.* 1170–1247) finished his *De rebus Hispaniae*, a Latin chronicle based on Christian and Muslim sources, and vernacular translations of it soon appeared. Another vernacular work, the *Anales toledanos segundos*, was compiled, probably by a converted Moor, between 1244 and 1250.

V The Galician-Portuguese Lyric[1]

Except in the north-east, all lyric and satirical courtly poetry in
Romance written in the Iberian Peninsula from the end of the twelfth
century to the middle of the fourteenth century was composed not
in Spanish but in the Galician dialect of Portuguese. This poetry is
therefore commonly described as 'the Galician-Portuguese lyric'. The
term should be understood, as far as its poets are concerned, more as a
linguistic one than an ethnic one. Thus a considerable number of the
poets who wrote in Galician-Portuguese were Castilians. The court of
Alfonso the Wise of Castile (1252–84) was a major centre of poetic
composition, both secular and religious, in Galician-Portuguese. It
should be noted that the form of the dialect used by the poets does not
reflect the evolution of the Galician-Portuguese vernacular during the
one and a half centuries of the dominance of this lyric genre. It was a
largely static and traditional literary language that existed as an instrument of expression for this poetry.

The reasons why Spanish poets until the late fourteenth century chose
to adopt a language other than their own for composing non-narrative
poetry have been much debated. It should be noted, however, that the
same thing occurred in Italy, where the Sicilian dialect became for a
time the language of the courtly lyric. Catalan-speaking poets, too,
wrote exclusively in Provençal until the fifteenth century – in that case
because of the priority and great prestige of the Provençal lyric and the
fact that the transition from their own language to Provençal was fairly
easy for Catalan speakers. It is thought that, because of the importance
of the shrine of St James at Santiago de Compostela (in Galicia) as a
cultural and international pilgrimage centre from an early date, a
courtly lyric tradition in Galician (but soon strongly influenced by the
Provençal tradition) developed there before it had time to do so in the
centre of the Peninsula. It was natural that, when Castilian poets
borrowed its forms and themes (and its music) they should also borrow
its language. Moreover, Galician was the official language of what was
then a politically and culturally important part of the dominions of the
Castilian crown.

Nearly 1,700 secular Galician-Portuguese poems survive. There is
documentary evidence that many more have been lost. About 160
separate poets (*trovadores*) have been identified.

The poetry of the Galician-Portuguese schools falls into three main

[1] This section has been written by the Editor.

categories which the poets themselves called *cantigas de amigo, cantigas de amor* and *cantigas de escarnho* or *de mal dizer* – as well as some minor ones which need not concern us here. The *cantigas de amigo*, of which some six hundred survive, are poems in which the singer is a girl who speaks about her lover and her love. She is either alone or in conversation with her mother – more rarely, with her sister, or even occasionally with the *amigo* himself. In the *cantigas de amor*, even more obviously and closely influenced by the Provençal lyric, it is the poet himself *qua* lover who speaks of his feelings for his lady, and his thoughts about her, in the complicated rhetoric of courtly, frustrated, love. The *cantigas de escarnho e de mal dizer*, of which a large number have survived, are satirical songs plainly much influenced by the Provençal *sirventés*.

All these poems have survived in three large manuscript collections or *Cancioneiros* (Songbooks). The earliest (late thirteenth or early fourteenth century) is the *Cancioneiro de Ajuda* which contains 310 *cantigas de amor* only. The earliest poems contained in the Ajuda manuscript belong to the late twelfth century. Most are contemporary with the Portuguese King Afonso III (1248–79). The other two manuscripts were both written later and in Italy. One, the *Cancioneiro da Vaticana*, is of the fifteenth century. It contains over 1,200 collected poems belonging to all three main categories of poem. The *Cancioneiro Colocci-Brancuti*, the most important of them, which once belonged to the sixteenth-century Italian humanist Angelo Colocci, has over 1,600 poems. The three *Cancioneiros* do not carry for their poems the musical notations which are a notable accompanying feature of the codices containing Alfonso the Wise's *Cantigas de Santa Maria*. We know, however, that it was the custom for both the words and the music of the work of an individual poet to be written on parchment rolls for performance and circulation. A fourteenth-century fragment of such a roll, containing some of the work of Martin Codax (*fl.* 1250), of Vigo, survives.

All the poetry with which we are here concerned was intended for sung performance to a tune (*som*) played on a lute, harp or viol. A firm distinction was usually made between the *cantiga de refrã* (i.e. a song carrying a refrain, like a Spanish *estribillo*), the refrain sometimes being fully incorporated into its structure, sometimes separate from it, and a *cantiga de meestria*, which had no refrain. In the *cantigas de refrã* some preference is shown for units of three stanzas (*cobras*). The *cantigas de meestria* tend to have seven-line stanzas while the *cantigas de refrã* prefer those of four lines (excluding the refrain itself). But there are many variations. In the Galician-Portuguese poems line-length varies between lines of five and fourteen syllables but the most popular lines of the *trovadores* were the octosyllable, usually with a strong internal stress on the fourth syllable, and a 'masculine' decasyllabic line (with a final stressed syllable). The seven-syllable line is also frequent.

The poems that have attracted most interest from critics and scholars are the considerable number of *cantigas de amigo* whose form shows an extraordinarily marked parallelistic structure of language and imagery. Whole lines may be repeated in each stanza with only, at its most extreme, the replacement of one word by a synonym, as in Martin Codax's complete poem:

> Ai ondas que eu vin veer,
> se mi saberedes dizer
> porque tarda meu amigo
> sen mi?

> Ai ondas que eu vin mirar
> se mi saberedes contar
> porque tarda meu amigo
> sen mi?

Such poems, and those where the parallelism is more complex, give a superficial impression of immobility and, indeed, from a narrative point of view scarcely advance at all. But the immobility is part of the poet's art in these works, and this structure as a means of conveying a single, profound emotion and nothing else can be extraordinarily effective. The parallelistic structure, peculiar to Galician-Portuguese poetry, almost certainly derives from women's popular song and dance routines where the repetitions were originally demanded by the collective movements of the dance.

The settings for the *cantigas paralelísticas* are redolent of sea-shore and the countryside. Thus in the type known as a *barcarola* the girl may be watching a ship putting to sea bearing her lover away or returning to the shore with him after an absence from her. The *bailadas* are concerned with invitations to groups of young girls to perform a dance so that their young men may see them. The *alvoradas* or dawn-songs are self-explanatory; it has been noted that the Galician-Portuguese *alvoradas*, unlike the Provençal *albas*, however, tend to concern themselves with lovers meeting at dawn (e.g. when the girl goes to wash at a fountain) rather than with partings at the day's coming. Quite a substantial proportion of these poems are *cantigas de romaria*, taking place against a background of pilgrimages to local shrines but concerned with love, not religion. Whatever the popular origins of the *cantigas de amigo*, however, their simplicity should not be over-stressed. Those that have come down to us often reveal, when closely examined, a high degree of stylistic sophistication. They often, too, show traces of Provençal thematic, stylistic and lexical influence. Towards the end of the period the Portuguese king Dinis (1279–1325) tried to revive the ancient parallelistic lyric tradition but his work in this area, though often finely and delicately written, lacks the conviction and freshness of the earlier poems.

The *cantigas de amor* are normally both metrically and intellectually much more complex than the *cantigas de amigo*. They rely on their audience's awareness of the doctrines of courtly love and the poetic rhetoric used to convey the poet's experiences of a courtly love situation. A feature which makes the content of such poems markedly different from the lyrics of Provence is that the woman whom the poet loves is normally unmarried or, if married, is shown as afraid of her husband. Modern readers tend to dismiss the *cantigas de amor* as monotonous in situation and language, too artificial and intellectually overcomplicated, but they plainly had a great attraction for the court poets of the thirteenth and fourteenth century for whom lyric poetry and the music that went with it represented a highly stylized and subtle rhetorical art. Now that editions of the works of separate individual poets are becoming available it is easier to see that the work of the different authors is a good deal more distinctive than used to be supposed when the poems were only available in great miscellanies or in anthologies.

The *cantigas de escarnho* and the *cantigas de mal dizer* differ in that the satire in the *cantigas de escarnho* is expressed in terms of double-meanings and that of the *cantigas de mal dizer* by direct statement. These works are sometimes obscene and their mode of expression often violent and crude. A poet like the thirteenth-century Pero da Ponte does not baulk at graphic allusions to homosexual acts. This frank and casual sexual aspect of some of these satirical *cantigas* needs to be borne in mind when we consider the apparently very restrained attitudes to sex of the *cantigas de amigo* and *cantigas de amor*. Many poets wrote both kinds of poetry. The doctrine of courtly love itself is sometimes mocked in the satirical poems. Satire in them is often trivial or takes the form of entirely personal abuse. It does not spare the great and the powerful, sometimes accusing them of cowardice in war, of hypocrisy, and worse. The theme of the penniless *hidalgo* seeking to keep up

appearances (so much to the fore in later Spanish and Portuguese literature) makes its first appearance in some of these poems. They are thus
of some interest to social historians, though recent investigations suggest
that their comments were often written in a spirit of jest and should
not, perhaps, be taken too literally.

Alfonso X of Castile's court, as we have seen, was a centre where the
Galician-Portuguese lyric was cultivated. Of his own poems in the
secular tradition very few survive and most of these are satirical works.
But Alfonso was also a patron of the Provençal poets of his time and
praised those Galician-Portuguese poets who could write 'come
proençal'. His 430 *Cantigas de Santa Maria*,[1] mostly written in the
1270s, where he proclaimed his intention to abandon the role of courtly
poet-lover and 'servir nova dona' (i.e. the Virgin), are largely narrative
poems which are based on religious legends and miracles associated
with the cult of the Virgin Mary. Among his sources were Gautier de
Coincy's *Miracles de la Sainte Vierge*, miracle collections in Latin and
the legendary material of the kind contained in Vincent of Beauvais's *Speculum historiale*. Many of the *Cantigas* therefore deal with
miracles that occurred outside Spain though many, too, belong to the
Spanish Marian tradition. They reflect, at their best, the simple, re-
assuring, religious *naïveté* of the Marian cult despite the complex
metrical structure employed in them by the king. He sometimes uses
lines of fifteen or sixteen syllables associated with rhythms not found
elsewhere in Galician-Portuguese poetry and with complicated rhyme-
schemes. Some of the *Cantigas*, too, are very long – up to twenty-six
stanzas. The theme and the narrative nature of these poems, as well as
their highly complex form, make them unique among surviving
Galician-Portuguese poetry. Not all may be the original work of
Alfonso himself. The fact that he elected to use for his new purposes the
traditional language of the medieval courtly lyric rather than Castilian –
given his efforts to exalt the Castilian vernacular in other fields of
writing – testifies to the strength of the Galician-Portuguese tradition.
Only during the fourteenth century did the poets whose native language was Spanish gradually come to use that language under the influence of direct contacts with northern French, Provençal and Italian
poetic influences. Changes in musical as well as poetic taste and, possibly, also the increasing political bitterness between Castile and
Portugal, as well as marked changes in the social background of
Castilian poets, perhaps also played their part. The Galician-Portuguese

[1] For the music of the *Cantigas de Santa Maria*, see Chapter 12, section II, p. 549.

tradition came to seem out of date and was abandoned though not despised. The Marquis of Santillana, in his *Carta* (*c.* 1449) on poetry and the history of the poetic art in Spain, praised the work of the Galician-Portuguese school for its subtlety and the sweetness of its language.

VI The Thirteenth Century: Alfonso the Wise

The balance in favour of Castilian as opposed to Latin as the language of scholarship and administration was decisively tipped by Alfonso X, the Wise (reigned 1252–84), who continued and greatly extended the cultural policy of his father, Ferdinand III. It was this royal intervention into areas that had for so long been the province of churchmen that gave one of the Peninsular vernaculars, Castilian, an official seal of approval which was to ensure its emergence as standard Spanish. Alfonso and his brother Fadrique had developed literary interests in their youth. By 1253 Fadrique had commissioned the translation from Arabic into Castilian of *Sendebar, o libro de los engaños et los asayamientos de las mujeres*. This was the *Book of Sindbad*, which may have originated in Sanskrit and come into Arabic via Persian. It consists of *enxiemplos* or tales told by seven wise men to delay the execution of a king's son, who has been falsely accused by his stepmother. It is thus a forerunner both of the misogynist and of the fable-book traditions.

On succeeding to the throne in 1252, Alfonso gathered a school of Latin, Arabic and Hebrew scholars in Toledo, and later established subsidiary schools in Seville and Murcia. He himself intervened in the composition of the works produced at his court: in the initial planning and possibly in the choice of sources, and certainly in the final stages of redaction, when we are told that he corrected the grammar and style so that all should be 'en castellano drecho'. Alfonso's principal political problem was the unification of his kingdoms and he clearly regarded it as vital to foster Castilian as the national language. His immediate preoccupations were the same as his father's: to reform the chaotic state of the law, which had become ever more pressing in the reconquered territories. As well as the translation of the *Fuero juzgo*, Ferdinand III had commissioned a new legal work, *El Septenario*, and the redaction of it continued at Alfonso's court. It constitutes an incomplete first draft of the first section of the great *Siete partidas*, which were begun in 1256 and finished in 1263. As a temporary measure, Alfonso issued the *Fuero real* (1255), which provided a code of law for newly conquered towns and, where necessary, a supplementary code for the older towns.

The *Siete partidas*, which were not promulgated until 1348, constitute a complete reform of canonical, constitutional, civil and criminal law, based for the most part on the Roman code. As well as arrogating absolute legislative power to the king, they provide a doctrinal and ethical basis for each law.

In 1255 Alfonso recruited scholars in Toledo, Burgos, Murcia and Seville who were to complete the fourteen *Libros del saber de astronomía*, which were based on the Ptolemaic system. Some of the works on astronomy, particularly the *Alfonsine Tables*, were later translated from Castilian into Latin and were used throughout Europe.

In the latter half of his reign, Alfonso turned to historiography, and in 1270 (possibly earlier) work began on the *Estoria de España*, usually called by scholars *La primera crónica general* because it was the first vernacular chronicle that gave full coverage of historical events throughout the whole Peninsula. Its sources included Ovid, Suetonius and Lucan, the works of Orosius and St Isidore, various medieval chronicles and epic material, and some Arabic histories. Before Alfonso's death the first part of the chronicle (up to the end of the Visigothic domination of Spain) was in a finished state and the remainder of the chronicle was already compiled, but some minor revisions and the final redaction of the latter part were carried out in the fourteenth century. One of the reasons for the comparatively slow progress on the *Primera crónica general* was probably the immense energy expended on the *General estoria*, begun in 1272. This enormous work provides a history of the world up to the parents of the Virgin Mary, and draws on the Bible, with intercalations from Jewish and Muslim histories, and many classical and medieval works. The *Lapidario*, compiled between 1276 and 1279, is a translation of a number of Arabic texts, and deals with the properties of precious stones and their astrological connections. In the same decade, the *Libro de Calila e Dimna* (or *Digna*) was translated from an Arabic version of an Indian original. It consists of a series of exemplary tales, some of which are told by two jackals. Some of the tales reappear in later Spanish fable-books. One of the last works of Alfonso's reign was the *Libros de ajedrex, dados e tablas*, completed in 1283 in Seville, which is intended for the recreation of 'men and women, old and sick, free or imprisoned, on land or sea'. It provides much information on various types of chess (including 'great chess') and on early forms of draughts, dice and backgammon.

Alfonso's achievement was to synthesize the knowledge of his day, greatly enlarging it with Oriental material and presenting it in a straightforward Castilian prose which made it available to all literate men. In his attempts to find national unity he firmly established Castilian as the national language, and by his encouragement of Christian, Muslim and Hebrew scholars he founded a new cultural patrimony for the whole of his dominions, which was not bounded by racial or religious bigotry.

VII The Late Thirteenth Century

During the last part of the thirteenth century a number of didactic prose works were written. The *Poridat de las poridades* consists of advice on good government, pseudo-Aristotle's letters to Alexander, tracts on physiognomy and hygiene and a lapidary; it derives directly from the Arabic source while the other European vernacular versions are based on the Latin *Secretum secretorum*. The *Libro de los buenos proverbios* consists of maxims from the classical and Oriental philosophers, while the *Bonium* or *Bocados de oro* recounts the voyage to India of a king who is in search of wisdom. The *Libro de los cien capítulos* in reality consists of only fifty chapters of general didactic advice, based on the *sententiae* of the ancient philosophers and illustrated with biblical examples. A summary of this work was made at the end of the thirteenth century and was entitled the *Flores de filosofía*.

The fragmentary poem, *Diálogo de Elena y María*, was composed during the last third of the thirteenth century and is written in irregular octosyllabic rhyming couplets in the Leonese dialect. It consists of a debate between Elena and María on the respective merits and demerits of a knight and an abbot. They decide to take their dispute to King Oriol's court, which is dedicated to love and entirely inhabited by birds. The poem had precedents in a twelfth-century Latin *Phyllis et Flora* and especially in a French *Jugement d'amour* whose disputants also appeal to a court of birds.

The thirteenth century thus witnessed the beginning of the decline of Latin culture in Spain and the rapid rise of vernacular literature which, by the end of the century, was principally in Castilian. By 1260, the monastic and ecclesiastical hold over the new vernacular literature was broken, and was replaced during the rest of the century by royal patronage. There was a clear movement of literary production from the monasteries of the north to the newly conquered central and southern territories, and this was accompanied by linguistic changes.

There were changes, too, in literary taste, from the religious and biblical to the didactic and classical. New themes were also discovered in Oriental literature.

VIII The Fourteenth Century

In the fourteenth century there began a slow decline in French literary influence on Castile and there emerged the first signs of the influence of Catalonia.[1] Royal patronage continued, though not on the scale of the Alfonsine court, and there was an emergence of secular noble writers. These changes are reflected in the literary topics chosen: rather than lives of saints, songs in praise of the Virgin and exhortations to penitence, we now find stories of adventure, a jocular poem on love and treatises on courtly behaviour. Books of tales and works on moral philosophy continued to be in vogue.

It is somewhat misleading to call the *Libro del cavallero Zifar* (*c.* 1301) the first Spanish romance of chivalry, because its hero is not presented as a typical knight-errant. The general lines of the first part of the work resemble the Byzantine novel: a family is separated by a series of misfortunes and after many sufferings they are reunited. But the structure of the work is much more complex (in this it resembles the *Libro de Alexandre*): the ancient curse on Zifar's family which has lost them an empire is partially removed by his exemplary life and his attainment of a kingdom (parts I and II). But it is not until his son Roboán regains the empire in part IV that the family's honour is fully restored. Thus two separate tales of adventures are interlaced into one theme. Unlike the heroes of most later romances of chivalry, Zifar becomes a 'knight of God' and his principal virtue is patient humility. The sources of the work are not known with any certainty: some of the episodes appear to derive from the Breton cycle of romances, others from the Christian legend of St Eustace and from Oriental sources. The names of the chief characters may be distortions of Arabic words, and the third part, which entirely consists of moral advice given by Zifar to Roboán, is based on the *Flores de filosofía* and other philosophical writings.

La gran conquista de Ultramar, a novel of the Crusades, also dates from the early fourteenth century. It derives principally from the *Roman d'Eracle* and its continuation (1295), which in its turn was a French translation of Guillaume de Tyre's *Historia rerum in partibus transmarinis*

[1] For an account of Catalan literature and culture during the Middle Ages, see Chapter 7.

gestarum, and from the Crusade cycle (*Chanson d'Antioche, Chanson de Jérusalem*). The Spanish author made a number of interpolations, including material concerning the Chevalier au Cygne and Godefroy de Bouillon, which probably came from a lost French *Isomberte* and from *Les Enfances de Godefroi de Bouillon*.

The *Vida de San Ildefonso* (*c.* 1304) is a *cuaderna vía* poem, quite competently composed by a priest of Úbeda (prov. of Jaén). Although it was probably inspired by Berceo's hagiographical poems, it fails to measure up to their standard. Another poem of this period written in the same metre is the *Proverbios de Salamón*, which describes in a lively manner the vanities of the world, the levelling process of death, the judgement of sinners and the qualities of the virtuous man.

Also from the early part of the fourteenth century is the *Castigos e documentos del rey don Sancho*, a book of philosophical advice partially exemplified by tales. The *Libro del consejo e de los consejeros* by 'Maestre Pedro' is a book of *sententiae* which was attributed to Pedro Gómez Barroso (*c.* 1270–*c.* 1349) who was uncle and tutor of Pero López de Ayala. Much of it is a gloss of Albertanus of Brescia's *Liber consolationis et consilii* (1246). A Latin chronicle was written in Alfonso XI's reign by Gonzalo de Hinojosa, Bishop of Burgos (d. 1327) – the *Chronica ab initio mundi usque ad Alphonsum XI*, which does not follow the model of the vernacular chronicles compiled in Alfonso X's court.

A partial translation of the French Grail cycle was made around 1313 by Juan Bivas. It consisted of three parts: *Libro de Josep Abarimatía, Estoria de Merlín* and *Demanda del Santo Grial*, all based on the post-Vulgate *Roman du Graal* (*c.* 1230–40) (formerly known as the Pseudo-Robert de Boron), not on the Vulgate version. Only fragments have survived in Spanish of the first part, but much of the second is incorporated in the *Baladro del Sabio Merlín*, printed at the end of the fifteenth century, and the third was printed in the form of the late *Demanda del Sancto Grial* at the beginning of the sixteenth century. In Portuguese the first and third parts have survived almost complete. Two separate versions of the Tristan cycle existed in Spain: there is a late fourteenth-century fragment and the *Tristán de Leonís* (printed in 1501); and the Aragonese *Cuento de Tristán de Leonís* (end of the fourteenth century). There are three fourteenth-century references to a lost version of the *Amadís de Gaula* story, which originated in Spain but which was clearly influenced by the Arthurian legend. In 1954 a manuscript fragment dating from the early part of the fifteenth century was discovered, but none of the original version has been found.

The legend of Troy is a recurrent theme in medieval literature and in thirteenth-century Spain had figured in the *Libro de Alexandre* and in the Alfonsine histories. The first work devoted exclusively to the legend is the *Historia troyana polimétrica*, which probably dates from the first half of the fourteenth century (though Menéndez Pidal thought it to be *c.* 1270). It is in a mixture of prose and verse, the prose largely based on Benoît de Sainte-Maure's *Roman de Troie* (*c.* 1150), but most of the material in its eleven poems appears to be original, with echoes of Ovid. Six different metres are used, the commonest being the four-line octosyllabic rhyming *abab*; the others are the six-line octosyllabic rhyming *aabccb*, the ten-line stanza of four and eight syllables arranged $a^4b^4a^4b^4c^8d^4e^4d^4e^4c^8$, the four-line heptasyllabic rhyming *abab*, octosyllabic couplets, and the *cuaderna vía*. Cassandra's prophecy (poem no. II), Agamemnon's arguing for the killing of Hector (poem no. III) and Troilus and Breseyda's farewell (poem no. VII) are particularly fine. There is a clear attempt to match the choice of metre to the subject-matter in each case.

The greatest Spanish work of the fourteenth century was composed by Juan Ruiz (dates not known), Archpriest of Hita (prov. of Guadalajara). It has been given the title of *Libro de buen amor* on the evidence of the text itself (cf. stanzas 13 and 933). The poem survives in three manuscripts, and there appear to have been two versions, the first of 1330 and the second of 1343. Most of the work is written in the *cuaderna vía*, though a number of stanzas have sixteen-syllable lines. Despite these variations Juan Ruiz was the most skilful exponent of this verse form, which he used with ease and fluidity and a great wealth of rhymes. He also demonstrates his ability with the *zéjel* (an Arabic form) and other metres. He himself talks of this in the prologue: 'conpúselo otrosí a dar algunos lecçiones e muestra de metrificar et rimar et de trobar'. In this prose prologue, which takes the form of a parodic sermon on the text 'Intellectum tibi dabo', he offers his poem as a warning of the dangers of 'loco amor' or sensual love, but adds that 'because it is a human thing to sin, if anybody (which I don't advise) wishes to indulge in *loco amor*, here they will find some ways to it'. This is followed by songs addressed to the Virgin. He then gives a warning on the dangers of misinterpreting his book, and illustrates these with the tale of the Greeks and the Romans. But at the end of the tale he adds to the confusion by concluding that 'there is no evil word if it is not evilly taken. . . . Understand my work properly and you will have a fine lady.' (Stanza 64.) He then launches on the first love affair, in which he claims to have been the unsuccessful lover (there are other examples of this pretended auto-biographical form in medieval European literature). This first rebuff leads him to reflect on destiny and the stars. The poem continues with two more affairs and a debate between the 'Arçipreste' and Don Amor (Love), which is broken by a long section on the seven deadly sins. There follows advice from Don Amor and from Venus. The central portion of the work consists principally of the Doña Endrina story (based on the Latin *Pamphilus de amore*), in which the go-between Trotaconventos plays a major part, thence dominating the work until her untimely death; the *serrana* ('hill-woman') episodes; the battle between Carnival and Lent; and the Doña Garoça story. In most of these main sections the poet uses popular tales to reinforce points of argument. The poem ends with the Arms of the Christian, a eulogy of short women, further instructions on understanding the book (he tells us jocularly in stanza 1632 that it contains many lessons of sanctity but few jokes), more songs to the Virgin and, lastly, the satirical song of the clerics of Talavera de la Reina, near Toledo.

The sheer diversity of the pieces[1] that make up the *Libro de buen amor* and the complex way in which they are interwoven, together with the author's deliberately unhelpful and jocular guides to the book's interpretation, have led to considerable disagreement among the critics over its purpose and meaning. For some it has seemed a burlesque art of love of Goliardic inspiration, for others its message is overridingly didactic, though presented humorously, yet others see it entirely as parody, even in the apparently moralistic passages. These divergent interpretations have hinged in particular on the meaning of the words 'buen amor', since Juan Ruiz deliberately makes puns on the phrase, thus obscuring the meaning. He also makes much of the fact that the wise will take a wise meaning, while the fool will take a foolish one, so that even over the modern reader the archpriest may still be having the last laugh.

Don Juan Manuel (1282–1348) was the grandson of Ferdinand III and nephew of Alfonso X. He exercised enormous political power and for some time was co-regent of Castile during the minority of Alfonso XI. He took part in the battle of the Salado (1340) and in the capture of Algeciras from the Moors (1344). Despite his political and military activities, he managed to find time to write several books in a model of Castilian prose style. Of his three most important works, the earliest was the *Libro del cavallero et del escudero* (1326) in fifty-one chapters,

[1] For an account of Juan Ruiz's knowledge of musical instruments, see Chapter 12, section II.

fifteen of which are missing. He appears to have taken the framework of the book from the *Llibre del Orde de Cavayleria* by Ramón Llull (1235–1315). A young squire, on his way to court, meets an ancient knight, who instructs him in the rules of chivalry. On his return from court where he has been knighted, the young man again seeks out the old knight who now instructs him concerning the angels, the heavens, the elements, the planets, mankind, and all manner of things. Much of the philosophical advice, however, appears to have originated with Juan Manuel. The second important work was the *Libro de los estados* (1327–32), which was based on some Latin or vernacular version of the Buddhist legend of Barlaam and Josaphat. In Juan Manuel's version, Prince Johas has been isolated from the world and its miseries by his father, the pagan King Morován, because of an adverse horoscope, until one day in the street he witnesses the dying moments of a man. Greatly troubled, Johas begs his mentor Turín for an explanation which he is unable to provide, and the king sends Turín to seek out Julio, a holy man. Julio's preachings convert the king, the prince and the mentor to Christianity, and the remainder of the work consists of a series of philosophical questions and answers which are mainly concerned with the salvation of the soul.

Don Juan Manuel's third important work, and also the best known, is the *Libro de Patronio o el Conde Lucanor* (1330–5), which is in five parts. The first part, which constitutes most of the book, contains fifty-one exemplary tales told by Patronio, Count Lucanor's adviser, to illustrate his solutions to the count's problems. The tales, which are taken from various Oriental and European sources, are skilfully told, though the framework produces a monotonous effect. The second part consists of a hundred proverbs, and the third of philosophical advice. The fourth part has great interest, because Juan Manuel deliberately used an obscure or cryptographical style to hide the meaning from the uninitiated. The final part consists of theological discussion.

In addition to these three major works, Juan Manuel wrote the *Crónica abreviada* (*post* 1337), a summary of his uncle's *Primera crónica general*. He also wrote the *Libro de los castigos o Libro infinido* (1334, 1342–4), a book of moral advice dedicated to his son; the *Libro de las armas* (1342), concerning his lineage and coat of arms; and the *Tratado de la Asunción de la Virgen María* (*post* 1342), which was his last work. His poetry is lost. All Don Juan Manuel's writings are didactic, written for the edification of those who knew no Latin, as he specifically states. His intense regard for style has a Renaissance ring, and his pride in it led him to suggest to readers who think they have found some fault in his writing that they first consult the corrected copies he left in the monastery of Peñafiel before blaming it on the author; these master copies are unfortunately lost. His chief preoccupations are ethical, the nature of friendship and one's behaviour to one's fellow men, and theological, the salvation of the soul.

In 1348 Rodrigo Yáñez composed the *Poema de Alfonso XI*, the language of which exhibits Leonese features. It consists of 2,455 four-line stanzas in octosyllables rhyming *abab*, but survives in a faulty state. It appears to derive from some prose chronicle. Its author was also acquainted with the *Libro de Alexandre* and the *Poema de Fernán González* (see above, pp. 208–9 and 211). The poem recounts the Andalusian campaigns of Alfonso XI and the battle of the Salado (1340). It transforms the king into an epic hero but it is by no means a production of high quality. Probably dating from the mid-fourteenth century, though the manuscript is from the end of that century, is the *Mocedades de Rodrigo*, which is a late reworking of an epic poem dealing with the Cid's youthful exploits. The reworking was carried out by a cleric, who was attempting to gain support for the diocese of Palencia at a time when it was in severe difficulties; the poet recalls the royal and papal favour enjoyed by the diocese in its early days and tries to claim the Cid as its patron. Much novelization of the Cid's early career is introduced. The faulty state of the extant version may be the result of dictation by a *juglar*, but the poem does not seem to have possessed much literary quality.

The *Poema de Yúçuf*, a *cuaderna vía* poem, was composed in the second half of the fourteenth century, or perhaps much later. It is an *aljamiado* text, i.e. a Spanish work transliterated into Arabic characters, and it seems to be the work of a Morisco from Aragon. In just over 1,200 lines it tells the story of Joseph, for the most part following the account in Sura XII of the Koran. Although the poem is the outstanding work in *aljamiado* literature, it does not rival the best of the *cuaderna vía* poems. In the same period Sem Tob, Rabbi of Carrión (prov. of Palencia), wrote his *Proverbios morales* – 686 four-line stanzas of heptasyllables, rhyming *abab*. It is not only the first Jewish poem written in Castilian but also the first example in Spanish of gnomic poetry (poetry consisting of moral maxims). The work, which the author dedicated to Peter I (reigned 1350–69), is a collection of philosophical advice taken from the Scriptures and from Oriental works. Sem Tob also wrote a debate and a liturgical poem in Hebrew. In the same manuscript as the

Proverbios morales is another poem, the *Doctrina de la discrición*, an early Spanish catechism.

Juan Fernández de Heredia (*c.* 1310–96) was an Aragonese nobleman who was Grand Master of Rhodes for the order of Knights Hospitallers. His literary output was immense. It included the *Grant crónica de Espanya* (based in part on the *General estoria*) the *Crónica de los emperadores*, *Crónica de Morea*, and the *Flor de las ystorias de Orient*, derived from a French source. His philosophical works include an Aragonese version of the *Secretum secretorum* (see p. 219), the *Libro de actoridades*, and the *Rams de flores*, based on the *Summa collationum* of John of Wales. Heredia had travelled in the East, but spent most of his literary career at Avignon, where he had access to Italian humanistic works. In the second half of the fourteenth century, the *Crónica de San Juan de la Peña* was compiled in the monastery of the same name in Upper Aragon. Latin and Aragonese versions of this have survived.

Castile in the second half of the fourteenth century suffered a series of political disasters: usurpation of royal power, civil war, regicide, wars with Portugal, Aragon and Navarre, in some of which England and France played a direct part. The major literary figure of this period was deeply involved in these events. Pero López de Ayala (1332–1407) was a courtier, diplomat and politician who became Chancellor of Castile. In 1354, Ayala was in the service of the Infante Ferdinand of Aragon and later served Peter I, Henry II, John I, Henry III and, briefly, John II. He was twice taken prisoner in battle: by the Black Prince at Nájera in 1367, and by the Portuguese at Albujarrota in 1385. He had a good knowledge of Latin works and translated into Castilian Boethius's *De consolatione philosophiae*, the first eight books of Boccaccio's *Fall of Princes* and parts of Livy. Though appalled by the breakdown of political and social order, he was unable to think in Machiavellian terms of a new political principle, and appears to have thought in pragmatic terms of the personal motives of the individuals who surrounded him. Despite his busy political career, his literary output was considerable. His chronicles cover the reigns of Peter I, Henry II, John I and the first five years of Henry III. He transformed the concept of the chronicle by concentrating on the secret motives and psychological quirks of the protagonists of history, which, for him, was made by the clash of personalities. His brief, incisive pen-portraits inspired two famous collections devoted to this literary form in the fifteenth century.

Ayala also wrote a highly esteemed treatise on falconry, the *Libro de la caça de las aves*, and a number of poems, some of which are contained in the *Cancionero de Baena*. His best-known poetic work is his *Rimado de palacio*, a long verse sermon on the evils of contemporary society, written for the most part in the *cuaderna vía*, though short Galician-Portuguese metres are also used. The *Rimado* opens with a treatment of the ten commandments, the seven deadly sins, the seven corporal works of mercy, the five senses and the seven spiritual works of mercy, which give it a strongly medieval spirit. But it then passes to the government of the republic and the ills of contemporary society. There follow a number of songs to the Virgin. The last part of the work consists of a long versification of the *Moralia* of St Gregory. What marks off the *Rimado* most from the earlier medieval poems is the strong expression of personal emotion, which earlier hardly appeared as a literary topic. It foreshadows, too, the later medieval and Golden Age fondness for satirical verse.

As well as political disasters, the fourteenth century also witnessed social crises with the spread into Spain of the Black Death, outbreaks of which occurred in 1348, 1362 and in the 1370s. Thus the last works of the century are pessimistic; in this way Spanish late medieval literature is at one with the temper of the late European Middle Ages. The *Danza de la muerte* consists of seventy-five stanzas of the verse form known as *arte mayor*, rhyming *ababbccb*. The poem is related to the European tradition of the *danse macabre* and presents the allegorical figure of Death inviting a member of each rank of society to join in his dance; in turn each tries vainly to decline and regrets the things of the world that he has to leave behind. The *Libro de miseria de omne* is a *cuaderna vía* poem dating also from the end of the century. The manuscript was found in a ruined tower in a village in La Montaña (prov. of Santander) in 1919. This pessimistic work is based on a famous treatise by Pope Innocent III, *De contemptu mundi*. It deals with the miseries of mankind, and includes some satirical comments on contemporary society. Finally the *Revelación de un ermitaño*, written in twenty-five stanzas of *arte mayor*, rhyming *abbaacca*, recounts the dream of a hermit. He dreams that he is in a dark valley where he finds the putrefying corpse of a man; nearby he sees a white bird (the soul) which is berating the corpse for its sins. There follows a short dispute between the body and the soul. A demon then appears to claim the soul, but an angel wards it off. Before leaving with the angel (a second version has an unhappier ending), the soul speaks of the vanities and vices of the world ('Todo es niebla, viento e roçio'). The poem ends with the warning 'pulvis eris'.

Although fourteenth-century literature ends on this religious note, these poems really constitute the death-throes of ecclesiastically inspired literature in Spain. Royal patronage had also petered out, and it was with the aristocracy and upper middle classes that the chief literary productions were to lie in the fifteenth century, apart from the popular ballads and songs which were the principal entertainment of the lower classes after the decline of the epic (but see note on p. 245).

IX Poetry 1400–1474

By the end of the fourteenth century the epic was entirely outmoded and had been replaced in popular entertainment by the ballads, which were called *romances* in Spanish from the late fifteenth century onwards (and the collections of them *romanceros* from after the middle of the sixteenth). Very few of the extant versions of ballads can be confidently dated before 1400, since their diffusion was almost exclusively oral until they were taken up by the court poets in the 1460s. The so-called *romances viejos* commonly touch on the more unlikely incidents in the lives of epic figures such as Mio Cid, Bernardo del Carpio and the seven Infantes of Lara, and it is feasible that in their earliest form they overlapped with the late versions of epic poems in the fourteenth century, but the oral and popular nature of both genres has ensured that we have little information on this important transition in Spanish literary history. Like the epic before it, the ballad was at first ignored, sometimes actively despised, by the increasing band of aristocratic secular poets, but the Castilian court of Henry IV accorded it literary respectability, and the form was to achieve even greater esteem among Golden Age writers and widespread distribution in printed *pliegos sueltos* (chapbooks).

The Spanish ballad metre was normally of octosyllabic lines with alternate assonance, the vast majority having the same assonance throughout, though a few, perhaps the oldest, show changes of assonance (some editors have regarded the pairs of octosyllabic lines as hemistichs of a sixteen-syllable line assonating *a a a a*, etc.). They sometimes exist in various versions, and their length may vary considerably (the most aesthetically successful are often quite short, containing between twenty and thirty lines of octosyllables). The *romances* are classified by their chronology and literary background: *viejos, juglarescos, artísticos* (or *artificiosos*), *fronterizos, noticieros*; and by their theme: Carolingian, Arthurian, historical, novelesque. The best of the *romances viejos* and a number of the novelesque, by a process of trimming known as *fragmentismo*, can create an effect of dramatic tension, of pathos, or of child-like incantation ('Rosa fresca, Rosa fresca, / tan garrida y con amor') hardly surpassed by the more 'literary' poetry of the period. The ballad reached its aesthetic peak in the sixteenth century, but the oral tradition continues unbroken into the twentieth in the remoter parts of Spain and South America and among the Sephardic Jews in North Africa and Asia Minor; its literary elaboration, carried out by Lope de Vega, Góngora and others in the late sixteenth century, was taken up again with great success in the twentieth by Antonio Machado and Lorca.

From the thirteenth to almost the end of the fourteenth century, as we have seen, Castilian lyric poets wrote their verses in a literary form of the Galician-Portuguese dialect, but from the late fourteenth they turned towards Castilian for this purpose. The transition can be seen in the *Cancionero de Baena*, a collection of *canciones* (lyric poems) and *decires* (narrative, panegyric or satirical poems) presented to John II of Castile in 1445. It contains 612 poems by more than fifty-four poets, of whom the earliest group flourished at the court of John I (1379–90) and the later group from the end of the fourteenth into the fifteenth century. Included in the earlier group are poems of Pero López de Ayala and Pero Ferrúz, who are the oldest of these poets, a testament written in *arte mayor* by Gonzalo Rodríguez, Archdeacon of Toro (*fl.* 1380–90), and five love poems of Macías, whose personal anguish later made him the model of the unhappy lover for the later poets and the hero of Lope de Vega's play *Porfiar hasta morir*. The most versatile of this early group was, however, Alfonso Álvarez de Villasandino (d. *c.* 1424), the best-known poet in the reigns of Henry II, John I and Henry III; his satires, lyrics and panegyrics contain apparently genuine autobiographical details of a dissolute life.

For their *canciones*, these poets employed the octosyllabic line with full rhyme and varied stress pattern, sometimes with regular insertion of the *pie quebrado* (broken half-line) for special effect, but for the *decires* they used either the octosyllable, or the dodecasyllabic *arte mayor* divided into two hemistichs each with one fixed beat. Of the later, intellectual generation of poets represented in the *Cancionero de Baena*, the best and one of the most influential was Francisco Imperial, son of one of the many Genoese merchants who had settled in Seville. Imperial was familiar with the classical and the Italian poets, particularly Dante (though the famous allegory, *Dezir de las siete virtudes*, based on parts of the *Purgatorio* and the *Paradiso* and attributed to Imperial, has been, per-haps wrongly, regarded as anonymous). A number of the later poets were *conversos*:[1] Juan Alfonso de Baena himself, Ferrán Manuel de Lando, who defended the new Italian poetic style against the attacks of Villasandino, and Ferrán Sánchez Calavera, author of the impressive *Dezir de las vanidades del mundo*, which adumbrated Jorge Manrique's *Coplas*. Other important *cancioneros* followed the *Baena*: the *Cancionero de Palacio* (1460s), the *Cancionero de Stúñiga* which for the most part contains the work of the Neapolitan court poets of Alfonso V of Aragon (all very much, however, in the Spanish tradition) and, later on, the *Cancionero general* (Valencia, 1511) compiled by Hernando del Castillo.

The two greatest poets of John II's reign (1406–54) were Santillana and Mena, who took opposite sides in the political disputes over the actions of Álvaro de Luna, Constable of Castile, who was executed in 1453. Íñigo López de Mendoza, Marquis of Santillana (1398–1458), was born in Carrión de los Condes (prov. of Palencia), the son of Admiral Diego Hurtado de Mendoza and nephew of the Chancellor Pero López de Ayala. He spent part of his youth at the Aragonese court where he came under Catalan and Italian literary influence. Later he had an active political and military career: appointed *adelantado* of the frontier of Jaén, he took part in the battle of Olmedo (1445), for which he was elevated to the marquisate. An admirer of the standard classical authors and an assiduous collector of Latin works for his great library, he is not thought to have known Latin. He therefore encouraged and patronized Castilian translations of Virgil, Ovid and Seneca. Among his prose works is the *Carta* or *Prohemio al condestable don Pedro de Portugal* (c. 1449), in which he attempts a critical history of European poetry and reveals his admiration for the French poets of the fourteenth and fifteenth centuries and his great enthusiasm for Italian poetry. His important corpus of verse includes religious, didactic and allegorical poems, attempts at writing sonnets in the Petrarchan style and courtly-love poems. The last include works of great delicacy and beauty and contain some of his finest compositions. His Dantesque allegorical *decir*, the *Comedieta de Ponza* (1436), concerns the naval defeat of the Aragonese by the Genoese near Gaeta, in which Alfonso V, his brothers John, King of Navarre, and Prince Henry were captured. The *Bías contra Fortuna* (1448) is an intellectual consolation for the political imprisonment of the poet's cousin. Other politically inspired poems include *Favor de Hércules contra Fortuna*, which attacks Álvaro de Luna, and *Doctrinal de privados*, which moralizes on Luna's fall from power and

[1] Jews converted to Christianity, or descendants of such converts.

death. Among his *decires* on the subject of love are the *Triumphete de amor*, inspired by Petrarch's *Trionfo d'amore*, *El sueño*, based on Lucan and the *Fiammetta* of Boccaccio, and the *Infierno de los enamorados*, a guided tour of the suffering lovers in Dante's *Inferno*.

Santillana's great contemporary was Juan de Mena (1411–56), who was born in Córdoba and studied at Salamanca and in Rome. On his return he was appointed royal chronicler and secretary. His prose works include the *Omero romançado* (or *Iliada en romance*), translated from the *Ilias latina*, and a commentary on his own octosyllabic poem, *La coronación* (1438), which, in a highly Latinized style, manages to criticize contemporary society and present an apotheosis of Santillana. Mena's greatest work was *El laberinto de Fortuna* (1444), an allegory in which the poet is transported to the palace of Fortune where he sees three wheels representing the past, present and future, only the second being in motion. Each wheel contains seven circles representing the seven planets, into which the various episodes are set. Despite the medieval nature of the allegory, Mena incorporates strongly classical and humanistic elements. The poem is addressed to John II and its implications are entirely political: the good party consists of God, Álvaro de Luna, Fame and Mena; the evil party includes Fortune, the nobility and factional strife. The aim was to win the king over more firmly to Luna's policies. The poem marks the apogee of the complex, elaborate poetic style of the fifteenth century and the peak of Latinization of Castilian vocabulary and syntax for poetic purposes. Towards the end of his life, when all his political hopes had faded with Luna's execution and John II's death, Mena composed the incomplete *Coplas contra los pecados mortales* (or *Debate de la Razón contra la Voluntad*), in which he returned to his simpler style for an ascetic account of the battle within man between reason and will, inspired by the *Psychomachia* of Prudentius (see p. 192 above).

This simpler style is also to be found in some of the work of Gómez Manrique (*c.* 1415–90), who was the major poet in the reign of Henry IV (1454–74). Although well known for his invective *decires*, his verses on statecraft and his love poems, Gómez Manrique's best compositions were the elegiac *Coplas para el señor Diego Arias de Ávila*, and the allegorical *Planto de las virtudes e poesía*, dedicated to the memory of Santillana. He was also author of an important liturgical drama, the *Representación del nacimiento de Nuestro Señor*. His nephew, Jorge Manrique (*c.* 1440–79), was to compose the most famous Spanish lyric poem of the later Middle Ages. Born the fourth son of Rodrigo

Manrique, Count of Paredes, Master of Santiago and Constable of Castile, he had an active military career like so many of the aristocratic poets of the period. All his poetic work followed the fifteenth-century Castilian tradition: he wrote lyrical *canciones* and amatory *decires* in the elaborate style, showing outstanding poetic skill. For his great poem on the death of his father, *Coplas que fizo por la muerte de su padre*, he chose the simple arrangement of octosyllables interspersed with the half line (*pie quebrado*) in full rhyme (the stanza arrangement being $8^a8^b4^c8^a8^b4^c8^d8^e4^f8^d8^e4^f$), and he exploited the delaying or cadence effect of the *pie quebrado* like no other poet. The themes of the poem stem entirely from medieval (and, in part, classical) tradition: life seen as a journey, the great men of the past, the *ubi sunt* topic, the dead man's qualities compared to those of famous men, personification of death, death the leveller, the temporary consolation of fame, the permanent consolation of salvation in Christ. What makes this such a great poem is the intense, yet restrained expression of personal emotion, so rare in this earlier literature, together with the simple directness of the language used, which has never failed to touch all Spanish-speakers, the skill with which a personal bereavement is given universal meaning, and, not least, the sheer technical competence of the poet. It is important to observe that after all the experimentation with Latinized language, Italian metres and forms, classical topics and imported themes, it was when it reverted to its simplest form, clearest language and oldest themes that Spanish poetry produced its finest masterpiece – as though refined in the fire to achieve its greatest purity.

X Prose Literature 1400–1474

In a number of respects fifteenth-century prose writings clung to past tradition. In didactic prose, collections of tales were still composed, but a new tendency was to draw on Latin sources, in preference to Oriental ones. Clemente Sánchez de Vercial (*fl.* 1406–34), Canon of León Cathedral, wrote, in addition to a liturgical manual and a guide for priests, the *Libro de los exenplos por a.b.c.*, in which the alphabetical frame replaces the frame-story that had been normal in this type of literature earlier. By far the largest of such collections (456 chapter divisions, 548 different *exempla*), Vercial's work draws on Valerius Maximus, the *Disciplina clericalis*, the *Dialogues* of Gregory the Great and other Latin sources, and it has a strong ecclesiastical bent. Intended according to the author's foreword as *solaz* (entertainment) for those who knew no Latin, it may also have served as a source-book for vernacular sermons. The best of the *exempla* collections was *El libro de los gatos*, which consists of sixty-five tales (fifty-eight chapter divisions), without framework. Most of it is an adaptation of the thirteenth-century Latin work entitled *Fabulae* or *Narrationes* by Odo of Cheriton, an English monk who lived for a time in France and who seems to have travelled in Spain. The *Gatos* is particularly critical of powerful prelates and has a crisp brevity unusual in this genre.

The most interesting of the aristocratic didactic writers was Enrique de Villena (1384–1434), who was of royal blood, but who was unsuccessful in his attempts to advance his career at court. His interests were wide and his work includes the *Arte cisoria* (1423) on cookery, the *Libro del aojamiento e fascinología* (1422–5) on magic (which helped to increase his notoriety as a dabbler in the black arts), and the only partially extant *Arte de trovar* on poetic composition. He is most remembered for his allegorical work *Los doze trabajos de Hércules* (1417), in which he used the classical episodes in order to analyse contemporary society. He also translated Virgil and Dante into Castilian, thus participating in the large amount of translation carried out in the fifteenth century; other translators took on, among others, Thucydides, Ovid, Cicero, Livy, Sallust, Petrarch and Boccaccio.

The most widely known didactic work of the fifteenth century is the *Arçipreste de Talavera, o Corbacho* (1438) by Alfonso Martínez de Toledo, Archpriest of Talavera (1397/8–1468). Of a probably influential Toledan family, Martínez held a benefice in Toledo by the time he was seventeen (although he was temporarily deprived of it later). By 1436 he was royal chaplain and Archpriest of Talavera. He seems to have travelled in Italy, and certainly was familiar with Catalonia and Aragon, where he may have perfected his restrained Italianate prose style. The *Corbacho* is a compendium of popular sermon material, and sets out to attack courtly love, which the author regards as lust. The first part deals with the degrading effects of lust on the bodies and souls of lovers, and the archpriest includes lively accounts of terrible cases that he himself witnessed in Catalonia: l'Argentera the strangler, the murderous mistress of Yrasón the painter, the sword merchant Juan Orenga, emasculated by his mistress (all in ch. xxiv). The second part recounts, with racy monologues, the vices of evil women in a humorous and ironic manner for the most part free from misogynistic bitterness. The third part consists of an analysis of the complexions or humours of men and their capacity for love, and the final part includes a disputation between Poverty and Fortune, based on Boccaccio's *De casibus virorum illustrium*, and an attack on astrology. Martínez's other sources included Andreas Capellanus's *De amore*, Juan Ruiz, the *Disticha Catonis*, the Decretals of Gregory IX, St Augustine, Ramón Llull and the *Vita Christi* of Francisco Eiximenis. The so-called 'elegant' style in which much of the work is couched has Latinized vocabulary, use of hyperbaton, repetition, rhymed prose and other rhetorical tricks, yet it has sufficient restraint to make it acceptable to a wide reading public. The striking use of 'popular' style, especially in the monologues, is by no means free of the same rhetorical devices, which here heighten the effect of what appear to be market-place tirades. It was this stylistic achievement that was later to be taken up in *La Celestina*. Martínez's inclusion of interesting case-histories ensured that his work would achieve a success denied to the ordinary moralistic tract and that it would fall into the hands of the lovers he most earnestly wished to turn from their sinful ways.

Chronicle-writing evolved into a considerable art in the reign of John II: the *Crónica de Juan II* incorporates the work of a number of chroniclers; the *Crónica del Halconero* of Pedro Carrillo de Huete, the king's falconer, makes use of many contemporary documents, some of which are transcribed in the text. Even after Luna's downfall, the *Crónica de don Álvaro de Luna* defends his policies (it was probably the work of one of Luna's servants, a certain Gonzalo Chacón). Some apparently historical works were really romances of chivalry: such was Pedro del Corral's *Crónica sarracina* (c. 1430), a fictitious account of the Moorish invasion of Spain. A biography that has in parts the tone of a novel of chivalry is the *Victorial* of Gutierre Díez de Games (c. 1378–c. 1448), which recounts the life of Díez's patron, Pero Niño, Count of Buelna, in particular his naval exploits against the English and the Mediterranean pirates. The *Libro del paso honroso* by Pedro Rodríguez de Lena, which has come down to us in an abridged version published in Salamanca in 1588, describes an actual event of the year 1434, when Suero de Quiñones, with the king's permission, held the bridge over the river Órbigo (prov. of León), on the road to Santiago, against all who wished to pass, simply as a gesture to his lady. During the numerous tourneys Suero and eight of his nine companions were injured and of his sixty-eight adversaries one was killed and many wounded. This incident gives us an interesting glimpse of the social values of the period and helps to explain the enormous vogue to be attained by the sentimental romances and the romances of chivalry – a situation in which life tried to emulate, even to surpass, literary models.

The unhistorical nature of the *Crónica sarracina* and other such works was denounced as 'trufa o mentira paladina' by Fernán Pérez de Guzmán (*c.* 1377/9–*c.* 1460), the most percipient historian of the period. He and a number of his kinsfolk were political opponents of Álvaro de Luna, and after 1433 Guzmán seems to have taken no further part in politics, either choosing or being obliged to remain in his village of Batres, where he dedicated himself to historiography. He undertook a number of translations, the most important being the *Mar de historias*, a vernacular version of Giovanni della Colonna's *Mare historiarum*, which consists of a series of brief biographies of classical heroes, Christian saints, medieval historical and fictitious figures, emperors and princes. The pen-portrait had already been tried by Guzmán's uncle, Pero López de Ayala, and on the basis of a pseudo-classical and a vernacular model Guzmán perfected this literary form in his *Generaciones y semblanzas* (1450, 1455), in which he provides physical and moral portraits of his more illustrious contemporaries, recognizing – and here he was an innovator in the period – both their good and their bad features. His view of the responsibilities of the historian to the chief actors in the events and to posterity is almost modern in its scrupulosity; a sign of this approach can be seen in his refusal to publish the portraits before the deaths of the persons depicted. The first version of his work therefore contained only thirty-two portraits, those of Luna and John II being added in 1455. His judgements of his subjects were based on a strongly held concept of Christian patriotism, and it is this firmness of principle that distinguishes him from the diplomatic discretion of his successor in this genre, Hernando del Pulgar (*c.* 1425–*c.* 1494). Pulgar was royal chronicler and writer of a collection of twenty-four pen-portraits entitled *Claros varones de Castilla* (1486), which includes descriptions of the most important figures of Henry IV's reign. Despite his silence on certain matters of which he is likely to have had detailed knowledge, Pulgar shows greater insight into his subjects than Guzmán. Both these historians wrote in a clear humanistic prose, but Pulgar had more pretensions to a rhetorical style.

The fifteenth century saw the composition of a number of books of travels but some of these were fictitious accounts. In 1403, Henry III appointed Ruy González de Clavijo (d. 1412) head of an embassy to Tamburlaine the Great, Emperor of the Mongols, which took six years to make the journey. On his return, Clavijo wrote his *Embajada a Tamorlán*, a full and factual account of the mission, with interesting and detailed descriptions of strange sights and unusual customs. Pero Tafur, one of the earliest of tourists, describes in his *Andanças e viajes* his journey during the years 1436–9 to Morocco, Italy and the Holy Land and his return by the land route, but his descriptions do not altogether eschew fantasy. *The Travels of Marco Polo* had been translated into Aragonese in the fourteenth century, and in the fifteenth they were translated into Castilian also, as were the fictitious *Voyages of Sir John Mandeville*. The reading public's taste for such descriptions, however fanciful, which had been strong in the thirteenth and fourteenth centuries (e.g. the wonders of the Orient in the *Libro de Alexandre* and much of the *Cavallero Zifar*), became insatiable in the fifteenth and sixteenth centuries, and, as for the authors who supplied this need, all the legends and fantasies of the past became grist to their mill.

Even more numerous than the travel-books were the prose romances, commonly based on French material, which were to achieve considerable circulation from the 1470s onward with the foundation of printing-houses in various Spanish towns. In addition to the epic and Arthurian romances, there was an important genre of sentimental romances, which take the form of analyses of the emotions of unhappy courtly lovers, often presented in allegorical or epistolary form. There is a strong Italian inspiration in this genre, principally Boccaccio's *Fiammetta*. The earliest was the *Siervo libre de amor* by Juan Rodríguez de la Cámara (or del Padrón) (end of fourteenth–mid-fifteenth century), some of whose poems appear in the *Cancionero de Baena* and other collections. His apparently truthful account of his own unfortunate love-affair contains a brief story, 'Estoria de dos amadores Ardanlier e Lyessa', based on the tragic life of Inés de Castro. He was also author of a treatise on nobility, *La cadira de honor* (or *Tractado de la nobleza e fidalguía*), and of the feminist *Triunfo de las donas*. The best known of the writers of sentimental romances was Diego de San Pedro, *hidalgo* in the service of the Girón family who seat was at Peñafiel (and whose descendants later acquired the dukedom of Osuna). We have two of his romances, the first being the *Tractado de amores de Arnalte e Lucenda* (first printed 1491, but written much earlier), in which Arnalte's unrequitable passion for Lucenda takes the conventional courtly form of a masochistic acceptance of suffering. San Pedro is best remembered, however, for his very successful *Cárcel de Amor* which was printed in numerous editions in Spain from 1492 (though written somewhat earlier) and elsewhere in Europe in the sixteenth century.

The author, as 'el Autor', plays a role in the action as go-between for the lovers, Leriano and Laureola. The work opens allegorically with Leriano being dragged to the Gaol of Love by a wild man who represents Desire. The Princess Laureola is falsely accused of unchastity, is condemned to death by her royal father, and is rescued by Leriano, who cannot now be permitted to see her again and who dies by refusing sustenance. His death scene is a travesty of the Eucharist, and thus makes a strong parallel between his type of love and love of God. The style is elaborate and courtly, though not as artificial as the author's earlier *Arnalte*, and in the final lament of Leriano's mother, it achieves a moving simplicity. The combination of tragic love and chivalric action, the clash within Laureola between honour and emotional inclination, Leriano's noble bearing throughout his sufferings and demise, all help to explain the work's success.

By the fifteenth century, we can see that the idea of literature and of its purpose had become much closer to the classical view. The shackles placed on it by monks and churchmen had been thrown off, and technical advances in paper manufacture, movable type and optics were to ensure a widespread distribution of the written word undreamt of in the earlier period.

XI Fifteenth-Century Lay Humanism[1]

An upsurge of interest in classical literature and thought is an evident feature of the Spanish fifteenth-century cultural scene. It is particularly associated with the patronage of a handful of prominent laymen of whom the Marquis of Santillana (1398–1458) was the most important. The famous library he collected, partly as a result of purchases of manuscripts made in Italy, had had its forerunners in the library of the Aragonese historian, Juan Fernández de Heredia (*c.* 1310–96), Grand Master of the Order of St John of Jerusalem, and that of Enrique de Villena (see p. 233 above). Other examples of noble bibliophiles and *littérateurs* who flourished during or after Santillana's time were Pedro Fernández de Velasco (1399–1470) and Carlos, Prince of Viana (1421–61), son of John II of Aragon and author of a translation of Aristotle's *Ethics* that remained a standard work well beyond the fifteenth century. These men between them made or sponsored a very large number of translations of the major classical authors into the Spanish vernacular. Santillana, in particular, also set out to make known in Spain the works of the great Italians of the Trecento – Dante, Petrarch and Boccaccio. The fact that they, and many of those who worked as translators under

[1] This section has been written by the Editor.

their patronage, were laymen and that this Spanish interest in the classics coincided with the great flowering of Italian fifteenth-century lay humanism has sometimes led scholars and critics to identify the two movements in an inadmissible way. The Italian humanists themselves, who were in the best position to judge, did not recognize the classicizing movement in contemporary Spain as reflecting in any close sense the pursuit of *studia humanitatis* as this was understood in Italy. Spanish fifteenth-century humanism was important, but it was important in its own way and, in fact, closely paralleled similar movements in France, Burgundy and England.

One of the reasons sometimes put forward to sustain the view that Italian humanism exercised a direct influence in Spain involves drawing assumptions from political relationships in the fifteenth century between the Crown of Aragon and Italy. Since Alfonso V of Aragon transferred his court permanently to Naples in 1443 and certainly there became the patron of many Italian humanists and the owner of a famous library of humanistic books, the conclusion has been drawn that the ideas, attitudes and methods of the Italian humanists must have found their way from Naples, through Catalonia, into the Iberian Peninsula. In fact it has so far proved impossible to document any such movement. Alfonso's Italian biographer, Il Panormita, contrasted the king's interest in humanism with what he described as the general indifference of Spaniards to scholarship and serious letters in the sense Italians now understood these. What we know of the literary interests of the Aragonese and Catalan knights and others who served Alfonso V in Naples confirms that they remained firmly attached to the reading traditions of the Iberian Peninsula and were remarkably unaffected by Italian humanism, or even by more strictly literary Italian influences.

Spanish fifteenth-century interest in the classical world, while genuine enough, was more concerned with assimilating it to enrich the medieval world-picture than with permitting it to open up new perspectives. The highly Latinized prose style of many of the vernacular translations made at this time from the classics should not mislead us. This represents a desperate but superficial attempt to manipulate the vernacular to make it more capable of conveying something of the complexity of Latin thought. As also occurred in France, when, in the sixteenth century, the need for vernacular translations of the major classical writings was again felt, most of the fifteenth-century ones were cast aside. The poet Juan de Mena (see p. 231 above) is often presented as a humanistic author and the immense influence of Latin on his themes, language and poetic style is evident enough. But his attitude to classical literature and the classical world remains for the most part firmly rooted in the Middle Ages; real evidence of genuine under-standing of the ancient world acquired from his classical reading occurs only occasionally and in a transient manner. The Spanish scholars whom Italian humanists respected were, in fact, men whose attitudes were firmly rooted in the scholastic tradition like Alonso de Cartagena (1384–1456), Bishop of Burgos, who engaged in a famous controversy with Leonardo Bruni about the latter's translation of Aristotle's *Ethics* into Latin, and the polymath writer and scholar Alonso de Madrigal, 'el Tostado' (*c.* 1400–55).

What was entirely absent from the work of the Spanish lay patrons of classical learning in the first half of the fifteenth century was that philological and textually sensitive approach to classical literature as well as that emphasis on a mastery of classical Latin considered in Italy indispensable for any serious humanist endeavour. Santillana did not know Latin and he did not think it necessary to learn it; he read the classics in Italian translations or in Spanish translations specially com-missioned by him. Italians therefore praised his amateur endeavours to master the classics but they did not accept him as a humanist. The Florentine humanist Vespasiano da Bisticci thus wrote of him after his death: 'he was not a man of letters, but he understood Italian very well' – a phrase that, applied to this great bibliophile, enthusiast for classical and Italian letters and gifted poet, usefully reminds us of the severity of humanist standards. Those who worked at the business of supplying vernacular translations for Santillana and others were well aware that they were being asked to undertake a task that could only provide, be-cause fifteenth-century Spanish was not yet sufficiently flexible or subtle, emasculated versions of the Latin originals. Alonso de Madrigal thus protested that it was impossible to translate the *Universal History* of Eusebius effectively into 'fabla castellana', and many other translators make the same complaint. The point did not impress Santillana who expressed himself satisfied if he could secure access to the content, if not to the form, of the great works of classical literature and thought.

That the ideals of Italian humanism could not easily be exported to Spain, just as they proved incapable of being exported to France or England at this time, should not surprise us. Neither the social nor the economic background that made Italian humanism possible existed in fifteenth-century Spain where, moreover, strongly held medieval notions about social hierarchy prevented learning, scholarship and literature receiving the prestige readily accorded to them in Italy by men of rank. The Spanish nobility generally were strongly indoctrinated with a belief that it was both socially improper and psychologically dangerous for those whose business was to defend the state by the sword to involve themselves seriously with letters, which were traditionally the business of priests. The ancient topos of the opposition between arms and letters was still held, outside Italy, to reflect a real truth about society. Santillana, indeed, was praised by the lettered precisely because, so they said, he was the first man of such high rank in Castile who had dared to devote himself both to chivalry and to learning. He was, however, severely criticized by his peers (and, it seems, by ecclesiastics, too) for this departure from tradition.

This medieval belief that the practice of arms was incompatible with a concern for letters continued to be strongly held by the Spanish nobility fifty years later when Peter Martyr wrote home to Italy from the Spanish court that the young noblemen there whom Queen Isabella had engaged him to instruct in humane letters 'declare their abhorrence of letters, which they believe to be a hindrance to a soldier's career'. All through the fifteenth century scholars attempted to convince kings and magnates, on the whole with only limited success, that their prestige would be enhanced, not diminished, by a dedication to learning and letters. We should not be misled by the fact that a handful of magnates did defy this assumption. Most did not, and since, under Spanish social conditions, humanism needed noble patronage if it was to flourish, the consequences of this hostility were important. The suspicion of lay humanism was probably reinforced by racial and religious suspicion. The scholars upon whom men like Santillana relied to act as translators were often *conversos*. *Converso* enthusiasm for scholarship and learning may well, in the long run, have been counterproductive.

In the second half of the century there are signs that a professional lay humanism more akin to that of Italy did make some headway in Spain. It certainly began to be recognized that the idea of a vernacular humanism dependent on translations from the classics was a contradiction in terms. The poet Fernando de la Torre now commented rather patronizingly of Santillana: 'what polished things we have seen from unlettered men!' Juan de Lucena, in 1463, caused Santillana to make an imaginary posthumous declaration that his lack of Latin had made him something less than a whole man. A *converso* humanist of Saragossa, Gonzalo García de Santa María, regretted that he had, as he said, wasted valuable years of his life making vernacular translations from the Latin for the benefit of the ignorant. But Italian scholars and Spanish scholars who knew what Italian humanism was all about still considered, when the Catholic Monarchs came to the throne, that humanism only had the thinnest of roots in Spain. Antonio de Nebrija (1444–1522) was, significantly, the first serious Spanish student of classical philology to come out of Spain. When he returned home from Italy about 1470 after ten years of study there it was to denounce the barbarous Latin used in Salamanca University and to complain, as a Spanish patriot, of the well-merited contempt he said Italian humanists felt for Spanish cultural traditions.

If it is plain that Spanish fifteenth-century humanism was a very different article from the humanism of Italy, that does not mean that it should be dismissed as a factor of no significance. It represents what could be done towards opening Spanish culture to a greater awareness of the thought and literature of the ancient world given the particular social structure and the dominant religious and political attitudes of fifteenth-century Spain. To expect Italian humanism to develop in Spain (or in fifteenth-century France, Burgundy or England) would be to ignore its social and economic roots. Spanish humanism was bound by the nature of Spanish society to be conservative and tentative. It insisted on retaining the closest links with the Christian tradition and with Christian morality and piety and was much interested, in a rather vague way, in Senecan stoicism partly because it believed that Seneca was a Spaniard. His ideas, in any case, appealed to a people who thought of themselves first of all as soldiers. Boethius, too, was a writer much favoured by Santillana and his successors. As well as its many volumes of classical works Santillana's library was notably well stocked with ethical and historical books. Rodrigo Sánchez de Arévalo (1404–70), jurist, diplomat and one of the most learned Spaniards of his day, who had lived long in Italy, was actively opposed to the teaching of pagan *studia humanitatis* in the schools, demanding that youth should first be firmly indoctrinated against the damaging effects of classical philosophy and literature by a thorough grounding in religion. Alonso de Cartagena allowed the study of pagan letters but only on condition that the student safeguarded himself from being corrupted by them by frequent readings of the Christian Fathers. It was not surprising, therefore, that Spaniards in the fifteenth century felt safer with the great Italians of the Trecento – with Dante (Santillana's greatest literary discovery), with the Latin works and the religious poetry of Petrarch and with some of the writings of Boccaccio. They certainly felt more at home with the identification made by some Italian fourteenth-century scholars between humanism and Christian ethics than with the more ambiguous attitudes of the fifteenth-century Italian humanists to religious and ethical issues. The point is of some importance if we are to understand the history of ideas in sixteenth-century Spain and, in particular, what was to happen in that area in the time of the Catholic Monarchs and the early years of Charles V's reign.

Bibliography

GENERAL

CASTRO, A. *La realidad histórica de España*. Rev. ed. Mexico City, 1962.

CURTIUS, E. R. *European Literature and the Latin Middle Ages*. London, 1953.

DEYERMOND, A. D. *The Middle Ages. A Literary History of Spain*, Vol. 1. Ed. R. O. Jones. London, 1971.

GREEN, O. H. *Spain and the Western Tradition*. 4 vols. Madison and Milwaukee, 1963–6.

LÓPEZ ESTRADA, F. *Introducción a la literatura medieval española*. 3rd ed. Madrid, 1966.

EARLY LATIN AUTHORS

COCHRANE, C. N. *Christianity and Classical Culture*. 2nd ed. Oxford, 1957.

FONTAINE, J. *Isidore de Séville et la culture classique dans l'Espagne wisigothique*. Paris, 1959.

PÉREZ DE URBEL, J. *San Isidoro de Sevilla: su vida, su obra y su tiempo*. 2nd ed. Barcelona, 1945.

THOMPSON, E. A. *The Goths in Spain*. Oxford, 1969.

CHRISTIAN AUTHORS OF THE ELEVENTH AND TWELFTH CENTURIES

DAVID, P. *Études historiques sur la Galice et le Portugal*. Coimbra, Lisbon and Paris, 1947.

GONZÁLEZ PALENCIA, A. *El arzobispo don Raimundo de Toledo*. Barcelona, 1942.

RICO, F. 'Las letras del siglo XII en Galicia, León y Castilla'. *Ábaco*, 2 (1969), 11–91.

The Mozarabic Lyric

DRONKE, P. *Medieval Latin and the Rise of the European Love-Lyric*. 2 vols. 2nd ed. Oxford, 1969.

GARCÍA GÓMEZ, E. *Las jarchas romances de la serie árabe en su marco*. Madrid, 1965.

STERN, S. M. *Les Chansons mozarabes*. Palermo, 1953.

THE THIRTEENTH CENTURY

LORD, A. B. *The Singer of Tales*. Cambridge, Mass., 1960.
MENÉNDEZ PIDAL, R. *Poesía juglaresca y orígenes de las literaturas románicas*. 6th ed. Madrid, 1957.
MICHAEL, I. (ed.). *Poema de Mio Cid*. Madrid, 1976.

Poema de Mio Cid
DE CHASCA, E. *El arte juglaresco en el 'Cantar de Mio Cid'*. 2nd ed. Madrid, 1972.
MENÉNDEZ PIDAL, R. *La España del Cid*. 5th ed. Madrid, 1956.
RUSSELL, P. E. 'San Pedro de Cardeña and the Heroic History of the Cid'. In *Medium Aevum*, XXVII (1958), pp. 57–79.
SMITH, C. (ed.). *Poema de Mio Cid*. Oxford, 1972.

Lost Epics
MENÉNDEZ PIDAL, R. *Reliquias de la poesía épica española*. Madrid, 1951.
REIG, C. *El Cantar de Sancho II y cerco de Zamora*. Madrid, 1947.

Gonzalo de Berceo
ANDRÉS, A. (ed.). *Vida de Santo Domingo de Silos*. Madrid, 1958.
DUTTON, B. *'La vida de San Millán de la Cogolla' de Gonzalo de Berceo. Estudio y edición crítica*. London, 1967.
—— (ed.). *Los Milagros de Nuestra Señora de Gonzalo de Berceo*. London, 1972.

Libro de Alexandre
MICHAEL, I. *The Treatment of Classical Material in the 'Libro de Alexandre'*. Manchester, 1970.

The Galician-Portuguese Lyric
DRONKE, P. *The Medieval Lyric*. London, 1968.
NUNES, J. J. *Cantigas d'amigo*. Vol. I: *Introdução*. Coimbra, 1928.
TAVANI, G. *Poesia del Duecento nella Penisola Iberica*. Rome, 1969.

Alfonso X
CATALÁN MENÉNDEZ-PIDAL, D. *De Alfonso X al conde de Barcelos*. Madrid, 1962.
MENÉNDEZ PIDAL, R. (ed.). *Primera crónica general . . .* 2nd ed. Madrid, 1955.
PROCTER, E. S. *Alfonso X of Castile*. Oxford, 1951.

THE FOURTEENTH CENTURY

Libro del Cavallero Zifar
RIQUER, M. DE (ed.). *El Cavallero Zifar*. Barcelona, 1951.

Arthurian Romance
BONILLA Y SAN MARTÍN, A. (ed.). *Libros de caballerías*. N.B.A.E. Madrid, 1907–8.
ENTWISTLE, W. J. *The Arthurian Legend in the Literature of the Spanish Peninsula*. London, 1925.

Amadís de Gaula
MOTTOLA, C. The '*Amadís de Gaula*' in Spain and France. New York, 1962.
PLACE, E. B. (ed.). *Amadís de Gaula*. 4 vols. Madrid, 1959–69.

Juan Ruiz, Archpriest of Hita
GYBBON-MONYPENNY, G. B. (ed.). '*Libro de buen amor*' Studies. London, 1970.
LECOY, F. *Recherches sur le 'Libro de buen amor'*. Paris, 1938.
LIDA DE MALKIEL, M. R. *Two Spanish Masterpieces: the 'Book of Good Love' and the 'Celestina'*. Urbana, 1961.
ZAHAREAS, A. N. *The Art of Juan Ruiz, Archpriest of Hita*. Madrid, 1965.

Don Juan Manuel
GIMÉNEZ SOLER, A. *Don Juan Manuel, biografía y estudio crítico*. Saragossa, 1932.

Mocedades de Rodrigo
DEYERMOND, A. D. *Epic Poetry and the Clergy: Studies on the 'Mocedades de Rodrigo'*. London, 1969.

Pero López de Ayala
RUSSELL, P. E. *English Intervention in Spain and Portugal in the Time of Edward III and Richard II*. Oxford, 1955.

POETRY 1400–1474

Ballads
MENÉNDEZ PIDAL, R. *et al*. (eds.). *Romancero tradicional*. 4 vols so far publ. Madrid, 1957–.
SMITH, C. C. (ed.). *Spanish Ballads*. Oxford, 1964.

Cancioneros
LE GENTIL, P. *La Poésie lyrique espagnole et portugaise à la fin du moyen âge*. 2 vols. Rennes, 1949–53.

Marquis of Santillana
LAPESA, R. *La obra literaria del Marqués de Santillana*. Madrid, 1957.

Juan de Mena
LIDA DE MALKIEL, M. R. *Juan de Mena, poeta del prerrenacimiento español*. Mexico, City, 1950.

Jorge Manrique
SALINAS, P. *Jorge Manrique, o tradición y originalidad*. 2nd ed. Buenos Aires, 1952.
SERRANO DE HARO, A. *Personalidad y destino de Jorge Manrique*. Madrid, 1966.

PROSE LITERATURE 1400–1474

Enrique de Villena

COTARELO Y MORI, E. *Don Enrique de Villena: su vida y obras.* Madrid, 1896.

Alfonso Martínez de Toledo

El Corbacho. Ed. Martin de Riquer. Barcelona, 1942.

—— Ed. J. González Muela. Clásicos Castalia. Madrid, 1970.

WHITBOURN, C. J. *The Arcipreste de Talavera and the Literature of Love.* Hull, 1970.

Historiography

TATE, R. B. *Ensayos sobre la historiografía peninsular del siglo XV.* Madrid, 1970.

Fifteenth-Century Humanism

DI CAMILLO, OTTAVIO. *El humanismo castellano del siglo XV.* Valencia, 1976.

ROUND, N. G. 'Renaissance Culture and its Opponents in Fifteenth-Century Castile'. In *Modern Language Review,* LVII (1962), pp. 204–15.

RUBIO BALAGUER, J. 'Sobre la cultura en la corona de Aragón en la primera mitad del siglo XV'. In *IV Congreso de historia de la corona de Aragón, ponencias,* 7 (1955), pp. 5–16.

RUSSELL, P. E. 'Arms versus Letters: Towards a Definition of Spanish Fifteenth-Century Humanism'. In *Aspects of the Renaissance: A Symposium,* pp. 47–58. Ed. Archibald R. Lewis. Austin and London, 1967.

SCHIFF, M. *La Bibliothèque du Marquis de Santillane.* Paris, 1905. Reprinted Amsterdam, 1970.

SORIA, A. *Los humanistas de la corte de Alfonso el Magnánimo.* Granada, 1956.

Note (see pp. 199 and 228 above)

Attention must however be drawn here to a recent major contribution to knowledge about later medieval liturgical drama in Castile – CARMEN TORROJA MENÉNDEZ and MARÍA RIVAS PALÁ *Teatro en Toledo en el siglo XI.* '*Auto de la pasión' de Alonso del Campo.* Anejos del Boletín de la Real Academia Española: Anejo XXXV, Madrid, 1977. This study, based mainly on documents found by its authors in the Archivo de Obra y Fábrica of Toledo cathedral relating to the period from the late fourteenth to the early sixteenth century, shows that Toledo was an active centre for the production of religious plays during this period and goes a long way towards undermining the traditional assumption that liturgical drama did not flourish in medieval Castile.

7 Medieval Catalan Literature

PAUL RUSSELL-GEBBETT

I Origins

The Catalan language existed as such from the ninth century at the latest. As from that time lyric songs and dances (devotional, erotic, satirical) and narrative poems (hagiographic, epic, propagandistic, burlesque) surely lived in the mouths of the people and were transmitted orally. But these were not strictly literature, although some of them were later to underlie and inform literature. Catalan literature proper does not begin until the twelfth century, if we discount the eleventh-century *Cançó de Santa Fe*, a hagiographic work of some sensitivity which may or may not have been composed in one of the great monasteries of Roussillon and whose language may or may not be the *rossellonès* of the time.

To the twelfth century belong the first examples of (anonymous) 'literary' prose, which makes a typically didactic appearance in the *Homilies d'Organyà*, an eight-folio fragment of a sermonary, and in a few lines of a translation of the *Forum judicum*. The language of both texts is a Provençalized Catalan, rather different from that of most of the vernacular notarial documents which survive from this period, and reflects the prestige of South French culture in Catalonia. This prestige, which has an obvious historical *raison d'être*, is most patent in the work of the poets, and a more or less correct Provençal is the language of poetry until the fifteenth century.

Two of the first Catalan troubadours known by name are Guerau de Cabrera (d. by 1170) and Guillem de Berguedà (*fl.* 1170–92). The former's chief claim to fame is his much-imitated *Ensenhamen* ('lesson') addressed to the *joglar* Cabra, wherein we learn not only what should be the skills of these medieval 'pop' performers (dancing, singing, reciting, playing musical instruments, etc.) but more importantly what more or less literary material they should possess in their repertoires. It is clear from the poem that cultured circles were acquainted with all the major historico-legendary and exemplary tales which we are accustomed to regard as having been disseminated via northern French – *matière de Bretagne, fabliaux, gestes* – and we might therefore surmise for many of them twelfth-century Provençal versions. Cabrera's poem (and later imitations of it) is of great interest for literary history. Guillem de Berguedà, pragmatic, cynical and violent, was one of the most accomplished composers of the politico-satirical *sirventès*. His best-known works are his *chansoneta* attacking Ponç de Mataplana, with its refrain 'A Marques, Marques, Marques / d'engan etz farsitz e ples', and his unusually sincere and moving *plany* on the exemplary death fighting the infidel of the same personage: *Consiros cant e planc e plor*.

These poets belong to the golden age of Provençal literature, when the itinerant court of Alfons II 'el Cast' (1162–96) was frequently in his disputed southern French domains, and attracting to it – as his opponents did to theirs – Catalan and Provençal poets and *joglars* capable not only of providing amusement and not too seriously meant instruction but also of composing and interpreting verses supporting the king's and his supporters' persons and policies. The *sirventès* was as much a part of courtly verse as were those compositions treating of 'ideal' love or debating moral topics, and it was often a good deal less barren.

II The Thirteenth Century

In the following century the Catalan Ramon Vidal de Besalú (*fl.* 1212–52) wrote the first Provençal *ars poetica*: *Las razos de trobar*. This is a disquisition on the nature and utility of poetry, and a grammar of the poetic language illustrated with excerpts from the work of poets who flourished in the *belle époque* before 1200. This first codification of the *saber de trobar* for long remained, in Catalonia, southern France and northern Italy, the authoritative work on the subject. It is interesting that Ramon Vidal mentions a traditional poetry to be found in the mouths of the people, and that as a poet he himself cultivated most especially the narrative forms more proper to the *joglars* – whose activity of course antedated that of the troubadours.

The major poetic figure of this century is, however, the prolific Guillem de Cervera or Cerverí de Girona (*fl.* 1250–80); he is the last of the 'classical' troubadours, and in his mastery of all the forms and genres of *trobar ric* as well as *trobar leu* he is in a sense their epitome. But Cerverí is also a very personal poet, no doubt partly because he was a *joglar* made good. His verse, usually didactic and moralizing, often expresses in dignified personal terms his disillusionment with the political actions of his protectors, with the gulf between public and private morality, between the ideal and the real; a tone of resigned melancholy pervades his fine *Sermó* and his more traditionally moralizing *Proverbis*. He also cultivated the forms and themes of the popular song (a visit to the court of the Castilian Alfonso X 'the Wise' may have shown him their artistic possibilities), and at the other extreme he could be as hermetic and baroque as any of his contemporaries. He was a great professional, with a copious and varied output, and there is no one to compare with him until the fifteenth century.

While the language of poetry remains Provençal, that of prose is in the thirteenth century an almost pure Catalan. Official or didactic prose is represented by the *Usatges de Barcelona* and the *Consolat de Mar*, respectively the earliest European feudal code and the first vernacular compilation of maritime law. Two other juridical texts reflecting Catalonia's expansion are the *Libre dels costums de Tortosa* and the *Furs de València*. More nearly literary are two anonymous translations of religious works: Jacobus de Voragine's *Legenda Aurea* and St Gregory's late sixth-century *Dialogorum libri IV*. The latter especially has a liveliness in its use of dialogue and a flexibility of style that argue a longish tradition in the translation from Latin of devotional material; that Catalan translations of the Bible had been made is evidenced by the fact that in 1234 James I 'el Conqueridor' ordered their destruction. Collections of proverbs and aphorisms from classical and Oriental sources were popular, and to Cerverí's *Proverbis* we might add the Jewish royal doctor Jafuda Bonsenyor's *Libre de paraules e dits de savis e filòsofs* and more than one collection by Ramon Llull. Their vogue continues into the next century, which sees some burlesque items amid the increasingly second-hand moralizings.

Historiography, translated and original, flowers in the expansionist thirteenth century. The *Crònica d'Espanya* (1263) by Pere Ribera de Perpejà is an adaptation of the Archbishop Jiménez de Rada's *De rebus Hispaniae*, and, between 1267 and 1283, was produced the Catalan version of the Latin *Gesta comitum barcinonensium et regum Aragoniae*, begun between 1162 and 1184. But neither of these can compare as vividly narrated lived history with the four 'great' chronicles, two of which belong to this century – those of James I and of Desclot.

James I's *Libre dels feyts d'armes* exists now only in an early fourteenth-century version, although it seems originally to have been composed in two instalments during the king's lifetime (1213-76) and with his active participation. In vivid yet natural language, some of it clearly a prosification of Catalan or Provençal *gestes* now lost, the captain-king recounts in the first person the epic events of a long reign – and most notably the conquests of Mallorca and Valencia, campaigns which the reader lives with the narrator. There is singularly little overstatement or idealization, no rhetorical posturing but much direct speech and dialogue; the king is allowed to emerge as a real person, with his strengths and weaknesses, his cruelties and kindnesses, and it is this truth to life, this humanity, which gives the autobiographical *Libre dels feyts* its value as a work of literature. There is something of the epic poem in the *Libre dels feyts* and something of the technique of the *joglar* in its telling.

The second great chronicle, Bernat Desclot's *Libre del rei En Pere d'Aragó e dels seus antecessors passats*, was probably written between 1283 and 1288; it treats for the most part of Peter III (Pere 'el Gran', 1276-85) and of the Crown of Aragon's struggles with the French and in Italy. Like the *Libre dels feyts*, Desclot's work contains material originating in rhymed works, although in the sections concerned with contemporary events more professionally respectable sources are evident: eyewitness accounts, official documents, etc. To some extent the style reflects these two types of sources, but it is always more carefully, clearly and ambitiously structured, richer and more varied (except in the matter of dialogue) than James I's. If James I's work is epic, Desclot's is rather more chivalresque, almost novelesque in spite of its historical seriousness – the times were such. There are some fine literary portraits, some good rhetoric, and much meticulously detailed description.

Cerverí, James I and Desclot are major figures in medieval Catalan literature, but their contemporary Ramon Llull (?1232-?1315) is a man of truly European stature. One might say that Llull is a literary figure almost in spite of himself, in that the majority of his 243 extant works are essentially didactic in intention. His whole much-travelled and combative life, after a late conversion, was dedicated to the propagation of the true faith and the extirpation of error by means of logical demonstration, and it is this logical demonstration that his works seek to provide. That he writes many of them in Catalan is an illustration of his seriousness of intent; that some of them may justifiably be classed as literature is a consequence of a number of factors: his ability to transform *a l'estil diví* the forms and genres of profane literature, his varied use of allegory, debate, symbol and *exemplum*, his ability to create a language capable of communicating his doctrine both with precision and passion.

Llull's best-known literary work is undoubtedly his allegorical social *romanç* the *Libre de Evast e de Aloma e de Blanquerna son fill* (1283–6). Here the youth Blanquerna rejects the marriage proposed for him by his parents and embraces the religious life. He ascends (unwillingly) the ecclesiastical hierarchy through his vehemently expressed faith and his uncommon gifts as a teacher and administrator, and after attaining to the dignity of Pope and reorganizing the Church finally abandons the apostolate and becomes a hermit. This, the first romance novel, is clearly an imagined autobiography, wherein the protagonist Blanquerna's gifts of faith, perseverance and intellectual power are justly rewarded, and he is thereby given the means to carry out the utopian programme of social reform and spiritual regeneration that it was Llull's life's ambition to effect. It is a deeply religious and fervently didactic work which contrives at the same time to portray quite vividly the society of the time; Blanquerna's encounters with old men and maidens, monks and minstrels, cardinals and canons, knights and esquires – all at once real and symbolic – tend all to the one end – the demonstration that God exists and that it is man's duty to love and serve Him and His creatures with an unswerving faith backed and propagated by reason and intelligence. The book owes much in its episodes to the motifs of courtly verse and the *roman courtois*, but the ambitious overall design is Llull's alone; it is Llull's intellectually most accessible major work, and probably his best known, partly because it incorporates the *Libre d'Amich e Amat*.

The *Libre d'Amich e Amat* is an aid to the right contemplation of God, a divine *breviari d'amor*. It takes the form of a mystical dialogue in 366 short verses between man (*Amich*) and his Creator (*Amat*), with an often personified *Amor* as the intermediary; the setting is a nature replete with symbolic values. This is Llull at his most lyrical, conveying a profoundly spiritual emotion in some of the most artfully simple and melodious prose in the Catalan language, quite often dialogued and rhymed, heavily metaphorical. In comparison with this mystical work most of Llull's 'real' poems (in Provençal) are sadly wooden, but this is to be expected in a writer who used rhyme so often as an aid to easy memorization.

Other prose works of interest are the *Libre de l'orde de cavalleria* (c. 1275), concerning the right formation of the Christian knight and later used by Don Juan Manuel and in the *Tirant lo blanc*; *Fèlix* or *Libre de meravelles* (1288-9), an extended and subtle disputation, full of interlocking exempla and much influenced by Vincent de Beauvais's *Speculum historiale*; and the *Libre de les bèsties* (incorporated in the *Fèlix*), a collection of apologues showing an obvious debt to the *Calila e Dimna* and the French *Roman de Renart*. These are some of the many works wherein Llull attempts to reshape and redirect the thought and society of his time, and in so doing subjects the language to a discipline and a creative process which leave it immensely the richer. His role in the creation of the literary language has rightly been compared to that of Alfonso X in the case of Castilian.

One other fine stylist demands mention, the Valencian visionary Arnau de Vilanova (?1240-1311). A man of great breadth of culture, prestigious as a royal and papal physician, he became convinced of the imminent coming of the Antichrist and called for an urgent reform of the Church and the religious life in such treatises as the *Confessió de Barcelona* (1305) and the *Raonament d'Avinyó* (1310). Neither Vilanova nor Llull was altogether popular with the lords spiritual of the thirteenth century.

III The Fourteenth Century

The fourteenth century is a period of consolidation, of gradual assimilation of many influences, and of continued ideological disquiet. By its close, and thanks in large measure to the love of learning of Peter IV (Pere III 'el Cerimoniós', 1336-87), the literature of Catalonia appears less medieval and some writers have begun to handle with style and assurance the new humanism. But it takes time.

Lyric poetry remains throughout in the straitjacket of Provençal tradition, written still in a foreign language and handling outmoded themes in the manner prescribed by the *Razos* of Ramon Vidal. New preceptive works such as Jofre de Foixà's *Regles de trobar* (1293-5), Catalan versions of the Provençal *Leys d'amors* (1328 onwards), even Jaume March's *Libre de concordances* or *Diccionari de rims* (1371) and Lluís d'Aversó's *Torcimany* – both composed at the instigation of Peter IV – accept the pre-eminence of Provençal. An attempt to resuscitate the glories of troubadour verse had led in 1323 to the founding of the *Sobregaya companhia dels set trobadors de Tolosa*, at whose *jocs florals* Catalan poets competed, and in 1393 John (Joan) I misguidedly established a similar company in Barcelona. Given the independence of

Catalan prose, the manifest artificiality of latter-day 'troubadour' verse and especially Catalonia's political involvement in the Italy of Dante and Petrarch, this adherence to an outworn tradition seems almost enigmatic.

A very few courtly poets stand out. Llorenç Mallol shows an early thematic influence of Petrarch; Guillem de Masdovelles (1375–1440) has some good political verse; Pere March (1338–1413), father of Ausias March, analyses the wretchedness of the human condition and his brother Jaume the effects of love, largely deleterious, upon both mind and body. As regards form, the Provençal hendecasyllable with its inhibiting caesura predominates. The artistic results of the Toulouse and Barcelona consistories were depressing indeed, and any freshness of approach is to be sought elsewhere than in official institutions – as for example in the isolated example of the famous Ripoll Manuscript 129 (after 1346) whose poets seem to follow in lighter measures the popularizing tendency of Cerverí.

While the lyric is stifled by preceptive pressures, narrative verse flourishes. The most diverse subjects are handled in swift-moving *noves rimades* (couplets of short lines, commonly eneasyllables) and *codolada* (combinations of short lines of varying length), both of which had become traditional, and it is in these forms that many French *romans* and *fabliaux* are Catalanized. To some extent they occupy the place of the short story or novel of a later age, when the influence of Boccaccio had rejuvenated and refined the art of story-telling, but their popularity particularly for satirical purposes endures into the fifteenth century and beyond. Jaume Roig's *Libre de les dones* or *Spill* (1456) is a notable later example of their use in misogynistic literature.

Two more fine chronicles were produced in this century, those of Ramon Muntaner (1265–1336) and Peter IV (Pere III). Muntaner's work, begun in retirement in 1325, has one overriding aim: to glorify the divinely appointed and divinely inspired kings of Aragon, recording their political and warlike achievements so that they may serve as an example to future rulers. His chronicle is both a *speculum historiale* and a record of his own life spent in the enthusiastic service of his revered kings and country; it is inspired throughout by an exalted, and endearing, love of his country and of all who serve it – from kings and captains to the feared *almogàvers*. Muntaner served the *casal d'Aragó* as a gifted military commander and administrator in the Mediterranean and Near Eastern campaigns, as a man of confidence, and finally and exultantly with his pen. In fine prose (*lo pus bell catalanesch del món*), often dialogued, frequently apostrophizing his hearers and involving them in the unfolding of his story, he describes battles and sieges, jousts and festivities; he analyses military and political strategies, relating events in different parts of the empire; and he tells us of his own considerable contribution. His literary culture is evidenced by his comparing his kings and captains to epic and chivalresque heroes, and his narrative technique is at times reminiscent of the Arthurian romances, but his chronicle remains always firmly based in reality, and as the only Western record of the Aragonese adventure in the East it is of great importance historically.

Like Muntaner, Peter IV conceived of history providentially, and as having an exemplary value; he saw in it a means of justifying his actions to posterity, and this is what the chronicle which bears his name sets out to do. It was composed with the assistance of collaborators (notably one Bernat Descoll) between 1375 and 1386, written in the first person and in the style which had become traditional (dialogued, emotive, sprinkled with personal reflections and picturesque anecdotes), but written also with great attention to both stylistic detail and objective truth. The not very sympathetic personality of the proud and authoritarian king, fighting with great political acumen for the unity of a kingdom threatened by rebellious barons and bourgeoisie, is clearly and honestly delineated, and this is the most 'modern' and scientific – and the last – of the major Catalan chronicles. Peter IV, who saw the utility of history, saw indeed the value of culture in all its manifestations. He promoted, as we have seen, the writing of poetic treatises; apart from his own chronicle he ordered the compilation or translation from the rediscovered classical sources of other historical works; and at his instigation versions of all manner of 'scientific' treatises were produced.

One major medieval encyclopedic writer remains, the Valencian Francesc Eiximenis (c. 1340–c. 1409), whose vast production and European popularity even after the Renaissance are an index of his importance. A Franciscan, educated in a number of European universities, living in an age of diverse religious and socio-political preoccupations and of incipient humanism, he remains steadfastly medieval in outlook and technique; his major work, Lo Crestià (1379–92), is the last of the medieval summae. In this work, of which only four of a planned thirteen books are extant, he explains with immense erudition and a plethora of exempla the principles of the Christian faith and the norms by which a Christian should live. While on the one hand he recalls

Ramon Llull, on the other he has something in common with his contemporary Sant Vicent Ferrer (1350–1419), the most entertaining – and
apparently effective – of sermonizers. Eiximenis can take an oft-told
tale and make it live, setting it in a contemporary situation and dressing
it in the most authentic of contemporary language; it is this masterly
use of the anecdote, richly adorned, full of ironic humour, that makes
him readable to the profane. We must not forget, however, that these
elements are only accessory – albeit pedagogically very apposite – to
Eiximenis's profoundly serious reforming work.

In so far as Peter IV promoted culture generally he promoted
humanism, but it is in the reigns of his successors John (Joan) I and
Martin I (Martí 'l'Humà') that humanism really gathers impetus; at
about the turn of the century translations (often second-hand via
French) existed of one or more works of Quintus Curtius, Sallust, Livy,
Palladius, Seneca, Boethius, Cicero, Ovid, Virgil, Lucan and of
Petrarch's and Boccaccio's Latin works. Even then medieval habits died
hard, and for most translators and imitators the interest of these writers'
works lay still in the teaching they contained rather than in the way
that teaching was put over; the idea that prose was necessarily for instruction rather than occasionally for pure enjoyment was slow to die.
That it did die must be attributed in part to Bernat Metge and Antoni
Canals.

Bernat Metge (mid-fourteenth century–1413) is the first Catalan
Petrarchist, in that his *Història de Valter e Griselda* (1388) is a translation
of the Italian's *De rerum senilium* – Petrarch having translated it from
Boccaccio's *Decamerone*. This might have been yet another translation
of yet another essentially medieval tale had not Metge quite deliberately, and successfully, contrived to reproduce the humanist's
Latin in a no less elegant Catalan. He created a new literary language,
seen at its most developed in his major work *Lo Somni* (1398). The
Somni's content is in a way still medieval: four dialogues concerning the
immortality of the soul, the contemporary socio-political situation, the
vices and virtues of woman and of man; but the writer's elegantly
sceptical attitude (he takes part in the dialogues) is less complying than
the medieval. The shape may still appear medieval, but many of the
sources Metge uses, combining them in a harmonious whole, are
'modern': Cicero's *Somnium Scipionis* and *Tusculanae*, Valerius
Maximus' *Factorum dictorumque memorabilium*, the *Aeneid*, Ovid's *Metamorphoses*, Dante's *Divina Commedia*, Boccaccio's *Corbaccio* and *De claris
mulieribus*, Petrarch's *Secretum* and *De remediis utriusque fortunae*. The

style, finally, is humanistic prose at its finest, beautifully constructed and balanced periods with a careful use of absolute constructions, hyperbaton and neologism. The *Somni* is a new phenomenon, it is literature for a minority, for pleasure.

The theologian Antoni Canals (mid-fourteenth century–1419) contributed to the spread of humanism as an elegant translator, but with an evangelizing end, of Valerius Maximus' *Factorum dictorumque* (1395), Seneca's *De providentia* (between 1396 and 1407) and of part of Petrarch's *Africa* in his *Rahonament entre Scipió e Aníbal*. A contemporary of Eiximenis and Sant Vicent Ferrer, he shared his fellow Valencians' preoccupation with the reading public's growing scepticism, fed by their infatuation with the pagan classic writers, but unlike them he used the would-be humanists' own weapons to combat them. The prologues to his translations and to his original religious works (e.g. the *Scala de contemplació* of *c.* 1393) make it clear that for him the pagan philosophers if read aright support rather than undermine scriptural teachings.

IV The Fifteenth Century

The establishment of the royal court in Naples by Alfons V 'el Magnànim' (1416–58), a lover of humanism and patron of humanists, is thought by some scholars to have contributed to a more complete and artistically more successful assimilation of Italian culture in the Catalan literature of the second half of the century. It is, however, notable that as far as the Catalan vernacular is concerned the preference was still for the great figures of the Trecento (and of course still for the Latin classics). That the effects of close contact between the Catalans and the works of *contemporary* Italian humanists were not greater and not sooner apparent in vernacular literature was probably due in large measure to the reinstatement in the closed society of the court of a renewed Latin as the language of culture. Hence in the first half of the century the original productions of Metge and Canals lacked successful imitators, and relatively few translations were made (one was the Mallorcan Latinist Ferran Valentí's version of Cicero's *Paradoxa*). In the second half of the century the only major Italian fifteenth-century humanists of whose works Catalan versions are known to have been made were Leonardo Bruni, Pier Candido Decembrio and Leone Battisti Alberti – and their influence was minimal. The court's absence in Italy and its preoccupation with Latin might thus appear to have had an initially retardatory effect upon the development of 'modern' Catalan prose literature.

Nor was there any thoroughgoing rejuvenation of the form and content of lyric verse in Alfons V's reign. Although the three major poets were all attached to the royal court the influence of the troubadours upon their verse – of the best troubadours, since they sought inspiration in twelfth- and thirteenth-century models and not in those of the Toulouse and Barcelona consistories – was more powerful than that of Dante or Petrarch. Poets such as Gilabert de Próxita (*fl.* late fourteenth century–early fifteenth century), Andreu Febrer (*c.* 1380–*c.* 1440) and Jordi de Sant Jordi (*c.* 1399–*c.* 1424) show only sporadic and rather minor traces of Dantesque or Petrarchan influence, although Febrer did in later life translate the *Divina Commedia* into Catalan verse; they remain basically medieval. They do share traces of a new sensibility in the treatment of erotic themes, and their hendecasyllable occasionally approaches the flexibility of the Italian masters, but they are far from being Dantists or Petrarchists; they were cultured nobles, men of sufficient taste and discernment to imitate the best of the traditional models and of sufficient feeling to allow their real emotions to inform their work. They did one of the things that Petrarch himself did – found inspiration in the work of men such as Arnaut Daniel and Bertran de Born, and Jordi de Sant Jordi in particular did it very well. But for his untimely death he might have left something more than some of the most sincere and delicate of fifteenth-century verse.

The great poet of the century is however Ausias March (1397–1459), whose verse synthesizes uniquely the lyric tradition of the troubadours, scholastic philosophy and the *dolce stil nuovo*. From the troubadours he inherited the moralizing tendency apparent in the work of his father Pere March (*c.* 1338–1413) and others of the Toulouse and Barcelona schools; he inherited from the same source his verse form (the hendecasyllable), his sparingly used technical armoury of imagery and conceits (his similes were later much imitated), his typically medieval topics (attacks on love, on woman, on the world). To scholasticism he owes philosophical rigour and Christian integrity in his analysis of a self embodying so many painful contrasts and conflicts, partaking of the nature of both angel and animal, compounded of body and soul, selfishness and abnegation, virtue and vice. To the Italians, and especially to Dante, he is indebted for his idealization of a real love. He wrote in Catalan, the first poet to free himself entirely of Provençal linguistic influence.

March's 125 poems are intellectually very demanding; they contain an implacable analysis of the nature of human love, of the poet's and the beloved's thoughts and actions in their loving and the implications these have for the health of their souls. Love, religious faith and death are the mainsprings of March's verses, many of them concerned with a real illicit love for one Teresa Bou. Man's nature aspires to perfection, but his senses contrive to render its attainment impossible. Human love, potentially ennobling if purely spiritual, cannot remain pure; the senses inevitably triumph, the more easily because woman (by medieval definition) is incapable of spiritual love. A man's search for perfect human love is thus eternally frustrated by its very object, and this is the cause of the poet's torment. It is also the cause of a stoic joy, for pleasure can be found in an ennobling suffering; suffering in this context arises out of a willed rejection of the promptings of the body, and is an affirmation of man's spirituality. Release from suffering can be found only in death, longed for because it dissolves the bonds of the flesh (but not of love), feared because it is the end of life, of the exercise of the will and the understanding, and also because it brings God's judgement. In a series of poems written after Teresa died (towards the end of the poet's life) Ausias March is tormented by doubts and fears about her fate, by the thought that if she is in Hell it may be through his fault. His attitude to death is of course equivocal: he vilifies death for having destroyed the lovers' union, but death has spiritualized their love and the poet can embrace it intellectually without doubt or fear. Death will eventually unite them, and they will be able to experience together for the first time a perfect love. But will death bring also damnation?

This sombre and tormented poetry, deeply religious and intensely personal, humanistic in its preoccupation with human dignity, obsessive in its analysis of human emotion, remains strangely modern. It was imitated by the great Castilian poets of the Golden Age, and translated by (among others) Montemayor and Quevedo.

Febrer, Jordi de Sant Jordi and March were all Valencians; Valencian too was the last major poet of the fifteenth century, Joan Roíç de Corella (*fl.* 1460–1500), theologian and humanist. His fame as a humanist writer rests principally upon his elegant adaptations of classical myths from Ovid's *Metamorphoses* and *Heroides*, Seneca's tragedies and Boccaccio's *De claris mulieribus*; they take the form of short prose tales, of sentimental allegories, couched in an ornate classicized Catalan – *valenciana prosa*. Two successful examples are the *Plant dolorós de la reina Ècuba* and the *Història de Leànder i Hero*, but his most original and personal work in this style is the *Tragèdia de Caldesa*. The *Tragèdia*, composed like the *Leànder i Hero* in a decorated but always elegant rhetorical prose with intercalated verse, tells the apparently true story of Caldesa's unfaithfulness to Roíç de Corella. Although in this work the customary emotional and formal exaggeration of the prose set pieces seems to correspond to a real bitterness, and thus to confer upon it an unwonted sincerity, it is in his verse that the writer appears most sincere. It expresses more effectively because more economically his anger at Caldesa's betrayal. As a poet Roíç de Corella is as original as his predecessor Ausias March, but very different: less tortured, less introspective, more luminous and more musical within (still) the bounds of a basically Provençal hendecasyllable. Roíç de Corella is an elegant optimist. He also wrote theological works of some merit.

In the mid-century the Valencian doctor Jaume Roig (*fl.* 1434–78) wrote in 16,359 lines of *noves rimades* the *Spill* ('mirror'), at once an extended anti-feminist treatise and a forerunner of the picaresque novel. It enjoyed considerable popularity, and contributed greatly to the flowering of satirical literature in Valencia. The tale begins with the youthful narrator's being disowned by his newly widowed mother and setting off penniless to make his own way in life, and we follow him on his travels and in his encounters with a variety of human types and in particular with women – uniformly greedy, vain, egotistic, stupid and hypocritical. The young man is befriended by a number of protectors, and eventually (at the end of the first book) returns home as a prosperous knight after fighting against the English in France. The second book of the *Spill* tells of his disastrous marriages and near-marriages, ending with a bitter attack upon nuns. The third takes the form of a long anti-feminist disquisition by the uniquely experienced Solomon, who appears to the narrator in a dream to dissuade him from a projected marriage to a relative. The fourth and last book tells of the narrator's decision to give up his search for a wife and to settle down in Valencia to a life of good works. Jaume Roig admits before invoking the Virgin Mary that one earthly woman escapes all his strictures – his own wife.

More a novel than a poem, it is a metrical *tour de force* – over 1,600 lines like the following: 'Per llurs husances / axí diverses / he tan perverses / obres e manyes / són alimanyes; / serp tortuosa / són e rabosa, / mona, gineta, / talp, oroneta . . .' (The subject is woman.) Lexically extremely rich, syntactically no more forced – but for different reasons – than the humanistic prose of a Roíç de Corella, the work's originality lies in its novelistic technique and its vividly contemporaneous satirical descriptions of real people in real situations. It is of course a partial portrait only, but the more valuable for being one of a side of life that was neglected by the still essentially noble and courtly literature of Catalonia, by the contemporary poets and those refined spirits who cultivated the sentimental and the eternally popular chivalresque genres, by the religious moralists and the humanist translators and adaptors who equated art with beauty, by such indeed as the unknown author of *Curial e Güelfa*.

The anonymous novel *Curial e Güelfa* is a courtly amalgam of sentimental, humanistic and chivalresque elements within a typically Byzantine framework: the union of two lovers after many vicissitudes. It is a historical fiction, set in the late thirteenth century, and the author has used the chronicle of Desclot to lend it a certain verisimilitude, but otherwise it follows a typical enough course: Curial forced to leave the court and prove his love for Güelfa (who enters a nunnery) by chivalrous deeds, the love of a grateful lady Laquesis – which must be resisted – Güelfa's jealousy when rumours reach her ears, her maid becoming Curial's esquire, a defeated knight adopting a life of contemplation, Curial shipwrecked, the noble Tunisian maid Camar committing suicide for love of him, etc. There are allegorical episodes and a mythological dream, Aragonese and Catalan knights with Peter III 'el Gran', noble French ladies conversing saucily in a convent, psychological analyses recalling Boccaccio's *Fiammetta*, the *què us diré* audience-involvement trick of Muntaner, an anticipation of the Moorish novel – all betraying a multiplicity of influences upon a clearly widely read author. The style is precise and elegant, faintly Italianate. Such realism as the book possesses is a courtly realism, and this is a gentle book for the amusement of gentlefolk still living in a medieval world and accepting medieval values.

Much more vital, more rumbustious, is the chivalresque *Tirant lo blanc*, begun in 1460 by the Valencian Joanot Martorell (c. 1414–68), a member of the minor nobility related by marriage to Ausias March. The *Tirant* was in part reworked by Martí Joan de Galba prior to its printing in 1490, but the lack of any extant manuscripts makes it impossible to assess the precise nature and extent of his contribution. The novel was translated very early into Spanish and Italian, and used by Ariosto and Bandello; Cervantes's approval of the work is well known.

The *Tirant* is a long and complex work, the unifying figure being the eponymous hero. The first ninety-seven chapters are set in England, whither the young Breton noble Tirant goes to take part in the festivities and joustings attendant upon a royal wedding. In England he learns the theory of chivalry and after being knighted by the king excels in knightly pursuits, dispatching a number of noble adversaries. This first part of the book shows a debt to the thirteenth-century Anglo-Norman *Guy de Warwycke* (probably via a later French prosification), to Llull's *Libre de l'orde de cavalleria* and Honoré Bouvet's late fourteenth-century *Arbre des batailles*; it reflects Martorell's known inclinations, for he was himself much given to the exercise of arms. Chapters 98–114 find Tirant intervening in the affairs of Sicily and fighting against the infidel in Rhodes and elsewhere in the Mediterranean and Near East; the novel's setting has shifted to the real-life theatre of a conflict in which the Crown of Aragon was deeply involved, and Tirant has become a Christian knight and defender of the true faith. Chapters 115–296 are concerned with Tirant's fighting for the Emperor of Constantinople as captain-general. He routs the Grand Turk and the Sultan, conquers North Africa, and returns to Constantinople as the saviour of the Byzantine Empire. There he marries the emperor's daughter Carmesina and becomes the Caesar of the Empire. In the fourth and last part of the book, commonly supposed to be the work in whole or in part of Martí Joan de Galba, Tirant falls ill and dies, Carmesina dies of grief and the emperor likewise. Such is the brief outline of the story, wherein apart from the influences already mentioned (of a generally chivalresque doctrinal nature) there are visible those of Cerverí de Girona, Muntaner – especially in the Eastern episodes – Metge's *Somni* (heavily plagiarized) and the Italian humanists – whose major works were by Martorell's time available in Catalan translation. From these diverse elements and his own gifts of invention and narration Martorell constructed the novel which so excited Cervantes's admiration.

The traits which especially and unexpectedly distinguish the *Tirant lo blanc* are its comicality, its robust, Boccaccio-like sensuality, the very human dimension of its characters. The portrayal of the eccentric Byzantine court is a delight, for the scenes of amorous intrigue and dalliance which a moralizing writer (an Ausias March or a Jaume Roig) might have made seem decadent and disgusting are drawn here with a graceful and amused salacity that is quite disarming. Lovers may initially address each other in long humanistic *parlaments* worthy of (and possibly imitated by) a Roíç de Corella, but when they have accepted each other there is in their conversation and their behaviour an exuberant and healthy sexuality in which everyone joins, a Renaissance enjoyment of life quite unattended by any feelings of guilt. All this seems entirely natural. Martorell's benevolent and twinkling eye is evident too in the suitably comic names he gives some of his characters, and in the farcical situations that he creates: the terrifying giant Kirieleison de Muntalbà who dies of grief over the tomb of his dead lord, the sailor Cataquefaràs and the king Veruntamen, Carmesina's sexy maid Plaerdemavida, the aptly misnamed Viuda Reposada in her red drawers about to take a bath, the emperor chasing the ladies-in-waiting and the empress in love with a page. The author succeeds in showing that underneath their courtly disguise his characters are eminently human, and enjoy life; caricatured they may be, but the caricatures are not too far from reality – and no one is a symbol. Tirant is of course a perfect Christian knight, but he owes his success in battle at least partly to the fact that he does not easily run out of breath; when he has been in a fight he has to rest from his wounds like anyone else; when he has to leave Carmesina's bed precipitately he jumps out of a window and breaks his leg; and eventually he dies in bed from an illness. The setting of the major part of the novel in contemporary history, in the Mediterranean and Aegean theatre of war, also lends an air of verisimilitude to the novel.

The style is many-faceted, and Martorell alternates skilfully between the latinate *parlament* and the colloquial language of everyday conversation, full of life and vigour.

V Decadence

The *Spill, Curial e Güelfa* and *Tirant lo blanc* are three works which would seem to usher in a Golden Age of Catalan literature – but they are an end rather than a beginning: the Golden Age never materialized.

The fact that Catalan literature never took root among the people (there is no anonymous epic, no balladry, no theatre) but was above all a courtly phenomenon is the basic reason for its rapid decline. The union of the Crowns of Aragon and Castile, bringing with it the loss of a court in Barcelona, left a cultural vacuum, and the Italian viceregal courts were peopled increasingly by Castilians. That Catalan culture which had contributed so much to the spread of humanism in the Peninsula, and to which Castilian literature was indebted, became tributary to the Castilian.

Bibliography

GARCIA SILVESTRE, M. *Història sumària de la literatura catalana.* Barcelona, 1932.

MOLAS, J. *Literatura catalana antiga.* Vol. I: *El segle XIII.* Vol. III (1): *El segle XV.* Barcelona, 1961 and 1963.

OLWER, L. N. D'. *Literatura catalana: perspectiva general.* Barcelona, 1917. (Revised as *Resum de literatura catalana,* Barcelona, 1927.)

RIQUER, M. DE. *Història de la literatura catalana.* 3 vols. Barcelona, 1964.

——— *Resumen de literatura catalana.* Barcelona, 1947.

ROMEU, J. *Literatura catalana antiga.* Vol. II: *El segle XIV.* Vol. III (2): *El segle XV.* Barcelona, 1961 and 1964.

RUBIÓ BALAGUER, J. 'Literatura catalana'. In G. Díaz-Plaja (ed.), *Historia general de las literaturas hispánicas.* Vol. I, pp. 643–746. Vol. III, pp. 727–930. Barcelona, 1949 and 1953.

RUIZ I CALONJA, J. *Història de la literatura catalana.* Barcelona, 1954.

TERRY, A. *Catalan Literature.* London and New York, 1972.

8 Spanish Literature (1474–1681)

P. E. RUSSELL

I Introduction

The period of literature dealt with in this chapter begins with a political event – the accession of the Catholic Monarchs at the end of 1474. It ends, conventionally, with a date from literary history – the death, in 1681, of the last of the great writers of the seventeenth century – Calderón de la Barca. These dates are as arbitrary as dates imposed on literary history usually are. Nevertheless there are valid grounds for starting our period in 1474, though these are not the ones sometimes given: for example, the influence of Italian humanism and the Italian Renaissance did not make itself decisively felt in any of the arts in Spain during the reign of the Catholic Monarchs (see Chapter 6, section XI). But in their time the spread of printing radically altered the situation and potential influence of writers, providing them with readers and the possibility of fame on a scale impossible in the days when literature was disseminated in manuscript form. During the reign of Ferdinand and Isabella, Spanish culture generally, including literature and ideas – particularly religious ideas – became, too, strongly influenced by new though still medieval patterns of thought and taste originating in the Low Countries and in Germany.

The first two subheadings in this chapter are both associated with historical events – the reign of the Catholic Monarchs and the reign of Charles V. The reason for associating literature in the first half of the sixteenth century with the reign of Charles V is that, in literature and ideas as in politics, a certain internationalist, 'European' outlook which was never to return then prevailed. This sometimes led to results surprising to those who think of Spain as a place where orthodox thinking and a respect for traditional authority were deeply rooted.

The third subheading ('The Counter-Reformation') is concerned with the time of Philip II (1556–98) when Spain took up the militant defence of the new orthodoxies of the Council of Trent as well as of her own position as the dominant power in Europe.

After the death of Philip II it ceases to be appropriate to associate the literary history of Spain with particular reigns or specific external, non-literary forces. Literature became associated with the court – now established permanently in Madrid – as such rather than with the concerns and politics of individual rulers.

It is common among critics of Spanish literature of this period to refer to it as 'the Golden Age'. The use of the term seems to have its origin in a passing metaphor used in 1827 by a minor Romantic writer, Martínez de la Rosa. Like many attempts to encapsulate a complicated cultural phenomenon in a single lapidary phrase, this one, partly because of its emotive implications and its association in classical mythology with an age of peace, innocence and happiness, is probably more misleading than helpful. The use of such a term also implies, perhaps, that the literature of the whole period has a general unity which it does not, in fact, have. Some critics prefer the term 'Golden Century' ('Siglo de Oro') but are unable to agree among themselves when this started and ended. It would, however, now be merely eccentric to reject the term 'the Golden Age' outright as a descriptive phrase but the reader should regard it simply as shorthand for 'literature written during the sixteenth and seventeenth centuries'.

In the account that follows space has dictated a number of omissions. The literature of the Golden Age was poetically particularly rich but minor poets are not mentioned unless some distinctive feature of their work has seemed to justify their inclusion. Regretfully, too, any discussion of the many important historical chronicles written by Spaniards, both in Latin and in the vernacular during the period, has also had to be omitted, though a number of these are of interest to students of literature and ideas as well as to students of history. The drama between 1474 and 1681 has not been distributed among the subheadings under which prose, poetry and ideas are discussed because the history of the theatre at this time is more autonomous and less dependent on influences outside the dramatic tradition itself than are other forms of literature. Drama is therefore dealt with *en bloc* in the final subheadings of the present chapter.

II Literature in the Time of the Catholic Monarchs (1474–1516)

Forty-two years elapsed between the accession of the Catholic Monarchs, Ferdinand and Isabella, in 1474 and the death of Ferdinand in 1516 (Isabella had died in 1504). The air of novelty that seems, at first sight, to mark the arts during this period often turns out, when analysed, to be traceable to shifts of emphasis in and new influences from the medieval world-picture. These new intellectual influences and new ideas, plainly discernible in literature, painting, sculpture and architecture, mostly, in fact, came from northern Europe, not from across the Mediterranean.

Italian humanism was not, of course, totally without influence. An Italian humanist with wide influence in Spain was Pietro Martire d'Anghiera – Peter Martyr – (1459–1526) who arrived in 1487 and was invited by Queen Isabella to teach the Latin language and Latin literature to the young noblemen who served her there (see p. 240 above). Italian humanism, in so far as it was acceptable in Spain at all, had to come to terms with the entrenched beliefs and values of Spanish society at a time when Spaniards were full of national pride and self-confidence. It is perhaps significant that, in the end, Martyr became a priest, having concluded that, in Spain, that was the only way a man of letters could win respect. Antonio de Nebrija (1442–1522) was among all contemporary Spanish scholars the nearest in spirit to the Italian humanists because he was essentially, like them, a philologist who understood the importance of linguistic skill and textual criticism as the essential basis for the serious study of ancient texts. Lexicography, orthography, archaeology, cosmology and history were also among his concerns. His *Introductiones latinae* (1481) was an attempt to provide an up-to-date and scientific Latin grammar for students. His *Grámatica sobre la lengua castellana* (1492), using Latin models, sought to give a standard descriptive account of Spanish phonetics, orthography and syntax. But Nebrija was by no means an uncritical admirer of Italian humanism or of Italy. He expressed the view, to be repeated a good deal in sixteenth-century Spain, that there was something corrupting about Italian culture, and he eventually announced that he would devote the rest of his life to biblical scholarship at the University of Alcalá and did so. The general quality of Nebrija's scholarship has perhaps sometimes been overrated. His violent temperament, his ardent patriotism and his pride sometimes overcame his scholarly scruples.

It is noticeable that, in the time of the Catholic Monarchs, the most respected and most read Italian writers in Spain were the great figures of the Trecento, not those of the more radically humanistic Quattro-cento. Thus Dante's *Inferno* (1515), Boccaccio's *Decameron* (*Las cient novellas*, 1496) and Petrarch's *De remediis utriusque fortunae* (1510) were translated into Spanish, as was Petrarch's vernacular allegorical poem the *Trionfi* (1512). But Petrarch's more famous *Rime* were not.

Spanish interest in learning and scholarship in the time of the Catholic Monarchs clearly felt most at ease when it was motivated by religious and theological purposes. The Franciscan cardinal, Francisco Ximénez de Cisneros (1436–1517) – the most powerful political servant of Ferdinand and Isabella – founded a new university at Alcalá de Henares (opened 1510) to improve standards of theological training and to foster theological scholarship in Spain. Alcalá was, however, a centre of rather modest intellectual innovation in a general way. Its opinions were rather critical of traditional medieval scholastic theology, preferring the teaching of William of Occam (1280–1349), which accepted that there was an inescapable divorce between faith and reason and also tended to stress the importance of both intuitive know-ledge and the individual's personal experience. In an age when all men's thoughts were still largely dominated by religion, such innovations in the specialist field of theology naturally had wider consequences than we might suppose.

The scholars whom Cisneros appointed to teach at Alcalá were often men of real ability, some of whom won themselves a European reputa-tion. A surprising number were *conversos*. Their monument is the famous Polyglot Bible, splendidly printed at Alcalá (1514–17), which gave the Hebrew, Chaldean and Greek texts of the Old and New Testaments alongside the text of the Latin Vulgate version traditionally used. The Polyglot Bible made it plain to scholars that the Vulgate translation was often seriously in error. Cisneros was a harsh prophet of Spain's Messianic destiny, an unrelenting enemy of the Spanish Moors and Jews alike and a keen supporter of the Inquisition. But he also lent an ear to the Dutch reformer Desiderius Erasmus (1466–1536), and was not unsympathetic, either, to the prophetic dreams which enjoyed wide sympathy among some churchmen at this time and which foretold an imminent *Renovatio mundi* which would both transform the Church and overturn the established political order in the world to introduce the Christian millennium. Such heady ideas, which also had their roots deep in medieval tradition, help to explain the mood of religious zeal that characterized Spanish life, at court as much as anywhere else, during the time of the Catholic Monarchs.

These developments among the intellectual élite were paralleled by a striking ground swell, among all classes (clergy and laymen alike), of emotional, anti-intellectual, religious attitudes whose origins have not yet been fully explained. The Franciscan preachers of the Strict Observance certainly played a considerable part because of their influence both at court and with the people at large. But the movement also owed quite a lot to the popular pietism that flourished at this time in northern Europe and was fed by vernacular versions of the New Testament and by Spanish translations of handbooks of private pietism like the *Imitation of Christ* (Sp. translation first printed 1490) – said to be the most widely read printed book in all Europe – and the *Vita Christi* of Ludolph of Saxony, translated by the Franciscan poet Fray Ambrosio Montesino (d. *c.* 1520). Poetry was particularly affected by this new religious spirit.

The secular poetry of the age is well represented in the *Cancionero general* (1511), edited by Hernando del Castillo, which contains the work of some two hundred poets, mostly of the fifteenth century. Their love poetry remains entirely faithful to the late medieval traditions of the genre. It is concerned with the permutations of courtly love, often presented in a style that lays much value on a rhetoric of paradox and conceit. The best poems of Juan del Encina (1468–1530) are to be found in his much reprinted *Cancionero* (1496). He was a skilled musician and his short, graceful lyrics, often developments of popular poems, were written to be sung. A large number of the melodies Encina wrote for them survive. They remind us that, in the time of the Catholic Monarchs (and, indeed, for a long time afterwards), lyric poetry in Spain as elsewhere was normally composed to be sung, and this essential fact often explains why poetry took the paths it did.

A feature of Spanish poetry at this time, too, was the imaginative and artistic skill that went into the writing of satirical verse and parody – also a feature of poetry in the Golden Age generally. One of the most original poets of this kind was Rodrigo de Reinosa (*fl. c.* 1490–*c.* 1520) whose works survive only in the little chapbooks (*pliegos sueltos*) through which medium printers distributed cheaply collections of popular poems and other literature. Reinosa's most ambitious and most successful piece of comic satire is his *Coplas de las comadres* in which, in dialogue form, he gives new life to the medieval literary tradition of anti-feminism, painting the snobbery, malice, deceits, envy and worse of a number of low-class women, some of whom are bawds and petty witches. The social background in which the *comadres* live is skilfully suggested. Reinosa's chief originality lay in his ability to listen to popular language and to convert it into controlled literary dialogue.

The great fifteenth-century poet and bibliophile, the Marquis of Santillana, had thought the ballads sung by the people to be, because of their lack of formal complication, fit only for the illiterate. In the time of the Catholic Kings, however, ballads came to be accepted at court and by men of letters as well as by court composers of chamber music. These professional musicians provided the ballads with far more complicated musical settings than those used by the people. Ballads were now sung at court by trained singers to lute and viol (*vihuela*) music. In adapting them for their new role the traditional themes of popular Spanish balladry were, however, kept, as was their characteristic form and style. The acceptance by the court of Ferdinand and Isabella, and by the cultured classes generally, of the ballads as part of the national literary tradition was to have notable consequences for the history of Golden Age literature generally. This phenomenon, like the acceptance of popular lyric poetry – religious and secular – reveals how far away general literary taste in Spain in the time of Ferdinand and Isabella was from the literary standards of the Italian humanists who had regarded popular literature as barbaric – and trivial as well. But it helped to make Spanish literature truly national and conserved a source of poetic inspiration in terms of themes, forms and techniques that (even if its worth has been somewhat overvalued) maintained an almost continuous link between professional literature and folk literature.

Prose romance was extensively cultivated during the reign of the Catholic Monarchs. One of its forms was the courtly romance, misleadingly described by some critics as the 'sentimental' romance or, even more misleadingly, as the 'sentimental novel'. These often oddly Kafkaesque studies, which have a very small centre of gravity, deal with the feelings and actions of lovers caught up in extreme situations deriving from the dialectic of courtly love and are set in a narrow context of tense melodrama, violence and gratuitous cruelty and often acquire a nightmare quality for which the English label 'sentimental' seems particularly inappropriate. Diego de San Pedro (*fl. c.* 1490) was the most famous Spanish writer of courtly romance. More important than his *Arnalte y Lucenda* (1491) was his *Cárcel de amor* (1492) which went into well over twenty editions in Spanish and was translated into various other languages. Its account of the ill-fated relationship of Leriano and Laureola explores the dialectical possibilities to be extracted from a study of a pair of lovers doomed to frustration and unhappiness, and eventually death, by the operations of the code of courtly love. Like most of these works, it is set in an atemporal and geographically merely notional context – as are the romances of chivalry, a genre with which, in its treatment of love, the courtly romance has considerable affinities. In a curious way the *Cárcel de amor*, presenting a royal father who sees family honour and reputation as more important than paternal love, anticipates the treatment of extreme problems of honour that made Calderón famous nearly 200 years later. The tragedies of the courtly romances are essentially fake tragedies arising out of a casuistical treatment of the doctrines of courtly love but they do attempt to present a detailed analysis of the feelings of characters enmeshed in the love situation.

The time of the Catholic Monarchs also saw, thanks to the invention of printing, the emergence of the medieval romance of chivalry as the most avidly read of all the forms of secular literature available to Spanish readers; chivalric romance was to go on enjoying this position in Spain through most of the sixteenth century. The popularity of the genre reflects the continuing allegiance in real life of the ruling élites of Europe to the twin medieval ideologies of chivalry and courtly love. A feature of the romances of chivalry is their ritualistic character; the very repetition of situation and event in one romance after another, which modern readers are liable to find tedious, was clearly an important source of satisfaction to their earlier readers. Another feature of the best of them is the depth of emotion they achieve in portraying the feelings of their larger-than-life warriors and lovers in the latters' struggles against the forces of evil, symbolically presented, that constantly threaten their prowess and honour and the purity of their love. One may suspect that part of the sense that the romances were in some way immoral that troubled sixteenth-century churchmen so much may have arisen from a feeling that these books stirred their readers' emotions in a way that trespassed on areas of feeling the Church wanted reserved for religious emotions. The first chivalric romances printed in Spain at this time were nearly all Arthurian or Carolingian tales that had previously been translated into Spanish to circulate in manuscript form – *El baladro del sabio Merlín* (1498), the *Demanda del Sancto Grial* (1515), *Lanzarote del Lago* (1515) or the Carolingian *Paris e Viana* (c. 1494) and *Enrique fi de Oliva* (1498). Popular, too, was the *Estoria del noble*

Vespasiano (*c. 1490*) – concerned with the Jews and Pontius Pilate – and *Oliveros de Castilla y Artus del Algarbe* (1499). The first chivalric romance known to have been printed in Spain was, in fact, the Catalan *Tirant lo blanc* (1490), a very popular book for a century or so, which, however, interpreted the chivalric ethic and the love motif with an attention to historical reality and an erotic emphasis that separate it from the general tradition. It was not imitated by others. The most famous romance of chivalry printed in the time of the Catholic Monarchs was *Amadís de Gaula* (first surviving edition 1508, but probably preceded by a lost edition of 1496). Already in existence in the fourteenth century, it consisted, in the early fifteenth century, of three books and was rewritten at the end of that century by García Rodríguez de Montalvo, who set out to update the famous story stylistically and linguistically. Rodríguez de Montalvo himself added a whole new book. Though in *Amadís de Gaula*, as in all the chivalric romances, action predominates at the expense of reflectiveness, the work, written in an elevated but concise and consistent style, is distinguished by its controlled inventiveness, guiding its readers without confusion through a labyrinth of interwoven adventures. Those who, in the real medieval world, were sacramentally received into the order of chivalry undertook to protect women and children, the unfortunate and the weak, to defend virtue, to be unfailingly loyal and courageous, and to wage war on the wicked, the arrogant and the disloyal – undertakings which in real life were, of course, like the precepts of Christianity, constantly broken. The romances represented, in some sense, a fictional fulfilment substitute through which people could live the ideals that human frailty denied them.

During the time of the Catholic Monarchs the publication began of the series of sequels to *Amadís* (e.g. *Sergas de Esplandián*, 1510, *Florisando*, 1510, *Lisuarte de Grecia*, etc.). A rival cycle – the *Palmerín* cycle – started with the publication of *Palmerín de Oliva* (1511). The work of creating new romances went on in Spain through most of the sixteenth century and nearly all found foreign translators. The romances never, as is often said, lost the attention of Spanish readers. Towards the end of the sixteenth century, however, they were no longer expensively printed but circulated instead in cheap chapbook selections. The tales nevertheless still delighted. They provided themes for a number of seventeenth-century playwrights and poets. The vogue of the romances of chivalry, in Spain as elsewhere, serves to remind us of the hold that certain medieval ideas and medieval life-styles still had on Renaissance

Europe. Even if we find the romances of no great interest today it is important for students of Golden Age literature not to forget that these works represented a substantial amount of the secular reading of many of the writers of that time whose works we still regard highly.

The general pattern of Spanish literature in the time of the Catholic Kings is, we have seen, mainly one of innovation within distinctively medieval traditions and attitudes. Yet by far and away the most important literary work written in Spain at this time lies largely quite outside any medieval literary or religious traditions and had, in any significant sense, only the slenderest historical links with anything previously found in Spanish literature. In 1499, printed at Burgos, there appeared the first version of the story of Calisto and Melibea (*Comedia de Calisto y Melibea*) – a prose work written entirely in dialogue or monologue form which, though divided into sixteen 'acts' of varying length, was plainly not intended for the stage. Its plot is quite simple. It traces the multiple personal disasters that ensued when a young nobleman, Calisto, lost all reason and sense of responsibility as a result of a violent physical passion he conceived for a noble young lady, Melibea. Rejected by her, he turned, on the advice of an unfaithful servant, Sempronio, to a notorious convicted procuress and witch, Celestina, to secure her aid in procuring Melibea. Celestina, using witchcraft as well as the knowledge of the sexual psychology of women collected by a lifetime's experience in her trade, was successful and the lovers, in the *Comedia*, briefly enjoyed the physical fruits of their passion, forgetful of all social and family obligations. But death overtakes all the main figures in the work. Celestina herself is murdered by Calisto's two servants, Sempronio and Pármeno, because her avarice blinds her for once to what is going on in the minds of others. Sempronio and Pármeno are hastily put to death for the murder. Calisto falls to his death when leaving his assignation with Melibea. Melibea commits suicide from grief, causing her mother's death from shock. The work ends with the lamentation of her father Pleberio against the death-dealing force of passion and the irrational operations of human destiny, expressed in an ambiguous form that hints that God himself is the destroyer of his own creatures. But the originality and power of the work lies not in its plot but in the unprecedented depth of its analysis of character and in the unconventional way in which the subject-matter is treated. In 1502 the work appeared under a new title – the *Tragicomedia de Calisto y Melibea*. Five new acts had been interpolated between Acts

XIV and XV of the original *Comedia* and other additions made to the 1499 text. In the *Comedia* Calisto had fallen to his death immediately after he and Melibea had sexually consummated their passion for the first time. One of the consequences of the interpolation of the five new acts was to extend the period of their love-making by a month – a change said to be demanded by the readers of the *Comedia*. This change altered the whole balance of the work by removing the swift dénouement. It also permitted the introduction of a splendidly drawn new character, the braggart soldier Centurio – to modern readers probably the only wholly comic character in the tale. The change of title was also explained as a response to the views of the readers of the *Comedia*, who thought it improper to categorize as comedy a work that ended tragically.

Most of the original *Comedia*, as well as the additions that went into the making of the *Tragicomedia*, were the work of a law graduate, Fernando de Rojas (d. 1541), who wrote it while still studying at Salamanca University. The influence of Roja's legal training on the content of the book is greater than has usually been recognized. Rojas, however, only claimed to be the work's co-author, declaring that he had found a manuscript of the first act (by an unknown author) in Salamanca. Act I is of enormously greater length than the subsequent acts. In it all the main characters are introduced and clearly delineated and the plot firmly launched. This act differs linguistically and in other ways from that part of the book for which Rojas claimed authorship and, though Rojas had a penchant for mystification, it is quite likely that the author of Act I was, as he asserted, not himself. Fernando de Rojas – a *converso*, that is a Christian of Jewish descent – was a native of Puebla de Montalbán (prov. of Toledo), and some of his near relatives were in serious trouble with the Inquisition on heresy charges. But he himself was a successful lawyer in the important town of Talavera de la Reina and held public office there before he died over forty years after his book was first published. Despite the European fame of the work he never wrote anything else.

The external ambiguities that surround the *Tragicomedia* are accompanied by ambiguity about the author's (or authors') intentions. One major cause of ambiguity is certainly the dialogue form. Except, perhaps, in the last part of the final act (in the monologue of Pleberio), no author's spokesman is present. The author, whose use of both dramatic and comic irony is masterly, hit on the idea of overcoming this exclusion by putting traditional moral and other opinions in the mouths of his characters, even when their actual acts or intentions were flagrantly at variance with their utterances on such matters – a device that, of course, adds to the ambiguity.

The model for the form (and to some extent for the content) of the *Tragicomedia* was a minor literary genre used by the Italian humanists of the fifteenth century – the humanistic comedy in Latin. This, closely connected with the universities, was written in the tradition of Roman comedy. But the genre, a lightweight one, is totally transcended in the Spanish book which explores human psychology and the forces that form and motivate behaviour to a depth not previously achieved in literature. Another important influence is that of Petrarch's Latin works but it has been noted that Rojas glosses his borrowed Petrarchan material in a more pessimistic way than Petrarch himself did. In the text of the book there is, remarkably, no suggestion that Christian teaching or Christian belief has anything to offer its characters. Indeed, the only figure from the Christian world who plays a role in it is that of the devil summoned by the witch Celestina from Hell to assist her in the procuring of Melibea. Priests, monks and nuns do not appear in the work as named characters but are mentioned as among the bawd Celestina's most enthusiastic customers. Another unusual feature of the book is its openminded attitude to its characters, who are not depicted as either wholly good or wholly bad. Even in the case of Celestina herself, it is pointed out that she is what she is because of the milieu of hunger and poverty into which she had been born. There is a complete avoidance of any desire to make the characters conform to traditional literary types and they often show unexpected traits of character or unexpected insights into themselves. Instead of presenting Pleberio to us as the vengeful, honour-conscious, noble father that both literary tradition and contemporary social opinion demanded, Rojas is content to show Pleberio as simply broken by grief over the death of a loved daughter whose breaches of the sexual code he treats as the consequence of forces outside her control. The work is, however, not by any means all serious. The straightforwardly comic, as well as irony, plays an important part in it and its earliest readers certainly found it funnier than the modern reader easily can. But its laughter is very much a form of unconscious whistling into the wind of·impending disaster. A close study of the book discloses that it was very carefully structured, the author having a clear idea of what was going to happen to his characters well in advance of events.

The *Tragicomedia* has sometimes been described as 'realistic'. It is true that it conveys, in a very vivid way, the *illusion* of reality lived in an everyday social milieu. Through the device of making the characters from time to time mention some new fact or series of facts relating to their past history they are gradually provided with fully explained roots in society as individuals. But we are not offered a naturalistic depiction of reality. Thus, though a lot of the dialogue is full of popular turns of phrase and popular proverbs and *exempla*, a very great deal of it, too, is written in highly unnaturalistic speech that achieves its effects by the use of the techniques of Latin rhetorical theory. Exactly how far this famous book indirectly reflects the social situation in Spain in the time of the Catholic Monarchs is a point on which critics are unable to agree. In addition to the suggestion of a close association with the situation of the *conversos* at that time it has also been seen as reflecting general economic and social changes of a wider character that occurred then. But its great popularity outside Spain – long after the reign of Ferdinand and Isabella, as well as during it – and the comments of foreign readers, suggest that it was seen as a universal work of literature that happened to be written in Spanish. It was enormously influential in sixteenth- and seventeenth-century Spanish literature, being repeatedly reprinted and imitated. The direct imitations (in which, as in the case of chivalric romance, the purpose is to continue the story either forwards or backwards) notably tend to stress the comic side of the *Tragicomedia* and to put the emphasis on its low-life characters. The subtlest aspects of Rojas's literary art escaped his imitators. The best of these imitations is probably Sancho de Muñón's *Tragicomedia de Lisandro y Roselia* (1542), but several of the others represent, during the time of Charles V, an important tradition of realistic writing too often ignored by students of fiction in the sixteenth century partly because its form – the dialogue – was later supplanted by narrative prose fiction and, no doubt, partly because of an assumption that imitations are necessarily an inferior kind of literature. This was not a point of view that would have been understood by sixteenth-century readers or critics.

III Literature and Empire (1516–1556)

The accession to the Spanish throne in 1516 of Charles of Habsburg (Holy Roman Emperor from 1519) provides an illustration of the way in which political change at the top can have a major effect on the climate of ideas and, through them, on literature. Charles's accession was regarded with some dismay by many Spaniards. Brought up at the

Burgundian court, unable to speak Spanish and, when he first visited Spain in 1517, surrounded by Flemish and other foreign counsellors, he and his officials were seen as a threat to Spanish national pride and liberties and to traditional Spanish values. The Spaniards, who wanted a Spanish king, found themselves, instead, confronted by a ruler whose representative in the Cortes of Castile called him emperor of the world, whose closest advisers were dedicated to Caesarism and who thought of Spain mainly in terms of her financial and military value to the operations of imperial policy in Europe. The fears of the traditionalists were confirmed in the cultural field by the sudden and surprising enthusiasm that now developed among an important minority of Spaniards, under the aegis of the imperial court, for the ideas and attitudes associated with the name of the Dutch humanist Desiderius Erasmus (1466–1536), a figure soon to be regarded by the orthodox as the man who had done most to open the way for the spread of Lutheranism in Europe.

To understand the meaning of the Spanish Erasmian movement it is necessary to study not just the writings of Erasmus's Spanish disciples but the works of Erasmus himself, for many of the latter, translated into Spanish, enjoyed great popularity in Spain. The ground for Erasmian reformism had been prepared by the spread, in the time of the Catholic Monarchs, of that popular, emotive pietism (itself much influenced by contemporary religious thought and practice in northern Europe) discussed in the previous section. Erasmus's work was concerned with supplying a coherent intellectual and doctrinal framework of ideas in tune with these pietistic tendencies of his age. What he stood for was a Pauline Christianity, drawing its authority from the Gospels. This stressed the need for the individual Christian to find his own way to God by private prayer and meditation and by the study of the Scriptures – in vernacular translation if needs be. Erasmus, too, rejected the notion of any kind of separation between the everyday life of a Christian and his religious life. He attached no great importance to the institutional traditions of the Church or to outward religious observances. These opinions were set out in his famous treatise, *Enchiridion militis christiani* (*The Manual of a Christian Knight*), published in Latin in 1515. This book became a best-seller in Spain after its appearance in Spanish in 1526 in a translation dedicated to the Inquisitor-General, Alonso Manrique. It ran to at least eight editions there by 1530. The *Enchiridion* contained the famous phrase *monachatus non est pietas* ('piety does not reside in a monk's cowl') which summed up his relentless criticism of the religious orders (including the Franciscans) whom he accused of hypocrisy, greed and vanity.

The political appeal of Erasmus's ideas to Charles V and his entourage lay in the humanist's attacks on the papacy for its corruption, its desire to play the part of a temporal power and its readiness to use war as an instrument of political policy. Christian rulers who regarded it as valid to make war on each other were also denounced in the *Querela pacis* (1516; Spanish translation 1520).

But Erasmus's writings challenged many other traditional assumptions. He ceaselessly satirized the methods and ideas of the scholastic theologians who still controlled theological and philosophical thinking in Europe's universities, regarding their disputations and preoccupations as irrelevant to the business of the Christian life. For him true wisdom was to be found in the Scriptures and it was to them, not to Aristotle or the theologians, to whom the Christian must turn, in the final resort, for divine wisdom and authority. Yet Erasmus was no fundamentalist. He was a student of the languages, thought and literature of the ancient world. But, in his view, the only justification for humanistic studies was that, properly used, they could help to make better Christians of modern men.

Erasmus introduced a new kind of committed literature to Europe, since everything he wrote was intended to serve a propagandist purpose and much of his writing had the immediacy of journalism; yet his attention to form and style and to the writing of convincing dialogue, as well as his sense of fictional reality, plainly represent literary values too. His favourite tool for making known his opinions was the dialogue. Here, in a rapidly sketched realistic setting, he would put to work various speakers, some representing his views, others those of his opponents, to discuss dialectically the matters in hand. Irony is a constant feature of Erasmus's style of polemical writing. He did not trouble to play fair with the representatives of the opinions or institutions he wished to criticize. He wrote in rapid, concise, unadorned prose – the antithesis of the rounded Ciceronian periods of the Italian humanists.

Both the Spanish court and the new University of Alcalá gave powerful protection to the views of Erasmus from about 1520 onwards. Priests and scholars of *converso* origin were notable among the Spanish Erasmians because, perhaps, they were prime targets for the suspicion and dislike of the traditionalists in Church and State. But, despite the angry protests of the Dominicans and other religious orders, the

Erasmians, who numbered high officials of the Inquisition and some imperial secretaries among their ranks, at first encountered little resistance.

The greatest Spanish thinker produced by the Erasmian movement was Juan Luis Vives (1492-1540), regarded by other European humanists of his day as the equal of Erasmus himself, or of Budé. But Vives was a citizen of Europe rather than of Spain. When he left his native Valencia in 1509 to study in Paris it was for good. He was of *converso* origin – a fact he took great pains to hide – and it has recently been established that his father was burnt for heresy in 1524 while, in 1529, the bones of his long-deceased mother were dug up and incinerated because the Inquisition found her guilty, *post mortem*, of being a Judaizer. Vives was, perhaps, not very outstanding as an abstract thinker but, in the Erasmian way, his experimental and inductive approach to particular problems often produced ideas and intentions well ahead of his time. His *De anima et vita* (1538) thus exalts the power of man's will which, when guided by reason, he describes as mistress and lord of all human acts. Vives claimed that the will was totally at liberty to decide freely between alternative courses of action – an opinion that explains his lack of sympathy for Lutheranism. His treatise *De subventione pauperum* (1526), remarkably for his times, urged that the poor and the aged deserved both sympathy and charity – while, at the same time, expressing his belief in the therapeutic value of hard work, even for the old. He was even more ahead of his times when he denounced as inhumane the accepted view that madmen were figures of fun and demanded compassion and kindness from society for them. One of his most influential treatises was his *De institutione foeminae christianae* (1524) – first translated into Spanish in 1528. This work's attitude to women before and after marriage deviated from traditional misogynist attitudes. It challenged the view that the sole or principal function of marriage was procreation, seeing it as a special spiritual relationship. In this book Vives made his severest attacks on chivalric and other romances and on literature of entertainment generally, including *La Celestina*. In his *Adversus pseudodialecticos* (1520) he continued the Erasmian attack on scholasticism and on the barbarous Latin of the schools. The treatise *De disciplinis* (1531) surveys the whole field of contemporary learning and its defects. Vives's attitude to pagan literature and learning both harked back to the *eruditio moralis* of early Italian humanism and foreshadowed the attitudes of the Jesuit *Ratio studiorum* to classical studies. The pagan authors should, he said, be approached like meadows, beautiful to the eye but bearing some noxious plants against which the visitor should carry a proper provision of antidotes.

Spanish Erasmianism at work on behalf of the political aims of Charles V can be seen in the works of one of the imperial secretaries, Alfonso de Valdés (c. 1490–1532). His *Diálogo de las cosas acaecidas en Roma* defended the sack of Rome by Charles V's armies in 1527, presenting this event as a judgement of God on the papal curia 'and on all churchmen in general' for their belligerency and corruption and for ignoring the warnings of men like Erasmus. The *Diálogo de Mercurio y Carón* (c. 1529) is, basically, also a defence of imperial policy in Europe but the scope of the piece is extended to embrace a general satirical and doctrinal attack on the dedication of establishment Christianity to an outward observance of religious practices rather than to 'true' Christianity. The style of Valdés's satirical writing owes much to Erasmus, particularly in its successful attempt to imitate the tone of private conversation and in its ability to maintain an ironical and comic stance even when his characters are making points about which Valdés himself felt very deeply.

His brother, Juan de Valdés (d. c. 1541), was a much more radical figure who devoted himself largely to strictly religious matters and who spent his life, after 1531, as a religious exile in Italy. His *Diálogo de doctrina cristiana* (Alcalá, 1529) – the only work of his printed in Spain in his lifetime – was dedicated to the Marquis of Villena. It preaches the Erasmian doctrines of interior Christianity but with additional overtones that suggest an underlying sympathy with some Lutheran doctrines, particularly that of justification by faith. The work contains some savage attacks on the clergy and particularly on the Dominicans, whose preachers are described as misusers of the Scriptures and deceivers of the people. In Italy he wrote his *Ciento y diez consideraciones divinas* (c. 1540, first published in Italian in Basle in 1550), a work (the Spanish original is lost) which was destined to exercise considerable influence on some areas of Protestant thought in Europe. Here the illuminist tendencies of the *Diálogo de doctrina cristiana* were much further developed. A work in a much more conventional Erasmian vein was his *Diálogo de la lengua* (written in Naples c. 1535), intended to help his Italian friends improve their Spanish. It reveals a desire to formulate a norm for cultured Spanish that would be concise, simple and free from all forms of stylistic affectation while, at the same time, subtle and plastic enough to cope with any intellectual demands made on it. He offered as an example of the best in existing Spanish prose the translation of Erasmus's *Enchiridion*, whose translator had, in fact, made considerable use of the language of vernacular preachers. Valdés found some merits in some of the Spanish romances of chivalry (which he admitted to having read avidly over a long period when he was a young man). He also wrote some penetrating praise and criticism of *La Celestina*. A feature of this book is the authority which it gives to popular Spanish proverbs as examples of the language in its pure and natural state.

Space does not permit a discussion of the work of the other Erasmian scholars and the other minor Erasmian figures. Mention should, however, be made of an extraordinary piece of prose fiction, *El Crotalón*, written about 1552 but not published until modern times. It has sometimes been attributed, probably wrongly, to the mildly Erasmian humanist Cristóbal de Villalón. The *Crotalón*, cast on the author's own authority in the form of a Lucianesque dialogue in twenty-one prose *cantos* in which a cock tells a shoemaker all he has seen of life and comments on it, is a confused, very prolix and often derivative but powerful piece of fictional writing where the emphasis is on description. The *Crotalón* is, at times, violently anti-clerical in a crude and bitter way that the Spanish Erasmists usually avoided. Another book of the time, *El Viaje de Turquía*, perhaps written by an Erasmian doctor and scholar, Andrés de Laguna (*fl. c.* 1551–9), is notable for its convincing account of Turkey and the eastern Mediterranean which the author knew only from books. It shows a determination to tell the truth about the Turks in a way that challenged the comfortable religious and patriotic myths of Spaniards. The author's Erasmianism is revealed whenever anything pertaining to Christianity is discussed. It contains some first-rate pieces of comic writing.

The novelty and the very unexpectedness of the Erasmian movement in Spain, usually thought of as a conservative bastion of orthodox religion, should not cause us to overrate its significance, though the existence of the movement disposes of any notion that Spain, in the early decades of the sixteenth century, was unaffected by the religious upheaval that then convulsed Europe. But as soon as Charles V, in the mid-1530s, had been forced by the rise of Lutheranism to reach an accommodation with the papacy and consequently withdrew his support from the Erasmian reformers, it was only a question of time before the immense underlying strength of orthodox religion in Spain reasserted itself. The Indexes of 1551 and 1559 largely put an end to the availability of Erasmus's works and those of his followers in Spain.

What this suppression could not do was to change at once the intellectual and literary attitudes of the generation which had been formed by the Erasmian movement.

It would be a grave error to presume that Spanish thinkers who were actively opposed to Erasmian ways of thinking in the time of Charles V were all merely obscurantists. Thus Fray Luis de Carvajal's defence of monasticism against Erasmian attack (*Apologia monasticae religionis*, 1528) was a telling and intelligent attack on Erasmian doctrines and on the personal position of Erasmus himself. There were other orthodox thinkers of religious and lay secular importance to the history of ideas whose work lay in other fields. Such a one was the Dominican Fray Francisco de Vitoria (1486–1546), scarcely the founder of international law he is sometimes claimed to be, but certainly a notable contributor to that subject and to the problem of the rights of the Spanish crown in the Indies and the rights of the Indians. Vitoria's methods of argument were scholastic but it was a new scholasticism purified by humanism, based directly on the *Summa theologica* of St Thomas Aquinas and concerned to serve practical social ends. Unlike Vitoria, his fellow Dominican, Fray Bartolomé de Las Casas (1474–1566), who devoted his life to the cause of the Indians of America against the Spanish colonists, knew at first hand what American conditions were like. His *Destrucción de las Indias* (1552) gave rise to violent polemics.

The name of the humanist Juan Ginés de Sepúlveda (1491–1573) is indissolubly linked with that of Las Casas because he was the latter's chief opponent in the arguments that convulsed governmental and religious circles in Charles V's time about the Spanish crown's rights to make war on the American Indians and to enslave them. Sepúlveda's real importance in the history of Spanish thought, however, lies elsewhere. After studying at Alcalá he went to Italy where he worked under Pietro Pomponazzi and became one of the leading authorities on Aristotle in Europe, pointing out errors in the existing commentaries and himself translating various books of Aristotle anew from Greek into Latin. His international repute as an Aristotelian scholar is shown by the fact that many of his works were first published in Italy or in Paris. Just as the Erasmians had thought that Plato should be numbered among the precursors of Christian thought, so Sepúlveda expressed the opinion that Aristotle must be numbered among the saved.

For the moment, though, it was more Plato who attracted the interest of laymen and whose thought had a good deal of direct influence on literature. Historians of ideas claim as Spanish, on somewhat dubious grounds, the exposition of Platonic ideas known as the *Dialogues on Love* by the Portuguese Jewish doctor, Jehudah Abravanel (*c.* 1470–1521), better known as Leone Ebreo. His family had fled to Spain in the 1480s after being involved in a conspiracy of the magnates against John II of Portugal. But Jehudah, as a professing Jew, was forced to leave Spain in 1492. The *Dialogues* (completed by 1502) were first published in Italian in Italy after his death (*Dialoghi d'amore*, 1535). The three dialogues, between Philo (Love) and Sophia (Wisdom), are uncompromisingly metaphysical in character. Though it was Leone Ebreo's purpose to reconcile the doctrines of Aristotle and the medieval Jewish philosophers with the doctrines of Plato, it is with Platonism, and in particular with the Platonic doctrine of love as the element that binds the universe together, with which he was most concerned. The work was to be very frequently cited and quoted from by Spanish poets and other writers, including writers of pastoral romance. An influential and highly urbane source of information about the Platonic doctrines of love was Castiglione's *Il Cortegiano* (see pp. 285-6 below), a work made available in Spanish thanks to the poets Juan Boscán and Garcilaso de la Vega.

It would be a mistake to suppose that, in the time of Charles V, Spanish readers' tastes were all on the high level so far discussed in this section. The emperor himself was a devotee of chivalry and a keen reader of chivalric romance. The latter's popularity as literature of entertainment continued unabated in Charles's reign. Continuations of the *Amadís* cycle were published (e.g. *Amadís de Grecia*, 1530; *Florisel de Niquea*, 1532), as were those of the *Palmerín* cycle (*Platir*, 1533). The most famous of the *Palmerín* volumes, *Palmerín de Inglaterra*, was first written in Portuguese (Spanish translation, 1547). There were many others. More difficult to understand today is the immense popularity, not only in Spain but in all Europe, of the prose writings of Antonio de Guevara (1480-1545), Bishop of Mondoñedo. His *Libro áureo del emperador Marco Aurelio* (1528) was later incorporated into his *Reloj de príncipes* (1539). The *Reloj* was intended for the instruction of princes and moved on the level of fairly commonplace moralizing that Guevara specialized in. In these as in his other works Guevara exploited the fashion for classical erudition by purveying it indiscriminately in large quantities; quite often, indeed, it was simply invented by him. His mind was essentially medieval, his notions of the ancient world being derived from a disorderly reading of various works, including some discarded sources like Walter Burley. The apocryphal, anecdotal quality of Guevara's writing as well as his brilliant capacity to invent lies are also to be seen in his *Epístolas familiares* (I, 1539; II, 1541), supposedly directed by Guevara to various important people. They are not real letters but rhetorical exercises enabling him to comment on a great miscellany of historical, scholarly and other matters. Guevara's popularity was due in part to his convoluted style. This was far removed from the stylistic ideals of the Erasmians. It is characterized by the use of antitheses, inversions, amplifications and digressions derived, probably, from traditional preachers' rhetoric. Another more reliable popularizer of the ancient world was Pedro Mexía (1497–1551) who also enjoyed a European reputation in his day. But his contemporary fame rested mainly on his *Silva de varia lección* (1540), a work reprinted some seventeen times in sixteenth-century Spain. The existence and popularity of encyclopedic works like those of Guevara and Mexía (as well as others of non-Spanish origin) should be remembered. These compilations (sometimes helpfully indexed) made it easy for authors in a hurry to display an erudition acquired with the minimum of effort.

New ground was broken in the history of Spanish prose fiction with the anonymous publication (1554) of a little work called *Lazarillo de Tormes*, the earliest of the Spanish tales of roguery (or delinquency, as a recent critic has it). *Lazarillo de Tormes* is the immediate though distant ancestor of the picaresque novel that came into being in Spain at the end of the sixteenth century. It is not true to suppose that realistic prose fiction depicting lower-class as well as upper-class life was not available to the reader of Charles V's time. This existed in the ever-popular *La Celestina* and its imitations. Francisco Delicado's *La lozana andaluza* (1528) is also an original work of realistic prose fiction in dialogue. The dialogue form in which these works were all cast, however skilfully handled, placed limits on the scope and tone an author could allow himself. The originality of *Lazarillo de Tormes* lay in its adoption of an autobiographical narrative form, the protagonist himself supposedly relating what had happened to him since childhood. The book, like many others written in Spain in the time of Charles V, achieved European fame.

The tale is an account of how an inexperienced boy from the lowest ranks of society learns by hard experience to trick and cheat his way upwards to what seems to him to be success and security as town-crier of Toledo – in reality a post regarded as socially despicable. In exchange for this final security he has to submit complacently to being cuckolded by an archpriest. Structurally the work is episodic, being written in short (sometimes very short) *tratados*, each concerned with some of Lazarillo's experiences with a series of masters. It is not realistic in the sense that everything is accounted for. The work plainly reflects sixteenth-century European interest in rogues and beggars and much of its material is taken from popular literary tradition – including the name of the protagonist, his career as the boy of a blind beggar, the fraudulent *buldero* and the famous character of the penniless *escudero* whose servant he becomes and who, though starving, is so concerned with his honour and his public persona generally that he is forced to live a miserable life of starvation, pretence and deceit. The author shows some genuinely sympathetic understanding of Lazarillo's plight and of that of some others among the book's low-class characters. The style of the book, described by its author as 'crude', is direct, concise, colloquial and ironical and was certainly in part responsible for its success, though its anti-clericalism's appeal at this time should not be discounted. *Lazarillo de Tormes*, amid the taste for chivalric romance and pastoral romance and for writing like that of Guevara and Mexía, shares with *La Celestina* and that work's better sequels and imitations, a certain sense of social awareness, a readiness to flout literary and other conventions and a striving for verisimilitude that make it immediately sympathetic to the modern reader.

It was – as in France and England at approximately the same time – in terms of lyric poetry that the literary tastes of the Italian High Renaissance first found their way effectively into the Spanish literary tradition. This event is associated with the name of a prolific but essentially minor poet, Juan Boscán (c. 1492–1542), and his close friend Garcilaso de la Vega (1501–36), one of the greatest and most influential poets who wrote in Spanish in the Golden Age.[1] Garcilaso, an aristocrat and a soldier in the imperial service, finally broke by his example the old Spanish prejudice that the aristocratic profession of arms was incompatible with a serious dedication to letters. His insistence in his verse that he divided his time between the sword and the pen discloses his awareness that he stood for something new in Spanish poetry. Garcilaso spent the last years of his life in Naples. His work in disseminating in Spain the ideals of the Italian Renaissance was not carried out only through the medium of poetry. From Italy (c. 1533) Garcilaso wrote to Boscán urging his friend to translate into Spanish Castiglione's famous manual *Il*

[1] Garcilaso's poems, with those of Boscán, were first published posthumously in 1543.

Cortegiano (1528) which set out the qualities of the perfect Renaissance courtier – a man cultivated in all the arts as well as skilled in arms. Book IV of Castiglione's book, moreover, contains an account of the doctrines of Platonic love placed in the mouth of Pietro Bembo (1470–1547). They are set out in a singularly attractive and emotive form calculated to appeal as much to the aesthetic emotions of the reader as to his intellect. Boscán's translation, *El Cortesano* (1534), was reprinted at least twelve times in sixteenth-century Spain. The prologue which Garcilaso wrote for it demonstrates how far the poet, as a result of his stay in Italy, had come to reject the literary traditions of his native Spain. He wrote: 'I know not why it has always been our misfortune that hardly anyone has written anything in our language except that which could very well be dispensed with.'

In the early sixteenth century Italian lyric poetry was dominated by a return to the pure Petrarchan tradition based on imitation of Petrarch's *Rime*. This Petrarchan style is instantly recognizable by its fondness for antithetical images to express the lover's experience of love – e.g. 'icy fire', 'sweet enemy' – and a series of consecrated images and epithets for describing the woman's beauty. The *Rime* had received no great attention in Spain (despite an abortive attempt by the Marquis of Santillana in the fifteenth century to write Petrarchan sonnets), partly because the traditional Spanish lyric metres were too short and too rigid to be capable of carrying the complex and subtle imagery and the musicality of Petrarch's lyrics. Boscán and Garcilaso dedicated themselves to the task of introducing the Petrarchan hendecasyllable (eleven-syllable) line into Spanish poetry along with its companion line, the heptasyllable (seven-syllable) line, together with the main verse forms that Petrarch used – such as the sonnet and the *canzone*. The far-reaching character of the technical revolution in Spanish prosody that was involved should not be underestimated. The Petrarchan metres were based on the rhythms of the Italian language; to use them in Spanish, Spanish poets would have to accustom their ear to the sound of stresses falling in unusual places and to a rhythmic flexibility not known in the Spanish octosyllabic line. The reactions of traditional Spanish poets to the innovations of Boscán and Garcilaso underline their revolutionary nature. Cristóbal de Castillejo (c. 1490–1550) denounced the Italianizers as unpatriotic men who wrote incomprehensible, foreign-sounding gibberish. He also complained that their poetry was excessively melancholy in content.

Boscán's historical importance is unquestioned, but he was not a good enough poet to become an effective interpreter of the tradition of the Petrarchan *Rime* in Spanish. The traditional rhythms of Spanish poetry – notably a tendency to end lines with a stressed syllable – too often impose themselves on his hendecasyllables and heptasyllables. He was also unable to master the imagistic concision and refinement of the Italian poet and too readily slipped into the purely rhetorical manipulation of intellectual conceits about courtly love which had been a feature of late medieval love poetry in Spain.

Garcilaso's *œuvre* is small in quantity. There is, too, a considerable difference in tone and quality between the poems he wrote before and those he wrote after he left Spain in 1532. Of the three eclogues which represent Garcilaso's major poetic effort, that known as *Égloga* II was almost certainly written before *Égloga* I. There are five *canciones* but only four of these follow the Petrarchan *canzone* form; '*Canción V*' is an ode in imitation of Horace. There are at most some forty sonnets. As a sonneteer Garcilaso was somewhat uneven but a number of his later sonnets, quite pagan in tone, are unsurpassed in Spanish. A handful of other poems complete such of his work in the vernacular as has come down to us. His friend the young poet Luigi Tansillo praised Garcilaso not only as a distinguished wielder of both pen and sword but also as a skilled lutanist. The Spanish poet's musical ability needs to be remembered in connection with the musical quality of his Spanish verse and the frequency with which aural images rather than visual images predominate in much of it. Some of his poetry was, in fact, set to music in sixteenth-century Spain.

Garcilaso's first and third *Églogas* are concerned with his ill-fated passion for 'Elisa', the pastoral name he uses in them to refer to a lady, Isabel Freire, whom he loved. He could not marry her because he had, in 1525, married another noble lady of the imperial court. Elisa herself, in 1529, also made what Garcilaso considered an unsuitable marriage and eventually died in childbirth during his exile in Naples. In *Égloga* I the Petrarchan tradition is mingled with the Renaissance pastoral tradition in the manner of Sannazaro's *Arcadia* (1504) to recount the history of the poet's love for Elisa. The monologue of the first shepherd, Salicio, deals with the period when the poet felt himself rejected by Elisa in consequence of her marriage. The monologue of Nemoroso describes the poet's feelings of despair after he had received the news of Elisa's death. The contrast between the pastoral world, full of memories of the time when the lovers were happy together, and the present emotions of the frustrated Petrarchan lover is here handled in masterly fashion, the unhappiness of the jealous Salicio and the grief of Nemoroso being presented as conditions of disharmony contrasting with the innate harmony of nature as conceived by the pastoral tradition. At the end of the poem, however, the poet finds a solution through art to his grief for his loved one when he visualizes himself as eventually rejoining Elisa in a pastoral heaven where, however, the lovers will differ from their earthly selves only by now being certain of immortality and eternal happiness together. *Égloga* II is immensely long (1,886 lines) compared with the poet's other two pastorals and seems to have been undertaken as an exercise in pastoral writing. Some of it was cast in dramatic pastoral dialogue evidently intended for stage performance. The poem is packed with Renaissance poetic themes and topics that would serve later Spanish poets well, but it is a work of uncertain intention and structure. *Égloga* III, perhaps written as late as the year of Garcilaso's death (1536), abandons Petrarchism entirely and presents the pastoral and the theme of Elisa's death entirely in Virgilian and Ovidian terms. Concern for formal perfection is uppermost here. This abandonment of Petrarch in favour of imitation of Latin models is also to be seen in the so-called *Canción* V and in some of the later sonnets. It was no doubt a consequence of Garcilaso's classical studies while in Italy.

Garcilaso's best poetry presents a deceptively relaxed stylistic appearance but close analysis reveals that it is always carefully controlled and structured, the structure carrying a unified and carefully selected complex of images to produce a planned effect. The musicality of the Garcilasan line has been noted already; he even made some use of the stress systems of Latin verse in the *Églogas* while the verse form of *Canción* V (the *lira*) represents a serious attempt, in the vernacular, to reproduce the effect of the metre of the Horatian odes. There is a freshness and a sense of absence of bookishness about Garcilaso's verse, as well as an avoidance of attitudinizing, that marks it off from the work of his successors and was no doubt due to the sense of liberation and fulfilment that his contact with the literature of the Italian Renaissance gave him. Though the total amount of verse he left was not large it had been correctly noted that, in it, we can find prefigured not only the themes and topics but also even stylistic features that anticipate, sporadically, the style of the *culterano* poets of the seventeenth century. Garcilaso's position as the founder of the Renaissance tradition of Spanish poetry was recognized in Philip II's time when he was canonized by the publication of elaborate commentaries on his work. The most notable of these was the *Anotaciones* of Fernando de Herrera

(1580). Garcilaso had written at a time when it was still believed that, as Pietro Bembo had insisted, the prime function of the poet was to create beauty and to give aesthetic pleasure. His failure to show any serious Christian concern in his work troubled some of his admirers in the second half of the sixteenth century.

No Spanish poet of Charles V's time approached the stature of Garcilaso, but perhaps the most interesting of the minor poets of this time was Gregorio Silvestre (1520–69), who, though of Portuguese origin, was for a long time organist of Granada Cathedral. His works were not published until 1582. Silvestre wrote in the traditional Spanish metres a number of moving religious lyrics which were intended for singing in Granada Cathedral. Some of these rather unexpectedly reveal, however, a marked awareness of the themes of the Italianate lyric. Silvestre was for a long time, nevertheless, an opponent of the metrical reforms associated with Boscán and Garcilaso – probably because of his concern with traditional music and singing. At the end of his life, however, he turned to the new metres with enthusiasm and wrote many sonnets in both the Petrarchan and classicizing styles. But, even so, Silvestre's poetry is usually religious or didactic in intention. He was the first sixteenth-century Spanish poet to stress particularly the theme of necessary disillusion with whatever this world has to offer – *desengaño*. Silvestre's poetry thus anticipates the age of the Counter-Reformation, a fact which perhaps explains why his work was first published and twice reprinted in the time of Philip II. Jorge de Montemayor (*c.* 1520–61) was a Portuguese *converso* by origin but he spent his life in Spain and wrote in Castilian. He, too, was a professional musician as well as a soldier and seems to have been killed in a love quarrel in Italy. He is best known for his pastoral romance *La Diana* (see p. 301 below). His *Segundo cancionero espiritual* (1558) is the most interesting part of his poetic work. It is markedly influenced by the Psalms and reveals a serious attempt to accommodate the style, language and imagery of the Psalms to the Italian hendecasyllable.

It is plain that the European rather than purely Spanish outlook that characterized the court of Charles V for most of his reign had some quite radical effects on the climate of thought and literary taste. It was not just a question of Erasmianism. In the 1530s the Spanish viceregal court at Naples, to which Garcilaso de la Vega was attached, was obviously now at last wide open to the ways of thinking and writing favoured by the Italian High Renaissance, and it was through that channel that these influences were successfully transmitted to Spain. A good deal of Spanish poetry and some early Spanish drama of this period was written in Italy, and many Spanish books were published there. Spanish belief in the natural superiority of Spanish cultural values over others was plainly modified by the influence of Caesarism and a certain sense of belonging to a European empire. But the change was only partial and Spain, in any case, opened its cultural frontier to the values of the Italian Renaissance in the 1530s at a time when the heyday of the Renaissance was almost at an end. In 1545 the sessions of the Council of Trent began and Charles V, now driven by the exigencies of international politics to become the defender of orthodoxy, also found himself forced more and more to treat Spain as the keystone of his empire and, in its defence, to call on Spanish traditionalism and Spanish patriotism.

As far as pure literature is concerned, however, there is one aspect of empire in the time of Charles V which is almost unrepresented at this time – that is the new Spanish empire in America. The great amount of writing carried out by historians, by lawyers, by political theorists, by priests and missionaries, on American themes goes almost unreflected in prose fiction, in poetry, in the drama. This fact ought to cause us less surprise than it sometimes does. Literature is the most traditional of the arts and a moment's reflection reveals that American themes could have no role to play in the kind of literature we have been discussing. A serious role for America in Golden Age literature was only to be found when the Counter-Reformation's cult of the heroic found a host of themes from the history of the Spanish conquest of America suitable as subjects for epic poetry.

IV Literature and the Counter-Reformation

The decrees of the Council of Trent were promulgated in Spain in 1564. The great questions, as it then seemed, which had been argued about in Europe for so long were now settled as far as Catholic Europe was concerned: man's eternal future was not totally predestined; aided by divine grace, he could exercise his free will (*libre albedrío*) to decide his soul's destiny; he could not be saved by faith alone but must, through good works and by leading a Christian and moral life, deserve salvation; God was not unknowable to man and faith needed the support of reason. The main source of theological authority was St Thomas Aquinas and, since St Thomas had largely followed Aristotle, Aristotle was the principal authority in matters of philosophy and should be accepted wherever what he had to say did not conflict with Christian revelation. To question most of these opinions was now heretical and it was the business, in Spain, of the Inquisition and the new Inquisitorial censorship to see that neither by word of mouth nor by the printed word could any heresies be circulated in Spain.

It should be noted, however, that nowhere did the decrees of the Council of Trent require literature to be didactic, only that no books should be *ex professo* obscene or lewd. The point is of some importance since historians have rightly detected in European literature, more or less contemporaneously with the Tridentine decrees, a new emphasis on the need for creative literature to have a didactic or moral purpose. But this movement in fact antedated the decisions taken at Trent. It was based on an interpretation of the literary theories of Aristotle – principally as these are set out in the *Poetics*, a work which was much studied and commented on, particularly in Italy, from 1548 onwards.

Another example of a new authoritarian approach to literature was, too, the restoration to a place of high importance in literary studies of the art of formal rhetoric. This supplied guidance and rules, originated by Greek and Latin rhetoricians, about literary style. Rhetoric was mainly concerned with telling writers how to achieve particular stylistic effects. As far as methods of thinking were concerned, the theologians of the Counter-Reformation returned to the strictly formal methods of argument, based on Aristotelian logic, that had been used by the scholastic philosophers. But neo-scholasticism was now purged of the absurdities criticized by Erasmus and his disciples.

It is important for any understanding of what happened to literature in the age of Philip II neither to ignore nor to exaggerate the role of the censorship of books. The censors readily detected and suppressed any direct statements of doubtful orthodoxy. But their attitude to their task was very literal. They were not much concerned with trying to work out the implications of statements that contained nothing heretical in themselves. Though, particularly from the 1580s onwards – when censorship became rather more rigorous – the censors increasingly concerned themselves with morality as well as dogma, they left 'literature of entertainment' largely untouched. In the Philippine period, indeed, the censorship was frequently accused of being insufficiently concerned with morality. However, the existence of the censorship was never out of the minds even of those writers concerned solely with entertaining their readers. Authors' prefaces increasingly contained declarations of intention stressing the moral and orthodox purposes of a work. Such declarations tended to become a ritual commonplace and it should not be too readily assumed that they necessarily represent the whole truth that was present in an author's mind.

A number of the great scholars and writers of the age were in trouble with the ecclesiastical authorities. The Inquisition, particularly at the University of Salamanca, conducted in the 1570s a deliberate and damaging campaign intended to enforce total orthodoxy among university teachers. A central figure in this campaign, and the most prominent of its victims, was Fray Luis de León (1527–91), the Augustinian poet, philosopher and theologian, who spent most of his life as a teacher at Salamanca. Luis de León is best known today as a poet of genius and the author of a prose masterpiece, the *Nombres de Cristo*. But, in his own time, he was highly regarded, too, as a Hebraist and theologian who wrote as easily in Latin as he did in Spanish.

Luis de León's prose works included the *Exposición del Cantar de los Cantares*, a translation into the vernacular of the Song of Songs. This was a literal translation from the Hebrew together with a commentary explaining the work's symbolism. It was naturally never published. The same was true of his commentary on the Book of Job (*Exposición del Libro del Job*), his swansong, finished just before his death. Fray Luis, who wrote much of this book in prison, found the message of Job particularly consoling. The work reveals Fray Luis's feeling for the Hebrew mystical tradition. His *De los nombres de Cristo* (1583) is a classic of Renaissance Platonism directed towards a religious purpose. It is in the form of a dialogue between three friends (among whom Marcelo speaks for Luis de León) that takes place on the farm of La Flecha, near Salamanca, during a summer vacation. The subject is, *per se*, a somewhat unpromising one for lay readers – a discussion of the various names by which Christ is known in the Scriptures. But the *Nombres de Cristo* is no simple scholastic or theological treatise. It is based on the Platonic theory of names. Fray Luis explains that a name is not simply an acoustic label; by its etymology, its sound and even its appearance, it is a true symbol or substitute for the thing named – a pale reflection of the object itself. A reading of the *Nombres de Cristo* serves to explain and illuminate Luis de León's poetry. It was bold to write at this time such a work in the vernacular at all. Fray Luis makes no attempt to conceal his regret about the decision of the Council of Trent to ban the Scriptures in the vernacular, while accepting the reasons for the ban. It was, he said, sad evidence of man's sinfulness and corruption that what was intended to be his medicine and cure (direct access to the

Scriptures) had become his poison. The book was an important event
in the development of Spanish prose for Fray Luis showed the vernacular to be capable of dealing simply and yet fully with highly difficult
intellectual concepts, though he also used rich and complex imagery in
it as well, for Fray Luis shows himself here totally open to the emotive
as well as the intellectual appeal of Platonic ideas.

Platonism is also the basis of many of Luis de León's best poems.
They were first published (Madrid, 1631) by Francisco de Quevedo.
The themes and imagery of the poems are frequently cosmic as Fray
Luis, drawing on Platonic and Ptolemaic theories of the universe,
imagines the soul returning upwards through the circles of the planets
to be restored at last to the empyrean from which it had come and
where all is light, harmony, purity, certainty and perfect peace. There
was the starry night to remind the earth-bound watcher of the harmony
of the universe into which his soul seeks to escape while the Platonic
theory of the music of the spheres is repeatedly used to conjure up bold
images of God as a practising musician, the creator of cosmic harmony.
Luis de León proclaimed repeatedly his yearning for peace and solitude,
and his view of the world in which he lived was, understandably,
highly pessimistic. He liked to think of death as life-giving, since it
freed the soul from the prison of the body, leaving it able to return to
the divine Idea from which it had come. But he was no mystic. These
aspirations to be free at last in death from the burdens of love, hate,
hope, jealousy and fear are the utterances of one who could have lived
a contemplative life but did not choose to do so and who never despised
the values of the human intellect.

Horace was a major influence on his poetic style, though usually not
on his basic subject-matter. He wrote in the *lira* metre (introduced into
Spanish by Garcilaso de la Vega) in an attempt to imitate in the
vernacular the rhythms of Horace's *Odes*. Horatian topics and images
frequently occur. Despite Fray Luis's love of music his verse is not
particularly musical or graceful; it is dramatic, exclamatory, questioning – each stanza tends to be complete in itself, though contributing to
a complicated edifice of structure and theme. Luis de León's verse,
despite its preoccupation with peace and harmony, conveys a sense of
tension and disquiet as, by sheer force of imagery and metre, the poet
pulls the reader into the ambit of his experience.

It would be a mistake to think of Luis de León as a man who
achieved intellectual and artistic greatness because he was dubiously
orthodox by the standards of his time. In an age when many chose

a safe mediocrity he brought, rather, an exceptional mind and an exceptional vision to support his own particular interpretation of the ideals of the Counter-Reformation. Another Salamancan scholar who successfully resisted attempts to curb his intellectual liberty was the outspoken humanist Francisco Sánchez, 'el Brocense' (1523–1600), who was accused of undermining the principles of formal logic on which scholastic theology was based and censured for criticizing Aristotle's theories of rhetoric. He demonstrated that a scholar who was not a theologian and had sufficient courage to defend independent opinions unconnected with theology or religion could not be interfered with by the Inquisition. El Brocense, in his *Doctrina de Epicteto* (1612), con-tributed to the development in Philippine Spain of an interest in the philosophy of neo-stoicism.[1] His commentary (1573) on the emblem-book (*Emblemata*, 1531) of the Italian Alciati also foreshadowed that remarkable interest in emblem literature (an emblem was an enigmatic symbolic picture under which was a short interpretative text, often in verse) shown by seventeenth-century Spanish writers of all kinds.

But, on the whole, after the 1570s, Spanish scholars learnt, at least in print, to toe the official line. Original contributions to sixteenth-century thought tended to come from men whose professional training seemed unlikely to make them dangerous. The educationalist Pedro Simón Abril (c. 1530–c. 1595), in his pedagogical treatises, had denied any value to human imagination and fantasy, which he considered to belong to an inferior human faculty men shared with some animals. This view was decisively challenged in one of the most original pieces of thinking printed in Philippine Spain – Juan Huarte de San Juan's *Examen de ingenios para las ciencias* (1575) which made a profound im-pression on contemporary European thinking. Huarte was a doctor and his conclusion was that there was a direct relationship between an in-dividual's physical and psychological make-up and his aptitudes and talents. Common sense dictated, he declared, that a man's profession should be chosen in the light of his psychological potential. These ideas, which seem obvious to us today, were highly novel in their time.

This initial period of the Counter-Reformation's establishment in Spain, for all its stress on human reason and its distrust of individual religious initiatives, witnessed the rise to fame of the two great Carmelite mystical writers, Santa Teresa de Jesús (1515–82) and San Juan de la Cruz (1542–91). *Theologia mystica*, often called by the Spanish mystics *ciencia de amor* or *cier.·ia sobrenatural*, had close affinities

[1] See section XI, below.

with neo-Platonist philosophy, which envisaged the ultimate reunion of the soul, purged of its physical prison, with the divine Idea from which it had originally come. Mysticism flourished in late medieval Europe. Among mystical writers then were the Fleming Jan van Ruysbroeck (d. 1381), author of *The Seven Steps of the Ladder of Spiritual Love* (from whom San Juan de la Cruz's metaphor of the *fuente escondida* seems to be taken). English mystical writers were Richard Rolle (d. 1349), author of the *Incendium amoris*, Walter Hilton (d. 1396), author of the *Scale of Perfection*, and the author of the anonymous *The Cloud of Unknowing*. Any reader who turns to these and similar medieval writers after studying Santa Teresa and San Juan de la Cruz will find himself in largely familiar territory, both in respect of the experiences offered and the imagery used in the attempt to convey them. The channels through which the mystical tradition reached Santa Teresa and San Juan are insufficiently known.

Santa Teresa's main prose works (her poetry is of little interest) are her spiritual autobiography (the *Vida*, 1561–2) and *Las moradas* (1577),[1] otherwise known as the *Castillo interior* – the castle within which are many chambers and in whose innermost chamber 'there take place between God and the soul matters of great secrecy'. Also of great interest are her *Cartas*, which are remarkably intimate and personally revealing. The *Vida* discloses that, as a girl, Santa Teresa was an avid reader of chivalric romance. It gives in great detail an account, written as far as possible in familiar, everyday language, of her mystical experiences as she traversed the traditional mystical way, a journey culminating, on several occasions, in the mystic marriage. Santa Teresa stresses the physical as well as mental suffering she underwent on her journey – fevers, failures of the pulse, levitation and periods of paralysis involving danger of death. The erotic imagery used at times to give (as she believed) some indirect hint of mystical rapture, can be startling. The moment of the mystical marriage itself is likened to the sensation of an arrow penetrating her entrails and burning them with delicious fire. Santa Teresa was fully conscious of the inherent contradictions involved in an attempt to convey in words an experience which, in fact, involved the suspension of all the individual's self-awareness – including the faculty of memory and the ability to think. 'Not thinking' and 'not knowing' are, in the language of mysticism, the paradoxical prerequisites of the attainment of direct knowledge of God.

There is nothing else in Spanish literature like Teresa's prose style, which is totally personal to her. Words and ideas pour from her pen

[1] Both first published 1588.

with a disregard both for logic and for conventional syntax. She often loses her train of thought in the middle of a sentence and does not bother to pick it up again. She frequently leaves out essential parts of her argument. Equally frequent are huge parenthetical digressions inserted into the sentence, which often never gets finished. Much use is made of popular language and vulgar forms of contemporary pronunciation and orthography.

The poetry of San Juan de la Cruz,[1] though concerned with conveying similar experiences and nurtured in the same tradition, is very different in style and effect. San Juan was a trained theologian and biblical scholar – a scholastic thinker who turned to mysticism. Both sides of him can be seen in the stylistic contrast between the text of his poems and the long prose exegesis to which he submitted some of them. The *Cántico espiritual* draws largely on the imagery of the Song of Songs. Here, in some forty stanzas written in the *lira* metre first introduced by Garcilaso de la Vega, the poet presents his readers with a dialogue between the soul ('La Esposa') and her bridegroom ('El Amado') – God. Other famous poems are the much shorter *Llama de amor viva* and the *Noche oscura del alma*, both also dealing with mystical ecstasy. In some of these works San Juan divinizes extensively the conventional language of courtly love, with its fondness for antithetical metaphor: mystical love is thus described as a wound that gives delight, as a flame that consumes without causing pain. In the *Coplas hechas sobre un éxtasis de alta contemplación* San Juan tried to convey the state of the mystic when he had sloughed off all individual feeling and intellection so as to achieve a knowledge beyond all understanding. The secrecy and privacy of the mystical experience is constantly insisted on by San Juan. His poems usually avoid any expository structure and seek to convey ecstasy by means of concise, concentrated, symbolic imagery. Exclamations are frequent. Nouns predominate, the role of the adjective is restricted, verbs are used sparingly and copulative conjunctions often omitted. A certain irregularity of metre contributes an appropriate impression of breathlessness.

San Juan believed that spiritual experience needed to be expressed in poetry free from affectation or the ensnarements of style. The poet was, like Santa Teresa, at all times conscious that he was trying to present experiences that involved total separation from the everyday world of human experience. He wrote in a letter of 1586: 'these waters of in-

[1] *Obras espirituales* first published 1618.

terior delights are not born on earth; the mouth of desire must open itself towards heaven.' His task was both easier and more difficult than Santa Teresa's – easier because he had all the resources of poetry and poetic tradition to help him, more difficult because he had to universalize what was in Santa Teresa's prose a personal record of a personal experience. The poetry of San Juan at its best is never naïve or faux-naïve; his poetic and his mystical intuitions are usually skilfully and subtly brought together. Some influence of the secular poetry of his age has been demonstrated, but this element should not be exaggerated. Much of his imagery can in fact be found in biblical sources. Most readers today prefer to take advantage of the saint's own statement that each may take the poems in his own way and that there is no need for any to feel bound by the (often disconcertingly arid) commentaries of their author. No poet, it may be added, seems so far away from the secular poetry of his time nor so unbound to any particular historical epoch.

There was a good deal of non-mystic religious writing during the Philippine period which was highly thought of then but is likely to seem of scant interest today. This is true even of the work of Fray Luis de Granada (1504-88) who, in his day, was universally acclaimed and read in Protestant as well as in Catholic countries. His best-known works are the *Guía de pecadores* (1556) and the diffuse, popularist, devotional theology offered in the *Introducción del símbolo de la fe* (1583). Fray Luis was a famous pulpit orator who wrote in Latin an important treatise on religious oratory (*Libri sex ecclesiasticae rhetoricae*, 1576) which was based on the stylistic precepts of Cicero. His Castilian prose style, oratorical, improvising and characterized by rotund Ciceronian periods, is a useful reminder that, in an age when pulpit oratory was a major concern of priests and their congregations, such oratory often had a direct influence on the way religious prose was written. Historically interesting also was the curious *a lo divino* movement in literature that developed for a time in Philippine Spain. The business of taking the melodies of popular secular songs and writing religious lyrics to replace the secular ones had long been a favourite Spanish practice. This work was now carried on more intensively as part of a formal programme for desecularizing literature. Sebastián de Córdoba made an elaborate attempt to divinize all the poetry of Boscán and Garcilaso in his *Obras de Boscán y Garcilaso trasladadas a materias christianas y religiosas* (1575). Efforts were made to divinize chivalric romance. Juan López de Úbeda (d. 1596) published a *Vergel de flores divinas* and a *Cancionero general de la doctrina cristiana* in which he offered peasants, servants and children religious songs that he hoped they would sing instead of their traditional profane ones, a notion that oddly predates similar efforts made in nineteenth-century Europe. The *a lo divino* movement represented one more manifestation of that ancient puritanical tradition that held that Christians should not spend their time reading anything but moral and religious works.[1]

Secular poetry in Spain during the last half of the sixteenth century underwent substantial changes, due mainly to the growing influence of Italian neo-Aristotelian poetic theory and to the example of post-Tridentine Italian poets. The most influential, in Spain, of the Italian interpreters and systematizers of Aristotle's literary theories was Giulio Cesare Scaligero whose *Poetices libri septem* (1561) was a major formative influence on the views about poetry held by Fernando de Herrera (1534–97) – the chief Spanish secular poet and literary critic of his time. One feature of the new poetic attitude was its insistent classicism: 'I do not hold anyone to be a good poet unless he imitates the excellent poets of antiquity,' wrote El Brocense (p. 294 above) in his annotated edition of Garcilaso de la Vega (1574); he complained that Spain was full of poetasters who lacked the professional knowledge, the linguistic skill and the scholarship to be real poets – a complaint echoed by Francisco de Medina in his prologue to Herrera's *Anotaciones* (1580), also of the works of Garcilaso. The new poetics were, in every way, authoritarian: Herrera did not hesitate to correct what Garcilaso had actually written when he thought the latter had fallen below what was required of a great poet. In the *Anotaciones* what Herrera sought to do, following neo-Aristotelian precepts, was to show that Garcilaso had both the learning and the familiarity with the great poets of the past to enable him to follow them as models, and, at times, to surpass them. Herrera's *Anotaciones* were, until the appearance in 1596 of Alonso López Pinciano's *Philosophia antigua poética*, the main source through which neo-Aristotelian critical theory was disseminated in Spain. Herrera's debt to Scaliger in this work was even greater than its author admitted.

Herrera's own poetic output was extensive. Part of it (*Algunas obras*) was published in 1582, in his lifetime. More appeared in the *Versos* (1619) but a considerable number of poems were not published until the present century. That Herrera, who was born and lived in Seville,

[1] For examples of *a lo divino* work in music at this time, see Chapter 12, section VII, p. 554.

was in many ways a great poet must be admitted, but he is also a hard poet for the modern reader to like. He had poetic imagination, a great feeling for language, an acute sense of metre and rhythm. He was, also, a true professional, constantly polishing and repolishing his work, perhaps to excess. But there is something over-contrived and therefore chilling about much that he wrote. His love sonnets, *églogas* and *canciones* are mostly designed to celebrate his Platonic love for Leonor de Milán (d. 1581), Countess of Gelves and wife of a man who was his close friend. They are quite deliberately Petrarchist in content and manner and equally deliberately intended to show that Herrera was capable of surpassing Petrarch. The rhetoric of courtly love is basic in these poems. The poetic history of his love is, however, also carefully interpreted in terms of neo-Platonic doctrine and his love lyrics constantly draw, with some intellectual rigour, on the now rather hackneyed Platonic dialectic. Herrera's Platonism is, however, curiously frigid. Nowadays he perhaps seems greater in poems like his *Égloga venatoria* where the element of subjective experience is less and where his undoubted mastery of colourful, descriptive, rhetorically sensual imagery and his feeling for classical mythology combine to produce something less conceptual and less enigmatic than much of his love poetry. Nature, as presented by Herrera, is a highly painted and perfected artefact – an imitation but in no sense a mirror-image of the real natural world.

Herrera sought very deliberately to create a new language of poetic diction in Spain in accordance with neo-Aristotelian beliefs that poetry is an art for a cultured, humanistic minority and needs a refined language of its own. He thus adopted a more Latinized syntax (aiming at a great degree of compression in poetic statements) and sought to enrich the language of poetry by introducing words (*cultismos*) borrowed directly from the Latin. These were often deliberately placed by him at key rhythmic sites in his lines. Herrera also skilfully employs the various stylistic devices of the rhetoricians to achieve particular effects. He believed that poetry should have grandiloquence and strength and manliness, and criticized the Italian poets for a certain effeminacy. Herrera is often called 'classical', but this is plainly misleading. Though he is steeped in classical literature, the attitude and tone of his poetry is not classical, for, by classical standards, it is basically restless, tense and over-dramatic.

No account of poetry at this time would be complete without

¹ See also Chapter I, section VII, p. 26.

reference to the great popularity of the learned heroic epic, cast in the Virgilian epic mode, but also much influenced by the Italian Renaissance epic. Under the influence of Torquato Tasso's famous *Gerusalemme liberata* (1581) Spanish poets, too, turned increasingly to epic treatment of religious themes; earlier they had tended to write about national history and national heroes. The best of the Spanish heroic epics of this time is that of Alonso de Ercilla (1533–1594) whose *Araucana* (published in three parts, 1569, 1578, 1589–90) was an account of the colonial war in Chile against the Araucanian Indians, in which Ercilla himself had taken part.

The humanist censors of chivalric romance had, from the time of the Erasmians onwards, their own idea of what a model prose romance ought to be. They found it in a long Greek prose romance written, probably in the second century A.D., by Heliodorus and called the *Ethiopian History* or *History of Theagenes and Chariclea* – from the name of the two lovers whose remarkable adventures and vicissitudes it recounts. No doubt some of the reputation this labyrinthine tale enjoyed was due to its impeccably classical origins. But it is also a work of very considerable literary merit. Its proliferating adventures are skilfully interlocked and justified. The consistently elevated style is sensitive and imaginative. It also retails in an easy way a good deal of ancient history and moral philosophy. The unfailing constancy and courtesy of the lovers, as well as their extreme propriety, make it a thoroughly moral tale. The *Historia ethiopica* delighted the Erasmians and continued, well into the seventeenth century, to delight Catholic and Protestant readers alike. The first Castilian translation appeared in 1554. The neo-Aristotelian critics were unstinting in their praise of the *Historia ethiopica*, which they categorized as an epic, though written in prose. It often provided models and source material for the pastoral romances and for the short stories of the time. The *Historia ethiopica* also, of course, catered well for the demand increasingly made of all literature as the sixteenth century wore on – that it should be marked by a concern to arouse what the theorists called *admiratio*, wonderment or surprise. Here one may postulate a connection with the not unsimilar aims of contemporary Mannerist painting such as in El Greco or Tintoretto.

As far as the average reader of prose fiction was concerned, the popularity of chivalric romance in the second half of the sixteenth century was probably overtaken by the fashion for pastoral romance, a form of writing in which pastoral and other forms of love poetry were linked by prose passages which provided a narrative background to the poems and explained them. The pastoral romance was essentially a development from Sannazaro's famous *Arcadia* (see p. 287 above), which was published in Spanish in 1547 and twice thereafter. Though the prose narrative part of the Spanish pastoral was now greatly developed beyond its role in the *Arcadia*, these hybrid works were still assigned to the category of poetry: Cervantes calls them 'libros de poesía'. Realistic critical criteria are therefore wholly inappropriate to them. In Sannazaro the rediscovery of Arcady, closely associated with the classical myth of the lost Golden Age, has the immediacy and the power to move of a new and deeply felt vision. The Spanish pastoral romances, at their best, seem artificial, contrived and trivial in comparison. Yet to ignore them is, as in the case of romances of chivalry, to be guilty of turning our backs on a large area of the literary and artistic taste of the age. The most famous of the Spanish pastoral romances, *Los siete libros de la Diana* (1559) by Jorge de Montemayor (see p. 289 above), was printed about twenty-five times in Spanish before the end of the Golden Age and read in translation in many languages. Such popularity speaks for itself. Love of an elevated kind is the theme of the pastoral. It is often, but not always, presented as an irrational force in human relationships, bound to lead to suffering but also to ennoble its victims. Pastoral romance, which belongs to the category of *romans à clef*, specializes in setting up a complicated cat's cradle of amorous relationships. It often adds gratuitously to the complications by, for example, disguising women as men. It has, too, a taste for the visually sumptuous – rich clothing, splendid Renaissance palaces and beautiful gardens, as well as a by now highly conventionalized Arcadian natural landscape, are described. White magic and beneficent female magicians help to solve the problems of the lovers.

The prose style of these books is intended to suit the theme: it is always elevated, rhetorical, rather long-winded and unsharp, setting a premium on melodiousness. A serious defect, even in the best pastoral writing, is that writers are unable to produce the sheer quantity of verse they demand of themselves at a sufficiently distinguished level. Like Montemayor, they are liable, therefore, simply to paraphrase Garcilaso and other pastoral and Petrarchist Spanish poets. As was the case with chivalric romance, readers could not bear to believe that these stories ever ended and wanted continuations, even if they were as poor in quality as was Alonso Pérez's Second Part of the *Diana* (1564). A much better tale is the *Diana enamorada* (also 1564) of Gaspar Gil Polo (d.

1585), where much of the verse is of some distinction, though the plot as such hardly exists here. *La Galatea* (1585), of Miguel de Cervantes, borrows for its adventures from Heliodorus and Montemayor and, for its dissertations on love and beauty, from Leone Ebreo. In 1580 an attempt to divinize the pastoral romance was made by a Cistercian monk, Bartolomé Ponce, in his *Clara Diana a lo divino* – a transposition *a lo divino* of Montemayor. Lope de Vega tried his hand at the genre in his *Arcadia* (1598) which portrays in pastoral guise amorous life at the ducal court of the Albas at Alba de Tormes.

The modern reader may find more to his taste the two or three so-called 'Moorish' prose romances, though these, in fact, appealed to exactly the same kind of sixteenth-century reader who liked chivalric and pastoral romance. This genre became well known outside Spain because of the inclusion in Book IV (of the 1561 edition) of Montemayor's *Diana* of the *Historia de Abindarráez y la hermosa Xarifa*. The best version of this tale is that of Antonio de Villegas (printed in 1565). Those who appear in the tale, Christian and Moor alike, see life through the mirror of chivalry and romantic love. The *Historia de Abindarráez* is brief and concise, well organized, and concerned with a single sequence of events. Its model is clearly the romantic Italian *novella* or short story. Its underlying theme is freedom; Abindarráez, captured on his way to see Xarifa by Rodrigo de Narváez at the beginning of the story, is allowed his freedom in order to visit her, in exchange for a vow thereafter to return to captivity. He redeems his promise, even though there was no constraint on him other than honour to do so, and discovers that he will always live in spiritual captivity to Narváez because of the latter's generosity.

The theme of the chivalrous Moor was established in greater breadth by Ginés Pérez de Hita (*c.* 1544–*c.* 1619) whose *Guerras civiles de Granada* (1595–1619) is a blend of history and fiction. Part I (*Historia de los zegríes y abencerrajes*) draws on chronicles, frontier ballads (and the author's own not very scholarly knowledge of Moorish customs) to make an exotic tale of romantic love, courage, chivalry and betrayal against a background of Moorish refinement and splendour. Paradoxically the taste for Hispano-Moorish themes was given further impetus because another Moorish romantic tale, the *Historia de los dos enamorados Ozmín y Daraja*, was incongruously inserted by Mateo Alemán into his gloomy picaresque novel *Guzmán de Alfarache* (Part I, 1599; Part II, 1604).

The popularity of *Guzmán de Alfarache* exceeded, when it first appeared, that which awaited *Don Quijote*. There were more than twenty Spanish editions of Part I by 1604. It was soon translated into the major European languages. Modern readers who find the book rather hard going will do well to remember these facts. To readers at the end of the sixteenth century Alemán's book plainly represented the opening of a new frontier in the history of prose fiction, and one much to their taste. It was the first large-scale fictional autobiography of an unpleasant rascal. Apart from *Lazarillo de Tormes* nearly fifty years before it is, too, the first Spanish fictional narrative that, in contradistinction to the romances, fits the definition of a novel as this was defined by eighteenth-century English critics – that it be a picture of real life and manners, and of the times in which it is written. Unlike *Lazarillo de Tormes*, however, *Guzmán de Alfarache* is enormously long. Unlike it, too, it is a work brimming over with bitterness and pessimism. Where the author of *Lazarillo* largely avoided moralizing, moralizing occupies a substantial portion of Alemán's book.

The narrative, written in the first person like *Lazarillo de Tormes*, is supposedly an account of Guzmán's unregenerate life of evil-doing, written by him after he has reformed. This device explains the dualistic character of the work. It makes it possible for Guzmán both to describe, often with a good deal of chilly enthusiasm and even self-satisfaction, his career as a malefactor, and to make morally improving comments, often of very great length, at the same time. There is nothing classical about the structure or tone of Alemán's book. It is loose and amorphous and the distinctions between the unreformed or the reformed status of the picaresque narrator and the persona of the author himself are not always maintained clearly. Guzmán is, at the beginning, depicted as the child of corrupt and evil parents and it is suggested that this fact pre-disposed him to a life of crime. Not only do his picaresque wanderings take him to various parts of Spain (Madrid, Toledo, Alcalá de Henares, Saragossa) but he also spends a good deal of time in Italy where he is, *inter alia*, jester to the French ambassador (a post he regards as one of humiliation) and servant to a cardinal. Long periods of time are in-volved in some of these episodes. It is while with the cardinal that he receives an education in the arts which, later, will enable him to study for seven years with success at the University of Alcalá de Henares. Guzmán is thus both intelligent and university-trained. He is, however, at all times (before his reformation) an instinctive thief, swindler and cheat, always rewarding kindness with ingratitude, incapable of pity and very frequently choosing a path of crime when there is no need whatever for him to do so. There is, too, a frank enjoyment of cruelty and hurtfulness. This is not an account of the life of a criminal in a society which is, itself, basically moral. Society and its institutions are shown consistently, like man himself, as fatally flawed by original sin. In an age when social criticism was usually confined to safe generalities Alemán sometimes offers us unexpected glimpses of the truth behind the Philippine establishment façade as when he tells us that the lower classes in Andalusia hate the nobles with a hatred 'as natural as the hatred a lizard feels for a snake'. But seventeenth-century European readers did not think the picture of human society was particularly Spanish, still less did they associate it with the religious dogmas of the Counter-Reformation. Ben Jonson's introductory verses to the English translation (1622) make it clear that the work was thought to be an excellent portrayal of the nature of human society generally.

Alemán's pessimism was plainly fed by his extensive reading. He is never at a loss to find supporting evidence for it in the Bible or some other source. Characteristically he does not allow all to end well once Guzmán has, after a period as a galley-slave, decided to become a reformed character. He is then promptly tortured and flogged for a crime he had, for once, not committed and he buys his way to a pardon by denouncing to the authorities a plan of his fellow galley-slaves to mutiny. They are executed. Alemán, in this book, however, does not (and could not) preach predestination or determinism. But he does not confine himself to presenting man and society as inherently false and deceitful. He suggests that deceit is a function of the natural world too.

The style of *Guzmán de Alfarache* was greatly praised – among others by Baltasar Gracián (1601–58) in his *Agudeza y arte de ingenio* (1642). Gracián called Alemán 'the best and most classical Spanish writer' and said his book combined Greek inventiveness, Italian elegance, French erudition and Spanish wit (*agudeza*). His style tends to be staccato, interrogative and scattered with aphorisms, but it is very varied. Extremely concise expression that foreshadows *conceptismo* alternates with a more rhetorical, Ciceronian type of prose. Alemán has a gift for the vivid image that will make his point though his depiction of every-day reality lacks the objectivity and pictorial quality of Cervantes. It should not be overlooked that Europeans in Alemán's time listened a great deal to sermons and liked doing so. There is a good deal of the preacher's art and approach in *Guzmán de Alfarache*. Alemán's book suggests that, faced with a world that is totally corrupt, men had better attend mostly to their own personal moral and spiritual salvation. This was to become one of the main themes of seventeenth-century Spanish writing. Tridentine theology, with its stress on man's freedom of choice and the power of divine grace, might have seemed to justify some degree of optimism. But, in practice, a note of transcendental pessimism soon became a prominent feature of Counter-Reformation literature – not only in Spain.

V Cervantes

In the prose fiction of Miguel de Cervantes Saavedra (1547–1616) the creation of purely literary values as an end in themselves is paramount. At its best, Cervantes's work, though often drawing directly on its author's close observation of everyday life and his own extraordinarily varied autobiographical experiences, is transmuted by art so that it acquires a universality and a timeless quality that frees it from bondage to the particular epoch in which Cervantes lived. Nevertheless his biography is of considerable importance not only since it helps to explain his originality as a writer but also because no other Golden Age prose writer so insistently presented his own persona *qua* author to his readers. Cervantes's father was a wandering, unsuccessful and hard-up doctor, though with pretensions to nobility; all his life Cervantes, too, was to be a wanderer dogged by poverty and the personal and domestic humiliations that went with it. Allusions to the destructive consequences of poverty are common in his works. He was for a time a rather elderly pupil (1563) at a school in Madrid run by Juan López de Hoyos, a schoolmaster who sympathized with the pedagogical ideas of Erasmus, but he seems to have had no further formal education, though he was a voracious and, by his own account, undiscriminating reader. The fact that his intellect was not disciplined according to the rigid university patterns of the day must probably be accounted an important factor that contributed to his originality as a writer and to his empirical and experimental intellectual attitudes.

In 1569 Cervantes left Madrid, probably to avoid prosecution on a wounding charge. He went to Italy and enlisted in the Spanish army there, not returning to Spain for twelve years. They were formative ones; he was a soldier with Don John of Austria's fleet at the great victory over the Turks at Lepanto (1571), losing the use of his left hand there as the result of a wound. He spent the next few years on garrison duty in Italy. At this time, or perhaps before it, Spanish romances of chivalry – as is plain from *Don Quijote* – figured prominently among his favourite reading and few of these works went unread or un-remembered by him.

In 1575 Cervantes completed his service and set out for Spain by sea. His ship was captured by Algerian corsairs and he spent the next five years as a Christian captive in the hands of the Turks in Algiers – an experience which also looms large in his works. He was finally ran-somed and returned to Spain expecting to be properly rewarded by the crown for his many services to it. He was to be bitterly disappointed. He now tried for the first time to break into the Madrid literary world. Since pastoral romances were the fashion he wrote and published one of these (*La Galatea*, 1585) but, since he was no poet, the work had scant success. He turned his hand somewhat more fruitfully, by his own account, to the theatre – then still dominated by the traditions of Juan de la Cueva and Lope de Rueda. In 1587 his continuing poverty com-pelled him to give up his literary life in Madrid, and he became a royal tax-collector in Andalusia. This employment required him to travel the roads of southern Spain constantly, visiting its small towns and villages to assess and collect dues. The consequences of these rural experiences, not normally part of the life of Spanish authors at this time, are to be seen at their most formative in *Don Quijote*. But misfortune continued to dog Cervantes. He was imprisoned two, or probably three, times because of trouble with his accounts, and learnt to know at first hand what life was like in a Seville prison. After 1590 there followed a number of years of residence in Seville which are not accounted for but the evidence for which is to be seen in many of his works. He appears at this time to have established rather ambiguous contacts with the organized, marginal, society of criminals and rogues which notoriously flourished in the Andalusian capital and whose argot (*germanía*) he be-came familiar with. In works like his short story *Rinconete y Cortadillo* he depicts and satirizes this society with an ironical good humour that contrasts notably with Mateo Alemán's bitter treatment of criminal life. When the First Part of *Don Quijote* appeared (1605) Cervantes had already left Seville for Valladolid. Three years later he was in Madrid and from then until his death in 1616 he was mostly resident in the Spanish capital. He was now famous (but by no means universally admired) as the author of *Don Quijote*. In 1613 he published his col-lection of twelve short stories, the *Novelas ejemplares* – several of them reworkings of tales that he had drafted a number of years earlier. In

1615 he followed this with a volume of his plays – *Ocho comedias y ocho entremeses* – which represented a second and foredoomed attempt to break into the theatrical world. The *comedias* reveal only too well in their structure and development that Cervantes's genius as a writer of prose narrative was not paralleled by any sense of the theatre (*vide* p. 351). The one-act *entremeses* – farces – are a different case. Cervantes's ability to write humorous dialogue, his gift for social satire and his delight in literary sleight-of-hand make these playlets enjoyable reading today. In 1615, too, the Second Part of *Don Quijote* appeared and repeated the popular success of the First Part. In 1614 a spurious Second Part, by an unidentified author calling himself 'Alonso Fernández de Avellaneda', who had possibly seen part of Cervantes's manuscript, appeared. It was the work of an admirer of Lope de Vega who objected to Cervantes's attacks on Lope's work and character and maliciously conceived the idea of stealing the second thunder of the creator of *Don Quijote*. Though a much cruder work than Cervantes's masterpiece, this anonymous imitation is, in fact, not without literary merits. Cervantes's literary ambitions, even in old age, seem not to have been satisfied by the knowledge that he was now famous throughout Europe as the creator of a new literary form – the comic novel. Just before his death in 1616 he completed his long romance in four books, *Los trabajos de Persiles y Sigismunda* (1617), which largely forsakes realism and irony (except in part of Book III) in favour of the romantic and remotely sited labyrinths of Byzantine romance in the style of Heliodorus (p. 300 above). Only in the *Prólogo* to this work do we find any trace of the characteristic Cervantine style of earlier days. Here, in his best ironical and comical vein, he consciously takes leave of the world, a few days before his death, with a black but good-humoured jest. He died in Madrid on 23 April 1616. No one troubled to mark his grave with a stone or memorial.

In this final *Prólogo*, and elsewhere, Cervantes is fond of depicting himself, though not without a tone of irony, as a merry fellow, but his temper, shaped by poverty, and many disappointments, frustrations and humiliations, was certainly less easy than that suggests. Avellaneda's description of him as a choleric and discontented old man resentful of the success of other writers and not slow to criticize them may not have been without some foundation. His frequently expressed fear of the damage hostile gossip could cause – perhaps unconsciously reflected in Don Quixote's continual anxiety about the machinations of evil wizards – is suggestive, though this topic was a fairly common one in Golden Age literature. Cervantes probably, too, underestimated the extent to which *Don Quijote* was felt to call in question, albeit obliquely, a great many sacred cows of his time. His best work, nevertheless, has an open, experimental and tentative character, very unlike most writings of the early seventeenth century. It used often to be said that he was the creator of the modern (i.e. nineteenth-century) novel but, in fact, these particular qualities make *Don Quijote* much more like a twentieth-century experimental tale. But there were limits to Cervantes's independence of mind. He seems always to have been over-respectful towards the authority of neo-Aristotelian literary theory – anxious to prove that he knew all about it and could satisfy its requirements when he chose to – hence the *Persiles y Sigismunda* and his insistence on turning out verse even when, as he himself admitted, he had no talent for writing serious poetry; neo-Aristotelian criticism denied on principle the highest critical accolade to those who were not poets.

Cervantes's fame today rests on the *Novelas ejemplares* and on *Don Quijote*. The seventeenth-century reader would certainly have added *Persiles y Sigismunda* to this list; at least six editions of that work were printed in 1617, not counting the first one, and more quickly followed. The *Novelas*, it has been noted, fall into two broad categories, though the two types sometimes intermingle. One type, more obviously derived from the Italian romantic *novella* tradition, deals with complicated and unusual plots involving love, friendship, honour, rape, adventure and so on, with much use of disguise, coincidence and mistaken identity. The Italian short-story writers Bandello and Giambattista Cinthio (1504–73) (and also Heliodorus) were his models here. These tales are written in an elevated but easy style and, despite some of their subject-matter, are entirely without the indecency of some Italian tales on similar themes. Examples are *El amante liberal*, *La española inglesa*, *Las dos doncellas*. There is ample evidence that, in the seventeenth century, many readers preferred this type to the more 'realistic' *Novelas* and it is mainly on these tales that any justification rests for Cervantes's claim that his collection of long short-stories was 'exemplary', in the sense that they show right triumphing and morality rewarded. The exemplariness of the other type of story is sometimes decidedly more elusive (as Avellaneda unkindly pointed out in 1614). The best that apologists for a moral intention can do about some of the tales which depict in detail the contemporary Spanish scene – like *Rinconete y Cortadillo*, *El coloquio de los perros* or *La ilustre fregona* – is to accept at their face value Cervantes's assurances that the social and other vices they depict should be avoided, while noting that nothing much is done in them to make vice unattractive. It is nevertheless plain enough that Cervantes's narrative genius was at its most creative in the *Novelas* when he turned to the task of converting into art, in the relatively narrow confines of the short story, what he had seen and discovered in his long experience of the grass-roots of contemporary Spanish society. A notable feature of Cervantes as a writer of short stories, even in the more romantic ones, is the stress he puts on the description of environment, and, of course, on dialogue – of which he was a master. He also, in the second type of tale, carried out various experiments such as that which was responsible for the splendid *Coloquio de los perros* in which, through the mouths of two talking dogs, various aspects of Spanish society are scrutinized satirically. His statement that he was the first Spanish writer to compose short stories is correct and none of his successors in this genre succeeded in equalling him. It is to the *Novelas ejemplares* that we must turn if we wish to examine Cervantes's literary artistry at its most polished and flawless. In *Don Quijote* unrevised spontaneity, leading to a considerable number of contradictions and inconsistencies, is the rule.

Part I (1605) and Part II (1615) of *Don Quijote* run to some fifty-two and seventy-four chapters respectively. The book thus compares in length with some of the longer chivalric romances whose reputation Cervantes claimed it was his purpose to destroy by ridicule. *Don Quijote* was universally admired throughout Europe for nearly three centuries as a brilliantly original piece of sustained comic writing whose author rang the changes on every form and style of humorous literature from farcical burlesque and parody to high comedy – the latter, in particular, marked by the deployment of a subtle and teasing irony. This view was utterly reversed by nineteenth-century Romantic criticism which made of the knight not an amazing and enigmatic madman but a tragic figure – a symbol of the inevitable defeat of human idealism. This Romantic view has largely coloured criticism of Cervantes's book ever since. Such an interpretation would certainly have surprised its author and his pre-nineteenth-century readers.

The special subtlety and ambivalence of the humour in *Don Quijote* lay particularly in Cervantes's comic exploitation of the fact that madmen, in their lucid intervals – as he himself pointed out, again citing examples he had known in real life – behave and talk sense in a way that makes them indistinguishable from (or even more perceptive than) those who are sane, and that, contrariwise, those whom society regards as sane can easily be brought, by contact with madness, to behave as if they were not.

Cervantes repeatedly declares that his intention in writing the book was to discredit the romances of chivalry and, indeed, it is, in essence as well as in structure, a parody of these works. Don Quixote is portrayed as having been rendered mad by reading the romances. Certainly Cervantes presumed that his readers would themselves be very familiar with these works. But Cervantes's actual attitude to the romances is, from the beginning, characteristically vacillating and ambivalent. It immediately becomes apparent that he must once have spent a great deal of time avidly reading great numbers of these works with enjoyment; he recalls their contents very accurately. It should also be noted that *Don Quijote* is strictly parody, not satire, and, in fact, really does nothing to challenge the chivalric romance's *raison d'être*; Don Quixote, unlike the heroes of the romances, is not noble (he is an *hidalgo*, not a *caballero*), he is not young, he is not skilled at arms, he is totally lacking in the qualities demanded of the courtly lover – all essential qualities or experiences of the heroes of the romances; he entirely lacks the mythical stature and the mythical ambience authors of the romances contrived for the latter. Sancho, too, has few of the characteristics of the squire in the romances, where a squire was a future knight. It seems likely that Cervantes was, in fact, less preoccupied about the shortcomings of chivalric romance than he pretended to be. What he was concerned with was the possibilities for parody these works offered him. He was also delighted by the new creative literary possibilities which opened up for him when he located his mad knight not in the mythical world of the romances but in contemporary Spain, and when he exploited – perhaps the major innovation in his work – the fact that, on their peregrinations, it was reasonable to presume that Don Quixote and Sancho must have spent a great deal of their time conversing with each other. Dialogue in the romances was usually ritualistic and its scope strictly limited.

The structure of *Don Quijote* is extremely loose. In both parts the sequence of adventures seems to have been organized in advance only in the broadest fashion and the narrative has a distinctly improvised air. Attempts have been made to suggest that, in Part II, Cervantes sought to present his two main characters in greater depth; Don Quixote, it has been said, is there less mad and less credulous, while Sancho Panza is allowed both to grow as an independent character and to become more like his master. There is some truth in this view, but these developments are by no means consistently maintained: in large parts of Part II both characters are treated as if they were still as they had been early in Part I. The desire to create and exploit an endless series of comic situations and to allow literary inventiveness full rein takes complete precedence over consistency in the development of the two main characters.

It is through the discussions that Don Quixote and Sancho have with each other, and with the great gallery of secondary and minor characters who pass through its pages, that *Don Quijote* mainly achieves its status as a work of social satire, though Cervantine irony and the ambivalence produced by the fact the observations of Don Quixote and Sancho are, respectively, those of a madman and a bumpkin (as well as the underlying humorous intention) make the satire far from committed. Socially Cervantes reveals himself in this book as an apostle of humanity, common sense and the *via media*, but his rationalism is not always liberal. On many issues, including the desirability of censorship, his opinions are strict. Much has sometimes been made of the fact that the form taken by Don Quixote's madness involves much mistaking of the identity of real people and objects by substituting for them hallucinatory realities drawn from memories of chivalric romance. Never once, however, does Cervantes attempt seriously to probe the metaphysical problems of illusion and reality that these experiences might seem to raise. Cervantes was no philosopher. He plays with illusion and reality mainly to tease his characters (and his readers) and for the opportunities for literary surprise and inventiveness – and comedy – such playing allows.

In Part I Cervantes, as he afterwards admitted, had doubts whether the comic story of Don Quixote and Sancho Panza alone could sustain his readers' interest: this part, therefore, contains a substantial number of serious long short-stories in the form of interpolated tales told by characters met by the two travellers. These have little or no connection with the main plot and are romantic tales in the Italian or Byzantine manner – idealistic novelettes in the pattern of some of the *Novelas ejemplares*. When he came to write Part II Cervantes admitted that these interpolated and extraneous tales had been adversely criticized by readers of Part I and he undertook not to repeat the mistake. The promise is not really honoured. Cervantes's irrepressible desire to tell stories not called for by his main plot is still much to the fore and the integration of these, in Part II, with the adventures of Don Quixote and Sancho is often more formal than real.

Cervantes called his most famous book an *historia* – in the tradition of the chivalric romances. But, essentially, *Don Quijote* is *sui generis*, and, apart from Avellaneda's imitation, no Spanish author of his time subsequently tried to copy it. Unwittingly, however, Cervantes certainly succeeded in doing rather more than he intended. Thus Don Quixote and Sancho, seen as figures of ridicule, passed immediately into popular Spanish folklore; they evidently contrived to achieve some sort of social significance as types. The two characters and their world, as we have seen, also proved capable of drastic reinterpretation with the coming of the Romantic sensibility – a sign, at least, that Cervantes, when he created them, had intuitively if not consciously tapped some deep springs in the human consciousness. It should be noted, though, that the only way in which the totality of what Cervantes wrote in *Don Quijote* – and the ways he wrote it – can be accounted for is by accepting it as a funny book and its author as more concerned with the sheer pleasure of comic creativity than with anything else.

VI Patterns of Thought and Taste in Seventeenth-Century Literature

Spanish literature in the seventeenth century conveys the impression that it is the product of a stable and well-integrated culture – an impression that is strengthened if we include the drama, where all classes most obviously came together to participate in a common cultural experience. Though the tone of this literature is often pessimistic, Spaniards had no doubts about the importance and quality of contemporary writing in Spanish. A decided note of nationalism now enters into their appraisal of it. The exuberant literary creativity of Spain at this period sometimes surprises historians for it was also a period of crumbling Spanish political and military power, of serious and unconcealed economic decline and of a good deal of political and social unrest at home. Little of this is directly reflected in literature.

Spanish seventeenth-century literature was greatly concerned with stylistic problems. These will be discussed in the following section. There were a number of other widely held preoccupations of a general kind that characterize it. One was a keen sense of the need for a writer to contrive to astonish or surprise the reader, to arouse his *admiración*. A much-stressed theme, too, was that of *desengaño* – a desire to persuade men, through the medium of literature, of the need not to be deceived by the attractions the world had to offer. Associated with the theme of *desengaño* was literature's concern with the difference between the appearance of things and the reality that lay behind the appearance. There was, also, much stress on the enigmatic and the cerebral so that the reader had to work hard to interpret what was offered him. This literature is usually doctrinal or, at least, feels obliged to affect to be doctrinal. It is markedly sententious.

In a formal sense, writers tend to abandon closed, symmetrical, organized structures and to prefer fluid, open-ended, apparently improvised ones. A concern for visual decorative effects is also characteristic, particularly in poetry. But this emphasis on the visual was not, at least in theory, intended merely to supply decoration for its own sake: it was supposed to aid the reader to grasp more fully both the concepts and the emotions the poet wished to communicate. Seventeenth-century Spanish writers, too, like to stress the interrelationships between literature and the other arts, particularly painting and music. Pagan mythology, interpreted allegorically or symbolically in a Christian or at least in a moralizing sense, is much used.[1] Allegory generally is restored to favour as a literary form after a long period when the influence of classical literature had caused it to be discredited. There is a notable lack of interest in creating realistic 'characters' in the Cervantine sense. Writers give the impression that they do not wish to be constrained by any obligation to make the personages they created 'lifelike' in any strict sense. These now tend to be either types, personifying virtues or vices, or caricatures, or dehumanized, larger-than-life symbols.

Some characteristic features of thought and taste in literature are almost certainly related to the commanding position the Jesuit Order came to have in the intellectual and cultural life of seventeenth-century Spain. This was due in large measure to the prestige of the Jesuit schools and colleges which had begun to dominate Spanish secondary education in the second half of the sixteenth century and which, after the death of Philip II (who had disliked the Jesuits), moved into the sphere of higher education too. Establishments like the famous Jesuit Colegio Imperial at Madrid rivalled the ancient universities, despite the violent opposition of the latter to competition from the Jesuits, whom they accused of teaching undesirable novelties. In fact the pedagogic innovations of the Jesuits were admired even by their Protestant enemies, and the attachment of those who had been educated by the

[1] For similar treatment of mythology in painting, see Chapter 11, section VI and section XII.

Jesuits to their former teachers and the latters' way of looking at things was well known. In the Jesuit colleges every effort was made to turn students into passable Latinists so that, in the seventeenth century, educated Spanish laymen were probably better able to read and to write in Latin than they had ever been. They were also taught how to use their own language effectively. Doubts about the propriety of Christian students' studying pagan authors were finally set at rest by the doctrine of the Jesuit humanists that Christians had an undoubted right to make use of 'the spoils of the Egyptians' for their own purposes. The Latin texts studied in the colleges were, however, carefully expurgated; the classical humanism of the Jesuits was not designed to encourage dangerous thoughts or to stir up immoderate enthusiasm for the ancient world. Despite its 'new look' Christianity, and the charges of novelty levelled against it, the Jesuit Order's ultimate aims were, as Loyola had demanded, uncompromisingly committed to the defence of orthodoxy.

It is obviously difficult to document the extent of this Jesuit influence on Spanish seventeenth-century thought and taste. Certainly the Jesuits played an important role in the censorship of books and, in this way, exercised some general influence on literature and other forms of writing. The stress the Jesuits put on the study of rhetoric in the colleges almost certainly played a part in the restoration of rhetoric to a commanding position in the act of literary creation; many of the commonly used manuals of rhetoric were written by Jesuits. The marked interest in casuistry found in some Spanish writing may well also be connected with the special interest the Jesuits had in this subject. Casuistry is that branch of ethics that resolves problems of conscience by showing how the general rules of religion and morality may be interpreted to meet the needs of special individual cases where particular circumstances or conflicting duties are present. At its worst casuistry became concerned not with the moral question 'Is this act right or not?' but with the question 'Can this act be justified by special pleading?' The process by which casuistical justifications were found could all too easily degenerate into mere logic-chopping and hair-splitting. Casuistry was, however, a popular subject in seventeenth-century Spain – and not just among priests. The *Summula casuum conscientiae* (1626) of the Jesuit Antonio de Escobar was a best-seller.

The Jesuits certainly played a direct part in fostering Spanish interest in neo-stoicism (see section XI below). Their interest in emblem literature as a tool for religious and moral propaganda contributed to the vogue of emblem literature generally. Emblem literature consisted of sequences of allegorical or symbolic pictures whose interpretation was not readily apparent from the picture itself. The meaning was elucidated in a short poem which appeared below it. The theory behind emblem literature was that the emblem itself taught a moral truth intuitively while the verses supplied a laconic explanation to confirm this. Emblems were employed by seventeenth-century painters, too – e.g. by Zurbarán. They were much used in Jesuit colleges for instructive purposes. This literature appealed to the contemporary taste for what was enigmatic, and its influence is sometimes discernible on the form and style of writing generally. Baltasar Gracián's *Oráculo manual* has thus been described as a collection of emblems lacking only the emblem pictures themselves. The sonnet, a form often used for the textual interpretation of an emblem, sometimes took on the characteristics of an emblematic poem without the presence of the emblem itself. The Jesuits were also interested in the related cult of the prose *empresa*, or motto. This was another form of enigmatic literature derived from heraldry.

The Jesuits were very sympathetic towards the baroque style in the visual arts. Their long-standing belief in the usefulness of these arts (painting, sculpture and architecture) for purposes of religious propaganda found baroque art's air of novelty, its stress on magnificence, its cult of the emotions, its dramatic quality and its desire to disturb particularly appealing. Many of the characteristics of Spanish seventeenth-century literature mentioned above have their parallels in contemporary baroque art. As a result it has become fashionable to describe much Spanish seventeenth-century literature as 'baroque' and to stress these analogies with the visual arts. As a descriptive term the word should, however, be used with caution. It is usually less helpful than one might suppose to describe literature in terms of the visual arts as this can amount to no more than saying that a literary work reminds one of a piece of painting, or sculpture or architecture. The label 'baroque' often tends to blur rather than to elucidate a critical statement since there is, as yet, no agreed definition of baroque art itself and no general agreement about the meaning of the term when applied to literature. Its use may distract the reader's attention from what is important in strictly literary terms about the work under discussion. That there are, however, some general coincidences of taste between literature and the visual arts in the seventeenth century is undeniable.[1]

[1] The reader should refer to Chapter 11, particularly to sections XI–XIV, for information about Spanish baroque art. A confrontation of seventeenth-century

VII *Culteranismo* and *Conceptismo*

The phenomenon of *culteranismo*, which gave rise to many polemics among Spanish poets and readers of poetry from the second decade of the seventeenth century onwards, is closely associated with the name of Luis de Argote y Góngora (1561–1627), the master of the *culterano* (as well as other) styles. The phenomenon of *conceptismo*, which found its best poetic expression in the highly strung poetry of Francisco de Quevedo y Villegas (1580–1645), gave rise to few if any polemics though it was, in its less obvious way, no less removed from the Renaissance poetic tradition than was the poetry of Góngora.

Conceptismo was by no means only, or even mostly, a matter of poetic style. It was very much a feature of seventeenth-century prose style, practised by Quevedo himself, by the Jesuit Baltasar Gracián (1601–58) and by many others. But, in a historical sense, Góngora and Quevedo were only partly the initiators (by example) of the two styles particularly associated with their names. A development towards *culteranismo* and *conceptismo* had long been hinted at by sixteenth-century writers of treatises on rhetoric and poetics, notably in Italy. *Conceptismo* may be seen ultimately as arising out of the argument that had gone on since Erasmus's time between those who regarded Cicero as the model for prose-writing and those whose preference was for the style of Seneca.

It is often said that it is impossible to distinguish clearly between *culteranismo* and *conceptismo*. In a sense this is true because *culteranismo* often has recourse to *conceptista* figures: Gracián, in his famous if very obscure treatise on *conceptismo* (*Arte de ingenio*, 1642; second edition with revised title *Agudeza y arte de ingenio*, 1648), very frequently cites Góngora as a master of *conceptismo*. But, at least in theory, we can identify the different intentions of the two styles. Quintilian (A.D. c. 35–c. 100) – increasingly the main authority on classical rhetoric – had clearly distinguished, in his *Institutio oratoria*, 'figures of thought', through which the orator sought to stir his hearer's intellect, from 'figures of speech', which were designed to appeal to his senses (notably the ear) or had a purely decorative function. *Conceptismo*, in rhetorical terms, was a matter of figures of thought, *culteranismo* of figures of speech.

---

literature with, for example, Spanish painting of the period, reveals that the painters were much concerned with forms of painterly baroque expression for which no literary parallels can naturally be found. For baroque music, see Chapter 12, section VIII.

Góngora himself used the adjective *culto* to define his 'new' style. This Italianism appears in Garcilaso de la Vega, applied to the poet Bernardo Tasso. In Garcilaso's time it meant simply 'polished', 'artistically skilled'. In the later part of the sixteenth century the word came to mean what was opposed to 'the vulgar' – hence 'erudite', as well as polished. But it also now had connotations of nobility. The *culto* style was appropriate to the nobleness of a poet's status. The polemics between Góngora and his opponents make it seem a simple matter to discover the latter's objections to the *culterano* style. They protested against the great number of lexical novelties it introduced into the vocabulary of poetry; against an excessive use of metaphor and, particularly, the habit of developing metaphor from metaphor ('aun las mismas metáforas metaforiza'); against the continuous rejection of the normal Spanish word order and its replacement by the freedom in the sequence of word and phrase characteristic of Latin poetry – the use of transpositions, inversions and the like. There were also complaints about the excessive length of Góngora's poetic sentences and phrases, about his use of exaggerated hyperbole, about his reliance on the plurivalent meanings of words, about his excessive repetition of the same words and phrases. It was also noted that *culterano* poetry broke with the Aristotelian categories by mingling 'high' themes with 'low' ones, humble words with sublime ones. What all this really meant was that *culterano* poetry offended by seeking to approximate Spanish poetic diction and style more closely to those of Latin poetry than had been attempted before.[1]

In terms of traditional Spanish rhetorical and poetical precept the criticisms made of *culterano* poetry by its enemies were valid. Góngora's defenders accepted traditional classical authority and mostly contented themselves with showing that there was both practical and theoretical precedent for all the innovations of *culteranismo* in classical Latin poetry and poetic theory, as well as in the writings of sixteenth-century Italians. Certainly, in some respects, *culteranismo* in poetry was not, historically speaking, the novelty Lope de Vega claimed it to be. It remained firmly within the general thematic and stylistic traditions of European Renaissance poetry and the impression of novelty derived from the fact that Góngora and his followers selected and concentrated exclusively on certain features of the tradition. That it seemed, however, for a time a shockingly new invention is beyond doubt.

[1] See Chapter 1, section VII, pp. 27–8 for additional information about the *culterano* style.

The first formal all-out Spanish defence of the case for unrestricted obscurity in poetry was the *Libro de la erudición poética* – published posthumously in 1611 – by Góngora's fellow Córdoban, Luis Carrillo y Sotomayor (*c.* 1582–1610), some of whose often interesting poetry was even more obscure than that of Góngora himself. A difficulty about Carrillo and about other defenders of *culteranismo* is their vagueness when answering the charge that, despite the alleged connection between philosophy and poetry, their poetry was short on content. None ever succeeded in explaining clearly what it was that was supposed to lie hidden within the dazzling outer skin (*corteza*), to use Góngora's term, of their work. In any case the arguments for and against the *culterano* style really turned out in practice to be beside the point. Góngora and his fellows were the literary spokesmen for a general change in taste that could not be halted by criticism or logical argument. This is demonstrated by the speed with which many of the most vociferous opponents of *culteranismo*, like Lope de Vega, Juan de Jáuregui and many others, ended up by adopting it.

Conceptismo's concern was not to present intricate surfaces but to appeal, it was claimed, to the intellect. It is useful in this connection to contrast one of Góngora's stark, undecorated, *conceptista* sonnets like *Menos solicitó veloz saeta* with his *culterano* writing. As its name reveals, *conceptismo* was concerned with the *concepto* or thought. But this word, too, had undergone a semantic change in later sixteenth-century Italian treatises on poetic style. It then became closely associated with the idea of 'wit' (Italian *acutezza* > Sp. *agudeza*), in the sense in which this term was used by the English metaphysical poets such as John Donne. Gracián, in his famous stylistic treatise, was much concerned with the phenomenon of *conceptismo* which he tried to analyse, declaring the conceit itself to be an intellectual act and *agudeza* (wit) the form in which the *concepto* was clothed to make it beautiful. The definition was unsatisfactory; it was always easier to sense *conceptismo* than to define it exactly.

An obvious feature of the *conceptista* style was its reliance on a rhetorical figure treated as a figure of abuse in classical treatises on rhetoric – *catachresis*. Catachresis involved bringing into a relationship, as a result of a deliberate intellectual act, things that in nature are widely separated. John Dryden described catachresis as 'something more desperate than a metaphor. It is the expressing of one matter by the name of another which is incompatible with it and sometimes clean contrary.' *Conceptismo*, too, made continuous use of the plurivalent meaning of words by means of the pun or *equívoco*. Clearly here again the desire of the seventeenth-century reading public to be astonished by their reading was an important factor in creating the *conceptista* taste. Writers such as Gracián found in Martial, Lucan and Seneca classical authority for the validity of *conceptismo*. For Quevedo, Seneca in particular was esteemed as a stylist. As he wrote: 'Most witty [*agudíssimo*] and admirably skilled was Seneca; his style, by the brevity of its aphorisms, works like a sea-strait, hemming into narrow spaces the currents of deep seas of knowledge.' Extreme concision of expression packed with enigmatic meaning which the reader must decipher is another characteristic of *conceptismo*. Emblems, *empresas* and hieroglyphs were also seen as examples of the style of *conceptista* writing. The movement was not particularly Spanish though it seems likely that its vogue in Spain was furthered by the approval given to it at this time in the Jesuit colleges. Gracián's writings on the subject are superficially so similar to those of the Italian Matteo Pellegrini, his contemporary, that it used to be supposed, incorrectly, either that Pellegrini borrowed from Gracián or vice versa. We must not, however, be misled by all this talk about 'concepts' to any false notions about the strictly intellectual quality of *conceptista* writing. It appealed to subtle, alert, minds capable of being amused and surprised by unexpected correlations of ideas but its creativity was, in the last resort, concerned with stylistics, not with expanding in any significant way the frontiers of thought.

VIII Seventeenth-Century Poetry: Góngora

Góngora was the most talked-about Spanish poet of his day and, judged by his effect on other poets, also the most influential one – the creator of a poetic style that was to last in Spain even beyond the end of the seventeenth century. No other poet of those times, either, was forced to explain his motives – or to have them explained for him by others – as Góngora was. Despite that, doubts remain as to what he was really about in the poems which made his name famous outside as well as inside Spain. Góngora's biography does not help to solve these doubts. He was a native of Córdoba and resided there until in 1617, already in his late fifties, he made a disastrous move to Madrid hoping to capitalize at court on his fame. Opinions have differed as to the extent to which Góngora's special sensitivity to light and colour may be connected with his Andalusian background. What is certain is that Andalusian popular music and song interested him greatly and inspired many of his short poems written in the traditional metres of oral poetry – *seguidillas*, *villancicos*, *letrillas*, ballads and the like. These are often works of great charm and lyric intensity, like the famous *La más bella niña* or *Las flores del romero*. Góngora continued to write such poems even when he had become famous as the apostle of poetic obscurity. His sensitivity to music, popular and serious, is important. Verbal melody is a characteristic of his poetry and this he considered to be a particular and desirable quality of the work of Andalusian poets. The Platonic theory of music plays some role in his most ambitious poems.

In many *letrillas* and sonnets Góngora puts the linguistic inventiveness and command of metaphor for which he was famous to serve his highly penetrating comic wit at the expense of his literary enemies, or others who had displeased him. An important aspect of Góngora's work, too, is his disconcerting capacity for humorous self-parody. In 1618, in the middle of the great quarrel about poetic style which he had started, we find him, in his *Fábula de Píramo y Tisbe*, guying his own *culterano* style for comic effect in a poem so erudite and complicated that it, too, was considered to need an explanatory commentary. Góngora was, in fact, always a poet who wrote in many different styles. In a revealing and startlingly modern phrase Góngora (1587) described himself as suffering from poetry as people suffered from an illness ('mal de poesía').

There was no sudden conversion to *culteranismo*. Strong tendencies towards *culto* writing can be discerned in some of his works from the 1580s onwards, while many examples of non-*culterano* writing occur up to the end of his life. As has been mentioned too, Góngora was also a master of the *conceptista* style. Some of his sonnets, stark and stripped of all decorative purposes, show Góngora using his erudition and his command of metaphor in a way that scarcely seems to belong to the *culterano* writer at all. Góngora's fame rests today, for most readers, on his major poems in the *culterano* manner. These are the ballad *En un pastoral albergue* (1602) – based on the famous episode of Angelica e Medoro in Ariosto's *Orlando Furioso* – the *Fábula de Polifemo y Galatea* (1613), the *Soledad primera* (1613) and the unfinished *Soledad segunda* (1614). Insufficient regard has, perhaps, been given to the fact that Góngora never finished the latter and, as far as we know, never began to write the two further *Soledades* he had planned. There are two other long poems worth attention. One is the *Oda a la toma de Larache* (1611) and the other the *Panegírico al Duque de Lerma* (1617). These are occasional poems (poet-laureate stuff) whose doctrinal content is nil. That Góngora found it possible to devote to them the full range of his gifts as a *culterano* poet is one of several factors that force one to ask whether, as he and his supporters asserted, the meaning beneath the dazzling surface of *culteranismo* was really so important to him as they said. It should be noted, too, that not a few critics have concluded that Góngora scored his greatest successes not in the well-known poems mentioned but in his sonnets. Many of these are certainly memorable in a way that the longer poems are not. The discipline of the sonnet form compelled the poet to limit the fecundity of his poetic imagination, his proliferating imagistic extravagance and his tentative, exploratory instincts as a poet. The requirement that the sonnet should end with a generalized moral or intellectual conclusion also makes this naturally ambiguous writer declare unambiguously what he is up to.

The principal features of *culteranismo* as a style have already been discussed (section VII above) and need not be repeated here. Like Paul Valéry, a modern defender of poetic obscurity, we can see that one feature of Góngora's work is his continual rejection of the immediate solution to the needs of poetic utterance suggested by the ruling linguistic and imagistic conventions of his day. This aspect of Góngora's poetry is what establishes a chasm between his work and those who followed him; the latter were mostly content simply to take over and follow somewhat automatically the new style he had created.

But, as has already been pointed out, the novelty of Góngora's style must not be exaggerated. He felt that the whole amalgam of Petrarchism with the Latin poetic tradition that, in Spain as elsewhere, had long dominated poetry was played out and that something new was required. But Góngora, a child of his age and his country, could not, in any really basic sense, break away from the traditions of Renaissance poetry. As indeed his defenders were quick to point out, authority for what he had done was to be found in that tradition. What we get in *culteranismo* is the selection of certain rather sparsely used features inherent in the tradition and a systematic concentration on them. The tradition is re-jigged, not abandoned.

A major problem is concerned with Góngora's claims that works like the *Soledades* have a hidden meaning available to those capable of penetrating beneath the surface. The Spanish poet-critics who rehabilitated Góngora in the 1920s took the action of the *Soledades* and their narrative content to be no more than a pretext to enable the poet to escape into the task of creating a poetic world independent of the real world and its problems. An examination in a seventeenth-century context of Góngora's continuous presentation of allusions to and

images from classical mythology, in particular, necessarily raises grave
doubts about the validity of such a view of Góngora's work. Contemporary commentators make it plain that the mythological allusions in
Góngora's work could all be interpreted either allegorically, emblem-
atically or symbolically in the manner suggested by the treatise on
mythology called *Philosophia secreta* (1585) by Juan de Moya (*c.* 1513–
97), so that they had a moral purpose. The opening passages of the
Soledad primera, moreover, lend themselves to allegorical interpretation
when they introduce an unnamed youth cast up naked by the sea on a
beach to begin the journey which will be the subject of the poem. The
turbulent sea, Góngora hints, can be interpreted as the sea of error from
which the youth, a refugee from unhappy love, has now escaped as
from a spiritual desert (*Libia de ondas*) to the *terra firma* of an ordered
world. All that follows can, too, be given moral, symbolic or emblematic meaning if we wish. Yet questions remain about the relevance of
this two-level, doctrinal meaning: as Lope de Vega and other critics
suggested, the basic themes that emerge from such an interpretation are
themselves so well worn that they seem inappropriate to the enormous
effort of poetic creation that has gone into this poem. Given the nature
of contemporary poetic theory, the allegorizing tendencies of the
Counter-Reformation and the need of poets to explain their work in
strictly intellectual and logical terms, it is improbable that Góngora can
ever have formulated for himself an art-for-art's-sake poetic aesthetic.
But it is hard to read his famous *culterano* poems, with their continual
emphasis on poetic means rather than ends, without suspecting that his
'mal de poesía' may instinctively have carried him in that direction.
There are indications in the very ambiguity of some of his explanatory
utterances and, perhaps, in the fact that he never finished the *Soledades*,
that he himself was baffled by the road along which his muse had taken
him.

The *culterano* style left a deep impression on Spanish poetry after
Góngora. That Góngora's poetic genius had opened new frontiers is
shown by the way many of those who had bitterly criticized *culto*
poetry at the time it first came to public attention ended by adopting it.
Thus Lope de Vega (1572–1635), from about 1621, began to write
(though not, of course, continuously) in a style sometimes indistinguishable from that of Góngora and marked by evident reminiscences of Lope's reading of the famous Gongorine poems. An example
is the poems published in *La Circe* (1624). Juan de Jáuregui totally

surrendered in his *Orfeo* (1624) to the style he had tellingly assailed a few years earlier. Góngora's influence also changed the style of one of the best of the minor poets of the seventeenth century, Juan de Tassis y Peralta, Count of Villamediana (1582–1622), the flamboyant author of some of the most savage and bold verse political lampoons of his day. After writing good sonnets in the tradition of Garcilaso, Villamediana, after 1616, became a disciple of *culteranismo*. His impressive *Fábula de Faetón* can stand comparison with Góngora's treatment of mythological themes. It is noticeable that it was in the presentation of such themes that *culteranismo* exercised its greatest impact on seventeenth-century poetry. A very unusual follower of Góngora was the Hieronymite monk Adrián de Prado (*fl.* 1620), whose *Canción a San Jerónimo* (1619), in which he pictures St Jerome in the Syrian desert, uses startlingly bold new images to describe the desert landscape and its creatures, and the saint himself, likened to 'algún seco tronco'. Adrián de Prado, in what is one of the most original of Spanish seventeenth-century narrative poems, does not hesitate to employ images relating to the human anatomy's less poetic features to describe grim natural landscapes.

A poet who, while not a Gongorist, merits careful attention in any history of seventeenth-century poetic taste is the Antequeran poet Pedro de Espinosa (1578–1650) who, before he became a hermit in 1606, wrote two remarkable descriptive poems, crammed to overflowing with vivid, colourful imagery, the *Fábula de Genil* and *La navegación de San Raimundo* which inevitably recall the exuberant, convoluted, rich, dazzling and capricious images of baroque visual structures. The *Navegación de San Raimundo* ostensibly describes the saint's journey from Mallorca to the mainland, but this religious theme is overwhelmed in a welter of sea imagery largely drawn from classical mythology which includes crowded imaginative descriptions of the marine deities and others who inhabit the submarine caverns of the ocean. The *Fábula de Genil* also invokes a similar vision of the underwater mythological world as well as of the river as it moves through the countryside. For all their pullulating imagery connected with movement the poet's great attention to detail gives these poems a visual quality of violent activity caught and made static that recalls the impression made by baroque sculpture. Espinosa, without anticipating the syntactical and lexical characteristics of *culto* poetry, does anticipate the total abandonment of limit which inspired Góngora's attitude to natural description. It should be stressed, however, that the brilliant artefacts of nature created by Espinosa, as is normal with *culterano* description, seem to owe next to nothing to any direct personal responses of the poet to nature, nor do they attempt to stimulate such responses in the reader. For this reason, too, suggestions that *culterano* description is sensuous in its appeal seem unconvincing. It is intended to astonish and to dazzle, to supply (by reminiscences drawn from the poet's reading associated with deliberate acts of the creative imagination) a new vision of the natural world whose interest lies precisely in the fact that it is invented by the poet.

IX Seventeenth-Century Poetry: Quevedo and Lope de Vega

Prose as well as poetry were the media used by Francisco de Quevedo. We shall be concerned here only with the poet. In his thousand-odd poems Quevedo, however, often dealt with the kind of material he was concerned with in his prose works, as well as with topics that were exclusively reserved for his verse. Thus his interest in neo-stoicism (pp. 334–7 below) is responsible for his very free verse translations of Epictetus and Phocylides (*Epicteto y Focílides en español*, 1635) – the only poetic work he published in his lifetime. His *jácaras*, black comic satires, written in *germanía* (the slang of the criminal classes), at the expense of the criminal community, reflect the sort of low-life caricatures he created in his famous picaresque novel, *El Buscón*, and in other works. His contemporaries correctly thought of his satirical writing as much influenced by the Roman satirist Juvenal: Lope de Vega, indeed, described him as a 'Juvenal en verso'. His verse, like his prose, was also constantly influenced – more than is supposed – by Seneca and Martial.

Despite his continual propagandist writing for his own version of the moral philosophy of Christian stoicism ('sufre, absténte'), Quevedo for most of his life was heavily and willingly involved in public affairs. A pitiless censor of the shortcomings of others, he was also very willing to admit to his own moral failures, though not to have them pointed out.

Quevedo's satirical and burlesque poetry – like his love poems – achieves its unique quality because of the poet's mastery of the *conceptista* or 'metaphysical' style whose main qualities have already been discussed. But in Quevedo this style, demanding as it is on the reader, does not, as Góngora's often does, give the impression that it has been contrived with slowness and care. Quevedo's harsh, staccato, exasperated, compressed, lapidary manner of writing (which, though less obviously, is a feature of his love poetry as well as of his satirical writing) seems to have flowed naturally from his pen – as it does, too, in the prose works.

As a satirist Quevedo does often recall Juvenal. Like the Latin satirist, his moral attitudes were over-simple; he idealized the past without, apparently, ever asking himself if there was any evidence that it was really any better than the present. His view of the world, too, was over-conservative, like Juvenal's. The derision, bitterness, violence and pitiless quality of his satire, whether aimed at the traditional classes of men who were the targets of the satirists or against individuals, is essentially caricature, often scatological, intended not to improve but to destroy. It was characteristic of Quevedo that, as part of his campaign against *culteranismo*, he should edit and publish the poems of a poet of another age, Luis de León (1629), while, at the same time, not sparing his attacks on other contemporary poets for being too traditional. Despite his praise of the old values, too, he played his part in devaluing them. In his ballad on Hero and Leander (as in his prose *Sueños*) classical mythology is deliberately degraded and ridiculed.

In his serious poetry Quevedo was obsessed yet fascinated by the idea that all men and women are under sentence of death, doomed by time if not by fate. The clock and the hour-glass provide the imagery for some of his finest poems on this theme. Characteristically, when he wishes to describe himself alone with his books, it is the fact that their authors are dead which supplies him with opportunities for *conceptista* wit: 'vivo en conversación con los difuntos / y escucho con mis ojos a los muertos.' His love poetry is still in the later Petrarchist tradition but the now hackneyed imagery and language are whipped into startling new postures by the use of catachresis and other *conceptista* devices. Quevedo's ability to bridge the gap between disparate ideas or situations by an act of wit is fully displayed in a work like his sonnet *En crespa tempestad del oro undoso*, where the sight of Lisi's unfastened, wavy, golden hair (again a hackneyed image) leads the poet into a brilliant series of interlocked sequences of forced metaphor in which the hair becomes, simultaneously, a sea in which the lover swims like Leander, the gold that men desire, and the sun's rays that burn and kill the over-ambitious like Icarus and so on. Such highly compressed and carefully organized poetic statements, always logically defensible and often ending in a tercet with emblematic implications, have little to say on a casual reading but demand the participation of the reader's intellect before they become intelligible. When they fail, as they sometimes do, they are little more than sets of clues to be solved like crosswords. They

are, when they come off, fully capable of producing genuine excitement as the poet suggests a whole series of new natural or metaphorical
relationships. Calderón's definition of poetry as 'una gala del alma o
agilidad del entendimiento' is singularly applicable to Quevedo, who
belongs to the same school that produced the English 'metaphysical
poets'. But Quevedo's poetic world seems to be, perhaps, more tightly
enclosed in its century than theirs. Ironically, while his satirical verse in
this style (when it was not simply ephemeral) is fully capable of arousing
the modern reader's feelings, it is by no means clear that his love poetry
can still do so.

The new *culterano* and *conceptista* styles did not, of course, triumph un-
challenged in seventeenth-century Spanish poetry. Respect for the
'classical' values of poetry and for classical poetic decorum could hardly
disappear without trace in an age when the great Latin poets were read
in the colleges as a matter of course, and when treatises on poetics and
rhetoric were studied which roundly condemned some of the practices
of the new-style poets. Court poetry, too, was – at least to some extent
– still written to be sung, and neither of the new styles readily lent
themselves to that. Bernardo de Balbuena (1568–1627), the writer of
heroic epic, admitted (1624) that many readers of such poetry were only
concerned with its verbal melodies or the superficial meaning of its
plot; it may be supposed that they responded in the same way to the
lyric. The poet Francisco de Trillo y Figueroa (1620–c. 1680) also
emphasized the prime importance of poetry's musical appeal. The importance of poetry as melody at this time should not be underestimated. The two Aragonese brothers, Lupercio Leonardo de Argensola (1559–1613) and Bartolomé Leonardo de Argensola (1562–1631),
strict disciples of Horace in theme and style, enjoyed much authority
and popularity. Gabriel Bocángel y Unzueta (1603–58), in the prologue
to his *Rimas y prosas* (1627), strongly denied that 'lo culto' must be
identified with 'lo escuro' – poets must be learned and elevated but
could very well be clear too. He called the 'verso hinchado y extraña
locución' of Gongorism a mere deceiving of the ears. But the traditionalists, simply because they did go on doing what had long been
done in poetry (even if often appropriating some of the new themes
and topics characteristic of seventeenth-century literature), lack the
power to excite us much today. In a real sense they were anachronistic.
Even a famous poem like the Horatian *Epístola moral a Fabio* (c. 1610),

probably attributable to the Sevillan poet Andrés Fernández de Andrada, was perhaps over-valued for its easy intelligibility in the days before modern critics had learnt to appreciate what Góngora or Quevedo were about.

The verse of Lope Félix de Vega Carpio (1562–1635), while it can often be called traditionalist, presents problems of assessment to the critic. It is often forgotten that Lope was almost as prolific a poet (in all the genres of his time) as he was a playwright; indeed, many of his lyrics were written for his plays. As is the case with the latter, sheer quantity and marked unevenness in execution make any critical synthesis of his poetic work difficult. What must be accepted, alongside the excitements of *culterano* and *conceptista* writing, is that in the first three decades of the seventeenth century the lyrics of Lope de Vega were immensely popular in Spain both among serious connoisseurs of poetry as well as with readers who just liked reading poems. Thus his volume of 200 sonnets in the Petrarchist mould, the *Rimas [humanas]* (1602), was sent to England from Madrid around 1613 by a member of Shakespeare's circle with the comment that Spaniards esteemed Lope as a writer of sonnets as greatly as Englishmen esteemed the sonnets of Shakespeare. The writer of these words, Leonard Digges, plainly did not think the comparison inept.

A special feature of Lope de Vega as a lyric poet in the Italianate–classical tradition is the unusual extent to which he openly used verse as a vehicle for only very thinly disguised emotional autobiography in a country where reserve about such matters was the rule and the courtly tradition demanded secrecy and disguise. A high proportion of Lope de Vega's lyrics, however, fail to satisfy simply because he wrote too much too easily and was over-ready to rest a poem on some good lines or to resort to rhetoric in lieu of, rather than as an aid to, a search for the exact expression of a feeling or an idea. The same is true of the hundred religious sonnets that make up the *Rimas sacras* (1614); his work here is popular in tone, often supplying religiosity instead of serious religious feeling, too effusive and easy. Three different main styles have been detected in his lyric work: (i) highly mannered love poetry in the later Petrarchist tradition, notable for its use of antithesis and rhetorically symmetrical language; (ii) the work he wrote in imitation of Góngora, despite his attacks on the latter; and (iii) his 'philosophical' poems, in which the poet seems determined to prove wrong those of his critics who claimed his poetry lacked depth of thought. A fourth category should be added to these: Lope's employment of the themes, styles and metres of folk poetry, which he regularly handled with real feeling and genius, meriting in this field comparison with Góngora. Nor can Lope be entirely thought of in his serious work as a poet incapable of achieving perfection. When he decided to take proper trouble over a poem and was genuinely moved he could write masterpieces. Examples are to be found in occasional sonnets or, for example, in the universally admired two *barquillas* (where the theme is the old topos of man's life as a journey in a boat) inserted into his strange half-autobiographical novel *La Dorotea*.

X Prose Fiction After Cervantes: the Picaresque Novel

The most striking thing about seventeenth-century prose fiction in general after Cervantes is the fact that it was scarcely influenced at all by the works which modern criticism regards as Cervantes's masterpieces. It was influenced to some extent by his more romantic *Novelas ejemplares* and by the kind of taste for the Byzantine adventure story represented by the *Persiles y Sigismunda*. But any debt to Cervantes was usually unacknowledged by the prose writers who succeeded him – as if their awareness of his genius was so oppressive to their own mediocrity that it seemed best to pretend he was not there. Cervantes, in some of his *Novelas ejemplares*, by turning to fiction based on direct observation of contemporary Spanish social realities and to commenting on the dilemmas of men and women as social animals as well as private individuals, had, of course, opened the way to a potentially limitless source of narrative fiction. But in this he was evidently far in advance of the times. Seventeenth-century writers of long short-stories and short novels instead found a ready response from Spanish readers for the type of tale sometimes categorized as the *novela cortesana*. This term is somewhat misleading, except in so far as it suggests that the milieu (and concerns) of these stories is with high life rather than low life. They have quite considerable similarities of content and tone with the run-of-the-mill *comedias* on which the contemporary theatre depended. They are usually written according to a ready-made formula for a public who wanted best-sellers that would not break with expected patterns but must hold the reader's attention and supply that ingredient of surprise indispensable for all literature. The formula usually excluded posing any really awkward questions, social or moral.

An exception to the general mediocre level of the *novela cortesana* is the minor but still interesting María de Zayas y Sotomayor (1590-

c. 1661) – *Novelas ejemplares y amorosas* (Part I, 1637; Part II, 1647) – one of the very few Golden Age women writers. She inveighs, in a surprisingly outspoken way, against the status of women in contemporary Spanish upper-class society. But her stories themselves suggest that perhaps all this was more directed to winning the sympathy of a predominantly feminine readership than because she really dissented seriously from conventional values, for she very often portrays her women as creatures of passion, not reason, foolishly ready to abandon everything, whatever the cost, for love. María de Zayas's attitudes are sometimes oddly cynical; she did not hesitate to depict melodramatic horrors and unladylike crudities to titillate her readers. In the tale called *La inocencia castigada* an innocent woman, walled up for six years by her husband, is described, when eventually discovered and released, as having her clothing and flesh partly consumed by the worms that had bred in her excrement.

Lope de Vega, determined as usual to show himself the master of all the literary trades, had published one *novela* before Cervantes published his – *El peregrino en su patria* (1604). It speedily went through six editions. It is about the endless travels of some pairs of lovers and the obstacles they have to overcome. Quite different problems are presented by the fictionalized piece of amorous autobiography, *La Dorotea* (1632), into which Lope clearly put a great amount of creative effort, and which has enjoyed some critical approval in the twentieth century as a kind of experimental novel and as a piece of literature exhibiting the characteristics of the 'baroque' age. *La Dorotea* is entirely in dialogue form, written in five 'acts' divided into a widely varying number of 'scenes'. Its formal model was the dialogued novel in the now antiquated tradition of *La Celestina*. Into this work Lope put some of his most sincere and deeply felt memories. It contains, as has been mentioned, some of his finest lyric poems, and it is written with a care unusual in Lope. But the ambiguity of *La Dorotea's* thematic framework and temporal stance is disturbing. Moreover, in a work where love is supposedly presented as a personal experience, Lope all too often offers his readers, instead, passages borrowed from Marsilio Ficino and other authorities. Unjustifiable digressions are frequent – there is an enormous one on *culterano* poetry. The book's worst shortcoming, in artistic terms, is its lack of any consistent viewpoint. As in the case of Cervantes, Lope's *Dorotea* makes one regret that the Golden Age did not accept real autobiography – particularly when its subject was love – as a serious literary genre.

Any discussion of the picaresque novel in the seventeenth century raises immediate problems of definition. If we take the genre to embrace *any* work of prose fiction in which attention is directed to the *pícaro* and the society in which he lived, the number of works to be considered is large and would, for example, have to include some of the *Novelas ejemplares* of Cervantes as well as some of the *novelas cortesanas* just discussed. If the term is restricted to those tales which, like *Lazarillo de Tormes* and *Guzmán de Alfarache*, strictly adhere to the autobiographical viewpoint (the decisive innovation in the art of realistic prose fiction discovered by the author of *Lazarillo de Tormes*) the definition of genre is more useful, though complicated by the fact that some seventeenth-century authors of picaresque stories use autobiography merely as a stylistic device, without seriously attempting to identify themselves with the *pícaro's* experiences or point of view.

The popularity of the Spanish picaresque novel not only in Spain but in Europe generally has been correctly connected with that interest in the life of the underworld of criminals, rogues and vagabonds that finds expression everywhere in various non-fictional forms of writing at this time. Literary attitudes to what in Spain was known as *la hampa* (the 'underworld') were ambiguous, vacillating between stern disapproval of an alternative society that was thought to be a menace to order and morals, and amusement at the tricks and antics of its members.

In *La ilustre fregona* Cervantes wrote a famous half-critical, half-sympathetic description of the life of the *pícaro*, adding the comment that many well-to-do fathers sought their missing sons in such communities and that these youths 'feel such sorrow when they are dragged away from that life as if they were being taken away to be executed'. Some of the attraction of the genre for seventeenth-century readers must have resided in the opportunities they offered the comfortably-off for vicariously enjoying such liberty. But in the larger cities like Madrid, Seville and Barcelona there was, in the seventeenth century, also a marked decline in law and order and in the moral climate generally. The new stress on the *pícaro* from the beginning of the century doubtless has something to do with people's awareness of this historical phenomenon. But the point should not be pressed too far; the *pícaro* of literature plainly was not identical with the *pícaro* of real life. The literary *pícaro* is not compelled by economic circumstances to be a rogue; he freely and repeatedly chooses to be one. The writers of picaresque novels usually thought of their protagonists as voluntary rogues, not as the helpless victims of economic or social misfortune. No picaresque novel ever sought to arouse a reader's compassion or sympathy for the *pícaro*.

Far and away the best of seventeenth-century Spanish picaresque novels was Francisco de Quevedo's remarkable *Historia de la vida del Buscón* (1626), a work of real genius. This is a comparatively short narrative of twenty-three rapidly moving chapters, free of digressions and author's comment, which keep strictly to the genre's autobiographical brief – the word 'Buscón' in the title means 'thief' or 'swindler'. The work was written some years before 1626 and various manuscript versions of it had long been in circulation. After its publication it was exceedingly popular, particularly in the 1620s; ten Spanish editions are known between 1626 and 1648. Quevedo's address to the reader stressed his book's capacity to amuse. He claimed some potential moral improvement could also, if the reader wished, be gleaned from the warning example of Pablos's life. But Quevedo did not rate the chances of this too highly, for, showing a more acute sense than some other writers of picaresque novels about the morally regenerative powers of such works, he remarked, 'I doubt if anyone buys a funny book [*libro de burlas*] in order to break with his depraved nature.'

El Buscón, too, shows more insight into psychological motivation than is usual. Pablos's father was a professional thief, his mother a witch and repairer of virgins (in the Celestina tradition), his uncle a public executioner. Quevedo goes to some trouble to show that this deplorable domestic background, and the scorn it earned him, left Pablos with an acute sense of his inferiority and a driving determination to climb socially. But, as was the case with Guzmán de Alfarache, it is implied that the background itself predisposes him to evil ways: Pablos is incapable of employing honest means of social climbing.

The book follows Pablos's career from his early days in Segovia, where he went to school – and, given his background, rather inexplicably became the protégé and private servant of a respectable young nobleman. It then deals with his time at the University of Alcalá, a subsequent stay in Madrid and, after a brief return to Segovia, his adventures in Toledo, where he acted in *comedias* and courted a nun. At the end of the book we find him in Seville as a card-sharper in the company of a band of *rufianes* (professional bullies). To avoid arrest for murder he sails for America with his mistress to see, as he puts it, if by changing continents his luck would improve. Quevedo makes him conclude the work, of which a second part was promised, by commenting that this notion proved unfounded since no one improves himself by changing only his location, not his manner of life.

What distinguishes *El Buscón* is its style. In it Quevedo uses his mastery of the *conceptista* style in prose to present a surrealist vision of life by means of forced metaphor and complicated playing on the plurivalent meanings of words. Here, as in the *Sueños*, Quevedo's art is one of penetrating caricature. The famous account of Pablos's stay in the house of the miserly Licenciado Cabra, who ran a boarding-school for young gentlemen in Segovia and starved them (chapter III), is, for its wit and grotesque realism, one of the most famous passages in Golden Age literature. Quevedo's descriptions of the practical jokes of which Pablos was victim or instigator totally lack any kind of pity or compassion. The book wins our allegiance through the sheer artistry of its author's use of language and the consistency of his vision.

No other subsequent picaresque novel approaches the quality of *Guzmán de Alfarache* or *El Buscón*. *La pícara Justina* (1605), perhaps by an unidentified doctor called Francisco López de Ubeda, has as its protagonist the first of the female *pícaras*. It seems probable that it was, in fact, a *roman à clef*, a disguised satire about highly placed real people at Philip III's court between 1601 and 1605. Somewhat more worthy of attention is *La vida del escudero Marcos de Obregón* (1618) by the musician and poet Vicente Espinel (1550–1624). *Marcos de Obregón* is not, strictly speaking, a genuine picaresque novel since it is supposed to have been written by an old squire (*escudero*) recounting his rather humdrum career for the instruction of youth. A lot of it is genuine autobiography dealing with real people but, to make this fairly unexciting life more spicy, Espinel interpolated bits of purely fictional autobiography into his story. As a result, the temporal framework of the novel and the continuity of its narrative dissolve into ambiguity. Once again we must be astonished at the failure of Spanish seventeenth-century writers of prose fiction to learn any lessons about their craft from Cervantes's example.

Of other picaresque tales the most interesting is a late one, *La vida y hechos de Estebanillo González, hombre de buen humor* (1646), described as 'compuesto por él mismo'. It is the autobiography ('relación verdadera') of a professional court jester who served Ottavio Piccolomini, one of the famous Catholic generals in the Thirty Years War, and the Cardinal-Infante Don Fernando, Philip IV's governor in the Low Countries. Estebanillo's wanderings as rogue, cowardly cabin-boy, fake doctor, pimp, army deserter, assassin, camp-follower and jester take him all over Europe. The book follows the *Guzmán de Alfarache* tradition in that it is supposedly written after Estebanillo, as a reward for his services as a jester to great households, has received a licence to open a gaming-house in Naples. Estebanillo tells his tale without shame and without a trace of finer feelings, religious concern or moral awareness. His successful career, he explains, is based on his cynical cheerfulness and his ability to make great men merry. The book is not artistically of great merit; all its emphasis is on action intended to make the reader laugh; little attempt is made to describe the varied milieux where events take place. But it does maintain a consistent viewpoint. Its author was a reader of Cervantes, whom he often cites.

The interest of the times in the life of vagabonds, rogues and criminals finds many other outlets in Spanish seventeenth-century literature. The popularity of *jácaras*, poems about the criminal fraternity written in the fraternity's private language – *germanía* – has already been mentioned. Picaresque elements penetrated the *novela cortesana*. Scenes from urban low life were, too, one of the staples of the dramatic inter-lude or *entremés*, a *sine qua non* of any theatrical programme at this time. One of the best of these is that called *La cárcel de Sevilla*, probably written at the end of the sixteenth century or early in the seventeenth century by a lawyer of Seville, Cristóbal de Chaves. It is a remarkably vivid and technically accomplished playlet describing prison life in Seville, in particular the preparations for a public hanging and the gallows humour of the victim-to-be, his fellow prisoners and his last visitors. A very readable account of the traps awaiting the unwary stranger in Madrid is the *Guía y avisos de forasteros* [*que vienen a la corte*] (1620) attributed to one 'Antonio de Liñan y Verdugo'. Its author may have been a Mercedarian friar, Alonso Remón. The book consists of fourteen 'novelas morales y ejemplares escarmientos'. Though its author, like others of his time, was, to modern tastes, sometimes tire-somely fond of quoting authorities and over-zealous in his moralizing, it is a work of considerably more stylistic as well as historical merit than better-known seventeenth-century stories. The picaresque novel's im-portance, even if the artistic worth of some individual examples has been over-valued and its comic intentions sometimes insufficiently stressed, lay in the fact that, by definition, it concerned itself with the literary depiction of society at its lower levels and therefore pointed the way towards more realism in prose fiction and away from romance.

XI Seventeenth-Century Thought: Neo-Stoicism

Spanish thinking after Trent was, as we have seen, dominated at its highest levels by theology and by the methodology of neo-scholasticism. There was, however, one area of thought – neo-stoicism – which considerably influenced some seventeenth-century Spanish writers (notably Quevedo) and where they found themselves relatively free to speculate outside the context of theology and neo-scholasticism. Neo-stoicism is so-called because it represented a bold attempt, made in the second half of the sixteenth century, to reconcile the thought of the ancient stoics with Christianity. The neo-stoic movement was a European one, affecting both Catholic and Protestant countries and writers.

Francisco de Quevedo defined his concept of stoicism in his first and best-known treatise on the subject, *Nombre, origen, intento, recomendación y descendencia de la doctrína estoica* (1635):

> La doctrina toda de los estoicos se cierra en este principio; que las cosas se dividen en propias y ajenas; que las propias están en nuestra mano, y las ajenas en la mano ajena; que aquéllas nos tocan, que estotras no nos pertenecen, y que por esto no nos han de perturbar ni afligir; que no hemos de procurar que en las cosas se haga nuestro deseo, sino ajustar nuestro deseo con los sucesos de las cosas, que así tendremos libertad, paz y quietud.

This idea that man will obtain freedom and peace only if he makes himself incapable of being affected by all outside influences which he cannot control is, though somewhat crudely put by Quevedo here, one of the basic tenets of stoicism.

The attempt to reconcile stoicism and Christianity is particularly associated with the Belgian humanist Justus Lipsius (1547–1606) – with whom Quevedo was in correspondence from 1604, as were many other Spaniards – and the Frenchman Guillaume du Vair (1556–1621). In his *Guide* (*Manductionis ad stoicam philosophiam*, 1604) – dedicated to Juan Fernández de Velasco, Constable of Castile – Lipsius stresses the role of the will in achieving stoical freedom, defining it as 'a certain and immutable judgement without which human tranquillity is impossible'. He also asserts, boldly, that stoical wisdom is the same thing as piety. Du Vair, who also wrote about constancy, asserted in his *De la philosophie des stoïques* (c. 1580) that stoicism was a philosophy of reason because it stood opposed to the unreason of accepting any moral or philosophical code based on the senses. But we should beware of crediting European sixteenth- and seventeenth-century neo-stoicism with too much belief in the efficacy of reason. Reason was only a step on the road to stoical perfection. Reason's role was to teach the will, but it was the will that finally governed the acts of the stoic at all times.

Because of Seneca's supposed 'Spanish' origins, there had always been a certain predisposition in Spain towards stoic ideas. They had been much to the fore in another age of decline – the fifteenth century. The attempt to reconcile stoicism and Christianity had, too, a special attraction for the Jesuits, who certainly went out of their way to propagate the neo-stoicism of Lipsius and to protect him. Lipsius, at one stage, had become a Lutheran, concluding that Lutheran opinions about predestination fitted stoical ideas more closely than orthodox ones. The Jesuits not only won him back to Catholicism (1591) but ensured that neither he nor his writings were suspect because of his lapse.

It was in fact not really possible to produce a satisfactory reconciliation of stoicism and Christianity. The ancient stoics had said that all things were subject to destiny. Lipsius was obliged to deny this in the name of God's omnipotence, taking, instead, the orthodox view that the chain of natural causes can be broken by secondary causes – of which, he said, the human will is one. Seneca had asserted that evil existed to conserve the universe. This was unacceptable to Christians. Lipsius fell back on near-Lutheran reasons to explain why God permitted evil to befall those (like children) who could not be expected to use evil fruitfully as stoic reason dictated: the fact was incomprehensible and one must simply believe obediently in divine justice, despite appearances. It was, however, not too difficult to equate Christian man's free choice with the stoic will and stoic contempt for the things of the world with Christian *desengaño*. Stoic *virtus* and Christian *virtue* were conveniently associated semantically. Neo-stoicism was clearly an élitist moral philosophy that must be meaningless to the masses. In addition to the two works already mentioned, Quevedo's verse translation of the *Manual* of Epictetus and of the *Carmen admonitorium* of the pseudo-Phocylides (1633) represent his main writings about stoicism. Jesuit interest in neo-stoicism is reflected in the *aprobaciones* to these works written by P. Juan Eusebio Nieremberg (1595–1658), the famous Jesuit ascetic writer, who, apropos of Quevedo's translation of Epictetus, remarked 'cuán cerca andaban los estoicos de la doctrina cristiana, veráse en estos avisos de Epicteto y en su sentimiento'.

Quevedo's treatment of his stoic and neo-stoic sources was, however, not scholarly nor, sometimes, even quite honest. He had evolved a theory that Seneca and Epictetus, since they lived in the time of the persecution of the Christians, could have heard the Apostles – insinuating, therefore, that their writings may have been directly affected by Christianity. He also asserted that stoicism, anyway, undoubtedly stemmed from the Book of Job and therefore had respectable biblical authority before the pagans developed it. In his verse translation of Epictetus he therefore makes the latter seem much more like Job than he really is. Quevedo, it is plain, urgently wanted to believe in the possibility of a reconciliation of stoicism and Christianity. His attachment to stoic doctrines sometimes made his essentially conservative mind take up attitudes at variance with consensus opinion. In his satire *Las Zahurdas de Plutón* he makes a devil tormenting an *hidalgo* in hell observe: 'tres cosas son las que hacen ridículos a los hombres: la primera la nobleza, la segunda la honra, la tercera la valentía.' More surprisingly, he attacks Aristotle and Counter-Reformation neo-scholasticism for its concern with things that do not matter – 'silogismos y demostraciones . . . lógicas mal dispuestas y menos importantes . . . filosofía natural (así la llaman, siendo fantástica y soñada)'. Elsewhere he denounced contemporary writers and thinkers, in the name of neo-stoicism, for their imprisonment in the thought of the Greek and Roman world ('no nos preciamos sino de creer lo que aquéllos dijeron'). But it would be rash to pay too much attention to these insights by seeing them as part of a coherent intellectual system for, both in his life and his writings, contradiction and the expression of for him only momentarily valid ideas was a feature of Quevedo.

The influence of neo-stoicism on Baltasar Gracián is much less easy to define or detect and awaits full investigation. Gracián nowhere sets out to act as a propagandist for neo-stoicism as a moral philosophy and his habit of not indicating the sources of his ceaseless borrowing from other writers, ancient and modern, does not at once make it plain that a work like *El Criticón* (1651–7) is, in fact, larded with reminiscences of Seneca – though not all of these bear directly on stoic ideas. Moreover it is true that the very worldliness of Gracián's doctrinal purposes in works like *El héroe* (1637) or *El oráculo manual y arte de prudencia* (1647) endows them with a purpose that is the antithesis of neo-stoic attitudes. It is, however, plain that stoic and neo-stoic ideas were familiar to Gracián. Gracián makes much of the neo-stoic idea that wisdom is the same thing as piety; his frequent stress on *sabiduría* should, perhaps, be seen in that light. He also makes the stoic point, for example in *El Criticón*, that virtue (supported by justice, prudence, fortitude and temperance) is the supreme prize. Thus, while Gracián cannot be described as a neo-stoic writer, it is probably true to say that he at least adapted neo-stoic precepts for his own rather limited doctrinal purposes.

Neo-stoicism's traces can be seen quite often in seventeenth-century Spanish literature and scholarship. Calderón's concept of his near-passionless *Príncipe constante* (the adjective is suggestive) and his frequent theme that man's greatest victories are those he wins over himself have neo-stoic overtones. But, simply because it was much talked about, the value of seventeenth-century neo-stoicism must not be exaggerated. It was a negative and selfish creed and, despite its sixteenth- and seventeenth-century apologists, one that was fundamentally at odds with Christian tenets. Its popularity at this time, though, probably reflects an underlying intellectual discontent with traditional orthodox Christian teaching about moral conduct. Neo-stoicism in Spain, closely connected with *conceptismo* because of Seneca's influence as a stylist, always, however, hovered on the brink of being a style of writing rather than a system of thought.

XII Didactic and Satirical Prose: Quevedo and Gracián

In seventeenth-century Spain prose satire again became, as in the time of Erasmus, a major vehicle for propounding general political theory and for disseminating general doctrines about individual and social morality. The tone of seventeenth-century social and moral satire was, however, poles apart from Erasmian satire. Humanistic optimism about the progress of man and society had been replaced by a thoroughgoing pessimism constantly stressing the need for total disillusionment about what this world had to offer man. In these respects there is a noticeable and not fortuitous coincidence with satire in post-Tridentine Italy, for Spain's two major prose satirists after Cervantes – Quevedo and Gracián – were influenced by two Italian writers of the previous generation, Giovanni Botero (1544–1617), the Jesuit political moralist, and the much-read Traiano Boccalini (1556–1613), whose absolutist, conservative and paternalist political and moral attitudes (and pessimism) have often been seen as typical of Counter-Reformation thinking. Since Boccalini was a great hater of Spain and did not conceal the fact in the *Ragguali di Parnaso* ('Reports from Parnassus') of 1605 and in his other writings, his popularity in Spain as a writer is indicative of the extent of his appeal to Spanish literary and ideological taste. In the *Ragguali* Boccalini uses the device of allegory, siting his satire in the city of Parnassus. His declared purpose is, by means of a narrative that will have an impact on the reader 'like a play of luminous rockets', to cast an unaccustomed light which would serve to illuminate in an unusual way the ridiculousness, the imbecility or the cruelty of human behaviour. Boccalini was much imitated in Spain by writers other than Quevedo and Gracián. Even if the genius of Quevedo and Gracián makes them unique as Spanish seventeenth-century moralists and satirists, it is useful to remember that they had many contemporary imitators and rivals who wrote in the same vein. Sententiousness was a major feature of Spanish seventeenth-century prose writing of all kinds.

Six major prose satires were written by Quevedo though he also wrote a considerable number of less important ones. His five *Sueños* were first published in 1627; some had been written long before then and had previously circulated widely in manuscript. In 1629 the censorship forced him to change the titles of four of these works because they referred to Christian concepts in a context of satire. The *Sueños* (modified title given in brackets) are: *El sueño del juicio final* (*Sueño de las calaveras*); *El alguacil endemoniado* (*El alguacil alguacilado*); *El sueño del infierno* (*Las zahurdas de Plutón*); *El mundo por de dentro*; *El sueño de la muerte* (*La vista de los chistes*). *La hora de todos y fortuna con seso* (1636) follows the same pattern but includes serious political satire (of foreign countries) among its somewhat disorderly assemblage of targets and is the most ambitious piece of satirical writing Quevedo attempted in this genre. In all these works, Quevedo, through the device of a dream or vision or allegory, is concerned with securing a bipartite view of men and society: as they seem to be and as they really are. The origin of this literary form goes back to the *Dialogues of the Dead* and the *Dialogues of the Gods* of the Greek satirist Lucian (A.D. *c.* 115–*c.* 200). Interest in this kind of contrasting double vision was, as we have seen, a particular concern of the age and, as in Quevedo, it is often associated with the idea of death, which will do away with human hypocrisy and disguise. We meet the objects of Quevedoesque satire in hell or at the moment of death and judgement. The purpose of this approach, with its notion of the two realities (appearance and truth), is made clear in *El mundo por de dentro* where we see an expensive and sad funeral cortège accompanied by the sorrowing widower and a host of mourning friends. The credulous onlooker is speedily disillusioned by his more experienced escort:

¡Desventurado! Eso todo es por de fuera y parece así; pero ahora lo verás por de dentro y verás con cuánta verdad el ser desmiente a las apariencias.

The whole funeral is hypocrisy and deceit; in reality the mourning friends are annoyed at having to waste their time, the widower looks sad because he resents the expense of his wife's illness and funeral. He is already planning to marry his mistress. Gracián's major work, *El Criticón*, is also mainly concerned with rubbing in the contrast between appearance and reality within a framework of allegory. The metaphysical basis of the distinction is, of course, never questioned. It is possible that the constant discrediting of observed reality may have furthered attitudes inimical to the development of any empirical and scientific outlook, though it seemed to be a useful tool for the Christian moralist desiring to fix men's minds on death and the importance of the hereafter.

What makes Quevedo's satires live today is not their moral message but their frenetical, exasperated style in which ideas and images tumble after each other in no very visible logical order or artistic structure. In them he seems consumed by a hatred of the human race that leads him to paroxysms of cruel and often scatological imagery and linguistic *tours de force* resting on the exploitation of those aspects of the *conceptista* style already discussed in connection with his picaresque novel, *El Buscón* (see pp. 331-2 above). When Quevedo writes in *El sueño del infierno* that 'la honra está junto al culo de las mujeres' he neatly manages to satirize with brutal realism what lay behind the fine words of the honour cult of the *hidalgo* class (a favourite target) by associating it with his misogyny, another favourite theme. The same sort of technique is used to destroy the Renaissance dream of the pagan divinities. Mars is described as the 'don Quijote de las deidades'. Jupiter is seen 'vestido de sí mismo [i.e. naked], hermoso para los unos y enojado para los otros, el sol y las estrellas colgando de su boca.' Scribes are seen, at the sound of the Last Trumpet, 'huyendo de sus orejas, deseando no las llevar, por no oir lo que esperaban.' Even the angelic Last Trumpeter himself is not spared from the down-grading ridicule that constantly poured from Quevedo:

Parecióme pues que veía un mancebo que, discurriendo por el aire, daba voz de su aliento a una trompeta, afeando con su fuerza en parte su hermosura.

It is noteworthy that Quevedo himself drew attention to the connection between his vision and that of the grotesque paintings of Hieronymus Bosch (c. 1450–1516) who also expressed in paintings of hell his encyclopedic disgust with humanity.

Quevedo claimed a serious moral purpose for his satires, asserting that there were 'muchas verdades duras y secas' to be found under all the wit and laughter. But his remark to the reader at the beginning of *El Buscón* (see p. 331 above) suggests that his intuition told him that satire, the traditionally approved literary medium for improving men and society, did not really work – an intuition perhaps responsible for the continuous tone of exasperation that is a mark of Quevedo as a satirist. Gracián, in *El Criticón*, did not credit his great predecessor's satire with much improving value; he said of Quevedo's work in this genre: 'estas hojas de Quevedo son como las del tabaco, de más vicio que provecho, más para reír que aprovechar.'

The objects of Quevedo's satire (in keeping with classical theory) are usually types, not individuals, and they are often present simply, perhaps, because they were consecrated targets. When he does turn his attention to satirizing persons of importance, such as the (unindividuated) minister who has feathered his nest at the expense of the governed, witticisms and stylistic pyrotechnics serve to divert attention from the real matter in hand – peculation of public money – rather than to draw attention to it.

A notable feature of the *Sueños*, too, is the way here, as elsewhere in his writings, Quevedo identifies himself with the aristocratic viewpoint. He is against upstarts of all sorts, among whom he numbers pretentious *hidalgos*. He hates lackeys who have some learning. He hates men who 'do' nothing, such as academics. He claims to rate arms above letters. Living in an age when Spain was beset by difficult financial and economic problems this highly intelligent man chose to regard bankers and traders as contemptible usurers. Any study of the writings of Quevedo (not only the satires) immediately discloses that inconsistencies and contradictions of this kind, particularly contradictions between his mental processes and his instincts and feelings, are an essential feature of Quevedo. There was much of the journalist about him, so that he recorded, post-haste, immediate reactions which might well be at war with the ideas fairly carefully put forward in his more serious works. Yet the very exasperation and despair of Quevedo's satires is what gives them their unique, surrealist artefact reality as well as their stylistic distinctiveness. These same qualities could also sometimes lead Quevedo to enunciate, in passing, genuine new ideas, as when for example he observes, apropos of death, that what man thinks he fears is what he most desires, or when, like Gracián later, he attacks his culture's dependence on classical authority: 'cautivos en las cosas naturales de los griegos y latinos, no nos preciamos sino de creer lo que dijeron.' No other Spanish writer of the sixteenth or seventeenth century so clearly as Quevedo gives the impression of a really exceptional intellect and creative ability partly frustrated by the very orthodoxies to which he willingly subscribed.

Many modern readers, confronted by writing so alien in theme and style to contemporary tastes, are tempted to take the view that the Aragonese Jesuit Baltasar Gracián (1601–58) is an even clearer case of a writer of genius driven by the stultifying orthodoxies of his order and his age to waste his intellect on matters of no significance. That there may be some substance in the charge cannot de denied, but it must also be said that the great and immediate success of the Spanish Jesuit's works outside Spain and the demand for translations of them suggests that he spoke in some very immediate way to the intellectual élites of seventeenth-century Europe.

Gracián's Jesuit training is, perhaps, a less important factor than has sometimes been supposed, though it certainly helped to give him his familiarity with Latin and with Latin literature and may well have launched that extraordinary knowledge of contemporary rhetorical theory that he displays (in a not very well-organized or clearly thought-out way) in his *Agudeza y arte de ingenio* (see p. 316 above). How far his Jesuit instructors in theology and moral philosophy contributed to the development of a mind that clearly revelled in subtleties for their own sake and which had marked élitist social and cultural tastes is quite uncertain. It must not be overlooked that the Aragonese Jesuit province to which Gracián belonged was not intellectually distinguished and that he himself was officially regarded as a bad Jesuit whose works were thought to have done harm to the order. A much more important influence on his way of thinking was probably his close friendship, during his long stay in Huesca, with Vincencio Juan de Lastanosa, a rich, powerful and cultured bibliophile and man of letters. Lastanosa's home was a regular meeting-place for a number of scholars and writers who formed a kind of learned 'academy' of a type common in seventeenth-century Spain. Several of Gracián's publications were printed under the patronage and doubtless at the expense of Lastanosa.

The books that concern themselves with political theory (mostly in terms of what qualities the successful ruler should have), and with Gracián's peculiar doctrines of conduct and behaviour, are *El héroe* (1637), *El político Fernando* (1640), *El discreto* (1646) and *El oráculo manual* (1647). His masterpiece, the long and ambitious allegorical satire he called *El Criticón*, was published in three parts (1651, 1653, 1657), despite the opposition of his superiors. When he disobeyed orders and insisted on continuing it they sent him to an obscure exile in the small Aragonese town of Tarazona where he died.

Gracián's concept of an *héroe*, whose necessary qualities are set out, in his first treatise, under the headings of twenty desirable *primores* (excellences), gives a decidedly new twist to the Counter-Reformation cult of the hero figure. Though Gracián attacked Machiavelli in *El Criticón* there are, in *El héroe* and the other treatises, many elements at least popularly associated with Machiavellian doctrines. Gracián's hero is a great man whose field may be politics or, indeed, simply the cult of 'virtue', as well as the more conventional fields for great deeds. He is recommended, *inter alia*, never to reveal all to anyone, to take care to cultivate a natural grace (*despejo*) that will enable him to win hearts, to fake some imperfections that will help him to avoid jealousy and put others off their guard, to find ways of winning the sympathy of powerful men, to be of limitless courage but not rash, to try to attract attention by finding new kinds of excellences in which to excel, and so on. At the very end of this catalogue, which lays much stress on the role of courage as well as fortune in determining success ('todo héroe tiene por padrinos el valor y la fortuna'), Gracián concludes with a somewhat perfunctory comment: 'ser héroe del mundo poco o nada es; serlo del Cielo es mucho. A cuyo gran Monarca sea la alabanza, sea la honra, sea la gloria.' The influence on *El héroe* of Giovanni Botero's *Detti memorabile di personnagi illustre* (1608) is plainly visible.

El discreto is divided into twenty-five chapters in which Gracián, using a variety of different structural approaches, sets out to establish the *realces* or 'qualities' needed to make a distinguished, cultivated and respected man – an *honnête homme* in the seventeenth-century sense. The emphasis is all on the task of deliberately and calculatingly constructing one's personality as a work of art. The final aim of *el discreto*, according to Gracián, is to know how to be a philosopher, sipping from everything, like a solicitous bee, either 'the honey of sweet advantage or wax to serve the light that comes from disillusion'. The *Oráculo manual* is, perhaps, the most startling of Gracián's shorter treatises. It consists of

300 maxims about personal conduct, each followed by an explanatory commentary. There appears to be no particular order about the maxims, which derive from a variety of sources such as Seneca and Tacitus (whose studied ellipses and use of antitheses and word-plays, as well as his political wisdom, appealed to Gracián's taste), Botero, Boccalini and others. In this treatise Gracián pushes his ideas on how to behave to achieve worldly success further than before. A life of ceaseless calculation in all dealings with one's fellows is proposed: one must never score at the expense of a superior; a stoic suppression of one's own passions and indifference to the passions of others must be cultivated; the search for personal reputation must be constant ('deseo de reputación nace de la virtud; fue y es hermana de gigantes la fama'); one must never make mistaken assessments of other people; think like the minority but take care to speak like the majority; avoid, out of compassion, becoming directly involved in the misfortunes of others; even with one's best friend avoid total disclosure, and so on. Gracián repeats the Quevedoesque warning against confusing *realidad y apariencia*: 'son raros los que miran por dentro y muchos los que se pagan de lo aparente'. The last maxim summing up all the rest is 'En una palabra, santo'. It is here suggested by Gracián that what he has really been teaching in the *Oráculo* is virtue, the only yardstick for measuring ability and greatness, which 'vivo el hombre, le hace amable, y muerto, memorable'. Neo-stoic notions of *virtus* seem here to be confused with the traditional Christian view of virtue. Religion is scarcely referred to in these treatises and their teaching is sometimes, even with the aid of casuistry, plainly contrary to traditional Christian ethics. We should not, however, exclude the influence on Gracián as a moralist of a simple wish to satisfy the desire of the seventeenth-century reader to be astonished and shocked.

A major difficulty for the modern reader in approaching these treatises (and the much more important *Criticón*) is Gracián's style. The primacy of sententious utterance is a major feature of Gracián's *conceptismo*. Clipped, short sentences are the rule, the phrase ideally containing no inactive grammatical elements. To this end, too, articles and the verb 'to be' are frequently omitted and adjectives and adverbs very sparingly used. The two-part structure of Gracián's sentences has been noted. They are notably either parallelistic ('tantos son los gustos como los rostros, y tan varios') or even more often make use of antithesis ('emprendo formar con un libro enano un varón gigante'). The characteristic *conceptista* exploitation of the plurivalent meaning of words is common. Reliance on the device of catachresis (see p. 318 above) is, of course, frequent – particularly in *El Criticón*. Gracián is fond of transposing the normal word order of Spanish, but this is not carried to extremes (as in Góngora). There is, though, in Gracián's use of words, a continuous and deliberate preference for the unexpected instead of the expected term. This may take the form of creating a new word from the Latin (e.g. *incomprensibilidad*) or, incongruously, the use in this highly refined diction of a low or even obscene term; the vocabulary of gamblers is, for instance, often in evidence. Gracián's use of imagery reveals scarcely any sensitivity to the external world of the senses; his metaphors – in accordance with the procedures of *conceptismo* – are cerebral, bookish in inspiration and frequently emblematic in function. Gracián described emblems, *empresas*, hieroglyphs and the like as 'la pedrería preciosa al oro fino del discurrir'.

The *Criticón* is a long and dense allegorical tale. It was plainly written slowly and with great care. Its three parts deal with the four ages of man. Gracián describes the subject of his book as 'filosofía cortesana', so making clear that the work is for the élite only. The title *Criticón* indicates that the work will be a critical analysis of human behaviour. The term *crisi* (here used instead of *capítulo*) describes each individual package of experience and deduction that goes to make up the equivalent of a chapter. The book is so densely packed with episode and comment that any succinct account is liable to leave a false impression of its scope. The two main characters, Andrenio ('untutored man') and Critilo ('the wise man'), whose worldly pilgrimage together is the subject of most of the *Criticón*, encounter each other when Critilo is cast ashore on the island of St Helena and finds living alone there the young savage Andrenio, whom he teaches to speak. Andrenio's earliest memories are of being fed by wild animals in a dark cavern on the island. The light of human reason, he explains, eventually broke in on his mind and he began to ask Cartesian questions: '¿Soy o no soy? Pero pues vivo, pues conozco y advierto, ser tengo. Pero ¿si soy, quién soy?' When he escapes from his cave and sees the spectacle of the order of nature, Andrenio is led to postulate the need for a Creator. The allegorical approach is thus plain from the beginning. The two are found by some passing ships and taken from the island to Spain. On the way Critilo recounts his personal history to Andrenio: he had fallen in love with Felisenda (Happiness) and had met disaster through imprudence. The travellers reach Spain and begin a long series of peregrinations in an allegorical world which, however, is not separate from but mixed up with the actual contemporary European world – as was usual in this type of literature. The juxtaposition of real people and real places with allegorical figures and allegorical locations constantly incites the reader to interpret everyday reality allegorically. Andrenio takes things to be what they seem and reacts accordingly; Critilo's role is to point out to him the realities that lie behind the appearances, revealing the ferocity, wickedness and hypocrisy of the world. Part II takes the pilgrims first to Aragon, where Gracián takes the chance to pay generous if rather parochial tribute to Lastanosa and his friends. They then visit the convent of Hipocrinda (Hypocrisy). In this *crisi* Gracián permitted himself some highly pointed attacks on clerical dissimulation, hypocrisy and simony. In Part III the pilgrims encounter a guide, 'El Descifrador', who knows how to explain the enigma of the world and who shows them human 'diphthongs' (beings made up of contradictory qualities) and 'parentheses', men who add quantity, not quality to life. After visiting, in Italy, the 'Cueva de la Nada' – into which disappear all those who could have done something valuable with their lives but did not – they are shown from a hill-top in Rome the revolving Wheel of Time, all change and yet all repetition. The long tale now approaches its end. Death appears surrounded by her jovial dancing ministers – allegorical figures of the excesses of man's appetites, which deliver them to her. She seems terrifying to Andrenio but smiling to the wise Critilo. Death orders a term to be put to the pilgrims' lives. But they are saved by securing admission to the 'Isla de la Inmortalidad'. The book concludes with the comment that, if the reader wishes to know what they saw and enjoyed there, let him take 'el rumbo de la virtud insigne, del valor heroico, y llegará a parar al teatro de la fama, al trono de la estimación y al centro de la inmortalidad'. Fame, secured by noble virtue and heroic courage, is the way to esteem and immortality in Gracián's world. Despite the novelty of his style his final message is, like Quevedo's, a reaffirmation of the social and ethical values of aristocracy.

Seventeenth-century critics seem to have been untroubled by the fact that nowhere does Critilo teach Andrenio the dogmas of the Christian faith, leaving him to discover truth solely by the teachings of experience and reason. A good deal of Gracián's satire is directed, like Quevedo's, at the traditional targets, but some, too, is at the expense of institutions, such as the Church, not often attacked in seventeenth-century Spain. Gracián does, as his most distinguished modern critic has declared, show a remarkable facility (within the narrow limits imposed by his particular satirical and moralistic approach) for exploring the motivation of human behaviour. But Gracián's attitudes on the political and moral issues he discusses, despite his outspokenness and his willingness to shock, break no new ground. He shares Quevedo's contempt for the world of trade and commerce, disliking Seville, for example, because 'está apoderada de ella la vil ganancia'. The value of his moral teachings, his theories on conduct and his political commentaries is undermined from the start by his own pessimism about the human condition and by his sense that man's penchant for wickedness and self-deception is incurable: only a few élite minds may hope to see the truth.

As an achievement of the creative imagination *El Criticón* is plainly remarkable. But Gracián's writings are nearly always without insights that extend further than those commonly held in his own age. His total silence about Cervantes in the *Criticón* is revealing since he there praised other and much lesser Spanish writers. Confronted by something really new, Gracián, one may suppose, felt uncomfortable – as the rigidity that lies behind the brilliant pyrotechnics of his style suggests. Overwhelming bleakness and an impression of a strangely static world are the lingering impressions left by Gracián's work, though one may admire his courage and his readiness to push his theories of morality and style to conclusions that would have been beyond the daring of lesser men.

XIII Sixteenth- and Seventeenth-Century Drama: the Beginnings

Secular drama in Spain until after the middle of the sixteenth century was a largely private affair put on in palaces for the entertainment of princes, noblemen and prelates. It was often the work of amateurs whose main interest was in other branches of literature. They had to try to learn that serious or comic dramatic dialogue is spoken movement, not poetic declamation, and that, even more difficult, dramatic narrative is not the same thing as other forms of literary narration. Religious drama had, of course, a solider staging tradition behind it and, in Spain as in other countries, a degree of professionalism existed among those who wrote religious plays and those who acted in them. But medieval religious drama existed to edify, it relied on well-known stories and it was self-sufficient. Not until the early Spanish dramatists such as Encina became acquainted at first hand with the contemporary secular theatre in Italy was secular drama in a real sense to get started, and the Italian roots of the Spanish *comedia* as created by Lope de Vega are still plain enough. It should be noted, though, that unlike the situation in other countries, liturgical drama continued to flourish in Spain as a separate genre even until beyond the end of the seventeenth century while, thanks to the preoccupation of seventeenth-century Spain with religious themes and religious propaganda, religious or theological subjects sometimes took over the *comedia* itself.

Juan del Encina (*c.* 1468–*c.* 1530), musician and lyric poet (see p. 269 above), tried his hand at various forms of dramatic writing. He was the author of some fifteen *églogas* intended for private staging and was the first Spanish dramatist to have his plays and playlets printed (1496). Comic peasants figure largely in some of these charades meant to amuse Encina's patron, the Duke of Alba, and the ducal household. Others of Encina's plays follow the traditional patterns of medieval religious drama. Some, however, move into a very different world. In 1513, during a visit to Rome, Encina wrote his most ambitious play, the *Égloga de Plácida y Vitoriano*, an Italianate pastoral play which was performed there. It has thirteen scenes and has sentimental and even tragic pretensions. But *Plácida y Vitoriano* (banned by the Inquisition in 1559, presumably because it parodied the liturgy), like Encina's other Italianate *églogas*, remains episodic in structure and lyrical rather than dramatic in tone. His main legacy to later secular drama was the stock character of the comic shepherd, speaking a stylized form of the sub-dialect of Leonese spoken in the Salamancan countryside and known as *sayagués*.

The comparative poverty of Spanish drama in these early years (compared, for example, with that of Italy) has often led Spanish critics to appropriate that part of the work of the great Portuguese playwright Gil Vicente (*c.* 1465–*c.* 1536) that was written in Spanish. But the contexts, the concerns, the themes and the tone of many of the very large number of plays he wrote (and most of the very large gallery of characters who people his multi-faceted world) are distinctively Portuguese. Vicente wrote festival plays (like the *Nao de amores*, 1527) for the wealthy Portuguese court of those days – which could sponsor lavish costuming and stage machinery. His patriotic plays were written for the same audiences. He also wrote morality plays in the medieval tradition but gave these a humanity and reality they had never before had: his trilogy known as the *Barcas* (*Barca do Inferno*, *Barca do Purgatório* and *Barca da Glória*, 1517–19) infuses with new life the old theme of the transport of the judged souls of the dead to Hell, Purgatory or Heaven. Vicente had the gift of writing sprightly, individualistic and 'actable' dialogue and so of creating real personalities, particularly when his intention was comic or satirical. He also had an acute ear for popular Portuguese music and song, much of which finds its way into his plays, giving them a moving, lyric note. Unlike his Spanish contemporaries he did not think of peasants and low-life types (even negro slaves) only as buffoons, but could treat them and their plight with some sympathy. Normally his satire is good-humoured, but his anti-clerical satire is biting. Vicente has therefore been suspected of Erasmian tendencies but, in fact, his satire seems to belong entirely to traditional medieval anti-clericalism and gives no hint of the positive aspects of Erasmus's thought. Vicente manipulates themes, plots and characters with a complexity and ease unknown to the contemporary Spanish dramatists, but, though a delight to read and living proof of what could be done with the traditional drama in the hands of a man of genius writing for a court that had ample funds to spend on dramatic spectacle, Vicente did not really open any important doors for the future of drama. That was to be done by the most important of the early Spanish dramatists, Bartolomé de Torres Naharro (c. 1485–c. 1520), sometimes described as the founder of Spanish romantic comedy.

Torres Naharro lived and wrote in Italy. His *Propalladia* (Naples, 1517) contained six of his *comedias* and a prologue setting out his theory of comedy ('an ingenious arrangement of notable incidents, ending happily'). He wrote in five acts (*jornadas*). He divides his comedies into two types: *comedias a noticia* (based on the dramatic portrayal of the lower levels of contemporary social reality) like his *Comedia Soldadesca* and *Comedia Tinellaria*; and *comedias a fantasía*, romantic comedy which did not pretend to be a reportage of everyday life, though seeking 'the colour of truth'. Each play has an *introito* in which a rude shepherd introduces the work and gives a summary of the plot in some detail according to the traditions of Latin comedy; the dramatist was perhaps not yet confident of his ability to present a self-explanatory dramatic action. Torres Naharro's work is not as sophisticated as is sometimes suggested but, at his best, he does reveal a genuine dramatic sense and an awareness of what dramatic structure is, and could manage real dramatic dialogue. In a very surprising way, too, this expatriate early sixteenth-century playwright prefigures some themes and characters that were to become standard features of the theatre of Lope de Vega and his generation. Thus, in his most accomplished play, the *Comedia*

Himenea, which has many echoes of *La Celestina*, the heroine plays fast and loose with family honour and is about to be killed by her brother on that account ('que la vida / por la fama es bien perdida') when a happy ending is contrived by her lover's agreement to marry her. Torres Naharro, too, introduces prototypes of characters who would dominate the *capa y espada* plays of the seventeenth-century *comedia* – the *galán* and the *dama* he courts, the *gracioso*, the lady's conniving female servant and others. His dialogue is, however – under contemporary Italian influence – far more suggestive and crude than anything the later Spanish *comedia* could tolerate. Torres Naharro's plays were reprinted about eight times in the sixteenth century and were therefore well known in print in Spain. In 1559 they were placed on the Index of prohibited books. It has been assumed that Lope de Vega must have read Torres Naharro; he may have done so, but Italian influence on the making of the classical Spanish *comedia* is not to be explained by so simple a cause.

The best of the religious dramatists during the first half of the sixteenth century was Diego Sánchez de Badajoz (*fl.* 1533–49), twenty-eight of whose plays, which he called *farsas*, in 'gracioso, cortesano y pastoril estilo', were published in 1554. Ten of them were intended for the Corpus Christi festival at Badajoz. His deployment of allegory in these makes him a precursor of the *auto sacramental* of Calderón (see section XVI). In his *Farsa militar* a friar, after resisting the routine temptations of world, flesh and Devil, is undermined by an appeal to his ambition and vanity, a treatment which also reminds us of some seventeenth-century *comedia* themes. The importance of comic negro characters in Sánchez de Badajoz's plays is noteworthy, reflecting the importance of the city of Badajoz in the slave-trade between Portugal and Castile. As a comic type, speaking his pidgin Portuguese, the negro was destined for a permanent role among the stock characters of the Golden Age theatre.

About the middle of the sixteenth century new developments occur. Italian professional actors begin to appear in Spain. The presence of one Mutio 'italiano de la comedia' is recorded in 1538 and, thereafter, there are references to Italian players and companies – a fact which needs to be remembered in connection with the Italianization of the secular drama that now began. The first Spanish professional actor of whom we have notice is the playwright Lope de Rueda (*c.* 1510–65) who flourished from about 1540 onwards, performing in inn-yards and patios under contract to local town councils, or in the houses of the wealthy. Unlike previous drama, Rueda's plays were in prose and were broken into six to ten *scenas*. He also wrote *pasos* – short one-act interludes of knockabout farce dependent today on their mastery of popular language but owing much in Lope's time to the skill of his actors at playing such parts. His *comedias* are drawn from Italian sources. The best of these is the *Eufemia*, described as 'muy exemplar y muy graciosa' in the editions printed after his death. These works recall Italian prose plays like *Gl'Ingannati* (1531) or the comedies of Aretino. There is no real attempt at characterization. In the *Comedia Armelina* the god Neptune appears in the action, but only as a figure of fun. Lope de Rueda's dialogue is always the work of a man who knew what stage dialogue ought to be but the links between his *scenas* are rough and, to get his plays across, much obviously was left to the ability of the actors themselves – a feature of the relationship between script and player perhaps too much ignored by modern students of the *comedia* generally. His career marks the establishment of acting as a whole-time profession in Spain. From the 1560s public theatres (sponsored by charitable brotherhoods) came into existence in Madrid, Seville, Valencia and other cities, thus creating a continuous demand for plays and assured employment for players.

It was for the new theatrical market in Seville that Juan de la Cueva (c. 1550–1610) wrote. His *Comedias y tragedias* were collected by him for publication in 1584. They were performed in Seville between 1579 and 1581. After 1581 he abandoned the theatre for other forms of writing. Fourteen of Cueva's plays survive and it should be noted that only three of these deal with topics from Spanish history; in these Cueva exploited the perennial popularity of the old heroic ballads about Spanish history, sometimes quoting the ballads themselves on stage. He presents epic narrative episodically, often failing to exploit the dramatic qualities inherent in his source material. All his plays betray a marked Senecan influence (perhaps through Cueva's knowledge of the plays of Giambattista Giraldi, an admirer of Senecan drama). This accounts for the violence, passion and rhetorical tone he tends to adopt. Cueva reduced the number of acts to four and wrote only in verse. He puts a great many characters on the stage (*El infamador* has twenty-two, who include Nemesis – 'diosa de las venganzas' – Venus, Diana, Morpheus and two 'wild men' all thrown in alongside the usual stock characters of comedy – the *galán*, the *dama* and the inevitable bawds, pimps, *rufianes* and servants).

Modern readers may find it difficult to understand how such an apparently bad dramatist, who still essentially thought of a play simply as narrative placed on a stage, was successful. It has recently been noted, however, that all Cueva's works were written in a very short period which coincided historically with the period when Philip II was taking over Portugal. It is suggested that this was a project of which Cueva disapproved and that his plays refer more or less obliquely to it. It is likely that the extent to which the themes (particularly the historical themes) used in the Spanish Golden Age theatre generally alluded indirectly to current affairs may have been underestimated. The point is, however, difficult to establish since the historical events Spanish Golden Age dramas often chose to treat of must often have had contemporary political implications, whether the dramatist wished it or not.

Another dramatist who was active during Cueva's time was Cervantes who, in the prologue to his *Ocho comedias y ocho entremeses nuevos* (1615), says he wrote some twenty or thirty plays for the Madrid stage in the 1580s, claiming that he reduced Cueva's four acts to three and was the first to put abstract allegorical and moral figures on the secular stage. Only two of these plays survive. *El cerco de Numancia* has been much praised at least for its thoughtful treatment of the famous siege of the Spanish city by Scipio Africanus. But its verse is banal, it is full of Senecan rhetoric and it proves (as do the later *comedias* of Cervantes written in imitation of the new style of Lope de Vega) that Cervantes never began to understand how to construct a dramatic plot as opposed to telling a narrative story. The one-act comic *entremeses* (nearly all in prose) have a wit, a technical skill and a concentration lacking in Cervantes's *comedias*. In one respect Cervantes's failure as a dramatist is to be regretted: his ranging imagination, interest in man as a social animal, and the great variety of themes and subjects he sought to deal with eclectically might, had they been successful, have made the Spanish seventeenth-century theatre broader-based than it became under Lope de Vega's influence.

XIV Seventeenth Century Drama: the *Comedia*

The seventeenth-century Spanish *comedia*[1] was written according to a dramatic formula originally worked out by Lope Félix de Vega Carpio (1562–1635) at the end of the sixteenth century. It was the existence of this formula that enabled Spanish playwrights to supply the great

[1] The term *comedia* in seventeenth-century Spain included *all* full-length plays whether or not they had happy endings.

number of plays that the theatres consumed. Though aspects of the formula were considerably modified by Pedro Calderón de la Barca (1600–81) and also, particularly after 1632, by the building in Philip IV's new Buen Retiro palace of a court theatre that catered for a somewhat new kind of audience, the original Lopean formula continued to dominate Spanish playwriting even into the eighteenth century. The existence of the formula makes it inappropriate to treat Spanish seventeenth-century drama strictly in terms of individual authors. That drama was, to a considerable extent, an atelier art. There was much collaboration in writing plays. Scripts were frequently altered and amended by managers. It is often impossible, on the basis of theme and style alone, to assign a *comedia* of unknown authorship with certainty to any particular dramatist. The pre-Calderonian *comedia* will, therefore, mainly be treated in general terms here. Mention of the work of individual major dramatists will be limited to indicating any special features exhibited by their plays, or any important innovations in the tradition introduced by them.

The secular Spanish theatre for which Lope de Vega had to cater was served by custom-built, municipally owned theatres (*corrales*), established in rectangular courtyards overlooked by the backs of houses whose rear windows thus served as boxes. The stage was placed at the far end of the yard. Round the two sides of the yard itself were a few rows of seats. In front of these was the *patio* where the majority of the audience stood to watch a play in the open or, at best, under a canvas covering. Women of the lower classes were segregated at the back of the theatre in the *cazuela* (stewpan). There was no proscenium curtain to screen the open stage, though there was a curtain at the back which could be drawn aside to 'discover' a room, tent, etc. Behind the stage proper was an upper gallery that was brought into use to represent a mountain, a tower, a balcony and the like. Scenery at first was rudimentary and the use of stage machinery limited, though these aspects of the theatre were to change greatly when the court theatre came into existence, and there was increasing use of machines and props even in the municipal theatres by the 1620s: Lope de Vega complained in 1623 of the development in them of machinery and other attractions for the eyes that more and more made *comedias* something to see rather than to hear. Plays were put on in the afternoon. The noise and music-hall boisterousness of audiences, particularly of the *mosqueteros* (or groundlings) in the *patio*, was notorious, but it was these same groundlings whose approval or disapproval could make or break a play. Regular theatres (at first run by religious brotherhoods but soon taken over by the municipalities) existed before the end of the century in Madrid, Seville, Valencia, Barcelona, Toledo and other cities. They were served by companies of professional actors and actresses numbering from about sixteen to twenty players. From 1600 companies had to be licensed by the crown but many unlicensed ones existed.

Very little is known about the style of acting in Spain at this time but we can be sure it was highly rhetorical. The formulaic style of the *comedia*, too, probably meant that a great deal was expected of individual actors in bringing out the full possibilities latent in what were, perhaps, often viewed more like modern film scripts than fully fashioned plays. The Italian *commedia dell'arte* with its tradition of improvisation had been well known in Spain in the period when permanent theatres were being established and may well have left its mark on the acting tradition. In the second half of the seventeenth century an account of a famous contemporary actor, Damián Arias de Peñafiel, stressed the perfection of his diction and gesture. He was expert at holding the audience in suspense by long pauses; on one occasion, a contemporary reported, he read a letter on stage which so filled him with emotion that he eventually tore it to shreds before beginning to declaim his next lines with immense vigour. There are accounts of actors writhing on the stage in death agonies and actresses tearing their clothes to pieces in moments of special emotion.

The great number of plays written in seventeenth-century Spain raises economic questions. What remuneration could an author expect for writing a play? In 1601 Lope de Vega received 500 *reales* (45·3 ducats) for a new *comedia* and one may assume Lope's fame already earned him more than was usual. At this rate he would have needed to write about twenty-two plays a year to earn even the thousand ducats which made a Castilian farmer of the time think himself well-off. Such amounts were a good deal less than contemporary English playwrights like Shakespeare expected to get for a play. Poor remuneration must, therefore, be regarded as one reason for the large number of plays written and the need not to spend more than a few days on each. Lope de Vega's output ran to hundreds and hundreds of plays (he listed the titles of 219 he said he had written by 1604 and soon after his death in 1635 was said – no doubt with some exaggeration – to have written 1,800 *comedias* in all as well as several hundred religious *autos sacramentales*; some 300 *comedias* certainly attributable to him have survived). Eighty out of several hundred plays by Tirso de Molina

(c. 1581–1648 – real name Fray Gabriel Téllez) are known. As for the pay of actors themselves, a very well-known actor, in 1595, signed a contract to perform for a whole year in the company of Gaspar de Porras for 3,000 *reales* (337·5 ducats) and Agustín de Rojas in 1602 accepted 2,800 *reales* for a similar period. Later on these figures rose considerably.

Lope de Vega set out a number of facts about his formula for writing *comedias* in his *Arte nuevo de hacer comedias* (c. 1607), an ironical poem in which he seeks to show that he was perfectly familiar with classical precepts about the drama. With his tongue very much in his cheek, he affects to regret that the vulgarity of his audiences has forced him to be successful by ignoring the precepts. A good deal of the *Arte nuevo* is concerned with the practical aspects of writing to a formula. The author of *comedias* should first write out a draft of the play in prose. The work should be divided into three acts, the first setting the situation, the second developing it and the third supplying the dénouement. It is very important not to disclose the final outcome until the end of the play otherwise the audience will walk out. He stresses the importance of making sure that the utterances of the characters are always appropriate to the social categories to which they belong. Other points of interest made in the *Arte nuevo* are that anything in a *comedia* that can be construed as satire (i.e. relevant to a contemporary Spanish situation) must be cautiously handled so that the satire is not too obvious. As to subject-matter, Lope in the *Arte nuevo* only singles out the theme of honour, which he describes as particularly useful because this theme always gets an active response from all parts of the audience. Rather surprisingly, he recommends a certain use of double-meanings and ambiguity in the dialogue on the grounds that this is liked by the unlettered who, he claims, enjoy working out the meanings for themselves. In the *Arte nuevo* what is stressed is how to give pleasure to an audience, but there is an underlying assumption that some degree of instruction as well as pleasure is understood to be involved.

Lope's account of his formula in the *Arte nuevo* may be enlarged by a process of induction from his plays themselves. As far as technique is concerned he normally used a sub-plot not separate from the main plot (as it had often been in the sixteenth century) but related to it and usually comic in intention. He also systematized the figure of the *gracioso*, a comic servant figure who both mirrors and mocks the situation and assumptions of his master; he is a coward where his master is bold; as lover he duplicates the love situation in which his master is involved but regards the rhetoric and airs of aristocratic love as ridiculous. He is meant, of course, to be funny. What is noticeably missing from the Lopean formula is any interest in depicting individual character in depth. There are very few memorable characters (as opposed to memorable acts and events) in the Lopean *comedia*. This is plainly to be seen in a play such as *El duque de Viseo* (*c.* 1608) which Lope himself called a *tragedia* because it ended in disaster for most of the principal figures except for the king. Time and again the student of Elizabethan drama or French classical tragedy notes a situation which, in those traditions, would have given rise to a probing soliloquy or dialogue adding to the individuality of the characters and examining in depth the moral and philosophical implications of the theme and of the situation in which he found himself. In Lope there is almost none of this. From one event we move rapidly on to the next with little introspective reaction from those involved.

The Lopean *comedia* attached importance to moral doctrine. The plays usually illustrate a didactic point with some care, but they often give the impression that doctrine was attended to after what simply seemed good material to make a play had been chosen. Lope frequently and deliberately, however, altered his historical or other source to make it illustrate a general point he wanted to make. Doctrine was certainly not unimportant to his audiences. This is shown by the markedly sententious character of some of the utterances put in the mouths of his characters. But neither the sententiousness nor the doctrine attempts to make broad new or disturbing points. The most it may do is, obliquely, to take one side in a current dispute. One such that is several times dealt with is whether seigneurial justice should be abolished and replaced by the uniform imposition of the king's courts (*Peribañez y el comendador de Ocaña*; *El mejor alcalde, el rey*).

In many of the plays there is an evident desire to achieve an unexpected dénouement that will surprise while, nevertheless, fitting into the traditional order of things. An element of casuistry is often introduced to justify this unexpected result. What has sometimes been identified as 'poetic justice' is a feature of the Lopean *comedia*: those who have committed crimes or errors usually get their just deserts. These are often, but not always, death. Sometimes, as in the violent and shocking *El castigo sin venganza* (1631), the operations of poetic justice can only be discerned by a great deal of reflection which the text does little to assist. The Senecan thrills offered by Lope in *El castigo sin venganza* include forcing the offending son, Federico, to murder his father's wife (who is also the woman Federico loves) by a trick and then having him executed for the murder.

The Lopean formula, of course, largely but not entirely excluded realism in the modern sense of the term. The seventeenth-century Spanish audience got more direct contact with everyday life in the comic or farcical interludes (*entremeses*) interpolated between acts I and II of every *comedia*. The *comedias*, always written in verse, turned away from the world as their audience knew it in favour of the romantic world of seventeenth-century literary convention. At least on the most obvious level, the *comedia* was profoundly escapist – not in the sense that 't evaded problems but in the sense that it substituted 'safe' problems for difficult or dangerous ones and proceeded to solve them in an oversimple if often procedurally casuistical way. That was certainly one of the reasons it was so popular. This determination to present only a theatrical reality is very well seen in the *comedia*'s treatment of peasant life – a frequent theme. It is plainly idealized – e.g. as in Rojas Zorillas's *Del rey abajo ninguno*. The same is true of the *comedia*'s treatment of upper-class sexuality which, even when seduction or rape is involved, is studiously presented in the language of poetic or courtly love. Lope and his followers, it must be remembered too, wrote for a theatre whose conventions seemed designed to exclude giving the audience any sense that the play was a slice of real life. The routine introduction of a comic *entremés* between acts I and II and a sung ballet between acts II and III, together with the music, dancing and, sometimes, the comic turns on the stage after the ending, must all be taken into account when assessing the impact of a *comedia* on its audience. It was essentially a literary performance that no one could mistake for real.

The themes of the plays were taken from all over the place. The corpus of Spanish balladry provided a number, of which Lope's *El caballero de Olmedo* is perhaps the most famous. Here the dramatist could be sure his audience at all levels would know in advance, through the ballad, what would happen in the play. A number of plays illustrate a truth drawn from a popular proverb – e.g. *Las paredes oyen* and *La verdad sospechosa*, both by Juan Ruiz de Alarcón (*c.* 1581–1639). Chivalric romance, often wrongly said to be dead in Spain by the end of the sixteenth century, supplied a number of plots. History (though only rarely ancient history) provided many subjects for Lope and his followers. Spanish medieval history was particularly favoured – as in Lope's *Peribáñez* or *Las mocedades del Cid* of Guillén de Castro (1569–1631) or Tirso de Molina's *Antona García*. But subjects were also sometimes taken from more recent Spanish history; one such is Calderón's famous *El alcalde de Zalamea*. These historical plays were always performed in modern dress and the subjects were chosen not only to exploit the audience's interest in the national history but sometimes because they could be used, after altering the facts if necessary, to make a general point relevant to the seventeenth-century Spanish world. Subjects of biblical and hagiographical origin were also frequent – e.g. *La venganza de Tamar* of Tirso de Molina, Calderón's *El gran duque de Gandía* (written on the occasion of the canonization in 1671 of the subject of its title, Francisco de Borja, a former general of the Jesuit Order). The Italian *novella* of Bandello or Geraldo Cinthio among others – given the taste of Spanish audiences for tales about romantic love and honour – also provided much material; Lope's *El castigo sin venganza* and *El castigo del discreto* and Rojas Zorrilla's *Los bandos de Verona* are examples. Spanish literature, too, provided material. Rojas Zorrilla made use of Cervantes's *Persiles y Sigismunda*. Mythology, based mainly on Ovid, also supplied many subjects, particularly in the time of Philip IV, when stage machinery became extremely complex and mythological subjects could be presented in an effectively spectacular way. Calderón was to specialize in this important area of the *comedia*.

The themes of the Spanish *comedia* are not wide-ranging though the great variety of plots chosen might at first suggest the opposite. Seventeenth-century Spanish drama, like Spanish seventeenth-century literature generally, has no Utopian vision and does not contemplate, still less wish for, serious social or economic change. The Spanish *comedia*'s attitude to the monarchy was strongly absolutist: individual kings may behave improperly and be implicitly criticized for that but the institution of the monarchy itself is always beyond criticism. The *comedia*, too, never seriously calls in question the permanency of the existing social hierarchy or the natural superiority of the nobility over all the other social classes. It is, in fact, largely concerned with the doings of the nobility. The members of the lower classes who appear, among other things to provide comedy, are usually the servants of the nobles. Merchants, functionaries of plebeian blood and similar middle-class persons are largely excluded from the Spanish plays and the general temper of the *comedia* is hostile to the middle class and its ideas. Naturally, too, a very large section of Spanish seventeenth-century society – the clergy, monks and nuns – only appears in these plays in the best possible professional light.

Spanish seventeenth-century drama's extraordinary obsession with the aristocratic doctrine of personal honour and reputation is difficult to account for. More than fifty of Lope de Vega's plays deal in a substantial way with the honour theme. Honour, seen chiefly as reputation, is presented in all these works as the most prized possession a man of noble blood has. His continuous concern for it is the chief way in which he is shown as differing from the plebeian, who is without honour (at least in the eyes of the nobles). Women of noble birth have honour, too, but husbands are perpetually aware that their reputation is chiefly at risk because of the fragility of women of whatever class and the readiness of other men of noble blood (despite preoccupation with their own honour) to seduce women. The code of honour as portrayed in the theatre demanded that the offended man should mercilessly avenge any attack on his reputation, particularly in domestic situations, even if no more than an indiscretion had been committed. A number of plays (*El castigo sin venganza* of Lope de Vega and Calderón's wife-murder plays such as *El médico de su honra* or *A secreto agravio secreta venganza*, for example) exploit, too, a problem that was inescapable given the origins of the honour code: how to avenge a private or domestic affront to one's honour and reputation without, in fact, advertising to the world that an affront had taken place.

The early seventeenth-century dramatists almost never criticize the validity of the code of honour as such, even when it takes extreme forms. They do, occasionally, criticize the view that men who are not of noble blood (particularly if they are 'Old Christian' peasants) are by definition without honour, asserting instead the rights of all virtuous men to self-respect and respect from others; *Fuenteovejuna* is an example of such a play, but there are others.

The history of the honour theme in the Spanish theatre goes all the way back to Torres Naharro (see pp. 348–9 above). The formal concept itself is medieval but the reasons for the extreme preoccupation with personal and particularly with marital honour shown by the Spanish seventeenth-century drama are still incompletely elucidated. Sixteenth- and seventeenth-century Spanish casuists are fond of discussing the circumstances in which, despite the Christian commandment forbidding homicide, reasons may be found to justify a man killing his wife; a casuistical approach to the problem is patent in some treatments of this theme, which clearly deal with exceptional cases. Jesuit emphasis on the cultivation of personal honour and reputation may have continued to give the theme a certain degree of respectable authority. But doubtless it also involved important psycho-sexual urges in Spanish society. That the theme of honour was a safe recipe for success with Spanish audiences is attested by Lope de Vega. Yet there is no reason to suppose that Spanish drama closely mirrored the facts of everyday social life more in this than in any other respect. An occasional case of real-life wife murder may well have been stimulated by the honour plays themselves.

Various attempts have been made to categorize the different types of *comedia*, the most useful of them dating from the seventeenth century itself. The *comedia de enredo* was so called because it made use of a complicated plot, relying much on disguise. Tirso's play *Don Gil de las calzas verdes* is an example of such a plot; Lope de Vega's *El castigo del discreto* is another. The *comedia de capa y espada*, the most popular category of all, involved persons of noble blood, wearers of the sword and the cloak, and sword-play in streets or public places, particularly at night. A typical example is *El acero de Madrid* of Lope de Vega or Calderón's *La dama duende*. The *comedia de teatro* depended for its effects on an expensive *mise en scène* and the use of stage machinery – as in Tirso's *El burlador de Sevilla*. The *comedia de figurón*, which appeared during the seventeenth century, centred round a grotesque caricature who causes annoyance and trouble to others and is himself the victim of merited mischance – Rojas Zorrilla's *Entre bobos anda el juego* is an example. The nature of the *comedia de santos*, also a prolific genre, is obvious. The genre known as a *tragicomedia* illustrates poetic justice meted out in tragic or near-tragic circumstances as the punishment for serious imprudence or some other grave deviation from the rational order of society. It has been said with some truth that the best of the *comedias* fall within this category. Lope de Vega, Tirso de Molina and others sometimes describe individual works of theirs as *tragedias* but these never satisfy classical canons of tragedy and are in fact technically still tragicomedies.

The formula for the Spanish *comedia* as created by Lope de Vega provided drama distinguished by rapidity of movement, lightness of touch and an excellent sense of the theatre. Its inventiveness was remarkable and caused its repertoire to be pillaged by the dramatists of other countries. Perhaps modern criticism has tended to stress its doctrinal aims in the pre-Calderón period at the expense of other elements that seventeenth-century audiences certainly thought important, notably its ability to amuse through its *graciosos*, comic peasants, *figurones* and the like, and its capacity to astonish by the unexpected.

Most of even its best plays were written strictly with the author's eye on the needs of a drama whose ephemeral character was generally accepted. Very many plays written for the seventeenth-century Spanish theatre, even by masters like Lope de Vega, were mere pot-boilers. The sheer theatricality of the *comedia*, however, provided delight, amusement, escape, fantasy and a varying degree of doctrinal instruction for a society that enjoyed wit and sententiousness and liked to have its prejudices confirmed by playwrights.

XV Seventeenth-Century Drama: Some Followers of Lope de Vega

The outstanding feature of the work of the many lesser or minor dramatists who followed Lope de Vega is the closeness with which they generally follow his formula. A contributory factor here was certainly that the companies of actors themselves were by now made up of actors and actresses who had specialized in the characters established by the Lopean formula – *dama, galán, gracioso, barbón* (grey-beard), *dueña* and so on, and playwrights were obliged to provide parts to fit the roles for which the actors were trained. The individual companies, too, developed their own particular traditions and specialities and the authors of plays commissioned by managers had also to take those into account. This is probably one of the reasons why the authors sometimes disconcertingly wrote *comedias* decidedly different in tone and content from what may seem to be their more typical work.

Such factors make generalizations about an individual's work provisional and tentative. Nevertheless three outstanding features of the Lopean formula dominate the work of Lope's followers. One is their preoccupation with the theme of honour. Another is their attitude to love. Common to nearly all those who followed Lope de Vega (including Calderón), too, is the belief that the last scenes of a play should involve a kind of final judgement where everything is satisfactorily resolved and order restored. Some modern criticism of the Spanish *comedia* has supposed that the doctrinal aspects of the plays can only be fully understood if we take it that the audiences were expected to carry away from the theatre an awareness of what would happen to the characters after the events described on the stage had ended. The general structure and the circumstances of the staging of Spanish plays (see p. 356 above) seem designed, however, to ensure that, from the audience's point of view, the whole matter was at an end when the play ended.

Guillén de Castro (1569–1631), one of the older contemporaries of Lope de Vega, specialized in the high-life ethical dilemmas that were to become a feature of the Spanish *comedia*. His best-known but not necessarily best play, *Las mocedades del Cid* (in two parts), presents a series of these – love versus duty, justice versus vengeance, honour versus human feelings, the whole set in a context of blood and violence as well as melodrama. Spanish medieval history is here deliberately presented anachronistically. Juan Ruiz de Alarcón y Mendoza (*c.* 1581–1639), a Mexican-born hunchback, is, for once, something of an odd man out in the history of the *comedia*. Twenty *comedias* of his were published (1628 and 1634). In his best-known plays he gets very near turning the traditional formula into a true comedy of manners, writing against lying, laziness, evil gossip and, in *El semejante a sí mismo*, against religious hypocrisy. In these works (but not in all of his plays) he cultivates a low key and irony. García, the protagonist of *La verdad sospechosa*, is good-looking and has all the natural advantages but he is a congenital liar who is eventually hoist with his own petard when he, in consequence, loses the woman he loves and is forced to marry another he does not love. Alarcón sometimes puts himself into his plays. Thus in *La verdad sospechosa* he is the *gracioso* whose advice to the protagonist, García, is unheeded, and in *Las paredes oyen* he appears (ennobled) as Don Juan. Alarcón's plays were not very popular with Spanish audiences. Perhaps, too, their doctrine was insufficiently wrapped up in the fantasy, violence and distance from everyday life the audience liked.

Tirso de Molina was, after Lope de Vega and Calderón, the most important seventeenth-century Spanish dramatist and, though very busy travelling and writing for the Mercedarian Order to which he belonged, he found time to write several hundred *comedias*. Some of his work was printed in five parts between 1624 and 1633. One feature peculiar to Tirso is the number of plays he wrote in which women play a dominant role. In *Antona García*, set in the 1470s, the heroine is a warlike Amazon with superhuman physical strength. In *La prudencia en la mujer* (set in the fourteenth century) the queen-regent, defending the throne of the infant king, her son, measures courage and prudence against the treason of disloyal grandees. This play also has in full measure the element of violence and melodrama that, in Tirso, is unexpectedly associated with his generally detached and ironical attitude of mind towards humanity and its problems. Tirso de Molina's best-known plays today are *El condenado por desconfiado* and *El burlador de Sevilla y convidado de piedra*, both written in the 1620s. Tirso's authorship of the first of these plays has been contested, probably wrongly. Both have theological themes and there is a relationship between the theological points each seeks to make. Both are concerned with faith, free will, grace and the role of good and evil works in deciding man's salvation or condemnation after death. Both plays, in presenting their points, set out to startle and astonish the audience, *El condenado por desconfiado* introducing the Devil as a character on stage. A hermit, Paulo, after many years of a severely religious life, comes to doubt if he will be granted salvation because he has a dream in which he sees that his end will be the same as that of a bandit. As a result of this lack of faith Paulo falls into the sin of despair and becomes a bandit himself. The other main character is the professional bandit, Enrico, against whose salvation all the cards seem stacked. He has raped women, burnt children alive and led a totally irreligious life. But he has proper feelings towards his father and it is filial piety that, despite the risk of capture, makes him visit his father on the latter's deathbed. He is arrested as a result of his visit and sentenced to death. The Devil and an angel dispute with him for his soul, the Devil promising he can help him escape the executioner. Enrico eventually rejects the Devil's offer, repents and is hanged, but his soul is saved. The theme also appears in Antonio Mira de Amescua's (*c.* 1574–1644) *El esclavo del demonio*, where, of course, the Devil is shown as incapable of keeping his promise. Enrico's salvation showed that the dream Paulo had had thus did not predict his own damnation or justify the lack of faith and despair that overtook him as a result of it. He is not saved. What we have here is one of those casuistical extreme special cases which so appealed to the seventeenth-century Spanish mind, but the play's implication (that a last-minute conversion could redeem a life of great wickedness while a life devoted to religious and good works could be nullified by a fairly understandable lapse into despair) may have been among the reasons why, in 1625, Tirso was officially rebuked by a royal commission because of the scandal he caused 'on account of the profane plays he writes which offer incentives to evil and bad examples'. *El burlador de Sevilla*, at any rate, puts the other side of the case, demonstrating this time that the sinner who persists in refusing grace in the belief that there will always be time to make use of it may find that God will not grant the necessary respite. Tirso's play is particularly carefully written. But Tirso's Don

Juan has none of the subtle implications or complicated features of the later Don Juan myth. He is brutal, violent and unfeeling, abusing four women and the laws of friendship and hospitality. He also murders an old man, profanes the sacrament and defies heaven. A destroyer of the personal and family honour of other men and women, he nevertheless contrives to regard his own behaviour as a manifestation of noble honour. Despite its serious and eventually supernatural theme, the pull of the Lopean formula was so strong that Tirso felt obliged to introduce the usual comic scenes, even just before Don Juan dines in a private chapel with the statue of the murdered *comendador*, Don Gonzalo, and (as a result of this final act of temerity), his hand in that of his ghostly victim, falls dead and unconfessed in a violent *coup de théâtre*. In its decidedly seventeenth-century Spanish dramatic context it is an effective doctrinal play and one of the mere handful of pre-Calderonian works that are truly memorable.

Francisco de Rojas Zorrilla (1607–48) and Agustín Moreto y Cabaña (1618–69) are usually regarded as disciples of Calderón rather than of Lope de Vega but it is not entirely clear why. Rojas Zorrilla was another cultivator of violence on the stage in the Senecan manner. In *Morir pensando matar*, which comfortingly suggests that God makes criminals destroy each other, the king makes his guilty queen drink from her father's skull. *Del rey abajo ninguno* – Rojas Zorrilla's most famous play – does present a version of the honour theme that is reminiscent of Calderón. Here the protagonist, Don García, falsely believes that the king has tried to seduce his wife. Since in all matters of honour the king alone is untouchable, Don García concludes he is obliged, in default of a male victim, to murder the wife he loves and who has committed no fault ('sólo por razón de estado / a la muerte te condeno'). All is well when García discovers that his wife's attacker was the royal favourite since, apart from the king, a man may avenge himself on anyone. He does so. Rojas Zorrilla's *Entre bobos anda el juego* is a pleasing example of the genre known as a *comedia de figurón* (see p. 359 above), the *figurón* here being depicted in the person of the grotesquely comic Don Lucas del Cigarral. The play defends the right of a woman to choose her own husband for love against the determination of her father, a poor knight, to marry her to the rich but detestable *figurón*. The moral, though, should again not be taken very seriously, as everyone knew that arranged marriages were the rule.

Agustín Moreto, another playwright-priest, also exploits the *figurón* tradition in plays like *El lindo Don Diego* – who is a self-loving fop suggested to Moreto by Guillén de Castro's *El Narciso en su opinión*. In *El desdén con el desdén* the heroine, Diana, disdains the love of men – or affects to. One of her lovers pretends to share her hatred and she inevitably falls in love with him. Tricks and ruses handled with grace and lightness of touch are an integral part of much but not all of Moreto's work, which sometimes seems already to look ahead to eighteenth-century comedy. Moreto's *El licenciado vidriera* is not very close to Cervantes's famous *novela* and, in fact, is about ingratitude. Cervantes's hero, Tomas Rodaja, was a poor student. Since such a hero was impossible on the Spanish stage Moreto had to turn him into Carlos, who is poor but noble. To show madness on the Spanish stage was also indecorous; Carlos merely feigns madness. In Moreto's *No puede ser* satire is directed against the practicability of the honour code. Moreto boldly suggests that, if a woman is determined to jeopardize her honour, she will find means of outwitting the men who try to prevent it. A version of this play was put on in London in 1668. Its English author, Thomas Sydserf, described it as a comical trifle but added that, like most other plays, 'useful moralities' could be found in it – a valuable reminder that, in fact, it would be next to impossible successfully to write a play devoid of some moral implications. The desire to find important doctrinal messages in the Spanish *comedia*, together with modern disapprobation of Moreto's habit of rewriting the plots of his predecessors (no cause, in seventeenth-century Europe, for criticism of any writer) have combined to cause his work to be underestimated today. Moreto was often an excellent author of pure comedy. In many of his works reason takes precedence over the elements of fantasy and passion which had been an integral part of the Lopean formula.

XVI Seventeenth-Century Drama: Calderón

Pedro Calderón de la Barca (1600–81) was not simply a writer of *comedias*. He was also a notable creator of a new type of religious *auto sacramental* (see below, pp. 371–3) and, in the last decades of his long career, he wrote works for the court theatre in which spectacle, instrumental music and singing played a large part; his *Púrpura de la rosa* (1660) introduced into Spain the pattern of Italian opera. Calderón is undoubtedly the most important and intellectually most rewarding dramatist who wrote for the Spanish stage in the seventeenth century. He has also always been, for foreigners, the most highly regarded Spanish playwright – though often misinterpreted by them – since his rediscovery by European Romanticism. In the Spain of his day he was recognized early on as something new among dramatic writers. In the 1690s, Francisco Bances Candamo (1662–1704) – himself the last writer of any importance in the *comedia* tradition – regarded Calderón as the true creator of a worthy drama in Spain:

> fue quien dio decoro a las tablas y puso norma a la Comedia de España, así en lo airoso de sus personajes como en lo compuesto de sus argumentos, en lo ingenioso de su contextura y fábrica, y en la pureza de su estilo.

This was going rather far: though Calderón introduced significant changes of emphasis and tone into the Lopean formula, drawing out latent possibilities in it, most of his work is still written within the Lopean tradition. What he now added was a much more tightly organized structure, a depth of ideas and a poetic density lacking in the earlier *comedia*. His work retains, however, a belief in the need for comic relief, even in the most serious plays; the *gracioso* continues to be almost indispensable, though the latter's role and the comic scenes associated with him are usually more closely integrated into the main theme than in Lopean *comedia*. As with the latter, Calderón, except on rare occasions, such as in *El alcalde de Zalamea* (?1636), is not interested in creating autonomous 'characters' as such; the personages in his more serious plays exist to serve and illustrate the dramatist's dialectical purposes; Calderón makes extensive use, particularly in his monologues, of neo-scholastic methods of reasoning, and his personages argue syllogistically. He also had a special gift for expressing in poetic imagery of a high order both the meaning of the intellectual concepts with which he was concerned and their emotive significance. Calderón's intellectual range as such is, in fact, quite narrow. What is new is the rigour of his dialectic and the undoubted primacy of theme in Calderón's mind, at least in his serious works.

Calderón was a pupil of the Jesuits at the Colegio Imperial in Madrid and doubtless learnt there his theology and his mastery of rhetorical precept and practice. He refused to obey his authoritarian father's wishes that he should become a priest and turned to the theatre to make his living, beginning his dramatic career in 1623. The domestic background to Calderón's youth was far from happy and it is probably no accident that, not only in *La vida es sueño* but in some other plays, a conflict between father and son is involved. Some episodes of violence marked his independent life as a young man. Despite his theological interests, Calderón did not become a priest until quite late in life (1651). After 1651 he restricted himself to writing plays for performance in the royal palace and to the composition of *autos sacramentales*. Calderón's first published plays appeared as early as 1636–7 (twenty-four plays). By the time of his death in 1681 he had written more than 120 *comedias* of various types and more than seventy *autos sacramentales*. Most of what are today his best-known works were, in fact, written in the 1630s, before he was forty.

The famous plays which posterity has selected as his masterpieces give a very one-sided impression of Calderón's total contribution to the seventeenth-century theatre. Thus a genre to which he contributed substantially was the *comedia de capa y espada*, good examples of which are *El maestro de danzar*, *No siempre lo peor es cierto* and *El astroólogo fingido* – all three among the works of Calderón adapted for the English Restoration theatre – or *La dama duende* and *No hay cosa como callar*. The latter is often considered Calderón's best work in this genre because its implications are rather less trivial than most. The subject-matter of these *comedias* is defined by one of the characters in *No hay cosa como callar*: '¿Qué he de hacer en tan extraño / lance de amistad y celos / de amor y honor?' They depend, as the genre demanded, on conflicts of love, honour and jealousy in which disguise, coincidence, the assumption of a false identity and the exploitation of a variety of dramatic tricks create bewildering situations for the usually very thinly drawn characters. In *No hay cosa como callar*, though it still remains essentially light comedy, the chief *galán* – Don Juan – is this time a thoughtless and selfish sexual philanderer who is reduced to lying to try to cover up his tracks and in the end finds his fate is in the hands of one of the women he has tricked; all the upper-class characters in the play find it suits their book to keep silence about what has passed. But the wounded *gracioso*, at the end of this play, is allowed to sound an unwonted sour note by reminding the audience of the selfish disregard of the characters for anything else except their own affairs.

Calderón's work was profoundly affected by the establishment of a permanent court theatre in the new Buen Retiro palace in the 1630s. This was built to make possible in Madrid the production of plays depending on complicated spectacular effects achieved by elaborate stage machinery and expensive sets. An Italian stage engineer, Cosme Lotti, came to Spain to teach Italian stagecraft to the Spaniards. At performances at the Buen Retiro we read of chariots drawn by fish vomiting water, real ships moving across the water and gods flying through the air; metamorphoses occurred before the eyes of the spectators. The stage sets were of extraordinary richness, employing elaborate perspectives and, judging by designs which have survived, dwarfing the actors. Music and singing also came to be an essential part of the court theatre. The *zarzuela* (named after the royal palace of the Zarzuela) was a performance partly spoken, partly sung, for which Calderón wrote a number of works (*El laurel de Apolo*, 1658, is an example) before progressing, in 1660, to writing full-scale operas.[1] When writing his mythological plays, Calderón was plainly influenced by the need to provide opportunities for the engineers and designers of sets to exercise their talents. But his presentation of mythological themes in no way represents an assertion of pagan values on the Spanish stage. In accordance with the approach to mythology in contemporary poetry and painting, Calderón, as he makes explicit in plays like *La estatua de Prometeo* (*c.* 1672), interprets mythology allegorically (and symbolically) so that, in this particular play, the conflict between passion (Palas) and wisdom (Minerva) ends with the triumph of reason. We are also reminded for good measure, as elsewhere in Calderón, of the hidden God who is the real master of the forces pagan error has mistaken for gods. It has been shown that, behind all the apparent superfluity of scenes and the complexity of these mythological plays, Calderón's characteristic concerns and style as a dramatist survive. But, like English masques of the period, when they are separated from the spectacular *mise en scène* for which they were written, only those who have an awareness of what that was like can, perhaps, really appreciate them today.

The first of the plays on which Calderón's reputation now rests, *El príncipe constante* (1629), is concerned with a Portuguese prince, Fernando, who, in real life, was handed over as a hostage to the King of Fez (1437) by his own brother, Prince Henry the Navigator, to guarantee the return to Fez by the Portuguese of the North African port of Ceuta after Henry's defeat at the hands of the Moroccans. Fernando was then abandoned to his fate when the Portuguese failed to honour their promises. But Calderón's play has nothing to do with historical fact – at least as regards Fernando's known behaviour in captivity. It is taken from hagiographical sources which had successfully turned the reluctant captive into a royal Christian martyr who chooses slavery and death rather than a freedom which meant the return of Ceuta to Islam.

[1] For a note on the musical aspects of the staging of Calderón's works, see Chapter 12, section VIII, p. 558.

Fernando is set up to personify the Christian virtue of defiant fortitude as defined by St Thomas Aquinas and he illustrates in extreme form a characteristic of Calderón's treatment of major themes. Protagonists are often shown as they struggle to attain truth or to carry through a course of action. Personal struggle of this kind is basic in Calderonian drama. But, except perhaps in honour plays, no intrinsic doubt is allowed in Calderón. The nature of truth is certain. Doubt is the result of error, ignorance or sin.

La devoción de la Cruz is also an early play (before 1633), in which the Cross figures as a symbol of divine clemency towards all sinners. It is a melodramatic work, including an abduction from a convent and an incest motif – the latter, in fact, not infrequent in the Spanish Golden Age *comedia*. Here Eusebio kills the elder brother of Julia whom he then abducts from a convent only to discover that she is his twin sister and the man he has killed his own elder brother. Eusebio and Julia both become bandits. It is also the case that their father, Curcio, had killed their mother, suspecting his honour had been affronted despite her oath on the Cross that she was innocent. Both twins, born just before her death, bear the mark of the Cross. It falls to Curcio to arrest and kill his criminal son – for whose criminality he, ironically, was ultimately responsible. Eusebio has been very wicked indeed but, despite that, his unfailing devotion to the Cross saves him. Though dead and even buried he is miraculously resuscitated long enough to be confessed and granted salvation. Julia the ex-nun, also now penitent, is saved from her father's vengeful sword. It is left to the father to point out to the audience that they have seen a happy ending.

El mágico prodigioso (1637), a *comedia de santos*, is the tale of a pagan scholar, Cipriano of Antioch, who loves a Christian girl, Justina. He is tempted by the Devil who appears to him as a philosopher and is angered by Cipriano's interest in Pliny's god, understood as a pagan intuition of the Christian God. Cipriano eventually agrees to surrender his soul to the Devil in exchange for possession of Justina, but the Devil is unable to move Justina whose Christian free will is proof against his powers. The impotent Devil is reduced to trickery: Cipriano, thinking to possess Justina, finds himself confronted by a skeleton instead. The skeleton, a symbol of *desengaño*, observes, 'Así, Cipriano, son / todas las glorias del mundo'. The Devil has to admit the existence of the Christian God and the latter's omnipotence, but reminds Cipriano he himself by virtue of their pact, is nevertheless the Devil's slave. But Cipriano is saved when he, too, calls on the Christian God. Cipriano and Justina are both martyred in Antioch as Christian saints. A tremendous storm marks their execution and the Devil appears on the scaffold where the new martyrs' severed heads and trunks are lying and, forced by God's superior power to do so, confesses to the people the truth of what has happened. The real prodigious magician is God.

Calderón cannot be acquitted of having, in this play, catered in part for a credulous, miracle-loving section of his audience by offering them hagiography and legend in a form calculated to impress rather than persuade. Calderón, in his days at the Colegio Imperial, would have learnt not to despise such incentives to piety and religion. The presence of the *graciosos* with their comic relief, too, remains a troubling tribute by Calderón to the demands of Spanish theatrical tradition. But *El mágico prodigioso*, in particular, also carries a strong vein of intellectual argument supported by moving poetic dialogue, which makes it possible also to treat the miracles as metaphorical expressions of well-known theological truths.

La vida es sueño (1635) – Calderón's most famous play – was intended for the municipal, not the court theatre. It is a more acceptable play for modern times than the two just discussed. It contrives to illustrate (again by presenting an extreme case) the orthodox view of free will and grace, this time without miraculous interventions, but solely as a result of the teachings of experience and reason. Segismundo is the son and heir of Basilio, King of Poland. Basilio is an expert astrologer who has divined that the stars foretell that his son will be a disastrous and impious prince. He therefore imprisons him in a remote cave, bringing him up in total ignorance of his birth. We first see Segismundo in chains suffering the deprivations and miseries of imprisonment for no reason known to him. Basilio, however, has second thoughts about his son's imprisonment: perhaps it was wrong, after all, not to have remembered that destinies foretold by the stars can be altered by acts of Christian free will. Segismundo, drugged, is now brought to the palace and liberated, but nothing is said about the past or his change of circumstances, so that he cannot be sure whether he is only dreaming he is free or not. In fact he now behaves with a violence that suggests the destiny foretold for him is correct. But, as he himself informs Basilio, since he has always been treated like a beast – deprived of liberty, the experience of life and the honour due to a prince – he has now become one. His sight in the palace of the beautiful Rosaura, whom he had first seen from his prison tower, convinces him that he is not dreaming. He is, however, returned in chains, as too dangerous for freedom, to the tower where he had first been held and is persuaded he had only dreamt he had been freed. Basilio is now convinced that, if allowed liberty, he would prove to be the monster his horoscope predicted. The army, however, mutinies against Basilio because Segismundo's exclusion would place a foreign prince on the throne on Basilio's death. The soldiers free Segismundo. Segismundo has now largely learnt his lesson: whether the world is real or is a dream, what matters is to do good works. He defeats Basilio in battle. Basilio is only the more certain of the truth of predestination and the impossibility of interfering with its dictates. But Segismundo survives the test to which his victory over his father puts him. He hands the throne back to Basilio, giving him a lesson at the same time on the errors his belief in destiny and his lack of faith in men's free will have led him to commit. *La vida es sueño* is the most splendidly poetic of all Calderón's plays. In it the conceits, the exploitation of continuous, *culterano* metaphor and the controlled use of poetic imagery to point up the underlying theme reach a level of continuous excellence that Calderón never quite reached in his other best-known plays. In no other play is the author's ability to be inspired poetically as well as dramatically by the contemplation of theological truths so effective. It is one of the few Spanish *comedias* whose dialogue (especially the great soliloquies on which the structure rests) sticks in the mind. The dream theme represents yet another manifestation of Golden Age literature's preoccupation with appearance and reality.

A great deal has been written about *El alcalde de Zalamea* (?1642) and Calderón's two wife-murder plays, *El médico de su honra* (1635) and *A secreto agravio secreta venganza* (1636), all of which deal, as do various others, in an unconventional way with the honour code. Calderón seems not to have noticed, or at any rate to have drawn no lessons, from the fact that, in the first-named play, his personages are more nearly individual and idiosyncratic characters in their own right than was usual with him. The situation dealt with – that a peasant has the right to avenge his family honour, here when it has been outraged by an army officer of noble birth – was one treated various times, but much less uncompromisingly, by Lope de Vega and others. The mayor, Pedro Crespo, using and abusing his judicial functions, executes the noble captain of the troops quartered in the town who has violated his daughter. The act is eventually accepted by the king, as the final arbiter of justice. Pedro Crespo is shown as an ignorant if manly peasant. But he insists that, as regards his honour, he is the equal of the gouty and crusty general, Lope de Figueroa, with whom he establishes a kind of friendship. The general is portrayed as a somewhat comical figure, a break with the social decorum of the Spanish *comedia*. *El médico de su honra* and its successor are very different. They deal with extreme cases of honour and the essentially casuistical nature of their themes is made plain by the form of the arguments put in the protagonists' mouths, when they discuss whether or not a husband's honour requires and justifies wife-murder. In both cases the wife has not committed adultery, merely been imprudent, or guilty in thought only. Calderón's attitude to the events he describes is not one of approval, but it certainly falls far short of unambiguous condemnation. The Spanish *comedia*, it can hardly be too often repeated, dealt only distantly with the facts of everyday life, and these honour plays, in their negative way, should perhaps also be seen as 'idealizations' of reality. One can imagine that many a husband (and perhaps even many a wife who was the victim of a husband's indifference) found in such plays a kind of catharsis. Nevertheless admirers of Calderón's plays perhaps do no service to his reputation by seeking to justify works, however well written, that catered, or seemed to cater, for the more ignoble instincts of a seventeenth-century Spanish audience and which, perhaps, Calderón himself thought of more as interesting exercises in casuistry on the stage than as models either to be followed or to be disapproved of.

The *auto sacramental* was a characteristically Spanish manifestation of the liturgical drama which was inherited from the sixteenth century and was brought to artistic fruition by Calderón. The *auto* was allegorical in form. It was intended for performance in the street and was an essential part of the popular religious festivities and processions associated with the feast of Corpus Christi. The function of the *autos sacramentales* was always to illustrate the meaning of the Eucharist. As an *auto* had to be performed on the same day in several parts of the city the stage sets and stage machinery for them were erected on large mobile carts – at first two carts were involved but, later in the seventeenth century, these were increased to four. When they reached the site where a performance was to take place a stage was quickly erected, the carts being stationed on either side of it and towards its rear. One should not deduce from the part played by carts that there was anything primitive about the staging of a seventeenth-century *auto sacramental*. The carts carried very elaborate scenic constructions and supporting stage machines. Since the theological content of an *auto sacramental* in Calderón's time was difficult for the unlettered to follow easily, from the beginning spectacular visual effects were relied on to hold their interest and to help to convey the doctrinal message of the *autos*.

It has been suggested that a knowledge of Calderón's *autos sacramentales* is essential if we are to understand what he was about in his *comedias*. This view, provided we consider only the famous doctrinal *comedias*, has a good deal to commend it, though, in fact, the connection – for example – between *La vida es sueño* and the *auto* Calderón wrote using the same theme is not particularly close. But there is a certain underlying tendency to present the characters in the *comedias* in a semi-allegorical way that recalls the *autos*. Calderón's methods of expounding scholastic doctrines are alike in both genres. If, however, the *comedias* have some of the characteristics of the *auto sacramental* it is also true that the latter is influenced by the *comedia* formula – e.g. in the *gracioso*-like figure of Albedrío even in a very late *auto* like *Andrómeda y Perseo* (1680). There are also not infrequently passing superficial *costumbrista* allusions in the *autos* such as those found in Calderón's routine *capa y espada* plays.

Calderón, in the *autos*, impresses, at his best, by the vigour and clarity with which he sets out orthodox theological dogmas in a language which makes subtle use of poetic imagery to support and develop his theme. A good example of a fairly early Calderonian *auto sacramental* is *El gran teatro del mundo*, where the traditional metaphor of the world as a theatre is exploited allegorically. The Producer (*autor*) is God, the Prompter is the law of Efficacious Grace. The other personages include the World, a king, Beauty, a rich man, a peasant, a poor man and Discretion (dressed as a nun and understood here as personifying religion). The characters, called upon to make their final exit (death), are judged according to the way they have performed their roles in the comedy of life. Only the poor man – who has never had any worldly possessions or pleasures to lose – and Discretion are unafraid of death, the latter because she has devoted all her life to preparing for it. In the end, however, only the rich man is damned – their good works are held to have saved the king and the others. *La cena de Baltasar* is a powerful work which deals with the dogma of the Redemption. Belshazzar's feast is treated as a profanation of the communion rite. Apart from the king himself, other figures in the *auto* are Idolatry and Vanity (Belshazzar's constant companions), Death, the prophet Daniel (God's spokesman) and Thought – presented as a madman and described by himself as 'inquieto y violento'. Belshazzar is killed by Death before the eyes of the audience and the idolatrous feast is succeeded on stage by an altar and the eucharistic vessels. Idolatry, now reformed, adores the sacraments. Calderón's later *autos* are usually more complicated and less easy to follow. An example is *El pintor de su deshonra* which puts on the stage a Painter, the World, Love, Lucifer, Guilt, Grace, Knowledge, Nature, Innocence and Free Will. The Painter is, in fact, God and it is in relation to him that the honour theme is introduced; unlike man, who avenges a slight on his honour by killing, God takes vengeance by pardoning the offender.

Reliance on ever more impressive spectacle ('lo aparatoso de las tramoyas') and on music and singing ('lo sonoro de la música') is more and more noticeable in the Calderonian *autos* as the century advances – just as it is in his *comedias*. He now sometimes turned, as in the latter, to mythological themes – e.g. in *El divino Orfeo* (1663) or *Psiquis y Cupido* (1665), for the presentation of which stage effects of great complexity were required and in which music played an integral part.

The Spanish *comedia*, remarkable to modern readers for its moral and social orthodoxy (and despite the fact that some of its most gifted writers were priests), was always under attack in the seventeenth century, particularly from the Jesuit Order, though in their colleges, in Spain as elsewhere, the Jesuits had made the writing and performance of improving dramas (nominally, but not always in practice, written wholly in Latin) an essential part of the Jesuit educational curriculum. On several occasions the theatres, despite royal patronage, were threatened with closure and they were in fact closed for some years in the 1640s. One of the objections to the *comedia* put forward by its critics was the immoral life of the players themselves. Objection was also made to the predominant role of love on the stage at a time when the teaching of disillusion with all worldly pleasures should be, it was said, the main concern of moralists. But the critics went further: the *comedias* were held to encourage social disturbance and civil war, even heresy. Even the great Lope de Vega was described in 1620 as a wolf feeding himself on the souls lost by attendance at performances of his plays and, in 1649, at the height of the attack on the theatre, as a man who had done more damage to Spain through them than Luther had in Germany through his heresies. This undercurrent of ecclesiastical hostility may have helped to deter any playwright who felt tempted to make radical changes in the traditional (and therefore fairly unassailable) formula originally created by Lope de Vega. But the lukewarm reception accorded by Spanish audiences even to the limited dramatic innovations of Ruiz de Alarcón suggests that Spanish seventeenth-century theatre audiences, in any case, did not want anything new. The partly illiterate character of these audiences and the view taken by professional actors themselves of the nature of the drama, of course, ruled out any development towards classical comedy and tragedy in the municipal theatres; the unclassical aesthetic tastes of the seventeenth-century cultured minority excluded any such development in the court theatre. Equally, a drama (like Shakespeare's) that would allow playwrights to philosophize speculatively or to ask and leave unanswered awkward transcendental questions was unthinkable in Counter-Reformation Spain. After a long period of creative richness Spanish drama was, after Calderón, destined to carry on its hallowed traditions in a dying fall until the eighteenth-century Enlightenment tentatively introduced Spaniards to new ideas about the nature, purpose and form of dramatic writing.

Spanish seventeenth-century drama very plainly reveals, as do many other branches of Golden Age literature generally from the time of the Catholic Monarchs onwards, the characteristic penetration of literature by popular influences. But these influences, except in minor genres like the *entremés*, were very far from being exercised in the direction of depicting man in his everyday social environment. As far as the seventeenth century is concerned, the notion that Spanish literature generally had the natural inclination towards realism (in the nineteenth-century sense) often claimed for it is palpably absurd. No such preoccupation is to be detected in the major work of Lope de Vega, Calderón, Góngora, Gracián or Quevedo. Cervantes, who might seem to be the exception who proves the rule, was, in fact, hesitant about his achievements in the field of literary realism and, as we have seen, secured little recognition either in his lifetime or after his death from other Spanish writers – particularly for the part of his work which had taken that particular path.

To the modern reader a great deal of Spanish seventeenth-century writing seems designed to keep at bay, in one way or another, the impact of the economic, monetary and social disintegration that more and more came to face Spaniards everywhere in their everyday life. There are, however, very few signs that Spanish writers, even at the end of the Golden Age, were troubled by this. The general theory about the nature of art to which they subscribed ruled out by definition realism as a significant art form. They did not want literature, in a literal sense, to mirror life. Its task was to improve on life, to look for the universal which lay behind the particular. Nor was it interested in the problems of man as a social animal since it regarded all human problems as essentially ones concerning man as an individual.

Bibliography

NOTE

The bibliography that follows lists only books and articles dealing in more general terms with aspects of literature, ideas and taste between 1474 and 1681. Some special emphasis has been given to books and articles in English. For bibliographical information regarding individual writers (up to date as far as 1971) see R. O. Jones, *The Golden Age: Prose and Poetry*, and Edward M. Wilson and Duncan Moir, *The Golden Age: Drama* (both London, 1971). For biographical information about individuals the *Diccionario de literatura española*, edited by G. Bleiberg and J. Marías, 4th ed. (Madrid, 1972), is useful. The most ambitious of the many modern histories of Spanish literature is the *Historia general de las literaturas hispánicas*, edited by Guillermo Díaz-Plaja. Vols II and III (2nd impression Barcelona, 1968) deal particularly with the Golden Age. The usefulness of the individual contributions to this work varies considerably. Some will be found decidedly old-fashioned in their critical attitudes, but others are helpful.

GENERAL

BATAILLON, M. *Erasmo y España: Estudios sobre la historia espiritual del siglo XVI.* 2nd Spanish ed. Mexico, 1966. (Essential reading for any serious student of the intellectual as well as the religious history of sixteenth-century Spain – and for many aspects of sixteenth-century literature.)

CASTRO, A. *La realidad histórica de España.* 3rd ed. Mexico, 1966. (For the student of Golden Age literature the interest of this work lies mainly in the conclusions it draws from the fact, or presumption, that a number of well-known Spanish writers belonged to the *converso* minority (i.e. were of Jewish ancestry). The author often pushes his interesting thesis beyond what an objective interpretation of the historical evidence permits and it should therefore be handled with caution.)

GREEN, O. H. *Spain and the Western Tradition.* 4 vols. Madison, 1963–6. (Concerned largely with the history of ideas, themes and topics as these appear in literature.)

JONES, R. O. *The Golden Age: Prose and Poetry. A Literary History of Spain*, vol. 2. London, 1971.

KRAILSHEIMER, A. J. (ed.). *The Continental Renaissance 1500–1600.* Harmondsworth, 1971. (Sections on Spain by R. W. Truman.)

MARAVALL, J. A. *La cultura del Barroco.* Barcelona, 1976.

MENÉNDEZ Y PELAYO, M. *Historia de las ideas estéticas en España.* 5 vols. Madrid, 1947. (Though in many ways now outmoded, still assembles much material for the history of aesthetic ideas in Spain not easily accessible elsewhere.)

PARKER, A. A. 'An Age of Gold: Expansion and Scholarship in Spain'. In *The Age of the Renaissance*. Ed. Denys Hay. London, 1967.

PORQUERAS MAYO, A. (ed.). *El prólogo en el Renacimiento español*. Madrid, 1965.

—— *El prólogo en el manierismo y barroco españoles*. Madrid, 1968. (Anthologies of authors' prefaces: useful for those wishing to have access to writers' officially declared intentions when writing their books, as well as for the historian of Golden Age theories of literature.)

INTELLECTUAL HISTORY

The following works may be found useful as an introduction to the intellectual history of Spain in the period 1474–1681. See also under 'Religious Thought'.

BATAILLON, M. See under 'General' above.

BELL, A. F. G. *Francisco Sánchez, el Brocense*. Oxford, 1925.

—— *Juan Ginés de Sepúlveda*. Oxford, 1925.

—— *Luis de León: A Study of the Spanish Renaissance*. Oxford, 1925. (An apologetic and one-sided view of the Spanish 'Renaissance' but contains much useful and detailed information.)

BLUHER, K. A. *Seneca in Spanien: Untersuchungen zur Geschichte der Seneca-Rezeption in Spanien vom 13. bis 17. Jahrhundert*. Munich, 1969. (Basic for an understanding of Spanish Golden Age neo-stoicism.)

CASTRO, A. *El pensamiento de Cervantes*. 2nd ed. Madrid, 1972.

ETTINGHAUSEN, H. *Francisco de Quevedo and the Neostoic Movement*. Oxford, 1972.

EVENNET, H. O. *The Spirit of the Counter-Reformation*. Cambridge, 1968. (A good general approach to the Counter-Reformation.)

FRAILE, G. *Historia de la filosofía española*. Madrid (B.A.C.), 1971. Revised ed. Pp. 213–398 deal with the history of philosophy in Spain in the Golden Age. A useful reference book.

GUY, A. *La Pensée de Fray Luis de León: contribution à l'étude de la philosophie espagnole au XVIᵉ siècle*. Limoges, 1943. (There is an abbreviated Spanish translation by Pedro Saínz Rodríguez, *El pensamiento filosófico de Fray Luis de León*, Madrid, 1960.)

HAYDEN, H. *The Counter Renaissance*. New York, 1950. (A massive study of the important anti-authoritarian, anti-scholastic and anti-rationalist currents in Renaissance writing. Though not directly concerned with Spain, contains much information that is highly relevant to Spanish literature and thought. The 'Counter-Renaissance' here must not be confused with the 'Counter-Reformation'.)

KAMEN, H. *The Spanish Inquisition*. London, 1965.

REKERS, B. *Benito Arias Montano*. London, 1972.

ZANTA, L. *La Renaissance du stoïcisme au XVIᵉ siècle*. Paris, 1914. (Still a useful approach to this theme.)

RELIGIOUS THOUGHT

BATAILLON, M. See under 'General' above.

BOEHMER, E. *Spanish Reformers of Two Centuries from 1520: Their Lives and Writings*. Strasbourg and London, 1874–1904.

GROULT, P. *Los místicos de los Paises Bajos y la literatura española del siglo XVI.* Madrid, 1976.

HATZFELD, H. *Estudios literarios sobre mística española.* 2nd ed. Madrid, 1968.

HAWKINS, D. J. B. *A Sketch of Mediaeval Philosophy.* London, 1946. (Chapter IX contains a useful summary account of sixteenth- and seventeenth-century Spanish neo-scholasticism and of the dispute between the followers of Domingo Báñez and Luis de Molina about free will.)

HAYMAN, A. *The Christian Renaissance: A History of the 'devotio moderna'.* Grand Rapids, 1924.

KNOWLES, D. *The English Mystical Tradition.* London, 1961. (Discloses the closeness of the connection between Spanish sixteenth-century mysticism and medieval European mystical writing generally.)

PEERS, E. A. *Studies of the Spanish Mystics.* 3 vols. London, 1927–60.

RICART, D. *Juan de Valdés y el pensamiento religioso europeo en los siglos XVI y XVII.* Mexico, 1958.

THEORY OF LITERATURE AND LITERARY CRITICISM

COLLARD, A. *Nueva poesía: Conceptismo, culteranismo en la crítica española.* Waltham (Brandeis University), 1967.

GALLEGO MORELL, A. *Garcilaso y sus comentaristas.* Granada, 1966. (Useful for the theory of poetry of Fernando de Herrera and his generation.)

GRACIÁN, B. *Agudeza y arte de ingenio.* Ed. E. Correa Calderón. 2 vols. Madrid, 1969.

LÓPEZ PINCIANO, A. *Philosophia antigua poética.* Ed. Alfredo Carballo Picazo. 3 vols. Madrid, 1953. (The most interesting of the Spanish Golden Age expositions of neo-Aristotelian critical theory.)

OROZCO DÍAZ, E. *Manierismo y barroco.* Salamanca, 1970. (Attempts to establish a theory of the Mannerist and baroque styles with reference to Spanish Golden Age literature.)

PRAZ, M. *Studies in Seventeenth-Century Imagery.* 2nd ed. 1964; reprint, Rome, 1975. (Essential for an understanding of emblem literature and its history in Spain.)

RILEY, E. C. *Cervantes's Theory of the Novel.* Oxford, 1962. (Contains much information about sixteenth-century critical theory, with particular reference to prose.)

—— 'Aspectos del concepto de "admiratio" en la teoría literaria del siglo de oro'. In *Homenaje a Dámaso Alonso*, III, pp. 173–83. Madrid, 1963.

SHEPARD, S. *El Pinciano y las teorías literarias del siglo de oro.* 2nd ed. Madrid, 1970.

WEINBERG, B. *A History of Literary Criticism in the Italian Renaissance.* 2 vols. 2nd impression. Chicago, 1963. (Because of the dependence of Spanish sixteenth- and seventeenth-century critical theory on Italy, essential for any detailed understanding of critical theory in Spain with reference to all the literary genres.)

WELLEK, R. 'The Concept of Baroque in Literary Scholarship'. In *The Journal o, Aesthetics*, V (1946), pp. 77–109.

WOODS, M. J. 'Sixteenth-Century Topical Theory: Some Spanish and Italian Views'. In *Modern Language Review*, LXIII (1968), pp. 66–73.

POETRY

ALONSO, D. *Poesía española, ensayo de métodos y límites estilísticos.* 5th ed. Madrid, 1970. (Garcilaso, Luis de León, San Juan de la Cruz, Góngora, Lope de Vega, Quevedo.)

BLECUA, J. M. *Sobre poesía de la edad de oro (ensayos y notas eruditas).* Madrid, 1970.

PIERCE, F. *La poesía épica del siglo de oro.* 2nd ed. Madrid, 1968.

RODRÍGUEZ-MOÑINO, A. *Construcción crítica y realidad histórica en la poesía española de los siglos XVI y XVII.* Madrid, 1965.

ROSALES, L. *El sentimiento del desengaño en la poesía barroca.* Madrid, 1966.

TERRY, A. *An Anthology of Spanish Poetry, 1500–1700.* 2 vols. Oxford, 1965–8. (Valuable, if succinct, historical and critical notes on the poets anthologized.)

WARDROPPER, B. W. *Historia de la poesía lírica a lo divino en la cristiandad occidental* Madrid, 1958.

WHINNOM, K. 'The Supposed Sources of Inspiration of Spanish Fifteenth-Century Narrative Religious Verse'. In *Symposium* (Winter, 1963), pp. 268–91. (Important for Spanish poetry in the time of the Catholic Monarchs.)

WILSON, E. M. 'Spanish and English Religious Poetry of the Seventeenth Century'. In *Journal of Ecclesiastical History,* IX (1958), pp. 38–53.

PROSE

(a) General

MENÉNDEZ Y PELAYO, M. *Orígenes de la novela.* 4 vols. 2nd ed. Madrid, 1962. (Though later investigations have often caused its judgements and information to be superseded or modified in detail, this encyclopedic study still remains the essential starting-point for a general historical approach to the romances of chivalry, the sentimental romance, the Moorish tale, the pastoral romance, the sixteenth-century short story and *La Celestina* and its imitations. It does not deal with the picaresque novel or with seventeenth-century prose fiction.)

(b) Chivalric Romance

ENTWISTLE, W. J. *The Arthurian Legend in the Literatures of the Spanish Peninsula.* London, 1925.

RIQUER, M. DE. *Caballeros andantes españoles.* Madrid (Austral), 1967. (Concerns itself with the activities of the real-life *caballeros andantes* in late medieval Spain.)

THOMAS, H. *Spanish and Portuguese Romances of Chivalry.* Cambridge, 1920. (A bibliographical and descriptive study. Does not attempt to discuss the general critical and literary problems posed by chivalric romance.)

(c) La Celestina

There are many studies on various aspects of *La Celestina.* Among those of a more general character are:

DUNN, PETER N. *Fernando de Rojas.* Twayne's World Authors Series. Boston, 1975.

MENÉNDEZ Y PELAYO. *Orígenes.* See (a) above. Vol. III, ch. X, and Vol. IV, ch, XI. (Specially useful for its account of some of the sixteenth-century imitations of *La Celestina.*)

LIDA DE MALKIEL, M. R. *La originalidad artística de 'La Celestina'*. Buenos Aires, 1962.

MARAVALL, J. A. *El mundo social de La Celestina*. Madrid, 1964.

(d) The Picaresque Novel

BATAILLON, M. *Pícaros y picaresca*. Madrid, 1969.

CHANDLER, F. W. *Romances of Roguery*. Vol. I: *The Picaresque Novel in Spain*. New York, 1890: reprinted 1961. (Still useful.)

JOSÉ, DELEITO Y PIÑUELA, *La mala vida en la España de Felipe IV*. Madrid, 1948. Though criticized as superficial contains a great deal of useful information from contemporary sources about low life in seventeenth-century Spain.

PARKER, A. A. *Literature and the Delinquent*. Edinburgh, 1967.

RICO, F. *La novela picaresca y el punto de vista*. Barcelona, 1970.

(e) The Pastoral Romance

AVALLE-ARCE, J. B. *La novela pastoril española*. Madrid, 1969.

(f) Cervantes

Studies on Cervantes are innumerable and the best tend to concentrate on particular aspects of his work. Some that deal with it in more general terms are:

AUERBACH, E. 'The Enchanted Dulcinea'. In *Mimesis*. Princeton, 1953. New York, 1957.

CASTRO, A. *El pensamiento de Cervantes*. See under 'Intellectual History' above.

DURÁN, M. *La ambigüedad en el Quijote*. Xalapa, Mexico, 1961.

ENTWISTLE, W. J. *Cervantes*. Oxford, 1940.

FORCIONE, A. K. *Cervantes, Aristotle and the 'Persiles'*. Princeton, 1970.

LEVIN, H. 'The Example of Cervantes'. In *Contexts of Criticism*. Harvard, 1957. Reprinted New York, 1963.

RILEY, E. C. *Cervantes's Theory of the Novel*. See under 'Theory of Literature and Literary Criticism' above.

RUSSELL, P. E. 'Don Quixote as a Funny Book'. In *Modern Language Review*, LXIV (1969), pp. 312–26.

SCHEVILL, R. *Cervantes*. London, 1919. (Still valuable for Cervantes's biography and for its account of his less-studied works.)

(g) Seventeenth-Century Prose-Writing

There are few general studies of Spanish prose-writing in the seventeenth century, most critical work in this field concerning itself with individual writers. In addition to the works listed under 'Intellectual History' (Evennet, Hayden, Zanta) see, however, also:

PRING-MILL, R. D. F. 'Some Techniques of Representation in the *Sueños* and the *Criticón*'. In *Bulletin of Hispanic Studies*, XLV (1968), pp. 270–84.

RAMÍREZ, A. *Epistolario de Justo Lipsio y los españoles (1577–1606)*. Madrid, 1966. (Lipsius's copious correspondence with Spanish scholars is not specially helpful for the history of neo-stoicism in Spain, but his letters and those of his Spanish correspondents (supplied here in Latin with Spanish translations) are valuable for their insights into the attitudes and interests of Counter-Reformation humanism and scholarship.)

WILLIAMSON, G. *The Senecan Amble*. London, 1951. (Though this study is concerned with the stylistic influence of Seneca and Lipsius on English prose style, much of its material is broadly valid for Spain too, in the absence of any general Spanish study of the subject.)

DRAMA

AUBRUN, C. V. *La Comédie espagnole (1600–1680)*. Paris, 1966. (The most useful and factually informative modern general study of the Spanish *comedia*.)

BANCES CANDAMO, F. *Theatro de los theatros de los passados y presentes siglos*. Ed. D. W. Moir. London, 1970. (A late seventeenth-century defence of the Spanish *comedia* by a practising dramatist.)

CASTRO, A. 'Algunas observaciones acerca del concepto del honor en los siglos XVI y XVII'. In *Revista de Filología Española*, III (1916), pp. 1–50, 357–86.

CHAYTOR, H. J. (ed.). *Dramatic Theory in Spain*. Cambridge, 1925.

CRAWFORD, J. P. W. *Spanish Drama before Lope de Vega*. 3rd ed. Philadelphia, 1967.

FLECNIAKOSKA, J.-L. *La Formation de l'"auto" religieux en Espagne avant Calderón (1550–1635)*. Paris, 1961.

FROLDI, R. *Lope de Vega y la formación de la comedia*. Salamanca, 1968.

JONES, C. A. 'Some Ways of Looking at Spanish Golden Age Comedy'. In *Homenaje al Prof. William L. Fichter*, pp. 329–39. Madrid, 1971.

PARKER, A. A. *The Approach to the Spanish Drama of the Golden Age*. Diamante VI. London, 1957.

RENNERT, H. A. *The Spanish Stage in the Time of Lope de Vega*. 2nd ed. New York, 1963.

SALOMON, N. *Recherches sur le thème paysan dans la 'comedia' au temps de Lope de Vega*. Bordeaux, 1965.

SÁNCHEZ ESCRIBANO, F., and PORQUERAS MAYO, A. *Preceptiva dramática española del renacimiento y el barroco*. 2nd ed. Madrid, 1965.

SHERGOLD, N. D. *A History of the Spanish Stage from Medieval Times until the End of the Seventeenth Century*. Oxford, 1967. (The major historical study of all aspects of Spanish stagecraft in the Golden Age.)

SHERGOLD, N. D., and VAREY, J. E. *Los autos sacramentales en Madrid en la época de Calderón: Estudios y documentos*. Madrid, 1961.

SULLIVAN, H. W. *Tirso de Molina and the Drama of the Counter Reformation*. Amsterdam, 1976.

VALBUENA PRAT, A. *Literatura dramática española*. Barcelona, 1930; reprinted 1950.

—— *Historia del teatro español*. Barcelona, 1969.

WARDROPPER, B. W. *Introducción al teatro religioso del siglo de oro*. 2nd ed. Salamanca, 1967.

WILSON, M. *Spanish Drama of the Golden Age*. Oxford, 1969.

WILSON, E. M., and MOIR, D. *The Golden Age: Drama 1492–1700. A Literary History of Spain*, Vol. 3. Ed. R. O. Jones. London, 1971.

His parody is lively and amusing and consciously follows the satirical side of *Don Quijote*, whereas his realistic descriptions owe something to the picaresque tradition; but the novel is shapeless and long-winded and there are too many critical and moral comments on the subject of oratory for modern tastes.

II The Enlightenment

By about the middle of the reign of Charles III, around 1770, the intellectual and cultural life of Spain had been largely stabilized. By this time a substantial body of men of culture and talent had arisen in every aspect of public life. They are the Spanish representatives of the period of the Enlightenment, of *las luces* or *la ilustración*, and belong to a class which, though mainly aristocratic in origin, was more concerned with talent and dedication than with rank: the men Cadalso called *hombres de bien*. It is a grave mistake to treat the age of Enlightenment as one of cold and sterile rationalism, only of interest in the degree to which it foreshadows Romanticism. For the next twenty years solid progress was made, especially in the more practical intellectual pursuits, and Spain produced a respectable number of writers and scholars comparable with, if not equal to, other Western countries. There is no space here to mention them all, but the work of the Valencian scholar Gregorio Mayáns (1699–1781) and Enrique Flórez (1702–73) earlier in the century was followed by the literary researches of Tomás Antonio Sánchez (1725–1802). The Jesuits expelled by Charles III have a special role in erudition. Juan Francisco Masdeu (1744–1817) embarked upon a *Historia crítica de España*, while Lorenzo Hervás y Panduro (1735–1809) and Esteban de Arteaga (1747–98) wrote pioneering studies on philology and aesthetics respectively.

The man who represents in the highest degree this dual concern for the practical and the beautiful is Gaspar Melchor de Jovellanos (1744–1811), who divided his busy life between writing and dedicated public service. Jovellanos played a significant part in Charles III's reforms. Then, caught in the political intrigues of the subsequent reign, he was exiled for several years to his native Gijón and to Majorca. He finally emerged once more in 1808 as a leader of the patriotic resistance against the French invaders.

His voluminous and varied writings are invariably lucid and thorough. Many of them are political or economic in nature, including his famous work, the *Informe sobre la ley agraria* (1795), a classic of clear exposition, and his last treatise, the *Memoria en defensa de la Junta Central* (1810), but he also wrote a memoir on public entertainments, an *Elogio de las Bellas Artes* (1782) and numerous essays on educational, social and linguistic questions.

Jovellanos's purely literary work is more mixed in quality. His play *El delincuente honrado* (1774), an example of the penetration of pre-Romantic sentimentality into neo-classical tragedy, is of little intrinsic merit. His poetry, on the other hand, has definite interest; though he writes in the typical modes of the time, he was able to endow some of his verse, his *Epístolas* especially, with the high seriousness characteristic of his whole personality. A great diarist and letter-writer, characterized by an alert intelligence and an excellent prose style, Jovellanos is one of those figures whose importance through his personal example and integrity transcends his actual works.

Typical of his age in a somewhat different way was José de Cadalso (1741–82), an army officer killed in an action against Gibraltar. A member of the *tertulia* of La Fonda de San Sebastián, Cadalso wrote plays, Anacreontic poetry and a critical satire, *Los eruditos a la violeta* (1772), but his reputation rests essentially on two violently contrasting books. His posthumous *Cartas marruecas* (1789), which purport to be the letters sent by a Moorish visitor to Spain, Gazel, to his tutor Ben Beley, with a Spanish friend Nuño supplying incidental comments, were once dismissed as a pallid imitation of Montesquieu's *Lettres persanes*, but are now seen as his principal work. Cadalso uses the device of the imaginary traveller to provide an intelligent moral commentary on Spain past and present. He vigorously decries educational stagnation, aristocratic pretensions and enervating modern luxuries and affectations hailing from France. Somewhat stoic in his attitude, he displays a very military cult of heroism and an unqualified admiration for the *conquistadores* and the sixteenth century in general. At the same time, in a very eighteenth-century fashion, his ideal of patriotism is public service.

Cadalso's other, once more popular, work, the *Noches lúgubres* (1790), is the most noteworthy example of pre-Romantic tendencies. The macabre idea of disinterring the body of his dead lover which occurs to Tediato may be autobiographical or merely literary, but at all events concealed in the rationalist baggage of the eighteenth-century intellectual was a time-bomb of sentiment liable to explode disconcertingly.

The specifically poetic activities of the 1770s and 1780s had become centred on Salamanca, where a flourishing group of poets led by the Augustinian friar Diego Tadeo González (1733–94) with José Iglesias de la Casa (1748–91), Cadalso and, to some extent, Jovellanos, revived a fragile pastoral convention infused at times with sentimentality; the characteristic form was the Anacreontic ode inspired by the minor seventeenth-century poet Villegas. Two students from the university later became attached to the group: Juan Pablo Forner (1756–97), best known for the fierce critical and satirical spirit displayed in his *Exequias de la lengua castellana* (1782) and his *Oración apologética por la España y su mérito literario* (1786); and Juan Meléndez Valdés (1754–1817), who was destined to be heralded as the restorer of Spanish poetry and who is the principal poet – the only one of real if minor distinction – in a non-poetic century.

Under the influence of Cadalso, Meléndez Valdés wrote *anacreónticas* of considerable charm on the trite epicurean themes, but without succeeding in overcoming the essential triviality of the genre. Where Meléndez Valdés offers something new is in his attitude to nature. From treating nature simply as a rhetorical or sensual background to man, Meléndez, in common with his European contemporaries, began to become concerned with all natural phenomena. If at times this gives rise to a mere listing of natural objects, at others it brings out a genuine and sympathetic scrutiny of nature. Meléndez produced his finest descriptions in his *romances* (ballads), a genre he defended enthusiastically; here a new awareness of the realities of country life supersedes to some extent the bucolic distortions of simple peasants and idealized love. Though sentimentality is never far away and Meléndez not infrequently indulges in lachrymosity and occasionally topples over into pure Romantic emotionalism (*El náufrago, Doña Elvira*), he finds in his best lyrics (*La lluvia, La tarde, A un árbol caído*, for example) a precarious balance between observation and sentiment. Urged on by Jovellanos, he embarked on more grandiose themes for which he was little suited. Meléndez Valdés's essential achievement was to establish an authentic, simple poetic style – an effective expression of a new sensibility which was infiltrating into the conventions of the time.

One other writer stands out in the later eighteenth century, Leandro Fernández de Moratín (1760–1828), son of the neo-classical theorist. Moratín wrote some competent neo-classical verse and a prose satire *La derrota de los pedantes* (1789), but until the recent publication of his remarkable diaries and letters which have made of him a far more interesting and rounded figure, attention had centred almost exclusively

on his five original plays. In these the influence of Molière, whose
École des maris and *Médecin malgré lui* he translated brilliantly, is
apparent without being enslaving.

His comedies reveal an obsession with one or two themes: the ease
with which people deceive one another or deceive themselves; the
consequent need for sincerity; the importance of education (of women
and of public taste); the difficult relations between old and young.[1]
Certain fixed types occur: unpleasant elderly females, gullible and
ignorant like *la tía* Mónica in *El Barón* (1803), garrulous and domineering like Doña Irene in *El sí de las niñas*; well-intentioned old men such
as Don Pedro in *La comedia nueva* and Don Diego in *El sí de las niñas*;
young girls driven to deceit, willingly and calculatingly, like *La
mojigata*, a sort of female Tartuffe, reluctantly and innocently as with
Doña Paquita in *El sí de las niñas*.

His concern for the theatre comes out clearly in *La comedia nueva o
el café* (1792), a rather too explicit though sprightly satire of the
extravagant melodramas associated with Luciano Francisco Comella
(1751–1812) and at the same time, in the figure of Don Hermógenes,
of pretentious pedantry.

The theme of his best play, *El sí de las niñas* (1805), the dangers of a
marriage between an elderly man and a young girl, had been anticipated by his first play, in verse, *El viejo y la niña* (1790). Written in
natural dialogue, with tenderness and wit, and well constructed within
the neo-classical framework of one night spent within the four walls
of an inn, *El sí de las niñas* is undoubtedly the best play written in
Spain since Calderón's time; its faults are the faults of the age: it is a
little too obvious and a little too tame.

The writers of the time of Charles III were, of course, deeply
sensitive about the backwardness of their country, and at the same time
almost aggressively optimistic about its immediate prospects. Our
appreciation of the later eighteenth century in Spain has suffered unduly
from the fact that its expectations were not to be fulfilled.

The first factor which imperilled the Spanish Enlightenment was, of
course, the French Revolution. Secondly, Spain's progress was impeded
by the mediocrity of Charles IV and the political intrigues of his reign,
but the most destructive blow was delivered by the French invasion
of 1808 which imposed an agonizing burden of choice upon men whose
ideals were basically those of the invaders but who were nevertheless

[1] It has been pointed out that there are no characters of between twenty-five and
fifty-five in his plays.

staunch patriots. It is significant that the two writers of most talent – Meléndez Valdés and Moratín – both in their prime, accepted the French regime, as did the only genius of the age, Goya, who gives an unsurpassed portrayal of the stages of the transformation from the placid bucolism of the eighteenth century to the turbulence and agonies of the nineteenth. An age of crisis for the whole of Europe, in Spain the natural evolution, cultural and historical, of the country was fatally distorted. In literature, the promise of the 1780s and 1790s was blighted, and although the literary currents proved remarkably enduring they were shadows of what they might have been. The gradual spread of sensitivity within the writers of the time, which might have evolved into an authentic Romantic imagination, was stifled by the impelling demands of the moment. The final disaster which dealt a death-blow to all hope of continuity with the past was the long tyranny of the restored Ferdinand VII. Spain suffered almost half a century of disruption, which disfigured her entire social and cultural development.

In the years immediately preceding the Napoleonic invasion, Meléndez Valdés's example had been followed by Nicasio Álvarez de Cienfuegos (1764–1809), who accentuated the pre-Romantic aspects of his older friend's work in poems on melancholy and sepulchral subjects. He gave a new urgency to stilted classical diction, but in doing so often descended into empty rhetoric, especially in his political poems. His development was cut short by the French invasion, as a result of which he died in exile in France. The most influential literary personality of the War of Independence, Manuel José Quintana (1772–1857), on the other hand, survived successive generations of poets quite unchanged. A civic poet, who deliberately concerned himself almost exclusively with purely external events, he wrote odes in praise of printing and vaccination, and addressed Juan de Padilla as the opponent of Spanish absolutism before the French invasion caused him to turn his attention to heroic exhortation in *Al armamento de las provincias españolas* and *A España después de la revolución de marzo*. Extravagantly praised in the nineteenth century as one of the greatest Spanish poets, Quintana can now be seen as representing a most unwelcome return to the most bombastic sort of rhetorical expression.[1] Within the same tradition is Juan Nicasio Gallego (1777–1853), author of the strident patriotic verses *El dos de mayo*.

Meanwhile, a second poetic group had arisen in Seville which harked

---

[1] Among his many prose works are his *Vidas de españoles célebres*, which correspond to the same nationalistic impulse as his odes.

back to the sixteenth century and which was influenced by the strong colour sense of Francisco de Rioja. Its leader was Alberto Lista (1775–1848), who, after the Peninsular War, exercised very considerable influence as an eclectic teacher and critic. Other members, also priests, were José María Blanco y Crespo (Blanco White) (1775–1841), who later played a vital role among the Spanish exiles in England, and José Marchena (1768–1821), who became a revolutionary and *afrancesado*.

Ferdinand VII's absolutism, exercised (with the brief respite of the 'Trienio Liberal' of 1820–3) from 1814 to 1833 (see Chapter 5, section IV), caused two waves of emigration which deprived Spain of its most vigorous intellectuals. It was the time of the 'lost generation'. Cultural life within the country hit rock-bottom, its level being eloquently conveyed by the famous statement from the University of Cervera: 'lejos de nosotros la funesta manía de pensar'.

Two events during this bleak period have some significance. The first is the vigorous defence of the Spanish Golden Age theatre, especially Calderón, sustained from 1814 onwards by the Prussian consul in Cádiz, J. N. Böhl von Faber, against José Joaquín de Mora and Antonio Alcalá Galiano. The traditionalist Böhl thus introduced into Spain the new literary theories of the Schlegel brothers which represent an important anticipation of Romantic theory, while his liberal opponents still held to neo-classical principles. The second event is the establishment in Barcelona of a review called *El Europeo*, edited by Buenaventura Carlos Aribau, Ramón López Soler, two Italian exiles and an English scientist. During its short life, 1823–4, the review brought into Spain various novel tendencies: German Romantic theory, Byron and Walter Scott.

The émigrés of 1823 were, however, nothing if not active abroad, especially in London. They were exposed to Romantic trends and influences and it is a commonplace of Spanish literary criticism that the exiles brought Romanticism back to Spain on their return at the death of Ferdinand VII in 1833. The undoubted weakness of Spanish Romanticism compared with the great movements in Germany, England and France derives largely from this enforced hibernation. Conditions in Spain, although very different from the industrially expanding rest of Europe, had evolved considerably, with the rapid growth of a strong commercial class, since the eighteenth century.

III Romanticism and After

The most exhaustive study of Spanish Romanticism is by the late Edgar Allison Peers (*A History of the Romantic Movement in Spain*, 1940). This lengthy work, beyond praise for the vast quantity of material it makes available, is less reliable from the critical point of view. Peers not only believed that Romanticism was a recurrent feature of world literature, a dubious proposition which raises more problems than it solves, but also firmly held that Spain and her literature are essentially Romantic. He accordingly saw in the Romantic movement a restoration of the true Spanish tradition and grossly overestimated the value of Romantic writers. As we have seen, however, there was little continuity with eighteenth-century pre-Romanticism and consequently little preparation, culturally or socially, for the sudden inrush of new ideas which correspond broadly with what Peers calls the 'Romantic Revolt'. The returning émigrés had adopted the prevailing literary fashion, and Madrid, following Paris, gave a tremendous vogue to Hugo, Dumas and Byron; and Romanticism was fleetingly associated with liberalism in the cafés, particularly 'El Parnasillo', where politics and literature were discussed. The attitude of revolt lasted a very short time. As early as Larra's funeral in 1837 a very different kind of writer – Zorrilla – made his début; Romantic radicalism barely survived the death of Espronceda in 1842 and was certainly dead by 1845.

If the 'revolt' was extremely short-lived, what Peers calls the 'revival' had in it much that was not Romantic at all; its main strength was a patriotic and traditionalist feeling which found its main inspiration in the historical novels of Sir Walter Scott.[1] The 'revival' sought to drive out the rebellious attitude while fitting the unobjectionable ideas into the conventional pattern; after 1845 it merged with the indeterminate 'eclectic' attitude which Peers described so fully.

Let us now proceed to trace the main events and achievements of Romanticism from 1830 onwards. The movement was most noisily effective in the theatre. The erstwhile neo-classical Francisco Martínez de la Rosa (1787–1862) turned towards Romanticism during his exile in France. *Aben Humeya*, written and produced in French in 1830 and in Spanish in Madrid in 1836, is full of Romantic atmosphere and exotic effects but has little revolutionary spirit; only slightly more forceful is *La conjuración de Venecia*, also written about 1830 and performed

---

[1] The best of the unsatisfactory crop of imitations in Spain was Enrique Gil's *El señor de Bembibre* (1844).

in Madrid in 1834, which counts as the first Romantic or near-Romantic play to be staged. Larra's *Macías* (1834) likewise has some Romantic features but in form can hardly be considered fully committed. The series of fully-fledged Romantic dramas begins in 1835 with *Don Álvaro o la fuerza del sino* by Ángel de Saavedra, later Duque de Rivas (1791–1865). Clearly related in tone and attitude with Hugo's *Hernani*, *Don Álvaro* is a vigorous though quite preposterous piece of work, constructed round a highly artificial code of honour and a rigidly imposed concept of destiny; it also includes some lively *costumbrista* scenes.[1] *El trovador* (1836) by Antonio García Gutiérrez (1813–84) is more lyrical if equally incredible and Juan Eugenio Hartzenbusch's (1806–80) *Los amantes de Teruel* (1837) more lachrymose and sedate; the three heroes, Don Álvaro, Don Manrique and Marsilla, show a clear evolution from ill-starred rebellion towards a less defiant and more sentimental attitude until finally, in the popular, swashbuckling *Don Juan Tenorio* (1844) by José Zorrilla (1817–93), we reach the supreme case of having it both ways; the arrogant rebel repents and is saved by the innocent love of Doña Inés, one of his victims. These Romantic plays are essentially period pieces. They are lacking in structural coherence, show little discrimination in their use of theatrical effects and are unsubtle in their characterization; the qualities they have are more appropriately displayed in opera, as Verdi demonstrated so effectively.

The type of play which retained most appeal after 1840 was the historical or legendary drama. Most of Zorrilla's plays, for example, take their subjects from Castilian history in order to extol, at the most superficial level, national qualities of bravery, honour and religion.[2]

Romantic drama did not in fact hold the field exclusively. Manuel Bretón de los Herreros (1796–1873) mostly followed Moratín's lead but with a much more bourgeois spirit and considerable *costumbrista* elements. He enjoyed great popularity. Among his best-known plays are *Marcela o ¿a cuál de los tres?* (1831) about a flirtatious girl and her three suitors; *Muérete y verás* (1837); and, above all, *El pelo de la dehesa* (1840)

---

[1] The most interesting of Rivas's later plays was *El desengaño en un sueño* (1842), inspired by Shakespeare and Calderón.

[2] *El zapatero y el rey* (in two parts, 1840–1) on King Peter I ('el Cruel'); *El puñal del godo* (1842) on King Roderick, the last Visigothic king; *Sancho García* (1842) on an early Count of Castile; and *Traidor, inconfeso y mártir* (1849) on King Sebastian of Portugal are the most notable.

in which the sterling qualities of a country bumpkin from Aragon are finally vindicated.

Similar in type was *El hombre de mundo* (1845) of Ventura de la Vega (1807–65) which looks forward to the later *alta comedia* or realist drama of Adelardo López de Ayala (1828–79), who, like all the playwrights here mentioned, continued to use verse even in plays with modern themes like *El tanto por ciento* (1861). The only real dramatic achievement of the period was *Un drama nuevo* (1867) by a genuine man of the theatre, Manuel Tamayo y Baus (1829–98); it is a well-constructed play, this time in prose, in which the 'new drama', created by Shakespeare, mirrors the tragedy of the actor Yorick in real life. The second vogue enjoyed by some Romantic dramatists, notably García Gutiérrez, in the 1860s, with reasonably competent historical plays such as *Venganza catalana* (1864) and *Juan Lorenzo* (1865) anticipates the recrudescence of melodrama, with occasional touches of positivism or social awareness, in the works of José Echegaray (1832–1916). Writing in prose or very stilted verse, Echegaray delighted in extreme situations, arbitrarily imposed by rigid interpretations of duty or honour and culminating in sensational tragedy. At the end of the century, Joaquín Dicenta (1862–1917), in *Juan José* (1895), gives Echegaray's techniques a new turn, in a more serious but wooden drama of social injustice.

After this incursion into the not very distinguished history of the theatre up to the late nineteenth century, we return to Romantic poetry. In Ángel Saavedra's verse we witness a development from neo-classical narrative to a sustained effort at evoking the emotional attitude of the Middle Ages which in *El moro expósito* (1834), for example, is prefaced by what is usually considered the Romantic manifesto by Alcalá Galiano. This very long poem in *romance heroico* employs an excess of rather artificial local colour; its best feature is a certain plastic descriptive force deriving from Rivas's strong pictorial sense. His *Romances históricos* (1841) date for the most part from after his return to Spain and his succession to the ducal title. Some years earlier, Agustín Durán had made available many of the old ballads in his *Romanceros* (five volumes, 1828–32).[1] Later, in 1854, Rivas published three more long narrative poems under the title *Leyendas*. Rivas's ballads mark an important stage in the revival of this narrative form but though written with verve and energy they are encumbered with diffuse descriptive

[1] Durán also contributed to the revindication of the national theatre in his *Discurso sobre el influjo que ha tenido la crítica moderna en la decadencia del teatro antiguo español* (1828).

detail of the sort the gaunt old ballads took for granted. The tone of the ballads, moreover, is now unequivocally nationalistic, confirming Courtney Tarr's thesis that 'Romanticism in Spain soon yields to Spanish Romanticism'. And so instead of bringing Spain – as it did for a moment – into contact once more with contemporary currents, Romanticism threw her back on the imitation of her own literary past.' This is the direction Zorrilla is to follow with an even less critical fervour and greater prolixity in his *Leyendas*. Zorrilla, more than any other writer, exemplifies what happened to Spanish Romanticism. His sentimental medievalism, picturesque descriptions, exaltation of conventional Catholic values and facile versification made him extremely popular but the verbosity and imprecision of thought and emotion in his poetry end by bringing narrative verse into disrepute. As Zorrilla himself so ingenuously put it, he had learned from his early years 'el arte de hablar mucho sin decir nada'.

José de Espronceda (1808–42), by contrast, represents in life and poetry the extrovert Byronic aspect of Romanticism to the exclusion of all others. Schooled by Alberto Lista, political conspirator, revolutionary exile, ardent pursuer of Teresa Mancha, he is ideologically typical of the rejection of conventional values; yet he retained in all his poetry considerable traces of neo-classical diction and was never able to break away entirely from a rhetorical style. Espronceda also began an epic poem *Pelayo* in his adolescence and paid homage to the taste of the age by writing a historical novel, *Sancho Saldaña*, and some undistinguished plays. His two major poems, *El estudiante de Salamanca* (1836–40) and the unfinished *El diablo mundo*, show different aspects of Romantic cosmic defiance. In the first, Espronceda re-creates admiringly the arrogant Luciferine rebel against authority of all kinds; Don Félix de Montemar accepts no curb on his freedom, shows no compassion for his victim, the excessively innocent Doña Elvira, and refuses no challenge to his pride; defiant to the last, unlike Zorrilla's Don Juan, he is finally swept off to hell. Coherently constructed and narrated with rhetorical verve and with some interesting metrical experimentation, it has been called the classical work of Spanish Romanticism. *El diablo mundo* is a somewhat pretentious Faust-like story of a man ('Adán') who miraculously regains youth and absolute innocence and who is progressively corrupted by the world. As important as the story itself is the attempt at creating a cynical, throw-off style in the manner of Byron's *Don Juan*. Included as one of the 'Cantos' of the poem is his best-known composition, the *Canto a Teresa*, in which an exaggerated picture of idealized love is capped by a bitter denunciation of his lover. The trouble is one is never altogether sure with Espronceda, inclined to whip up his emotions artificially, of the degree of pose involved in his attitude. Other poems treat of grandiose, cosmic themes (*Himno al sol*); of patriotic liberalism (*Al dos de mayo*); of sensationalist subjects about victims of society (*El reo de muerte*); or society's scapegoats (*El verdugo*). More effective for my taste are his vigorous songs *Canción del pirata* and *El mendigo* in which Espronceda transfers his urge towards freedom into relatively objective channels, even if it is startling to find a pirate proclaiming 'Sólo quiero / por riqueza / la belleza / sin rival'.

Lesser Romantic poets were the Valencian priest Juan Arolas (1805–49), Nicomedes Pastor Díaz (1811–63), author of lugubrious poems like *La mariposa negra*, Enrique Gil y Carrasco (1815–46), more delicate in feeling and subject-matter, and the sentimental and discursive Cuban poetess Gertrudis Gómez de Avellaneda (1814–73).

The Spanish Romantic movement had not developed the distinctive power of the imagination we associate with Romanticism[1] or achieved any deeper understanding of hidden mental processes. This weakness was to be remedied in the work of Gustavo Adolfo Bécquer (1836–70) who came on the scene a generation later. Immediate post-Romantic poetry – apart from Zorrilla, who was for some years absent in Mexico and France – had meanwhile taken off in two main directions: first, a reaction against Romantic emotionalism, in Ramón de Campoamor (1817–1901); second, a revival of civic poetry, in oratorical style, in Gabriel García Tassara (1817–75); and later in Gaspar Núñez de Arce (1832–1903). From his *Doloras* (1845) onwards, Campoamor was the representative poet of the nineteenth-century bourgeoisie in his debt to positivism made acceptable by complacency; his short poems (*doloras, humoradas, pequeños poemas*) are marked by scepticism, obvious irony and a tone of condescension. His style – and this is his positive feature – turns away correspondingly from Romantic rhetoric. Some critics have sought recently to rehabilitate Campoamor, but his self-satisfied deflating of all emotion seems to me irredeemable.

In Bécquer and the lesser contemporary poets – among whom Eulogio Florentino Sanz (1825–81), translator of Heine, and Augusto

[1] 'The Romantic reaction, naturally, was to stress imagination and vision, i.e. the less conscious side of artistic creation, the uniqueness of the poet's individual experience, and the symbolic rather than the decorative or descriptive value of images.' W. H. Auden, *The Enchaféd Flood* (London, 1951), p. 58. See also C. M. Bowra, *The Romantic Imagination* (Oxford, 1950), pp. 1–24, 272–92.

Ferrán (1836–80), author of *La Soledad* (1860), have a particular importance – who share some of his characteristics we see the confluence of two traditions: the discovery of the German lyric, considered to be intimate, direct and inspired by folk-poetry (from the key-figure, Heine, the bitter post-Romantic sarcasm also derives); and the Spanish popular lyric of the *coplas* and *cantares*. These two currents account for the short, direct personal *Rimas* cultivated by Bécquer, of which Núñez de Arce's famous sneer, 'suspirillos líricos de corte y sabor germánicos', derogatory tone apart, is a quite accurate definition.

The *Rimas* on poetry apart, the essential stimulus is love. Some poems (*Poesía eres tú*) have a startling ingenuousness, and many show a disconcerting desire to leave the material world, to disintegrate into pure spirit. Most of the *Rimas*, however, are of bitter disillusion – Bécquer goes through the whole gamut of Romantic attitudes: self-pity; recrimination; meditation on death; escape into dream or the unconscious. There are sarcastic moments and on occasions an unexpected touch of objectivity (e.g. XLII, XXX, L, XLI). It is a mistake to exaggerate the apparently artless spontaneity of the *Rimas*; they are written according to a consistent, if extremely naïve, view of poetry. Characterized by a phenomenally exuberant fantasy, Bécquer's problem lies in reducing it to words by rational means. When he managed to achieve this, he gave his poems a firm logical structure, with strong parallelistic features, the most typical form being an eight-line poem in assonance using eleven- and seven-syllable lines.

In his review of Ferrán's *La Soledad*, Bécquer provides a superb definition of his poetry: 'natural, breve, seca, que brota del alma como una chispa eléctrica . . .' The *Rimas* thus are direct and concentrated, eliminating, with few exceptions, cause and circumstance. Their diction is simple and modern and all the senses are brought into play in the images employed, with light images very prominent among them. There is a measure of fusion or synaesthesia: 'con palabras que fuesen a un tiempo, / suspiros y risas, colores y notas'.

Historically, Bécquer's *Rimas* reveal a remarkable telescoping of poetic tendencies from neo-classicism onwards. Brought up in the classicizing tradition of Seville, Bécquer went on to produce the purest expression of the intimate and imaginative side of Romanticism and anticipate in directness and concentration some symbolist characteristics. Despite his intrinsic *naïveté*, his reputation is now higher than that of any other nineteenth-century poet.

Bécquer's *Leyendas* show the same imaginative powers and the dangers of letting his imagination loose, especially in *El rayo de luna*. He favours remote or exotic subjects – Oriental, medieval, supernatural – and is attracted by the evocative quality of music (*Maese Pérez, el organista*). The ethereal *Leyendas*, though less successful than the *Rimas*, give a further dimension to nineteenth-century prose.

Rosalía de Castro (1837–85) is the other poet of the time whose reputation stands high today. She has some similarities with Bécquer and was probably influenced by him. The principal figure in the revival of the Galician lyric, she has an intense regional concern and a deep feeling for nature. Popular poetry is also a strong influence, especially in *Cantares gallegos* (1863). In *Follas novas* (1880) impressive personal lyrics appear with her characteristic melancholy, ingrained pessimism (*Saudade*; 'desengano sin cura nin consolo') and human compassion. She uses a wide range of metres and moralizes, somewhat facilely at times, especially in the Castilian poems called *En las orillas del Sar* (1884).

It will be convenient to deal here with the Galician revival. Apart from Rosalía de Castro, it counts on two good poets: Eduardo Pondal (1835–1917), a melancholy poet of nature, and Manuel Curros Enríquez (1851–1906), whose *Aires d'a minha terra* (1880) are more vigorous and combative. The blind Valentín Lamas Carvajal (1854–1906) wrote poignantly on rural themes in verse and prose. Some prose writers have used Galician, but without much success; prominent Galicians like Pardo Bazán and Valle-Inclán preferred to use Castilian. Galician literature was stimulated by the establishment in 1906 of the Academia Galega and by the later Seminario de Estudos Galegos. García Lorca paid tribute to the lyrical qualities of the language by writing some poems in it. Since the Civil War Galician has been discouraged, but writing continues, especially in verse.

IV *Costumbrismo* and the Realist Novel

I have left till now a distinctive feature of the Romantic period, *costumbrismo*, because of its far-reaching implications for later developments in fiction. The Romantic cult of local colour, the rise of newspapers to cater for a new middle-class readership and the opportune stimulus of the French writer Jouy all contributed to foster a new form, from the 1830s onwards: the short article or satirical sketch on popular customs. Its success is traditionally attributed to three men: Ramón de

Mesonero Romanos (1803–82), who depicted in an engaging if somewhat pedestrian style typical scenes from Madrid; Serafín Estébanez Calderón (1799–1867), from Málaga, who purveyed in his *Escenas andaluzas* (1847) picturesque but static descriptions in stylized, archaic prose; and finally Larra. Mariano José de Larra (1809–37) was, of course, much more than a *costumbrista*. One of the most remarkable journalists and essayists Spain has produced, 'Fígaro', as he was known,[1] dominated a relatively new medium from his early youth until his suicide at the age of twenty-eight. After a partly French upbringing (his father was an *afrancesado* doctor) he brings an apparently cold, critical gaze to bear on the institutions and people of his country. But he also had the strong passions of a man of his time. His Romanticism is more obvious in his literary productions – *Macías* and the historical novel *El doncel de don Enrique el Doliente* (1834) – which reflect the desperate passion leading to his suicide but for which he did not find an adequate form of expression. His essays, by contrast, even when they are most deeply personal, have a tightly controlled style and a logical structure.

These consist of literary criticism, including perceptive first-night reviews of many of the Romantic plays; amusing yet mordant political satire mainly against the Carlists; and articles on manners. The last are undoubtedly the best. The satire of manners is never simply superficial or picturesque; it eschews local colour and in such articles as *El castellano viejo*, *El café* or *Empeños y desempeños* 'Fígaro' shows how personal defects – self-delusion, pretensions, dishonesty, uncouthness – mirror social failings. He also gives expression to his deep-felt pessimism in such articles as *El día de difuntos* or *Noche buena de 1836* or when he gloomily identifies himself with Quevedo in *El mundo es máscaras*. His treatment of the problem of Spain provides a link between Feijoo and Cadalso and the Generation of 98, and his sardonic satire of Spain, the country of *quasi*, a 'nueva Penélope' – 'la España no hace sino tejer y destejer' – has lost little of its vigour or its relevance today.

It has generally been held that the *cuadro de costumbres* gave rise to the *novela de costumbres* and from the latter developed the regionalist and finally the realist novel, the most vigorous and prolific literary form of the later nineteenth century. And though some doubt has been cast on the direct causal relation between these forms, the historical importance of the work of Cecilia Böhl de Faber, better known as

---

[1] The habit of using *noms de plume* was frequent at the time. Thus Mesonero Romanos was 'El curioso parlante' and Estébanez Calderón 'El solitario'.

Fernán Caballero (1796–1877), is undisputed. The daughter of the Prussian consul in Cádiz (see p. 390 above), she published late in life the first major *costumbrista* novel, *La gaviota* (1849), which incorporated directly observed description of Andalusia into a narrative pattern. In this simple story of the failure of the worldly ambitions of a fisher girl, and even more strongly in her later novels (*Clemencia*, 1852; *La familia de Alvareda*, 1856), the topic of the struggle between the corrupt, liberal town and the pure, traditional country emerges; Catholic morals are extolled and of course virtue is rewarded and vice punished. Somewhat similar in situation, though inferior in quality, is Antonio de Trueba (1819–89), author of *Cuentos de color de rosa* as well as of the folk poetry of *El libro de los cantares*.

After Fernán Caballero fiction grew apace, in part because of the vogue of serial publication in instalments or *entregas*; apart from numerous hack-writers four novelists who published their first important work in the 1870s stand out.

The next stage of development corresponds to another Andalusian a full generation younger than Fernán Caballero: Pedro Antonio de Alarcón (1833–91). His longer novels have greater narrative skill than Fernán Caballero's works, but are no less obviously 'thesis novels', concerned with illustrating a traditionalist moral viewpoint: the rake Fabián Conde is finally redeemed by his Jesuit confessor Father Manrique in *El escándalo* (1875); we are shown Venegas's devotion for 'el niño de la bola' in the novel of that title (1880) and witness the struggle for his soul against the embittered free-thinker Vitriolo. At the same time, Romanticism weighs heavily: highly dramatic confrontations and purple patches abound, and there are many examples of sentimentality.

Alarcón was undoubtedly more successful in his shorter works, especially *El sombrero de tres picos* (1874), in which his talents as a narrator are guided by the requirements of a racy folk-tale. The story of an elderly local official, the *corregidor*, who attempts to seduce the beautiful miller's wife, and his subsequent discomfiture is very lightly treated, in a neat parallelistic fashion, which made it eminently suitable for the masterly conversion into a ballet at the hands of Falla. Also popular for its vigorous portrayal of the protagonist, a rough diamond softened by feminine ingenuity and guile, is *El capitán Veneno* (1881).

Juan Valera (1824–1905) was an Andalusian aristocrat of great charm, urbanity and culture who enjoyed a most distinguished diplomatic, political and social career. In literature he cultivated various genres and is one of the most talented essayists, raconteurs and letter-writers Spain has known, but he never lost the air of a gifted amateur or dilettante, which caused him to be treated – and to treat himself – as something of a lightweight. Unlike Alarcón or Pereda, he had no social or moral purpose to serve and roundly declared that the aim of the novel was to be *bonita*, to amuse and to idealize; but his novels are none the less the serious expression of his own characteristic brand of urbane cynicism. They deal in particular, discreetly but constantly, with the problems of love. In his first and best novel, *Pepita Jiménez* (1874), the apparent religious vocation of the seminarist Luis Vargas gradually gives way to love for the young widow Pepita, while in *Doña Luz* (1879) the elderly missionary Father Enrique conceals until after his death his love for the protagonist. In *El comendador Mendoza* (1877) and again in the later *Juanita la larga* (1895) and *Genio y figura* (1897) he deals with the love of an older man for a younger woman.

Valera's novels have some regionalist flavour, but with a difference: local colour is developed, not for its own sake, but as part of the work as a whole. Valera constructs his novels most carefully, though they are leisurely enough to include frequent philosophical disquisitions; in *Pepita Jiménez*, for example, he makes remarkably fine use of the epistolary form. He also passes for the finest stylist of the nineteenth century; his language is rich and fluent, cultured and ironic. As his letters show all too clearly, Valera was unwilling to risk sacrificing his position in society by saying wholeheartedly where he stood; his novels, sophisticated and intelligent as they are, suffer accordingly.

The clearest case of a thoroughgoing regionalist is found in the work of José María de Pereda (1833–1906), an *hidalgo* from Santander who devoted his life to writing in praise of the sterling qualities of the rural life of that region, La Montaña. His first important work, the descriptive sketches *Escenas montañesas* (1864), is followed by stalwart defences of traditionalist values: *De tal palo tal astilla* (1880), for instance, is a refutation of Galdós's attack on religious fanaticism, *Gloria*. His two best novels come somewhat tardily. Though just as uncompromising, they are less polemical and more positive in their portrayal of the rural hierarchical society Pereda appreciated so much. *Sotileza* (1885) is a novel of the coast, set in the harsh, authentic atmosphere of the fishing quarter of Santander, whereas *Peñas arriba* (1895) deals with the Montaña; the narrator, Marcelo, is gradually won over by the rough healthy life of the Cantabrian village, and eventually replaces his uncle Don Celso as its patriarch.

Pereda has all the solid merits of an unconditional attachment to a region which we see in the Brontë sisters and Thomas Hardy. He provides excellent descriptions, truly reflects country speech patterns and constructs clear, if very slow-moving, plots. The world he evokes is not so much idealized as seen at its best; the trouble is not that it is false but that it is antiquated. Once considered the conservative counterpart of his liberal antagonist and friend Galdós, Pereda now appears as a worthy writer who insisted on burying his very considerable talents in the past.

Benito Pérez Galdós (1843–1920) in fact stands head and shoulders above his contemporaries as a major international figure directly comparable with Balzac and Dickens, whom he much admired, and in Spain only surpassed by his no less admired Cervantes. Although he was younger than the novelists described so far, his earliest novels *La fontana de oro* (1870) and *El audaz* (1871), on political events of the immediate past, antedate theirs. In 1873, however, Galdós embarked on a different method of chronicling near-contemporary history in the *Episodios nacionales*, which clothe a scrupulous narration of historical events with a somewhat thin fictional story. The first two series, of ten volumes each, were completed by 1879; they deal respectively with the War of Independence, starting off with the battle of Trafalgar, and the reign of Ferdinand VII. Many years later, in 1898, Galdós took up the form again and wrote three more series, chronicling Spanish history up to the Restoration. The *Episodios* have the immeasurable importance of displaying recent history to Galdós's fellow countrymen and reveal admirable qualities of fairness, toleration and balance. Though they are certainly patriotic, the early *Episodios* have certain anti-heroic qualities, as when the battle of Bailén is reduced to a desperate individual struggle for water. As an art form, however, they are not entirely successful: the history is often too demanding, the author too obtrusive, while the fictional side is feeble or improbable; and the characters are inevitably generalized rather than particularized.

Between 1876 and 1879 Galdós wrote four straight novels, which he later called *novelas contemporáneas de la primera época*. They are essentially *novelas de tesis*, written from the liberal standpoint. *Doña Perfecta* (1876) portrays the struggle between bigotry and liberalism in a provincial setting, *Gloria* (1877) the confrontation of Catholic and Jewish fanaticism, and *La familia de León Roch* (1879) a·marriage ruined by religious intransigence.

Galdós's great novels date from 1881, with *La desheredada*, and continue in unbroken succession until *Misericordia* (1897): twenty novels in all. The four very late novels after *Misericordia* show a falling off and need not concern us. In these works the clear-cut conflict of the earlier novels has given way to a more balanced portrayal of society. Galdós is very much concerned to reflect change within social classes. He pays special attention to the Madrid middle class, essentially administrative and commercial, and to the rise and fall of individuals, such as the reluctant ascent into the aristocracy of the skinflint money-lender Torquemada. His characters are set firmly in their environment and conditioned by it, but at the same time respond individually to their circumstances. Isidora in *La desheredada* and Rosalía in *La de Bringas* (1884) bring about their own downfall; Torquemada is faced with the problems of death – his son's, his wife's and his own – for which he is not adequately prepared; even the character for whom there is the least escape, the *cesante* Villaamil (*Miau*, 1888), aggravates his problem by his own attitude. On the other hand, Benina, in *Misericordia*, representing the increasing spirituality of his later work, cheerfully makes the most of her situation in a spirit of perfect charity. Galdós's concept of reality embraces a wealth of abnormal types, a strong sense of the ironies of life, a considerable vein of fantasy and a preoccupation with dreams and subconscious states of mind. He has characters racked by passion (the priest Polo in *Tormento*, 1884; the aptly named hero of *Ángel Guerra*, 1890–1), pushed into despair and suicide (Rafael, in *Torquemada en el purgatorio*, 1894; Villaamil) or derangement or insanity (José Ido del Sagrario and, above all, Maxi in *Fortunata y Jacinta*, 1886–7). At times, he shows clear signs of surpassing realist techniques, as when the hero of *El amigo Manso* (1882) recounts his story from beyond the grave; or when a figure invented by Benina turns out really to exist; but Galdós's twentieth-century characteristics can easily be exaggerated.

Galdós has the unwarranted reputation of having a mediocre style. He is, in fact, an excellent narrator and making wide use of dialogue demonstrates an unrivalled capacity for capturing living speech of all kinds: popular idiom (Fortunata, Izquierdo in *Fortunata y Jacinta*), administrative jargon (in *Miau* and *La de Bringas*), the sentimental speech of lovers (*Fortunata y Jacinta*), schoolboy slang (Luisito in *Miau*), the strange language of a Middle-Eastern beggar (Almudena, in *Misericordia*), and so on.

Finally, a few words must be said about *Fortunata y Jacinta*, Galdós's finest and longest novel, a largely unrecognized European masterpiece.

Sub-titled *Dos historias de casadas*, it concerns essentially four people and their respective environments: Jacinta Santa Cruz and her husband Juanito; the working-class girl Fortunata, Juanito's mistress, married to Maximiliano Rubín, a pharmacist from the lower middle class who compensates for his puny physique by an extremely rich imaginative life. Around these central figures revolves an immensely live world of well-developed characters interlocked in an amazingly skilful manner. Yet the basic structure and significance of the story are beautifully clear. Fortunata has a child by Juanito whereas Jacinta is barren; when the former dies, her child is adopted by Jacinta, thus renewing the inbred blood of the new aristocracy of wealth.

Zola's definition of naturalism in his *Roman expérimental* (1880) had important repercussions in Spain. These doctrines of biological and social determinism influenced Galdós to a limited extent from *La desheredada* onwards, but were far more important for the novelists who immediately follow. The Countess Emilia Pardo Bazán (1851–1921) brought the subject into the limelight in her articles *La cuestión palpitante* (1883) in which she defended Zola's doctrines, with certain reservations, reconciling them with Christianity. Naturalism in Spain meant essentially a readiness to deal more radically with social themes, to examine attentively the seamy side of life and to treat sexual themes more directly and less idealistically. Pardo Bazán found her true subject in the abject rural life of her native Galicia in *Los pazos de Ulloa* (1886) and its sequel *La madre naturaleza* (1887) in which the degeneration and collapse of an aristocratic family is powerfully if stolidly documented. An important critic concerned with the latest literary currents in Europe, Pardo Bazán also wrote observant evocations of Galicia and lively short stories.

Leopoldo Alas (1852–1901), better known as 'Clarín', was respected and feared in his lifetime as a devastating critic. His reputation today rests essentially on his works of fiction, especially his one long novel *La Regenta* (1884) which is only rivalled in the Iberian Peninsula by *Fortunata y Jacinta* and the novels of Eça de Queirós. Clarín depicts leisurely but mercilessly the three aspects of the provincial capital Vetusta, transparently Oviedo: the sinister, ambitious clerics, the depraved, frivolous aristocracy and the mean and ignorant political intrigues of the Casino. The book contains two masterly character studies. Doña Ana Ozores, 'la Regenta', has something in common with Emma Bovary; frustrated in an unsatisfactory marriage, she seeks refuge in a false mysticism under the influence of the Magistral Fermín de Pas (the second admirable portrait) only to discover that beneath his driving ambition lies sensual passion, and to fall eventually into the arms of the ageing 'Don Juan' of Vetusta, Álvaro de Mesías, who then kills her husband in a duel.

The portrayal of its ineffectual hero Bonifacio in Alas's shorter novel *Su único hijo* (1890) has some interest, but apart from *La Regenta* his best work is found in his short stories, the finest of which (*¡Adiós 'Cordera'!, Zurita, El señor, Pipá*, etc.) have a deep human compassion within a firm construction.

Armando Palacio Valdés (1853–1938), author of such popular novels as *Marta y María* (1883), *José* (1885) and *La hermana San Sulpicio* (1889), merits less attention, for his graceful narrative skill cannot conceal his basic superficiality.

Much younger but still naturalistic in technique is Vicente Blasco Ibáñez (1867–1928). His radical political activities and his inferior commercial production of later years obscured his very real achievement in his early Valencian novels, *Flor de mayo* (1895), *La barraca* (1898) and *Cañas y barro* (1902), which have a strong narrative line against an authentic, rapidly sketched, yet colourful background of the Valencian *huertas*.

V The Catalan *Renaixença*

One of the most important incidental effects of Romanticism was the revival of regional consciousness and regional languages. In the case of Catalonia the impulse was especially strong, based as it was on solid economic strength, which had made Barcelona in the nineteenth century the most dynamic city in Spain, as well as on nostalgic memories. In this it was unlike most regional revivals, including the Galician one. This summary cannot hope to do full justice to modern Catalan literature. It should, therefore, be remembered that this literature has produced at the very least half a dozen authors in the front rank of writers in Spain and that Barcelona as a cultural centre had had an importance rivalling, and at times surpassing, that of Madrid.

Prepared to some extent by isolated writing in Catalan and an unbroken popular tradition, by the great vogue of historical novels in Catalonia and by such writers in Castilian as Manuel de Cabanyes (1808–33) and Pablo Piferrer (1818–48), the effective *Renaixença* or linguistic revival dates from the *Oda a la pàtria* published by Aribau in 1833: a remarkable if circumstantial poem given the disuse of the language for literary purposes for nearly 300 years. The next stage is represented by the work of Joaquim Rubió i Ors (1818–99), 'lo gaiter del Llobregat', who revived the ancient troubadour tradition, which was consolidated by the re-establishment of the medieval Court of Love, the *Jocs Florals*, in 1859 and the increasing support of scholars like Milá y Fontanals.

At a time when poetry in Castilian was in the doldrums, a major poet in Catalan, Jacint(o) Verdaguer (1845–1902) – 'Mossèn Cinto' – brought a powerful rural tradition to enlarge an impoverished vocabulary. His epic poems *L'Atlàntida* (1877) on the imaginary continent Atlantis, and *Canigó* (1886) on the symbolic Catalan mountain, have, notwithstanding the rather ingenuous anthropomorphism of their conception, a genuine feeling for nature and a cosmic vision. Verdaguer also wrote beautiful, simple religious lyrics.

The popular theatre in Catalan was restored by Frederic Soler, 'Serafí Pitarra' (1839–95), in fine satirical sketches and consolidated by Angel Guimerà (1845–1924), the most important dramatist of his time, who gave a powerful expression to rural drama. His *Terra baixa* (1897), translated into Castilian by Echegaray, became the model for this class of play.

The novel emerged in the 1880s with the naturalistic treatment of urban themes in the works of Narcís Oller (1845–1930) in *La papallona* (1882), *Febre d'or* (1890) and *Pilar Prim* (1906), novels which compare favourably – Galdós apart – with contemporary works in Castilian. A more rural course is followed by Marià Vayreda (1850–1903), and, continuing well into the twentieth century, by the short-story writer Joaquim Ruyra (1858–1939) and Víctor Català (Catarina Albert) (1873–1966), author of *Solitud* (1905).

VI Nineteenth-Century Ideological and Critical Tendencies

This is perhaps a convenient moment to give a summary account of the history of ideas and criticism during the nineteenth century. Two Catholic apologists stand out in the first half of the century, the right-wing polemicist Juan Donoso Cortés (1809–53) and the Catalan priest Jaime Balmes (1810–48), author of a more balanced defence of Catholicism and a philosopher noted for the emphasis he placed on common sense.

The most original and influential philosophical tendency of the century was the somewhat amorphous movement known as *krausismo*. Introduced into Spain by Julián Sanz del Río (1814–69), this doctrine, based on the idealistic concepts of a little-known German philosopher, Christian Friedrich Krause (1781–1832), was far more important for its practical consequences in education than for its abstruse tenets. The essential figure was Francisco Giner de los Ríos (1839–1915), an outstanding teacher of exceptional integrity who founded in 1876 the Institución Libre de Enseñanza, the most significant educational venture in Spain of modern times, which, with its complementary Residencia de Estudiantes, exercised a decisive influence on successive generations of intellectuals. *Krausismo*, as its historian Juan López Morillas has defined it, was more than a philosophy, an *estilo de vida*. Founded on a secular and liberal basis, it placed great emphasis on moral integrity and on the formation of the whole man, fostering, among other things, *excursionismo* to discover Spain's forgotten provinces.

Not far removed in his ideas from the *krausistas* was Joaquín Costa (1844–1911), a self-formed lawyer and political economist who led a hard-hitting campaign for the regeneration of the country based on Europeanization and agrarian reform. Better known for his unremitting reformist zeal than for his actual works, Costa coined some of the key slogans of the age: 'Escuela y dispensa' to mark his essential priorities, and 'Cerremos el sepulcro del Cid con siete llaves para que no salga' to shut off Spain's imperial past.

The great scholar Marcelino Menéndez Pelayo (1856–1912) was in a different camp politically and devoted some of his enormous intellectual energy, especially in his early works *La ciencia española* and *Historia de los heterodoxos españoles*, to Catholic apologetics and to the patriotic urge to justify and extol Spain's past glories. Taught in Barcelona by the distinguished scholar Manuel Milá y Fontanals (1818–84), Menéndez Pelayo covered in his voluminous work every period and genre, and although some of his prejudices, notably those concerning Góngora and Calderón, have since been effectively demolished, there are still few subjects within Hispanic culture for which he does not remain the starting-point.

VII The Generation of 98 and Early Twentieth-Century Prose

The nineteenth century in Spain may conveniently be thought of as coming to an end, early, with the Spanish–American war of 1898[1] just as it began, late, in 1808, with the French invasion. Two opposing

[1] For an account of this war and a historical view of its aftermath, see Chapter 5, section VIII.

literary movements, the so-called Generation of 98 and *modernismo*, appear at this time, but it is a mistake to draw too sharp a distinction between them.

The 'Generation of 98' is a loose term to embrace a group of men who were spurred on to reassess and regenerate Spain, especially Castile, as a result of the disastrous war in which Spain lost her last overseas colonies. Much less of a coherent group than its chief propagator 'Azorín' claimed, they are exposed, though their response is very different, to the same European influences – Darwin, Spencer, Hegel, Renan, Nietzsche among them – and they have a similar reaction to the Bourbon restoration of 1875, which had given political stability for the first time in the century but at the expense of a sham constitution and rigged elections. Much of the iconoclastic zeal of the Generation derives, in my view, from its disgust at the Restoration settlement. Despite the claims of political and social reform that are sometimes made for it, the Generation of 98 is essentially a literary movement. Its attitude to Spain is a subjective one, summed up in Unamuno's phrase 'me duele España', and its achievement lies in the personal revelation by non-Castilians of the Castilian landscape, evoked and admired with a Romantic upsurge of emotion; and a freeing of the language from the ballast of nineteenth-century rhetoric.

Among the men normally attached to the Generation there is a significant age difference between Miguel de Unamuno (1864–1936) and Ángel Ganivet (1865–98) – with whom despite his early death it is convenient to deal here – and three other writers: 'Azorín' or José Martínez Ruiz (1873–1967), Pío Baroja (1872–1956) and Ramiro de Maeztu (1874–1936). Ramón del Valle-Inclán (1866–1936) and Antonio Machado (1875–1939) – who are dealt with later – are sometimes included in the Generation. The great scholar Ramón Menéndez Pidal (1869–1968) who devoted his main efforts to studying the history, literature and language of Old Castile, may also be associated with the Generation.

Unamuno was, on the one hand, a contemporary of Ganivet's and, on the other, an elder member of the Generation. Ganivet, cutting off his career by suicide, left only an admirable evocation of his native Granada, essays on writers of the north of Europe, two original novels about a somewhat burlesque *alter ego*, Pío Cid, and an interpretation of Spain, the *Idearium español* (1897), in which he proclaims, on dubious geographical and philosophical grounds, Spain's independent, virginal spirit and the present need of concentrating her energies within her own territory. Ideologically in a limbo between strong spiritual aspirations and a lack of faith, seeking refuge somewhat desperately in Senecan stoicism, Ganivet faces problems similar to those of the later Unamuno. Unamuno before 1897, however, was a progressive Europeanizer (see his *En torno al casticismo*, 1895, and his interesting correspondence with Ganivet, *El porvenir de España*) who, after a religious crisis in 1897, came to formulate his own heterodox and existentialist philosophy, his *Sentimiento trágico de la vida*, a doctrine of constant and fertile conflict between the two irreconcilable forces of reason and faith, a conflict which is at the root of all human endeavour, for consciously or unconsciously every man is striving to justify survival after death. More important than the philosophy itself are the literary consequences. In my view his greatest literary achievement lay in his novels. After an extensive novel on the second Carlist war set in his native Bilbao, *Paz en la guerra* (1897), Unamuno developed a highly original form of narrative. First, in *Niebla* (1914) – called a *nivola*, not a *novela*, to mark its distinctive nature – a famous confrontation takes place between the character Augusto Pérez and 'Unamuno' himself. Though the latter tells Pérez peremptorily that he is going to kill him off, we are left with the doubt as to whether he did not commit suicide as he intended and as his friend Víctor Goti proclaims in his defiant prologue. Uncertainty and ambiguity run right through Unamuno's later novels, in which the leading characters seek to justify their existence by extremes of assertiveness: domineering 'aunthood' (motherhood combined with virginity) in *La tía Tula* (1921); bitter envy in *Ábel Sánchez* (1917); the arrogance of a self-made man, *Nada menos que todo un hombre* (1920). *San Manuel Bueno, mártir* (1933) is a miniature masterpiece in which the tragic doubt about survival racks the spirit of a saintly village priest, viewed at some distance through the memoir of one of his parishioners.

Unamuno also wrote copiously in verse (*Poesías*, 1907), including a long meditative poem *El Cristo de Velázquez* (1920) and a day-to-day poetic diary during and after his exile in France, the posthumous *Cancionero*. Unamuno's poetic technique, at the farthest pole from *modernismo*, is clumsy and anachronistic, but his vigorous thought and sentiment break through. His plays are interesting for his ideas, especially *La esfinge* (1897) and *El otro* (1926), but show no conception of stage technique. His essays make a vast contribution to the 'literature of confession' so infrequent in Spain; and he evokes powerfully the Spanish landscape. Unamuno is often irritating and tedious in his reiterations, but his role as *excitator Hispaniae* and a mover of souls is a central one in twentieth-century Spain.

'Azorín', born in Monóvar, Alicante, became, after an early revolutionary period, a sensitive and original interpreter of Castile. Essentially static, he captures the emotional effect of the minute and transient detail, extracting in Ortega's phrase 'primores de lo vulgar'. Of his countless works – for he wrote far too much – the best are the semi-philosophical novels of his early maturity (*La voluntad*, 1902; *Antonio Azorín*, 1903; *Las confesiones de un pequeño filósofo*, 1904) in which he analyses the paralysis of will of his generation, and the evocations of Castile and its literature which follow: *Los pueblos* (1905), *La ruta de Don Quijote* (1905), *Castilla* (1912), *Clásicos y modernos* (1913), etc. 'Azorín''s style, with its short sentences, simple statements and word order, repetitions, evocative adjectives, archaisms and diminutives, represents the most extreme reaction against the oratorical tradition.

Essentially independent and negative in his view of life, his Basque friend Baroja is characterized by a burning hatred of sham. The only quality he esteems is uncompromising honesty. Many of his novels include extensive philosophical discussions, but these lead nowhere: in *Camino de perfección* (1902) Ossorio is finally obliged to submit to the environment he loathes; and *El árbol de la ciencia* (1911) ends in suicide. In the rest what dominates is action. Baroja's heroes are generally vagabonds, rebels (anarchists in the trilogy of *La lucha por la vida*, 1904–5) or sailors (*Tierra vasca*, 1900–9), often apathetic, pessimistic men pushed on from adventure to adventure. Impelled by this same urge, Baroja wrote a series of twenty historical novels, *Memorias de un hombre de acción*, on the famous conspirator Eugenio Aviraneta. The episodic structure of his novels, which have no overall plan, conveys admirably his outlook: a chunk of raw life begins and ends abruptly – purposeless, brutal, incomprehensible. His style, much criticized for its carelessness, is in reality a most effective instrument; he writes in short, jerky sentences, clearly expressed in unaffected, workaday Spanish. Probably the most important Spanish novelist of this century, Baroja has had great influence on the post-Civil-War novel.

The work of the third member of the trio, Maeztu, was confined to essays on mainly political subjects, some literary criticism and two widely differing appraisals of Spain, *Hacia otra España* (1899) and *Defensa de la hispanidad* (1934), which mark his development from a Nietzschean radical to a traditionalist leader.

A novelist hardly connected with the Generation of 98 is Gabriel Miró (1879–1930). A 'levantino' like 'Azorín', he wrote dense lyrical descriptions of the region, using a figure called Sigüenza as his mouth-piece (*Libro de Sigüenza*, 1917; *El humo dormido*, 1919), and also trans-posed scenes from the life of Jesus to the Alicante region, endowing them with intense plastic qualities by means of meticulous static description. His finest novels are *Nuestro padre San Daniel* (1921) and its sequel *El Obispo leproso* (1926), set in Oleza (Orihuela). They deal with the conflict between the constricting forces of tradition, and the spontaneous natural joy represented by Father Magín. These conflicts, personal not political, are developed most subtly by means of sensual im-agery taken from nature and lovingly elaborated with conscious artistry.

Ramón Pérez de Ayala (1880–1962), of a later generation, is far more intellectual. Side by side with his learning, his power of abstrac-tion and his studied prose goes a somewhat aesthetic sensuality. Of his three major novels, *Luna de miel, luna de hiel* and its continuation *Los trabajos de Urbano y Simona* (1923) deal in a rather ridiculous way with the disastrous effects of a total lack of sex education on a young couple about to marry. *Tigre Juan* and *El curandero de su honra* (1926), another double novel, reverses the conventional Calderonian marital honour situation: Tigre Juan turns, not on his adulterous wife, but on himself. Ayala's best novel – a major achievement – is the one where his intellectualism is given freest rein: *Belarmino y Apolonio* (1921), the story of two philosophical shoemakers who represent opposing systems of thought and expression, the one introspective, hermetic, ultimately incapable of communication, the other extrovert, rhetorical and dramatic.

José Ortega y Gasset (1883–1955) was basically a philosophic writer but he exercised a profound influence over an extremely wide range of subjects: no Spanish intellectual writing since 1930 can be altogether free from the impact of his work. A staunch Europeanizer, he intro-duced modern German philosophy into Spain and founded the highly influential periodical *Revista de Occidente*. His thinking emphasizes man's situation in history and in society, and he formulated early in his career the phrase 'Yo soy yo y mi circunstancia'. He developed a theory of perspective which attempts to bring together rationalism and relativism: every age has its own distinctive values, absolute for itself, but invalid for other epochs. Hence his insistent concern for the present – our perspective – and his constant reiteration of such expres-sions as *vital, vigente, a la altura del tiempo*.

Ortega's concern with the present informs his best-known books, *España invertebrada* (1921), *El tema de nuestro tiempo* (1923) and *La rebelión de las masas* (1930). In the first, Ortega is perceptive in discerning the salient features of the modern situation of Spain (separatism, a 'go it alone' attitude) but it is vitiated by grave historical shortcomings, a most dubious notion of Teutonic superiority and a certain idealization of force.

Ortega gave his attention, brilliantly but not always systematically, to many other subjects: to historiography, where he inclines to sweeping generalizations, to the role of the university or the library, to art, to contemporary literature. He coined the phrase 'deshumanización del arte' to describe, with superficial accuracy, the aestheticism of the twenties and foretold the decline of the novel. He wrote clear-cut, polished, pungent Spanish, with undertones of the spoken word (he was a brilliant lecturer) and a tendency to let metaphor run away with him.

Eugenio d'Ors (1882–1954), sometimes linked with Unamuno and Ortega as one of the three intellectual mentors of the twentieth century, is not in the same class. His defence of classicism, precision and order, his élitist aesthetics, and his sensitive interpretations of art have a certain historical and intrinsic importance, but are flawed by his pedantic solemnity and his insufferably affected style. His early and best work, in Catalan, will be dealt with separately (pp. 424–5 below).

Ramón María del Valle-Inclán began to write as the most forceful, aesthetically aggressive writer of his time, akin to Huysmans or Oscar Wilde. His best-known early work, the *Sonatas* (1902–5) on the four seasons, describes the mannered, erotic adventures in Galicia, Mexico and elsewhere of the Marquis of Bradomín, 'feo, católico y sentimental'. In the trilogy of the *Comedias bárbaras* (1907–8, 1922) Valle-Inclán portrays admirably the heroic struggle of the proud patriarch Don Juan Manuel Montenegro against his sons, villagers and old age, and in a contemporary trilogy of novels *La guerra carlista* (1908–9) he shows admiration for another lost cause.

After the First World War he changed to a bitter pessimism projected scathingly on everything he had previously idealized: rural Galicia, Mexico, Carlism. After some transitional plays of great concentrated power (e.g. *Divinas palabras*, 1920), he perfected, in *Luces de Bohemia* (1920), a distinctive dramatic form, the *esperpento*, which he defined as a mathematical deformation of the classical norms by means of distorting mirrors. The most famous, *Los cuernos de Don Friolera*

(1921), has the qualities of a puppet-show; viewed from outside by a couple of extravagant intellectuals, alienation, in the Brechtian sense, is complete. Don Friolera, old, bald and unheroic, is obliged by the army code of honour to try to kill his apparently faithless wife; he fails, and the emptiness of mechanical rules of behaviour is starkly revealed through the antics of the puppets.

The powerful novel *Tirano Banderas* (1926) relates the fall and death of a Latin American dictator with grotesque distortion, vigorous dialogue and a complex time sequence.

The problem of Spain is implicit in all Valle-Inclán's later writing – for this reason Pedro Salinas termed him the 'hijo pródigo' of the Generation of 98 – and in the unfinished *Ruedo ibérico* (*La corte de los milagros*, 1927; *Viva mi dueño*, 1928; *Baza de espadas*, posthumous) he dealt mercilessly in *esperpento* language and technique with the intrigues, amours and pettiness of Isabella II and her court on the eve of her expulsion in 1868.

Valle-Inclán created for himself a most vivid individual style: direct, colloquial, and with invented words of his own. He is one of the great innovators, in both the novel and the drama, of the twentieth century.

VIII The Poetry and Drama of the Early Twentieth Century

An account of the poetic movement known as *modernismo*, which began in Spanish America, will be found in Chapter 10, section IX. Here suffice it to say that *modernismo* in general is comparable with the aesthetic *fin de siècle* movements in other countries:[1] the Pre-Raphaelites, *art nouveau* in the arts; decadentism, Celtic twilight, etc., in literature. It is no less a reaction against typically nineteenth-century values – realism, positivism, commercialism, etc. – than the Generation of 98. Whatever the role of Rubén Darío (1867–1916) in the development of the movement in Spanish America – whether he is considered the leading light or merely the popularizer – there is no doubt that as far as Spain is concerned he was the acknowledged leader. Although he had some slight precedent in the exuberant and colourful poetry of Salvador Rueda (1857–1933) it was Darío who caught the imagination of the younger poets following the publication of *Prosas profanas* (1896) and Darío's second visit to Spain in 1898: he brought before them, at a time of complete poetic prostration, a new exoticism and flexibility

[1] Catalonia had its own distinctive form of modernism (see p. 424 below).

and opened out to them the whole range of nineteenth-century French influences, from Victor Hugo to the symbolists. It is more than possible that Darío merely set fire to already dry timber which would have burst into flames anyway, and there is no doubt at all that a quick reaction ensued against Darío's special brand of exotic flamboyance, but for the first time a writer from the New World exercised a decisive influence on the course of Spanish literature.

Among the immediate supporters of the new poetry were the now almost forgotten Francisco Villaespesa (1877–1936), founder of one ephemeral review after another, Juan Ramón Jiménez (1881–1958), Manuel Machado (1874–1947) and Antonio Machado.

Juan Ramón Jiménez is an extreme example of a life dedicated to poetry. At first he wrote (*Arias tristes*, 1903) melancholy descriptions of nature (*paysages d'âme*) in which the facets chosen – deserted gardens, dry fountains, moonlit nights – together with musical motifs, reflect his own soul. Later, he came to formulate a complete and unbending dedication to a concept of pure poetry which was to be 'todo verdad presente, sin historia'. This purity is first sought in the *Diario de un poeta reciencasado* (1917), his poetic impressions of his transatlantic voyage to join his future wife. 'Ni más nuevo al ir, ni más lejos,' he declares: 'la depuración constante de lo mismo.' This stripping-down reaches the extreme of the two-line poem in which he asserts triumphantly that he has – momentarily – reached his goal of beauty:

> ¡no le toques ya más,
> que así es la rosa!

He now writes a poetry of pure symbols, in which words have acquired a special transposed value: *rosa*, *mar*, *oasis*, *árbol*, etc., are no longer real objects but aspects of his spiritual life. In his later period, especially after he left Spain in 1939, Jiménez opened out his range of subjects without fundamentally changing his poetic vision. In *Animal de fondo* (1949) his quest for an aesthetic god is complemented by the god's need of the poet. He also wrote a charming story of his Andalusian childhood and a donkey (*Platero y yo*, 1914) and some tart impressionistic sketches of his contemporaries: *Españoles de tres mundos* (1942). The most concentrated of the great European symbolists, Jiménez received the Nobel Prize in 1956 at the end of his life when his type of poetry was already out of favour.

Antonio Machado's early poetry shares with Jiménez's a strong introspective impulse, but there is a more urgent concern with fatality and death in his probing of dream and childhood memory. His inner exploration reaches its peak in the *galerías* of *Soledades, Galerías, Otros poemas* (1907); the fixed symbols – the road, fountain, sea, flowers – he uses are the fruit of long and careful meditation. By 1907, however, Machado was dissatisfied with self-absorption: he had begun to analyse himself more closely ('pobre hombre en sueños, poeta, / siempre buscando a Dios entre la niebla'), to take themes from the outside world and above all to attach a fundamental importance to time: *la palabra esencial en el tiempo* becomes his definition of poetry. His out-ward-looking attitude is strengthened during his residence in Soria with *Campos de Castilla* (1912), in which apparently prosaic topographi-cal description becomes infused with a personal involvement: *Campos de Soria* starts objectively: 'Es la tierra de Soria / árida y fría . . .' and by the end has a highly subjective emotional charge: '. . . conmigo vais / mi corazón os lleva!' Machado also attempts with less success to revive narration in *La tierra de Alvargonzález*. His critical love for Castile and his sharp implied criticism of aspects of traditional attitudes link him with the Generation of 98. Tragically affected by the death of his young wife, he wrote some of the most moving poetry in the language. His later work is more fragmentary and philosophical, and he created an 'apochryphal philosopher' Juan de Mairena, in whose name he continued to write profound comments on existence and poetry throughout the Civil War. His slowly elaborated poetry, meditative and dense and at its best extraordinarily precise, and his sense of personal commitment have given him in recent years an enormous, possibly even excessive, reputation; but he is undoubtedly one of the finest poets of the twentieth century.

Antonio's brother Manuel remains much closer to a decadent variant of *modernismo*, fusing Paris and Andalusia in charmingly super-ficial impressionistic pieces inspired by Verlaine. His poetic commentar-ies on paintings and his occasional use of national themes are interesting, but he is essentially a minor poet.

The twentieth century brings also a certain renovation to the theatre, but it never attains the same level as poetry or the novel. Galdós, from 1892 onwards, tried his hand on the stage, dramatizing some of his novels (*Realidad, Doña Perfecta*) and having a momentary *succès de scandale* with *Electra* (1901), an anti-clerical piece which provoked a disturbance. But the theatre was not Galdós's forte and his efforts did not produce any decisive effect. The real transformation was due to

Jacinto Benavente (1866–1954), often associated with the *modernistas* but in reality independent of them. Benavente rescued the theatre from the exaggerations of Echegaray. His typical plays (*Gente conocida*, 1896; *Lo cursi*, 1901) are drawing-room comedies, set in Madrid, with some local colour, little action, no melodrama and some satirical edge. On occasion, he opts for a foreign setting and introduces a tragic note, as in *La noche del sábado* (1903), and in two plays, *Señora ama* (1908) and *La malquerida* (1913), he is more ambitious, attempting serious rural drama; these are effective but somewhat unconvincing. *Los intereses creados* (1907) is rightly esteemed among Benavente's best; he skilfully uses a *commedia dell'arte* background to make the fairly obvious cynical point that everyone has his price. Benavente's best plays date from before the First World War; they give the effect of an adroit sameness and a lack of strong convictions.

Gregorio Martínez Sierra (1881–1947) had greater affiliations with the *modernistas*. His plays, in which his wife's collaboration is evident, are sentimental and now dated; the best known is *Canción de cuna* (1911). He also translated Rusiñol (see p. 424 below) and was an important producer.

More successful, in their limited way, were the brothers Álvarez Quintero (Serafín, 1871–1938, and Joaquín, 1873–1944) who exploit Andalusian *costumbrismo* in their light, unpretentious pieces. A distinctive Spanish form which deserves a special mention is the *género chico*: short sketches or *sainetes*, or libretti for *zarzuelas*, full of Madrid atmosphere and slang, in which Carlos Arniches (1866–1943) excelled.

A playwright, also associated with *modernismo*, who dramatized historical legends in verse was Eduardo Marquina (1879–1946), starting with *Las hijas del Cid* (1908) and continuing with *En Flandes se ha puesto el sol* (1910), but his discreet versification cannot conceal the fact that he is writing in a defunct form. By contrast, a writer whose reputation is tending to grow, although his works have hardly been seen in Spain itself, is Jacinto Grau (1877–1958). Criticized at times for being too literary and for defects of style, he showed originality in his treatment of the biblical parable in *El hijo pródigo* (1918), while his best play *El señor de Pigmalión* (1921) is linked with both Cervantes and Pirandello.

IX The Poetry of the 1920s and 1930s

In the 1920s a brilliant group of poets appeared: there was nothing comparable in the other genres. Known variously as the generation of 1925 or 1927 or the generation of the *dictadura* (Primo de Rivera's), it consisted of the following poets, listed in order of birth: Pedro Salinas (1891–1951), Jorge Guillén (1893–   ), Gerardo Diego (1896–), Dámaso Alonso (1898–   ), Federico García Lorca (1898– 1936), Vicente Aleixandre (1898–   ), Emilio Prados (1899–1962), Rafael Alberti (1902–   ) and Luis Cernuda (1902–63). By the late twenties they were joined by Manuel Altolaguirre (1906–59) and in the thirties by Miguel Hernández (1910–42).

Certain general features characterize the whole generation: a broadly symbolistic interpretation of poetry; a devotion to the poetry of Juan Ramón Jiménez if not to his person; a very literate, even erudite approach by poet-professors; a cult of Góngora and the popular tradition; a lack of political or social involvement; and tragic and irrevocable dispersal with the advent of the Civil War.

Guillén published widely in reviews before he finally brought out the first edition of *Cántico* in 1928, followed by the extensive revision and augmentation in the successive editions (1936, 1945), until the definitive version of 1950. He has been wrongly accused of cold cerebralism in *Cántico* in imitation of Paul Valéry. Although he uses an intellectual technique of abstraction which derives from 'pure poetry', what he is expressing is a spontaneous delight in living. To be, for Guillén, is to feel; to feel is to consent, and hence the urge to 'consumar la plenitud del ser en la fiel plenitud de las palabras'. To this end Guillén employs a sharp technique of breaking up normal syntax into evocative units: single-word exclamations, apposition, sudden questions, intensification of abstracts ('¡cuánto Abril!') within a terse expression and tight metrical form. He distinguishes clearly between *ser* and *estar* and calls up the moment of reawakening, regaining awareness of himself and his surroundings:

> Yo. Yo ahora. Yo aquí.
> Despertar. Ser. Estar.
> Otra vez el ajuste prodigioso.

Characteristic too of Guillén is the refusal to enter into metaphysics, to seek the ultimate reality of his experience: the amazingly concise three-word line – 'Mira. ¿Ves? Basta.' – is his response. Since *Cántico* he has written three sections (*Maremágnum*, 1957; *Que van a dar en la mar*, 1960; *A la altura de las circunstancias*, 1963) of a new book *Clamor*, in which he has allowed political and social considerations to enter.

Unlike his friend Guillén, Salinas seeks the archetype of emotion which lies beneath the love expressed in *La voz a ti debida* (1934), his best collection: 'Por detrás de ti te busco'. While Guillén marvels with his eyes open at the perfection of the world, Salinas found the visible world disordered and formless: perfection is reached only by shutting one's eyes, through the organizing power of dream. Names represent the process of classifying and intellectualizing; he aspires to a purer state where names have no validity: his highest joy is 'vivir en los pronombres'. Time is likewise a limiting factor. In conversational language, Salinas brings a wide range of everyday things within the scope of his metaphysical vision. Salinas was also a most distinguished scholar and teacher.

Few poets have a more deeply rooted frustration with life than Cernuda, for whom the two terms of *La realidad y el deseo*, the title he gave his collected poems, remain irrevocably apart, although the quest for an unattainable Arcadia – the Seville of his childhood, a glimpse of an impossible Eden in Mexico – never ceases. But with his pessimism goes a rare artistic integrity which made him search for simple, unobtrusive speech rhythms and to objectivize his despair; he loathed the self-assertion of an Unamuno or a Juan Ramón Jiménez. Influenced by Hölderlin, Bécquer and the English Romantics, he drew poetic strength from his despair in exile (in England, the United States and Mexico) and created towards the end of his life very fine, sober dramatic monologues on such historical figures as Lazarus, Caesar, Quetzalcóatl and Philip II. His evocative prose poems *Ocnos* (1942–9) are likewise impressive. Cernuda was also a scathing but highly sensitive critic.

By reason of his more appealing themes and his tragic death, Lorca is far better known abroad than his no less gifted contemporaries. In his early verse, influenced by children's songs, he sought to capture immediate visual impressions in simple vocabulary but complex metaphor. The *Romancero gitano* (1928) brought back narrative poetry with its stylized gipsies who represent uninhibited emotions against the cramping social convention personified by the Civil Guard. The ballads have a strong narrative line with the imagery confined to incidentals. They are also amazingly concentrated, for Lorca uses his very acute senses – he was an accomplished musician and painter – to forge condensed transpositions such as 'Sangre resbalada gime muda canción de serpiente' and 'el liso gong de la nieve'. And they ignore cause and effect, giving a purely sense impression of what is happening: 'y un horizonte de perros / ladra muy lejos del río'.

Before visiting New York, Lorca had a crisis of disillusionment curiously similar to Alberti's, and reflected in his *Poeta en Nueva York* (published 1940), with its powerful disjointed imagery of waste and violence, his own dissatisfactions as well as his passionate reaction to mechanized civilization. His *Llanto por la muerte de Ignacio Sánchez Mejías* (1935) gives admirable expression to his elegiac mood and his personal preoccupation with death.

Today his plays appear as important as his poetry, and perhaps more so. They represented a possible breakthrough in the mediocrity of the Spanish stage, for through the theatrical company La Barraca he directed in the thirties Lorca did far more than simply produce his own plays. Among these are several interesting experiments with animal plays, puppet farces and experiments with time (*Así que pasen cinco años*, 1931). His major work consists of a delightful ballet-like comedy *La zapatera prodigiosa* (1930) and a trilogy of rural tragedies. In these three plays, in which the theme of frustration is paramount, Lorca progressively cuts down the external poetic elements until he produces a stark clash of wills, very tightly organized, in *La casa de Bernarda Alba* (1936). Thus *Bodas de sangre* (1933) has powerful, supernatural forces – the moon, a beggar-woman representing death – and uses verse frequently; *Yerma* (1934) has less fantastic sequences and more prose. Each of the plays is very dramatic but Lorca was conscious of the dangers of letting loose his powerful lyric vein and most critics now agree that *La casa de Bernarda Alba* is his finest play.

Another playwright of the Republic who continued his work in exile was Alejandro Casona (1903–65), author of plays of fantasy such as *Los árboles mueren de pie* (1949).

In his early work Alberti dabbled with popular influences (*Marinero en tierra*, 1924) and Gongoristic language (*Cal y canto*, 1927) with adroit playfulness. Then a grave personal crisis provoked a volume of the most original and dense symbolism which has something in common with *The Waste Land*. In *Sobre los ángeles* (1928), he expresses in stark, unadorned vocabulary his anguish and desolation by means of countless 'angels', mostly hostile, who personify the violence, emptiness and confusion of his emotional state: there is an 'ángel superviviente' but he is 'alicortado'. Not long afterwards Alberti found stability in the Communist Party, which he has continued to support since the Civil War. His later work includes sensitive poetry on the theme of exile and an autobiography, *La arboleda perdida*, (1959) essential for the background of his poetry.

In *Espadas como labios* (1931) and *La destrucción o el amor* (1933) Aleixandre pours forth a torrent of sensuality in violent cosmic or natural imagery and rhythmic, impelling free verse. His irrepressible zest for life is expressed in a form radically opposed to Guillén's well-chiselled *décimas*, and Aleixandre expressly refuses to countenance any limit on energy. Behind the apparent lack of restraint, however, there is an able craftsman very capable of controlling the poetic effects of his frenzies. Like Dámaso Alonso, Aleixandre was influential in the immediate post-Civil-War period.

Much of the importance of Gerardo Diego, the anthologizer of the generation, lies in the experimental games with images and automatic writing which characterized *creacionismo*, introduced into Spain by the Chilean Vicente Huidobro, and the earlier *ultraísmo*, fostered by Guillermo de Torre. These ephemeral movements were significant in providing new insights for the major poets of the period. Related to these anti-rationalist tendencies was the indefatigable literary activity of Ramón Gómez de la Serna (1888–1963), the most important prose-writer of the period, famous above all as the inventor of the *greguería*, a short, witty metaphor on the most commonplace of subjects. The *greguería* had great contemporary significance, when its value and originality were rather overrated.

Prados and Altolaguirre were more isolated figures, the former devoted to somewhat solitary contemplation (the title *Jardín cerrado* (1946) is significant), the latter pursuing closely Juan Ramón's quest for experience beyond the senses.

Miguel Hernández was a remarkable poet whose career was truncated by the Civil War. Of peasant origins (from Orihuela) and largely self-taught, he drew inspiration from the poets of the Golden Age for a highly original poetry, fresh in vocabulary and imagery, in *El rayo que no cesa* (1936); his uninhibited love sonnets and his elegy on his friend Ramón Sijé are outstanding. A fervent Republican who died in gaol in 1942, his poetry on his suffering after the war, *Cancionero y romancero de ausencias*, is deeply moving.

X Literature after the Civil War

The Civil War of 1936–9 broke the continuity of a literature flourishing as never before since the Golden Age. The conflict itself gave rise to hardly any literature of intrinsic value. When it ended, the long isolation caused by the Second World War and the repression, restrictions and censorship imposed by an oppressive totalitarian regime tragically perpetuated the gap between victors and vanquished, exiles and writers within Spain. Moreover, the critical climate had changed and once a distinctive orientation started to re-emerge it was opposed to what it considered aesthetic and minoritarian attitudes.

In poetry the revival came more quickly than in other genres. The first poetic movement after the war, the 'Garcilaso' group, was frankly escapist, but the passionate animist poetry of Aleixandre and particularly the collection *Hijos de la ira* (1944) by Dámaso Alonso,[1] with its preoccupation with problems of personality, death, living in society, expressed in long reiterative lines of free verse, stimulated a revival in both subject and form. Gradually Spanish poets have become largely committed to a personal concept of poetry, often combined with a doctrine of socio-historical realism and a more or less implicit hostility to the Franco regime; they have turned their backs on the symbolist current of Juan Ramón Jiménez and have held up Antonio Machado, not altogether for the right reasons, as a model. Among the first poets to reflect this new attitude were Blas de Otero (1916–   ), a powerful but uneven poet who, making a direct confrontation with Jiménez's *inmensa minoría*, entitled one of his books *Con la inmensa mayoría*; Gabriel Celaya (1911–   ), rather older than the others; and José Hierro (1922–   ). Two younger poets, among many, who show particular distinction are José Ángel Valente (1929–   ) and Claudio Rodríguez (1934–   ). The movement towards personal preoccupations and human solidarity is a welcome and natural one and the search for a serviceable, conversationally based language for verse, influenced by Machado and Cernuda, is particularly salutary. In recent circumstances there was a danger of stridency and unrestrained protest, but on the whole these poets seemed well aware of this. Although no poet recognized to be of the first order has yet arisen in Spain since the Civil War, a great deal of observant, sensitive, human-orientated and clearly expressed poetry is being written.

[1] Dámaso Alonso is also supremely important, of course, as the major literary critic of his generation.

The novel, in poor shape before the Civil War, took longer to recover after it. A few writers, formed before 1936, wrote after its end in what seems an anachronistic style: Ignacio Agustí (1913–74) related in Galsworthian fashion the destinies of the Catalan industrial family Rius (*Mariona Rebull*, 1944; *El viudo Rius*, 1945), and Juan Antonio Zunzunegui (1901–   ), in a late flowering of documental realism, censures the corruption of the Madrid bourgeoisie (*Esta oscura desbandada*, 1952), or follows the wandering of tramps and ruffians in pre-war Madrid (*La vida como es*, 1954).

The Civil War only slowly became a subject for novels at more than a blatant propaganda level. The most popular and the most ambitious work is the mammoth trilogy of José María Gironella (1917–   ), *Los cipreses creen en Dios* (1953), *Un millón de muertos* (1961), *Ha estallado la paz* (1966), which is monotonously documentary and seen, despite an effort at impartiality, from the winning side. Also more of a reportage than a novel, though considerably more forceful, is the autobiographical and self-centred *La forja de un rebelde*, in three parts, by Arturo Barea (1897–1957), first published in English in 1941–4 and in Spanish in 1951. More artistically satisfying are the works of the other exiles. Max Aub (1903–72) has given, in five books, under the collective title of *Laberinto mágico*, an enthralling epic description of the course of the war, in a technique combining features of Galdós's *Episodios* and Valle-Inclán's *Ruedo ibérico*. Still little known in Spain, Aub also wrote, from his exile in Mexico, a fascinating biography of an imaginary Catalan painter, *Jusep Torres Campalans* (1958), in which he reconstructs the Barcelona of Picasso's youth. Ramón J. Sender (1902–   ), noteworthy for novels of social conflict before the war (*Siete domingos rojos*, 1932; *Míster Witt en el cantón*, 1936), wrote a surprisingly dispassionate parable *El rey y la reina* (1947), but the best of his somewhat uneven novels is, perhaps, the short *Réquiem por un campesino español* (1953). Francisco Ayala (1906–   ) has written short stories and novels, before and after the war; his novels *Muertes de perro* (1958) and *El fondo del vaso* (1962) deal with the horrors of life in an imaginary tyranny.

The revival of the novel within Spain begins with *La familia de Pascual Duarte* (1942) of Camilo José Cela (1916–   ), a work of brutal realism in which the condemned Duarte recounts in his memoirs, in a powerful, crude, rustic style, the succession of murders he has committed. He is not fundamentally wicked, but in invariably agonizing circumstances he cannot tame his primitive passions. Thus the novel has a certain fatalistic inevitability which has caused it to be called existentialist, while the accumulation of bloody deeds has given rise to the name *tremendismo*.

Cela's most ambitious work is *La colmena* (1951), which centres on a café in Madrid in three days of 1942. In what he calls a *novela reloj*, an immense crowd of people – so many they need an index – throngs through the microcosm of the café, all isolated and alienated from one another. Cela switches from character to character and scene to scene, with frequent interruptions, recapitulations and flashbacks. He characterizes his seedy characters with a phrase, and writes excellent dialogue, drawing on Madrid slang. It is altogether a most impressive, if depressing, portrayal of post-Civil-War Madrid, run down, aimless, with ambitions limited to money and lust. Cela's later novels do not achieve the same standard.

Another novel which caught the mood of the time, with its scarcities, prohibitions and dullness, was *Nada* (1944) by Carmen Laforet (1921–   ), but it no longer seems a particularly significant work.

In the 1950s a new type of novel begins to emerge; it has been called the 'social' novel, that is a novel which is concerned with social conditions as they are and which attempts to reveal them with complete objectivity.[1] A key work for its objective vision if not for its social commitment is *El Jarama* (1955) by Rafael Sánchez Ferlosio (1927–   ), a meticulously detailed account of a Sunday trip to the Jarama river – the scene of one of the battles of the Civil War – by a group of young working-class people; at the end of the day one of the girls is drowned. A second plane of reality is provided at the nearby inn where local villagers and a family from Madrid converse. Narration is reduced to the minimum, no character stands out above the others and the tenuous action is conveyed, as in a film, by the superbly captured dialogue. Ferlosio's only other novel offers a great contrast, but is also experimental: the fantasy *Alfanhuí* (1951).

Narrative objectivity reminiscent of the cinema also occurs in the novels of Jesús Fernández Santos (1926–   ), beginning with *Los bravos* (1954), but the social issues are clearer and in this, as in most other comparable novels, there is an implied criticism of society in the grinding poverty of the village described.

[1] The vogue of travel-books to the less-known and poorer regions of Spain, following Cela's *Viaje a la Alcarria* (1948), corresponds to this cult of objective realism. Examples are *Caminando por las Hurdes* (1960) by Antonio Ferres and Armando López Salinas, and Juan Goytisolo's *Campos de Níjar* (1960).

Of exceptional importance is the only completed novel of Luis Martín-Santos (1924-64), *Tiempo de silencio* (1962), which traces, with brilliant clinical analysis, the process by which a young doctor is caught up and ruined in a sordid Odyssey of Madrid low life.

Other recent works of fiction which seem to stand out as significant are: the later novels of Miguel Delibes (1920-), from *El camino* (1950), with its excellent penetration into child psychology, onwards – the best of them may well be one of the most recent, *Cinco horas con Mario* (1966); some of Ana María Matute's (1926-) many novels, especially *Fiesta al noroeste* (1953); the work of Juan Goytisolo (1931-) whose novels (the most important are *La isla*, 1961; *Fin de fiesta*, 1962; *Señas de identidad*, 1966; and *Reivindicación del conde don Julián*, 1970) reveal a constant examination of conscience and evolve to a new and searing vision of Spain; and the prize-winning *Tormenta de verano* (1961) by Juan García Hortelano (1928-) in which the discovery of a woman's body on a beach serves to lay bare the inadequacies of bourgeois society.

Contemporary drama is, at the moment of writing, in worse shape than the novel and has not enjoyed the same relative flourishing of the last decades. The most original dramatist to emerge in Spain is Antonio Buero Vallejo (1916-) whose plays follow the same pattern of awareness of social problems as does the work of novelists and poets. He has employed varied dramatic techniques. *Historia de una escalera* (1949) depicts the squalid life on a slum staircase at three distinct periods – 1919, 1929, 1949. *Hoy es fiesta* (1956) uses the same background of poor people who momentarily think they have won the lottery. *Las meninas* uses Velázquez's painting and times to comment on problems of government and corruption in high places. Unfortunately, Buero is an isolated figure who has to struggle against an apathetic commercial theatre. The important radical dramatist, Alfonso Sastre (1926-), has encountered even more difficulties because of the clear political implications of most of his plays, which are effective dramatic dialogues without great technical innovations. The contemporary Spanish theatre needs, even more than the other arts, a breath of fresh air or the winds of change.

XI Modern Catalan Literature

Twentieth-century Catalan literature built brilliantly on the solid base established in the previous century. By 1900 Catalan was the normal medium of expression for most native-born Catalans. Joan Maragall (1860–1911) was, without doubt, the greatest poet in the Spain of his time. He brought together a wide European culture and modern urban sensibility and a simple direct style based on the spoken language (*la paraula viva*), in which he wrote of domestic bliss, nature and Catalan legends. He took the subject of the legendary *Comte Arnau* to construct a complex myth of life as continuous endeavour and added the theme of redemption. His *Cant espiritual* is the expression of his deep contentment with the life of this world, unsurpassable in any future existence: 'Sia'm la mort una major naixença'. Maragall also wrote extensively in Spanish; his essays, sensitive and far-reaching, less known outside Catalonia than they deserve to be, are among the most important writing on the problem of Spain at the turn of the century.

Mallorca, too, produced two excellent poets, Miquel Costa i Llobera (1854–1922), a classical poet with a fine sense of style, and Joan Alcover (1854–1926), best known for his poignant elegiac poems.

The bustling, seething Barcelona of 1900 produced a distinctive type of modernism, in which the visual arts (Ramon Casas, the young Picasso, the architect Gaudí) and music (Albéniz, Granados) figured prominently: the typical rendezvous was the café 'Els Quatre Gats'.[1] Apeles Mestres (1854–1936) was an artist who in his poetry followed an original medieval inspiration. The typical *modernista* was Santiago Rusiñol (1861–1931), also a painter, who burlesqued exaggerations, including modernist ones, in his plays and stories. His best-known work, *L'auca del Senyor Esteve* (1907; as a play 1917), is both a satire and an elegy of an archetypal *petit bourgeois* of Barcelona, set in the form of popular broadsheet literature.

Barcelona was an important centre of innovation in the theatre, in which the *Teatre íntim* of Adrià Gual played a special part. Catalan translations of Ibsen, Maeterlinck and Hauptmann were staged, and prepared the way for the social dramas of Ignasi Iglésias (1871–1928).

In 1907 the Institut d'Estudis Catalans was founded and thanks to the philologist Pompeu Fabra the grammar and orthography of the Catalan language were standardized. The strengthened provincial government, the *Mancomunitat*, under Prat de la Riba, provided a strong cultural impulse, with Eugenio d'Ors ('Xènius') as its presiding authority. His *La ben plantada* (1911) sets out to be a lyrical evocation, in the guise of a girl called Teresa, of the essence of Catalonia; he commenced his *Glosari*, later continued in Castilian, as a means of

[1] See also Chapter 11, section XVIII.

commenting acutely and ingeniously on current issues; and he popu-
larized the term *noucentisme | novecentismo* for the new literature.

Intellectualized symbolism came to Catalonia early; from the first
decade of the century Guerau de Liost (Jaume Bofill i Mates) (1878–
1933) and Josep Carner (1884–1970) combined most effectively the
verbal meticulousness of symbolism with the urge to intellectualize
the language; Carner lived on to write moving poems from a long
exile (*Nabí*, 1946). Joan Salvat-Papasseit (1894–1924), a working-class
poet, avant-gardist and rebellious at first, came to write fine evocations
of everyday things and uninhibited love poetry. With Carles Riba
(1893–1959) the symbolist tradition reached its highest point. In
Estances (1919, 1933) Riba creates abstractions from his own passionate
experiences; later, in exile and on his return to Spain, he looked for
archetypes for his own distress in the classics. His concentrated, erudite
poetry, combining cerebral power and human passion, is among the
finest of his time. Josep Sebastià Pons (1886–1962), from Roussillon,
joined this intellectual tradition, while Josep Maria de Sagarra (1894–
1961) followed a more popular and hearty approach in poetry and
drama. Josep V. Foix (1894–) is a remarkably original surrealist who
conveys his personal experiences by hermetic but striking symbols,
either in sonnets or poetic prose, with long, elaborate titles.

In prose, the novels of Joan Puig i Ferrater (1882–1956), Carles
Soldevila and Miquel Llor should be mentioned, together with the
short stories of the Valencian Ernest Martínez Ferrando.

The restrictions after the end of the Civil War on the use of Catalan,
which had enjoyed full official status under the Republic, were a
severe blow. After some years of complete suppression, books in
Catalan reappeared but free development long remained artificially
hampered: there was still, even up until 1976, no daily newspaper
permitted in Catalan. Post-war literature has followed a similar course
to that described above for Spanish, though symbolist aesthetics survived longer, until Riba's death in 1959. The path to a more committed
literature was led in poetry by 'Pere Quart' (Joan Oliver) (1899–)
and by Salvador Espriu (1913–) who had developed a sort of 'paradise lost' around a mythical village Sinera (Arenys de Mar) and a
wider myth of Sepharad (Spain) in a highly significant volume of
poetry *La pell del brau* (1960). The most important later poet is
probably Gabriel Ferrater (1922–72). The Mallorcan novelist Llorenç
Villalonga (1897—) has used a conventional technique and much
psychological perception to describe the social changes produced in

semi-feudal Mallorca by the tourist boom (*Bearn*, 1961), and Mercè Rodoreda (1909–) has produced a first-rate novel, *La Plaça del Diamant* (1962), on a girl's life in a Barcelona suburb during the Civil War.

The essay flourishes in the prolific work of Josep Pla (1897–), who writes in idiosyncratic Castilian as well as in Catalan, and the Valencian Joan Fuster. Production of books in Catalan is once more running at a very high level and at the same time Barcelona has become a very important centre for writers in Spanish. There is now more fruitful interchange between the two cultures than for many years.

Bibliography

EIGHTEENTH CENTURY

DELPY, G. *Feijoo et l'esprit européen: essai sur les idées maîtresses dans le 'Théâtre critique' et les 'Lettres érudites'*. Paris, 1936.

GLENDINNING, N. *The Eighteenth Century. A Literary History of Spain*, Vol. 4. Ed. R. O. Jones. London, 1972.

SARRAILH, J. *L'Espagne éclairée du XVIIIᵉ siècle*. Paris, 1954. Spanish trans. Mexico, 1957.

SEBOLD, R. P. *El rapto de la mente*. Madrid, 1970.

BROWN, R. F. *La novela española: 1700–1850*. Madrid, 1953.

GIL NOVALES, A. *Las pequeñas Atlántidas*. Barcelona, 1959.

MARÍAS, J. *La España posible en tiempo de Carlos III*. Madrid, 1963.

MARICHAL, J. *La voluntad del estilo*. Barcelona, 1957. (Essays on Feijoo, Cadalso, Jovellanos.)

CAMPOS, J. *Teatro y sociedad en España (1780–1820)*. Madrid, 1969.

COOK, J. A. *Neo-Classic Drama in Spain: Theory and Practice*. Dallas, 1959.

MCCLELLAND, I. L. *Spanish Drama of Pathos*. 2 vols. Liverpool, 1970.

—— *The Origins of the Romantic Movement in Spain*. Liverpool, 1937, 1975.

NINETEENTH CENTURY

CASALDUERO, J. *Estudios de literatura española.* Madrid, 1962.

COSSÍO, J. M. *Cincuenta años de poesía española (1850–1900)*. 2 vols. Madrid, 1960.

DÍAZ PLAJA, G. *Introducción al estudio del romanticismo español*. 2nd ed. Madrid, 1942.

EOFF, S. H. *The Modern Spanish Novel*. New York, 1961.

JURETSCHKE, H. *El origen doctrinal y génesis del romanticismo español*. Madrid, 1954.

LÓPEZ MORILLAS, J. *El krausismo español*. Mexico, 1956.

LLORÉNS, V. *Literatura, historia, política: ensayos*. Madrid, 1967.

—— *Liberales y románticos: Una emigración española en Inglaterra 1823–1834*. 2nd ed. Madrid, 1968.

MONTESINOS, J. F. *Costumbrismo y novela*. 2nd ed. Madrid, 1965.

—— *Introducción a una historia de la novela en España en el siglo XIX*. 2nd ed. Madrid, 1966.

—— *Galdós*, 3 vols. Madrid, 1968–1972.

PATTISON, W. T. *El naturalismo español: Historia externa de un movimiento literario.* Madrid, 1965.

PEERS, E. A. *A History of the Romantic Movement in Spain.* 2 vols. Cambridge, 1940.

SHAW, D. L. *The Nineteenth Century. A Literary History of Spain.* Vol. 5. Ed. R. O. Jones. London, 1972.

VARELA, J. *Poesía y restauración cultural de Galicia en el siglo XIX.* Madrid, 1958.

ZULETA, E. DE *Historia de la crítica española contemporánea.* Madrid, 1966.

TWENTIETH CENTURY

General

BARJA, C. *Libros y autores contemporáneos.* Los Angeles, 1935.

BLANCO AGUINAGA, C. *Juventud del 98.* Madrid, 1970.

BROWN, G. G. *The Twentieth Century.* A Literary History of Spain. Vol. 6. Ed. R. O. Jones, London, 1972.

CLAVERÍA, C. *Cinco estudios de literatura española moderna.* Salamanca, 1945.

DÍAZ-PLAJA, G. *Modernismo frente a noventa y ocho.* Madrid, 1951.

GRANJEL, L. *Panorama de la generación del 98.* Madrid, 1959.

GULLÓN, R. *La invención del 98 y otros ensayos.* Madrid, 1969.

LAÍN ENTRALGO, P. *La generación del noventa y ocho.* Madrid, 1945.

LÓPEZ MORILLAS, J. *Intelectuales y espirituales.* Madrid, 1961.

—— *Hacia el 98: literatura, sociedad, ideología.* Barcelona, 1972.

MAINER, J. C. *Literatura y pequeña burguesía en España. 1890–1950.* Madrid, 1972.

RAMSDEN, H. *The 1898 Movement in Spain: Towards a Reinterpretation.* Manchester, 1974.

RIBBANS, G. *Niebla y soledad: aspectos de Unamuno y Machado.* Madrid, 1971.

SALINAS, P. *Literatura española siglo XX.* 2nd ed. 1948; reprinted Madrid, 1970.

SÁNCHEZ-BARBUDO, A. *Estudios sobre Galdós, Unamuno y Machado.* Madrid, 1968.

SHAW, D. L. *The Generation of 1898 in Spain.* London, 1975.

SOBEJANO, G. *Nietzsche en España.* Madrid, 1967.

TORRE, G. DE *Historia de las literaturas de vanguardia.* 3 vols. Rev. ed. Madrid, 1965.

TORRENTE BALLESTER, G. *Panorama de la literatura española contemporánea.* 2 vols. 2nd ed. Madrid, 1961.

TUÑÓN DE LARA, M. *Medio siglo de cultura española, 1885–1936.* Madrid, 1970.

Novel

ALBORG, J. L. *Hora actual de la novela española.* 2 vols. Madrid, 1958, 1962 and 1968.

GOYTISOLO, J. *Problemas de la novela.* Barcelona, 1959.

MARRA-LÓPEZ, J. R. *Narrativa española fuera de España.* Madrid, 1963.

NORA, E. G. DE. *La novela española contemporánea (1898–1960).* 3 vols. Madrid, 1958–62.

PÉREZ MINIK, D. *Novelistas españoles de los siglos XIX y XX.* Madrid, 1957.

SOBEJANO, G. *Novela española de nuestro tiempo.* Madrid, 1970.

VARELA JÁCOME, B. *Renovación de la novela en el siglo XX.* Barcelona, 1967.

Poetry

ALONSO, D. *Cuatro poetas españoles*. Madrid, 1962.

—— *Poetas españoles contemporáneos*. 3rd ed. Madrid, 1965.

AUB, M. *La poesía española contemporánea*. Mexico, 1954.

CANO, J. L. *Poesía española del siglo XX*. Madrid, 1960.

CASTELLET, J. M. (ed.). *Cuarto de siglo de poesía española, 1939–1964*. Barcelona, 1964.

CERNUDA, L. *Estudios sobre poesía española contemporánea*. Madrid, 1957.

CIPLOJAUSKAITÉ, B. *La soledad y la poesía española contemporánea*. Madrid, 1962.

DEBICKI, A. P. *Estudios sobre poesía española contemporánea. La generación de 1924–1927*. Madrid, 1968.

DEHENNIN, E. *La Résurgence de Góngora et la génération poétique de 1927*. Paris, 1962.

GONZÁLEZ MUELA, J. *El lenguaje poético de la generación Guillén-Lorca*. Madrid, 1954.

GUILLÉN, J. *Language and Poetry*. Cambridge, Mass., 1961.

LECHNER, J. *El compromiso en la poesía española del siglo XX*. 2 vols. Leiden, 1968.

MORRIS, C. B. *A Generation of Spanish Poets 1920–1936*. Cambridge, 1969.

ONÍS, F. DE (ed.). *Antología de la poesía española e hispano-americana*. New York, 1961.

TREND, J. B. *Lorca and the Spanish Poetic Tradition*. Oxford, 1956.

VIDELA, G. *El ultraísmo*. Madrid, 1963.

VIVANCO, L. F. *Introducción a la poesía española contemporánea*. 2nd ed. Madrid, 1970.

YOUNG, H. *The Victorious Expression*. Madison, 1964.

ZARDOYA, C. *Poesía española contemporánea*. Madrid, 1961.

Theatre

GARCIA PAVÓN, F. *Teatro social en España*. Madrid, 1962.

RUIZ RAMÓN, F. *Historia del teatro español*. 2 vols. Madrid, 1971.

TORRENTE BALLESTER, G. *Teatro español contemporáneo*. 2nd ed. Madrid, 1968.

CATALAN

GILI, J. L. *Catalan Grammar*. 3rd ed. Oxford, 1967. (Includes literary anthology.)

TRIADÚ, J. (ed.). *Anthology of Catalan Lyrical Poetry*. Oxford, 1953.

CASTELLET, J. M., and MOLAS, J. (eds.). *Ocho siglos de poesía catalana*. Madrid, 1969. (Bilingual Catalan/Spanish.)

RUBIÓ I BALAGUER, J. *Literatura catalana*. In G. Diaz-Plaja (ed.), *Historia general de las literaturas hispánicas*, Vols III–V.

—— *Un segle de vida catalana, 1814–1930*. 2 vols. Barcelona, 1961.

TERRY, A. *Catalan Literature. A Literary History of Spain*, Vol. 7. Ed. R. O. Jones. London, 1972.

10 Spanish American Literature

D. P. GALLAGHER

I The Colonial Period

Quite unselfconsciously, the first colonial chroniclers took up, during the decades of Discovery in the sixteenth century, many of the fundamental themes that were to interest other writers throughout the history of Spanish American literature. Like Spanish American writers after Independence in 1810, the chroniclers were impressed by the grandeur and variety of the landscape and by the exotic nature of the Indian. Like their successors they felt themselves to be engaged in an often unequal struggle against a hostile environment, yet they were passionately inspired by that environment's immeasurable possibilities and the prospects it opened up of constructing a new world. Usually they brought to bear a culture acquired in Europe upon a new, unprecedented context, the result being a curiously eclectic meeting-ground between two worlds which has characterized much Spanish American literature ever since. Thus the Inca Garcilaso de la Vega (1539–1616), a Spaniard born in Cuzco of an Indian mother, was able to combine such activities as the translating of León Hebreo with the writing of his *Comentarios reales* (1609), an account of the Inca Empire that culminates in its conquest by the Spaniards, and which freely mingles the thoughts of a Spanish Renaissance mind with the maternally transmitted legends of the Inca race. Similarly, Alonso de Ercilla y Zúñiga (1533–94), in his epic poem *La Araucana*, published in three parts (1569, 1578 and 1589–90), freely injected Renaissance concepts into descriptions of the *araucanos*, the nomadic warrior Indians of the south of Chile.

The admiration for Aztec civilization revealed by the conqueror of

Mexico, Hernán Cortés (c. 1484–1547), in his letters to Charles V (1519–26), is somewhat marred by his equally fervent readiness to destroy it, yet the championship of the Indian cause was taken up as early as the sixteenth century by Dominican friars in Hispaniola. Thus the *Brevísima relación de la destrucción de las Indias* (1552) by Fray Bartolomé de las Casas (1474–1566) contains lurid accounts of Spanish iniquities against the indigenous population, for whose advocates it has always remained an inspiration up until the present day.

It is indeed worth bearing colonial literature always in mind, if only because it reminds us of the extent to which certain themes that have characterized Spanish American literature are basic to the continent's context and inseparable from it. On the whole, though, colonial literature is very disappointing. The sheer emotion of discovery and the sheer magnitude of events described in works like the *Historia verdadera de la conquista de la Nueva España* (1632) by Bernal Díaz del Castillo (c. 1492–1584) endow them with a very great interest, and not only as historical documents. But when the sense of newness that had inspired the chroniclers began to diminish, so did the value and interest of colonial literature.

The crown was no help. In 1531 a royal decree was passed that prohibited the importation and circulation of romances in the colonies. Although the inventories of libraries and book-shop catalogues suggest that romances were indeed smuggled in from Spain, this was no help to a potential local author of prose fiction, for it was strictly forbidden to print works of fiction in the colonies. The result was two centuries of notorious literary barrenness – a seventeenth century in which the most fruitful literary activity consisted of the poor imitation of Spanish 'baroque' poetry, and an eighteenth century in which an emasculated Enlightenment manifested itself merely in poor imitations of French models. There was admittedly one somewhat miraculous exception, one Mexican poet whose talent stands out during these two centuries – albeit relatively speaking – Sor Juana Inés de la Cruz (1648–95). Her autobiographical essay *Respuesta de la poetisa a Sor Filotea de la Cruz* (1691) and her best poems, the *Sueños*, were to provide the first evidence of intellectual independence and vigour in Spanish America, her passion for intellectual freedom indeed often bringing her into conflict with the ecclesiastical authorities.

II The Literature of Independence

Although the repressive factors that served to inhibit the development of creative literature during the colonial period were automatically removed by the Emancipation, that event itself could hardly have been expected to produce good literature immediately. Repressed habits died hard, and the literature that was directly inspired by Independence is indeed as disappointing as colonial literature, despite the often extravagant claims that are made for it.

In the first place, the poets of Independence disguised the originality of the events they described in a neo-classical style they lazily imitated from the European Enlightenment. The disastrous effects of thus reducing a new experience to a borrowed form of expression can be examined in the work of the Ecuadorean poet José Joaquín de Olmedo (1780–1847), who had been urged by his friend the liberator, Simón Bolívar (1783–1830), to celebrate the triumphs of the Revolutionary War. Thus his *La victoria de Junín. Canto a Bolívar* (1825) is marred by a vocabulary that is often merely sonorous:

> El trueno horrendo que en fragor revienta
> y sordo retumbando se dilata
> por la inflamada esfera,
> al Dios anuncia que en el cielo impera . . .

Although Olmedo's work is of some interest historically, Spanish American literature has subsequently become too rich to justify the notoriously uncritical reception he has had among Spanish American literary historians. The same is true of another 'poet of the Independence', the Venezuelan Andrés Bello (1781–1865), a man who, though justly remembered as the organizer of Chilean education and in general as a publicist, philosopher and grammarian, wrote poems that are marred by the same stylistic limitations that can be discerned in Olmedo's. Thus in his *Alocución a la poesía* (1823) he fatuously addresses a sensible appeal for poets to draw their inspiration from the New World rather than from Europe in a borrowed style that undermines the appeal's purpose.

Bello is sometimes admittedly valuable for the ideas contained in his poetry, if not for his ability to express them. For he manages to foreshadow what have been some of the key concerns of Spanish American culture up to the present day. He was the first, for instance, to recognize a task that many Spanish American writers have felt to be central to their enterprise – the elementally Adamic one of simply naming a virgin continent. His *Alocución a la poesía*, moreover, fore-shadows such works as *Alma América* (1906) by the Peruvian poet José Santos Chocano (1875–1934) and *Canto General* (1950) by the Chilean poet Pablo Neruda (1904–73) in attempting an epic description of the whole continent. As in Neruda's vast poem, landscape descrip-tion is mingled with historical narrative and political propaganda, which in Bello's case is directed at the iniquities of Spanish rule.

Bello was the last champion of neo-classicism in Spanish America. His neo-classical faith could not but help to undermine his attempts to create an authentically American literature. Such a literature only emerged when writers aimed to discover autochthonous forms and an autochthonous language to match the unprecedented events they were describing. The history of Spanish American literature in the nineteenth century is largely the history of very partial successes in the achievement of this aim.

III *Gauchesco* Literature

The earliest partial success was that of *gauchesco* literature, impressively pioneered by the Uruguayan poet Bartolomé Hidalgo (1788–1822).

Who were the gauchos, and what sort of people were they? During the colonial period the inhabitants of the pampa, or flat grasslands of Argentina, had developed a very independent way of life based on the abundance of livestock in the River Plate area and on the sparsity of its human population. The vast plains of Argentina seemed to be their own, as was indeed an unlimited amount of free meat. From the end of the eighteenth century, however, and particularly after the Declara-tion of Independence, which brought with it the institution of free trade, livestock came to be in increasing demand, for the export first of hides and then of salted meat. The random killing of livestock and the traditional vagrancy of the rural population thus came under heavy pressure, and a sequence of laws against 'vagos y malentretenidos', though not unknown during the colonial period, was vigorously enforced. It was at this point that *gauchesco* literature emerged and appropriated the term 'gaucho' to describe the rural population in question, taking up the story of a people and a way of life that had entered into a period of intense crisis. The independence of the gauchos was undermined further because their recruitment into popular militias was necessary for the Wars of Independence and the civil wars that followed. Two birds were being killed with one stone at their expense because such recruitment was the most common punishment for unauthorized slaughtering of cattle and for vagrancy, intolerable in a country where the labour force was so scarce.

The initial purpose of Bartolomé Hidalgo's poetry was to boost the morale of the gauchos fighting in the Wars of Independence. What better way of doing this than to borrow the poetic traditions that had developed orally among them, and which he had encountered as an officer? Hidalgo's *gauchesco* poems thus originated as a result of contact between an articulate officer and the oral tradition of the illiterate ranks. They were also the outcome of an attempt to reach an audience on which a neo-classical ode would have had little impact but which, though illiterate, could easily memorize and transmit poems whose rhythm was familiar. Hidalgo imitated the metre and language of the gaucho *payadores* or wandering troubadours who performed in the rural inns, the *pulperías*.

Hidalgo's fame, though, rests not so much on his early *cielitos*, conceived as military propaganda, as on his *diálogos*, octosyllabic conversations between two gauchos – Contreras and Chano – which were written after Independence and which contrast the heady idealism of the emancipation with the civil wars that were later to undermine it. The *diálogos* display considerable social as well as political concern, for they lament the poor lot of the gaucho despite his ardent role in the fighting, and contrast it with the favourable one of city opportunists.

Another *gauchesco* poet, Hilario Ascasubi (1807–75), was directly inspired by the pioneering example of Hidalgo. Ascasubi, however, began to write his *gauchesco* poetry in very different circumstances, namely during the 'federalist' dictatorship of Juan Manuel Rosas (1793–1877)[1] when the liberal opponents of a repressive, nationalist regime were exiled either to Chile or, as was the case with Ascasubi, to Montevideo. Ascasubi's first work, *Paulino Lucero*, was originally published in the form of loose news-sheets between 1839 and 1851 and distributed among the Argentine exiles in Montevideo in an effort to stir them into action against Rosas.

Primarily *Paulino Lucero* is a work of propaganda, and it suffers all the shortcomings inherent in so circumstantial a purpose. Much of the propaganda is no more than mere primitive taunting, but it is easy to appreciate the extent of its effectiveness. The propagandist approach is, moreover, interestingly responsible for the injection of a new crudely

[1] Rosas was more or less in control of Argentina from 1829 to 1852.

grotesque realism into Spanish American literature, particularly in the descriptions of Rosas himself. Thus in *Coplas de Cielito y Pericón* interesting connections are established between the rising price of soap in Buenos Aires and the dictator's smell. In a poem of particularly grotesque impact, *Isidora la federala*, the dictator is portrayed as the drunken collector of the ears, heads and hides of dead *unitarios* – the political opposition – and, in *La refalosa*, *federales* lustfully indulge in the torture of *unitarios*. What better way to incite the *unitarios*, at whom these poems are addressed, to revenge?

A later work by Ascasubi, *Aniceto el Gallo*, is also circumstantial, for it describes his disappointment with Justo José de Urquiza (1801–70), the governor of Entre-Ríos province, who led the cause against Rosas to victory at the battle of Caseros (1852). But it lacks the spontaneity that characterized the poems of *Paulino Lucero*. More ambitious is Ascasubi's *Santos Vega* (published with the other works in Paris in 1872), a complex, undiluted narration in verse which combines *costumbrista* descriptions of the gauchos' life with a labyrinthine web of Romantic plots and sub-plots.

Santos Vega is an example of *gauchesco* poetry succumbing to the influence of Romanticism, being often little more than a *gauchesco* version of Argentina's most notable Romantic poem, *La cautiva* (1837) by Esteban Echeverría (1805–51). Unlike the English and French Romantics, Spanish American poets did not have to travel far in search of exotic adventure: the main theme of both *La cautiva* and *Santos Vega* – the *malón* or raid on cattle ranches by nomadic Indians who ravaged the pampas until the 1870s – is both exotic and autochthonous at one and the same time, in particular because the Indians had a habit of carrying off the young women – the *cristianas* – along with the livestock they habitually stole: hence the recurring Romantic theme of the *cautiva* in Argentinian literature.

By 1872, with the work of Hidalgo, Ascasubi and several others in print, a firm tradition of *gauchesco* poetry had been established. This tradition made possible the appearance that year of the first part of the finest work of *gauchesco* literature, *Martín Fierro* (1872–9) by José Hernández (1834–86). Hernández, an ex-federalist, wrote *Martín Fierro* as a gesture of political protest against the liberal presidency of Sarmiento, and particularly as a gesture of social protest at Sarmiento's exploitation of the gaucho, although repressive measures against the gauchos were taken as strongly under Rosas as under Sarmiento – Rosas after all had needed the gaucho militias too.

Martín Fierro is effective as a protest poem. It is interesting, too, as a *costumbrista* poem; Hernández, unlike Hidalgo and Ascasubi, was himself an *estanciero* (landowner) and knew rural Argentina better than he knew anything else. *Martín Fierro* is a great deal more, however, for apart from being a specific reaction to specific Argentinian laws and conditions, it becomes something else, an archetypal reaction against society in general. *Martín Fierro* implicitly appeals to the good old days when the inhabitants of rural Argentina lived freely, untrammelled by social organization, with free livestock to feast on and an undivided pampa to gallop on. And no better statement against society as such is made in the poem than when Sargento Cruz, in charge of a patrol sent out to capture Martín Fierro, is so moved by the outlaw's bravery that he changes sides, and helps Martín Fierro fight the patrol.

The essentially anti-social attitude of *Martín Fierro* very soon captured the imagination of Argentinians. When later, in the 1880s, novels by Eduardo Gutiérrez (1853–90) such as his *Juan Moreira* (1879), which was basically a variation on the *Martín Fierro* theme, were adapted for the popular theatre, it was not uncommon for the audience to intervene on the stage lest the outlaw be captured by the police. That Martín Fierro, an outlaw (and, indeed, a murderer), should have been almost universally recognized as the most sympathetic protagonist of Argentinian literature, may, to say the least, be sociologically significant. In an excellent study of this poem, Jorge Luis Borges (1899–) has suggested that *Martín Fierro* is linguistically the most authentic *gauchesco* work simply because it alone was written by a man who was actually brought up on the pampa. According to Borges, its language has an authentic gaucho flavour because it came naturally to Hernández. When dialect is imitated artificially, it is bound to be exaggerated for greater effect and Borges is probably right in saying that no real gaucho would have concentrated exotic vocabulary as hectically as the characters of, say, Ascasubi do. In *Martín Fierro* gaucho vocabulary is only employed where it is strictly necessary. The flavour of gaucho language is instead suggested rather by the poem's syntax and rhythm. Both the pampa and the skills of the gaucho's trade – throwing the *lazo* and the *bolas*, breaking in horses, branding livestock – are moreover taken much more for granted in *Martín Fierro*. The countryside in the other *gauchesco* poets is seen from the outside and its presentation seems geared to an urban reader. Only an urban writer or an urban reader would be likely to see horse-breaking, say, as an exotic activity worthy of lengthily documented description.

These points are worth considering when approaching the whole question of the authenticity of *gauchesco* poetry, particularly since extravagant claims are often made for the value of *gauchesco* texts as linguistic documents. In the first place we will never be able to establish the exact relationship between *gauchesco* literature and the authentic, oral, gaucho poetry of the time because that poetry was never recorded. Furthermore, the syntax of, say, Ascasubi's *Santos Vega* is far more complex than any gaucho would be likely to master. A somewhat learned syntax associated with an exaggeration of popular dialect make for a poetry that is an approximation to real gaucho speech rather than an accurate rendering of it.

At any rate the *gauchesco* poets did *attempt*, however exaggeratedly, to discover an autochthonous language competent to express autochthonous themes. Their work compares favourably with the efforts of such writers as Juan María Gutiérrez (1809–78), Ricardo Gutiérrez (1836–96) and Rafael Obligado (1851–1920) who believed that, though it was proper to treat specifically American themes in literature, these should be expressed in a polished cultivated Spanish.

IV River Plate Romanticism

The Romantic movement (from which the later stages of *gauchesco* poetry cannot, of course, be separated, including *Martín Fierro*, with its romanticization of the outlaw) flourished in the River Plate area more than anywhere else in Spanish America. It appears to have reached Argentina around 1830, the year of the return to Buenos Aires of Esteban Echeverría (p. 434 above), a young poet who had imbibed Romanticism for five years in Paris, and who was responsible for perhaps the first self-consciously Romantic poem in the Spanish language, *Elvira o la novia del Plata* (1832).

Although Echeverría was not as solely responsible for Argentinian Romanticism as is sometimes imagined, his influence was considerable, particularly in his insistence that literature should be both socially conscious and nationalist in aim. We have noticed the impact *La cautiva* had on the writing of Ascasubi's *Santos Vega*. More important is a startlingly mature short story, *El matadero*, apparently written about 1839, at the height of Rosas's power and circulated with powerful effect among friends, although not published until the 1870s. Written with a realism that was wholly new to Argentinian prose, it describes an orgy of butchering that follows the arrival of fifty head of cattle at a Buenos Aires slaughterhouse. Excitement brought on by witnessing the butchering causes the mob to turn on a stranger in the street simply because he is wearing European clothes and must therefore be an *unitario*. After beating him up they abandon him, assuming him to be dead.

The slaughterhouse is, of course, a symbol of the Rosas regime, for Rosas did indeed represent the cattle-interest in Argentina. But to condemn a regime by equating it with so necessary an institution as a slaughterhouse is somewhat unfair. At any rate Echeverría's realistic, colloquial prose, which reads naturally and is free of that excessive zeal to imitate dialect that marred much of *gauchesco* writing, was a healthy innovation. Moreover his *Dogma socialista*, published in the 1840s, is one of the most coherent statements of the liberal, anti-Rosas cause written at the time.

Another young victim of the Rosas regime was José Mármol (1818–71), whose first Romantic poems were written in 1838 on the wall of the cell in Buenos Aires where he was being held captive. Like Echeverría, he was a far better prose-writer than poet, and his career is vindicated with the writing of *Amalia* (1851–5), perhaps the most interesting novel written in Spanish America during the nineteenth century, despite its notorious imperfections.

The plot of *Amalia* is ludicrously melodramatic: it is the story of an *unitario*'s struggle to hide from Rosas's secret police in Buenos Aires after a failed attempt to escape to Montevideo, of his love for a beautiful widow, Amalia, and of his eventual murder, with Amalia, by the Mazorca, Rosas's storm-troopers, on his wedding day. Yet the novel most eloquently displays the full implications of the *unitario* cause. Its melodrama is, moreover, so professionally deployed that no novel of the period is more readable. An impressive level on which the novel functions is that of terror; *Amalia* presents a hair-raising portrait of the helpless loneliness of the few *unitarios* who remained in Buenos Aires in the face of a spectacularly thorough secret police. The contrast between the corruption of the police and the lovers' innocent emotions is tendentious, but it is effectively presented. *Amalia* is indeed an interesting forerunner of a twentieth-century novel that depicts a similar situation, *El señor presidente* (1946) by the Guatemalan novelist Miguel Ángel Asturias (1899–1974). Here again, an alarmingly small number of individuals attempt to sustain a life of decency in a society where characters either compromise and perish spiritually, or refuse to do so and perish physically.

That *Amalia* is a novel of propaganda is obvious – its lurid descriptions of Rosas himself are reminiscent of those in *Paulino Lucero*. Yet, in fairness, the portrait offered of the *unitario* exiles in Montevideo is not a rosy one. Their leaders turn out to be ambitious *caudillos* just like Rosas, and they are all at loggerheads with one another.

David Viñas (1929–), in his admirable *Literatura argentina y realidad política* (1965), has pointed out an interesting dichotomy of style in *Amalia*: Rosas's entourage is always described in the most concrete possible terms, in a language comparable to that of Echeverría's *El matadero*, whereas Amalia and her friends are sometimes described in an insipidly ethereal language; thus 'había algo de resplandor celestial en esa criatura de veintidós años'; 'Amalia no era una mujer; era una diosa . . .'

Much evidence could indeed be drawn from *Amalia* to support the theory that the assumptions of liberals tend to be somewhat unreal; few novels offer better opportunities for those Marxist critics who like to investigate the gaps that separate writers' apparent intentions from their real ones. The décor of Amalia's house is revealing enough; she has velvet wallpaper, luxuriously thick Italian carpets, a French bed of carved mahogany, a Cambray lace bedspread – indeed everything is both exquisite and imported in this house that is supposedly a bastion of 'democracy'. One begins to notice in *Amalia* that the rigid opposition between *civilización* and *barbarie* that was to characterize the fiction of liberal novelists until Rómulo Gallegos (1884–1969) is at best a double-edged weapon. One of the strongest arguments that Mármol, the democratic *unitario*, levels against the 'barbaric' Rosas is that his regime has made the rabble cocky. Servants are now insolent; worse, 'the negroes have become haughty'. When the Mazorca finally come to perpetrate their murder, their gesture is seen as 'plebeian impudence'.

Amalia suffers all the limitations of Romantic fiction: it is filled with melodramatic intrigues, cloak-and-dagger skirmishes and insipidly operatic love exchanges. There is no character development. Emotions are rigidly fixed. Conflict exists between one character and another, but never *within* a character. Yet Mármol captures the reader's interest by the careful manipulation of suspense. He writes a fast narrative never devoid of action. The novel is, moreover, sustained by the sheer infectious ingenuousness of its liberal faith. Indeed, in the long run, its extraordinary interest can be ascribed to a quality not intended by the author: its very innocence, which allows one to unravel the most unconscious assumptions of a nineteenth-century liberal mind.

A large number of interesting 'non-literary' works – histories, travelogues and philosophical and political essays – were published in the River Plate during this period, and some of them had important repercussions on literary activity. Most important in this respect was *Civilización y barbarie: vida de Juan Facundo Quiroga* (1845) by the Romantic publicist and statesman Domingo Faustino Sarmiento (1811–88), a book in which a passionate attack is launched on the Rosas regime. Like Mármol and Echeverría, Sarmiento presses the claims of a sometimes dubious *civilización* on his 'barbaric' country, though, more originally than them, he is often not able to suppress his admiration in practice for the barbaric gauchos he condemns in theory. Such honest ambivalence was to be shared by many subsequent deployers of the *civilización : barbarie* confrontation, in particular by Rómulo Gallegos.

V Mexico

Whatever the limitations of River Plate writers in the first decades after Independence, it is hard to find another region in the continent whose literature is capable of rivalling them. The only possible competitor is Mexico, though Mexican writing matured much later, perhaps because the political ferment that so inspired Argentinian writers in the 1830s and 1840s did not come to Mexico with comparable vigour until the 1850s. Until the liberal revolution of 1854 and the wars of the *Reforma* that followed it, Mexican literature was distinguished by little more than the fact that it was a Mexican, José Joaquín Fernández de Lizardi (1776–1827), who wrote the first ever Spanish American novel, *El periquillo sarniento* (1816). This novel itself was little more than a landmark, however. Like Lizardi's subsequent work it contains worthy attacks on the colonial heritage of laziness, corruption, bigotry and superstition in Mexico. But the picaresque adventures of its hero are marred by an almost unreadable didactic digressiveness.

In 1869, two years after the final triumph of the *Reforma*, the novelist Ignacio Altamirano (1834–93) founded a magazine, *El Renacimiento*, where he formulated the sort of literary programme that had been outlined in Argentina by Echeverría and Sarmiento some decades earlier. Thus Altamirano recommends that Mexicans cease slavishly to imitate European models: while free to learn technically from abroad, they should draw inspiration from the vast number of autochthonous topics available to them; Aztec civilization, for instance, or the Conquest, or the present-day Indians, the landscape, the Wars of Independence, the empire of Maximilian and so on. Like Echeverría he is aware of the novel's social potential. Because it is an accessible, uncomplicated genre he believes it to be exceptionally useful educationally. What better way, for instance, to teach history to the people and to develop in them a national consciousness than to write historical novels?

Altamirano's programme was indeed responsible for a wave of historical novels during this period. In most of these novels, by such writers as Juan Mateos (1831–1913) and Vicente Riva Palacio (1832–96), colonial history, not surprisingly, is violently revamped so that the Indians are seen as idyllically noble in contrast to their rapaciously brutal conquerors.

The most accomplished Mexican novel to have been inspired by the *Reforma*, Altamirano's *El Zarco*, was published posthumously (1901), though set during the 1860s. Although on the surface a Romantic novel, full of portents and melodramatic coincidences, *El Zarco* is nevertheless original because it functions more deeply as a criticism of Romantic fiction. Thus the novel's heroine, after entertaining Romantic fantasies about the bandit who abducts her, discovers him to be mean, cowardly and brutal: so much for the Romantic myth that idealized the bandit – a myth which had found its Mexican expression in a novel called *Astucia, el jefe de los Hermanos de la Hoja* (1865–6), by Luis Gonzaga Inclán (1816–75). Altamirano contrasts his bandits with the hard-working community of the town of Yautepec, whose sugar and banana plantations and orange groves they harass.

One interesting innovation in *El Zarco* is that, unlike many European Romantic novels and their uncomplaining Spanish American imitations, the hero is dark and the villain is blond (his nickname, 'El Zarco', means 'blue-eyed'), a healthy sign, perhaps, of a burgeoning cultural assurance and of the shedding of racial complexes.

VI Jorge Isaacs

No other Spanish American country throughout most of the nineteenth century produced literary movements coherent or talented enough to warrant the separate treatment that has been accorded above to those of Argentina and Mexico. However, mention should be made of individual achievements in some other countries: an important one was *María* (1867), a novel by the Colombian writer Jorge Isaacs (1837–95) which is perhaps the most quintessentially Romantic novel in Spanish American literature.

María, too, is a novel of many shortcomings and on the surface it looks meekly imitative. Its plot, which describes a spontaneously intense love foiled by the educational ambitions of a parent who insists that his son study in Europe, seems like a carbon copy of *Paul et Virginie* (1788). One feels that 1867 is a bit late for nature to be hectically reflecting the characters' moods or presaging their future. The novel's impact is also undermined by a long, out-of-place digression set in West Africa, the only excuse for which is the West African origins of a servant on the *hacienda* where the action of the novel takes place. *María* survives, however, because its plot, though blatantly unoriginal, is effectively placed in a context – that of the Cauca valley – that is unmistakably local, and the flavour of that context is forcefully expressed. The novel's engagingly unpretentious simplicity is, moreover, perhaps responsible for the fact that, along with *Martín Fierro*, it is the nineteenth-century work of literature that has made the deepest impression on the continent's popular consciousness up until the present day.

VII Cirilo Villaverde

Romanticism came earlier to Cuba than to Colombia, the Cuban poet José María Heredia (1803–39) being a distinguished precursor of the Romantics all over the continent. By the time that Cirilo Villaverde (1812–94) published the first part of his fine Romantic novel *Cecilia Valdés* (1839) the Cuban Romantic movement was in full sway, centred round a vigorous literary circle that had been founded in Havana by a writer of popular ballads called Domingo Delmonte (1805–53).

Cecilia Valdés is an example, as are all the novels mentioned to date, of the way in which the Romantic movement meant something different in each country it was imported into, responding each time to different local conditions and life-styles. Thus, whereas Argentina's finest Romantic novel is about the dictator Rosas, Cuba's finest Romantic novel is about slavery. We have seen how typically Romantic themes could, moreover, be found neatly, if accidentally, relevant to a local context – thus a typically exotic Romantic theme such as a white girl's capture by the Indians coincided perfectly with conditions in Argentina. Similarly, in *Cecilia Valdés* a typically melodramatic Romantic plot – that of the lovers who do not realize they are brother and sister – was turned by Villaverde into a critique of sexual relations between masters and slaves. For it is the oligarchic Don Cándido Gamboa's adventures with shapely negresses that cause his son, Leonardo, not to realize that his favourite mulatta, Cecilia Valdés, is his half-sister. There is a comparable plot in *Cumandá* (1879), by the Ecuadorean novelist Juan León Mera (1832–94).

Like *Amalia, Cecilia Valdés* is a social document of great importance. Its portrait of sexual relations in nineteenth-century Cuba serves eloquently to unravel significant aspects of the island colony's class structure. Thus sexual relations are stamped with the urge to, as the Cubans put it, *mejorar color*. Black women seek out mulattos as their partners; mulattas seek out white men: each offspring is a step up the race ladder. The process is a familiar one in all the European colonies in the Caribbean.

The novel's portrait of Don Cándido Gamboa is particularly interesting as social documentation. He is a man who lavishes the vast wealth he has shadily acquired in the slave-trading business on such commodities as a title of nobility, a particularly 'conspicuous' form of consumption. *Cecilia Valdés* is moreover an excellent novel of manners, charting the city's lively tropical street-scenes and, in contrast, the forced formality of its questionably enriched high society. Villaverde also treats us to detailed descriptions of those public dances where rich young men went to pick out their mulattas – there Villaverde is particularly sensitive to the tension and pathos that a clash of class cultures can provide.

VIII Alberto Blest Gana

Perhaps the finest Spanish American novelist of manners in the nineteenth century is the Chilean Alberto Blest Gana (1830–1920), who – several years before Pérez Galdós, in Spain, published his first work – wrote *La aritmética en el amor* (1860), the first Spanish American novel to show a decisive Balzacian influence. Two years later there followed his finest novel, *Martín Rivas* (1862), a realist novel whose maturity is remarkable when one considers that it was written several years before Isaacs wrote *María*.

The plot of *Martín Rivas* is not outstanding: the eponymous hero is an impoverished student living with a rich family whose daughter despises him until she realizes he is worth more than the frivolous dandies who surround her. What is admirable about *Martín Rivas* is rather the authenticity and perception with which Blest Gana portrays the Chilean upper and middle classes and charts both the subtle gaps that separate them culturally and the less subtle ones that separate them financially. He portrays mainly to criticize. The upper classes are obsessed with money and engaged in political opportunism. They adulterate their culture with servile imitations of French culture; some of them can scarcely even speak Spanish, their language being punctuated with such comic Gallicisms as 'rendir visita', 'yo quemo de impaciencia' or 'eso no hace nada'. The middle classes, or *medio pelos*, are no better: meanly ambitious, they will stop at nothing in order to rise socially.

Blest Gana consciously, sometimes aggressively, reacts against Romanticism in *Martín Rivas*. Romantic love scenes occur only to be satirized; potentially melodramatic episodes are treated with cold sobriety: thus Martín Rivas's escape from gaol (where he has landed on account of his liberal politics) is described in just one cool, unadventurous sentence.

Blest Gana pursued his *comédie chilienne* in such novels as *El ideal de un calavera* (1863) and *Los trasplantados* (1904). The latter explores the Jamesian theme of the impoverished European aristocrat's search for a rich American bride – this time a Spanish American one. In another novel, *Durante la reconquista* (1897), Blest Gana seeks to emulate Galdós's historical novels, the *Episodios nacionales*.

IX *Modernismo*

Until now, apart from the *gauchescos*, there has been more occasion, in this survey, to talk about prose fiction than about poetry. It was not until the 1880s, with the advent of the *modernista* movement, that poetry of some importance began to be written in Spanish America.

By 1880, some Latin American countries, notably Argentina and Mexico, were entering a period of rapid economic development and, therefore, of increasing material prosperity – in particular for those sectors of the population which profited from the boom in the export of raw materials to Europe. Governments believed orderly material progress to be more important than political freedom, and consequently intellectual curiosity, when not confined within the limits of the official 'positivist' orthodoxy, was not an exceptionally valued commodity. It is not, therefore, surprising that indifference to political issues should have characterized a large proportion of *modernista* poetry. This political apathy is often held by critics to have been a manifestation of the poets' rejection of their respective societies, their importation of the more sensual aspects of French symbolist poetry being, moreover, often portrayed as a bold challenge to the narrow-minded philistinism of the time. We shall see, however, that the *modernista* poets were probably not all that rebellious or anti-social.

The first stage of *modernismo* is characterized by the somewhat hollow borrowing of contemporary French poetic fashions – a practice that was pioneered by the Nicaraguan poet Rubén Darío (1867–1916) in his *Azul* (1888) and further developed by him in *Prosas profanas* (1896), the poems in these books being largely imitations of the Symbolists and the Parnassians.

From the Parnassians the *modernistas* inherit (and, more significantly, exaggerate) a cult of elegance. The poets themselves adopt aristocratic pseudonyms – thus the Mexican poet Manuel Gutiérrez Nájera (1859–95) calls himself the 'Duque Job', the Cuban poet Julián del Casal (1863–93) becomes the 'Conde de Camors' – and their poetry is adorned with delicately languid princesses and *marquesas*. 'Triunfos mundanos' are praised; a 'fúlgido palacio' provides the background. Even the poet's metaphors – and the points of reference of a metaphor are an excellent gauge of a poet's innermost assumptions – are aristocratic. Thus in Gutiérrez Nájera's *Ondas muertas* (1887) the water from a fountain is a

> niña que en regio palacio
> sus collares de perlas desgrana . . .

A poetry thus obsessed with foreign titles, jewels, palaces, silk, velvet and marble does not appear to constitute the challenge to its materialist, *parvenu* environment that it is often made out to be. Rather it is surely the literary equivalent of contemporary architectural attempts to turn Mexico City and Buenos Aires into the 'Athens of the New World' or the 'Paris of South America'. While the new rich were lavishing their newly earned sterling on the importation of luxury goods or on travel to Europe that led to hectic aping of European high society, so the 'new cultured' displayed a similar *arribismo* in their work: they imitate, and they imitate precisely the poetry that best reflects contemporary social aspirations. The result is sadly inauthentic. There is something almost comic about Rubén Darío, who was a Nicaraguan *mestizo*, declaring his love for diamonds on 'cuellos blancos' (only swan-white women are usually appreciated by *modernista* poets, who might have learnt something from Altamirano's blond villain), and his love for 'gentes de maneras elegantes / y de finas palabras . . .' (*Epístola*, 1906).[1]

A significant borrowing of the *modernistas* was eroticism. This usually consisted of the tantalizing contemplation of languid, blonde goddesses unlikely ever to be possessed, but occasionally *modernista* poets are more explicit, and it is perhaps not extravagant to say that the *modernistas* were useful in removing an important taboo in Spanish American literary practice.

We have seen that, in its first stage, *modernista* poetry was marred by its literary self-consciousness. To imitate the latest from Europe was more important than to react to a genuine creative impulse. Very occasionally – usually at a later stage when maybe they have got their experimenting out of their system – *modernista* poets write, however, in a manner which suggests that they really felt a need to write, that an intimate urgency is the cause of their poems. This is so in the case of an exceedingly moving, deeply personal poem, *Nocturno*, by the Colombian poet José Asunción Silva (1865–96). Some of Darío's later poems, moreover, reflect a new desire to test some of the clichés of *modernista* rhetoric and to measure them against a more rigorously thought-out reality. Thus in his *Soneto autumnal* he describes a Versailles that is spectacularly different from the elegant palace that had been evoked in his *Prosas profanas*. Cold weather and uncouth modern tourists are the main impressions he experiences on this occasion. The *modernista* illusion has disappeared – though not the aristocratic disdain.

In 1900 there appeared a work that was greatly to influence the *modernista* poets, *Ariel* by the Uruguayan essayist José Enrique Rodó (1871–1917). In this book, the sensitive, intuitive qualities of the Latins (the spirit of Ariel) are favourably contrasted with the pragmatic but philistine materialism of the United States (the spirit of Caliban) – a reaction against positivist philosophy and against the excessive admiration for the Anglo-Saxons' material progress which that philosophy

[1] Another kind of imitation contemporary to *modernismo* is that of French naturalism. Here the result is very different: Spanish American naturalists such as the Argentinian novelist Eugenio Cambaceres (1843–88) rebelliously dissect the materialistic societies that the *modernistas* ultimately appear to have revelled in, despite their occasional disavowals.

had led to in Spanish America. After reading Rodó, Darío became a fervent convert to a poetry that was both more patriotic and more public; Rodó's assertion of faith in the Latins was converted by Darío into the stridently hearty Hispanic exhortations of a poem like *Salutación del optimista* in his *Cantos de vida y esperanza* (1905). Alas, like his previous imitations of the latest French fashions, this poem, too, suffers the shortcomings of much poetry written to order and turns out to be a mere exhibition of clichés of little content: 'se anuncia un reino nuevo'; 'la celeste Esperanza'; 'la nación generosa, coronada de orgullo inmarchito'; 'la latina estirpe verá la gran alba futura'.

None of the poets mentioned were good poets, if one compares them with their contemporaries in Europe or their more mature successors in twentieth-century Spanish America. A great deal is owed them, however, simply because they brought Spanish Americans into contact with modern European poetry. For the time being that contact was bound to be overpowering, but it paved the way for a more evenly matched Latin participation some decades later, in the poetry of Neruda and of the Peruvian poet César Vallejo (1892–1938). And *modernista* cosmopolitanism – their readiness to write if necessary about China or India or Japan or Nordic mythology (as in the odd case of the Bolivian poet Ricardo Jaimes Freyre, 1868–1933) – may not bear the stamp of authority that would make it palatable to us today, but it did prepare the ground for the more authentic cosmopolitanism of contemporary Spanish American writing.

The *modernistas* introduced new themes into Spanish American poetry, as we have seen; they introduced new metres, making versification in Spanish more flexible and musical. The European symbolists taught them a great deal about the musical properties of verse, and also induced them to write a sensual, plastic poetry that was new to Spanish American literature. The *modernistas* were also the first professional writers in Spanish America, taking their task more seriously than writers before them had. They constituted, moreover, the first literary movement that operated on a continental scale, thus widening the horizons of literatures that had previously been obliged to develop within a narrowly local context.

X Peruvian Nationalism

While cosmopolitan *modernismo* flourished in other parts of Spanish America, in Peru a different kind of movement began to evolve that was both more nationalistic and more socially conscious. There, a writer called Ricardo Palma (1833–1919) was made responsible for the restoration of the National Library in Lima after its destruction during the War of the Pacific (1879–83) with Chile. From the archives of the viceregal period that Palma found in the library he collected material for an original anecdotal genre he called the *tradición*. This was a brief historical sketch, four or five pages long, which sought to capture the essence of a given historical event and which liberally mixed legend with fact. Palma's anecdotes are at once informative, appealing and symbolic. Writing in a popular, colloquial Spanish, concentrating often on the role of very ordinary men and women in historical events, and deriding the corruption of the viceregal regime, Palma paved the way – no doubt quite unconsciously – for the first coherently radical movement in Spanish American literature, inspired and founded by a man who ironically was also a *modernista* poet, Manuel González Prada (1848–1918).

González Prada shared many of the attributes of the positivists such as, for instance, a fervent belief in the natural sciences and an active contempt for metaphysics. However, he departed from positivist thinking on racial issues. Far from attributing the continent's backwardness to the racial inferiority of its Indians as the positivists did, he became the Indians' most ardent advocate since Las Casas. In 1886 González Prada formed in Lima a 'Círculo Literario' which aimed at creating a literature of social commitment. Although, for this purpose, he personally restricted himself mostly to the polemical essay, his 'Círculo Literario' was responsible for the emergence of one important novel, *Aves sin nido* (1889) by Clorinda Matto de Turner (1854–1909). This was the first Spanish American novel really to examine the Indian question from a social point of view, for the village in the *sierra* in which it is set is depicted as being viciously exploited by an Establishment comprising its priest, its governor and its judge. Albeit clumsily and tentatively, the pattern was set by Matto de Turner for the *indigenista* novels of the twentieth century.

XI The *Indigenista* Novel

In the wake of González Prada a great deal of polemic around the Indian question was sustained in Peru, Ecuador and Bolivia in the first decades of the twentieth century. On one hand, positivist contempt for the Indian died hard; at the other extreme advocates of the Indian sustained the view that he was the depositary of an utterly superior vitality that would lead him eventually to surpass the white man. More realistically, José Carlos Mariátegui (1895–1930), the founder of the Peruvian Communist Party, saw the Indian problem not as an ethnic one but rather as a class one. Inspired by this polemic there developed the so-called *indigenista* novels of, among others, Alcides Arguedas (Bolivia, 1879–1946), Jorge Icaza (Ecuador, 1906–), Ciro Alegría (Peru, 1909–67) and José María Arguedas (Peru, 1911–69), through which, for the first time, a literary movement sought coherently to champion in fictional form the rights of the Indian against the exploiting landowner.

The trouble with the *indigenista* novelists is that, like the *gauchesco* poets, they do not usually belong to the community they are writing about. They belong to the white upper or middle classes, a fact which is very evident in their novels. Thus in Alcides Arguedas's *Raza de bronce* (1919) we are treated to an elaborate description of an Indian marriage ceremony; in *Huasipungo* (1934), by Icaza, we are meticulously introduced to Indian burial practices. These novels offer the reader lavish details about cock-fighting (*Huasipungo*), coca-chewing (Alegría, *El mundo es ancho y ajeno*, 1941) and the administering of putrid urine as medicine (*Huasipungo*). The impression created is that these novelists are offering Indian customs and lore to the reader quite consciously as something exotic and alien – the Indians would take these things for granted – thus unwittingly detracting from the social impact that they aim for when they describe the Indians' miserable conditions of life.

Indigenista literature indeed presents much the same problems of distance between the author and his material that *gauchesco* literature presents, and which are perhaps common to all literary enterprises that feature the depiction of subjects that are alien to their author for reasons of race or class. How authentically can a writer present material that is basically alien to him? For whom, moreover, is he presenting it? When *gauchesco* literature was being written to exhort the gauchos to battle it could at least be claimed that the illiterate gauchos could memorize poems written in a metre and language familiar to them. But novels cannot readily be memorized and the chances of an Indian ever reading an *indigenista* novel were remote, not only because a majority of Andean Indians were – and still are – illiterate but, worse, because a large proportion of them speak Quechua, not Spanish. These novels were therefore unlikely to drive the Indians to revolutionary action, although this often appears to be one of their authors' aims. And the middle and upper classes whose conscience they might have hoped to stir tended, at the time, to read only European literature anyway.

The problem of language was the cause of another difficulty. The *indigenista* novels usually present dialogues between the Indians in a heavily Indianized Spanish. This is all right when an Indian is speaking to a landowner – he must then speak in Spanish and his Spanish would indeed be Indianized – but it is a dubious practice when portraying the Indians speaking among themselves, for to make Quechua-speaking Indians speak Indianized Spanish among themselves is like translating Pirandello into Italianized English. The exaggerated difference between the speech used in dialogue by the Indians and the often precious language used in the narrative descriptions found in these novels, moreover, reveals the extent of the abyss that separates the novelists' cultural attitudes from those of the Indians.

Most of these defects are avoided by a more recent Peruvian *indigenista* novelist, José María Arguedas. Arguedas was brought up in an *ayllu*, or Indian community, and learnt Quechua before learning Spanish. In his best novel, *Los ríos profundos* (1959), he presents us with an authentic expression of the Indian mind. No longer an outsider peering in on Indian life, his hero looks out at the world from an Indian insider's point of view. Arguedas has still, of course, to face the problem that he must write in Spanish – indeed he suffered a great deal of anguish on account of it. But his work certainly surpasses the novels of his predecessors. Similarly Miguel Ángel Asturias (1899–1974) has been relatively successful in such *indigenista* novels as *Hombres de maíz* (1949) and *Mulata de tal* (1963). The problem with Asturias's work is that it is hard in it to separate authentic expressions of the magical consciousness of his Guatemalan Indians – the descendants of the Mayas – from manifestations of magic that emanate from the writer's own mind as a result of his contact with the surrealist movement in Paris. For all his frequent clumsiness and lack of sophistication, Arguedas is far more effective because he is less pretentious.

XII Other 'Regionalist' Novels

A prominent feature of the *indigenista* novels is their vivid response to the natural landscape – a similar one in all three countries concerned since in all of them the Indian population is concentrated high in the *sierra*, in Andean valleys that are seldom lower than 8,000 feet and often twice as high. A comparable response can be discerned in other 'regionalist' novels throughout Spanish America contemporary with the *indigenistas*: in the novels, for instance, of the Venezuelan Rómulo Gallegos, of the Colombian José Eustasio Rivera (1889–1928) and of the Argentinian Ricardo Güiraldes (1886–1927). These works bear strong similarities to the *indigenista* novels in many respects, the difference being that in their respective countries the Indian element is of lesser, sometimes minimal importance, and the landscape is a different one. In Güiraldes's *Don Segundo Sombra* (1926), Gallegos's *Cantaclaro* (1934) and *Doña Bárbara* (1929) and in the first part of Rivera's *La vorágine* (1924) flat cattle-raising grasslands, known as the *pampa* in Argentina and the *llano* in Venezuela and Colombia, are described. On the other hand Gallegos's *Canaima* (1935) and the second part of Rivera's *La vorágine* are set in the jungle. But the bitter struggle against a hostile, undominated nature is always a similar one. Nature is the source of all hope for the future, for the continent's wealth stems from it. It is also the future's main obstacle, man's struggle with it being an equal and unpredictable one; sometimes, as is the case with the hero of *La vorágine*, he loses, devoured without trace by the jungle.

The elemental presence of nature evokes elemental responses from the characters. Man in these 'regionalist' novels is an archetypal being, his individual traits disappearing in the vastness of his elemental gestures. His natural obsession is to be fully a man, a *macho*. Gallegos, in particular, attempts to chart the dangers inherent in such primitive reactions, and characters like Marcos Vargas in his novel *Canaima* eventually destroy their impressive potential merely because the task of being simply a man, a brave, undefeated *macho*, is a limited and inconsequential one. However, in *Doña Bárbara*, Gallegos displays the same honest ambivalence towards *machismo* and towards the primitive instinct that Sarmiento displayed in *Facundo*. His hero, Santos Luzardo, seeks to stamp out *machista* violence on the *llano* but he himself is forced to adopt *machista* measures in order to achieve his aim; he finds himself delighting in his own competence as a forceful male.

Gallegos's dilemma is the dilemma of the liberal, and his novels display the shortcomings of a liberal position that has not changed a great deal since the times of Mármol. Indeed, as in *Amalia*, the concept of 'civilization' proposed is both arbitrary and questionable. In the first place, 'civilization' equals property. Luzardo is in fact a Caracas aristocrat who returns to the *llano* to recover land belonging to him that has been usurped by a mulatta upstart, Doña Bárbara, and which he himself has never attempted to administer. Further, 'civilization' equals upper-class manners; Doña Bárbara's daughter Marisela, who has been abandoned by her mother and brought up in the wilderness, is taken under Luzardo's wing. What does he teach her? To say 'hallé' instead of 'jallé', 'vea' instead of 'aguaite', and to behave in general like the 'señoritas de Caracas, todas bien educadas y exquisitas'. It is hard to feel very enthusiastic about a civilization whose panacea is elegant affectation.

The regionalist novels, like the *indigenista* novels, are also marred by the weakness of their language. They are written in a style notable more for its literary prettiness and for its sonority than for any real attempt expressively to match the vast themes that are being described. The novelists, moreover, make no attempt to evolve a suitable structure for their novels. They describe chaos and violence but contain them structurally in a conventional linear sequence.

These limitations are worth noting firstly because it is impossible to forget that the novels are roughly contemporary with Joyce's *Ulysses* (1922), Proust's *A la recherche du temps perdu* (1913–27) and Faulkner's *The Sound and the Fury* (1929), and secondly because, in the last thirty years, the Spanish American novel has finally, as we shall see, found its way to a language and structure capable of expressing the Latin American context. It has also abandoned the easy division of reality into Manichean opposites and discovered that conflicts exist not only between inexorably good or bad persons but also more complexly within a single person.

A special word about Güiraldes's *Don Segundo Sombra*: on the surface it is just one more *costumbrista*-regionalist novel which nostalgically resuscitates the *costumbrista* lore of the gaucho – horse-breaking, the rodeo, cattle-branding, cattle-driving, and so on. But *Don Segundo Sombra* is something more for it is a novel that somehow manages to transcend the local context and to stand up as an archetypal study in self-fulfilment and self-mastery. For all its limitations – and as documentation of life in the *pampa* the work is historically extremely dubious – it is perhaps the first Spanish American novel to create a myth of universal proportions.

XIII Spanish American Poetry in the Twentieth Century

Before we examine the contemporary Spanish American novel, which is so sophisticated an improvement on the work in this genre so far discussed, it is time to examine contemporary Spanish American poetry, which achieved maturity long before the novel did.

Two poets not yet mentioned, who were basically or orginally *modernista* poets, provide a bridge between *modernista* and contemporary poetry because their work both foreshadows some of the chief concerns of contemporary poets and directly influences them. They are the Uruguayan poet Julio Herrera y Reissig (1875–1910) and the Argentinian poet Leopoldo Lugones (1874–1938). Whereas the language of the *modernista* poets descended quickly into cliché, uncreative repetition depriving their work of substance, these two poets began to deploy a new intensity of expression. In their poetry one gets a sense of a mind thinking, and thinking creatively, aiming to renew the language of poetry, to re-express experience. Metaphor is no longer empty ornament. The distinction between poetry and prose is once again not merely one of metre and rhyme, but rather one of intensity of expression, compression of meaning.

In such books as *Los éxtasis de la montaña* (1904–7), *Los sonetos vascos* (1906) and *La torre de las esfinges* (1909), Herrera y Reissig attempts to renew his metaphors by aiming at surprise, hoping to jolt the reader with unexpected images, in the manner of the French poet Jules Laforgue (1860–87). Thus in *La torre de las esfinges*:

> La luna muda su viaje
> de astrólogo girasol,
> y olímpico caracol,
> proverbial de los oráculos,
> hunde en el mar sus tentáculos,
> hipnotizado de Sol.

Of course this is poetry that is merely outwardly descriptive. There is no urgent tension driving the poet to write it. And the metaphors startle more than they illuminate: we probably do not see the moon better if we see it as an Olympic snail. The same is true of Lugones, where the content of the metaphor is usually far more elaborate than the phenomenon it seeks to describe. Thus when, in *Metempsicosis* (1897), he compares a promontory to the neck of a sombre horse, he forgets about the promontory and gets carried away in a complex description of the horse. Yet in such books as Lugones's *Crepúsculos del jardín* (1905) and *Lunario sentimental* (1909) we do not find the lazily inexpressive phrases that we encountered in Darío. In Lugones's poetry every epithet counts. Thus in *Hortus delicarum* (1905) Lugones is capable of smelling 'un indulgente olor de violetas' where a *modernista* might have smelt 'un aromático olor de violetas'.

Herrera y Reissig and Lugones are among the most important direct precursors of contemporary Spanish American poetry. Their influence, for instance, on *Los heraldos negros* (?1919), Vallejo's first book, was immense. Another forebear of contemporary Spanish American poetry was the notorious *ultraísta* movement in Spain which burgeoned there under the aegis of Guillermo de Torre and was imported into Argentina by Jorge Luis Borges. It was the *ultraístas'* valuable role eclectically to absorb and then to disseminate most of the aesthetic adventures of the various movements of the European vanguard. It is possible to trace *ultraísta* affinities with cubism, futurism, Dadaism, surrealism and, through Borges's translations, with German expressionism. Their poetry, which futuristically denied all tradition and sought to reduce poetry to unconnected and all-embracing, all-expressive metaphors, was, however enthusiastic, essentially 'fashionable' poetry. However, the sheer provocativeness of the *ultraísta* manifestos and the outrageous novelty of their ideas could not fail to have stimulating repercussions.

Another important inspiration for the burgeoning of contemporary poetry was the work, and, more important, the aesthetic polemics of the Chilean poet Vicente Huidobro (1893–1948). His role was to spread ideas conducive to the free unleashing of the imagination, and he is significant as a foreshadower of Latin America's interminably rich literature of fantasy. For Huidobro, the founder (and perhaps sole exponent) of a movement known as *creacionismo*, believed that the justification for poetry was that it should impose upon itself no limits. Rather than imitate nature, poets should re-create it, including in their poems whatever disparate notions happened to cross their minds. According to Huidobro, the result would indeed be that poets would imitate nature more genuinely, creating originally and from nothing as nature does.

XIV César Vallejo

In ?1919 there appeared, in Lima, Vallejo's first book of verse, *Los heraldos negros*. Some of its poems, such as *Nochebuena*, betray an obvious *modernista* strain and could almost have been written by Darío. Others, such as *Bajo los álamos*, describe pastoral sunsets, as Herrera y Reissig did, and deploy images that closely follow, even in their detail, their precedents in Herrera y Reissig's work. Like Lugones, Vallejo strenuously aims to avoid commonplace words and comes up if necessary with the most outlandish of neologisms.

His debts are clear. What is fascinating about *Los heraldos negros* is that, although it is Vallejo's least important work, and is as yet immature – many of the poems were written in 1916, when Vallejo was twenty-four – for the first time in Spanish American poetry one can spot the appearance of a truly original voice, of a man who unmistakably has something to say and who has his own way of saying it. The voice is lonely, even gloomy: the experience of abandoning the humble *sierra* town of Santiago del Chuco where Vallejo was born and facing a hostile Lima is traumatic. Vallejo's ideal is indeed always to be his home village, in particular his protective, beautiful mother. Often this peaceful, nostalgic sector of Vallejo's consciousness is expressed, moreover, in the most unpretentiously direct poetry that has been written in Spanish America, a poetry in which Vallejo takes the risk of being unadornedly commonplace and manages instead to be exceptionally moving.

The peace of the mother-protected village is evoked in Vallejo's two other books: *Trilce* (1922) and the posthumous *Poemas humanos* (1939). But in *Trilce*, his most hermetic book, it becomes little more than a vulnerable flash of hope, drowned in the confusion of a man who has chosen to leave his sheltered home and then has not been able to cope. The poetry in *Trilce* is the poetry of a man who is racked by guilt merely because he has made the gesture of abandoning the simple innocence of childhood and opted for the labyrinthine complexity of manhood. Manhood proves to be an 'inútil mayoría', its reward merely the loneliness of orphanhood.

Trilce is largely a confessional book: it is the expression of a man who has delved deep into his unconscious, extracted its confused and multiple signs, and displayed them stridently on the page. Vallejo's unconscious freely reveals itself in *Trilce*, but in a censoredly oblique manner. Amidst the wildly disconnected images it is just possible to discern an extremely anguished eroticism, tormented by guilt. Thus in the fourth poem of the book, vibrant, intolerable noises assail the poet from nowhere in punishment for what appears to be some sexual crime. In general *Trilce* is a book full of inexplicable irritation ('Escapo

de una finta, peluza a peluza', poem XII), of subtly disturbing, unidentified sounds that are always close to unhinging the mind. Vallejo's
poetry is full, too, of ambiguous neologisms, of menacing, abstract
cadences. It is also a tensely dramatic poetry, where meaning is strug-
gling to surface, only to be quickly stifled, except when Vallejo has no
trouble in understanding, when the village makes a fleeting appearance.
Only the village is comprehensible: the rest is guesswork, the vain
grasping of signs that slip away.

If one or two other things later become comprehensible and certain
they are negative. In *Poemas humanos* there is an increasing concern
with the negative certainty that the social conditions of his country's
Indians are shameful, that the lives of his country's miners (which he
also describes in his novel *Tungsteno*, 1931) are bestial; the orphanhood
that Vallejo encountered as an individual on leaving his mother becomes
the orphanhood of the dispossessed in general.

Vallejo's social conscience was particularly stirred by the Spanish
Civil War, although there is a great deal of difference between Vallejo's
poetic reaction to that event and Pablo Neruda's. For, whereas Neruda
then tended to abandon his hermetically introspective poetry, opting
for a more exterior and public form of expression, Vallejo merely
added the Civil War to his consciousness. This neurotic, who took
more risks delving into the psyche than perhaps any other Spanish
American poet and whose work often reminds one of American
confessional poetry, of Sylvia Plath, say, was not suddenly cured by
the prospect of socialism – such a sudden cure might have made one
wonder at the sincerity of the neurosis and made it appear to have
been merely a literary pose. From the centre of his neurosis Vallejo
merely discerned, in the Civil War, a breath of fresh air, a possible
outlet, a hope for the 'communion' of men hitherto orphaned. This
yearning for 'communion' beyond his neurotic loneliness (which if
anything was becoming more acute) produces poetry of remarkable
intensity. It is this intensity that characterizes the long sequence called
España, aparta de mí este cáliz and the last poems of *Poemas humanos*,
written in the last months of 1937 in an unprecedented final burst of
creativity, as if Vallejo were aware of his impending death. They
are his most complete poems because in them he delves deeper into
his psyche than ever before and, at the same time, his field of vision
has expanded sufficiently to admit the possibility of an outlet.

XV Pablo Neruda

The other great poet of Spanish America is undoubtedly Neruda (1904–73), a man about whom so much has been written and who himself has been so extremely prolific that it is hard to know where to begin a brief discussion of his work that will do him justice.

As with Vallejo, it is possible to discern in Neruda's beginnings, for instance in his first book of poems, *Crepusculario* (1923), and even in the more authoritative and memorable *Veinte poemas de amor y una canción desesperada* (1924), the vestiges of the *modernista* movement. In the erotic *Veinte poemas*, however, relationships between the human body and nature are expressed in symbols that have, already, the flavour of a very personal inspiration.

In the two parts of *Residencia en la tierra* (1933 and 1935) Neruda delved deeply into his unconscious, like Vallejo in *Trilce*. Where the imagery that Vallejo finds there is starkly austere, however, Neruda's, in its portrayal of a disintegrating world, is almost playful in its surrealistic exuberance.

As we have noted, the Spanish Civil War inspired Neruda quickly to overcome his lonely alienation, the first example of a radically reformed, now public and exteriorized vision being his *España en el corazón* (1937). Neruda has said that he joined the Chilean Communist Party because he came to realize, in the Spanish Civil War, that, where so much was at stake, the Communists were the only force disciplined enough and coherent enough effectively to cope with the struggle against Fascism. It was at any rate as a Communist that he composed the bulk of his great epic poem, the *Canto General* (1950), a work in which, in the tradition of Bello and Santos Chocano (though immeasurably surpassing it) Neruda attempts to celebrate the geography and history of his entire continent, and to examine it, moreover, through the spectrum of a political doctrine that sought to transform it.

The *Canto General* is uneven, a feature of Neruda's work as a whole. Like Victor Hugo, Neruda has written some of the worst as well as some of the best poetry in his language. Thus, though in the *Canto* he is able to write unsurpassable poetry on practically anything, on a prehistoric stone, on the sad interminable rain of the Chilean forests, or on the advent of the *conquistadores*, he is capable also of political denunciation – against for instance the Chilean President Gabriel

González Videla, or the United Fruit Company[1] – which, though often deserved, rarely surpasses the most unimaginative ranting, acceptable for Ascasubi perhaps, but Neruda can do better.

One sequence, *A las alturas de Macchu Picchu*, stands out in the *Canto*, and certainly there is no finer poem in Spanish America. In the first part, Neruda obliquely summarizes the concerns of his previous poetry, and in doing so re-enacts its hermeticism, its calculatedly ambiguous syntax, its obsessive images. Then, inspired by the heights of the spectacular Inca citadel, he proceeds to reject his previous work, and the very language of the poem becomes more freely and confidently explicit.

In another important book, *Odas elementales* (1954), Neruda yielded one of his most original contributions to poetry in Spanish. It is often said that the originality of its poems lies in their structure: they are printed in lines of sometimes only two or three syllables, in order that the reader might reconsider the normal emphasis he would give to the words of a given sentence. Yet similar techniques can be found in the work of poets like Mayakovsky or Apollinaire several decades earlier. The poems are original rather because they direct the reader's sensibility to things that are not normally the subject of poetry. Thus, in the *Odas*, Neruda finds that the most insignificant thing – an onion, a tomato, an artichoke, a bird – can be seen to be miraculously significant, an indispensable component of an organic whole to which Neruda gestures in enthusiastic affirmation. Moreover, after the occasionally rancorous ranting of the *Canto*, he discovered in himself a generous humour, a new benignity which appeared to suggest that he had found his feet as a man and reached a definite maturity. Nowhere is this vein more evident than in *Estravagario* (1958), a playfully eccentric book that followed two more books of *Odas* published respectively in 1956 and 1957.

Neruda became almost a book-a-year man, and it would be pointless to discuss every one of his publications. Among his later works, perhaps the most important is the *Memorial de Isla Negra* (1964), a verse autobiography that is immeasurably helpful for the elucidation of his entire work, because Neruda was always, more or less obliquely, a poet in whom the autobiographical element was important.

Of all the poets writing in Spanish in this century, Neruda strikes one

[1] An American enterprise involved mainly in the exploitation of bananas in Central America.

as being the most talented partly because more than any other he gives the impression of being a 'natural' poet. Maybe poetry did come easily to him, but one of Neruda's most remarkable merits was that he was a hard-working professional who inspired Spanish American poets to overcome their haphazard amateurism. Neruda, like Vallejo, always believed that the poet must above all be an artisan, and it was in the difficult period of his artisanship in the 1920s that he laid the foundations of his later excellence.

XVI Other Contemporary Poets

It is difficult to generalize about the more recent generations of Spanish American poets because poetry has meant many different things to different poets. For the Mexican poet Octavio Paz (1914–) poetry is, for instance, not the mere expression of an existing world but rather a quest for something beyond it. The very act of writing a poem is a gesture that aims to attain a communion that will overcome the poet's basic solitude. The poet must break through his fundamental alienation, imposed equally by a capitalist society that is notorious for its insensitivity and by a Marxist society that subordinates his vitality to the interests of an impersonal and incomprehensible entity, the state. Paz pleads for a reaffirmation of the present, of the 'body sign' in an age where happiness is relegated to a mythical future. His poetry is the search for a fulfilment in the present, for the discovery of a blissful *instante* in which the body will triumph in communication with another body. His most coherent expression of these aims is a poem called *Piedra de sol* (1957), which is indeed one of the finest erotic poems in the Spanish language.

More recently, in his experimental poem *Blanco* (1967), he has attempted to emulate the structural achievements of the Argentinian novelist Julio Cortázar (1914–) in the latter's novel *Rayuela* (1963) by constructing his poem in such a manner that it can be read in different sequences and from different angles with the consequence that on each reading the meaning of the poem is modified. The poem is in the end a series of shifting *instantes* that subsume multiple sensations and deploy signs that point in many different directions.

Very different from Paz is the Chilean poet Nicanor Parra (1914–), the author of a kind of poetry he calls *anti-poemas*. Instead of embarking on existential adventures as Paz does, his poetry comments sardonically, in a conversational, aggressively 'unpoetic' language, on the trivial contradictions of everyday life. Other poets such as the Peruvian Carlos Germán Belli (1927–   ) and the Chilean Enrique Lihn (1929–   ) show a similar distaste for 'poetic' language.

One can discern yet another direction in the poets of the so-called *Orígenes*[1] group in Cuba, such as José Lezama Lima (1912–76), Eliseo Diego (1920–   ), or Cintio Vitier (1921–   ). Each of these poets displays personal characteristics foreign to the others, but all of them share a fervent Catholic faith, which they express in a poetry where all experience has a metaphysical connotation. The work of Lezama Lima, the most absorbing poet of the group, is notable for its long patterns of interrelated metaphors reminiscent of Spanish baroque poetry.

There is a younger generation of Cubans – among them such poets as Roberto Fernández Retamar (1930–   ), Heberto Padilla (1932–   ) and Pablo Armando Fernández (1930–   ) – whose difficult task it has been to bring to bear a sensibility that had already matured by 1959 on the unprecedented experiences of the Revolution.

XVII The Contemporary Political Novel

Fertile as Spanish American poetry quite clearly is today – and in a brief discussion of it one is clearly guilty of many omissions – it is in the novel that Spanish American literature has distinguished itself most spectacularly in the past few decades, having developed impressively and unrecognizably since the 'regionalist' period.

How did it all begin? Not quite as suddenly as some of the novels' exegetes appear to believe: the jump from Gallegos to Gabriel García Márquez (Colombia, 1928–   ) and Mario Vargas Llosa (Peru, 1936–   ) was not a miraculously unprecedented one. It is hard – and perhaps futile – to establish exactly where the roots of contemporary Spanish American fiction lie, but it is perhaps not extravagant to agree with the Mexican novelist Carlos Fuentes (1928–   ) that a great deal is owed to the novel of the Mexican Revolution. For it was in the novel of the Mexican Revolution that certain sophisticated developments occurred. Thus the work of Mariano Azuela (1873–1952) and Martín Luis Guzmán (1887–1976) for the first time offered a complex, ambiguous vision of Spanish American reality. Those writers asked questions – 'Is the revolution worth the violence?', 'Will it ultimately change anything?' – but they left them unanswered. It is never possible really

[1] From the name of a periodical they published in the 1940s and 1950s.

to establish who the real villains are. Perhaps the Mexican novelists learnt to write ambivalently – and therefore more authentically – merely because the events of the revolution themselves were so ambiguous. Thus Pancho Villa (1877–1923) was so equivocal a character that Guzmán's fictionalized biography of him, *El águila y la serpiente* (1928), had to be equivocal too.

Another pioneering feature, particularly in the novels of Azuela, was that they tentatively broke up conventional linear narrative. Thus in *Los de abajo* instead of being presented with a sequentially narrated story we are treated to a series of impressionistic flashes, as if the form of the novel were underlining the fact that the most an observer of the revolution can ever grasp of it is a series of disconnected fragments of evidence. Moreover Azuela's novels are written in a coolly deadpan language that responds toughly to the toughness of the events it seeks to describe – a far cry from the literary prettiness of the language of a Ciro Alegría or of a Gallegos.

The novel of the Mexican Revolution is thus a forerunner of a whole generation of contemporary novelists who seek to evolve a structure and a language suitable to express the political and social reality of the continent, an enterprise which, too, was partly initiated in Mexico, where the tentative technical innovations of Azuela were updated by Mexican novelists like José Revueltas (1914–76) and Agustín Yáñez (1904–), who appropriated such techniques as stream of consciousness and Proustian perspectivism to describe the revolution. Another precedent can be found in the work of the Argentinian novelist Roberto Arlt (1900–42), a writer who was perhaps the first to attempt to find another (subsequently very common) way out of the conventional realist mould in order to delve more deeply into his country's social and political problems: that of fantasy.

The first really impressive political novel to have been published in Spanish America is *El señor Presidente* (1946) by Miguel Ángel Asturias: a claustrophobic account of a savage (unidentified) dictatorship in Central America. The novel has many shortcomings – indeed many of its technical innovations distract from its purpose instead of enhancing it. Asturias's use of stream of consciousness, though innovatory in the Spanish American context, is generally clumsy, and his love of pun and onomatopeia unhelpfully irrelevant. Worse, Asturias is a man who (to paraphrase Borges) believes that good writing involves the use of every word in the dictionary.

Why then is *El señor Presidente* a landmark in Spanish American fiction? Because in it, despite the distracting effects of his technique, Asturias is able to communicate the horror of a particularly barbaric dictatorship without being dogmatic. In the wholly corrupted society he describes, where moral stature is a guarantee only of death, a man can become so confused that he is no longer able to distinguish between good or bad, even if he wants to. Necessarily recurrent self-justifications of his compromises with the *status quo* have blunted his moral judgement; hence the ambivalent nature of the President's henchman, Cara de Ángel, more a victim of circumstance than actively objectionable, capable of the most abject corruption yet sensitive enough to be brazenly nostalgic for a lost innocence which he is naïve enough to imagine he can recapture.

It is a pity that the scrupulous authenticity with which Asturias approached his subject in *El señor Presidente* was jettisoned in his subsequent political novels. Thus in his novels on the United Fruit Company, such as *Viento fuerte* (1950) and *El papa Verde* (1954), Asturias reverts to the Manichean mould: the Americans are unmitigated scoundrels, the Guatemalans innocent victims. It would seem that, for Asturias, villainy has complex roots and equivocal implications only when exercised by his compatriots.

Latin America is a continent that is generally supposed to have a brighter future than it has had a past. But in one country, Uruguay, the reverse is probably the case. Once a prosperous model of democracy and social welfare, Uruguay is now (1972) on the brink of bankruptcy, crippled by an outrageously top-heavy bureaucracy. What better way of depicting this condition than that chosen by Juan Carlos Onetti (1909–) in a novel like *El astillero* (1961), in which a man is appointed to manage a shipyard to which no ship has come for seven years, and where there are no workers left to manage? In a gesture of monumental but hopeless defiance, the manager spends most of the novel doggedly thumbing through the yellowing files, as if the motions of administration were the equivalent of administration itself. It is doubtful whether a documentary investigation into Uruguayan conditions could have expressed the curious sense of clinging gloom that *El astillero* (like other works of Onetti such as *El pozo*, 1939; *Tierra de nadie*, 1941; *La vida breve*, 1950; and *Juntacadáveres*, 1964) expresses. As in the novels of Roberto Arlt, fantasy has been summoned to furnish a social condition with a lastingly eloquent metaphor.

In Latin America (barring Cuba) revolutions come and go but politically and socially, little changes. It is therefore perhaps not surprising that some contemporary Spanish American political novels offer a cyclical view of history. Such a view is doggedly presented in *El siglo de las luces* (1962) ('las luces' = 'the Enlightenment'), a fine work by the Cuban Alejo Carpentier (1904–   ) which depicts the effects of the French Revolution on the Caribbean islands, and which placidly contemplates the relentless passage from monarchy to Jacobinism to Bonapartism back to monarchy. Ultimately, for Carpentier, it is not historical events that count but rather the perennial archetypes. Thus Esteban, the hero of the novel, finds that the archetypal experience of climbing a tree is more meaningful than the confusing and futile events that surround him.

A cyclical pattern can be discerned in one of the most interesting political novels written in Spanish America, Vargas Llosa's *Conversación en la Catedral* (1969). Much of this novel's cyclical vision is expressed in the book's very structure, for in it Vargas Llosa reshuffles the normal sequence of time. Thus we often read about the events of the Odría dictatorship in Peru (1948–56) after reading about the presidency of Manuel Prado (1956–62). The two presidents are thus seen to be interchangeable, despite the fact that Prado supposedly represents a return to 'democracy'. Everyone is indeed hopelessly lost in the structural labyrinth of the book, and *progress* out of it is impossible, a dilemma that is enhanced by the fact that we often read about *progressive* actions before reading about *regressive* ones that in fact preceded them. Vargas Llosa's labyrinthine structure eloquently expresses a labyrinthine yet stagnant Peruvian society, which not even the ruthlessly Machiavellian Minister of the Interior is able to manipulate and which the students of San Marcos University, for all their revolutionary efforts, are not able to change. Further, just as the characters are never able to see more than just a few steps ahead of them in the labyrinthine situation in which they are immersed, so the reader is forced to share their confusion as it is reflected in the perplexing – though ultimately coherent – structure of the book.

Conversación en la Catedral is a novel that unmasks Peruvian society by tellingly investigating the gap that separates its public face from its true face. The structure is again manipulated to this end, for at first the true face of Peru creeps to the surface only in quickly suppressed flashes, scarcely perceptible signs which often only an attentive reader will grasp. Such clues are eventually pieced together in coherent narrative sequences of revelation and denunciation, when they simply cannot be concealed any longer.

Thus Vargas Llosa's excellence lies partly in his success in evolving a structure for his fiction competent to deal with the social and political reality of his country. He had been evolving it heroically ever since the writing of his first novel, *La ciudad y los perros* (1963), where he sought to unmask the true face of a military school in Lima that lay concealed behind the brazenly respectable façade that it presented to parents and public, and *La Casa Verde* (1966), a novel in which structural juxtapositions are used to express the labyrinthine nature of Peruvian geography.

XVIII The Novel of Fantasy

Very often interpreters and critics of Latin American writing merely assert that most Spanish American novelists at some point or other draw on fantasy in their writing, but they do not usually ask themselves why. The influence of surrealism is sometimes offered as a crucial factor. Yet, barring Asturias, fantasy as deployed by Spanish American novelists does not on the whole have surrealist roots any more than that of say, Kafka, does. Another frequent explanation is the sheer towering influence of Borges. Yet Borges himself was launched into his career as a writer of fantasy by a writer of a previous generation, Macedonio Fernández (1874–1952). And it is anyway hard to believe that so insistent a habit can be attributed to the example of just one man. A key to the understanding of Spanish American literature of fantasy may be found in *Cien años de soledad* (1967), a remarkable novel by the Colombian writer Gabriel García Márquez which has captured the public imagination more than any other Spanish American novel, and which describes 'one hundred years of solitude' in an imaginary Colombian backwater called Macondo.

Cien años de soledad itself is a novel of fantasy, in the typical Spanish American manner, for real, wholly plausible situations imperceptibly take on a magical dimension. When least expected there is a rainstorm of dead birds, yellow flowers fall from nowhere to carpet the streets, dead men live, a girl emulates the Assumption of the Virgin Mary. And all this is described in an efficiently realistic prose that reads like a parody of historical narrative, full of dates and concrete details. This, we are made to believe, is the 'true' history of Macondo.

García Márquez also makes innumerable oblique references to other Spanish American novelists in *Cien años de soledad*, to Borges, Fuentes, Carpentier, Cortázar and Juan Rulfo (Mexico, 1918–   ). Sometimes he parodies them and sometimes he merely alludes slyly to one of their characters. He does this to remind us that *Cien años* is not only a fascinating novel in its own right: it is also a conscious meditation on past Spanish American writing, and particularly on the need that writing has felt to have recourse to fantasy. At one point in *Cien años* a strike in an American banana plantation is violently crushed, and the corpses of the strikers are whisked away by train, never to be seen again. And yet the citizens of Macondo are told that the strike was amicably settled. Worse, it is subsequently asserted in school textbooks not only that the strike never took place but indeed that the banana plantation never existed. Here at last, then, we have a context in which the presence of fantasy in Spanish American fiction can be understood. For where governments and foreign companies can cavalierly change reality, who can say what is real any longer? And is not the reality of Colombia more fantastic than any fairy-tale? The novel's descriptions of the interminable Colombian civil wars leave no doubt that it is.

Fantasy can therefore be used to symbolize the political situation of the sub-continent and also function as a reaction *ad absurdum* to it – this is what occurred in Onetti's *El astillero*. It has other roots, too, however. In a place like Macondo, a cultural backwater where education has scarcely penetrated, things that are perfectly normal to us may seem fantastic. The arrival of the first train, the feel of a block of ice exhibited in a gipsy fair, the cinema, the aeroplane – all these things are far more fantastic for the citizens of Macondo than the assumption of a local girl into Heaven, or the reappearance of a dead man. Fantasy, then, is a question of cultural assumptions: the frontier between fantasy and reality is situated differently according to one's environment. And in a continent where the Stone Age can survive not far from a vast city, it is not easy to agree on a continental scale on what is real.

A novel to which García Márquez repeatedly (though obliquely) refers in *Cien años* and which illustrates this proposition is *Pedro Páramo* (1955) by the Mexican writer Juan Rulfo. Here the novelist takes the medieval beliefs of a typical village in Mexico for granted: all the characters in the novel save the hero are dead, yet they have no difficulty in exercising conversation with the hero who is, moreover, initially unaware of their condition.

XIX Jorge Luis Borges

In the River Plate area fantasy does not have its roots in popular superstition because the area's population is largely one of European immigrants, although politics there are often certainly as fantastic as they are in Colombia – hence Arlt and Onetti. Perhaps Jorge Luis Borges (1899–) intuited another reason for the appeal of fantasy on the River Plate in such early poems of his as *Fervor de Buenos Aires* (1923), *Luna de enfrente* (1925) and *Cuaderno San Martín* (1929), in which the very presence of Buenos Aires on the vast pampa strikes him as fragilely implausible, a fantastically tenuous human encroachment that loses all its stability in reality as soon as one stands on a suburban street, looks down that street and sees it diminish weakly into the immense plain. The very presence of man and his feeble constructions seems fantastic. Borges has recourse to English idealist philosophy in order to dramatize this point: in *Amanecer* (*Fervor de Buenos Aires*) he wonders at the danger the very city's existence undergoes just before dawn, when nearly everyone is asleep, given that things only exist in the eye of the perceiver, that *esse est percipi*. You have to keep looking at Buenos Aires in order that it may not disappear!

Borges is rightly more highly regarded for his short stories than for his poems, and the best of these can be found in two books, *Ficciones* (1944) and *El Aleph* (1949).[1] Usually the stories function as metaphysical fables: Borges indeed shares the belief of the Vienna school that metaphysics is a branch of the literature of fantasy. Philosophical ideas – the more extravagant and conjectural the better – are paraded in order finally to be set at the mercy of reality. But that reality itself is presented so equivocally that it is ultimately impossible to discern where the author stands, or to decide where we stand. His stories are often presented as labyrinths – intellectual labyrinths in which questions are asked that point in innumerable, self-contradicting directions only to be left unanswered. The attitude of these stories is ultimately one of utmost scepticism: nothing can be asserted or believed where nothing is ultimately knowable. But it is also one of anguish, because assertion and belief are precisely what man yearns for.

According to the prologue of a more recent book, *El informe de Brodie* (1970), its stories are 'realistic' in the manner of the early Kipling, thus marking a new departure for Borges. This prologue, however, is one more example of Borges confusing his readers: 'el cuento

[1] The 1952 edition of *El Aleph* contains four new stories.

más fantástico del libro', as one Argentinian reviewer put it. The stories are indeed realistic in appearance, but all of them have a fantastic or metaphysical undercurrent. This is partly due to oblique allusions to his previous work in them, which invite the reader to bring to bear his memories of *Ficciones* and *El Aleph* on the new stories in order to furnish his interpretation of them with a wider dimension. Borges, who incidentally has always been notable for his interest in aesthetics and whose work is on one level a meditation on the whole Western literary tradition, has always emphasized the extent to which our reading of a book depends on what books we have read before it. Thus in the story *Pierre Menard, autor del Quijote* (in *Ficciones*) he illustrates the fact that Cervantes's novel is not the same book for a reader of Nietzsche that it is for a reader of *Amadís de Gaula*. Similarly, *El informe de Brodie* cannot be unaffected by a previous reading of Borges's earlier work, as a result of which its 'realism' will turn out to be something other than what it appeared to be.

Borges's most successful follower in Argentina has been Julio Cortázar, a writer of excellent short stories – collected in such books as *Bestiario* (1951), *Final de juego* (1956), *Las armas secretas* (1959), *Todos los fuegos el fuego* (1967) and *Octaedro* (1973) – in which reality slips into fantasy and which deploy a burlesque metaphysical humour to great effect. His best qualities as a humorist and as a writer of fantasy are evident too in his novels, *Los premios* (1960), *Rayuela* (1963), *62, modelo para armar* (1969) and *El libro de Manuel* (1973). *Rayuela* is interesting technically because it compresses the effects of Proustian perspectivism into the structure of a single volume. In Proust's *A la recherche du temps perdu* different viewpoints on a given character are offered in different volumes of the book. Cortázar's innovatory device is to recommend two (or more) readings of his novel, each time the chapters being read in a different sequence. Our attitude to characters and situations is thus altered according to the order in which we learn of them. In the second (or subsequent) readings we can also draw on fresh chapters at the end of the book that had been kept from us on first reading, and these fresh chapters again throw enough new light on the characters to make us revise our opinions about them.

XX The Search for Language [1]

An important aspect of contemporary Spanish American fiction has been its deep commitment to discover a live, authentic language, unlike the language used by the 'regionalists' of the 1920s and 1930s. They aim therefore to ensure that language no longer decorously covers up for reality but rather that it savagely unmasks it. There are some novelists who have been so conscious of the need for the novel to investigate and renew the habits of Spanish that language has been the fundamental concern of their work. Thus the Cuban novelist Guillermo Cabrera Infante (1929–) has written a novel, *Tres tristes tigres* (1967), in which language is so important that a whole section of the book is given over to parody: seven Cuban writers take up their pen to describe the assassination of Trotsky.

Cabrera Infante achieves through language what Vargas Llosa achieves through structure – the labyrinthine multiplicity that Vargas Llosa is able to express through structural juxtaposition is expressed by Cabrera Infante through a meticulous examination of words. Thus he finds that no word is a stable entity: all words point in innumerable different directions, a fact that is dramatized by the obsessive use of pun, anagram and palindrome in his novel, and by the disturbing jokes his typewriter occasionally makes when it reveals that the transposition of just two letters can turn a word into its opposite, *casualidad* becoming *causalidad*, *alienado* becoming *alineado*. There is one inventive character in the novel, Bustrófedon, who we are told is capable of making a whole dictionary out of a single word. Thus Bach for him becomes Bachata, Bachanal, Bachillerato, Bacharat, Bacaciones and so on.

Tres tristes tigres incidentally relieves the solemnity of a great deal of Spanish American fiction by being one of the funniest novels ever written in Spanish, deploying a humour that is obstinately, defiantly absurd. Thus the character Rine, a famous inventor in Havana among whose most notable discoveries are rubber streets for cars with asphalt tyres, and a candle that no wind will blow out. Why? 'Cada vela lleva un letrero impreso en tinta roja que dice "No encender" .'

Another writer for whom language is paramount is the young Argentinian novelist Manuel Puig (1932–). In two of his novels, *La traición de Rita Hayworth* (1968) and *Boquitas pintadas* (1969), he explores an area that has not been hitherto approached in the Spanish

[1] For a general discussion of the contemporary situation of the Spanish language in America from a linguistic historian's point of view, see Chapter 1, section IX.

American novel: the genteel lower middle classes of provincial towns in Argentina. In *Boquitas pintadas* the delicate aspirations of provincial teenage girls brought up on *radionovelas* and *fotonovelas* are expressed precisely in the language those girls would use, for a great deal of the novel is structured on their love letters, diaries and telephone conversations.

The language of these people is an unconscious parody of popular culture, and Puig maintains an ironic presence of his own in the novel, enabling him thus to investigate that culture's assumptions and implications through its language. A similar investigation into the linguistic habits of popular subcultures is indeed made in *Tres tristes tigres*, and one of the ways that Cabrera Infante is able to achieve the already mentioned multiple vision of his novel is by examining the many different kinds of Spanish spoken in Cuba, where sometimes the island's African strain is the principal distorting element in the language and other times it is the immense impact of the American presence in Cuba before the revolution. Cabrera Infante takes a look at another cultural problem in Spanish America: the low standard of translations of American novels which Cubans are (or were) brought up on, and which, because the novels were so popular, must obviously have had their effect on Cubans' use of language. Thus characters in these translations (which he parodies) say things in impossible Spanish like 'yo objeté', 'como es usual', 'no es nada de mi negocio', and so on.

It must be said that, although many of the concerns of both Cabrera Infante's and Puig's work are local ones, their novels are, unlike those of the 'regionalist' period, interesting far beyond their local context.

Spanish American writing during the past few decades of the century has most certainly come of age, first in poetry and finally in fiction. An important reason for the recent flourishing of the novel has been the spread of university education, which has helped considerably to widen the market for new writing. Gone, moreover, are the days when Spanish American élites read only European novels and despised the home product. *Cien años de soledad*, for instance, had by late 1970 already sold more than half a million copies. This change is important because it means that some writers can now devote themselves solely to writing if they want to and so attain the degree of professionalism necessary to achieve competent standards of expression. Outside the United States there are probably few regions of the world where the novel is at present flourishing as it is in Latin America. But then in Latin America, unlike Europe, there now exist many of the conditions favourable to the writing of a rich, productive fiction: a large, responsive market, a society that is changing rapidly and that is therefore likely to stimulate the writer, and above all perhaps a lack of the sort of distinguished precedents that elsewhere depress the novelist into feeling that everything has been said. Latin America is a region that novelists can feel to be as yet largely unwritten.

Contemporary Spanish American writing has come a long way since Olmedo and Bello. Writers are now sufficiently self-assured to borrow whatever techniques they might feel to be of use to them from Europe and the United States, in the knowledge that technically they have just as much to offer of their own, and that they have so much to say that they need not feel inhibited by the sort of crisis that leads some French writers to devote interminable pages to the description of, say, a tomato. The future potential of Spanish American writing can be measured finally by the fact that a writer like Vargas Llosa was born as recently as 1936, and a whole new generation of talented younger writers has already emerged beneath him.

Bibliography

ALEGRÍA, F. *Las fronteras del realismo: literatura chilena del siglo XX*. Santiago de Chile, 1962.

—— *Historia de la novela hispanoamericana*. Mexico, 1965.

ANDERSON IMBERT, E. *Historia de la literatura latinoamericana*. Mexico, 1961.

ARA, G. *La novela naturalista latinoamericana*. Buenos Aires, 1965.

ARCINIEGAS, G. *El continente de siete colores*. Buenos Aires, 1965.

BENEDETTI, M. *Letras del continente mestizo*. Montevideo, 1967.

—— *Literatura uruguaya siglo XX*. Montevideo, 1963.

—— *Letras de emergencia*. Buenos Aires, 1973.

BLANCO-FOMBONA, R. *El modernismo y los poetas*. Madrid, 1929.

BRUSHWOOD, J. *Mexico in its Novel. A Nation's Search for Identity*. Austin, 1966.

—— *The Spanish American Novel, A Twentieth Century Survey*. Austin, 1975.

CARILLA, E. *La literatura de la independencia hispanoamericana*. Buenos Aires, 1964.

—— *El romanticismo en la América hispánica*. 2nd ed. Madrid, 1967.

CASAL, L. 'Literature and Society'. In *Revolutionary Change in Cuba*. Ed. Mesa-Lago, C. Pittsburg, 1971.

COHEN, J. *En tiempos difíciles, la poesía cubana de la Revolución*. Barcelona, 1970.

CORTÁZAR, A. R. *Poesía gauchesca argentina*. Buenos Aires, 1969.

COULTHARD, G. R. *Race and Colour in Caribbean Literature*. Oxford, 1962.

FAURIE, M.-J. *Le modernisme hispano-américain et ses sources françaises*. Paris, 1966.

FERNÁNDEZ RETAMAR, R. *La poesía contemporánea en Cuba: 1927–53.* Havana, 1954.

FLORES, A., and SILVA CÁCERES, R. *La novela hispanoamericana actual.* New York, 1971.

FRANCO, J. *The Modern Culture of Latin America.* London, 1967.

—— *An Introduction to Spanish American Literature.* London, 1969.

—— *Spanish American Literature since Independence.* A Literary History of Spain, Vol. 7 (ed. JONES, R. O.). London, 1973.

FUENTES, C. *La nueva novela hispanoamericana.* Mexico, 1969.

GALLAGHER, D. *Modern Latin American Literature.* 1973.

GHIANO, J. C. *Constantes de la literatura argentina.* Buenos Aires, 1953.

GIACOMAN, H. edits a series of collections of critical essays on modern Latin American writers using a standard format and title (e.g. *Homenaje a Ernesto Sábato, variaciones interpretativas en torno a su obra.* New York, 1973.) Collections on the following have appeared: Carpentier (1970), Asturias (1971), Fuentes (1971), Cortázar (1972), García Márquez (1972), Vargas Llosa (with Oviedo, J.), (1972), Roa Bastos (1973), Yáñez (1973), Onetti (1974), Rulfo (1974). All are published in New York.

GONZÁLEZ, M. P. *Trayectoria de la novela en México.* Mexico, 1951.

GROSSMAN, R. *Historia y problemas de la literatura latinoamericana.* Madrid, 1972.

GULLÓN, R. *Direcciones del modernismo.* Madrid, 1963.

HARSS, L. *Los nuestros.* Buenos Aires, 1966.

HENRÍQUEZ UREÑA, M. *Breve historia del modernismo.* Mexico, 1954.

HENRÍQUEZ UREÑA, P. *Historia de la cultura en la América hispánica.* Mexico, 1947.

—— *Las corrientes literarias en la América hispánica.* Mexico, 1949.

—— *Ensayos en busca de nuestra expresión.* Buenos Aires, 1952.

JITRIK, N. *Ensayos y estudios de literatura argentina.* Buenos Aires, 1970.

—— *Escritores argentinos, dependencia o libertad.* Buenos Aires, 1967.

—— *El fuego de la especie, ensayos sobre seis escritores argentinos.* Buenos Aires, 1971.

JONES, C. *Three Spanish American Novelists – A European View.* Diamante XVII. London, 1967.

LAFFORGUE, J. (ed.). *Nueva novela latinoamericana.* Buenos Aires, 1969.

LAZO, R. *Historia de la literatura hispanoamericana.* Mexico, 1965.

—— *La novela andina: Pasado y futuro.* Mexico, 1971. (Alcides Arguedas, Vallejo, Alegría, Icaza, José María Arguedas, Vargas Llosa.)

—— *Historia de la literatura cubana.* 2nd ed. Mexico, 1974.

LEONARD, I. A. *Baroque Times in Old Mexico.* Ann Arbor, 1959.

—— *Books of the Brave, Being an Account of Books and of Men in the Spanish Conquest and Settlement of the Sixteenth-Century New World.* Cambridge, Mass., 1949.

LEUMANN, C. A. *La literatura gauchesca y la poesía gaucha.* Buenos Aires, 1953.

LICHTBLAU, M. A. *The Argentine Novel in the Nineteenth Century.* New York, 1959.

MENTON, S. *Prose Fiction of the Cuban Revolution.* Austin, 1975.

MOSES, B. *Spanish Colonial Literature in South America.* London, 1922.

ORGAMBIDE, P., and YAHNI, R. (eds.). *Enciclopedia de la literatura argentina.* Buenos Aires, 1970.

ORTEGA, J. *La contemplación y la fiesta.* Caracas, 1969.

—— *Figuración de la persona.* Barcelona, 1971.

—— *Relato de la Utopía, notas sobre narrativa cubana de la Revolución.* Barcelona, 1973.

PAZ, O. *Cuadrivio.* Mexico, 1965. (Darío, López Velarde, Pessoa, Cernuda.)

PICÓN-SALAS, M. *De la Conquista a la Independencia: Tres siglos de historia cultural hispanoamericana.* 2nd ed. Mexico, 1950.

PRIETO, A. *Estudios de literatura argentina.* Buenos Aires, 1969.

PRING-MILL, R. *Pablo Neruda, A Basic Anthology.* Oxford, 1975. (This has an extensive and authoritative introduction.)

RODRÍGUEZ-ALCALÁ, H. *Narrativa hispanoamericana. Giiiraldes, Carpentier, Roa Bastos, Rulfo.* Madrid, 1973.

RODRÍGUEZ MONEGAL, E. *Narradores de esta América.* Vol. 1, Montevideo, 1969. Vol. 2, Buenos Aires, 1974.

—— *El arte de narrar.* Caracas, 1968.

—— *Literatura uruguaya del medio siglo.* Montevideo, 1966.

—— *El boom de la novela hispanoamericana.* Caracas, 1972.

RQJAS, A. F. *La novela ecuatoriana.* Mexico, 1948.

RUTHERFORD, J. *Mexican Society during the Revolution: A Literary Approach.* Oxford, 1971.

SAMANIEGO, A. *Poesía peruana contemporánea.* Lima, 1968.

SÁNCHEZ, L. A. *Proceso y contenido de la novela hispano-americana.* Madrid, 1953.

SCHILLING, H. *Teatro profano en la Nueva España.* Mexico, 1958.

SCHULMAN, I. A. *Génesis del modernismo, Martí, Nájera, Silva, Casal.* Mexico, 1966.

SOLÓRZANO, C. *El teatro latinoamericano en el siglo XX.* Mexico, 1964.

SUÁREZ-MURIAS, M. C. *La novela romántica en Hispanoamérica.* New York, 1963.

TORRES-RÍOSECO, A. *La gran literatura iberoamericana.* Buenos Aires, 1945.

—— *Grandes novelistas de la América hispana.* 2nd ed. 1949.

VIDELA, G. *El ultraísmo. Estudios sobre movimentos poéticos de vanguardia en España.* Madrid, 1963.

VIÑAS, D. *Literatura argentina y realidad política. De Sarmiento a Cortázar.* Buenos Aires, 1971.

—— *Literatura argentina y realidad política.* Buenos Aires, 1964.

VITIER, C. *Lo cubano en la poesía.* Havana, 1970.

XIRAU, R. *Poetas de Mexico y España.* Madrid, 1962.

YURKIEVITCH, S. *Fundadores de la nueva poesía latinoamericana.* Barcelona, 1971. (Vallejo, Huidobro, Borges, Girondo, Neruda, Paz.)

ZEA, L. *El pensamiento latinoamericano.* 2 vols. Mexico, 1965.

ZUM FELDE, A. *El problema de la cultura americana.* Buenos Aires, 1945.

11 The Visual Arts in Spain

O. N. V. GLENDINNING

I The Beginnings

The painting, architecture and sculpture of Spain cannot easily be separated from the art traditions of other European lands. The idea that Spanish artists were always somehow especially independent of other traditions (and more particularly addicted to realism than these) was a commonplace in art history at one time, but it does not, nowadays, seem to be a tenable generalization about the visual arts any more than it is about Spanish literature, regarding which similar opinions long held sway. Styles of visual art travel from one province to another, or from one country to another, with the speed of merchants and the inevitability of invading armies. Because art speaks a more universal language than literature it passes most frontiers with even less difficulty.

Although little now remains of the earliest primitive art in Spain, the cave paintings at Altamira near Santillana del Mar (prov. of Santander) and those in Asturias, at Candamo and other sites, suggest that religious belief and ritual first guided art in the Iberian Peninsula as elsewhere in Europe. The artist helped his community to hunt by sympathetic magic; deer and other animals are often depicted with wounds in their sides or spears in vital organs. Subsequent contacts with other Mediterranean societies and different cultures encouraged decorative as well as socio-religious developments in art in Spain.

II Invasions and Cultural Contacts

The Greek and Phoenician invaders who occupied some coastal areas, the Romans, the Visigoths and later the Moors, all successively left artistic as well as institutional, ideological and linguistic marks in the Peninsula. The Romans' boldly patterned pavements and wall-paintings, the great theatres at Mérida and Tarragona, the aqueduct at Segovia, and bridges such as those at Salamanca and Alcántara, offered obvious lessons to their successors about scale and the beauty of organized form. The Romans' ability to create the illusion of three dimensions on a plane surface and their fascination with geometrical patterns are well reflected in pavements at Ampurias and at Itálica (near Seville).

The rich layers of civilized living which survive at Ampurias (prov. of Gerona) from long periods of Greek and Roman occupation and trading-port activity contrast with the bleak stone walls and cisterns of the Iberian and Greek settlements at Ullastret (also in the prov. of Gerona), on a hill once surrounded by water not many miles inland.

Visigothic architecture and design in Spain added Byzantine and Germanic touches to basically Roman forms and conventions. On the one hand, carved decoration with flowers and rope patterns as well as religious scenes now appeared on the pilasters and capitals of churches and palaces (the latter have sometimes been converted into the former, like Ramírez's palace at Naranco now the church of Santa María); on the other, Roman traditions are sometimes preserved in Visigothic work. A Roman cameo is embedded in the centre of a Visigothic cross in the treasury at Oviedo cathedral, and the mural decorations which originally covered every inch of the interior of San Julián de los Prados in the same city (built between 812 and 842) revived Roman designs used in mosaics at Andallón and fourth-century frescoes from Santa Eulalia de Bóveda.

Moorish decoration, which evolved as a result of the Muslim ban on representational images, led to a delight in contrasting details and brilliant colours, precise yet delicate, formal yet sensuous: a proper background for the ritual of baths as well as that of religion. Just as Visigothic art passed on Roman traditions, Moorish art in Spain sometimes borrowed from the Visigoths. Thus, in the former great mosque at Córdoba (begun by 'Abd ar-Rahmān I in 785) a maze of horseshoe arches and polychrome patterns spring from marble columns with Visigothic stone capitals, carved with a simplified leaf pattern deriving ultimately from the Corinthian order. The Moors also brought into Spain decorative elements picked up in countries they had conquered earlier. The pairs of birds set beak to beak in mirror images, which are the main motif on the Hispano-Mauresque 'Witches' textile (twelfth century, Museo Arqueológico, Vich), derive ultimately from the mythical animals which face one another on either side of the tree of life in Mesopotamian patterns. In due course Moorish work in Spain influenced architecture outside the Peninsula. The mosques of the Almoravids and Almohads at Algiers (1096) and at Tlemcen (1136) were based on the Córdoban model; that at Marrakesh had a minaret inspired by the twelfth-century Almohad Giralda at Seville. Eventually much Moorish art in Spain was subsumed into or associated with later Spanish work. The great mosque at Córdoba like some other Moorish mosques became Christian churches; the Alhambra at Granada had a Renaissance palace for Spanish kings built into its complex. While the Moors still held the south, *mudéjar* work for Christian patrons continued the Moorish style in areas from which they had withdrawn. Alfonso XI's palace at Tordesillas (prov. of Valladolid, *c.* 1340) has a patio with various kinds of Moorish arch in it, and in 1354 a Moorish architect called Mahomet de Bellico worked on the Chapel of the Trinity for the Royal Monastery at Sigena. Later, in 1402, a Moor from Borja called Mahomet carved the woodwork of the choir stalls in Huesca cathedral; even after the fall of Granada and well into the sixteenth century, Moorish–Christian styles of coffered ceiling decoration (*artesonado*) continued to be in demand for public buildings such as the universities of Alcalá and Salamanca and private palaces. Plaster or carved friezes, decorative tiles, ivory inlaid coffers bearing Moorish patterns were common in sixteenth-century houses in Toledo, Seville and other centres, and so continued to be part of the Spanish scene. At Saragossa, the construction of a public timepiece for the city – the Torre Nueva (a leaning tower when it was demolished at the end of the nineteenth century) – was contracted to Gabriel Gombao in 1504, and we know he employed one Christian, two Moors and a Jew to produce work that reveals some obvious *mudéjar* details. The artistic symbiosis of Christian and Moorish traditions is particularly strong in the *mudéjar* churches of the old kingdom of Aragon, which contained the greatest proportion of *mudéjar* (later Morisco) peasants and artisans in all Spain (before the conquest of the kingdom of Granada).

III Medieval Christian Art

Artists in Spain under the Visigothic or Moorish regimes or the various Hispanic Christian monarchies worked not only for God but also for the greater glory of the princes and prelates they served. Their art was intended to commemorate the wealth and power of the owner, as well as the ability or vision of the artist. Gold letters spelling out the name of the Visigothic king Reccesvinthus hang down from the seventh-century crown made for their monarch with jewels below them. The letters at the bottom of an eleventh-century carved ivory crucifix formerly at San Isidoro at León which read 'Ferdinandus Rex Sancia Regina' (i.e. 'Ferdinand I and his wife, Doña Sancha') are only marginally smaller than the words 'IHS Nazarenus Rex Iudeorum' ('Jesus of Nazareth, King of the Jews') above the head of Christ himself. The wooden casket with golden hasps and ivory decorations to hold the body of San Millán, which Sancho the Great is supposed to have commissioned from a sculptor called Aparicio in the early eleventh century, and which was embellished with carvings of princes, monks and other dignitaries, as well as with scenes from the life of the saint, may have been designed to encourage the idea of tribute to San Millán, in much the same way as was Gonzalo de Berceo's poem about the life of the same saint (see Chapter 7, p. 207).

Much art in churches or monasteries, however, fulfilled the fourth-century instruction of Pope Gregory the Great that images should be used to teach the Gospel to the illiterate masses. The great carved entrance for the Benedictine convent at Ripoll (prov. of Gerona), attributed to Gilabertus of Toulouse, which dates from the twelfth century; the statues and bas-reliefs on the porches of the cathedral at Santiago de Compostela, which were the work of Maestro Esteban and Maestro Mateo – probably neither of them Spaniards – at the same period, are full of doctrine as well as of decorative effects and show. On the Pórtico de la Gloria at Santiago there is a typically symbolic arrangement of figures. The Saviour is in the centre, and the evangelists with their beasts, the apostles, patriarchs and other saints stand around. Purgatory and hell are at either side, and angels with harps and dulcimers line the arch to represent heaven. Some of the carved patterns are as meaningful as the figures, and the vine scroll which runs along the top of the capitals conveys the message that Christ is the true Vine. As Émile Mâle has said, the 'artistic representation of sacred subjects [in the Middle Ages] was a science governed by fixed laws which could not be broken at the dictates of individual imagination.' What was represented was more important than the style of the artist himself.

If sculptures could be decorative sermons in stone, other works of art – paintings, tapestries and stained glass – had a similar function in churches. The tapestry of the Creation in the cathedral at Gerona (twelfth century) is a case in point. Around the figure of God at the centre of the tapestry runs the story of the Creation, with explanatory quotations in Latin from Genesis. Scenes representing the seasons of the year, the days and various human activities make up the square frame in which the circle of pictures of the Creation story is set. So the main point of the Creation story is its relevance to the life of man. Significantly the figure at the centre is Christ as well as God the Father. The quotation from Genesis, 'And God said let there be light and there was light', refers to Christ and the New Testament, not merely to the light of sun, moon and stars.

In the course of the twelfth century many areas which had been under Moorish domination were reconquered. The cathedrals at Salamanca, León and Pamplona were newly built at this period. The Segovian Romanesque churches and the old cathedral at Segovia (destroyed in the early sixteenth century) followed the nomination of Pierre d'Agen as bishop (1120) after the Reconquest, the cathedral being built between 1136 and 1144.

Appointments of foreign bishops like Pierre d'Agen and the influence of foreign-based monastic orders with their international organization and attitudes, as well as other political and economic contacts, helped to encourage the dissemination of international styles of art and architecture in Spain. The Romanesque is one such international style; for example the decoration found in the Catalan churches of the eleventh, twelfth and thirteenth centuries is very much in line with that elsewhere in Europe. The practice of filling the apses of basilicas with frescoes or mosaics spread with Greek and Byzantine artists into Italy (a major work is the cathedral of Monreale in Sicily, A.D. 1190) and thence elsewhere, and the arrangement of subjects varies very little from one place to the next. A common pattern in Catalonia places the Pantocrator – a representation of God but usually in the figure of the second person of the Trinity – in the semi-dome with the symbols of the evangelists or angels around him, and below him the Virgin and Child with the Magi and a frieze of figures of saints or sacred narrative, sometimes on two levels and sometimes on one only.

Catalan churches were also enriched by religious paintings on panels to serve as altar frontals. These often have Christ in a central position flanked by two tiers of apostles, and the decoration of the tympanum above doorways in cathedrals or monasteries frequently repeats similar patterns. The effects which some artists and sculptors of the period obtained in groups of figures is particularly noteworthy: the strongly patterned rows and piles of faces (there were no rules of perspective at the period) carved in the door of the chapter house in Pamplona

Cathedral (fourteenth century); the group of apostles in a panel in the cloisters of Santo Domingo de Silos (late eleventh century); and the extraordinary groups of mourners whose wavy hair contrasts with the straight stripes of their garments in panels from the tomb (c. 1300) of Don Sancho Saiz de Carrillo (now in the Museo de Arte Antigua, Barcelona).

Technical advances also spread from one country to another. The development from tunnel vaulting, in which enormous weights of stone were carried by side walls of great thickness, or by massive columns, to a system of roofing which used solid ribs to span the vault between columns and employed lighter materials to fill the spaces between, spread in this way from Durham in England (1093–1128). Subsequently the development of more slender columns with pointed ribs and higher vaults travelled across Europe between the twelfth and the fifteenth centuries.

The Cistercian Order played a particularly important role in transmitting this new 'Gothic' style of architecture. The nave of the Spanish Cistercian abbey church at Fitero (after 1200) repeats that at Pontigny in Normandy (c. 1150). And there were some Cistercians among the architects from Anjou as well as Burgundy who had brought elements of the Gothic style into Spain earlier. Angevin inspiration is found in high-domed lantern towers whose supporting ribs are decorated on the outside and have turrets at the corners: the prototype in Spain is the Tower of the Cock (Torre del Gallo) on the old cathedral at Salamanca and the stumpier versions of the same design at Zamora and Toro. Burgundian influence is found at late twelfth-century Ávila, whose architect Maestro Freuchal took Saint-Denis, Vézelay, Sens and Saint-Germain-des-Prés in Paris as his models.

Later Gothic buildings in Spain also provide variations on French themes. The five aisles rising in steps from side to central nave of Toledo Cathedral (begun 1221) and Burgos (1222) derive ultimately from Bourges, and were later applied to the new cathedral at Salamanca; the ground plan, radiating chapels and elevation of León (c. 1255) were inspired by Rheims and Amiens; and the chapels which ring the nave at Palma de Mallorca (late thirteenth century), Barcelona (begun 1298), Gerona (1312) and Castellón de Ampurias (fifteenth century) followed the single-nave example of Albi (1282). Despite this French influence, however, the proportions of the Catalan and Mallorcan cathedrals ultimately put them in a class of their own because the height of their side aisles is much greater than that of their French Gothic models. There is a sense of space across the building, as well as in length and height, which gives them a special character; the span (in excess of seventy-five feet) across the nave at Gerona is thought to be the widest vault constructed by Gothic builders anywhere in Europe. Varied fenestration also gives these cathedrals individuality. In Gerona the high windows keep the main body of the cathedral consistently in mysterious and religious gloom, through which the powerful columns stride. At Palma, on the other hand, the slender columns rise through an area bathed in light from large ogive windows on two storeys.

Building in the Gothic style was not, however, the prerogative of the Church, and the style is not really of necessity the embodiment of the lofty spiritual aspirations that August Wilhelm Schlegel and the Romantics postulated to account for it. It produced roofing and windows with a new delicacy of decoration in stone; previously decoration had only been possible by painting on the stonework or carving the solid surfaces of capitals. Aristocrats and kings used the style for castles and palaces and public buildings, as well as for the ecclesiastical constructions they patronized, so that it was not thought of as having uniquely religious functions. We find it in windows of the Hospital de los Caballeros at Cáceres (founded in 1486), in those of the Casa de las Conchas at Salamanca (1483), the porch and façade of the Benavente family's palace at Baeza (now a seminary) as well as in the Lonjas (mercantile exchanges) of Palma and Valencia, and even in occasional farmhouse windows in Catalonia, where the overall design of the building has nothing remotely Gothic about it.

Great numbers of European pilgrims to Santiago de Compostela, as well as architectural styles, travelled from France into Spain during all this period. The influence of the famous pilgrim route on literature and language is well known and its influence is to be seen in buildings on the route. This is the case in the cathedrals at Burgos and León (c. 1255). The whole character of the towns that developed along the road was sometimes determined by the pilgrim traffic. While the route was still threatened by the Moors, the towns had to be fortified or sited on easily defensible escarpments. Viana, in Navarre, was fortified in 1219; Puente la Reina, also in Navarre (founded in 1090), whose bridge was intended to facilitate the passage of pilgrims, and Santo Domingo de la Calzada, in La Rioja, are also walled. Churches on the route sometimes are manifestly much larger than normal local congregations required.

The king, the aristocracy and the Church continued to dictate the development of the arts and architecture in this medieval society. Nobles commissioned works which at the same time reflected their high status, demonstrated their piety and exalted the Church. One of the ways in which this was done was by incorporating a portrait of the noble donor in religious paintings. This custom, incidentally, lasted well into the seventeenth century. Valdés Leal painted an *Immaculate Conception with two donors* in 1661 (National Gallery, London), and, earlier in the same century, Quevedo found a place in hell in his *Sueños* for those who ostentatiously gave retables to churches in the hope of gaining forgiveness of sins in part-exchange. A fine example of a fourteenth-century commission of this kind carried out in the French Gothic manner in Spain is a large anonymous panel painting dated 1396 for the sepulchral chapel of the López de Ayala family at the Dominican convent of San Juan in Quejana (prov. of Álava), now in the Art Institute, Chicago. The practice of frescoing churches had already been replaced by the use of painted or sculptured retables, and these progressively increased in size and number of compartments during the fourteenth and fifteenth centuries. The statesman, poet and historian Pero López de Ayala commissioned the work – his father had founded the convent in 1374 – and the retable is of a size appropriate to the importance of the family, measuring twenty-two feet long by eight feet high. On the left, St Blaise blesses Pero López and his eldest son; on the right, St Thomas Aquinas (in his Dominican habit) blesses the donor's wife, Doña Leonor de Guzmán, and her daughter-in-law. In the central crucifixion panel Pero López and his sister Marí Ramírez are depicted kneeling at the foot of the cross; while at the sides there is also a nativity and a resurrection, with medieval knights and lances under the Gothic tomb out of which Christ resurrects. By comparison with panels of an earlier period the donor and his family are much more prominent here; they had played no part in the more didactic decoration of Romanesque churches. In this case the names of the Ayala family in the painting rise out of their mouths in gothic script.

The painting by Jorge Inglés ('George, the Englishman') of the retable in the chapel of the Hospital at Buitrago (founded by Íñigo López de Mendoza, Marquis of Santillana, poet and man of letters, and commissioned by him in June 1455) continues the same tradition with an only slightly smaller than life-size portrait of the marquis kneeling on one side, and of his wife on the other. The twelve angels painted on the second storey bear the donor's imprint, since they carry manuscripts in their hands of the twelve religious poems, the *Gozos de Santa María* written by Santillana.[1]

Portraits, however, were not the only way in which donors could make their presence and importance felt. Sometimes heraldic devices proclaim the status of the donor as graphically and as prominently as a portrait would. At the top of the Tree of Jesse retable in the chapel of Santa Ana in Burgos Cathedral, at the foot of the cross and in four other places, we find Bishop Luis de Acuña's arms. His portrait as donor also appears, and he spelt out his generosity to the cathedral authorities in no uncertain terms, speaking of 'the decorous and ennobling act which he had performed for the church in making his chapel of the Conception of Our Lady so large and beautiful, with such a rich retable on which he had spent more than a million and a half *maravedís*'.

Guilds, the military orders and the municipalities (*concejos*), who made increasingly important demands for works of art in the fifteenth century, were no less ostentatious in drawing their patronage to the attention of the worshipper. In Luis Dalmau's *Retable of the Councillors* (1445, Museo de Arte Antigua, Barcelona) – painted for the chapel of the municipal council in the Catalan capital – Christ is a dark figure carrying his cross behind the bright, red kneeling figures of the individual members of the council. The walls and turrets of medieval Barcelona rise proudly in the background, viewed through a window with the sea and mountains beyond.

Naturally the richness of clothes and jewels also reflects material power in many paintings of donors, especially since the sumptuary laws decreed that only nobles could wear the more luxurious materials. Brilliance of clothing at the period finds a place in courtly poetry, too; the *Arte de trovar* of Enrique de Villena (1384–1434), describing a poetic competition at the court of Ferdinand I of Aragon in Barcelona, particularly notes the richness of tapestries on the floor, cloth of gold on a platform, the brilliantly coloured, illuminated manuscripts and the jewel as prize.

In terms of art we also find these riches in the clothes of donors Jaime Huguet painted in 1442 for a triptych of St George, or translated into painting by Bartolomé Bermejo (*fl.* 1474–94) in his *St Michael* (in Sir Harold Wernher's collection at Luton Hoo). This painting has a rich gold background with leaf patterns and borders in red worked

[1] For Santillana's literary work, see Chapter 5, Section IX.

in it. The saint stands on a golden dragon in gold and jewelled armour – rubies and pearls – and wields a sword with his right arm. The serene face of the archangel is brilliantly lit, and a rich cloak of cloth of gold with a crimson lining to set off the armour unfolds behind him. His left leg and raised right arm form a central pivot around which his body curves, about to strike. The wings make a tilted ogive arch to the right, and the cloak makes a balancing pattern to the left, while on the ground below the dragon's tail curves to complete the elliptical design. Dominated by the whole construction, and yet obviously upsetting it, is the donor in the left-hand corner. His face looks upwards towards one leg of the saint and his hat runs parallel to the flying folds of the cloak above him. Bermejo, to judge from the composition, only worked him into the picture because he had to. The gold haft and bottom of the scabbard, the illuminated book of hours in his hand, the gold chain round the neck and patterned damask coat all denote the donor's wealth.

IV Foreign Influences during the Later Gothic Period

In the fourteenth and fifteenth centuries, painters and artistic styles travelled between countries as readily as did architectural theory and practice. The Archpriest of Hita's story (c. 1342) about Pitas Payas, who painted a lamb on his young wife's lower abdomen before going off to work in Flanders, and returned to find it had grown into a ram as the result of an inartistic lover's ministrations, is a delightful fancy which may itself have come from France rather than Spain. But the reality of the itinerant artist's travel in search of commissions reflected in the story was certainly as much a part of Spanish experience as that of other European countries.

On the eastern coastline of Spain artistic contacts with Italy grew naturally out of the Mediterranean trade in which the ports of Catalonia and Valencia participated; there is an evident awareness of the Sienese fresco painters' style and perhaps of Giotto in, for example, the work of Ferrer Bassa, notably in his murals for the convent of Pedralbes commissioned by Peter IV of Aragon, for which he began negotiations with the abbess in 1343. But Bassa's murals also show the difficulty this painter had in following his Italian models.

Italianate style is also a significant element in the three brothers Serra – Jacme, Pere and Joan – of Barcelona, the eldest of whom was mentioned in a will as the painter of a retable for a tomb in Saragossa as early as 1361. In Jacme Serra's work there are attempts at perspective – an Italian development – and Pere Serra's pupil, Luis Borrassá, shows an even clearer mastery of three-dimensional space in works like his altarpiece for the convent of Santa Clara at Vich.

The fifteenth century also saw the arrival in Spain of a number of artists from other countries, mostly from northern Europe, lured no doubt by the possibility of fat commissions. A French silversmith, called 'Rodrigo Fernai' in Spanish documents, made a silver cross for the parish church of St Tirso in Oviedo in 1406; a fine French sculptor, 'Johan Lome' of Tournai, began work on his masterpiece, the tomb of Charles the Noble of Navarre in Pamplona Cathedral, in 1416; a Florentine painter and sculptor named Dello di Niccola lived much of his life at the court of John II of Castile, where he died in 1421. More particularly a number of Flemish and German artists also came to settle and work in Spain in the fifteenth century. In Toledo, sculpture on the cathedral façade was begun by two Spaniards called Alfonso and Alvar Rodríguez, and continued by the Flemish sculptor 'Egas' shortly after 1466; one of his companions, who worked on the façade of lions, was John of Brussels, or Juan Guas. Guas was also a master-builder and responsible for work behind the high altar in the cathedral. He was engaged to supervise building at Toledo Cathedral between 1477 and 1488; designed the church of San Juan de los Reyes in Toledo (1479–80), the Infantado palace at Guadalajara (1480–3), and the chapel of San Gregorio at Valladolid (1488). Just over half a century after Guas's time, the windows of Toledo Cathedral were being painted by two Germans, known as Pablo and Cristóbal.

During the reign of the Catholic Kings, the unification of Spain, the defeat of the Moors and expectations of peace encouraged a great programme of public building with attendant commissions for artists both foreign and Spanish. In thanksgiving for the victory of Toro in 1476 against the Portuguese invaders and Castilian rebels, the Monarchs founded the church and monastery of San Juan de los Reyes at Toledo, Santo Tomás at Ávila, San Jerónimo at Madrid, and Santa Cruz at Segovia; and for Santo Tomás commissioned a series of paintings for two retables, ten of which, by Pedro Berruguete (c. 1450–1504), survive in the Prado Museum today. Although Berruguete follows earlier practice in using gold for some of the backgrounds of his scenes, and such traditional devices as Latin words coming out of the mouths of Christ on a crucifix and the kneeling figure of St Peter Martyr, he also shows that he had learnt, from a period in Italy around 1477, much about the use of perspective, notably in views through arches and the patterns of tiled floors, and the sense of space and play of light and shadow.

For Toro itself Queen Isabella commissioned a large retable, many of whose panels were the work of a Flemish sculptor, Juan de Flandes (*fl.* 1496–1518). In the south, work on Seville Cathedral, which developed particularly at the end of the fifteenth century, was also put in the hands of foreign artists. Arnault of Flanders (Arnao de Flandes) was employed on the windows there from 1504 to his death in 1557, at an initial basic salary of 5,000 *maravedís* (just over thirteen ducats), with an additional three *reales* (later four) for every foot of glass he completed. Decades later in the same cathedral, a Netherlander, Cornielis, was carving woodwork as late as 1584, having been previously employed from 1536 on the choir at Ávila, where he was paid eighteen ducats (6,750 *maravedís*) for each pair of stalls completed.[1] Work at Toledo Cathedral was carried on by the Dutch sculptor Diego Copin (de Holanda): first on the retable in 1500, and then from 1507 on the figures of kings and urns and other decorations for the chapel of the old kings.

These and other artists from the Low Countries and Germany brought a new and meticulous exactitude of realistic detail to Spain, to be seen to its finest advantage perhaps in the work of Gil de Siloé (*fl.* 1442–95) – a Fleming or German – and his school of sculpture. They also brought a new refinement and delicacy in decorative elements, which some later artists like Velázquez's father-in-law, Pacheco, found lifeless and 'dry'.

Particularly important is Gil's work in the Burgos area, especially in the Cartuja de Miraflores, in which Queen Isabella wanted to erect monumental tombs for her parents and her brother, the Infante Don Alonso. The Charterhouse itself had been founded in 1442 by John II, who had also chosen it as his burial place. A German architect, 'Juan de Colonia' (Hans of Cologne), who arrived in Burgos in 1442, drew the plans and work began in 1454. The tombs were designed in 1486 and executed between 1489 and 1493 in front of the high altar. Their base is an eight-pointed star fifteen and a half feet long, twelve feet wide and six feet high – a motif probably derived from the carved wooden *mudéjar* doors at the convent of Las Huelgas near Burgos. The delicacy of Moorish decoration in fact harmonizes remarkably well

[1] The ducat, a unit of account only after 1537, was tariffed at 375 *maravedís*; the *real* was worth 34 *maravedís*.

with the Gothic patterns which Gil weaves against this background. The carving of the canopies above the heads of the recumbent effigies and of the lace-work and jewellery worn by the two figures is of extraordinary finesse. Yet a sense of overall design is not sacrificed to the execution of detail. The four evangelists sit at the principal points of the star pattern, and their strong poses and the bold patterns of their garments impose natural yet dynamic rhythms on the whole. The same is true of the tomb of the Infante Don Alonso, whose kneeling figure is framed under a basket-handle arch by a fretwork border in a traditional medieval pattern of curling vine shoots and leaves, decorated with balancing cherubs and all kinds of animals.

In a similar way, Gil de Siloé and Diego de la Cruz, who worked together on the retable for the high altar at the Cartuja (1496–9), imposed a rhythm of medallions on the whole, however disparate the patterns of the various scenes within the medallions themselves might appear.

Naturally, famous artists travelled within the Peninsula. The Dutch based in Burgos, for instance, earned some commissions in Valladolid, as a result of the patronage of the Bishop of Palencia between 1486 and 1499, Fray Alonso de Burgos; the latter was also responsible for inviting the German, Simón de Colonia, to construct the superb façade for San Pablo at Valladolid, and for commissioning Gil de Siloé (with Diego de la Cruz) to make the retable for his chapel in the college of San Gregorio, in the same city, founded c. 1488.

V Co-Existence: the Italianate and the Plateresque

Side by side with these façades, patterned with Gothic designs – basket-handle arches and decorative ogees – another Valladolid building developed in a very different manner at the same period: away from detail and towards a sharper sense of the harmony of the whole. This was the Colegio de Santa Cruz, one of whose architects was a Spaniard. Lorenzo Vázquez (fl. 1490–1509), the man responsible for the main façade of the building, was one of the first Spanish importers of Italian Renaissance styles. Like many of the other artists and architects in Spain in the sixteenth century, who rather tardily took up Italian fashions – much as did Garcilaso in Spanish poetry – he almost certainly spent some time in Italy and may well have studied at Bologna. The ground floor of Santa Cruz was begun

in 1486 in the Gothic style, with flamboyant decoration in the stonework of pilasters and in the screens of the galleries in the courtyard;
but Vázquez transformed the design of the upper portions of the
façade in 1491, and simple classical pilasters decorate the surface of
the main supports on either side of the doorway at first-floor level.

Vázquez may also have designed the Medinaceli Palace at Cogolludo
(prov. of Guadalajara), which was built at much the same period
(1492–5). There the window arches in the façade are subdivided into
two as was the fashion in the Florentine palaces of the mid-fifteenth
century, which also used rustication and marked the floor divisions
with a decorative rib as does the Medinaceli Palace. The portal itself
is in Renaissance style too, although the decoration round the windows
is ogee, and Gothic in fact.

The impact of Italian styles and precedents in architecture can
subsequently be followed in Spain in the cruciform plan of the hospital
at Santiago de Compostela (1501–11) by Enrique Egas, whose heavily
sculptured porch is, however, the work of French artists; in Diego de
Riaño's new façade for the Town Hall at Seville (1527), and in the
rounded arch buttresses of Juan de Álava for San Esteban in Salamanca.
In sculpture, the classical manner is found in the work of Bartolomé
Ordóñez on the choir stalls of Barcelona Cathedral (1517–19) and
Diego de Siloé's for San Benito in Valladolid (1528) and for Granada
Cathedral. Italian sculptors also brought the style with them: Domenico
Alessandro Fancelli in his Monument to Prince Juan for Santo Tomás
at Ávila (1511), and Jacopo Florentino, in his exceptionally graceful
and balanced composition for the *Entombment of Christ* in the palace at
Granada. On occasion Italians and Spaniards collaborated on a work
in the Renaissance manner, as was the case in the choir stalls for El
Pilar in Saragossa, which were the work of Esteban de Obray from
Navarre, Nicolás Lobato from Saragossa itself, and the Florentine 'Juan
Moreto' (1542–8).

There was no immediate and total adoption of Renaissance styles,
however. Just as Castillejo and other poets continued to write in
established Spanish verse forms rather than Italianate metres and
Petrarchan fashions, so much architecture continued to be unaffected
by the recent importations. Diego de Riaño, for instance, submitted
designs to the chapter of Seville Cathedral in the Gothic, Graeco-
Roman and Plateresque styles, leaving his masters to choose the design
they preferred. Charles V at first disliked Gil de Siloé's Graeco-Roman
plan for Granada Cathedral, because it clashed with the Gothic style

of the chapel for the tombs of the Catholic Kings; and between 1515 and 1522 there was a dispute in Salamanca over the form of columns to support the nave of the new cathedral. Away from the major centres of taste the Gothic style continued to appeal for well over a hundred years. In the little village of La Pera (prov. of Gerona), a fine Gothic bell-tower with long ogive openings was completed in 1699, patterned no doubt on those built in the same area at an earlier period like the one at Figueras.

Plateresque decoration, which often overlaid basic forms with detail, sometimes adapted itself to the line of Renaissance-style buildings in arches or friezes, and sometimes blurred them with elegant but unclassical patterns. The name *plateresco* – which reflects a stylistic similarity to the work of silversmiths – was a term first used in the sixteenth century to describe the Gothic cathedral at León. Nowadays it refers to the detailed ornamentation which is carved on the stone surfaces of many late fifteenth- and sixteenth-century buildings with decorative rather than symbolic intent. It is sometimes thought that the style is particularly Spanish. Yet architects and masons merely applied to stone the kind of decoration which was common throughout Europe for the borders and title-pages of books, and frequently to be found in wood-carving, specially the retables, of the late fifteenth century and the early sixteenth century too.

Decorative friezes and carved pilasters had been a feature of Roman buildings, and similar carved motifs were not unusual in Italy in the late fifteenth and early sixteenth centuries, as in Giovanni da Venona's façade for Santa Maria dei Miracoli at Brescia, for instance. In Spain, Diego de Riaño's façade for the Town Hall at Seville and the Hospital de San Marcos at León follow classical traditions. Sometimes, however, Plateresque decoration becomes more important than the architectural forms it was originally intended to enhance. The decoration over the basket-handle arches of the main entrance to Salamanca University not only fills the main sections of the façade around the heraldic devices, but overspills the framework in which order and logic and the true Renaissance principles of harmony would confine it. Here the Gothic delight in symbolic or ornamental detail seems to persist, just as the poetic forms of earlier times persisted at the same period in the sixteenth century. For these and similar reasons the Flemish style of painting appealed to Spanish individual and collective patrons, who preferred to follow traditional fashions. Charles V employed Antoniis Mor (Moro), and, much later, painters like Alonso Sánchez Coello (d. 1590) and his pupil Pantoja de la Cruz (b. 1551) continued the Flemish style of detailed portraiture to the satisfaction of the royal family, while at the same time learning from portraits by Venetian artists also in the royal collections.

The easy co-existence of Gothic detail and Renaissance harmony of overall design in sixteenth-century Spain perhaps contributed to the success there of some Flemings who had been trained in Italy. A notable case in point is that of Pedro de Campaña (Kempeneer) who lived and worked in Seville in the middle of the century. His *Descent from the Cross* (1547–8) was painted in the Flemish manner for Hernando de Jaén and is in Seville Cathedral, and his *Purification of the Virgin* retable also for the cathedral, which included portraits drawn from life of the donor and his family, was clearly in the manner of Raphael. Later Velázquez's father-in-law in the early seventeenth century was to dislike the former as intensely as he admired the latter.

Uncompromisingly Italianate in conception is the great Diego de Siloé's (*c.* 1495–1563) cathedral at Granada, begun in 1528. Great clusters of columns with Corinthian capitals support the rounded arch structure of the nave, and the overall plan of a square nave and aisles with a vast semicircular apse added to the end for a high altar under a rotunda is magnificent and precise in its proportions. The rotunda itself has triumphal arches as frames for pictures at the first-floor gallery level, echoing perhaps the religious symbolism of the cathedral as a whole – a thanksgiving for the triumph of Christianity over Mohammedanism.

Equally Italianate, despite some Gothic elements, is Rodrigo Gil de Hontañón's façade for the university at Alcalá (1537–53), which is harmoniously composed around overlapping squares, with triangular pediments at the top of the central section and over windows on the ground floor.

VI Italian Renaissance Influences

Charles V and some of his nobles who were aware of the imitations of classical buildings elsewhere in Europe soon helped to establish the Renaissance style in Spain. A high point is certainly the royal palace at Granada. Its architect, Pedro de Machuca, had studied in Italy, and his paintings often had Italian conventions and manners in them. The square ground plan for the palace encloses a huge circular courtyard which has dimensions similar to those of Hadrian's villa at Tivoli. The circular courtyard was itself characteristic of the classical Roman *villa suburbana* as described by Pliny the Younger in his letters. The façades are probably derived from the palaces of Bramante and Raphael; the fenestration, with alternating rounded and triangular pediments, is particularly close to that of the first floor of Raphael's Palazzo Branconio dell'Aquila, enriched with double columns in the centre, and without the variations from one floor to the next which the Italians favoured. The ensemble then was a proper reflection of Charles V's classical status and grandeur: the imperial Caesar of his time, as poets often remarked.

Charles V had earlier supported Italianate styles in art when he first established his court in Valladolid. Already in December 1518 he had made Pedro Berruguete's son Alonso his court painter and sculptor. The latter had been trained and had worked in Italy, earning apparently the approval of Michelangelo, some of whose works he copied. An early important commission for the younger Berruguete was the retable for the Benedictine monastery of San Benito el Real at Valladolid (1526–32), although he was also under contract to execute frescoes with simulated golden mosaic backgrounds 'in the Italian manner' for the Capilla Real at Granada (1521), which were either barely begun or never completed.

The *Flight into Egypt* from the retable for San Benito, now in the Museo Nacional de Escultura at Valladolid, is typical of the energetic rhythms of Alonso Berruguete's painting and sculpture. A date palm curves massively in an almost Roman arch over the Holy Family; the Virgin Mary and Christ-Child are on the donkey's back, with St Joseph close behind. The painting is palpably an illustration of an anecdote about the Flight into Egypt related in the apocryphal Gospel of Pseudo-Matthew, in which the Christ-Child bids a palm tree whose fruit is out of Mary's reach to bend its branches to her. But Berruguete relates the story in a powerfully emotive way. There is a superb gradation of contrasts in parallel lines: peace in every gesture of the Infant Jesus, concern yet acceptance in Mary, and almost tormented consternation in Joseph, emphasized by the backwards tilt of his head and the energetic sweep of his garments.

Berruguete, in fact, sees the biblical story very much in human and dramatic terms. Perhaps he had learnt to omit the cruder traditional symbols of sanctity in Italy, and his use of distorted lines to express feeling follows precedents of classical sculpture and Italian practice. His powerful genius earned him the courtesy title of 'Magnificence' and he seems to have enjoyed a status which was not normal in the Peninsula at the time. His contract for a retable for the Colegio del Arzobispo in Salamanca (later the Colegio de Nobles Irlandeses), allowed him 'unusual latitude in the planning of the structure and the choice of subjects'.

Perhaps in the mid-sixteenth century among Spaniards only Gaspar Becerra (b. 1520) came near to enjoying a similar freedom. Vasari in Italy records some of his work as an apprentice between 1544 and 1546, and he sculptured the retable of Astorga Cathedral shortly after his return to Spain in 1588. Five years later he was given the title of royal painter by Philip II, and his commissions included the high altar for the church of the Descalzas Reales in Madrid, destroyed by fire in the nineteenth century, and frescoes for the Alcazar palace lost in the conflagration of 1734. Although time and men have destroyed a high proportion of Becerra's work, at least his frescoes of the myth of Perseus survive in the south-west tower of the Pardo Palace. Not only is Becerra's superb sense of design apparent in these paintings, but also his ability to appeal to the senses as well as to the intellect. A possible reason for the subject of the series is its appropriateness to a tower ceiling. Danaë was shut up in a tower by her father, and it was there that Jupiter came to her in a shower of gold, engendering in her the hero Perseus. But if common Spanish sixteenth-century interpretations of the Danaë, Perseus and Medusa stories are anything like those given at only a slightly later date by Pérez de Moya in his *Philosophia secreta* (1585), there must have been food for royal thought as well as sensual appetites in these ceiling pictures.

According to Moya, the Danaë story contains lessons about the conquest of wealth and its inherent dangers. Medusa and her sisters were beautiful because of their riches, and to capture them Perseus needed the qualities of a good general: swiftness of action (the flying horse Pegasus), ability to cut off supplies as well as destroy (the sword of Mercury), and discretion (the shield of Minerva). The removal of the Gorgon's head and the ensuing flight of the serpents show the ultimate power of prudence over the deceitful machinations of an enemy. At the same time the legend warns of the dangers of cupidity. The shower of gold (i.e. money) is responsible for the abandonment of virtue by Danaë in the first place.

The general subject therefore is one with an obvious relationship to kingship at a time when Spain's overseas involvement and expansion was in hand. Either, then, the scenes symbolized the desirability of God-inspired victories, or the dangers of cupidity – or the two subjects together.

Possibly artists enjoyed a greater freedom in the execution of mythological paintings than in religious or portrait subjects, although patrons often required a subject to be painted in a particular way. Other court painters working in different fields reflect, however, in a more obvious way, the pressures of patronage upon them. Any artist of real independence of mind had to fight constant battles with his masters in the sixteenth and seventeenth centuries. This was precisely the position of El Greco (c. 1548–1614). Probably attracted to Spain in the first instance by the grandiose plans of Philip II for the Escorial (which drew other artists from Italy, like Bartolomé Carducho and F. Zuccaro), and other known sources of patronage in ecclesiastical dignitaries, he was fairly frequently the victim of financial double dealing and misunderstanding.

VII El Greco

One of El Greco's earliest commissions in Toledo was *The Disrobing of Christ*, for which the contract was made shortly before 2 July 1577 with the cathedral authorities. El Greco appears to have based his treatment of the subject on St Bonaventure's *Meditations on the Passion*, which specifically mentions the presence of the three Marys at the disrobing, all of whom are portrayed in the painting. The clergy objected to their inclusion because their presence was not documented in the Bible, and subsequently tried to pay the artist much less than his representatives thought right (227 ducats instead of 900), alleging that it was as improper to place the heads of the crowd higher than that of Christ as to include the three Marys. Although El Greco originally agreed to modify the picture, he did not finally do so, and accepted 317 ducats in payment.

These petty objections to El Greco's painting show some of the consequences that the patronage system could have for the artist. The subject was no doubt related to the sacristy in which the painting was to be placed: a reminder to the priest as he put on or took off his vestments of the relevance of Christ's life to his calling. Yet El Greco clearly meant to extend the meaning of the painting, by linking Christ's imminent vilification and suffering in connection with the disrobing to his final suffering on the Cross. Furthermore, the Marys, who watch a carpenter making a hole in a piece of the Cross, express a positive compassion and concern, and so counterbalance the crowd of brutal and cruel people at Christ's back anxious to pluck the robe from Him. They add significantly to the exemplary quality of the painting, as well as to its dramatic, spatial and aesthetic organization. Equally the portrayal of the Roman centurion in sixteenth-century Spanish armour helped to make the spectators of the period feel responsible for the suffering of Christ: an involvement of the spectator with the subject of the painting which El Greco developed further in other works.

El Greco was obviously careful in his approach to commissions from Philip II, yet failed to please the monarch too. His *Allegory of the Holy League*, of which there is a small study (for the final version in the Escorial) in the National Gallery, London, is patently the kind of politico-religious painting that the king would have approved. The Doge of Venice, the Pope and Philip II himself kneel in the foreground, while an idealized figure which may be of Don John of Austria holds a sword behind them; above, angels adore the symbol of Christ's name (IHS), and below at the right the jaws of hell yawn. But if this almost medieval representation of the struggle of the forces of good and evil satisfied Philip, El Greco's painting of *The Martyrdom of St Maurice* (1580-2) did not, although the artist was paid 800 ducats for it. Possibly the originality of its colouring and the elongation of the figures (both of which find precedents in Italian art in the sixteenth century) were not to the king's taste; certainly he soon substituted a much duller painting of the same subject by an Italian artist, Romulo Cincinnato, for that of El Greco.

Despite the fact that some patrons found reasons to object to or dislike El Greco's work, the artist was fortunate in finding a number who were prepared to back it, regardless of its departures from the artistic and iconographic conventions to which they were accustomed. The quality of his portrait work was indubitable. Possibly also his obvious interest in and ability to convey spiritual values and problems in a moving way echoed the Counter-Reformation preoccupations of some patrons.

El Greco had already shown great ability as a portrait painter and a capacity to reflect the need for spiritual reform in religious paintings before he left Italy for Spain. His first version of *Christ Driving the Money-Changers out of the Temple* – with its obvious Counter-Reformation lesson for a materialistic Church – dates from 1560-5. Pope Paul IV (1555-9) had already accepted the relevance of the subject by having a scene of the Purification cast on the obverse side of a medal. In a version completed by El Greco a decade later, some contemporary artists, including Titian and Michelangelo, are portrayed in the foreground on the right, adding to its realistic qualities and strengthening the symbolic contrast in the composition between those on the right who watch with concern the process of purification, and those on the left whose contorted and half-naked bodies are the objects of Christ's scourge.

In later *Purifications* executed in Spain the symbolism of details is still further amplified. The Frick Collection's version of the subject (1595–1600) places an overthrown table in the foreground for the first time, which is biblically authentic; yet it also includes two bas-reliefs between the columns at the back which add greatly to the meaning of the painting. These two reliefs are acceptable on a realistic level but are also symbolic. On the left, Adam and Eve are being driven out of the Garden of Eden, and this clearly relates the materialism of the money-changers to the original sin of man. On the right we see the sacrifice of Isaac – an Old Testament parallel for Christ's sacrifice – which both explains the expression of pity rather than wrath on the face of Jesus in the painting, and reminds the observer of man's need for His sacrifice. The approach to the subject here is clearly more austere than in previous versions, and the sensual half-naked women on the left in the *Purifications* of El Greco's Italian period no longer distract the mind of the beholder. The progressive tightening of the composition advances still further in the *Purification* now in the National Gallery in London, where El Greco, following the Frick version in most of the details, substitutes a plain floor for the chequerboard marble-slab pattern of his earlier versions.

It is obviously impossible to say how far changes of emphasis and modifications of this sort in El Greco's treatment of subjects corresponds to the patrons' requirements as opposed to the artist's own wishes. It is equally impossible to guess how far his specialization in penitential saints corresponds to Counter-Reformation demands rather than to his personal involvement with doctrinal questions. It is evident, however, that the power of El Greco's art was not usually diminished by his contractual obligations, once he was established in Spain. Even in early stages of his Toledo career he seems sometimes to have been able to disregard some of the terms of a contract. Although his agreement for the altar-piece for Santo Domingo el Antiguo, Toledo (1577), required a shield – probably with the arms of the donor, Doña María de Silva – to be placed in a broken pediment over the main storey of the high altar, he eventually placed an elliptical Veronica there.

Similar modifications seem to have been made by the artist to his painting of the *Burial of the Count of Orgaz* (1586–8) for an altar in the church of Santo Tomé, Toledo. The original contract specified that the space below the picture was to contain an epitaph and a tomb painted in fresco, yet ultimately an inscription in Latin on a large stone plaque took the place of these. This clearly distracts the attention less than frescoes would from the painting itself. The only known dispute over this painting was over the price, and El Greco finally received 1,200 ducats, 400 less than his valuers had suggested. At the same time the ecclesiastical authorities did well not to object to a work so new in kind and manner at the time. The unification of levels in the *Burial of the Count of Orgaz* and its composition are highly original. The brightly coloured and strongly lit group in the foreground – St Stephen and St Augustine carrying the body of the count – echoes the brilliance of the Gloria above, while the row of black-clothed, white-ruffed mourners in the centre stripes a lozenge of darkness between the two areas of light. A pattern of hands draws the eye to the group in the foreground, and then via the upturned eyes of some of the figures below, through rising clouds and angels' wings, elongated bodies and unearthly light, into a vortex which ends in God the Father. El Greco uses conventional symbols where necessary to spell out the characters in the picture: a scene of the stoning of Stephen on the saint's cope, St Thomas's carpenter's square and St Peter's keys. Yet the composition shows the real point to be not miracles in themselves, but their relevance to man. The sixteenth-century onlookers, one a known friend of the artist, Alonso de Covarrubias, seem to stress the relevance of the scene. If the church had originally commissioned El Greco to celebrate a benefactor of the church and the monks of St Augustine, the artist himself appears to have sought to stress the meaning of a fourteenth-century story for his own times.

Although there were cases where particularly friendly relationships existed between El Greco and his patrons and the artist had some autonomy, even at the height of his fame in Toledo there were some instances in which his conception of a work could be seriously altered by his employers. A notorious case in point is his work for the Hospital of Charity at Illescas. The contract was originally drawn up and signed in June 1603 and its exact terms are not known. Clearly a careful iconographical scheme was agreed. The theme of the sanctuary was the Glorification of the Virgin, and El Greco's retable and pictures related everything to this. Yet two angels in sculpture on the tabernacle for the Host were removed before 1607 because the hospital authorities disliked them, so that the initial unified conception of El Greco himself was quickly broken in some of its details, and the passage of time has brought changes and additions of a kind which destroy still further the original design. El Greco's Madonna of Charity, for example, which was intended to occupy the rectangular space at the top of the retable, was first mutilated in the artist's lifetime, when the ruffs on the side figures were overpainted because the hospital authorities disapproved of them, and was subsequently removed from its original position altogether and placed (with an added semicircular piece at the top) in one of the lateral altars.

The financial dispute with the Hospital over payment was particularly bitter. The Hospital originally set a price of 2,430 ducats after an evaluation, which El Greco rejected as unreasonable, in 1605. Further evaluations by persons appointed by the Council of the Archbishop suggested figures of 4,437 or 4,835·52 ducats, which the Hospital refused to pay. Ultimately, in 1607, El Greco appears to have been driven to accept 2,093 ducats – less than the low price originally proposed by the Hospital.

Setbacks and injustices of this order must have tried the spirit of an artist as independent as El Greco, but he made money enough to live comfortably and, according to some, luxuriously; and perhaps he drew some encouragement from the vigorous support he received from some of his artistic and intellectual contemporaries. The poet Góngora and the poet and famous court preacher, Fray Hortensio Paravicino, praised his work in verse, and both recognized his particular ability to give life to his paintings. Paravicino also recognized that unusualness ('extrañeza') of El Greco's work which proved an obstacle to its appreciation, in the artist's own time and since. There is no doubt of his increasing boldness and originality of design through his career. Yet perhaps the daring elongations of figures and powerful compositions tend to distract attention from the quite remarkable ability of El Greco to convey emotion through facial expression. Symbolism sometimes contributes to the understanding of his paintings – the lamb with legs tied for sacrifice in his Nativity scenes, for instance, which foreshadows the death of Christ at the very scene of His birth – but their deeper meaning as often depends on the interpretation of faces. This psychological depth sets his paintings of the Holy Family more particularly apart from those of other painters of his time, who eschewed haloes and excessive idealization and yet failed finally to suggest the full range of human tenderness, maternal concern and dignity, far less otherworldliness, which El Greco contrived to do.

VIII Artists and Craftsmen

El Greco deserved to enjoy exceptional status and in part in fact enjoyed it. Most Spanish artists in the sixteenth century, however, were more often merely hired to do a particular job of work than to create original art. An artist began painting – like any other trade – as an apprentice aged between twelve and fifteen. He would in due course of time be examined and if he passed be admitted a master-painter in the guild. Subsequently his work for patrons would be assessed by the guild's *veedores* (overseers), who would determine the value of the work done and see that a just price was paid and that the job had been properly carried out in respect of materials and workmanship.

Under the general cover of art there were a number of smaller crafts or *oficios* in which a person could be examined. These lesser specializations appear to have increased in the course of the late sixteenth and early seventeenth centuries. In notarial documents of the early 1500s in Seville, for instance, we find painters, painters of religious images, gilders and illuminators. In 1622, however, Juan de Manzanares was examined 'in the art of painting the Roman', which apparently meant work done on ceilings, doors and windows; and Antonio Luque was examined not just as a gilder, but in a more limited way as 'a gilder of reliquaries and candlesticks'. In 1619 a landscape painter was specifically examined in his craft, for the first time in Seville. The artist in question was Flemish – one Adrián Escarabán – and he may well have been lured to Spain to cope with a growing demand for that kind of painting. Specifically 'Flemish landscapes' are mentioned in Cervantes's exemplary novel *La gitanilla* as commonly decorating rich men's houses at the period (*c.* 1613), although by 1633 Vincencio Carducho, in his *Diálogos de la pintura*, thought there was no lack of Spaniards in Madrid capable of rivalling skilled foreigners.

Clearly a major part of the work that artists were asked to do in the sixteenth century was of a religious nature. Armorial decoration accounted for another important aspect of work in Seville, and interest in the classics gave rise to mythological subjects. Juan Rodríguez

Madrigal commissioned Alonso Rodríguez Cebadero in 1514 to paint five panels for a bed with scenes from the story of Ulysses. No specifications were laid down for this particular job as they were in the case of heraldic or religious commissions, where the artist committed himself to use the precise colours, the number of figures and arrangement agreed on the basis of a preliminary sketch and laid down in his contract. In Juan de Paradiñas's contract for a retable for San Lorenzo in Seville, for instance, the figure of San Sebastián was to have a red cloak, green tunic and a red hat, and his canopy was to be of fine blue with a well-worked arch, and the back of the canopy to be a half-wall of mouldings with sky and landscape (*su cielo y lejos*) beyond. The retable was to be painted in oils – a relatively new medium in Spain, and one which had only been discovered in the early fifteenth century.

In the course of the sixteenth century the artist seems increasingly to have used his own knowledge and initiative, though as late as 1638 Pacheco, in his *Arte de la pintura*, obviously accepts that the person or persons responsible for a commission still exerted an influence. Jusepe Martínez in his *Discursos practicables de la pintura* (*c.* 1673) finds a proof of Ribalta's patience in the number of works he painted 'in which he followed exactly the intentions and instructions of those who paid him to carry out the work'. At the same time Pacheco also shows how the composition of painting or the manner of representing a particular scene is more properly the result of the artist's own study and knowledge – of the human body, of other painters' work, of the Bible and of theological writing when it comes to a religious subject.

It is difficult to tell whether Pacheco is describing the artist's situation as it was, or as he thought it ought to be. But it is clear that he felt that the artist was no longer a mere craftsman engaged in an *oficio mecánico*, but a person employed on a more honourable kind of work. The variety of knowledge that a painter had to have in order to draw made his work an *arte liberal*. If drawing were not in fact the basis of art, painting would be 'oficio común como los demás' ('the same as any ordinary craft').

The status-seeking passion of Spaniards in the sixteenth century, then, ultimately affected the artist, just as it affected the poet and composer too. Juan del Encina pointed out in his *Arte de la poesía castellana* (*c.* 1496) that the poet was a lord or captain, while the reciter or 'trobador' was a mere slave or common soldier, and, later, learned and difficult poetry was seen as a reflection of noble breeding by Fernando de Herrera in his commentaries on Garcilaso (1580) and Carrillo y Sotomayor in his *Libro de la erudición poética* (1611). In a similar way Pacheco thought it was important that kings and nobles and learned men did not think it beneath them to draw and paint. He pointed to the status already achieved by artists in Italy in the fifteenth century, and argued that God had been a painter too – although one of the religious who read his work in manuscript was less keen on the idea. The parallel between the Divine Creation and that of the artist underlined the originality of the latter (making it art and not mere imitative craft), and this became a seventeenth-century commonplace and the frequent basis of a conceit in poetry of the period. When looking at a lifelike portrait the soul of the person portrayed did not know whether it was in the real body or in the painting, so close was the artist's work to that of God!

The claims advanced by Pacheco reflect a new confidence in art in Spain and a new willingness on the part of the artist to stand up for his own ideas. An analysis of documents relating to artists in Seville suggests that the periods from 1500 to 1529 and 1590 to 1619 were particularly active ones in the Andalusian capital, so perhaps Pacheco and his son-in-law Velázquez received a special stimulus from a favourable market situation. The guilds also helped the artist to stand up for himself, and the one in Seville took care to prevent unqualified persons from poaching on its rich preserves. In May 1630, the painter Alonso Cano even petitioned that Zurbarán be prevented from undertaking work in the cloister and sacristy of San Pablo until he had passed his examinations for a painter's licence in Seville, so jealously were the rights of local artists guarded.

An increase in the demand for works of art at the end of the sixteenth century may well have contributed to the demands for greater status and the recognition of specializations. But the majority of people could still only afford the crude wood-cuts of a ballad or religious poem in broadsheet form; and the Church, the religious orders, the crown, the nobility and the municipal authorities remained the primary taskmasters of the artist. The first of these still had more commissions for the artist than anyone else. Even painters like Pacheco and Velázquez called themselves 'painters of religious images' ('pintores de imágenes') in the first place. The work of Juan Fernández de Navarrete (1526–79), Francisco Ribalta (1565–1628), Luis de Morales (d. 1586) and Luis Tristán (1586–1640) was mostly for the Church, and so was that of artists of greater renown like Zurbarán and Murillo.

IX Ribera and Zurbarán

For many of these artists Italy was still a major source of inspiration; Navarrete studied with Titian, Morales learnt from Florentine as well as Dutch painting, and Tristán inherited some of the Italian traditions via his teacher El Greco. Ribalta is thought to have made at least one journey to Italy. He was clearly interested in the work of Raphael, Carracci and Sebastiano del Piombo, and he made a copy of Caravaggio's *Crucifixion of St Peter*. Together with the Count of Benavente, a viceroy of Naples from 1603 to 1610, and the Count of Villamediana, who was in Italy from 1611 to 1617 (both of whom bought paintings by Caravaggio), Ribalta must have been one of the first to introduce the chiaroscuro manner of the Italian master into Spain, where it later excited the admiration of painters in Seville such as Pacheco and Velázquez. But Jusepe de Ribera (1590–1652) and Francisco de Zurbarán (1598–1662) developed as powerfully as any Spanish artists the strong contrasts of light and shade which were especially popular in Italian art in the second half of the sixteenth century.

Ribera, though born and probably trained in Spain, moved to Italy (*c.* 1610) as a young man of about twenty and finally settled in Naples. He worked on classical and religious subjects for the two main categories of patron – the aristocracy at the Spanish viceregal court and the Church – and displayed extraordinary ability at conveying the furrows of human features with expressive yet delicate and precise brush strokes. Lined faces and physical peculiarities seem to have had a particular attraction for him, and he rendered with complete fidelity, for instance, a phenomenal bearded lady suckling a child, including her history in Roman-style lettering on a plinth at her side – as if the subject were a classical one (Tavera Hospital, Toledo) – as well as executing etchings of grotesque male heads. Sometimes his 'character' faces are not only fascinating in themselves but have a contrastive function in a larger composition. The old lady on the left with a basket of fruit and emblematic rose in the painting of *The Holy Family with St Catherine* (1648) provides not only a tonal contrast with the foreground group of the Virgin and Child and saint, because she is mainly in the shadows, but also an earthy quality which throws the idealized conception of the three central figures into relief. Ribera's vision of sanctity is often more naturalistic than that of many of his contemporaries. His male saints may not convey inner torments as do those of El Greco, but they are men whose life has been hard, men who have experienced life rather than removed themselves from it. The tension of life that they express often flows over into the compositions of the paintings themselves. A bough leans leftwards across a dim landscape while a saint kneels looking to the right; and in the *Martyrdom of St Bartholomew* in the Prado, the straining arm and leg muscles of the men hauling St Bartholomew upwards, the saint's backward-leaning body with right leg bent under him, and the cascade of white cloud from the right, all contribute to a sense of the torture which the painting depicts.

No doubt Zurbarán learnt the Italian manner in Seville when he went there as a young man from Extremadura and was apprenticed to an artist called Pedro Díaz de Villanueva. To judge from Pacheco, Andalusian artists felt that both elegance and true naturalness stemmed from Italy. Even the way in which Zurbarán represents female saints in the dress of ladies of his time follows sixteenth-century Italian precedents. It was the normal practice of Raphael and Titian, though in Zurbarán it used to be put down to 'Spanish realism'. Sebastiano del Piombo's *Dorothea* (*c.* 1512), sometimes taken to be a portrait, does very much the same thing as Zurburán's Santa Dorotea in the Seville Museum: both are ordinary ladies yet carry the basket of apples and roses connected with the miracle that attended the saint's martyrdom. The humanization of religious subjects which El Greco particularly established in Spain is merely carried a step further by Zurbarán, no doubt with the intention of showing the links between the world of religion and everyday experience, and the relevance of the saints' lives to those who take their names at baptism.

Zurbarán's earliest-known important commissions fall between 1625 and 1629, and are all for religious orders in Seville: twenty-one paintings for the Dominican convent of San Pablo el Real; a Crucifixion for Trinitarians; twenty-two canvases for Mercedarians and four paintings for the church of San Buenaventura and the Franciscans. In the years that followed he worked for Capuchins, Carthusians and Hieronymites too.

His paintings of saints and of monastic dress bring out his fondness for simplicity of line and restraint in colour. But there is above all an interest in pose or, perhaps more accurately, in repose, in all his work, which is particularly appropriate to these monastic paintings. Whereas El Greco's saints express strong feeling, the pangs of suffering, penitence and emotion, Zurbarán's are more obviously contemplative, abstracted, quietly ecstatic. His driving principle seems to have been to suggest rather than explain: much in little. Thus he painted on a number of occasions a lamb with its legs tied (there is one signed and dated 1632). Obviously this is the sacrificial lamb, which is to be identified with Christ, yet only in one instance does he make this explicit by adding the Latin phrase 'Tamquam Agnus' ('like a lamb'), presumably recalling the phrase 'He was led like a lamb to the slaughter' in Acts 8:32, quoting Isaiah 53:1, or echoing the lamb described in the Book of Revelations 5:6. The painting here is an aid to meditation: a beginning rather than an end in itself. It is a visualization of an object related to a meditation such as was recommended by Fray Luis de Granada in his *Libro de oración* and by St Ignatius in his *Spiritual Exercises*.

The same could be said of some of his still lifes. In one in the Contini–Bonacossi collection in Florence, a pile of lemons on a silver dish stands on a table beside a basket of oranges, orange blossom and leaves, while a vase or drinking vessel and a carnation on a silver dish complete the composition on the other side. As is common in still lifes of the period, there is room for meditation on the transience of life and beautiful things here. The fruit blossom which precedes the fruit and the cut carnation which will die speak of the passage of time. There is contrast between the bitter and the sweet. And yet there is no obviously over-blown flower or fallen bloom or blatant symbolism; everything is pristine, orderly and harmonious, and it is only the slightly idealized light and the formality of arrangement which suggest that the painter may have intended us to look beyond mere reality here, perhaps to the traditional emblematic connection between the ideal beauty of the orange and God's grace or the Virgin Mary. Elsewhere quinces are juxtaposed to the mother of God in a painting by Zurbarán of the Virgin with the Christ-Child and St John, possibly because of the emblematic use of the quince to signify modest or self-effacing virtue. In other paintings more obvious lilies are placed on the table before St Anthony of Padua in a Vision of the Infant Christ appearing to the saint (c. 1628–30), and in a vase on a table beside the Virgin in a scene of the Holy Family at Toledo, Ohio, because they are traditionally associated with the saint and the Virgin as symbols of purity.

In this last painting the Christ-Child has just pricked his finger on a crown of thorns which lies on his knee, and still-life elements – books on a table, a bowl and a basket on the floor, two white doves – both contribute to the sense of the reality of Christ's life and to the meaning of it for the believer. The colours and composition – blues, whites, reds, browns and pinks arranged in strong and simple patterns – help to maintain the same delicate balance between physical worlds and their metaphysical implications.

X Architecture in the Reigns of Philip II and Philip III

The restraint and careful organization of Zurbarán's work is a graphic counterpart to much of the architecture of the second part of the sixteenth and early seventeenth centuries, under the initial austere direction of Philip II, notably at El Escorial. The king brought Juan Bautista de Toledo (d. 1567) from the viceregal court at Naples to Madrid in 1559, and work was begun on the combined monastery and palace in 1562. The grid plan, symbolically connected with St Lawrence, on whose feast the battle of St Quentin (1557) was won, and which the building was to celebrate, was Juan Bautista's, as also the unadorned fortress-like south front. The completion of the building, however, was largely in the hands of Juan de Herrera (1530—97), who did not eliminate decoration so entirely but kept it to the most chastely classical in all his works. Obelisks in slate or stone, round stone balls, double columns or pilasters and plain rectangular reliefs dress the surfaces and adorn the roofs of the Escorial itself, the Lonja (Exchange) at Seville (1582–99) and the ground and first floors of Valladolid Cathedral. Squares, rectangles, triangular pediments, circular motifs and rounded arches are the essence of his surface forms and internal organization everywhere. Sometimes the present-day viewer loses some of the sense of the grandeur and harmony of the original as a result of later modifications. The obelisks which Herrera placed on the central façade of the church at the Escorial as elsewhere on the towers, for instance, were subsequently replaced by statues; and on top of the austere base provided by Herrera for the main façade of Valladolid Cathedral, Churriguera, in the early eighteenth century, added broken pediments and all kinds of light-catching and shadow-creating effects with varying planes, while his huge decorative flattened scroll-ends at the side bear no relation to the forms below.

This relative austerity of Renaissance forms was to be found in architecture throughout Spain at this period, sometimes in very out-of-the-way places. Like the Gothic, Renaissance fashions spread widely under the influence of the buildings of monarchs, aristocrats and prelates, and perhaps also of furniture and book design, which turned from Gothic patterns to Plateresque or Renaissance style of decoration in title-pages of books, small chests of drawers (*bargueños*) and picture frames. For some the Renaissance or classical style could not spread fast enough, and the silversmith Juan de Arfe y Villafañe (1535–1602), when he was preparing a *custodia* for Seville Cathedral in 1587, spoke critically of the elaborate use of unclassical, ill-proportioned and meaningless decoration made by his contemporaries, which, according to him, they took from French and Dutch prints. The Escorial was Arfe's avowed ideal. And others followed Herrera as well.

In at least one case, a town was almost completely remodelled in the early years of the seventeenth century on Herreran principles. This was the small town of Lerma between Burgos and Valladolid, where the Duke of Lerma spent vast sums in transforming the remains of a medieval castle and its poor surroundings on newly acquired estates into a palace, square and park, more suited to a man of his status and to the king's favourite.

Francisco de Mora, a pupil of Herrera, was the principal architect of the Lerma scheme. The new palace (1605) was built round a spacious patio, adorned with Doric and Ionic columns, a rounded pediment over the main doorway, double pilasters on the corner towers with slate spires – not unreminiscent of the Escorial or of the Court Prison (now the Foreign Office) which Francisco de Mora's nephew, Juan Gómez de Mora, was to build in Madrid in 1629–34. The duke attempted to establish a sort of court for himself at Lerma, by building a spacious square in front of the palace and selling the new houses round it to socially desirable people.

But if the design of the Lerma palace and its surroundings was basically classical and severe, it was decorated with a richness that was more in keeping with the luxurious tastes of the reign of Philip III than of his more monastically inclined predecessor. The balconies and grilles of the first part of the palace were gilded by Vicencio Carducho (1576–1638), one of the court painters in 1605, and some of the later balconies were painted in blue and gold. Inside, many of the rooms were decorated with Talavera tiles, with chimney-pieces of polished jasper. There were rich Turkish, Chinese and Indian wall-hangings, and damasks, taffetas and brocades to cover tables, beds and cushions. Curtains to cover doorways included some from India with 'birds and landscapes and various other details'. Amongst the tapestries for the walls there were Triumphs *a lo divino* – the triumph of the Catholic Church was a commonplace subject for paintings and decorative work after the Counter-Reformation – 'The Seven Virtues' and a biblical group; classical series of the Wars of Troy, the Labours of Hercules and the Wedding of Mercury; historical subjects such as the Taking of Antequera and Hannibal's battles; and other series with plants, woodland scenes, 'marvels' and golden grotesques. The collection of paintings included portraits, landscapes, still lifes and mythological subjects by unidentified artists, a *Cleopatra* attributed to Bassano, paintings of the Five Senses by Bartolomé Carducho (Ribera painted a similar series before 1616 and the so-called *Blind Man of Gambazo* in the Prado, dated 1632, is probably one of a comparable group and represents *Touch*). A *Conversion of Mary Magdalene* attributed to Tintoretto, and a set of the twelve apostles by Rubens (before 1618), presumably those now in the Prado, were among the religious paintings.

Lavishness on this scale was unparalleled in Spain outside royal palaces, and Lerma seems to have ranked second only to the Escorial in the view of many visitors. It gives some indication of the developing taste of the period and the growing interest in objects which were decorative as well as significant, and sometimes not all that significant! Still lifes and landscapes were now increasingly in demand, and no longer necessarily part of religious scenes (mere backgrounds or fore-grounds) as they had originally been.

The pursuit of a comparable richness in architecture is well exemplified by the façade of the Angustias church at Valladolid by Juan de Nates (1597–1604). Nates does not look back to Plateresque decoration, which had tended to conceal or obscure the lines of buildings, but emphasizes forms and symbolic ends with statues in niches, Corinthian columns and varyingly faceted surfaces, which produce a slightly more elaborate texture than is to be found in Herrera's buildings. Elsewhere contrasts of brick and stone or the introduction of chaste reliefs achieve similar effects, as in Francisco Bautista's church of San Isidro at Madrid (1629), and even more obviously in the chapel of San Isidro at San Andrés (1642–69), also in the capital. Pedro de Torre, the architect, placed double pilasters with Corinthian capitals at the corners, a classical stone cornice at the top, and an echoing line of stonework at the base to frame the brickwork of the façades. Statues in niches at the base of the cupola also emphasize the basic lines of the structure and carry the eye upwards.

XI Significant Forms of the Seventeenth Century

Many seventeenth-century Spanish architects have an almost functional approach to decoration, much as we find in poets of the period like

Góngora and Quevedo, for whom richness of rhythm, sound and imagery were not merely ends in themselves but also aids to fuller comprehension of the ideas and emotions they expressed. By contrast with Plateresque decoration, which may underline forms but seldom relates to the purpose of a building, seventeenth-century decoration frequently has specific meaning in its context. The different orders of pillars were appropriate to different situations. The highest symbolic status was commonly accorded to the Corinthian column, which represented ideal beauty and was often identified with the Virgin Mary. It is frequently placed in the top storey of altar retables, as at the Escorial, with the Ionic and Doric below it. The corkscrew column, increasingly used in Spain in the seventeenth century, was an emblem of the highest virtues of Christ and the Blessed Virgin, according to Fray Juan Ricci.

In painting, too, decorative elements are not without deeper significance in some instances. But the pleasures of the senses are unashamedly pursued as well. Still-life painting gives some idea of the balance of sense and sensibility. Juan van der Hamen (1596–1632), who was of Flemish extraction, seems, for instance, to celebrate the delights of gastronomy in some of his still lifes. Even when some of the food depicted is cut into – conceivably implying the brevity of pleasure in material things in a conventional way – we feel that the object of the cut is to display the visually appetizing rather than to open up a moral perspective. Lope de Vega, in a sonnet, certainly emphasized van der Hamen's skill in representing flowers and fruit rather than any ulterior aim. Yet in *The Cook* (*c.* 1630), the juxtaposition of the fat live chef and plump dead birds is evidently suggestive, and the presence of money and playing cards in the painting (*copas* is the suit, naturally) seems to extend the meaning more palpably.

Slightly more austere in his approach to the still life is the Manchegan Fray Juan Sánchez Cotán (1561–1627). When he places crowns of exquisitely painted flowers on the head of the Virgin the symbolism is unquestionable. But it is less palpable perhaps in a still life pure and simple, such as the famous one in which an apple and a cabbage hang on strings on the left in a window opening, while a water melon, a piece cut from it, and a cucumber complete a curve of greens, yellows and pinks across the canvas (1602, San Diego Art Gallery, California). The cut melon could, of course, be symbolic, but chiefly the painting seems to be playing with a limited range of colours, lighting, and perhaps the position in space of the objects in relation to one another.

Much the same might be said of the work of Alejandro de Loarte (*fl.* 1622–6), although the conventional juxtaposition of a live stag-beetle on a table with hanging dead birds in one canvas shows that he sometimes felt inclined to carry the still life beyond the representation of the objects themselves. Flower painters such as Juan de Arellano (1614–76) and his son-in-law Bartolomé Pérez (1634–93) also knew and used the conventional patterns of dead and living things, perfect flowers and overblown or fallen blossoms. Yet they delight the eye rather than disturb the spirit with their compositions. Possibly the taste of the buyer and his easy or uneasy conscience affected the balance. Certainly Antonio de Pereda (1608–93) knew how to vary the mix of seriousness and delight. Some of his still lifes revel in the textures of rich materials, drinking vessels and fruits, like the one in the Louvre. In others a clock, also a favourite theme of poets at this time, obtrudes its blatant warning, amongst glasses, nuts and shell-fish (the canvas dated 1652 in the Pushkin Museum, Moscow), or an angel points out the futility of material wealth as in the *Dream of a Knight* (Real Academia de San Fernando, Madrid), or *Vanitas* (in the Vienna Gallery).

Many of these artists and their contemporaries excite the senses and the intellect by composition as well as by subject-matter. Padre Juan Bautista Mayno's (1568–1649) *Adoration of the Shepherds* (*c.* 1620, in the Villanueva y Geltrú Museum), which humanizes the angels as well as the members of the Holy Family in what was by now an almost conventional way, decoratively arranges the centre of the scene in a circular pattern of variously angled forms. Even more powerful is the arrangement of his painting of *The Retaking of Bahia* (1635, Prado Museum), where the left foreground contains an oval group of ordinary people, men, women and children, gathered around a wounded man, in striking contrast to the proud commander of the expedition, Don Fadrique de Toledo, on the right in the middle distance. The latter displays a tapestry in which Victory and the royal favourite, the Count-Duke of Olivares, crown Philip IV with laurels, before a circle of kneeling subjects paying homage. Unlike most of the representations of battle scenes painted for the Buen Retiro palace to celebrate recent Spanish victories, Mayno focused his picture less on the heroism of generals and nobles and the might of the crown than on the suffering that war brings to ordinary people, and the need for a Christian concern for its inevitable victims. He has used patterning techniques: contrasting colours, opposed circles and a strong diagonal from top left to bottom right, to achieve his effect.

XII Diego Velázquez (1599–1660)

At the period there was no greater master of composition in Spain than Velázquez; no one more expert at creating the illusion of reality with brush strokes either. Velázquez, like his master and father-in-law Pacheco, practised a good deal of drawing from life as a young man, and his early training was to good effect. There were social reasons for drawing well too. It was the ability to do this that made the artist an independent and individual creator rather than a slavish imitator of works by earlier artists; the ability made painting an art rather than a mechanical craft. Velázquez's youthful drawings had been executed with charcoal and white highlighting on blue paper; a young apprentice sitting for him in different poses, laughing and crying and so forth, and 'leaving nothing difficult out', as Pacheco put it. Yet clearly from the start Velázquez also acquired Pacheco's serious approach to the significance of a painting.

Works which are generally thought to belong to the early stages of Velázquez's career in Seville already support this view: the *Water-Carrier* now in the Wellington Museum at Apsley House, and the *Old Woman Frying Eggs* (National Gallery of Scotland, Edinburgh). Both these paintings juxtapose youth and age in a striking way, as well as organizing people and objects into decorative patterns: the lined water-pitcher and lined face of the carrier echo one another, as do the smooth glass and the smooth-faced boy on the left-hand side of the picture. The objects all show off the ability of the artist to capture reality, yet at the same time relate to one another in an elegant compositional order and contrast with one another in a meaningful way. The *Old Woman Frying Eggs* is even more clearly a meditation on the passage of time and the hardship of life. The woman's expression is momentarily abstracted, so is the boy's; and the eggs are caught at the precise moment when the white begins to solidify yet has not entirely done so.

Parallels and contrasts remain the essence of Velázquez's art. *Christ in the House of Martha and Mary* (c. 1620, National Gallery, London) is an early case in point. The world of Martha is prominent in the foreground on the left and in the still life of fishes on the table, while Mary is seen with Christ on a smaller scale at the right. An older woman attends both Martha and Mary, literally pointing to their contrasting situations. The spectator looks at Martha rather than at Mary and is compelled to identify with material rather than spiritual values in the first instance. The current theory about the painting is that Christ and Mary are seen in an interior room through a hatch or aperture. If this is the case the bright light of the inner room is meaningfully contrasted with the dark wall against which Martha and her older companion stand. An alternative theory, which holds that it would be inappropriate for Christ to bless Mary with the left hand, sees the inner room as a reflection in a mirror. In this case, the relationship of the spectator to the painting would be more complex still. Martha would be looking at the scene between Christ and Mary which *we* see reflected in the 'mirror'. In any event, although we are quick to identify with Martha, we are enabled to recognize the greater significance of the spiritual life. The same is true in *Christ at Emmaus* (Beit Collection, Blessington, Ireland), where the scene of Jesus with his disciples is again a small part of the painting, an event taking place in an inner room, while a mulatta girl stands behind a table in the foreground, with material things around her.

Velázquez is in fact constantly involving the onlooker in his pictures. This, a frequent device in Raphael, was common practice in the portrait, but rare in other types of painting in Spain. We can feel part of the broken circle of Spanish and Netherlandish troops looking on at the scene of *The Surrender of Breda* (1634, Prado, Madrid), and may identify with both victors and vanquished, though the erect lances and powerful horse on the right, and the dispirited pikes, halberds, men and horses on the left make it as clear which is which, as do the figures of Justinus of Nassau with the key and Spinola the Spanish general in the centre of the composition. Several faces look out at us to bring us into the picture.

The same is true in the *Old Woman Frying Eggs* where the boy looks, more or less, at us; and the *Water-Carrier* where a third face, between the carrier and the boy, drinks from a mug or glass and looks out at the spectator. It is also the case in *The Triumph of Bacchus* (Prado, Madrid). In this last instance, however, Bacchus looks less at us than abstractedly into the distance, perhaps as an indication of the forgetfulness associated with drunkenness. Throughout the *Triumph of Bacchus*, Velázquez again makes use of suggestive parallels and contrasts. The balding, drunken, ageing men juxtaposed to the young Bacchus seem to make Pérez de Moya's point that the abuse of wine brings on old age and decay. The semi-nakedness of Bacchus and his youth could also illustrate the carelessness characteristic of those given to drink, and their inability to keep anything prudently concealed. In fact, whereas it has often been held that Velázquez intended to mock the myths, it is equally possible that, like most of his Spanish contemporaries, he was using them to make indirect statements about human behaviour or experience, and emphasizing their relevance to seventeenth-century life.

Nowhere does Velázquez use the myths more subtly than in his painting of *The Fable of Arachne* (Prado, Madrid). This canvas used to be called *The Spinners* or *The Tapestry Factory*, and was thought to be a representation of a specific workshop in Madrid. Fortunately the real title is known from the inventory of Pedro de Arce who owned the painting in 1664, and from eighteenth-century lists of the royal collection; the full meaning of the painting becomes clearer in the light of the Arachne story. Most artistic representations of the subject pick on the moment in the story when Arachne, having refused to give due praise to the gods and overproud of her skill as a weaver, is turned into a spider by the goddess Minerva. Velázquez, in contrast, has chosen the moment when Arachne has woven the first tapestry with such genius that she seems likely to win her contest with the old woman (the goddess in disguise). He follows Ovid's *Metamorphoses* (Lib. VI, fabs 1–4) in making the subject of Arachne's first tapestry (showing how Jupiter bent before man (or woman) rather than vice versa) *Europa and the Bull*. The tapestry itself hangs at the back of Velázquez's painting in a brightly lit area, and those in Madrid in the artist's lifetime would have had less difficulty than we do today in recognizing it as a copy of Titian's *Rape of Europa*. Titian's painting hung in the Royal Palace in Madrid (it is now in the Isabella Stewart Gardner Museum in Boston), and had been copied by Rubens, so Velázquez has obviously paid Arachne a singular compliment by identifying her work with that of the greatest European painter of the sixteenth century. It seems clear that Velázquez intended to idealize the artistic prowess of man in identifying Arachne with Titian. Was he also implying that a greater artist than Arachne (or Titian) might come afterwards? It is impossible to say. Pérez de Moya certainly held that the story was a warning to artists that their work would be superseded by those who came after them, and perhaps Velázquez expresses in the canvas a confidence in his own skill to render space and light and the movement of the spinning-wheel that might well be considered to rival the art of Titian.

Velázquez, like the Venetian master he emulated, commanded a unique position as an artist in his time: respected and befriended by the king and his favourite, the Count-Duke of Olivares, and given high office in the royal entourage as well as a knighthood in the Order of Saint James. The obvious advantages he derived from his position at court were two visits to Italy – one of them to collect paintings and classical statues for the decoration of the palace at Madrid – and relatively rich financial rewards for his work. But he also seems to have enjoyed a surprising measure of freedom in the treatment of the subjects he painted. While other Spanish artists, for instance, suffered from the opposition of the Inquisition to paintings of the female nude – although Pacheco admitted that artists must use the female figure (the face and hands from life, the rest from art) – Velázquez was able to paint at least four nudes. One of these was the superb *Venus and Cupid* now in the National Gallery, London.

Obviously Velázquez's relative freedom was not bought without some concessions to the court, and by comparison with Rembrandt, for instance, he seems in some ways quite conventional, in all probability genuinely respectful of the hierarchy of court life. His paintings of the royal family are sometimes evidently idealizing, and seem to follow his father-in-law's line that prudence was necessary when portraying the king, despite the fact that realism was normally of prime importance in a portrait. In the equestrian portraits in particular (including that of the Count-Duke of Olivares), Velázquez implies flattery by following the emblematic tradition, and showing the riders' tight rein on their prancing horses: conventionally symbolic of a prince's statecraft. At the same time Velázquez was no servile flatterer. A picture like *Las Meninas*, in which the princess's dwarfs and attendants are represented on a level with the Infanta herself, and the king and queen are merely seen reflected in a mirror, appears to emphasize the humanity of members of the royal family rather than their hierarchical status. Yet even here the positions of the infanta and the king and the queen, and the lighting, indicate their central place in the order of the court, without the artist's having recourse to the heavy symbolism that is found in many portraits and prints of the period. Rubens's grisaille of the count-duke puts in the club of Hercules, the trumpets of Fame, the owl of Wisdom, cornucopia and laurels to underline the heroic stature of Olivares. Velázquez praises in less blatant fashion, yet shows that he, too, knew and accepted his place.

XIII Alonso Cano (1601–1667) and Bartolomé Murillo (1617–1682)

The phenomenal success of Velázquez is, of course, an index of the interest in Spain in the accurate representation of objects, play of light and space, and decorative arrangement. Lesser artists of the period are equally concerned with these matters. Alonso Cano, who worked as a sculptor and architect as well as a painter, was particularly good at combining accuracy with decorative effects. Initially he followed his father in the retable-making trade, and his earliest commissions were for work to be carried out in collaboration with Miguel Cano. The bulk of Alonso's work was religious although he was employed for a short time at the court by the king. Although his work was subject to the inevitable pressure of patrons, he managed to be independent in many ways in his artistic development. His retables at Santa María, in Lebrija, and La Magdalena, at Getafe, show his ability to relate sculpture and painting to architectural forms; the one at Lebrija (1629) is particularly original for its time. Its tall Corinthian columns with spiral patterns are twice the normal height, and the retable has one double storey and an attic instead of the more usual three equal divisions. The curves in the carving of the drapery give energetic movement to the statue of the Madonna and Child above the high altar, as well as to the life-size figures of St Peter and St Paul which stand on either side at the attic level. These curving patterns in clothes recur in much of his later work in both sculpture and painting, and a flying circle of material and two windswept swatches add a sense of drama and movement to St John the Evangelist's Vision of Jerusalem (1635–8), now in the Wallace Collection. Whereas stillness is of the essence in Zurbarán's work, Cano follows rather in the path of Velázquez, seeking life and exploiting contrasts – particularly the simple tensions between straight lines and curves. In The Miracle of the Well (Prado, Madrid), one of the most admired of Cano's paintings in his own time, the circular group of women and children round the well, the mouth of the well itself, its pulley and curving rope, are set off by the upright figure of San Isidro, the strong rectangles of the building in the background and the gently rising beam at the right from which the pulley hangs. Tension and rhythm are created by similar means in the Descent into Limbo (Los Angeles County Museum), where a barred window in the background, the lines of the dark opening of a door at the right, the pole of the banner in Christ's hand, the inclined upright of the cross, and the slope of an opened hatch in the floor mark a series of angles which set off the curves of the pendant, the serpent seen through the window, and the unclothed bodies of the group of figures in the foreground, including the superb, curvaceous, white and slightly bent body of a woman at the right.

Strong lines and dynamic groupings also characterize Cano's series of paintings for the sanctuary of Granada Cathedral, where he became prebendary after appointment by Philip IV in September 1651. His work for the chapter included statues, silver lamps and a lectern (1652–6) in which scroll patterns and repeated curving forms are used boldly to particularly good effect. This is also the case in his design for the façade of the cathedral in which rounded arches, circular windows, circles in relief and pilasters create patterns in different planes which sun and shadows heighten.

Bartolomé Murillo continues this interest in decorative effect, though he works with more restrained rhythms and often achieves contrast by using a wider variety of colours than Cano or Zurbarán. His compositional lines are often rigidly geometrical. In the painting of *St Elizabeth of Hungary* (Caridad Hospital, Seville) – which seemed a major work or a work of major morality to Spaniards in the nineteenth century when it was in the Prado – the saint is placed at the apex of a basically diamond-shaped group. Other heads on the left are on a line with that of St Isabel and weight the composition on the left-hand side, and all the figures are concentrated in the lower half of the painting, giving the ensemble a rather heavy, posed feeling, lacking in movement. *Christ Healing the Paralysed Man* (1673–4, National Gallery, London) is also a left-hand-side composition, and the early group of the Holy Family and donkey in the *Flight into Egypt* (c. 1645, Art Institute, Detroit) has an almost pentagonal arrangement which occurs again in the *Family Group* (c. 1660) in the Erik Bergmann collection (Monroe, Michigan). At the same time, Murillo's use of colour and lighting frequently brings his simplest compositions to life. The fine canvas of *St Ildefonso Receiving the Chasuble from the Virgin* (Prado, Madrid), for instance, basically depends on the elementary device of crossing diagonals. Yet here the strong line of light from top right to bottom left – very fashionable in the seventeenth century, thanks to Rubens – the brilliant colouring of the chasuble in the centre, and the decorative arrangement of angels' legs and arms leading the eye from the bottom of the painting to the Virgin, create various focuses of interest. Elsewhere brushwork gives vitality to a simple composition.

The Flower Girl (*c.* 1665-70, Dulwich College, London) is diamond-shaped. But the folds in the girl's clothing and in the headdress add considerable life to the work, and the cloud background is also looser and more vigorously executed than much of the earlier painting. Brushwork and lighting combine to excite the eye in the small painting of *Christ and St John as Infants* in the Prado. The rhythms of this painting expand naturally out of the single lamb in the bottom left-hand corner through the central group of the two holy children (caught in movement) up to a triad of cherubs in the clouds above. There is play on ideas to add interest to this painting too, since the Christ-Child and infant St John toy with prophetic symbols. The shell containing water which St John offers Jesus foreshadows His baptism; the slender wooden crook which Christ carries is in the shape of His cross. Particularly admirable in its combination of religious significance and pictorial effect is Murillo's series of paintings of the story of the Prodigal Son (Beit Collection, Blessington, Ireland). It is not known for whom Murillo originally produced this series illustrating the six main moments in the parable. The dangers of wilfulness, pride and riotous living, and the sinner's need for repentance and charity are some of the main lessons of the story (Luke 15:11-32). Murillo clearly saw charity as one of the main points of the parable when he used the Return of the Prodigal as a subject on its own as part of the decorative scheme for the Charity Hospital in Seville (1670-4), where it hung next to an Old Testament story also associated with the need for charity: 'Abraham and the Angels'. In his series of six Prodigal pictures, Murillo follows the progress of the son from opulence to beggary, from pride to repentance, through colour and design as well as through the episodes of the story itself. In the early scenes ('The Prodigal receiving his portion', 'leaving home' and 'feasting') a crescendo in the richness of the colours and the elegance of the environment points up the development of the story. The second half of the series uses greys and green and cold skies to accentuate the decline. The scene of the Prodigal feeding the swine has a wonderful sense of desolation and asceticism about it in tone and composition, to play on the emotions. The rocky, wilderness environment, and the black and white pigs, strike an obviously penitential note.

More complex rhythms occur in Murillo's later work. A bold swirl runs through a brightly lit group of figures in *The Birth of the Virgin* in the Louvre, and there is a particularly brilliant counterpoint of rhythms in the *Two Trinities*, sometimes called *The Holy Family*, in the National Gallery, London. The oval group of Jesus with Joseph and Mary in the foreground with the Christ-Child standing on a low rock in the centre becomes part of a larger oval. The figure of God the Father, above the Infant Jesus, and two cherubs form a decorative arch which echoes the pattern of heads in the foreground. At the same time there is a strong vertical line in the composition running from the first person of the Trinity through the Dove of the Holy Spirit to God the Son below.

Occasionally Murillo, like Velázquez, plays with the reality of painting in an interesting fashion. Velázquez inveigles the spectator into the reality of his canvases; Murillo perhaps more theatrically breaks out of it. He does this particularly effectively in the self-portrait now in the National Gallery, London. There he has depicted himself on a square canvas inside a simulated oval frame. The oval stands like a mirror on a ledge or table, on which lie a rolled-up drawing, pencil and ruler, and, on the right, a palette and brushes. Underneath the oval frame, hanging over the edge of the ledge, is a Latin inscription stating that the self-portrait was executed at his children's request 'pro filiorum votis ac precibus explendis'. The ledge then is the basic reality of the painting, and the self-portrait is a painting within a painting. Yet Murillo has depicted his right hand reaching out of the canvas, as it were, and resting on the simulated frame. Logically then he must be standing behind the ledge, with an empty frame in front of him. On the other hand, there appears to be no space between the ledge and the wall in which he could stand. The spectator is ultimately forced to recognize that here art deals in illusions, and is poetry not history.

Two other kinds of painting in which Murillo excelled must be mentioned here: low-life scenes, which like the picaresque novel had become popular in Spain in Velázquez's time; and landscape, for which there was also an increasing demand in the seventeenth century. Some landscapes of course were basically circumstantial pieces, such as the royal boar-hunts by Velázquez and his son-in-law Mazo. Murillo, however, in the small landscape with travellers which is in the Prado, produced something much more imaginative. The pattern of light curves into a road in the foreground and bends back into the mountains in the background with a typically baroque sweep.

Murillo often uses these strong diagonal lines of composition, which are commonly identified with baroque painting. In Spain Rubens employed them to great effect in both religious and mythological subjects, and many of these graced the royal collection in Murillo's time, some commissioned by Philip IV from the artist himself when he was in Spain, others acquired after his death. Another type of decorative painting to become popular in Spain in the course of the seventeenth century were the dynamically designed hunting scenes of Paul de Vos.

XIV Art and Architecture in the Second Half of the Seventeenth Century

Spanish artists clearly learnt the force of the diagonal from these precedents and from the example of Murillo, and diagonal composition is strong in Juan Antonio Escalante's *Dream of St Joseph* (c. 1665) and Francisco Herrera the Younger's theatrical *Triumph of St Hermengildo* (c. 1660–70) in the Prado. Diagonal structures also stand out in Juan Bautista del Mazo's (d. 1667) picture of *The Artist's Family* (c. 1658) in the Vienna Gallery, which aligns the groups of figures far less flexibly than Velázquez's *Meninas* on which it is clearly modelled.

The *Immaculate Conception* of Juan Carreño de Miranda (1614–85) in the Hispanic Society in New York takes Murillo's *Conceptions* one stage further. Murillo's Virgin (Prado no. 972) is gently borne up by a cherubic quartet bearing symbols of the Mother of God into a misty diaphanous light; Carreño de Miranda's is thrust heavenward by a pyramid of pushful cherubs towards an inverted pyramid of cloud and more cherubs. Carreño's Virgin in fact seems pinned to the crossing of the diagonals, and restrained by heavy swirling drapes.

A similar contrast could be made between Murillo's *Conceptions* and those of José Antolínez (1635–75). That in the Bowes Museum in Barnard Castle follows Murillo in giving the cherubs below the figure of the Virgin palms, lilies and other symbols, but differs from the older artist in the accentuation of rhythms. Two flying cherubs and a palm in the foreground echo the main diagonal from left to right, and the clouds mark a similar (almost corkscrew) pattern. Antolínez also chooses sharper colour contrasts than Murillo, who certainly favours variety but balances his tones with a fine sense of unity. Antolínez inclines to the garish. In the *Liberation of St Peter* in the National Gallery, Dublin, a flashy angel wears a tunic with narrow stripes of red, blue and yellow.

Equally theatrical is the work of Claudio Coello (1642–93) and Valdés Leal (1622–90). Perhaps Valdés's ability in dramatic and moralistic compositions explains his work for the Jesuits. In Italy Lord Chandos in 1620 had been impressed by the Society's interest in getting 'all possible inventions to catch men's affections and to ravish their understanding', and in Spain the Jesuits encouraged drama in art as well as in literature. Velázquez's *Adoration of the Magi* (Madrid, Prado) was probably painted for the Noviciado de San Luis of the Jesuits in Seville in 1619, and is strongly lit and rich in detail. Zurbarán's *St Francis in Meditation* (National Gallery, London) also owes something to the Jesuits and their advocacy of the contemplation of a skull as an aid to meditation on death, which led to the frequent representation of saints with skulls from the end of the sixteenth century onwards. Valdés himself painted seven scenes from the life of St Ignatius for the Jesuit house in Seville probably in 1665 (now in the Seville Museum). The group was originally hung in the patio of the house 'not only for the sake of religious decoration, but also as an example which people might follow, so that by abhorring the deformity of their souls they might become converted to a better life.' The painting of *St Ignatius Watching over his Arms before the Altar of the Virgin of Montserrat* apparently had a particularly strong moral impact, leading to at least one conversion in 1665, and Valdés later became a master of emblematic paintings for meditation. Two that were commissioned by the notorious Sevillian nobleman and convert Don Miguel Mañara for the Caridad in Seville followed Mañara's own *Discourse on Truth* for their subject-matter. But zigzag lines of composition and stage lighting play an important part in driving the message home. These are particularly noticeable in *The Triumph of Death* (1672). A skeleton carrying a coffin as well as the traditional scythe treads under foot a globe, a knight's armour, crowns, jewels and books, to extinguish life's candle. The words 'In ictu oculi' – from the service for the burial for the dead – remind the observer that 'we shall not all sleep, but will be changed in a moment *in the twinkling of an eye*, at the last trump' (1 Corinthians 15).

Architecture and retable design moved in a similarly theatrical direction towards the end of the seventeenth century. The concern for the harmonious and meaningful relationship between parts and the whole in the sixteenth century which underlay Plateresque high altars like Felipe Vigarny's in the Royal Chapel at Granada (1521), Damián Forment's detailed and Gothic but unified altars for the Pilar at Saragossa (1509–12) and Huesca Cathedral (1520–34), as well as more chastely Renaissance designs like Becerra's high altar for Astorga

Cathedral (1588-60), now gave way in many instances to structures which dazzled the eye without adding new emphasis to a biblical story. The large canvas of the Crucifixion and the sculptured group of the Descent from the Cross below it, in the High Altar for the Caridad at Seville (1670-3), make less of an impact on the spectator than the lines of the four corkscrew columns, and the scroll ends and flamboyant decoration in the attic part of the retable. There, architectural forms – more elaborate columns and a pediment – are concealed behind an elaborate shell structure containing a sculpture of the Virgin and attendant angels. Other carved angels fly (as it were from the 'wings') towards the altar from the pillars of the main arch across the altar steps. In San Esteban at Salamanca, José de Churriguera's retable is dominated by the patterns of foliage twisting round columns.

Although sculpture is often the most traditional of the arts, naturalness tended to make way for dramatic effect in it too in the seventeenth century. Basically naturalistic sculptors like Montañés and Gregorio Fernández (1566-1637) were not exempt from the baroque fascination with strong diagonals and swirling patterns. Fernández's *Pietà* (1617) in the National Museum of Sculpture at Valladolid, shows the body of Christ curving up from the ground on a shroud to rest on the Virgin Mary's knee. The panel of the Baptism of Christ above the altar of St John the Baptist in the church of Santa Paula at Seville (1637-8) has the strong diagonal line from bottom left to top right, and the upwards sweep that characterizes much baroque painting in Spain. The decorative development of retables naturally went on to influence the design of church façades, and the monastery of Sobrado de los Montes in Galicia, whose nave was completed in 1707-10, shows how elaborate column decoration and varied surface texture can be rendered in stone. The symbolic significance of decoration at this as at other periods should not be forgotten, however. Vine-leaves and grapes on retable columns remind the worshipper of Christ the true Vine, and the blood of His sacrifice in the Mass, while contributing to a decorative effect. People were then more accustomed to the use of symbolism in church decoration than they are today. The tortoise of idleness, the peacock of pride and the wolf of avarice are crushed beneath the triumphal chariot of the Sacrament in Antonio Palomino's painting for the choir of San Esteban at Salamanca (1705); and the same painter took fourteen manuscript pages to explain his 'idea' for the ceiling paintings in the chapel of Nuestra Señora de los Desemparados in Valencia, and the doctrinal relevance of the subjects in the composition.

The success of Luca Giordano (1632–1705), who was lavishly treated by Charles II in Madrid from 1692, did much to establish the popularity at court of similarly brilliant pieces with enigmatic meanings.

XV Tradition and Change in Eighteenth-Century Art and Architecture

As in literature, the early eighteenth century saw a continuation of late seventeenth-century decorative fashions. The change of dynasty in 1700 and the economic and political restructuring of the country which came shortly afterwards had no immediate impact on the arts. Pacheco had complained in the early seventeenth century that Madrid did not know what was going on in art in Granada – a situation very similar to that in poetry at the same period – and the eighteenth century saw no sudden improvement in communications. The main roads remained bad until the second half of the century, and travel within the Peninsula was not lightly to be undertaken. Poor roads together with varied monetary systems and customs barriers helped to keep provinces independent from one another. Divisions between the old areas of Aragon and Castile were also accentuated during the Wars of the Spanish Succession.

In architecture there was an obvious period of expansion after the signing of the Treaty of Utrecht (1713). The development of the Indies trade in Seville, and after 1717 in Cadiz, encouraged building in Andalusia. Important new cathedrals looking to Granada for inspiration in grandeur were begun at Guadix and Cadiz, both by Vicente Acero y Acebo (*fl.* 1714–38), and later continued by members of the Cayón family. In Seville much imposing work was carried out by Leonardo de Figueroa (d. 1730). For the church of San Luis there, he used great corkscrew columns (*salomónicas*) to adorn the lower part of the piers on which the cupola rests. At the Seminary of San Telmo (a training school for navigators), he interrupted the relative sobriety of an Herrera-type brick façade with the magnificent west entrance. This entrance rises three storeys in all – the last unfunctionally clear of the roof – and uses double columns profusely, richly carved with different patterns at each storey. Figueroa also varies the style of arch on each level, and on the ground and first floors the window opening and main doorway respectively have angles cut at the corners of the surrounds to break the simple symmetry of the rectangle. On the first floor there is a rounded arch above the central window and a basket-handle arch in front of it, rather like perspective 'flats' for a stage set. The Cartuja (Charterhouse) at Granada is another Andalusian building which conceals rather than emphasizes its basic forms at this period. In the sacristy all kinds of scrolls and fantastic shapes in plasterwork cover the pilasters. Although all the pilasters follow the same design the effect is one of restless undulating lines. Equally eye-catching is the splendid Obradoiro façade for Santiago Cathedral of Fernando Casa y Nóvoa (c. 1738): a set of complex variations on the rounded arch and Corinthian columns. In this instance, however, there is a functional element in the design too, since it allows light to flood the nave from the great west windows.

Not everything was for the eye alone in buildings of this period. Figueroa placed allegorical statues on plinths at the first- and second-storey levels on the west entrance of San Telmo, and the round balcony which overhangs the door is borne up on the backs of stone savages, appropriately enough for a building connected with the Indies trade. Symbolism continued to be an important element in ecclesiastical architecture in this as at earlier periods. In Toledo Cathedral the 'Transparente' behind the high altar which Narciso Tomé and his father started at the beginning of the century, perhaps in emulation of Bernini's Dove window and Gloria in St Peter's, Rome, is a case in point. Light floods down from a concealed source on to paintings, sculptures, a retable with strange peeled pillars, and an image of the Sacramental Host from which gilded rays emanate. The immediate impact – when the sun is shining – is spectacular in the full sense of the word. At the same time a high proportion of elements in the design relate to the Mass, since the whole object of the 'Transparente' was to encourage those who circulated behind the high altar during the Eucharist to meditate on the service itself. On either side of the altar and on the ceiling Old Testament parallels for the Mass are represented, and the sculptured tableau above the altar depicts Christ and the twelve apostles at the last supper. The Jesuits also continued to sponsor works of particular brilliance in the eighteenth century to capture the soul along with the senses. Pedro Duque Cornejo's florid, scroll-patterned altar for the Novitiate Chapel of San Luis in Seville (c. 1730) is a fine example, as is also the variegated upper storey of the façade and the cloister of the Clerecía at Salamanca by García de Quiñones (1750–5). The poet José Tafalla Negrete wrote a poem on a particularly spectacular temporary altar in a Jesuit church which attempted to match its high baroque art with equally elaborate verse:

> Famed and festive this design
> – in which refined and subtle line
> profusely mixed with splendour bright
> lucent flowers and fragant light,
> pious and exemplary,
> planned long days full zealously –
> at last the pompous display ends
> as heavy evening deathward bends.

Pedro de Ribera's elaborate portal for the Hospice of San Fernando in Madrid (1722) may have had a symbolic function too. Admittedly it takes the idea of creating illusions through art further than most buildings when it imitates the folds and tassels of curtains in stone. Yet the intention is to simulate an altar retable as well as to surprise with art, and so to remind the passer-by of the religious foundation and charitable nature of the institution. Less symbolic and more illusionary presumably were the imitation rocks at the bottom of the Goyeneche palace at Madrid. These were thought to be a typical example of pointless decoration by the neo-classics, and were expunged together with other surface decorations when the architect Villanueva (later responsible for the Museum of Sciences which became the Prado Museum) made the building suitably classical when it was taken over by the Real Academia de San Fernando.

If the decoration on the Goyeneche palace seems not to have been symbolic, that on other palaces and public buildings clearly was. The porch of the palace of the Marquis of Dos Aguas in Valencia, for instance, is entirely related to his family estates at the town of Dos Aguas, not far from the capital. Designed by Hipólito Rovira Brocandel in 1740–4, it transfers into a swirling pattern of alabaster emblems everything connected with the 'two waters' from which the marquis's home town takes its name (the rivers Júcar and San José). Swans, snakes and palm trees symbolize the rich produce of fertile river-valleys, and are also associated with the Blessed Virgin and religious virtues; carved gods pour water out of traditional urns depicting the two rivers in a conventional way. In a niche over the porch the Virgin with a rosary gives appropriately benevolent protection, since she is the patron of the town of Dos Aguas. Consequently the design has a religious as well as decorative function: the riches of the marquis, like the cornucopiae and downward-shining rays on the façade, stem from the Mother of God.

Breaks with previous practice were introduced in the eighteenth century in some cases, as at earlier periods, by foreign artists and architects who came to Spain to work. A German, Conrad Rudolf, trained in France, was responsible for designing a new façade for Valencia Cathedral in 1703 to a novel curved pattern, subsequently used by Jaime Bort Miliá for Murcia Cathedral (1741–54) and by Ventura Rodríguez for the church of San Marcos at Madrid (1749–53). Architects and designers from Italy and France were also brought to Spain by the king to enlarge the palace at Aranjuez, to build a new one at San Ildefonso, outside Segovia, and rebuild the Madrid palace when the old Alcázar there was burnt down in 1734. One of the Italians, Santiago Bonavia, may well have provided Ventura Rodríguez with the immediate model for San Marcos, since he used curved façades at Aranjuez (San Antonio, 1748), and elliptical forms too for San Miguel (1739–46) and the Royal Palace chapel in the capital (1740s).

These palaces not only introduced new architectural forms and manners into Spain; they also attempted to raise the status of the Spanish monarchy once more. La Granja at San Ildefonso was to be a miniature Versailles: the gardens were laid out by French designers, and French sculptors carved the figures for the various fountains. Expense was spared on neither exteriors nor interiors. Holes were blasted in the rocky hillside above the palace, and filled with earth to enable avenues of trees to be planted. A great collection of Italian and Dutch paintings was assembled to hang on the walls of the palace apartments. Some paintings were also commissioned for the new palaces, too, and often these express the power of the monarchy. Luis Egidio Meléndez (1716–80), a great specialist in still lifes, painted a series for Aranjuez representing all the produce of Spain, which individually seem beautifully balanced and harmonious compositions: a delight to the senses rather than a traditional warning of the ephemeral nature of material things. As a group, however, they acquire a political significance, and reflect the power of Spain much as Tiepolo's more obviously symbolic ceilings for the throne-room of the palace at Madrid. Tiepolo's work represents the nature of the Catholic ruler and the extent of Spain's home and overseas dominions, their peoples, flora and fauna; the elements and the chief rivers of the Peninsula are symbolized in sculptured medallions at the four corners of the ceiling by the French sculptor Michel, extending the message of royal power.

The Bourbon monarchs controlled the development of the arts in Spain more than their predecessors, principally by the creation of royal academies. There had, of course, been academies of arts in a number of centres like Seville and Saragossa in the seventeenth century. But these had been the result of the enterprise of individuals and guilds of artists and had no national status. Philip V approved the establishment of an Academy of Arts (Real Academia de San Fernando) at Madrid in 1744, and the statutes were finally accepted by Ferdinand VI in 1749; others followed at Valencia, Saragossa and Seville. The idea was to improve the standard of architects and artists, and to raise the arts in Spain to the level of other European countries. A desired economic by-product of the academies was the improved saleability of Spanish art, so that less would be bought from abroad. The ninety-eight students who enrolled at Madrid in 1752 included sons of silversmiths, carpenters, furniture makers, silk manufacturers, and there was one from the earthenware factory at Talavera; so the economic advantages of the training and the improved opportunities for commissions appear not to have escaped the attention of craftsmen who wanted their children to better themselves.

The Academies helped to establish a standardized taste in Spain on a national rather than a regional basis. Artists from the provinces often went to Madrid to study, and the general acceptance of neo-classic principles was clearly encouraged in that way. Provincial projects needed the approval of the San Fernando Academy. In the second half of the century the Academies attempted to eradicate vestiges of guild structures remaining in some areas, particularly after 1 May 1785 when the king made an order allowing artists to work freely in any part of the country without becoming members of local guilds. Provincial tastes did not entirely die out, however. At churches in Priego de Córdoba in the 1770s stucco work of the richness and decorative variety produced in Granada at the beginning of the century was still being devised. The basic design of farmhouses in country areas also remained largely unchanged, and earthenware patterns in the main centres of production did not alter much either in the course of the century.

Despite the continued domination of the arts by the patronage of king and Church in the eighteenth century, new opportunities for artists certainly arose at this period. As a result of the growing wealth of the merchant class a new kind of collector of paintings and *objets d'art* came into existence: one who had more respect for the artist's own views, was more or less his social equal, and was less inclined to dictate to him than the patrons of earlier periods. Artists still tried, naturally enough, to obtain a post in the king's employ, but there was an increasing market for the small picture – landscapes, still lifes and bourgeois portraits – and for prints, too, at the end of the century. Luis Paret (1746–99), for instance, who had been trained at the San Fernando Academy, although later a pupil of the French artist Charles de la Traverse, and who painted some brilliant small canvases of court subjects – *Charles III Dining* and a scene from one of the masked balls held in Madrid in 1767 (Prado, Madrid) – and many views of Spanish ports for the king, also undertook book illustrations for Sancha, the publisher. Paret's obvious delight in the world of the senses got him into trouble with the hierarchy on more than one occasion. He was exiled to Mexico in the 1770s for his involvement in princely amours, and later, in Bilbao, was reported to the Inquisition for possessing and lending a copy of the *Celestina*.

Faced with a changing society, the old despots necessarily became more benevolent, as can be seen from eighteenth-century developments in city and town planning. The Goyeneche family's rural town of Nuevo Baztán near Loeches (prov. of Madrid) was laid out by José de Churriguera (1665–1723) between 1709 and 1713, and a glass industry was established there in an attempt to diversify the sources of rural prosperity. Church and palace are inevitably at its centre, but three interconnected squares create some alternative focuses of interest, and there was no intention to create a private court with aristocratic hangers-on as Lerma had sought to build at Lerma a century earlier. The same concern for the social life of townspeople was reflected in La Carolina in the province of Jaén, built as a consequence of the plan to repopulate the Sierra Morena region after 1767. At La Carolina one main axis of the town led from the Plaza Mayor to the church and the intendant's residence. But the township had a number of other squares too, including one of hexagonal shape, a characteristic of the Sierra Morena towns.

In expanding cities important new civil developments can be followed in the course of the century. At Salamanca a new and very spacious Plaza Mayor was planned by Alberto Churriguera and begun in 1729; at Madrid the Puente de Toledo (bridge commissioned in 1719) and new barracks were built by Pedro de Ribera, who also laid out gardens by the Manzanares. A model suburb was built at Barceloneta outside Barcelona to serve the port between 1752 and 1775; and a

fine square was designed by Juan Antonio de Olaguibel for Vitoria in
1781–91. New suburbs developed in towns and villages as well as
cities to cater for the increase in population in the second half of the
century.

XVI Francisco de Goya (1746–1828)

In painting Goya mirrors the changing Spanish society of his day.
His initial training was in Saragossa, where there was a small but
relatively flourishing guild of painters in the eighteenth century. A
period of study in Italy followed – common for Spanish artists in the
eighteenth century as in earlier times – and this enabled Goya to
establish himself as an independent painter on his return. His early
commissions were for nobles in the Aragonese capital, like the Counts
of Sobradiel, and for churches in the area, notably N.S. del Pilar,
which was decorating its ceiling and cupolas (full of light at the
time, though less well lit today) and generally sparing no expense to
enrich the cult of the Virgin. From 1775 Goya began to work for the
Tapestry Factory at Madrid, where he came under the direction and
influence of Mengs, Charles III's favourite painter and an arbiter of
neo-classic taste in Spain.

Many of Goya's portraits and tapestry cartoons in the 1770s and
1780s follow Mengsian principles: arranging groups in the shape of a
pyramid and giving variety to the painting by placing people in different stances and making them all look in slightly different directions.
Very obvious pyramid groups occur in the *Kite-Flyers* and the portrait
of the Osuna family (both in the Prado), and, in the portrait of the
Count of Floridablanca (Banco Urquijo, Madrid), crossing diagonals
are marked by the arrangement of books on the floor as well as by
curtains at the left and the blue sash of the Order of Charles III which
the count is wearing. Sometimes a comparison between a preliminary
drawing and a finished painting enables one to see how far the aesthetic
doctrines accepted by the establishment influenced his work at this
period. The panel painting of a *Girl on a Swing* for the Duke of Osuna,
for instance, is a very carefully composed picture. The girl herself and
figures to left and right form a neat pyramid. The trees lean inward
to emphasize the diagonals, and there is a misty and idealized landscape
of mountains in the background. The preliminary drawing on which
the *Swing* is based concentrates on the figures of the man pushing and
the girl, and a dynamic rhythm and vitality is present which the

painting loses. More leg is shown in the drawing than the decorum of a painting for an aristocratic household finally permitted, and the moral and aesthetic restrictions imposed by the commissioned work are plain to see.

Occasionally, even in portraits, Goya's personality manages to break through the conventions. This is very clearly the case in the painting of the young boy *Don Manuel Osorio de Zúñiga* (1784, New York, Metropolitan Museum). The child's head is centrally placed and the diagonal from top left to bottom right follows a shadow down the wall in the background in a conventional way. But also in the background Goya has placed three cats, one of which stares with unconcealed excitement at the child's pet magpie held on a string in the foreground. This lively group in the left-hand corner necessarily distracts attention from the child, who seems oblivious of what is going on. A similar painting by Agustín Esteve of *Don Juan María Osorio-Álvarez* (*c.* 1786), with a linnet, clearly modelled on Goya's, eliminates this element, which suggests that it may not have met with complete approval.

An early break with tradition occurs in Goya's tapestry cartoon of *Winter*. The usual way of representing the subject was to show people wrapped in furs, a family by a fire or an old man with a beard. Goya shows none of these, and concentrates less on the delights of winter than on its rigours for the labourer. A group of country men muffled in cloaks against the wind and the snow make their way with a sow on the back of a mule across a desolate stretch of snow: a 'capricious' or original approach to winter for an artist according to one of Goya's contemporaries.

More obvious originality followed in the 1790s, when illness and subsequent deafness cut Goya off from easy contacts with people around him. There was no break in his work at court, which continued to please his royal masters – his paintings of Queen María Luisa are generally more flattering than those of his less talented contemporaries – but he began to paint some small pictures 'giving free rein to his imagination, normally restricted in commissioned work', as he himself observed. One of these showed a scene in a mad-house with two men fighting and a keeper striking them on the head; others may have been scenes from everyday life, or witchcraft or the theatre, paintings such as those he executed for the Alameda Palace of the Dukes of Osuna in the 1790s, which included the scene from *El hechizado por fuerza* now in the National Gallery in London.

Drawings and etchings also gave him an opportunity to develop new approaches in the 1790s. In some of his *Caprichos*, published in 1799, there were veiled and sometimes ambiguous attacks on the Inquisition, the monastic orders, the judiciary and the mindless nobility, as well as general moral criticism. The techniques of caricature were used, and so was ingenious word-play. Thus in No. 53, *¡Qué pico de oro!*, a group of open-mouthed admirers sit round a pulpit or professorial desk and listen to a lecture or sermon from a parrot. 'To speak like a parrot' in Spanish means to speak apparently intelligently but without real knowledge, so the representation of the speaker involves criticism. The phrase 'pico de oro', on the other hand, implies true wit and discretion in the orator, and Goya presumably uses it to express the audience's view and suggest that the 'parrot' has taken them in, too.

Goya's choice of etchings for the expression of these ideas is an interesting one. Prints after all were rapidly creating a wider public for art in other countries. The success of Hogarth's prints in England is a well-known case in point. When Goya refers to his art as 'idioma universal' (a universal language) in the preliminary drawing for No. 43, *The Dream of Reason Produces Monsters*, he is presumably implying, as Palomino had done before him, that art could speak to the illiterate majority as well as to the literate minority, and to people in many countries.

In fact the *Caprichos* did not reach the wide public that Goya may have hoped for, but he continued to make etchings and clearly sought to create a broader interest in art than had previously existed. The lack of a real middle class in Spain at this time necessarily limited the impact of his move, and we can see in Goya an artist who was in many respects revolutionary, and yet unable to reach many of those who might have profited from knowing his views. Furthermore, it was not easy to speak out against unconstitutional monarchy and political or religious tyranny in Goya's Spain. His most critical work is inevitably to be found in drawings and etchings he never circulated. In one of his drawings (for No. 77 of the *Desastres*) the Pope walks a tightrope, and the comment is 'Que se rompe la cuerda' (The rope is breaking); in another a woman has been imprisoned 'Por liberal' (for being generous, or, alternatively, a political liberal).

A measure of Goya's breadth of ideas and originality of views can be got from his *Disasters of War* series of etchings. Unlike many earlier artists faced with the subject, who saw only the generals or represented the horrors of war as a sort of distant stage spectacle or news item, Goya looked at the ordinary man in the war situation, in close-up. He did not suggest that the Spaniard's role in the war with France was necessarily a heroic one. The brutal treatment of a person by the Spanish populace, in Nos. 28 and 29, is seen now as a vile act, the consequence of irrational mob action, now as an understandable act ('lo merecía' – he deserved it). The punishment of criminals in war, in Nos. 34 and 35, is now explainable ('Por una navaja' – for killing with a knife) and now irrational ('No se puede saber por qué' – you cannot tell why these men were put to death).

Finally Goya's concern with the irrational and the bestial side of man finds extraordinarily powerful expression in some drawings of nightmares and in the series of so-called 'Black Paintings' originally on the walls of two rooms in his country house just outside Madrid, and now in the Prado Museum. The obsessive subjects here are age and cruelty; the universal and the human; time and violence. The hideous trio of the Fates spins out and weaves and breaks human life; two men bludgeon one another with clubs. In the series of etchings called the *Disparates* the same dark sense of man emerges, and Goya seems to use images taken from Carnival customs to point up the ways in which man overthrows the moral and rational order of life to express his vile nature.

In technique as well as in subject-matter Goya thrusts away the conventions in later work. In paintings like the first of the two sometimes held to represent the martyrdom of Jean de Brébeuf and Gabriel Lallement at the hands of the Iroquois Indians (*c.* 1812–18, Besançon Museum), the pyramided groups and balanced composition of the early work are set aside. Virtually the whole of the left part of the canvas is totally without incident, as it is again in No. 21 of the *Tauromaquia* etchings with devastating dramatic effect. Goya's friend Ceán Bermúdez tells us he sometimes used his fingers to paint with, much against Ceán's good advice. Yet the rational is never entirely missing in Goya's work either, nor is his faith in the possibilities of beauty in human beings and their capacity for good as well as evil, whatever their background. In most of his representations of ordinary people – the knife-grinder, the water-carrier and men working in a forge – there are no patronizing airs, as one feels there were in Murillo: rather the faith of a Velázquez or of the Enlightenment in the dignity of man, and a sense of the need for justice and tolerance.

XVII The Nineteenth Century

After such a change of values it is hard to see where others could go after Goya. Some merely followed, reworking Goya's subjects – particularly bullfights and Inquisition scenes – and carrying his carefree manner still further, as in the case of Eugenio Lucas; others, such as José Madrazo, Vicente López and José Aparicio, reasserted the neo-classical virtues. The latter's paintings of *The Hunger in Madrid* and *The Glories of Spain* show that this artist's neo-classicism was strongly linked to a belief in the union of Church and monarchy under Ferdinand VII in Spain. It is hardly surprising that more space is given to the explanation of these two paintings in an early catalogue of the Prado Museum (1828) than to most of Velázquez's. With the return of the liberals in 1833 and a new direction in Romantic taste – which had previously followed Schlegel in looking to ideals of monarchy, aristocracy and religion – Goya seemed very much to the point, particularly as a painter of Spanish *costumbres*: *majos* and *majas*, bullfights, sports and pastimes. Alenza and Valeriano Bécquer (the brother of the poet) followed him, like Lucas, in this. Subsequently, when impressionism spread to Spain from France, Goya's brushwork and bold juxtapositions of colours were relevant too.

Goya, above all, was the first of a line of painters who worked in part for the emerging middle classes. His portrait subjects had included fellow artists, architects, actors like Máiquez (Prado), La Tirana (Real Academia de San Fernando) and Doña Antonia Zárate (Beit Collection); businessmen like his daughter-in-law's father, Miguel de Goycoechea, and a banker relative by his son's marriage, Don Juan Bautista de Muguiro (Prado). This trend continued in Federico de Madrazo's fine bust portrait of the French painter Ingres (1833) and in his full-length portraits of the actor Arjona (1852) and the famous actress Teodora Lamadrid (1852), all three paintings now in the collection of the Hispanic Society of America. Madrazo's relative by marriage, Mariano Fortuny (1838–74), also painted some portraits, although he is chiefly known for landscapes, his Moroccan paintings, bullfights and other Spanish genre subjects. Later, however, portrait painting became an international affair as it had been in the sixteenth, seventeenth and early eighteenth centuries: Whistler painted the world-famous Spanish violinist Sarasate; the Basque Zuloaga painted the Cambridge historian and university teacher Oscar Browning (King's College, Cambridge).

Other types of painting that blossomed in the Romantic and post-Romantic periods were historical scenes and landscapes. Historical subjects could be allegorical. José de Madrazo's *Death of Viriato* (Prado, Madrid), depicting the murder of a patriotic hero at the instigation of his Roman enemies, obviously dealt indirectly with the supposed treachery of the *afrancesados* in Spain during the Peninsular War. In a similar way, at the same period, Martínez de la Rosa used a historical subject connected with the *comuneros* revolt in the sixteenth century to comment on the struggle against absolutist regimes in his play *La viuda de Padilla*. Subsequent historical paintings, of which many large examples now hang in the Museo de Arte Moderno in Madrid, took a more Romantic view of history, idealizing the past in the manner of the enormously successful historical novels of Fernández y González.

Landscapes gave nineteenth-century artists in Spain as elsewhere in Europe the opportunity to express more personal or poetic moods, or alternatively to satisfy a market for topographical subjects which was later to be met more easily by the photograph. Pérez Villaamil (1807–54) was a noted practitioner, and so was Martín Rico (1833–1908), whose paintings found their way into a number of foreign collections. A branch of this kind of work was regional painting – the equivalent in the fine arts of Pereda in the novel, or the plays of the brothers Quintero at a later date. The approach of the artist varied in much the same way as that of the novelist or playwright. He could approach regional life colourfully and perhaps patronizingly like Joaquín Sorolla (1863–1923) with vigorous and effervescent light in the impressionist manner; or he could approach it with more sombre tones and a sense of the harsh existence which was the more common experience of country life, as the two Basques Ignacio de Zuloaga (1870–1945, well represented in the Bilbao gallery) and Juan de Echevarría (1875–1930) appear to do. A third possible approach is a personal one: seeing in country life a reflection of the artist's own emotions, and this perhaps one finds in José Gutiérrez Solana (1886–1935).

As at other periods, patronage was an oppressive force to many artists, and a stimulus to others. The wealthiest Spanish collectors in the nineteenth century were primarily concerned with art as an investment. They bought old masters, or hired art historians to do so on their behalf, as was the practice of the banker José de Salamanca (later Marquis of Salamanca, 1811–83). Salamanca, who was responsible for the development of the middle-class quarter of Madrid (still known as the 'barrio' of Salamanca), and who built himself an imposing palace in the Paseo de Recoletos, amassed a vast collection of Spanish masters, whose sale was responsible for the loss of a great number of art treasures to Spain.

More modest middle-class patrons, however, permitted the fullest development of the artist's expression – particularly in Catalonia. The modest could of course tyrannize too. Picasso's father, an art teacher in Málaga and later in La Coruña and Barcelona, was condemned to painting endless pictures of doves because of an apparently bottomless middle-class demand. On the other hand many of the revolutionary painters of the turn of the century could not have established themselves at all without bourgeois patronage.

XVIII Gaudí

An outstanding patron of the arts in Catalonia was in fact an aristocrat: Count Eusebi Güell. It is hard to see how the highly original genius of the Catalan architect Antoni Gaudí (1852–1926) could have developed without the support of this rich and enlightened patron. Perhaps it was through Güell that Gaudí became familiar with the theories of Ruskin and Morris. Gaudí's zeal for craft and for religious spirit is certainly akin to that of Ruskin, and like Ruskin and Morris too, he believed in the traditions of the crafts. He constantly drew on the glazed tile tradition and the skill in brick construction and wrought ironwork common in Catalonia. Indeed his own ability as a carver and his skill as a builder also meant that he could evolve, test and modify forms he borrowed from earlier work or from his contemporaries. It was perhaps this craftsman's ability to work out his ideas in materials and improvise, as well as to calculate effects on the drawing-board, which led to Gaudí's extraordinary originality.

Gaudí's starting-point was, like that of most other architects of his time, the Gothic revival. As he himself wrote: 'Before the middle of this century [the nineteenth], tradition imposed the forms of the Renaissance. Since then, the tendency is to reject them in favour of those of the Middle Ages.' Gaudí thought that both styles contained elements worth preserving: the cupola and the decorative element in painting from the Renaissance, for instance. But modern application of the 'brilliant and reasoned' qualities of the Gothic style suffered in two ways in his view. Firstly, the public no longer understood the meaning of Gothic forms and symbols. Secondly, it was no longer proper to exploit craftsmen in order to achieve the perfection of details essential to early buildings.

In his approach to his great unfinished religious buildings like the chapel for the Güell colony and the Sagrada Familia in Barcelona, Gaudí's interest and belief in the Gothic can be clearly seen. The eastern portal or Portal of the Nativity of the Sagrada Familia – the only one so far completed – appeals to the old tradition of the retable façade, and is indeed very close in overall form to the retable behind the high altar in the cathedral at Castellón de Ampurias. One of the studies for the western portal also suggests a retable façade concept and seems an echo of the high altar in Santa María del Piño in Barcelona in general scheme. Details recall Gothic (and Romanesque) traditions too: the use of large script on the wall to spell out the significance of different parts of the building, such as the names of saints depicted in sculpture, the words 'Hosanna' and 'Excelsis' on the pinnacles of the Nativity façade, 'Sursum corda' and 'Sanctus' on the belfries. Ultimately, however, the main design for the Sagrada Familia develops away from the Gothic, first by the introduction of the tilted tree-like column, then by the use of warped surfaces often coated with brilliant tiles which accentuate contours – both elements tried out first in the crypt of the Güell colony chapel and in the Casa Milá.

Barcelona became in Gaudí's time the most important centre for new art and architecture in Spain for more reasons than just patronage. The vigorous revival of Catalan culture, set on foot earlier in the nineteenth century,[1] encouraged artists to develop in a more independent way than elsewhere in Spain. Furthermore, a prosperous bourgeois city such as Barcelona inevitably encouraged the development of anti-bourgeois art in the late nineteenth century as it did in other European centres: anti-bourgeois art ironically dependent on bourgeois financial support. Above all, Barcelona at the end of the century, despite its expansion, was still small enough to allow an artistic group with common aims to develop.

Artists and writers in Barcelona came together more particularly in the café called 'Els Quatre Gats', from July 1897, much as artists and writers in London at the same period gathered in the Café Royal. There were exhibitions, concerts and puppet-shows in Els Quatre Gats to encourage its role as an artistic centre. A literary and art review was born there in 1899. The leading painters were Santiago Rusiñol,

[1] See also Chapter 5, section VIII, and Chapter 9, section V.

Ramón Casas, Isidro Nonell and Miguel Utrillo (father of the more famous Maurice) – mostly Parisian in style and manner. But if many of these names are nearly forgotten today outside Spain, it was in their midst that a major twentieth-century master first appeared: Pablo Picasso.

XIX Pablo Picasso (1881–1973)

Picasso's drawing for Els Quatre Gats (signed P. Ruiz Picasso) is in the Toulouse-Lautrec manner, like a number of his earlier paintings – the *Woman in Blue*, for instance (1901, Museo de Arte Moderno, Madrid). His interest in bold design may have caused this early response to Lautrec, although the circus and music-hall subjects must also have attracted him. The interest in structure, however, long outlived the passion for Toulouse-Lautrec in Picasso's work. Els Quatre Gats must also have encouraged Picasso to take an interest in French art, and like many of the Barcelona group he soon went to Paris. He lived mostly in France after 1905, yet he never entirely lost his concern for things Spanish.

In France, Picasso, like Matisse, became fascinated with primitive masks in about 1909, and learnt from them what earlier artists had learnt from Japanese prints and Cézanne: the emotional charge of geometrical structures. Later, in the 1920s, he shared with other artists and with Stravinsky in music a delight in classical organization. Picasso seems to have had, like Gaudí, the ability to assimilate and transform various new styles and influences. Yet if the styles were usually shared with French artists – or with Spaniards working in Paris, like Juan Gris – Spanish subjects constantly recur. The bullfight, for instance, was seen initially (1902) as a pretext for sharp 'sol y sombra' contrasts; in the 1920s for statuesque groupings; in the thirties as a violent, sometimes pseudo-sexual conflict between horse and bull; and in the forties and fifties as a subject to be treated with fierce brush strokes and a sense of dynamic spectacle. The guitar and the mandolin pass through similar transformations, according to the stylistic preoccupations and drives of the artist at the moment at which they were painted, drawn or engraved.

Ultimately Picasso illustrates as well as any major twentieth-century artist the radical changes in the nature of art that have occurred in the last hundred years. For centuries the subject remained as important if not more important than the artist's vision. Latterly the painting itself, the patterns used, the imagination of the artist, or even the brush stroke, became the main point of art. Whereas originally a style was a means of conveying effectively the subject of a painting, which embodied emotion in itself, the style later became the prime expressive factor. This does not mean that art has stopped communicating; merely that it communicates what the artist wants or feels rather than what a patron or a restricting society demands. The way in which Picasso used things that are familiar to us to make us see the patterns they form and the tensions of different shapes and colours, rather than the objects in themselves, is of the essence of contemporary art, and of art in general since the coming of the photograph; to be more precise, since the popularization of the photograph at the beginning of the present century. Hence Picasso's willingness to take second-hand subjects and produce variations on art as well as variations on life. In the late 1950s Picasso painted between forty and fifty brilliant canvases based on Velázquez's *Las Meninas*, and others based on Manet's *Déjeuner sur l'herbe* and El Greco's *Portrait of an Artist*. These paintings are *about* painting. In the case of El Greco this is obvious; Velázquez shows himself at work on a large canvas in *The Maids of Honour*; and Manet's *Déjeuner* is a nineteenth-century parody of a classical group and so mocks academic approaches.

One can see why Picasso admired paintings such as these. At the same time his variations on them led to the accusation that he latterly lost his involvement with life. Nothing, in fact, could be further from the truth, since paintings are as much a part of life as the landscape the artist looks at, or the model who sits in his studio, or the studio itself. Picasso painted all of these things. With emotive line and colour, sometimes using violent myths or familiar symbols like the dove of peace or the minotaur, but often exploiting the ordinary tensions of life – the urges, delights and frustrations of the senses – Picasso expressed the beauty, irony, comedy and tragedy of life. In the paintings which have the greatest impact in our times he often linked imaginative symbols with specific beautiful, ironic or tragic human occasions. *Guernica* (1937), for instance, sets the bullfight struggle between violent bull and sacrificial horse as a symbol of tragic conflict amid burning houses and victims of air attack, expressing the brutality of war in general as well as the German bombing of a Basque town in particular.

XX Dalí and Miró

In Picasso's case the artist's symbols were often taken from traditional Spanish as well as universal stock. Other twentieth-century Spanish artists have exploited their own unconscious in a more determinedly personal and, at first sight, more hermetic manner. Salvador Dalí (b. 1904) has used basic surrealist techniques to this end: creating the atmosphere of dream, or juxtaposing things not normally found together, without seeking to lose a semblance of reality, rather like De Chirico or Magritte, and sometimes like them deriving humour from juxtapositions as well as psychic shocks. The development of Joan Miró (b. 1893) has led to a much more radical departure from the nineteenth-century emphasis on links between art and reality. His early paintings of the period 1916–17 were simplified landscapes and still lifes preoccupied with geometrical form in the Cézanne tradition, but viewed from unusual angles and with extraordinary springy rhythms. The fascination with lines and patterns – echoing Japanese style in the signature, print on the wall, and general execution in the *Portrait of E. C. Ricart* (1917) – becomes increasingly delicate between 1918 and 1920, contrasting tendril forms with bold lines and dog-tooth shapes. Progressively Miró simplified his patterns and moved further away from straightforward external reality, adding more elusive symbolic elements in the 1920s, when he spent much of the time in Paris. Gradually he eliminated the horizon line in his paintings, so that his increasingly abstract forms float or dance perplexingly in space. Sometimes words or lettering play a part in the paintings as in the witty canvas *This is the Colour of my Dreams* (1925), where the word 'Photo' in the top left-hand corner is accompanied by a blue blot at the bottom on the right hand, with the words 'ceci est le couleur de mes rêves' written underneath it: an obvious jibe at naturalistic art.

Miró's painting may mock photographic realism – symbolic forms, curves and patterns of colour are frequently given extraordinarily detailed titles like *People in the Night Guided by the Phosphorescent Tracks of Snails* (1940) – yet never loses its roots in nature. Bird and insect, sun and moon, man and woman, create a primitive yet poetic dualism in many of his works. There are disturbing conjunctions of colours, painful absences, in his works which set out to awaken responses rather than merely describe the visual world. Perhaps the whole object of the long titles is to get the subject itself out of the way, so that the painting itself can begin, and the imagination of the spectator can work more freely on the forms and colours with which it is presented.

Contemporary Spanish painters have continued the spirit of protest and the interest in elusive symbolism of Miró and the surrealists, yet attach a new importance to the paint in itself. Tàpies and Cuixart, who established themselves in Catalonia in the forties and fifties as masters of evocative abstraction with sombre tonalities, have developed an almost sculptural approach to the paint surface, texture taking precedence over pattern. Collage techniques, pieces of string, metallic tones, sand, plastic and marble dust stand conventional ideas about the nature of painting on their heads in Cuixart's work. In Madrid, Canogar and Feito also shape and groove their paint surfaces, and the old idea that a painting represented rounded objects and space on a plane surface is clearly cast aside. These painters give us real three-dimensional forms, not simulated ones. So the forms on the canvas no longer point, symbolically, to some reality outside themselves. The reality of the paint is enough in itself.

XXI Towards Modern Sculpture

The movement away from realism to elusive or evocative forms can be followed as clearly in sculpture as in painting. Naturalism and the imitation of the styles of classical antiquity run on from the seventeenth through the eighteenth century into the nineteenth. Francisco Salzillo (1703–83) and Agapito Vallmitjana (1833–1905) continued the realistic traditions of men like Pedro de Mena (d. 1688) and Pedro Roldán. Manuel Álvarez (1727–97) and Damián Campeny (1771–1855) worked expressively within the neo-classic manner. A rhythmic naturalism with some reminiscences of Rodin is evident in portraits and bull-fighting subjects by Mariano Benlliure (1862–1947), but a more primitive and virile force flows in the sometimes cubist lines of Manolo Hugué's work (1872–1945). A clear development from a simplified realism to abstraction marks the output of Ángel Ferrant (1891–1961), but there has only recently been any sign of real originality in Spanish sculpture, notably in Eduardo Chillida (b. 1924).

From his early simplified forms of human torsos Chillida soon moved to less explicit and more evocative shapes in iron or wood rather than stone. There are often reminiscences of natural forms in these. Winnowing forks seem the basis of *Silent Music* (1955); anchors or fishing hooks of *Vibration No. 1* (1955); and more obvious parallels occur in the series of sculptures with the title *Dream Anvil* (1954–8). But as the titles indicate Chillida prefers to express rhythms and open-ended movements rather than to capture explicit *things* in the world around him. The imagination and the solid reality of iron and wood combine magically in his work, in which there is an extraordinary tension between strong materials and springy movements, elegance and muscle, earthbound flight. If a Spanish critic seeks to define Chillida's sculpture as the 'spirit of the Basques', the French and the Americans and the Germans evidently find something more universal in it.

Bibliography

PRIMARY SOURCES

CARDUCHO, V. *Diálogos sobre la pintura* (1633). Ed. F. J. Sánchez Cantón. Madrid, 1923.

CASSIANO DAL POZZO. 'Descripción del Escorial por Cassiano dal Pozzo (1626)'. Ed. Enriqueta Harris and Gregorio de Andrés, Anejo de *Archivo Español de Arte*, No. 179 (1972).

CEÁN BERMÚDEZ, J. A. *Diccionario histórico de los más ilustres profesores de las bellas artes en España*. 6 vols. Madrid, 1800. Facsimile reprint. Madrid, 1965.

FORD, R. *A Hand-Book for Travellers in Spain and Readers at Home* (1845). 3 vols. London, 1966.

GARCÍA HIDALGO, J. *Principios para estudiar el nobilísmo y real arte de la pintura* (1693). Ed. A. Rodríguez-Moñino. Madrid, 1965.

GUEVARA, F. DE. *Comentarios de la pintura* (1560?). Ed. R. Benet. Barcelona, 1948.

HERRERA, J. DE. *Sumario y breve declaración de los diseños y estampas de la Fábrica de San Lorenzo el Real del Escurial* (Madrid, 1589). Facsimile reprint as annex to L. Cervera Vera, *Las estampas y El Sumario de El Escorial por Juan de Herrera*. Madrid, 1954.

HOLANDA, F. DE. *De la pintura antigua* (1548). Versión española de Manuel Denis (1563). Madrid, 1921.

MARTÍNEZ, J. *Discursos practicables del nobilísimo arte de la pintura*. Ed. J. Gállego. Barcelona, 1950.

PACHECO, F. *Arte de la pintura* (1638). Ed. F. J. Sánchez Cantón. 2 vols. Madrid, 1956.

PALOMINO, A. *El museo pictórico y escala óptica* (Madrid, 1715–24). Reprinted Madrid, 1947.

PÉREZ DE MOYA, J. *Philosophia secreta* (Madrid, 1585). Ed. E. Gómez de Baquero. 2 vols. Madrid, 1928.

PONZ, A. *Viaje de España*. 18 vols. Madrid, 1772–94; reprinted Madrid, 1947; Facsimile reprint, Madrid, 1970.

VIÑAZA, CONDE DE LA. *Adiciones al Diccionario histórico . . . de Ceán Bermúdez* (Madrid, 1889–94). Reprint, Madrid, 1970.

DOCUMENTS

Documentos para la historia del arte en Andalucía. 10 vols. Seville, 1927–46.

GARCÍA CHICO, E. *Documentos para el estudio del arte en Castilla.* 4 vols. Valladolid, 1940–50.

MARTÍ Y MONZÓ, J. *Estudios histórico-artísticos relativos principalmente a Valladolid.* Valladolid, 1901.

PARDO CANALÍS, E. *Registros de matrícula de la Academia de San Fernando de 1752 a 1815.* Madrid, 1967.

PÉREZ SEDANO, F. *Datos documentales inéditos para la historia del arte español.* Madrid, 1914.

SÁNCHEZ CANTÓN, F. J. *Fuentes literarias para la historia del arte español.* 5 vols. Madrid, 1923–41.

ZARCO DEL VALLE, M. R. *Documentos de la catedral de Toledo.* 2 vols. Madrid, 1916.

CATALOGUES AND GUIDES

AZCÁRATE, J. M. DE. *Monumentos españoles. Catálogo de los declarados histórico-artísticos.* 3 vols. Madrid, 1953–4.

BARCIA PAVÓN, A. M. DE. *Catálogo de la colección de dibujos originales de la Biblioteca Nacional.* Madrid, 1906.

CAMÓN AZNAR, J. *Museo Lázaro Galdiano.* Madrid, 1964. Text and slides.

GARÍN Y ORTIZ DE TARANCO, F. M. *Catálogo-Guía del Museo Provincial de Bellas Artes de San Carlos.* Valencia, 1955.

GAYA NUÑO, J. A. *Historia y guía de los museos de España.* Madrid, 1955.

—— *La pintura española fuera de España (Historia y catálogo).* Madrid, 1958.

—— *La pintura española en los museos privinciales.* Madrid, 1964. Text and slides.

GESTOSO Y PÉREZ, J. *Catálogo de las pinturas y esculturas del Museo Provincial de Sevilla.* Seville, 1912.

GUDIOL RICART, J. *Guías artísticas de España.* Barcelona, Aries, various dates.

GUINARD, P. *Peintures espagnoles dans les musées francais.* Paris, 1964.

Los monumentos cardinales de España. Madrid, Plus Ultra.

NATIONAL GALLERY CATALOGUES. *The Spanish School* by Neil Maclaren. Second ed. revised by Allan Braham. London, 1970.

NATIONAL GALLERY OF SCOTLAND, EDINBURGH. *Shorter Catalogue: a complete list of the Collection* . . . by Colin Thompson and Hugh Brigstocke. Edinburgh, 1970.

NATIONAL GALLERY OF IRELAND. *Catalogue of the Paintings.* Dublin, 1971.

OTERO PEDRAYO, R. *Guía de Galicia.* Vigo, 1954.

PEMÁN Y PEMARTÍN, C. *Museo de Bellas Artes de Cádiz. Catálogo de las pinturas.* Cadiz, 1952.

SÁNCHEZ CANTÓN, F. J. *Guía completa del Museo del Prado.* Madrid, 1967.

VELASCO AGUIRRE, M. *Catálogo de los grabados de la Biblioteca de Palacio.* Madrid, 1934.

WATTENBERG, F. *Museo Nacional de Escultura de Valladolid.* Madrid, 1963.

GENERAL STUDIES

ANGULO IÑÍGUEZ, D. *La mitología y el arte español del Renacimiento.* Madrid, 1952.

Ars Hispaniae. Historia Universal del Arte Hispánico. 19 vols. Madrid, 1947–66.

Art Treasures in Spain. Monuments, Masterpieces, Commissions and Collections. Introduction by Juan Ainaud de Lasarte. London and Sydney, 1970.

BERENGUER, M. *Arte en Asturias: de la cueva candamo al palacio ramirense del Naranco.* Oviedo, 1969.

CAMÓN AZNAR. I. *Las artes y los pueblos de la España primitiva.* Madrid, 1954.

DURLIAT, M. *L'Art catalan.* Paris, 1964.

GAYA NUÑO, J. A. *Historia del arte español.* Madrid, 1946.

GUDIOL, J. *The Arts of Spain.* London, 1964.

GUTKIND, E. A. *Urban Development in Southern Europe: Spain and Portugal.* International History of City Development, 3. New York and London, 1967.

KUBLER, G., and SORIA, M. *Art and Architecture in Spain and Portugal and their American Dominions 1500–1800.* London, 1959.

LAMBERT, E. *L'Art en Espagne et au Portugal.* Paris, 1948.

—— *L'Art gothique en Espagne aux XIIᵉ et XIIIᵉ siècles.* Paris, 1931.

LAFUENTE FERRARI, E. *Breve historia de la pintura española.* 4th ed. Madrid, 1953.

LOZOYA, MARQUÉS DE. *Historia del arte hispánico.* 5 vols. Barcelona, 1931–49.

MÂLE, E. *Arts et artistes du Moyen-Age (L'Espagne arabe et l'art roman),* Paris, 1939.

GÓMEZ MORENO, M. *El arte románico español.* Madrid, 1934.

MENÉNDEZ Y PELAYO, M. *Historia de las ideas estéticas en España.* 5 vols. Madrid, 1947.

RÁFOLS, J. F. *Modernismo y modernistas.* Barcelona, 1949.

TERRASSE, H. *L'Art hispano-mauresque, des origines au XIIIᵉ siècle.* Paris, 1932.

PAINTING AND DRAWING

ALPERS, S. *The Decoration of the Torre de la Parada.* London and New York, 1971.

ANGULO IÑÍGUEZ, D. *Pintura del Renacimiento.* Ars Hispaniae, 12. Madrid, 1954.

BERGSTROM, I. *Maestros españoles de bodegones y floreros del siglo XVII.* Madrid, 1970.

BREUIL, H., and OBERMAIER, H. *La cueva de Altamira en Santillana del Mar.* Madrid, 1935.

CATURLA, M. L. *Pinturas, frondas y fuentes del Buen Retiro.* Madrid, 1947.

GAYA NUÑO, J. A. *La pintura románica en Castilla.* Madrid, n.d.

—— *Arte español del siglo XIX.* Madrid, 1966.

—— *La pintura española de medio siglo.* Barcelona, 1952.

GUINARD, P., and BATICLE, J. *Histoire de la peinture espagnole du XIIᵉ au XIXᵉ siècle.* Paris, 1950.

JEDLICKA, G. *Spanish Painting.* Trans. J. Maxwell Brownjohn. London, 1963.

LAFUENTE FERRARI, E. *Breve historia de la pintura española.* 4th ed. Madrid, 1953.

LARCO, J. *La pintura española, moderna y contemporánea.* 3 vols. Madrid, 1964.

LASSAIGNE, J. *La Peinture espagnole des fresques romanes au Greco.* Paris, Geneva and New York, 1952.

—— *La Peinture espagnole de Velasquez à Picasso.* Paris, Geneva and New York, 1952.

MILBURN, A. 'Some Modern Spanish Painters', *Studies in Modern Spanish Art, and Literature presented to Helen F. Grant.* Ed. N. Glendinning. London, 1972.

OAKSHOTT, W. F. *Sigena: Romanesque Paintings in Spain and the Winchester Bible Artists.* London, 1972.

POST, C. R. *A History of Spanish Painting.* 14 vols. Cambridge (Mass.), 1930–66.

SÁNCHEZ CANTÓN, F. J. *Spanish Drawings from the 10th to the 19th Centuries.* London, 1965.

TORRES MARTÍN, R. *La naturaleza muerta en la pintura española.* Madrid, 1971.

ARCHITECTURE, SCULPTURE AND TOWN PLANNING

ALCOLEA, S. *Escultura española.* Barcelona, 1969. With English, French and German translations.

ANGULO IÑÍGUEZ, D. *La escultura en Andalucía.* 3 vols. Seville, 1927–36.

CAMÓN AZNAR, J. *La arquitectura plateresca.* 2 vols. Madrid, 1945.

CAPEL MARGARITO, M. *La Carolina, capital de las Nuevas Poblaciones.* Jaén, 1970.

CARO BAROJA, J. 'Una teoría de las ciudades viejas', 'Las nuevas poblaciones de la Sierra Morena y Andalucía' and 'Arte e historia social y económica'. In *Razas, linajes y pueblos.* Madrid, 1957.

CERVERA VERA, L. *El conjunto palacial de la Villa de Lerma.* Valencia, 1967.

—— *Bienes muebles en el Palacio Ducal de Lerma.* Valencia, 1967.

CHAMOSO LAMAS, M. *La arquitectura barroca en Galicia.* Madrid, 1955.

DURLIAT, M. *L'Architecture espagnole.* Toulouse, 1966.

GAILLARD, G. *Les Débuts de la sculpture romane espagnole.* Paris, 1938.

—— *La Sculpture romane espagnole de Saint-Isidore de Leon à Saint-Jacques de Compostelle.* Paris, 1946.

GÓMEZ MORENO, M. E. *Las águilas del Renacimiento español: Bartolomé Ordóñez, Diego Siloé, Pedro Machuca, Alonso Berruguete. 1517–1558.* Madrid, 1944.

—— *La gran época de la escultura española.* Barcelona, Madrid and Mexico, 1964.

HOAG, J. D. *Western Islamic Architecture.* London and New York, 1963.

LAMPÉREZ Y ROMEA, V. *Arquitectura civil española de los siglos 1 al XVIII.* 2 vols. Madrid, 1922.

LAVEDAN, P. *L'Architecture gothique religieuse en Catalogne, Valence et Baléares.* Paris, 1935.

MARÇAIS, G. *L'Architecture musulmane d'Occident: Tunisie, Algérie, Maroc, Espagne et Sicile.* Paris, 1954.

ORTIZ ECHAGÜE, C. *La arquitectura española actual.* Madrid, 1965.

PORTER, K. A. *Spanish Romanesque Sculpture.* Florence, 1928.

PROSKE, B. G. *Castilian Sculpture, Gothic to Renaissance.* New York, 1951.

RAHLVES, F. *Cathedrals and Monasteries of Spain.* Trans. J. C. Palmes. London, 1966.

ROSENTHAL, E. E. *The Cathedral of Granada.* Princeton, 1961.

SARTHOU CARRERES. *Catedrales de España, su pasado y su presente.* Madrid, 1964.

—— *Castillos de España, su pasado y su presente.* Madrid, 1964.

TORRES BALBÁS, L., CERVERA, L., CHUECA, F., and BIGADOR, P. *Resumen histórico del urbanismo en España.* Madrid, 1954.

OTHER ARTS

AINAUD DE LASARTE, J. *Cerámica y vidrio.* Ars Hispaniae, 10. Madrid, 1952.

FROTHINGHAM, A. W. *Spanish Glass.* London, 1963.

STAPLEY, M. *Spanish Interiors and Furniture* (Photographs by Arthur Byne). 3 vols. 1921–5. Reprinted in 1 vol. 1969.

WATERER, J. *Spanish Leather.* London, 1971.

STUDIES OF SOME MAJOR ARTISTS AND ARCHITECTS

Cano

WETHEY, H. E. *Alonso Cano. Painter, Sculptor and Architect.* Princeton, 1955.

Centenario de Alonso Cano en Granada. Estudios. Catálogo. 2 vols. Granada, 1969.

The Churrigueras

GARCÍA Y BELLIDO, A. 'Avances para una monografía de los Churrigueras'. In *Archivo Espanol de Arte* (1929).

Dalí

DALÍ, A. M. *Salvador Dalí vu par sa sœur.* Paris, 1960.

DESCHARNES, R. *The World of Salvador Dalí.* London, 1962.

JEAN, M. *The History of Surrealist Painting.* Trans. Simon Watson Taylor, London, 1960.

Gaudí

LE CORBUSIER, GOMIS, PRATS VALLES. *Gaudí.* Barcelona, 1958.

CASANELLES. *Antonio Gaudí: A Reappraisal.* London, 1967.

MASINI, L. V. *Gaudí.* London, Sydney, Toronto and New York, 1969.

SWEENEY, J. J., and SERT, J. L., *Antoni Gaudí.* London, 1960; 2nd ed. 1970.

Gil de Siloé

WETHEY, H. E. *Gil de Siloé and his School: Late Gothic Sculpture in Burgos.* Cambridge (Mass.), 1936.

—— 'The Early Works of Bartolomé Ordóñez and Diego de Siloé'. In *Art Bulletin.* XXV (1943).

Goya

GASSIER, P., and WILSON, J. *Goya. His Life and Work.* London, 1971.

GUDIOL, J. *Goya.* London, 1966.

HARRIS, E. *Goya.* London, 1969.

HARRIS, T. *Goya. Engravings and Lithographs.* 2 vols. Oxford, 1964.

HELMAN, E. F. *Trasmundo de Goya.* Madrid, 1963.

KLINGENDER, F. D. *Goya in the Democratic Tradition.* London, 1948. Rev. ed. 1968.

LÓPEZ REY, J. *A Cycle of Goya Drawings.* London, 1956.

—— *Goya's Caprichos: Beauty, Reason and Caricature.* 2 vols. Princeton, 1953.

SAMBRICIO, V. DE. *Tapices de Goya.* Madrid, 1946.

SÁNCHEZ CANTÓN, F. J. *The Life and Works of Goya.* Madrid, 1964.

—— and SALAS, X. DE. *Goya and the Black Paintings.* London, 1964.

El Greco

BORJA DE SAN ROMÁN, F. DE. *El Greco en Toledo.* Madrid, 1910.

CAMÓN AZNAR, J. *Domínico Greco.* 2 vols. Madrid, 1950.

COSSÍO, M. B. *El Greco.* Madrid, 1908. Definitive ed. Barcelona, 1972.

GUINARD, P. *Greco*. Paris, 1956.

HARRIS, E. 'A Decorative Scheme by El Greco', *The Burlington Magazine*, LXXII, 154 ff.

PROCOPIOU, A. G. 'El Greco and Cretan Painting'. In *The Burlington Magazine*, XCIV, 76 ff.

RUTTER, F. 'The Early Life of El Greco'. In *The Burlington Magazine*, LX, 274 ff.

WETHEY, H. E. *El Greco and His School*. 2 vols. Princeton, 1962.

Juan Gris

KAHNWEILER, D. H. *Juan Gris. Sa vie, son œuvre, ses écrits*. Paris, 1946.

Herrera

CERVERA VERA, L. *Las estampas y el sumario de El Escorial por Juan de Herrera*. Madrid, 1954.

RUIZ DE ARCAUTE, A. *Juan de Herrera, arquitecto de Felipe II*. Madrid, 1936.

Miró

BUCCI, M. *Miró*. London, Sydney, Toronto and New York, 1971.

DUPIN, J. *Miró*. London, 1962.

LASSAIGNE, J. *Miró*. Paris and Geneva, 1963.

PENROSE, R. *Miró*. London, 1970.

Murillo

BRAHAM, A. 'The Early Style of Murillo'. In *The Burlington Magazine*, CVII, 445–51.

CURTIS, C. B. *Velázquez and Murillo*. London and New York, 1883.

MONTOTO, S. *Bartolomé Esteban Murillo*, Seville, 1923.

MAYER, A. L. *Murillo*. Stuttgart, 1923.

Palomino

APARICIO OLMOS, E. M. *Palomino: su arte y su tiempo*. Valencia, 1966.

PÉREZ SÁNCHEZ, A. E. 'Notas sobre Palomino pintor'. In *Archivo español de arte*, XLV, No. 179, 251 ff.

Picasso

ARNHEIM, R. *Picasso's Guernica: The Genesis of a Painting*. London, 1962.

BLUNT, A. *Picasso's Guernica*. London, 1969.

—— and POOL, P. *Picasso. The Formative Years*. London, 1962.

DAIX, P. *Picasso*. London, 1965.

DUNCAN, D. D. *Picasso's Picassos*. New York, 1968.

JAFFÉ, H. L. C. *Pablo Picasso*. London, n.d. [1965].

OLIVIER, F. *Picasso and his Friends*. Trans. J. Miller. London, 1964.

PARMELIN, H. *Picasso says . . .* London, 1969.

PENROSE, R. *Portrait of Picasso*. London, 1972.

—— *Picasso*. London, 1971.

POOL, P. 'Sources and Background of Picasso's Art 1900–1906'. In *The Burlington Magazine*, CI, 176 ff.

RICHARDSON, J. *Pablo Picasso: Watercolours and Gouaches*. London, 1964.

Ribera

CHENAULT, J. 'Ribera in Roman Archives'. In *The Burlington Magazine*, CXI, 561 ff.

TRAPIER, E. DU GUÉ. *Ribera*. New York, 1952.

Solana

SÁNCHEZ CAMARGO, M. *Gutiérrez Solana, pintura y dibujo*. Madrid, 1953.

Sorolla

PANTORBA, B. DE. *La vida y el arte de Joaquín Sorolla*. Madrid, 1952.

Eight Essays on Joaquín Sorolla y Bastida. 2 vols. New York, 1909.

Valdés Leal

GESTOSO Y PÉREZ, J. *Biografía del pintor sevillano Juan de Valdés Leal*. Seville, 1917.

TRAPIER, E. DUGUÉ. *Valdés Leal, Spanish Baroque Painter*. New York, 1960.

Velázquez

ANGULO ÍÑIGUEZ, D. *Velázquez. Cómo compuso sus principales cuadros*. Seville, 1947.

CAMÓN AZNAR, J. *Velázquez*. 2 vols. Madrid, 1964.

HARRIS, E. 'A Letter from Velázquez to Camillo Massimi'. In *The Burlington Magazine*, CII, 162 ff.

LAFUENTE FERRARI, E. *Velasquez*. Paris, Geneva and New York.

LÓPEZ REY, J. *Velázquez. A Catalogue Raisonné of his Œuvre. With an Introductory Study*. London, 1963.

—— *Velázquez' Work and World*. London, 1968.

SALAS, X. DE. *Velázquez*. London, 1962.

SÁNCHEZ CANTÓN, F. J. 'New Facts about Velázquez'. In *The Burlington Magazine*, LXXXVII, 289 ff.

—— and RODRÍGUEZ MARÍN, D. F. *Cómo vivía Velázquez*. Madrid, 1942.

TRAPIER, E. DU GUÉ. *Velázquez*. New York, 1948.

TROUTMAN, P. *Velázquez*. London, 1965.

VARIA VELAZQUEÑA. 2 vols. Madrid, 1960.

Zuloaga

LAFUENTE FERRARI, E. *La vida y el arte de Ignacio Zuloaga*. San Sebastien, 1950.

Zurbarán

CATURLA, M. L. 'New Facts on Zurbarán'. In *The Burlington Magazine*, LXXXVII, 303 ff.

—— 'Zurbarán at the "Hall of Realms" at Buen Retiro'. In *The Burlington Magazine*, LXXXIX, 42 ff.

GUINARD, P. *Zurbarán et les peintres espagnols de la vie monastique*. Paris, 1964.

SORIA, M. S. *The Paintings of Zurbarán*. 2nd ed. London and New York, 1953.

12 Spanish Music

ROBERT STEVENSON

I Visigothic and Mozarabic Music

The first Hispanic writer profoundly to affect the course of musical history – Isidore of Seville (c. 570–636) – belongs to the early Middle Ages (see pp. 193–4 above). The musical dicta in his celebrated *Etymologies* continued to be copied and revered for at least a millennium.

From Isidore's epoch to the Muslim invasion (589–711) the Visigothic Church served as nursery for a body of liturgical chant no less extensive than the Gregorian repertory. At least seven bishops are credited by their biographers with having composed chants taken into the Visigothic repertory: Isidore's brother Leander (d. 599) of Seville; Eugenius II (d. 657), Ildephonsus (d. 667) and Julian (d. 690) of Toledo; Conantius (d. 639) of Palencia; Joannes (d. 631) and Braulius (d. 651) of Saragossa – the latter Isidore's favourite pupil. The ninth-century Azagra Codex preserves Eugenius III's neumes – in this codex staffless notations hinting at melodic contour but not pitches – for two laments, the first bewailing the Visigothic king, Chindasvinth (d. 652), the second his queen, Recciberga (d. 654).[1]

Unfortunately, the notation of these laments is by no means unique in failing to certify pitches. Of the surviving thirty or so manuscripts containing Visigothic chant (called Mozarabic chant after the Muslim invasion in 711), only one manuscript[2] contains any melodies that were transcribed after 1089 into heighted neumes. None the less, scholars such as Casiano Rojo and Germán Prado in *El canto mozárabe* (1929) and Louis Brou in an important series of articles during the 1950s have deduced many of the formal principles of Visigothic = Mozarabic

[1] BN Madrid, MS 10029, f. 51r–v.
[2] Real Academia de la Historia, Madrid, MS A56.

chant. Even without solving the mystery of the precise pitches, they have succeeded in showing that the Mozarabic neumes equivalent to the Gregorian *podatus, clivis, torculus, scandicus* and *climacus* can be found grouped into recognizable patterns in the manuscripts.

In contrast to the more restrained Gregorian chant which rarely requires more than forty notes on single vowels, even when the word is alleluia, Mozarabic composers did not shrink from melismas four, five or six times as lengthy. At the close of line 8 on folio 61*v* in the *Antiphoner* of León comes a 200-note vocal cadenza so elaborate that the scribe had to let it erupt from the bottom of the outer margin to the top, where it spills into the upper margin. Because vocalized on the second syllable of alleluia, rather than the last, this chant identifies itself as an office alleluia.

To judge from directions in the *Antiphoner* of León, the singers of Mozarabic chant on occasion turned to drama. For instance, a shaky voice (*voce tremula*) is prescribed at f. 166*v* for the singing of 'O my people, what have I done unto thee or wherein have I wearied thee' (Micah 6:3) during the early hours of Good Friday. A *sotto voce* delivery (*subtili voce*) is required at f. 164*v* for Jesus' words, 'Behold the hour cometh, yea is now come, that ye shall be scattered, every man to his own, and shall leave me alone' (John 16:32). But the singer of the first processional antiphon at Palm Sunday Mass must begin in a loud clear voice (f. 153*v*) audible above the approaching crowd, and on another occasion in mid-Lent town-criers' voices (*voces preconias*, f. 133) are stipulated.

The musical notations used by scribes who copied the Mozarabic repertory into the *Antiphoner* of León (dated 1069), into British Museum Add. MSS 20848 and 30850,[1] into two manuscripts originally from Toledo Cathedral[2] (35.1 and 35.2), into five manuscripts still at Toledo, and into about twenty other sources scattered from the Coimbra University Library to the Ruskin Museum in Sheffield, fall into two classes – neumes in the Toledo group of manuscripts flattening horizontally above the text, and those in the *Antiphoner* of León and kindred sources rising vertically above. Even though the Toledo copyists used fewer neume-types, the transcription into modern notation of any Mozarabic music, except twenty-one melodies for burial

[1] The latter MS is from the Benedictine abbey of Santo Domingo de Silos (prov. of Burgos).
[2] BN Madrid, MSS 10001 and 10110 – formerly in the Biblioteca Capitular, Toledo (35.1 and 35.2).

ceremonies and for the Maundy Thursday foot-washing event, involves considerable guesswork. This is so because upon Alfonso VI's suppression of the Mozarabic rite around 1085, the older books quickly fell into disuse. Only in the manuscript formerly in the monastery of San Millán de la Cogolla[1] were the old neumes that tell nothing but the number of notes sung to a syllable (if more than one note, the direction of note movement) scratched out, being replaced by neumes of the so-called Aquitanian type that permit exact transcription into modern notation.

True, at Toledo itself six parishes were allowed after 1085 to continue with the old Mozarabic rite. Five years after becoming Archbishop of Toledo, Francisco Ximénez de Cisneros (1436–1517) added to his other grand gestures the sponsoring of a 480-folio publication, *Missale mixtum secundum regulam beati Isidori dictum Mozarabes* (Toledo: Peter Hagenbach, 1500). The three local scholars then considered most learned in the obsolete rite – parish priests of the Churches of Saints Luke, Justa and Rufina, and Eulalia – aided Alfonso Ortiz, a canon of Toledo Cathedral, in editing this 'Mozarabic' missal. Cisneros also endowed the Mozarabic chapel in Toledo Cathedral, with the intention that thirteen chaplains, a sacristan and two acolytes should daily attend to the celebration of the sung mass and office in that chapel.

Even today, three huge manuscript choirbooks containing the Mozarabic liturgy survive from Cisneros's epoch for the use of the chapel. But how authentic was still the pre-1085 musical tradition rachitically surviving in a few parish churches at Toledo around 1500 remains an open question. José Subirá's *Historia de la música española e hispanoamericana* (p. 57) includes a fine facsimile of the *Alleluia: Laudem Domini* from one of these three choirbooks. Even at first glance, anyone can see that this is accentual melody organized into footfall beats. One pungent melodic figure recurs often enough to sound like a 'motive'. Except for notes 2 and 3, the first 16 notes of 'Alleluia' serve for 'Laudem Domini', thus structuring the music still more decisively.

From these same Mozarabic chapel choirbooks Dom Germán Prado extracted the first 'Mozarabic' chant included in an English language textbook – Carl Parrish's *A Treasury of Early Music*.[2] Not

[1] Real Academia de la Historia, Madrid, MS A56.
[2] New York, 1958, pp. 14–15. The chant has been recorded commercially (Haydn Society Records, P.O. Box 2338, Hartford, Connecticut, HSE-9100, N80P-5320, Vol. 1, Side 1, Band 3).

liking the heavy footfall of accented beats in Cisneros's restored repertory, Prado smoothed out the rhythm to make the chant in question, the antiphon beginning *Gaudete populi et letamini angelus*, look as Gregorian as possible. The *Antiphoner* of León includes this same antiphon (f. 175*v*), but of course in neumes undecipherable so far as pitches are concerned (and marked for the Easter Vigil rather than for Easter Day). Other pre-1085 Mozarabic music manuscripts containing this same *Gaudete populi* antiphon include British Museum Add. MSS 30846 (f. 1) and Real Academia de Historia, Madrid MS A56 (140*v* – one verse only). But the succession of neumes in the *c.* 1500 restored version does not even faintly resemble the succession in the León *Antiphoner* in any of the other two sources just named.

If the sphinx's riddle of Mozarabic musical notation still defies any really satisfactory answer, what certainties can the scholars agree upon? On paleographical evidence permitting new datings of Toledo, Biblioteca Capitular, MSS 35.2–35.5, Anscari M. Mundó convincingly showed in 1965 that pristine Mozarabic practices did indeed survive at Toledo until well after 1300.[1] According to Don M. Randel's *The Responsorial Psalm Tones for the Mozarabic Office*,[2] the Mozarabic Church never did develop any one monolithic musical practice uniform throughout the Peninsula. Musically, Spain was 'las Españas' long before Alfonso VI tried to impose liturgical unity by adopting an outside rite. Running like a multicoloured thread through all Spanish musical history from the Middle Ages to the present, a multiplicity of local traditions prevents the historian from ever fastening on one single style as typical of the whole.

Even if scholars never succeed in deciphering Mozarabic musical manuscripts to scholars' universal satisfaction, the evidence already available teaches yet another lesson. Far from lagging behind the rest of Europe, Visigothic composers actually anticipated musical forms developed elsewhere. For instance, the parallelistic form AA[1] BB[1] CC[1] DD[1] . . . , which, in conjunction with syllabic verse, came to be known as sequence and which in histories of music today still continues to be described as the 'invention' of Notker of St Gall (*c.* 840–912), was already current in the León *Antiphoner* repertory before 711. Dom Louis Brou found not only the sequence *Sublimius diebus* in the León source (f. 1*v*), but the *Alme Virginis* and two more sequences in Toledo.[3] Copied

[1] 'La datación de los códices', *Hispania Sacra*, XVIII (1965), pp. 20 f.
[2] Doctoral dissertation (Princeton University, 1966), p. 83.
[3] Biblioteca Capitular, MS 35.7, f. 45.

as early as the ninth century (according to *Hispania Sacra*, X (1957), p. 394), this book still continued in use a half millennium later.

II Hispano-Moorish Music

The Muslim invaders brought a host of new instruments to the Peninsula. To the twenty-five instruments given their Latin names in Isidore's *Etymologies* (III, xxi–xxii; XVIII, iv), the Moors added the instruments that came to be known in Spanish as *adufe* < *al-duff* = square tambourine; *ajabeba* (*exabeba*) < *al-shabbāba* = transverse flute; *albogón* < *al-būg* = metal cylindrical instrument with reed-mouthpiece and seven finger-holes; *añafil* < *al-nafīr* = straight trumpet four feet or more in length; *atabal* < *al-ṭabl* = drum; *canón* < *qānūn* = a psaltery; *panderete* < *bandair* = tambourine; *sonajas de azofar* < *ṣunūj al-ṣufr* = metal castanets. The *naker* (< *naqqāra* = small wood or metal kettledrum), the lute (< *'ud*) and the rebec (= *rabel* < *rabāb*) fanned out over all Europe. Seville became the centre of Moorish instrument-making, just as Córdoba was the centre of Arabic learning.

Moorish instrumental virtuosi also gained employment at Christian courts. For instance, Sancho of Castile (ruled 1284–94), Peter III of Aragon (r. 1276–85) and Alfonso IV of Aragon (r. 1327–36) engaged players of the *añafil, ajabeba, canón* and *rabel*. From Játiva, a recognized centre of Moorish minstrelsy, Peter IV of Aragon (1336–87) summoned Ali Eziqua and Çahat Mascum, his favourite players of the *rabel* and *ajabeba*. Even churchmen delighted in Moorish minstrelsy, so much so that the Council of Valladolid (1322) forbade any further hiring of Moorish musicians to enliven Christian vigils or any more *tumultum* caused by their mixing at Christian feasts. This ban is the more interesting because, as Don Quixote well knew when reproving Maese Pedro for his bells, mosques not only lacked bells but there never existed even in medieval Spain anything approaching 'mosque' music.

The Muslims who overran Spain in the eighth century not only introduced numerous instruments that, in Spanish, still bear names of Arabic origin but also brought with them various Arabian musical treatises that were translated into Latin at Toledo and thence disseminated northward. Al-Fārābi (*c.* 872–950), in particular, came to be quoted by numerous theorists from Vincent of Beauvais, Jerome of Moravia and Lambertus in the thirteenth century to Gregor Reisch (1467–1525) and Juan Bermudo (*fl.* 1549–55) in the sixteenth century.

One form of Moorish poetry, the *zajal* (Sp. *zéjel*), bears a close resemblance to the Spanish fifteenth-century *villancico*, and some scholars have argued strongly for an interrelationship. Some literary evidence also survives to suggest that the Moors in the kingdom of Granada (before its conquest in 1492) were the first to use letters of the alphabet to denote finger position on the guitar.

III Medieval Instruments

In his 6,912-line poem *El libro de buen amor* (*c.* 1343) – see p. 222 above – Juan Ruiz, who was very familiar with the popular musical instruments of his day, differentiates between two types of *guitarra*, one *latina* (line 1,228d, akin to the classical lyre), the other *morisca* (1,228a). He distinguishes also between the *rabé* (1,229a, 'rebec') and the *rabé morisco* (1,230a). The paramountcy of instruments in the music of Ruiz's Spain can be inferred not only from the large number mentioned by name but also from the fact that an instrumental accompaniment is always specified for motets and *chanzonetas* (1,232c, 1,241d). For Ruiz each instrument, moreover, had its own ethos. The *mandurría* he classed as a 'silly, whining' instrument but the *rabé* as the apt accompaniment for *Calvi garabí* (a tune alluded to as specifically Arabic in 1577 in Francisco Salinas's treatise *De musica libri septem*,[1] under the name *Calui vi calui/Calui araui*).

Among other string instruments Ruiz alludes to the *baldosa* (zither played with a plectrum), the harp, lute (*laúd*), psaltery and two types of *vihuela* – *de arco* (1,231a, 1,516a, played with a bow), the other *de péndola* (1,229d, played with a quill plectrum). By their names the following six instruments disclose their Moorish provenance: *albogue* (1,213b, 1,517a, 'pastoral recorder'), *albogón* (1,233a, 'large recorder'), *añafil* (1,096a 1,234a, 'Moorish trumpet'), *atanbal* (1,234a, 'kettledrum'), *atanbor* (894c, 895c, 898b, 1,227d, 'drum') and *axabeba* ('transverse flute'). He mentions also the following: *caño entero* and *medio caño*, *canpana*, *çampoña* (1,213b, 1,517a, 'syrinx'), *caramillo* (pipe made of reed), *cascabel* ('sleighbell'), *citola* ('citole'), *dulcema* (1,233a, 'shawm'), *flauta* (1,230c, 'recorder'), *gaita* (1,233a, 'cornemuse'), *galipe francisco* (1,230b, 'small French recorder'), *odreçillo* (1,000b, 1,233c, 'bagpipe'), *órgano* ('portative'), *pandero* and *panderete*, *çinfonia* (1,233b, 1,516b), *sonajas de açofar* (1,232b, 'metal clappers'), *tamborete* (1,230d, 'side drum') and *trompa*. All told, Ruiz's catalogue reaches no less than thirty-two

[1] Salamanca, 1577, p. 339.

instruments, plus five sub-varieties. This number is the more significant because in his whole body of poetry Chaucer alluded to only twenty.

Because various miniatures in a manuscript in the Escorial Library (*B.i.2*) picture Moorish instrumentalists at the court of Alfonso X of Castile (r. 1252–84), and because at Alfonso's court the chief collection of medieval Spanish monody was compiled, a few scholars during the 1920s went so far as to contend that the *Cantigas de Santa Maria*[1] – as this body of monody is called because it consists entirely of poems written in honour of the Virgin by or for Alfonso – derive from now lost Moorish songs. However, the thesis that Moorish melody finds an echo in any of the 423 Alfonsine *Cantigas* remains unproved — since not so much as a scrap of medieval Moorish music survives to show what it was like. The pioneer recording of a dozen of these *Cantigas* made by Noah Greenberg[2] captivates the listener with the infectious jangle of percussion and plucked instruments. For the instruments, Greenberg invoked the authority of the famous illuminations found in quantity in manuscripts of the *Cantigas*. But the curve of any *cantiga* melody, and indeed the basic musical ideas, can scarcely have been Moorish when every song in the entire collection celebrates the Virgin and her miracles.

IV Medieval Polyphony

Three widely separated sources of medieval polyphony survive in Spain. These are: (i) the twelfth-century *Codex Calixtinus* at Santiago de Compostela, containing twenty-one short pieces with Latin text;[3] (ii) the early fourteenth-century *Las Huelgas Codex* – belonging to the renowned royal convent for Cistercian nuns founded about 1180 on the outskirts of Burgos (of the 186 items in this codex, eighty-seven are duos, forty-eight are trios, one requires four voices, the rest are monophonic); and (iii) the mid-fourteenth-century *Llibre Vermell* at Montserrat in Catalonia with ten pieces (three *a 3*, two *a 2*, the others monophonic).[4] The *Codex Calixtinus* lists by name, as composers of the various pieces in it, fifteen pilgrims to St James's shrine. However, all but one (a 'Galician doctor') came from outside Spain. The most famous single piece in the codex, *Congaudeant catholici* (one of the

[1] For an account of the literary aspects of Alfonso X's *Cantigas de Santa Maria*, see Chapter 6, section V.
[2] New York Pro Music Antiqua, 'Spanish Medieval Music' (Decca DL 9416).
[3] *Codex Calixtinus*, ff. 131 and 185–90.
[4] ff. 21*v*–26*v*.

earliest trios known), is ascribed to 'Master Albert of Paris'. The *Las Huelgas Codex* also draws heavily on the French Ars Antiqua repertory, only 'Johan Rodrigues' in the manuscript representing Spain. Noah Greenberg's recording mentioned in the preceding paragraph includes Professor Denis Stevens's reconstruction of a twenty-three-minute mass in honour of the Blessed Virgin assembled from the troped chants at folios 1 (Kyrie), 4*v*–5*v* (Gloria in excelsis Deo), 5*v*–6 (Gradual), 34*v*–35 (Sequence), 8*v*–9*v* (Offertory), 11–12 (Sanctus) and 19*v* (Agnus Dei) of this manuscript – which has the unique distinction of being the only monument of early medieval polyphony to have survived until today in its place of origin.

The *Montserrat Codex*, like the *Calixtinus*, contains pilgrim music – but for a shrine of the Virgin. Four of the monodies are dance songs marked 'aball redon'. The *Llibre Vermell* contains also the oldest known 'Dance of Death' music – *Ad mortem festinamus*, illustrated in the manuscript by a skeleton lying in an open coffin. *Mariam Matrem*, *a 3* at f. 25, exemplifies the *virelai* form (an opening refrain preceding and following the strophes) which remained a favourite in non-liturgical Spanish composition for several centuries. *Mariam Matrem* also foreshadows later usage by giving the top voice the faster, free-flowing melody, and by assigning parts to contra and tenor that imply the use of instruments.

V Fifteenth- and Sixteenth-Century Polyphony

Fifteenth- and sixteenth-century secular composition with Spanish texts consists mainly of ballads (*romances*) and carols (*villancicos*). In these early ballads, the same music serves for each poetic quatrain. Because the subject-matter often treats of some bygone heroic exploit, the musical pace is suitably slow and dignified.[1] *Villancicos* follow the *virelai* scheme, a musical refrain enclosing the strophes. The pangs and joys of love, often in a fictitious country setting, allow for a wide variety of musical moods and tempi. So far as form is concerned, the younger composers in the *Cancionero musical de Palacio* (Palace Songbook) in the Royal Library in Madrid (MS 2-I-5) often allow a poetic strophe to end after the musical refrain has begun. The musician, poet and dramatist Juan del Encina (1469–1529), the leading composer in the *Cancionero musical de Palacio*, wrote texts (see p. 269 above) as well

[1] For an account of medieval Spanish ballad literature, see Chapter 6, section IX, and Chapter 7, section II.

as music for his *villancicos*, most of which date from 1492–8. *Villano* means 'rustic', and Encina's *villancicos* appropriately stress shepherds, village swains, country folk and courtiers masquerading as rustics. But the music for these works always betrays the polished hand of a composer equally at home with his patrons, the Duke and Duchess of Alba (Don Fadrique de Toledo and Doña Isabel Pimentel), or, later in his career, at the court of the Spanish Pope Alexander VI and of Alexander's successor, Julius II.

Surrounding Encina in the *Cancionero musical de Palacio* (the most important monument of Spanish secular polyphony in the Renaissance) swirl a galaxy of no less stellar personalities – among them Juan de Anchieta (*c.* 1462–1523), Francisco de Peñalosa (*c.* 1470–1528), Francisco de la Torre, Alonso de Alva, Francisco Millán, Gabriel Mena and Juan Ponce. Several of the older composers in the *Cancionero musical de Palacio*, Johannes Cornago (*fl.* 1466), Juan de Triana (*fl.* 1478), Juan Fernández de Madrid (*fl.* 1479), Juan Pérez de Gijón (*fl.* 1480) and Juan de León (*fl.* 1480), to name no others, crop up also in the *Cancionero Colombina* – a still earlier collection of Spanish secular polyphony now preserved in the Biblioteca Colombina in Seville.[1] The most influential foreign-born composer included in both the Palace and Colombina songbooks, Johannes Urrede of Bruges, served as Ferdinand V's chapel-master.

Other foreigners who visited Spain, and who left their mark, include Jean Ockeghem (1469), Alexander Agricola and Pierre de la Rue (1506). The influence of Flemish polyphony shines clearly in the masterful masses and motets of Anchieta and Peñalosa, especially of the latter who resided at Pope Leo X's court and whose many-faceted genius makes him the most important Spanish composer before Cristóbal de Morales (*c.* 1500–53). One Peñalosa mass parodies Urrede's extremely popular *Nunca fue pena mayor* ('Never was there greater sorrow'), the verses of which were written around 1470 by the first Duke of Alba, García Alvarez de Toledo – Urrede's employer before Ferdinand V appointed him chapelmaster (1477). Another takes the ubiquitous *L'Homme armé* theme for its subject, and another parodies the popular chanson, *Adieu mes amours*. But he declares his Spanish nationality by taking for themes of other masses *El ojo* and *Por la mar*. Juan de Anchieta, a close relative of Ignatius Loyola, leaves a less learned repertory, only one movement of a mass taking *L'Homme armé* for its theme, and he never tries to compete with Josquin des Prez's display of learning

[1] MS 7–I–28.

or feats of contrapuntal virtuosity. Both Peñalosa and Anchieta do frequently cite plainsong, but Anchieta often contents himself with mere chords as framework for the plainsong themes, whereas Peñalosa weaves his Gregorian themes in an intricate polyphonic web.

VI Renaissance Theorists

The same contrast between the learning of Peñalosa – who, while a canon in Seville Cathedral, simultaneously held a post at the papal court – and the plainness of Anchieta, who stayed mostly in Spain, can be seen between the erudition of the most famous Spanish Renaissance theorists – Bartolomé Ramos de Pareja (*fl.* 1482) and Francisco de Salinas (1513–90), both of whom wrote in Latin and resided lengthily in Italy – and the less involved and more concise teaching of the many Spanish theorists who wrote in their own tongue and never roamed abroad. Ramos de Pareja challenged Pythagorean traditional tuning when he asked that the major thirds of c–e, f–a, g–b be tuned in the 5:4 vibration ratio, and that the minor thirds of a–c, d–f and e–g be tuned in the 6:5 ratio (Pythagorean tuning called for the 81:64 and 288:243 ratios). He also argued for solmization through the entire octave instead of by hexachords, as had been the medieval practice. The reputation of Salinas, to whom his friend Luis de León wrote a famous ode about music, rests on his treatise, *De musica libri septem*, published at Salamanca in 1577 while Salinas was occupying the chair of music there. One of the clearest and most orderly solutions to the problems of tuning and temperament which the Renaissance had inherited from both classical antiquity and the Middle Ages, Salinas's masterly treatise also catalogues musical metres. To illustrate the varieties of possible metrical schemes, he includes numerous vernacular ballads and folk-songs. He is credited with having been the most avid folk-song collector of his century. Blindness makes his achievement all the more remarkable, as it does also the publications of the greatest Spanish Renaissance organist, Antonio de Cabezón (1510–66; *Obras de música para tecla, arpa y vihuela*, Madrid, 1578), and of the consummate vihuela player and composer, Miguel de Fuenllana (*Orphenica lyra*, Seville, 1554).

VII Renaissance Music

The vihuela – shaped like a guitar (figure 8, flat back) but equipped with six courses (all but the top course employing two strings) – inspired the publication of seven books between 1536 and 1576. Not staff notation but tablature is the system used in all these seven vihuela books, six horizontal lines denoting the six courses, and arabic numerals telling which fret to press. Only one of these publications, Diego Pisador's *Libro de música de vihuela* (Salamanca, 1552), betrays the hand of an amateur, all the rest from Luis Milán's pioneer *El maestro*, issued at Valencia, to Esteban Daza's *El Parnasso* (Valladolid, 1576) testifying to the high artistry of their compilers. Luis de Narváez (1538), Alonso de Mudarra (1546) and Enríquez de Valderrábano (1547) published their tablatures at Valladolid and Seville.

While each vihuelist shows his own individuality, Valderrábano can be chosen as representative. His *Silva de sirenas* divides into seven books. Books I, II, III and VI contain transcriptions of movements from masses, motets, chansons, madrigals, *villancicos* and *romances*; Book VI includes *fantasías* for solo vihuela. In Book II Valderrábano prints the part to be sung as well as played in red, the other parts in black. Book VI contains intabulations and *fantasías* for two vihuelas (printed upside-down to each other, the parts can be played by two vihuelists from the same open book); Book VII a pavane and variation-sets based on familiar subjects (*Conde Claros, Guárdame las vacas =* Romanesca, *pavana =* Folia). The composers providing Valderrábano with matter which he parodied in his *fantasías* include Charles V's chapel-master, Nicolas Gombert, and such other Flemish and French composers as Noël Bauldoin, Jean Mouton and Josquin des Prez. Italian lutanists also gave him occasional material, but Cristóbal de Morales proves his undisputed favourite among native-born Spanish composers.

Morales – born in Seville and reared in a cathedral served by the best Peninsular composers of the age (Peñalosa, Alva, Torre, Pedro de Escobar, Pedro Fernández de Castilleja) – successively gained posts as director of music in Ávila (1526) and Plasencia (1528) cathedrals. From 1535 to 1545 he sang in the papal choir at Rome, where, in 1544, he published two books of masses the first dedicated to Cosimo de' Medici, Duke of Florence (whose wife was the daughter of Pedro de Toledo, viceroy at Naples – where Morales had worked before entering the papal chapel), the second to Pope Paul III. However, even before 1544, Morales's music had been widely printed in Italy, and, throughout the remainder of the century, his fame was testified to by frequent reprints of his books not only at Venice and Milan but also at Antwerp, Augsburg, Louvain, Lyons, Nuremberg, Paris and Wittenberg. Upon his return to Spain, Morales successively headed the musical establishments in Toledo Cathedral (1545–7), the Duke of Arcos's private chapel at Marchena, and Málaga Cathedral (1551–3). His fame reached all the principal New World cultural centres; abundant evidence of sixteenth-century performances of his music still exists at the ancient Inca capital of Cuzco, at Bogotá (Colombia), at Puebla and at Mexico City.

Morales's best personal pupil, Francisco Guerrero of Seville (1528–99), owed him both his first musical post (at Jaén), and a musical technique unsurpassed in Philip II's reign. Guerrero's first book of masses (Paris, 1566), dedicated to Sebastian (King of Portugal), opens with a parody of Morales's *Sancta et immaculata* motet. In the same book the *Missa inter vestibulum et altare* again chooses Morales's motet of that name for parody. However, Guerrero proved himself equally at home with foreign sources when he used a Janequin chanson, a Verdelot madrigal and a Le Heurteur motet as the bases for other masses.

Although, in the 1580s, Guerrero twice visited Italy to supervise publications (a second book of masses and *Liber vesperarum*, Rome, 1582 and 1584; *Canciones y villanescas espirituales*, Venice, 1589) and, in 1588–9, journeyed to Palestine after which he published a travel account, *Viage de Hierusalem*, he spent the years 1554–99 principally at Seville, where, until 1573, he shared the titular direction of the cathedral music with the valetudinarian Pedro Fernández (native of Castilleja). Guerrero, unlike Morales and Victoria, composed copiously to secular texts. The largest collection of his profane songs, now in Madrid, was formerly in the Duke of Medinaceli's private library.[1] Contemporary Sevillian poets such as Baltasar del Alcázar and Gutierre de Cetina gave him his poetry. In later life, associating himself with the contemporary *a lo divino* fashion in contemporary Spanish poetry, he refitted many of his secular songs to sacred texts, publishing them at Venice in 1589 with the title *Canciones y villanescas espirituales*. His vast influence in the Spanish-speaking world falls only slightly behind Morales's, and, if manuscript and printed copies of his music count, exceeded even Victoria's.

The supreme glory of Spanish Renaissance music, Tomás Luis de Victoria (c. 1549–1611), began as a choirboy in the cathedral of his native town, Ávila, where the three chapelmasters during his youth were all 'principal' men in their profession – Gerónimo de Espinar (1550–8), Bernardino de Ribera (1559–63) and Juan Navarro. Antonio de Cabezón also played from time to time in the cathedral at Ávila,

[1] MS 13230, edited in *Monumentos de la musica española*, VIII and IX (1949–50).

where the Cabezóns maintained their family residence from 1538 to 1560. In 1565 Victoria entered the Collegium Germanicum in Rome, the Jesuit missionary training institution. From 1569 to 1580 Victoria held an organist's post in the Aragonese church at Rome, in 1571 he began teaching at the Collegium Germanicum, and in 1575 he was ordained in the church of St Thomas of Canterbury by the English bishop at Rome, Thomas Goldwell. His first book of motets appeared in 1572 at Venice, patronized by the German Cardinal-Archbishop of Augsburg. Several other works were published in Rome and Venice before Victoria's return to Spain about 1587, from which year until death he was chapelmaster and organist of the royal convent of the Discalced Clarist nuns in Madrid. In this convent then dwelt the Dowager Empress María, whose death in 1603 inspired one of Victoria's most admired masterpieces, his *Officium defunctorum*, published at Madrid in 1605. Now regarded as second only to Palestrina in the Roman polyphonic school, Victoria published twenty masses, fifty-three motets, thirty-three hymns, sixteen Magnificats, various antiphons, litanies and office for Holy Week music. As a motet composer he stands second to none, his *Vere languores* and *O vos omnes* ranking with El Greco's canvases as supreme expressions of the pathetic. However, his works include also a Battle Mass for Philip III and a number of joyous pieces that caused King John IV of Portugal to admire his exuberance.

Trailing somewhat behind Morales, Guerrero and Victoria, but a composer whose vespers music continued to be widely sung in Portugal, Mexico and South America as late as the eighteenth century, was Victoria's mentor, Juan Navarro – successively chapelmaster at Ávila, Salamanca, Ciudad Rodrigo and Palencia. His influence was principally exerted through a collection published at Rome a decade after his death, *Psalmi, Hymni ac Magnificat* (1590). The best available sample of Navarro's secular songs survives in the Medinaceli manuscript already mentioned (p. 554 above). This predominantly Andalusian collection[1] of Spanish-text madrigals, *villancicos* and *romances* preserves (in addition to seven items by Navarro himself, who was born in Seville) fifteen by the Seville-born brothers Pedro and Francisco Guerrero, twelve by the chapelmaster at Vila Viçosa, Ginés de Morata, and six by Rodrigo de Ceballos (active at Seville, Córdoba and Granada).

[1] Edited by Miguel Querol Gavaldá in *Monumentos de la música española*, VIII (1949) and IX (1950).

The composers in the so-called *Cancionero de Upsala*,[1] the printed part-books of which were discovered in Sweden by Rafael Mitjana, range from Encina to Gombert. However, their names must be learned from concordances, because, with one exception, these *Villancicos de diuersos autores* (Venice, 1566) lack composer ascriptions in the imprint. At least seven Peninsular composers did publish secular collections in their own names during the sixteenth century, thus dispelling the idea fostered by some scholars that Spanish vocal music during the Golden Age excluded the profane. Both quality and quantity entitle Juan Vásquez to first honours in his generation of secular composers (*Villancicos y canciones . . . a tres y a quatro*, Osuna, 1551; *Recopilación de sonetos y villancicos a quatro y a cinco*, Seville, 1560). In 1560–1 the Barcelona organist and canon Pedro Alberch Vila (1517–82) published there his *Odarum* (*quas vulgo madrigales appellamus*), but in partbooks of which only the altus survives. Mateo Flecha the Younger's *Il primo libro de madrigali a quatro & cinque voci* (Venice, 1568) mates with Italian texts (one exception), but *Las ensaladas* (Prague, 1581) by himself and his namesake uncle, Mateo Flecha the Elder, combine with Spanish texts. Juan Brudieu's *Madrigales* (Barcelona, 1585), edited anew in 1921, include eleven with Spanish text and four with Catalan text. Other secular collections, Pedro Valenzuela's *Madrigali* (Venice, 1578) and Sebastián Raval's *Il primo libro de canzonette a quattro voci* (Venice, 1593) and *Madrigali* (Rome, 1595), reflect with texts in Italian their composers' long residence abroad.

The Toledo-born Diego Ortiz spent his mature years at Naples, where he rose to be director of the Spanish viceroy's choir. Not to slight his native tongue, Ortiz's *Glose sopra le cadenze* (Rome, 1553) appeared with Italian and Spanish texts simultaneously. Teaching string players how to replace plain passages with cunningly ornamented florid passages, his treatise includes model treatments of an Arcadelt madrigal and a Sandrin chanson. Tomás de Santa María's *Arte de tañer fantasía* (Valladolid, 1565) tells the keyboard player how to ornament plain passages and also pioneers in giving fingering and interpretation instructions.

The theoretical masterpiece of the century in Spanish, Juan Bermudo's *Declaración de instrumentos musicales* (Osuna, 1555), goes beyond fingering and interpretation to survey every major problem of the epoch. Something of the didactic spirit informs also the pioneer anthology published by Luis Venegas de Henstrosa, *Libro de cifra nueva*

[1] Edited by Jesus Bal y Gay (México, 1944).

(Alcalá de Henares, 1557), for keyboard, harp and vihuela – a collection of 138 pieces classed as hymns (23), psalms, *tientos* (18), *canciones* (14), *fabordones llanos* (10) and *fabordones glosados* (10), *fantasías*, *romances*, motets, Kyries, and the like. Even the great Antonio de Cabezón, whose *Obras de música* (1578) appeared a dozen years after his death, left a body of ciphered pieces for 'keyboard, harp and vihuela' that he taught his pupils, rather than the virtuoso repertory with which he himself entertained Philip II during forty years of peripatetic court service. None the less, these 'crumbs from his table' establish him as perhaps the greatest Spanish organ composer in history, and evince at every turn his mastery of variation technique, of structural balance in the *tiento*, and an inimitable flow of gracious melody.

VIII Baroque Music

Francisco Correa de Arauxo (*c.* 1578–1654) published the most important monument of Peninsular baroque organ music, *Libro de tientos y discursos . . . intitulado facultad orgánica* (Alcalá de Henares, 1626), a collection rated by Higinio Anglés as the most revolutionary and brilliant of the era. Contemporary with Correa de Arauxo flourished not only Juan Bautista Comes (1568–1643) of Valencia and Juan Pujol (*c.* 1573–1626) of Barcelona, of both of whom there are modern editions (1888 and 1926–32), but also a cadre of vocal polyphonists who are now but dimly known for lack of scientific reissues – Sebastián de Vicanco (*Magnificats* published at Salamanca, 1607), Alonso Lobo (*Liber primus missarum*, Madrid, 1602), Sebastián Aguilera de Heredia (*Magnificats*, Saragossa, 1618), Sebastián López de Velasco (*Missas, Motetes, Salmos, Magnificat*, Madrid, 1628); other lights who did not publish in their own lifetimes include Gabriel Díaz Besson, Carlos Patiño and Diego Pontac.

In contrast with Victoria, who never sacrificed expressivity for technical display, his fellow townsman Sebastián de Vivanco (*c.* 1551–1622) pushed contrapuntal complexities to extreme lengths in his *Liber magnificarum* of 1607, and his ten masses abound in ingenious canons. Rather than resorting to the conventional parody techniques in such titled masses as *O quam suavis es* (= *Primi toni* based on his own motet of that name), *Doctor bonus* (= *Quinti toni*), *Crux fidelis*, *Assumpsit Jesus* and *In manus tuas*, he instead extracted single lines from his sources and stretched these single lines on the rack of successive, preconceived rhythmic patterns which shift from movement to movement. Not surprisingly, Vivanco ended a career that began at Lérida (and took him thence to Segovia and Ávila) as a university professor at Salamanca. On his major works he lavished all the artifice and cunning bestowed on Guerrero's *Ave sanctissima virgo* by Géry de Ghersem (parody mass at the close of Philippe Rogier's *Missae sex*).[1]

The dominant court figure in the reign of Philip III, Mateo Romero ('Maestro Capitán', *c.* 1575–1647), so thoroughly identified himself with Spain, although born at Liège, that it is he who outshines all others in the finest Peninsular collection of secular songs formed in the forepart of the seventeenth century, the so-called *Cancionero de Claudio de la Sablonara*, his twenty-two items contrasting with Juan Blas de Castro's eighteen, Gabriel Díaz Besson's eight, Álvaro de los Ríos's eight, Juan Pujol's seven and Manuel Machado's four. Seven other songbooks date from the early seventeenth century – those of Olot, Turin, the Biblioteca Casanatense in Rome, as well as Medinaceli MS 13231, *Romances y letras a tres vozes* and a stout *Libro de tonos humanos* in the Biblioteca Nacional at Madrid (M. 1262 and 1370), and Juan Arañés's printed *Libro segundo de tonos y villancicos* (Rome, 1624); but only *Romances y letras* and the first volume of a baroque anthology are as yet available in the 'Monuments of Spanish Music' series (Barcelona, 1956, 1970).

In the Peninsula, drama sung throughout is commonly supposed to have begun with Lope de Vega's *La selva sin amor* (1629), during the première of which instruments were carefully hidden from the spectator's view. Although the composer of the music for Pedro Calderón de la Barca's *La púrpura de la rosa*, first performed at the Coliseo del Buen Retiro (Madrid) on 17 January 1660, to celebrate Louis XIV's marriage to a Spanish infanta, must now be guessed at, he was probably the harpist Juan Hidalgo (d. 1685) who wrote the music for Calderón's second opera *Celos aun del aire matan* (three acts mounted at the Buen Retiro on 5 December 1660).[2] In both instances, singers from the Royal Chapel sang the mythological roles, tales from Ovid's *Metamorphoses* supplying the arguments. Apart from drama sung throughout, Calderón also invented the *zarzuela* (*El golfo de las Sirenas*, 17 January 1657), which in his hands was always a dignified exposition of some mythological subject, the numerous sung choruses and *coplas* alternating with spoken action lines. After Calderón, this type of

[1] Madrid: Joannes Flandrus, 1598.
[2] Act I of this opera was published in 1933 (Barcelona) from a defective score. The complete score survives only at Évora.

zarzuela declined and from 1700 to 1850 remained a moribund genre, only to be revived in the 1850s as a light entertainment type equivalent to the Gilbert and Sullivan operetta.

The vihuela of six courses gave way to the guitar of five in the baroque, Luis de Briceño being the first to publish a Spanish guitar method at Paris (1627) and also one of the first to popularize abroad the use of signs for whole chords. Once having learned what each sign meant in terms of a five-note chord, the player could stop reading the difficult tablature notation that had kept the vihuela an aristocratic instrument in the previous century. To specify the composers: Gaspar Sanz (1640–1710) published an *Instrucción . . . sobre la guitarra española* (Saragossa, 1674 and 1679) which caps a long series of guitar methods ranging from Juan Carlos Amat (Barcelona, 1586), Girolamo Montesardo (1606), Antonio Carbonchi (Florence, 1640), Nicolás Doizi de Velasco (Naples, 1640), through Lucas Ruiz de Ribayaz's *Luz y norte musical* (Madrid, 1677) and Francisco Guerau's *Poema harmónico* (Madrid, 1684). These guitar books make a treasury of popular dances of the period, Sanz's *Instrucción* alone containing over two dozen types. Along with antique *pavanas* and *gallardas*, he includes *zarabandas*, *chaconas*, *pasacalles*, *folías*, *gigas*, *canarios*, *alemandas*, *españoletas*, *marizá-palos* and *jácaras*.

The rhythms and sometimes the very titles of these dances invade the *villancicos* of the seventeenth and eighteenth centuries, which poured forth in profusion from every chapelmaster's pen at Christmas, Corpus Christi, Assumption and other feasts. Far from being confined in the *AB c c ab AB* structure typical of the Renaissance *villancico*, the baroque *villancico* emerged as a miniature drama replete with introduction, arias, recitatives, coplas for soloists, choruses and instrumental interludes. The richness of the baroque *villancico* repertory defies cataloguing, because even minor cathedrals in Spain often preserve hundreds of by now neglected and unrecognized provincial composers. Appreciation of the baroque *villancico* repertory has also been retarded by the charges that such moralists as Benito Jerónimo Feijoo (1676–1764)[1] levelled against it when decrying it as theatrical. Feijoo complained that *menuetes, recitados, arietas . . . canarios . . . gigas* and the like belonged in the playhouse, not the temple. He also decried the use of violins and other brilliant instruments, calling instead for a return to sixteenth-century sobrieties. His favourite whipping-boy, Sebastián Durón (1660–1716), after apprenticeship in Saragossa as

---

[1] For Feijoo as a figure of the Enlightenment, see Chapter 9, section I.

organist, moved to Seville (1680–5), then to Burgo de Osma and Palencia (1686–91), whence he was called to be organist and composer for the Royal Chapel at Madrid. Already while at Seville, he composed *villancicos* that spread to the distant reaches of present-day Bolivia, and at Lima before 1700 he was already recognized as the leading contemporary Spanish composer. His very success, whether in nearby Portugal (both Oporto and Lisbon manuscripts testify to his reputation there) or in Peru, made him Feijoo's most conspicuous target. However it was really Durón's having sided with the defeated Austrian pretender to the Spanish throne in the War of the Spanish Succession that largely accounted for the revolt against his music in Feijoo's time. His operas in the National Library in Madrid, his cantatas in the National Library in Lisbon and his *villancicos* in many leading Latin American libraries justify a reappraisal of Durón as one of the most enchanting composers that Spain has produced in any reign.

IX Eighteenth Century

The eighteenth century began with an attempted revival of the pure church style in a *Missarum liber* (Madrid, 1703) dedicated to Philip V by Durón's successor as organist of the Chapel Royal, José de Torres Martínez Bravo (1665–1738). Dedicated to the seven mysteries of the Virgin, the seven masses run from first to seventh tones in a manner reminiscent of Navarro's and Aguilera de Heredia's Magnificats. The leading native-born composer at mid-century, Antonio Soler (1729–83), left an abundance of masses, motets, psalms, Magnificats and *villancicos* to the Escurial Library, where as a professed Hieronymite he served as organist; but his universal fame today rests on his keyboard sonatas, twenty-seven of which were published at London in his lifetime. His theoretical writings, of which the fountainhead is *Llave de la modulación* (Madrid, 1762), reveal his study of the organ works of José Élías – who in turn was the principal pupil of the famous Valencian organist and composer Juan Cabanilles (1644–1712), and also his personal contact with Domenico Scarlatti, harpsichordist to Queen María Barbara.

After a lengthy pause in the production of native Spanish music for the stage, especially during the residence of Farinelli at the courts of Philip V and Fernando VI (1737–61), homegrown talent reasserted itself in the more modest vernacular genre known as the *tonadilla escénica*. The *tonadilla escénica* freed itself from the taint of mere entr'acte

(*entremés*) or finale (*sainete*) music to become, around 1760–90, a fifteen-
or twenty-minute playlet typically involving two to four singing
characters (a larger number was possible) treating a comic subject in
strains reminiscent of the music heard in street and tavern. Luis Misón
(d. 1766), Pablo Esteve (d. 1790) and Blas de Laserna (1751–1816)
contributed heavily to the *tonadilla* repertory, of which there are 2,000
pieces in the Biblioteca Municipal, Madrid, alone.

Only abroad did Spanish-born composers of pretentious operas
come into full glory during the century: Domingo Terradellas (1713–
51) and Vicente Martín y Soler (1756–1806) were the most successful.
A pupil of the celebrated Francisco Valls (1665–1747), chapelmaster
of Barcelona Cathedral, Terradellas studied also with the Francesco
Durante at Naples, where he moulded the style that enabled him to
compete advantageously with the best Italians of the day in settings of
Metastasio and Zeno. Punctuated by a journey to London in 1746 to
see his *Anibale in Capua* mounted, Terradellas's career belongs almost
entirely to Naples, Rome, Turin and Venice. To distinguish his style,
Terradellas made much more of crescendi than his predecessors, fore-
shadowing Rossini. Martín y Soler, on the other hand, takes credit for
being one of the first to capitalize in opera on the kind of valse that
was to become a rage in the nineteenth century. *Una cosa rara* (Vienna,
1786), Martín y Soler's *dramma giocoso* quoted by Mozart in *Don
Giovanni*, enjoyed fifty performances in eight years, and *L'arbore di
Diana* (Vienna, 1787) eighty-three before 1805. In 1788 he settled at St
Petersburg on Catherine II's invitation, remaining there until he died.

X Nineteenth and Twentieth Century

Another Spaniard followed Martín y Soler to Russia – Fernando Sor
(1778–1839). An opera, ballet, but principally guitar composer, Sor
returned from St Petersburg to Paris in 1826, where he shared with
Dionisio Aguado (1784–1849) the reputation of being the greatest
guitarist of the period. Pablo de Sarasate (1844–1908) rivalled Paganini
as violinist and composer. Among the dramatic composers of the nineteenth century, Ramón Carnicer (1789–1855), Baltasar Saldoni (1807–
89), Hilarión Eslava (1807–78), Tomás Bretón (1850–1923), Felipe
Pedrell (1841–1922), Isaac Albéniz (1860–1909) and Enrique Granados
(1867–1916) wrote operas that enjoyed varying degrees of success.
Carnicer, now best known as the composer of the Chilean national
anthem, wrote eight operas with Italian libretti (1819–38), Saldoni, of

little creative ability but a pioneer musical historian, wrote three to Italian texts, and Eslava, another musicologist, three also. On the other hand, Bretón's nine operas (1875–1914) adopted Spanish libretti.

Even more successful than his operas, Bretón's six three-act, six two-act and twenty-two one-act *zarzuelas* (1874–1916) include several masterpieces, *La verbena de la paloma* (1897), for instance. Francisco Asenjo Barbieri (1823–94) resembles Saldoni and Eslava in combining dramatic composition with musical research, but far exceeded either predecessor in both creative talent and musicological expertise. The first of a series of Barbieri's triumphs as a *zarzuela* composer, *Jugar con fuego*, which had its première on 6 October 1851, was followed by such great successes as *Pan y toros* ('Bread and Bulls') and *El barberillo de Lavapiés*. Barbieri eventually completed seventy-seven *zarzuelas*. His invaluable services to Spanish musicology were matched by those of Pedrell, who, however, lacked the popular touch as a composer and enjoyed no more than a *succès d'estime* with his *Els Pirineus* (Barcelona, 1902) – in which he aspired to be the Spanish Wagner.

At the turn of the nineteenth century, two Catalan composers overshadowed all their Spanish contemporaries – Isaac Albéniz (1860–1909) and Enrique Granados (1867–1916). The French musicologist Henri Collet rightly coupled them in a double biography (1925). Both started as pianists, both idealized Spanish dance measures, both gained their widest fame as local colourists, both essayed opera, both died at the same age. Both visited America, but Albéniz as an adolescent and Granados at the end of his life to hear his opera in three scenes, *Goyescas*, first performed at the Metropolitan Opera House on 28 January 1916.

After the success of Albéniz's *The Magic Opal* (London, Lyric Theatre, 19 January 1893), the older composer was commissioned by the banker-librettist Francis Money Coutts to compose *Henry Clifford*, a three-act opera based on an incident in the War of the Roses (Barcelona, 1895), and then *Pepita Jiménez*, based on Juan Valera's novel (Barcelona, 5 January 1896). But Albéniz's permanent fame rests on his piano suite *Iberia* (1906–9) comprising twelve pieces, most of which have been frequently recorded. Transcribed for orchestra by his fellow pupil at Brussels, Enrique Fernández Arbós (1863–1939), two pieces from *Iberia* now rank among the most admired masterpieces in the entire Spanish literature – *Fête-Dieu à Séville* and *Triana*. According to Manuel de Falla,[1] Albéniz owed his inspiration for *Iberia* to Debussy – who taught him and other Spaniards not to despise

[1] *La Revue musicale*, I (Dec. 1920), p. 210.

'comme quelque chose de barbare' the popular effects of Andalusian music.

Still more popular with the public because of its haunting tune is Albéniz's *Tango in D*, op. 165, no. 2, belonging to a suite called *España* (1890). Dedicated to the scion of the London publishing firm who managed the Saturday Popular Concerts, S. Arthur Chappell (1834–1904), this tango (now a household melody) belongs to the three years, 1890–3, when the Albéniz family lived in London in Brompton Road. Fritz Kreisler, Jacques Thibaud, Beniamino Gigli, Wilhelm Backhaus and at least twenty other world-famous artists had already recorded it before the day of the LP.

Albéniz's famous tango is a tango because he calls it that, but *habanera* would be equally appropriate. Similarly, Granados's much admired *Colección de tonadillas, escritas en estilo antiguo* is a set of tona-dillas only because he chooses to call it so. Mostly a delicious set of piano-accompanied solo songs to poetry by Fernando Periquet, this set has nothing to do with the tonadilla of Laserna and Esteve. Its delights are retrospective – the eighteenth century viewed through late nineteenth-century spectacles. Granados's Madrid-laid opera also charms us by evoking the same bygone late eighteenth century, in-habited by picturesque *majos* and *majas* of the type made famous in Goya's paintings. At the close, the bullfighter Paquiro kills his rival in love who is captain of the guard, Fernando – but only after their inamorata has tasted ecstasy in a garden scene, entitled *La maja y el ruiseñor*, that ranks as one of the supreme love scenes in the literature of the modern lyric stage.

In his *Danzas españolas*, especially nos 2, 5, 6, 8, 11 and 12, and *Zambra*, Granados forsakes Madrid for southern Spain and the gipsy. The gipsy again plays a crucial role in *El amor brujo* (Madrid, 1915), the most popular ballet written by Manuel de Falla (1876–1946, died at Alta Gracia in Córdoba province, Argentina). Falla's success, towering above all other Spanish twentieth-century figures, is attested by the LP catalogues, all of which rank him far ahead of Albéniz, Granados, Joaquín Turina (1882–1949), Ernesto and Rodolfo Halffter (1905– and 1900–), the latter a Mexican citizen in later life. Falla's two-act opera *La vida breve* (1904–5, first performed at Nice in 1913), *El amor brujo* (containing the all-time favourite Ritual Fire Dance), piano and orchestra *Noches en los jardines de España* (1911–15, premiered 1916), ballet in two scenes *El sombrero de tres picos* (1916–17, 1918–19), marionette play with music based on the well-known episode in *Don*

Quijote, El Retablo de Maese Pedro (first staged 1923) and Harpsichord Concerto (1923–6, 1928), have each been recorded not once but several times. Of his completed mature large works only the *Fantasía baetica* (1922), dedicated to and first performed (in New York) by Artur Rubinstein, has so far failed to win its audience. His oratorio, unfinished at death, *Atlántida*, a 'scenic cantata' to a text drawn from the Catalan poet who became a monk, Jacinto Verdaguer (1845–1902), consumed Falla's energies during his last twenty years. Columbus's New World discoveries mingle with 'the grandiose vistas and the bold aspirations described by Plato in his *Critias*' to make this posthumous torso (premiered in concert form in Barcelona, 24 November 1961, and in a staged setting at the Teatro alla Scala, Milan, the next year) a *mélange des genres* militating against its success with the international public that loves *cante jondo* but not the Calderonian *auto sacramental*.

Falla remained to the end a tonal composer. His successors profess a different creed. Chief among the Spanish serialists of the 1950s was Luis de Pablo (b. Bilbao, 1930), hailed by Federico Sopeña in *La historia de la música española contemporánea* (1958) as the 'most intellectual' of the younger group. Composing in opus numbers has not prevented his adopting titles and pursuing techniques that keep step with Darmstadt and Donaueschingen leadership. The concerts of the short-lived Grupo Nueva Música (1958–9) included, in addition to Luis de Pablo, works by Ramón Barce, Manual Moreno-Buendía, Fernando Ember, Enrique Franco, Manual Carra, Antón García Abril, Alberto Blancafort and Cristóbal Halffter. The last's repertory embraces works of widest stylistic variety, sometimes invoking the spirit of late Falla (*Antífonal pascual*, op. 4), sometimes of Webern (*Tres piezas*, op. 9, revised as *Concertino*, op. 13), and even sometimes exploring the post-serial world of Stockhausen. Widely travelled, briefly head of the Madrid Conservatory and always challenging in his musical insights, Cristóbal Halffter is already a name that will find its way into all future histories of Spanish music.

Gone from Halffter's music and that of all those round him are the folkloric delights expected by all foreign admirers of Albéniz, Granados and Falla. But the astringency and denationalization found in all the vanguardists itemized in Arthur Custer's 'Contemporary Music in Spain', *Musical Quarterly*, XLVIII/1 (January 1962), are the price that any living group had to pay for membership in the dominant musical currents of the 1960s.

Bibliography

ANGLÉS, H. *Gloriosa contribución de España a la historia de la música universal.* Madrid, 1948.

—— 'Hispanic Musical Culture from the 6th to the 14th Century'. In *Musical Quarterly*, XXVI (1940), pp. 494–528.

—— 'La música anglesa dels segles XIII–XIV als països hispànics'. In *Analecta sacra tarraconensia*, XI (1935), pp. 219–33.

ARAIZ MARTÍNEZ, A. *Historia de la música religiosa en España.* Barcelona, 1942.

AUBRY, P. 'Iter Hispanicum'. In *Sämmelbande der Internationale Musik-Gesellschaft*, VIII, IX (1906–10), pp. 337–55, 517–34; 32–51, 137–74, 175–83.

BIBLIOTECA CENTRAL, BARCELONA. *La música española desde la edad media hasta nuestros días. Catálogo de la exposición histórica celebrada en conmemoración del primer centenario del nacimiento del maestro Felipe Pedrell.* Barcelona, 1941.

BIBLIOTECA NACIONAL, MADRID. *Catálogo musical de la Biblioteca Nacional de Madrid, por Higinio Anglés y José Subirá.* 3 vols. Barcelona, 1946–51.

BORREN, C. VAN DEN. 'Publications musicologiques espagnoles'. In *Revue belge de musicologie*, VII (1953 [2–4]), pp. 146–64.

CHASE, G. *The Music of Spain.* New York, 1941. 2nd ed. New York, 1959.

CONSEJO SUPERIOR DE INVESTIGACIONES CIENTÍFICAS. *Monografías.* Instituto Español de Musicología. 1946– . (5 issued through 1950.)

—— *Miscelánea en homenaje a Monseñor Higinio Anglés.* 2 vols. Barcelona, 1958–61.

—— *Monumentos de la música española.* 1941– . (33 vols through 1971.)

CURT DE LAFONTAINE, H. T. *Music in Spain.* London, 1920.

DONOVAN, R. B. *The Liturgical Drama in Medieval Spain.* Toronto, 1958.

ESPINÓS MOLTÓ, V. *El Quijote en la música y la música en el Quijote.* Ediciones de conferencias 48. Bilbao, 1946.

EXIMENO, A. *Don Lazarillo Vizcardi: sus investigaciones músicas.* Sociedad de Bibliófilos Españoles. 2 vols. Madrid, 1872.

FALLA, M. DE. *Escritos: introducción y notas de Federico Sopeña.* Madrid, 1947.

FARMER, H. G. *An Old Moorish Lute, Being Four Arabic Texts from Unique Manuscripts in the Biblioteca Nacional, Madrid (no. 334) and the Staatsbibliothek, Berlin (Lbg. 516).* Glasgow, 1933.

FERNÁNDEZ-CID, A. *La orquesta nacional de España.* Dirección general de bellas artes. Madrid, 1953.

GEIGER, A. 'Spezielles über Form und Inhalt der spanischen Münchener Kodizes'. In *Zeitschrift für Musikwissenschaft*, VI (1924), pp. 240–65.

JACOBS, C. *La interpretación de la música española del siglo XVI para instrumentos de tecla.* Madrid, 1959.

KASTNER, S. *Contribución al estudio de la música española y portuguesa.* Lisbon, 1941.

MITJANA Y GORDON, R. 'La Musique en Espagne'. In *Encyclopédie de la musique et dictionnaire du Conservatoire*, Pt I, Vol. 4 (1920), pp. 1913–2351.

MUNDÓ, A. M. 'La datación de los códices litúrgicos visigóticos toledanos'. In *Miscelánea en memoria de Dom Mario Férotin 1914–1964*, pp. 529–53. Madrid, 1966.

PEDRELL, F. *Diccionario biográfico y bibliográfico de músicos y escritores de música españoles.* 2 vols. (A–F, G). Barcelona, 1897.

—— *Orientaciones* (*1892–1902*). Paris, 1911.

—— *Teatro lírico español anterior al siglo XIX: documentos para la historia de la música española.* 5 vols. La Coruña, 1897–8.

POPE, I. 'The "Spanish Chapel" of Philip II'. In *Renaissance News*, V (Spring, Summer 1952), pp. 1–5, 34–8.

—— 'Spanish Secular Vocal Music of the Sixteenth Century'. In *Renaissance News*, II (Spring 1949), pp. 1–5.

PRADO, G. 'Estado actual de los estudios sobre la música mozárabe'. In *Estudios sobre la liturgia mozárabe*, pp. 89–106. Ed. Juan Francisco Rivera Recio. Toledo, 1965.

QUIEVREUX, L. 'Flamenco and the Flamencos'. In *Guitar Review*, XX (1956), pp. 16–19.

REUTER, R. *Órganos españoles.* Dirección general de bellas artes. Madrid, 1963.

RIAÑO Y MONTERO, J. F. *Critical and Bibliographical Notes on Early Spanish Music.* London, 1887.

RIBERA Y TARRAGÓ, J. *Music in Ancient Arabia and Spain: Being 'La música de las Cantigas'.* Translated and abridged by Eleanor Hague and Marion Leffingwell. Stanford, 1929.

RUBIO PIQUERAS, F. *Música y músicos toledanos.* Toledo, 1923.

SALAZAR, A. 'El gran siglo de la música española: en el cuarto centenario de la muerte de Cristóbal de Morales'. In *Revista musical chilena*, IX (1954), pp. 14–28.

—— *La música de España: la música en la cultura española.* Buenos Aires, 1953.

—— 'Music in the Primitive Spanish Theatre before Lope de Vega'. In *Papers read by Members of the American Musicological Society at the Annual Meeting . . . 1938* (1940), pp. 94–108.

SOPEÑA, F. *Historia de la música española contemporánea.* Madrid, 1958.

SPEER, K. 'The Organ *Versos* in Iberian Music to 1700'. In *Journal of the American Musicological Society*, IX (Fall 1956), pp. 244–5.

—— 'The Organ *Verso* in Iberian Music to 1700'. In *Journal of the American Musicological Society*, XI (Summer–Fall 1958), pp. 189–99.

STARKIE, W. 'Cante Jondo, Flamenco and the Guitar'. In *Guitar Review*, XX (1956), pp. 3–14.

—— *Spanish Raggle-Taggle: Adventures with a Fiddle in North Spain.* London, 1934.

STEVENSON, R. *Juan Bermudo.* The Hague, 1960.

—— 'Music Research in Spanish Libraries'. In *Notes of the Music Library Association*, X (December 1957), pp. 49–57.

—— *Spanish Cathedral Music in the Golden Age.* Berkeley, 1961.

—— *Spanish Music in the Age of Columbus.* The Hague, 1960.

—— 'Espectáculos musicales en la España del siglo XVII'. In *Revista musical chilena*, XVII (1973), pp. 3–44.

SUBIRÁ, J. *Historia de la música española e hispanoamericana.* Barcelona, 1953.

—— *La música en la casa de Alba: estudios históricos y biográficos.* Madrid, 1927.

—— *La tonadilla escénica.* 3 vols. Madrid, 1928–30.

—— *Tonadillas teatrales inéditas: libretos y partituras, con una descripción sinóptica de nuestra música lírica.* Madrid, 1932.

TREND, J. B. *Luis Milán and the Vihuelistas.* London, 1925.

—— *Manuel de Falla and Spanish Music*. New York, 1929.

—— *The Music of Spanish History to 1600*. London, 1926.

—— 'Spanish Madrigals'. In *Proceedings of the Musical Association*. Session 52, 1925–6 (1926), pp. 13–29.

URSPRUNG, O. 'Musikkultur in Spanien'. In *Handbuch der Spanienkunde*, pp. 329–57. Frankfurt-a.-M., 1932.

VALLS, M. *La música española después de Manuel de Falla*. Madrid, 1962.

WAGNER, L. J. 'Flemish Musicians at the Spanish Court of Philip II'. In *Caecilia*, LXXXVI (Autumn 1959), pp. 107–14.

WARD, J. 'The Editorial Methods of Venegas de Henestrosa'. In *Musica disciplina*, VI (1952), pp. 105–13.

—— 'The Lute in 16th-Century Spain'. In *Guitar Review*, IX (1949), pp. 26–8.

NOTE

The twenty-six volumes of the *Anuario musical*, issued by the Instituto Español de Musicología of the Consejo Superior de Investigaciones Científicas 1946 through 1972, contain seven or eight articles in each issue that are indispensable reading for any serious student of Spanish musical history.

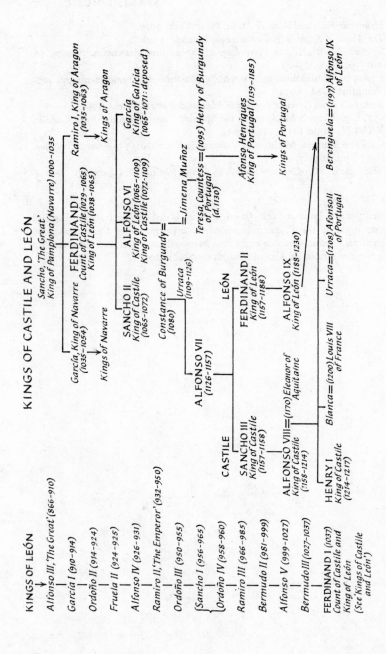

KINGS OF CASTILE AND LEÓN

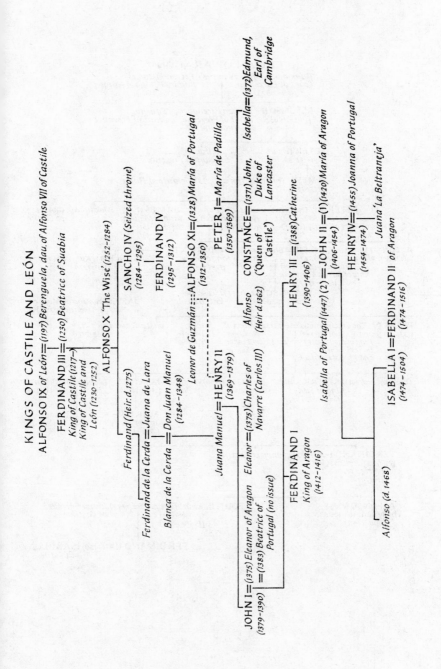

KINGS OF CASTILE AND LEÓN

ALFONSO IX of León == (1197) Berenguela, dau. of Alfonso VII of Castile

FERDINAND III == (1230) Beatrice of Suabia
King of Castile (1217–)
King of Castile and
León (1230–1252)

ALFONSO X 'The Wise' (1252–1284)

SANCHO IV (Seized throne)
(1284–1295)

FERDINAND IV
(1295–1312)

Leonor de Guzmán ::::: ALFONSO XI == (1328) María of Portugal
(1312–1350)

PETER I == María de Padilla
(1350–1369)

CONSTANCE == (1371) John, Duke of   Isabella == (1372) Edmund,
('Queen of   Lancaster   Earl of
Castile')   Cambridge

Alfonso
(Heir d.1362)

HENRY III == (1388) Catherine
(1390–1406)

Isabella of Portugal (1447) (2) JOHN II == (1)(1420) María of Aragon
(1406–1454)

HENRY IV == (1455) Joanna of Portugal
(1454–1474)

Juana 'La Beltraneja'

Ferdinand (Heir d.1275)

Ferdinand de la Cerda == Juana de Lara

Blanca de la Cerda == Don Juan Manuel
(1284–1348)

Juana Manuel == HENRY II
(1369–1379)

Eleanor == (1375) Charles of
Navarre (Carlos III)

FERDINAND I
King of Aragon
(1412–1416)

JOHN I == (1375) Eleanor of Aragon
(1379–1390)   == (1383) Beatrice of
Portugal (no issue)

ISABELLA I == FERDINAND II of Aragon
(1474–1504)   (1474–1516)

Alfonso (d.1468)

CROWN OF ARAGON

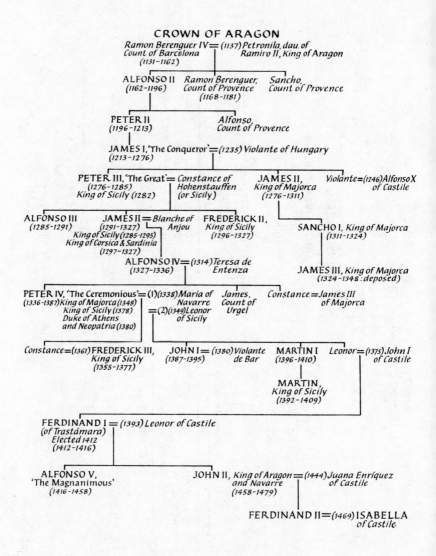

Ramon Berenguer IV = (1137) Petronila, dau. of
Count of Barcelona   Ramiro II, King of Aragon
(1131-1162)

ALFONSO II   Ramon Berenguer,   Sancho,
(1162-1196)   Count of Provence   Count of Provence
                 (1168-1181)

PETER II   Alfonso,
(1196-1213)   Count of Provence

JAMES I, 'The Conqueror' = (1235) Violante of Hungary
(1213-1276)

PETER III, 'The Great' = Constance of   JAMES II,   Violante = (1246) Alfonso X
(1276-1285)   Hohenstauffen   King of Majorca   of Castile
King of Sicily (1282)   (or Sicily)   (1276-1311)

ALFONSO III   JAMES II = Blanche of   FREDERICK II,
(1285-1291)   (1291-1327) Anjou   King of Sicily   SANCHO I, King of Majorca
                 King of Sicily (1285-1295) (1296-1327)   (1311-1324)
                 King of Corsica & Sardinia
                 (1297-1327)

                 ALFONSO IV = (1314) Teresa de   JAMES III, King of Majorca
                 (1327-1336)   Entenza   (1324-1348: deposed)

PETER IV, 'The Ceremonious' = (1)(1338) Maria of   James,   Constance = James III
(1336-1387) King of Majorca(1348) Navarre   Count of   of Majorca
King of Sicily (1378)   = (2)(1349) Leonor   Urgel
Duke of Athens   of Sicily
and Neopatria (1380)

Constance = (1361) FREDERICK III,   JOHN I = (1380) Violante   MARTIN I   Leonor = (1375) John I
King of Sicily   (1387-1395)   de Bar   (1396-1410)   of Castile
(1355-1377)

                                                               MARTIN,
                                                               King of Sicily
                                                               (1392-1409)

FERDINAND I = (1393) Leonor of Castile
(of Trastámara)
Elected 1412
(1412-1416)

ALFONSO V,   JOHN II, King of Aragon = (1444) Juana Enríquez
'The Magnanimous'   and Navarre   of Castile
(1416-1458)   (1458-1479)

                                 FERDINAND II = (1469) ISABELLA
                                                       of Castile

HOUSE OF HABSBURG

FERDINAND AND ISABELLA
(d. 1504)   (d. 1516)

Maximilian, Holy Roman Emperor = Mary of Burgundy
(1493-1519)

JOANNA 'The Mad' = (1496) PHILIP I 'The Fair'   Margaret
(d. 1555)   (d. 1506)

Catherine = (1509) Henry VIII

María = (1500) Manuel I of Portugal

Isabella (1526) = CHARLES V (I of SPAIN) Emperor (1516-1556)

Eleanor = (1519) Manuel I of Portugal

Catherine = (1525) John III of Portugal

Ferdinand I King of Bohemia and Hungary (1526-1564)

John = Margaret of Burgundy
(d. 1497)

John III of Portugal
(d. 1557)

María of Portugal (1) = (1543) PHILIP II = (2) (1554) Mary Tudor
(1556-1598)

Isabelle de Valois (1559) (3)
Anne (1570) (4) of Austria

Joanna = (1552) Prince John of Portugal
(d. 1554)

María = (1548) Maximilian II Holy Roman Emperor (1564-1576)

Don John of Austria
(d. 1578)

Don Carlos
(1545-1568)

Sebastian I of Portugal
(1554-1578)

PHILIP III = (1599) Margaret of Austria
(1598-1621)

Isabelle de Bourbon (1625) (1) = PHILIP IV = (2) (1649) Mariana of Austria
(1621-1665)

Louis XIII = Anna
of France (1615)
(1610-1643)

Anna

María = (1631) Ferdinand III, Holy Roman Emperor

Mariana = (1649) Philip IV

Leopold I = (1676) Eleanor of Neuburg
Holy Roman Emperor
(1658-1705)

Archduke Charles ('Charles III') (Pretender to the Spanish throne, 1700-1725)

Louis XIV of France = (1660) María Teresa
(1643-1715)

Baltasar Carlos
(d. 1646)

CHARLES II
(1665-1700)
(no issue)

Margarita

Louis, 'Le Grand Dauphin' = (1680) María Anna of Bavaria
(d. 1711)

PHILIP V (of BOURBON)
(1700-1746)

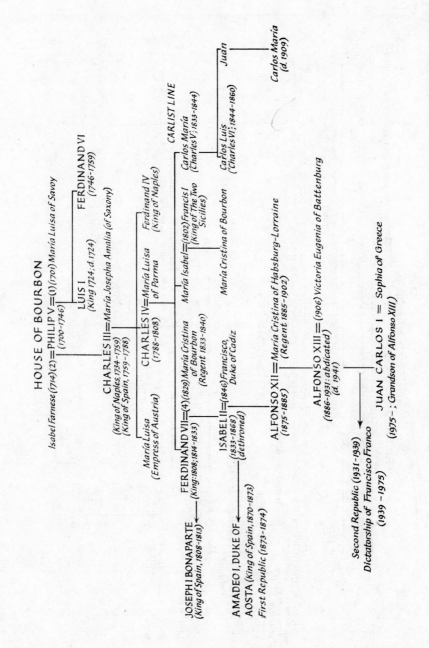

Index

(Figures in bold type indicate main references)